Global Sociology

Third Edition

Robin Cohen
& Paul Kennedy

With

Maud Perrier

Global Sociology

Third Edition

palgrave
macmillan

First edition 2000
Second edition 2007
Third edition 2013
Published by
PALGRAVE MACMILLAN

Palgrave Macmillan in the UK is an imprint of Macmillan Publishers Limited, registered in England, company number 785998, of Houndmills, Basingstoke, Hampshire RG21 6XS.

Palgrave Macmillan in the US is a division of St Martin's Press LLC, 175 Fifth Avenue, New York, NY 10010.

Palgrave Macmillan is the global academic imprint of the above companies and has companies and representatives throughout the world.

Palgrave® and Macmillan® are registered trademarks in the United States, the United Kingdom, Europe and other countries.

ISBN: 978–0–230–29374–8

This book is printed on paper suitable for recycling and made from fully managed and sustained forest sources. Logging, pulping and manufacturing processes are expected to conform to the environmental regulations of the country of origin.

A catalogue record for this book is available from the British Library.

A catalog record for this book is available from the Library of Congress.

10 9 8 7 6 5 4 3 2 1
22 21 20 19 18 17 16 15 14 13

Printed and bound in China.

For Selina and Sue

Brief contents

Contents

List of figures

List of tables

List of boxes

Global thinkers

About the authors

Robin Cohen is Emeritus Professor of Development Studies and former director of the International Migration Institute at the University of Oxford, UK. He was Professor of Sociology at Warwick for many years and retains an honorary professorship there. He has held full-time appointments at the Universities of Ibadan in Nigeria, Birmingham in the UK, Cape Town in South Africa and the West Indies in Trinidad, and also taught in the USA and Canada.

Robin is editor of the Routledge series *Global Diasporas*. His books include *Frontiers of Identity: The British and the Others* (1994), *Global Diasporas: An Introduction* (1997, rev. 2008) and *Migration and its Enemies* (2006). With Paola Toninato he has edited a large student reader, *The Creolization Reader* (2009). His major works have been translated into Chinese, French, German, Greek, Italian, Japanese, Portuguese and Spanish.

Robin's research is on international migration, diasporas, cosmopolitanism and creolization. His research on creolization was funded by the award of an Economic and Social Research Council Professorial Fellowship. He is principal investigator on the Oxford Diasporas Programme (2011–15) funded by the Leverhulme Trust, and is also helping to establish a research programme on 'super-diversity' in South Africa in association with the Max Planck Institute for the Study of Religious and Ethnic Diversity, Germany.

Paul Kennedy is Visiting Reader in Sociology and Global Studies at Manchester Metropolitan University, UK. He has taught and researched at the University of Ghana in Accra, Cape Coast University (also in Ghana), the Institute for Development Studies at Sussex University, Southbank Polytechnic and MMU. He was the director of the Institute for Global Studies at MMU from 2002 to 2007. He was a founding member of the Global Studies Association in 2000 and has acted either as its secretary or chairperson during most of the years since then.

His books include *Ghanaian Businessmen: From Artisan to Capitalist Entrepreneur in a Dependent Economy* (1980), *African Capitalism: The Struggle for Ascendancy* (1988), *Local Lives and Global Transformations: Towards World Society* (2010) and the edited volumes, *Globalization and National Identities* (2001) with Catherine Danks and *Communities Across Borders* (2002) with Victor Roudometof.

Recent research interests include work on green/ethical businesses, transnational professionals, especially architects, and social networks and life course changes among young educated continental Europeans working in Manchester.

Tour of the book

In this chapter we shall look first at some of th[e]
milestones in the discipline's development. T[he]
and universal claims, positioning the disciplin[e]
for a long time the primary concern was to co[l-]
lar nations and their societies. To an extent this
transnational outlook. Accordingly, we also exa[mine]
tive changes that have prompted some so[me]
approaches that make sense of the more co[mplex]
around us – a global sociology. Although seein[g]
becoming more and more common, not all so[cial]
forth be the sole preoccupation of the professi[on]
further developing a global sociology is, inde[ed]
insights into our evolving world.

KEY STARTING POINTS IN SOCIOLO[GY]

Sociology developed in nineteenth-century E[urope]
of knowledge, notably philosophy, history an[d]
capture the import and drama of industriali[zation]
that were rapidly transforming the modern wo[rld]

◀ **Chapter introductions**
Short introductions to the key topics covered in each chapter help guide you through the textbook.

as war, poverty, financial crises or inequality. In addres[s]
divided. Some centre their work on professional recogni[tion]
while others work with policy-makers. Others again feel t[hat]
and see that as a legitimate extension of their roles as socio[logists]
although there are some overlaps between these categori[es]
them, we now, in effect, practise four kinds of sociology
public (Table 1.1).

TABLE 1.1 Burawoy's four types of sociology		
Type of sociology	Common cognitive practices	Target
Professional sociology	Advanced theoretical and empirical work, using explicit scientific norms	Peers,
Critical sociology	Foundational and normative, driven by moral vision	Critica[l] debat[e]
Policy sociology	Empirical, concrete, applied and pragmatic	Policy
Public sociology	More accessible/relevant theoretical and empirical work, lectures and media appearances	Desig[n] comm[unity]

Source: Adapted from Burawoy (2005).

Figures and tables ▶
New and classic figures and tables summarize and elucidate the theory.

A PAUSE TO REFLECT

Some sociologists suggest that, despite showing [...]
it is difficult to exclude the values and beliefs they [...]
engaged in research on the human condition, we [...]
be bias in sociological research? Can this be mini[mized]
their values before they report their findings?

The search for sociological knowled[ge]
public policy become all too evident. Soci[al]
destructive, produce unintended consequ[ences]
their research often may challenge offici[al]
gist off guard. In revealing findings that c[atch]
ologists are expected to be even more met[iculous]
ples may make the argument clearer. Let [us]
nist views and most of the people you qu[estion]
greatly on the attentions of enraptured [...]

◀ **A pause to reflect**
Questions throughout chapters encourage you to think critically about what you have just read.

THE GREAT DEPRESSION (1929–39)
The most severe capitalist downturn ever known, although some have compared the global economic crisis beginning in 2007/8 with it. By late 1932, in the USA alone, around 15 million workers were unemployed. The crisis began in October 1929 when company share values on New York's Wall Street stock exchange crashed. A number of stockbrokers and investors jumped to their deaths from their skyscraper offices. A series of escalating bank and currency collapses soon turned the crisis into a global one. German Nazism and Japanese fascism were partly caused by the world economic collapse.

In the period up [...]
remained intelligent [...]
they rarely lifted their [...]
them. In front of their [...]
Great Depression, the [...]
ment of women on the [...]
social realities were fo[...]
or national contexts.

POST-1945: WIDE[NING]
COMPLEX WORLD

The end of the Secon[d...]
tional forces. Japan wa[s...]
trializing and non-Wes[tern...]
had brought the USA [...]
the locus of political a[nd...]
its part, the Soviet Union made enormous [...]
sending the first cosmonaut to space in 19[...]
weaknesses in the economy. The French, [...]

Definitions ▶
Short definitions of key terms in sociology, or background information on particular important events help you get to grips with each chapter.

KEY CONCEPT

The NEW INTERNATIONAL DIVISION OF LABOUR divides production into different skills and tasks spread across regions and countries rather than within a single company. From the 1970s onwards, as key production functions shifted away from the old industrial zones, hitherto agricultural countries, particularly in the Asia-Pacific region, rapidly joined the ranks of the new international division of labour.

THE NEW INTERNAT[IONAL]

Partly in response to the [...]
a team of German resear[chers...]
that a NEW INTERNATIONAL [...]
were reacting particular[...]
and other newly indust[rializing...]
deindustrialization of th[e...]
observe in Chapters 4 [...]
growing tendency for [...]
locate the more labour-[...]
developing countries, so [...]

Advocates of the NI[DL...]
ing processes in cheap labour havens did littl[e...]
ment prospects in the poor countries in quest[...]
the growing ranks of unemployed people in t[he...]
TNCs. While these theorists suggest that the [...]
countries' ability to dominate the world capi[tal...]
'global losers' in all countries. Like world syste[m...]
ery being able to overcome its relative econom[ic...]
from dependence on raw material exports to t[...]

◀ **Key concepts**
Succinct discussions of key concepts in sociology or related disciplines such as anthropology, politics and economics are useful for revision.

GLOBAL THINKERS 1 IMMANUEL M. WALLERSTEIN (1930–)

Immanuel Wallerstein [...]
the most important ac[...]
since the 1970s. At the [...]
(1974: 15), Wallerstein [...]

in the late fifteenth [...]
into existence what [...]
economy ... it was [...]
social system the w[...]
which is the distinct[...]

What was hidden behind Wallerstein's apparently simple declaration was [...]
understandings of the world:

- For Wallerstein, political structures (like empires and states) were gi[ven...]
  emphasis on interpenetrating trade networks that crossed state bou[ndaries...]
  labour, market share and raw materials drove the world system forw[ard...]
  emphasis on trade led many scholars to accuse Wallerstein of being [...]
  someone who overemphasizes the causal role of economic factors. [...]
  social movements and politics, he has never entirely shaken off this [...]

Global thinkers ▶
Analyses of the important research undertaken by key thinkers in sociology and related disciplines provide some background to current sociological thinking.

BOX 1.2 Post-1945 Western sociologists and the non-We

- **Barrington Moore** (1967, 1972) thought that a comparative histor
  understand why some societies prospered while others languished, a
  democracies and others dictatorships. In his ambitious comparative
  and China, he considered how the cultural foundations, historical tra
  through different kinds of peasantry and aristocratic systems of land
  interacted in constraining and/or shaping the direction, speed and c
  industrial societies.
- Other US sociologists like **Talcott Parsons** (1971) tended to talk in t
  'modernization', which involved the 'non-Western' world 'catching up
  'Western' world and Japan.
- German scholar **André Gunder Frank** (1967, 1969), who worked in
  influenced by the theories of 'dependency' and 'underdevelopment'
  popularized their work by writing in English and extended it in new
- Although the term 'Third World' originated with a French journalist,
  (1967) also drew from writings by Latin Americans, Asians and Africa
  characteristics of the Third World, one that was relatively poor, neith
  Western nor non-Western.

◀ Boxed text
Examples, case studies and timelines of key events help you to apply the theory to the real world.

Review ▶
Summaries of chapter content draw helpful conclusions and often look towards the future of the discipline.

pressure from their disgruntled, insecure c
have devised policies to regulate destructive
The continuing power of the banks to resist
far enough.

REVIEW

That sociology drew on Enlightenment th
pline with its strong positivist tradition. So
pline with several important streams. One
explores how subjective elements shape
dealing with human nature and social co
differences. Sociology therefore requires a
needs and has developed methodologies t
highly intimate data, but in ways that mini
inclinations. Nevertheless, stringent attemp
to the critiques of others do not preclude
different political, social, economic and m

In this book, we are particularly conce
discipline can be used to develop a global s

◀ Further reading
Annotated suggestions for further research, including books and journal articles, for those who want to learn more.

FURTHER READING

M. Davis's *Planet of Slums* (2006) provides an excelle
experiences of different groups across the wor

In *American Apartheid: Segregation and the Making*
Denton consider the consequences of deindus
workers.

A. Sen's *Poverty and Famine: An Essay on Entitlement*
detail, but it remains a classic work that is chall
time. (You can ignore some of the more techni
the argument.)

R. Wilkinson and K. Pickett's *The Spirit Level: Why Equ*
achievement. Using international data and con
show that greater equality benefits everyone, b
exercise, not a political tract, but it has importa

K. L. Thachuk, contains detailed material on all the for

L. Napoleoni's *Terror Inc: Tracing the Money behind Global T*
accessible discussion of the fascinating links betwee
and terrorism, replete with numerous examples.

Many chapters in *States of Conflict: Gender, Violence and R*
al., provide vivid case studies, coupled with careful a
complex subject.

Questions and ▶
assignments
Questions to test your understanding of chapter content, requiring you to conduct your own research and think independently.

QUESTIONS AND ASSIGNMENTS

1. How useful are official statistics to the sociological st
    demand and so limitless a supply, is it possible to stop
2. Show how patterns of social control have changed in
3. What are the new features of contemporary terrorism?
4. Using specific examples, examine how and why many
    family life reflect the realities of gender oppression an

◀ Companion website
Visit the companion website
www.palgrave.com/sociology/cohen3e for
comprehensive learning materials, including:
- Mind maps to help you link key
  topics, perspectives and themes
- Bonus chapters
- Glossary
- Useful web links
- Short pieces on key topics
  touched on in the book
- Self-test questions.
Lecturers can also find:
- Lecture plans for various modules,
  mapped onto the textbook
- Groupwork activities for use in seminars
- PowerPoint slides.

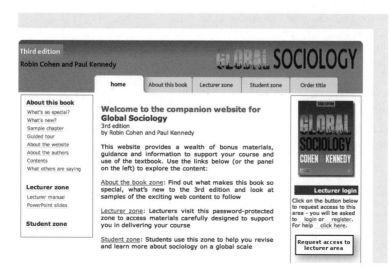

Authors' acknowledgements

Robin Cohen and Paul Kennedy would like express their deep gratitude to Selina Molteno Cohen who lent her expertise at the last crucial stages of the book. Paul Kennedy wishes to thank friends and colleagues, especially Stephen Edgell, Susie Jacobs, Phil Mole and Scott Boynting.

Maud Perrier provided some excellent support. In particular, Chapter 13 'Globalization, families and social change' was written by her and offers a new thematic dimension that was absent in earlier editions of this book. She is also actively engaged in helping to compile the website that supports this book.

The book was carefully piloted through the editorial processes at Palgrave Macmillan. At an early stage Emily Salz was involved, but we were then placed in the capable hands of Anna Reeve, Joanna McGarry and Amy Grant. Their observations were often pointed, but they were always deeply involved in making this book better. Thanks go to the team at Aardvark Editorial, including their eagle-eyed and helpful copy editor, Maggie Lythgoe. Any deficiencies that remain are attributable to the authors.

Finally, we wish to thank both the anonymous reviewers who commented on early plans for the new edition and those on the review panel whose detailed thoughts on the manuscript proved invaluable. Some of these reviewers used earlier editions of this book on their courses and we are grateful to them for their constructive comments and loyalty. The review panel are:

- Johanna Bockman at George Mason University, USA
- Simon Bradford at Brunel University, UK
- Victoria Gosling at the University of Salford, UK
- David Inglis at the University of Aberdeen, UK
- Daniel Levy at Stony Brook University (SUNY), USA
- Margery Mayall at the University of Queensland, Australia
- Shawn McEntee at Salisbury University, USA
- Alphia Possamai-Inesedy at the University of Western Sydney, Australia
- John Roberts at Brunel University, UK
- Silke Roth at the University of Southampton, UK
- Anne Scott at the University of Canterbury, New Zealand
- Michael Whittingham at Kingston University, UK

We are also appreciative of the friendly emails from students who have found something of merit in our efforts.

Publisher's acknowledgements

The authors and publishers are grateful to the following for permission to reproduce figures and tables:

AP/Press Association Images for Figure 20.2, '"No nukes" protest sign'.

The CIA World Fact Book for Table 4.1, 'Top 10 countries by value of exports (US$), 2010'.

Corbis for Figures 0.1, 'The Occupy Wall Street movement', 2.1, 'Moai at Ahu Akivi ceremonial site, Easter Island', 2.2, 'Nelson Mandela in March 1990 on his release from 25 years in prison', 3.1, 'Cleric and astronomer Nicolas Copernicus (1473–1543)', 4.1, 'Ford's Highland Park plant in 1913', 4.2, 'Chiquita banana plantation, Cahuita, Costa Rica, 1996', 4.3, 'A departing Lehman Brothers employee', 6.1, 'Amartya Sen (1933–)', 6.2, 'A starving Dinka child', 10.1, 'TNC marketing', 10.2, 'Corporate irresponsibility', 11.3, 'Maximilien de Robespierre (1758–94)', 12.1, 'Thomas Malthus (1766–1843), prophet of doom?', 12.2, 'Charles Darwin (1809–82)', 14.1, 'Mexican girls with blocks of chewing gum', 15.2, 'Mickey Mouse', 15.3, 'Tiger Woods at a tournament in Florida, USA', 17.3, 'Whirling Dervishes' and 19.1, 'The *Fuerza Joven* ('Young Force') of Bolivia'.

Fotolia for Figures 8.2, 'Women machinists in a Cambodian garment factory', 13.2, 'Japanese family-centred values', 21.1, 'Graffiti in Harlem' and 22.1, 'Petrovsky Passage, Moscow'.

Getty Images for Figures 5.1, 'A rally in Vilnius, Lithuania on 11 March 2012' and 19.2, 'An anti-war demo in London, 2011'.

Instituto Fernando Henrique Cardoso and Magdalena Gutierrez for Figure 1.2, 'Fernando Henrique Cardoso (1931–)'.

iStockphoto for Figures 9.2, 'The Martin Luther King Memorial, Washington' and 18.1, 'Raffles Hotel, Singapore'.

Jason Cohen for Figure 14.2, 'Mural in Cape Verde'.

Mary Evans Picture Library for Figure 9.1, 'Seven native Herero men chained together in German South West Africa (now Namibia)'.

Panos Pictures for Figure 6.3, 'Waste pickers in Guatemala City, Guatemala'.

Pearson Education Ltd for Table 7.1, 'Class schema in the UK', from Marsh, I., Keating, M., Eyre, A., Campbell, R. and McKenzie, J. (eds), *Making Sense of Society: An Introduction to Sociology* (1996).

Penguin and Bloomsbury USA for Figure 22.2, 'The relationship of health and social problems to income inequality', from Wilkinson, R. and Pickett, K. *The Spirit Level: Why Equality is Better for Everyone*, London: Penguin (2010) and New York: Bloomsbury USA (2010).

Princeton University Press for Table 18.2, 'Distribution of employment in New York, London and Tokyo, 1970s and 1980s', from Sassen, S. *The Global City* © 1991 Princeton University Press.

Robin Cohen for Figure 17.1, 'A Candomblé religious statuette for sale in a Brazilian market'.

Routledge for Table 13.1, 'Therborn's world family systems typology', in Therborn, G. *Between Sex and Power: Family in the World 1900–2000* (2004).

Sage for Tables 2.1, 'Changes in the speed of transport, 1500–1960s', from Dicken, P. *Global Shift: The Internationalization of Economic Activity* (1992) and 19.1, 'Global civil society events in April 2008', from Timms, J. 'Chronology of global civil society events', in Kumar, A., Scholte, J., Kaldor, M., Glasius, M., Seckinelgin, H. and Anheier, H. (eds) *Global Civil Society 2009* (2009).

Science and Society Picture Library for Figure 8.1, 'A woman suffragette *c.* 1910'.

Tulasi Srinivas for Figure 1.1, 'Mysore Narasimhachar Srinivas (1916–99)'.

Wiley for Figure 18.2, 'The hierarchy of world cities', from Friedman, J. 'The world city hypothesis', *Development and Change*, John Wiley and Sons (1986).

World Bank Development Research Group for Table 6.1, 'Number of poor people in the developing world', from Chen, S. and Ravaillon, M. *The Developing World is Poorer Than We Thought, But no Less Successful in the Fight Against Poverty*, Washington, DC (2008).

For their permission to use images of themselves in the Global Thinkers boxes, the publishers would like to thank:

Immanuel M. Wallerstein, Roland Robertson, Anthony Giddens, Walden Bello, Leslie Sklair, Sylvia Chant, Patricia Hill Collins, David Harvey, Nina Glick Schiller, Arlie Hochschild, John Urry, Manuel Castells (and Maggie Smith), Jürgen Habermas, Ulrich Beck, Zygmunt Bauman and Martin Albrow.

The publishers would also like to thank akg-images for the photograph of Max Weber, Corbis for the photographs of Karl Marx, Emile Durkheim and Michel Foucault, Claire Guttinger at the Collège de France for the photograph of Pierre Bourdieu, and the Holberg Prize, University of Bergen/Florian Breief for the photograph of Jürgen Habermas.

Every effort has been made to trace all the copyright holders but if any have been inadvertently overlooked the publishers will be pleased to make the necessary arrangements at the first opportunity.

Abbreviations and acronyms

9/11	11 September 2001 terrorist attack on twin towers in New York
AIDS	acquired immune deficiency syndrome
ASEAN	Association of Southeast Asian Nations
BIP	Border Industrialization Program
BRIC	Brazil, Russia, India and China (countries)
CCTV	closed-circuit television
CEDAW	Convention on the Elimination of All Forms of Discrimination against Women
CIA	Central Intelligence Agency (USA)
CNN	Cable News Network
CO_2	carbon dioxide
CPC	Communist Party of China
CSR	corporate social responsibility
DRC	Democratic Republic of the Congo
ECHR	European Court of Human Rights
EDL	English Defence League
EPZ	export-processing zone
ETI	Ethical Trading Initiative
EZLN	Zapatista National Liberation Army
EU	European Union
FDI	foreign direct investment
FTSE	Financial Times (and London) Stock Exchange (a stock index)
G7	group of seven (advanced industrial nations, now called the G8)
G20	group of twenty finance ministers and Central Bank governors
GATT	General Agreement on Tariffs and Trade (now the World Trade Organization)
GDI	gross domestic income
GDP	gross domestic product
GM	genetically modified
GNP	gross national product
GSM	global social movement
HIPC	heavily indebted poor country
HIV	human immunodeficiency virus
ICC	International Criminal Court
ICT	information and communication technology
IDP	internally displaced person
IGO	international governmental organization
ILO	International Labour Organization
IMF	International Monetary Fund
IMR	infant mortality rate
INGO	international nongovernmental organization
IPCC	Intergovernmental Panel on Climate Change
IQ	intelligence quotient

IT	information technology
LA	Los Angeles
MDGs	Millennium Development Goals
MPI	Multidimensional Poverty Index
NAFTA	North American Free Trade Agreement
NATO	North Atlantic Treaty Organization
NGO	nongovernmental organization
NIC	newly industrializing country
NIDL	new international division of labour (theory of the)
NRMs	new religious movements
OECD	Organisation for Economic Co-operation and Development
OPEC	Organization of Petroleum Exporting Countries
PV	photovoltaic
RBS	Royal Bank of Scotland
SEC	Securities and Exchange Commission (USA)
TNC	transnational corporation
TNI	transnationality index
TRIPS	Trade-Related Intellectual Property Rights
UN	United Nations
UNCED	UN Conference on Environment and Development
UNCHR	UN Centre for Human Rights
UNCTAD	UN Conference on Trade and Development
UNDESA	UN Department of Economic and Social Affairs
UNDP	UN Development Programme
UNEP	UN Environment Programme
UNESCO	UN Educational, Scientific and Cultural Organization
UNHCR	UN High Commission for Refugees
UNICEF	UN International Children's Emergency Fund
UNRISD	UN Research Institute for Social Development
USSR	Union of Soviet Socialist Republics
WHO	World Health Organization
WSF	World Social Forum
WTO	World Tourism Organization (in Chapter 15 'WTO' refers to this organization)
WTO	World Trade Organization (elsewhere in the book 'WTO' refers to this organization)
WUF	World Urban Forum

Introduction

Sociology involves the systematic study of the character of human interaction. Historical events, beliefs and social influences acting on an individual, family or wider social group often structure human behaviour. Their outcomes are experienced at a number of levels – local, national, regional and global. As we shall see later in this book, many sociologists are particularly adept at describing the patterns of social interactions at the community and national levels. Why do we argue that we now need a more macroscopic and comparative approach, a 'global sociology'? This expression was first used by Wilbert E. Moore in the 1960s when he argued that the world had become 'a singular system' in three senses:

1. There was 'a remarkable concurrence in the ideology of economic development'.
2. The 'pool of options' to achieve this was both limited in number and worldwide in scope.
3. 'The life of the individual anywhere is affected by events and processes everywhere' (Moore 1966: 481).

The processes that Moore observed have, however, accelerated and become more threatening. We now live within the orbit of the multiple, interlocking, sometimes dangerous and always challenging transformations, risks and crises that encompass our globe. Some are the product of earlier changes, such as imperialism or the spread of nation-state industrialization projects, while others are the result of recent forms of globalization. To understand these changes we require, in Albrow's (1987) telling phrase, 'a sociology for one world'.

RECENT GLOBAL CHANGES

In the body of the book, we examine these parallel transformations and sometimes crises taking place all around us in more detail, so here we provide only a brief outline of some important global changes arising over the past few years.

THE SHIFT IN ECONOMIC AND POLITICAL POWER

Although the USA remains the most powerful nation on earth militarily and economically, there has been a radical shift in power from the USA, Europe and Japan to other countries and regions. One would have to be living on Mars not to notice the extraordinary development of China. China is an unusual society in that the Communist Party enjoys the sole right to political organization, but competition in the economic sphere has been allowed to multiply, and sometimes run riot. This unusual combination of a political monopoly and a free market has lifted millions out of poverty, while China has been extending its influence to many parts of the world. India's rise to prominence is more modest than China's but, by contrast, it has mobilized its labour force, made significant advances in the information technology and service sectors, and become a large exporter of manufactured goods – all without foregoing its democratic traditions, which it inherited from the largely constitutional process of decolonization. Competition between parties for a popular vote, a free press and respect for the rule of law remain important parts of India's achievement.

While the progress made by China and India is headline news, the global shift of power has by no means stopped there. Oil-rich countries have often been able to capitalize on the shortage of crude supplies resulting from political insecurity, for example in Nigeria and Iraq, or major accidents, for example the damage to the British Petroleum oil rig in the Gulf of Mexico. Often, they have used their funds, called 'sovereign funds', to buy large holdings in Western banks. By 2010, little Qatar had the world's highest gross domestic product per capita (a conventional measurement of wealth using the number of people in the country as the divisor), a calculation helped by the fact that there are fewer than 300,000 citizens in Qatar (Chapter 3). The Qatari government has also allied itself to the democratic forces in the region providing, for example, hundreds of millions of dollars in military aid to the rebels in Libya.

Other major beneficiaries in the shift of world power include Brazil, which has finally realized its founders' dream that it would one day be a great power. A succession of competent and effective administrators and political leaders has finally welded together its vast resources, engineering and scientific skills and large population. Russia's success is patchier and more prosaic: it has used its reserves of oil and gas to demand more from its hapless customers to the west (Chapter 4). Together, Brazil, Russia, India and China are now referred to as the 'BRIC' countries. This is a convenient acronym, which reminds us of the new geopolitical realities, but it should not conceal the fact that there have been significant advances elsewhere. South Africa has shrugged off the constraints of the apartheid system, although the country also benefited from the apartheid government's fiscal conservatism. Turkey's economy is booming. Its rates of urbanization and industrialization are now so dramatic that its prime minister, Recep Tayyip Erdogan, re-elected in 2011, has announced several multi-billion dollar development projects, including new towns and a canal to bypass the Bosporus. Australia has made a successful transition from a mining and agricultural economy to one based on services, and appears to be one of the few developed countries to have emerged relatively unscathed from the recession beginning in 2007. Certain countries in tropical Africa, a region that seemed to be mired in poverty, are also showing significant growth spurts. Nigeria, for example, averaged an annual growth rate of 6% between 2004 and 2010, with little sign that the global recession has hindered its progress. Religious violence in the country may, however, damage its political stability, with ramifications for the economy and social structure.

GLOBAL WARMING AND CLIMATE CHANGE

The economic rise of China, India and a number of other countries has placed additional pressure on finite or shrinking world resources, especially water, fossil fuels, wood, minerals, agricultural land and food. Even without these hothouse economies, most environmental scientists agree that the warming of planet earth through human activities has increased greenhouse gas emissions, leading to climate change. Melting polar icecaps and glaciers, increasingly violent storms and more frequent droughts already provide grim indications of what may be in store. Equally worrying is the likelihood that climate change will aggravate or cause food shortages, environmental migration from low-lying or arid areas, and perhaps large-scale violence. It will also hit hardest those countries that are poor and least able to cope (Chapter 20). The remorseless pressure on the world's resources is likely to persist for at least the next four decades, with the continued growth of the world population – although the rate of increase has slowed – expected to peak at around 9.3 billion by mid-century (Chapter 12).

INCREASING INEQUALITY BOTH WITHIN AND BETWEEN SOCIETIES

For the past 30 years, technological change and more open markets have enabled transnational corporations (TNCs) and financial institutions to move or spread their operations more easily across countries. This has allowed them some leeway in negotiating their tax contributions used in the reproduction of family, educational and infrastructural investment within the countries in which they operate. At the same time, workers are often coerced into accepting a decline in job security or risk plants being relocated elsewhere (Chapter 10). In stark comparison, all but the most highly skilled workers have far less opportunity, if any, to move freely across borders. They also tend to be relatively immobilized by local, cultural and family ties (Chapter 7). There is a growing disparity between economic growth in the leading developing countries and the vast majority left behind, sometimes called the 'Fourth World', where, according to some scholars (for example de Rivero 2001), the possibility of serious economic development is now an illusion.

Unregulated economic globalization constitutes only one reason for growing inequality, but it is certainly a major one. Here, decades of neoliberal, open market economic policies are partly responsible. The dangers of world inequality are many and include the possibility of growing social conflict expressed in the form of racism, Islamophobia and/or genocidal wars that spill outwards, growing crime and violence (much of it against women), and unmanaged migration flows. To these we can add the problems occasioned by the heightened dependence of individuals, families, businesses and governments on credit to supplement inadequate incomes (Chapters 4, 6 and 7).

THE TREND TOWARDS INDIVIDUALIZATION

Hand in hand with the pressures towards globalization is virtually an opposite trend, namely a primary concern with self-realization as one's main purpose in life (Beck and Beck-Gernsheim 2002). Individualization enhances the capacity for self-criticism and greater openness to the world – as we show in Chapters 2 and 15 when we discuss reflexivity. Yet, an obsession with self-realization could equally engender and legitimize a narcissistic, hedonistic, selfish 'me-culture' that overwhelms any sense of social/moral accountability towards one's community or nation, let alone to people in other countries. Even family life, so long a bulwark against wider pressures, has radically changed, simultaneously becoming a site of pleasure, togetherness and intimacy and one of exploitation, oppression and inequality (Chapter 13).

Some thinkers (Kenway et al. 2006; Szerszynski and Urry 2006) suggest that the mass media, the internet and the consumerist world of branded goods offer arenas for creative self-expression while enabling individuals to think of 'themselves as global' (Urry 2000: 185). Equally, however, far from helping to extend people's horizons beyond the local, mass consumer culture, the leisure industry and celebrity lifestyles might reinforce personal vanity and immersion in a private realm of fantasy constructed solely around personal hopes and obsessions. We evaluate these contrasting positions with respect to consumerism in Chapter 14.

THE WORLDWIDE RECESSION

Problems in one economic sector and a few countries – caused partly by the willingness of banks to lend too much unsecured credit to too many borrowers with poor prospects of servicing their debts – started in 2007 and rapidly spread and engulfed banks and financial institutions in many countries across the world. Ultimately, in October 2008, virtually the entire global financial system came close to collapsing, with dire consequences for businesses when they could no longer secure the credit they needed to keep their workers in jobs. Ordinary citizens struggled to access sufficient funds to purchase household goods, cars or properties. We discuss the financial crisis, and its causes and effects, in more detail in Chapter 4.

While optimists thought that the recession was nearly over in mid-2011, the collapse of stock market values in August 2011 showed that many hitherto strong links in the world economy were, in reality, remarkably fragile. In major economies such as the USA, the UK,

Japan and Italy, the recovery remained weak, investor and consumer confidence was low, and unemployment levels were persistently high. The US and European governments alike acted to stave off a depression by bailing out failing banks and injecting massive fiscal stimuli to sustain demand. However, the attempt to pay off the resultant deficits by cutting pensions and welfare payments, and reducing social services, has led to continuing fiscal crises, notably in Greece, Italy, Portugal and Spain, and to considerable social unrest – especially in Greece, Spain, Ireland, Italy, France and the UK. Greece is perhaps the most extreme example of the contradiction between the demand for austerity required by its creditors (the International Monetary Fund and the leading Eurozone countries) and the politics of the street, where many Greek protestors refuse to accept cuts to their benefits, wages, pensions, education and health services.

The emergence from the recession is gradual and uncertain elsewhere too. The German economy looks comparatively strong. Sobered by the long memories of the Great Depression and the two world wars, German people tend to be savers, not spenders. The level of personal debt was low when the crisis hit, and because the rental market remained buoyant, there was no housing 'bubble'. By contrast, the Japanese economy has been flat for a long time and the effects of the tsunami and nuclear accident at Fukushima in 2011 have not helped. Modest growth is predicted for the intermediate future.

SOCIAL PROTEST AND THE AUDACITY OF HOPE

In the USA, the initial popularity of Barack Obama, sworn in as president in January 2009, largely contained radical politics. Many young people in the electorate, using the social media to reach their peers, embraced his optimistic message first articulated at his keynote address to the Democratic National Convention in 2004, when Obama asked his audience to embrace 'the audacity of hope':

> Do we participate in a politics of cynicism or a politics of hope? … It's the hope of slaves sitting around a fire singing freedom songs; the hope of immigrants setting out for distant shores; the hope of a young naval lieutenant bravely patrolling the Mekong Delta; the hope of a millworker's son who dares to defy the odds; the hope of a skinny kid with a funny name who believes that America has a place for him, too. Hope in the face of difficulty. Hope in the face of uncertainty. The audacity of hope! (Obama 2004)

The excitement of the occasion still shines through in the YouTube video (Obama 2004). He appeared to speak to and for a younger, culturally more heterogeneous group. Until the very last moment when US voters entered their voting booths, commentators were still unsure whether Obama's part-black origins would prevent him from being elected, despite his attractions as a candidate and the negative feelings towards an unpopular incumbent Republican president. In the end, Obama triumphed to general acclaim, or perhaps profound relief that the Bush era was over. For the rest of the world, this new president seemed to connect in an important way. His mixed heritage meant that everyone could claim a slice of him. In Kenya, his father's birthplace, the popular Senator Keg beer became known simply as 'Obama'. His speeches, particularly a beautifully crafted address given in the Grand Hall of the University of Cairo in June 2009, appeared to signal the beginning of a new dialogue between the West and the rest. This is an extract from that speech:

> There must be a sustained effort to listen to each other; to learn from each other; to respect one another; and to seek common ground. As the Holy Koran tells us: 'Be conscious of God and speak always the truth.' That is what I will try to do – to speak the truth as best I can, humbled by the task before us, and firm in my belief that the interests we share as human beings are far more powerful than the forces that drive us apart. … Part of this conviction is rooted in my own experience. I am a Christian, but my father came from a Kenyan family that includes generations of Muslims. As a boy, I spent

several years in Indonesia and heard the call of the *azaan* [the Muslim call to prayer] at the break of dawn and the fall of dusk. As a young man, I worked in Chicago communities where many found dignity and peace in their Muslim faith.

Inevitably, the 'audacity of hope' in which Obama asked us to believe has given way to considerable disillusionment. Obama has certainly recognized the power of the emerging economies and has sought to adjust to a more complex and plural world; the mind map of international relations emerging from Washington is less hierarchical and more plural and networked. Power is to be shared and negotiated rather than exercised unilaterally. However, after several years in office, finding peace in the Middle East is as elusive as ever, the war in Afghanistan continues, and there are still prisoners held in Guantanamo Bay, despite the president's promise to close the prison. Above all, Obama has had to show his electorate that he remains a strong president and a merciless enemy of al-Qaeda. In announcing the killing of Osama bin Laden on 2 May 2011, he vowed to continue the decade-long war against al-Qaeda and to defend the USA from any further terrorist attacks. In the US elections in November 2010, the Democratic Party suffered major losses at federal and state levels. Most commentators took this as a negative judgement of President Obama's handling of the economic crisis.

In the USA and most countries of the developed world, social protest has predominantly stayed within the confines of conventional politics, although there have been quite dramatic, and occasionally violent, street protests arising from movements protesting against financial greed, corrupt politicians and welfare cuts, particularly in Spain, Greece and Italy. This anger is also reflected in the Occupy Wall Street movement (Figure 0.1), supported by many of the young people who had put such trust in Obama's candidacy. One survey indicated that 64% of the protesters were less than 34 years of age (Captain 2011). By October 2011 protests had spread, with the help of Facebook and mailing lists, to 82 countries and 950 cities. Other social protests have included marches of tens of thousands of people against what was seen as a rigged election in Russia. However, anger at the state of the world is not only the preserve of the left. The far right has made significant gains in European elections in traditionally social democratic countries like Sweden, Denmark, the Netherlands and Belgium, where xenophobic passions have been inflamed. New migrants and established ethnic minorities provide convenient targets for those in the longstanding populations experiencing social dislocation, unemployment and uncertainty.

FIGURE 0.1 The Occupy Wall Street movement
This movement has galvanized opposition to corporate greed and the bailouts of the banks. Many younger people are involved, while a significant number are students frustrated at their job prospects.

THE ARAB SPRING

Somewhat unexpectedly, the audacity of hope can be recast as the leitmotiv of the events in the Middle East and North Africa commencing in December 2010 and subsequently dubbed 'the Arab Spring'. Starting purportedly (the story has been disputed) in Tunisia, where a vegetable seller resisted a local bureaucrat's orders, strikes, demonstrations and uprisings took place in Tunisia and Egypt (where the protesters achieved a measure of success), and in

Bahrain, Yemen, Iraq, Jordan, Morocco and Algeria. Minor protests have taken place elsewhere in the region. By mid-2011, there was a massive trial of strength between the government and the protestors in Syria, and a violent contest for power in Libya, which culminated in the brutal death of President Gaddafi in October.

The Arab Spring is of crucial significance for at least four reasons:

1. It signifies the power of the ideas of freedom, democracy and constitutional government in a region marked by decades of repressive, authoritarian government.
2. It demonstrates the power to mobilize people through the internet and social networking sites, such as Facebook, Twitter and YouTube.
3. It captures the anger of disillusioned young, educated people whose career ambitions have been thwarted and who remain a potent reminder that inequality and lack of opportunity can destabilize an existing political order.
4. There are some long-term implications for the balance of power between Israel and its neighbours and between the Middle East and Western countries more generally.

While we are in the midst of the uprisings it is difficult to predict their ultimate significance, but it is perhaps useful to reproduce the notably cautious note struck by Benantar (2011: 7):

> The Arab democratic uprisings are facing two major challenges. *The first* one is a genuine transformation: the revolts have to effect a real change of regimes, not just a change within current regimes. The democratic process is hard and long and the democratic learning curve a steep one. The Arab people have taken the first step, but the counter-democratic forces are still in power in many states including Tunisia and Egypt. *The second* one is the role of the major external actors which try to influence the Arab democratic process in order to preserve a kind of right of control over the emerging democracies. Many external powers prefer a limited democracy in the Arab world: sufficient to overthrow authoritarianism and to calm popular fervor but limited to the extent of being truly independent from foreign influence.

The Arab Spring has since spawned a wave of supposedly copycat protests in other parts of the world, but the resemblances are often imperfect. 'The Chilean winter' comprised the mobilization of students, angry at educational reforms, but also at the authoritarian style of the Chilean government. In Israel, 250,000 people took to the streets demanding a reduction in housing costs and in frustration at the neoliberal policies of the country. Interestingly, at least some elements of the protest movement want the Israeli government to open a more fruitful dialogue with its Arab neighbours. In the UK, demonstrations against the harsh policing of the black community turned into a destructive spree, accompanied by looting of popular consumer goods. In all these events, mobile phones (in particular) were used to direct and energize the protesters.

SOCIOLOGY'S CONTRIBUTION TO UNDERSTANDING GLOBAL ISSUES

In trying to explore the interactions, transactions and processes that arise at a global level, sociologists sometimes employ insights from other social sciences – notably economics, political science, anthropology and history. Certain theories and methods, however, are intrinsic to the discipline and many teachers insist that their students understand the evolution of the ideas of the pioneers of sociology. While there is a lot to be said for interdisciplinary and multidisciplinary perspectives, we think it is important first to gain some command of the fundamental theories, methods, findings and sensibilities of your chosen discipline. Before indicating the distinctive contribution of sociology, however, we will make a few remarks here about political science, economics and political economy.

Political scientists examine the policies and decisions that governments and political elites make in response to electoral outcomes and the lobbies of various interest groups; the main focus is on the national level. International relations – the branch of political studies that focuses on the global sphere – is primarily concerned with relations between competing nation-states in an inherently anarchic world. In both cases, the emphasis tends to be on large organizations and institutions – governments, parliaments, ministries, or intergovernmental organizations such as the United Nations (UN) or World Bank. How do the elites who manage and control these bodies win power, reach international agreements, formulate policies and make decisions? Scholarly work in this area has cast light on global political life, especially on new global attempts to solve world problems through intergovernmental laws and agreements. This focus on the macro level, however, gives us little understanding of how ordinary people and social groups can, could or actually do help shape global processes. This is a serious limitation for our purposes.

Economics is primarily concerned with the rational decisions that entrepreneurs make to maximize their profits and consumers make to satisfy their needs or wants. A market economy governed by competition and a price mechanism supposedly guarantees two benefits – maximization of social welfare for the majority and efficient deployment of scarce resources in the overall economy (Keen 2001: 39). Moreover, it permits individuals to seek their private and selfish goals. To understand how this supposedly works in practice, economists adopt assumptions about how individuals make rational choices. They then deploy theoretical arguments and models – some requiring highly complex mathematical formulations – to aggregate these assumptions so they can understand how an entire economy reaches equilibrium in the supply and demand for goods.

While economics has delivered some impressive results, particularly using multivariate and regression analyses, the discipline has also attracted fierce criticism, particularly in the wake of the recession commencing in 2007. At heart, the models and assumptions that most economists use depend on implausible, abstract individuals. It is difficult to take seriously the idea that individuals invariably make rational, informed decisions based solely on price, opportunity and market signals. Actual consumers often fall into debt through pursuing lifestyles shaped by powerful advertising. Similarly, speculative bubbles frequently occur when investors irrationally buy into or escape from markets in currencies, commodities, government bonds or equities. As Keen (2001: 239) suggested, instead of looking 'dispassionately at investment prospects and world economic conditions', investors are likely to 'look furtively and emotionally at each other' – displaying a kind of herd instinct – as they try to predict, then follow, how other investors will evaluate government policies, the strength of different companies and the lure of new opportunities. Unusually for a discipline whose practitioners have normally expressed considerable self-confidence in their theory and methods, some key economists are now seeking to reform their profession. A good example is the Institute for New Economic Thinking (INET), founded at King's College London in October 2009, with the financial help of George Soros, the well-known investor with a penchant for new ideas. According to its opening credo, the institute

> recognizes problems and inadequacies within our current economic system and the modes of thought used to comprehend recent and past catastrophic developments in the world economy. The institute embraces the professional responsibility to think beyond these inadequate methods and models and will support the emergence of new paradigms in the understanding of economic processes. (INET 2010)

Because it focuses on the power relations behind international trade regimes, national and global patterns of inequality, and the successes or failures of national economic development programmes, the subdiscipline of political economy is more useful for understanding global changes. We align ourselves with a number of key propositions in political economy and several of our earlier chapters reflect this perspective. Through sociology, however, one can go further. In particular, the discipline facilitates the examination of areas of human endeavour about which neither conventional economics nor political science can tell us much. This is partly because the scope of sociological research is not confined to one dimension of human experience, but encourages one to explore how these spheres interact with each other and with people's cultural and social activities. In addition, sociologists are interested in the everyday, personal micro relations, affiliations and social interactions of real – not abstract – social actors. Naturally, we are aware that these social relations are embedded in vast macro structures and institutions controlled by various political, financial and cultural elites and driven by impersonal forces such as market pressures. We are especially interested in how individuals perceive, react to or cope with incoming global forces or even how they learn to surf the vast waves of global life and mesh them in some small way into their private micro worlds.

Sociologists are vitally interested in investigating how the interpersonal, micro relations that social actors deploy help to shape global processes, whether they operate as individuals, in friendship groups, as small businesses, social networks or as families. Global social actors include migrants, tourists, consumers, professionals, students, criminal gangs, users of the internet and social networking forums, and cross-national marriage partners. In these and other ways sociology fills the gaps, opens to scrutiny and makes sense of those rather large empty spaces of missing knowledge that other social science disciplines mostly neglect. In the pages that follow we shall endeavour to show how you can better understand your world, at the personal, social and, especially, global levels.

THE ORGANIZATION OF THIS BOOK

This book is divided into four parts, with the following broad themes:

1. the *interpretations* that have been used to explain our increasingly globalizing world (Chapters 1–5)
2. the *divisions and inequalities* induced by global changes (Chapters 6–11)
3. the *experiences* of individuals, social groups, families and urban residents (Chapters 12–18)
4. the *dynamics and challenges* facing an emerging global society (Chapters 19–22).

INTERPRETATIONS

In Chapter 1, we discuss how sociology as a discipline evolved, what it explains and some of its limitations. We show that some of the building blocks of the discipline, such as the notion of 'community', worked well at a local level; while others, such as 'society', were more or less synonymous with the nation-state. As social, cultural, economic and political changes began to assume a global character, late twentieth-century sociologists had to adapt some of their ideas and perspectives to a global scale. In Chapter 2, we draw you into our understanding of two key concepts, 'globalization' and 'globality', necessary direction finders for our long intellectual journey. The first concept has now spread into common usage and is often found in magazines and newspapers. It refers to the ways in which the world is being knitted together by the increased volume and speed of cross-border transactions. Globalization, particularly of social and cultural activities, leads to the elaboration of a second and less well-rehearsed concept, the idea of globality. Whereas globalization refers to the objective, external ties that bind us together, globality alludes to the subjective, personal awareness that many of us share and are increasingly likely to share – a common fate.

A major theme of this book (and an abiding concern of sociology) is how social change arises and becomes diffused. Despite the ubiquity of contemporary means of transport, globalization and globality have not been dropped from the sky by passing aircraft. They are the outcomes of a long evolutionary process whereby small isolated societies and large civilizations came to relate to one another. In Chapter 3, we situate the moments when human-kind became increasingly capable of understanding itself collectively. Contacts arose from long-distance trade, from the spread of world religions such as Islam, Buddhism and Christianity, and from the force of colonialism and imperialism. The idea of a universal humanity was developed particularly by European Enlightenment thinkers who, although they recognized that there were 'backward regions', thought all were capable of reaching the end state of modernity.

In Chapter 4, we depict substantive changes in the world of work. Rapid and unprecedented technological change and intensifying international competition have led to economic insecurity and the internationalization of work. The more vulnerable position of women has led to the feminization of work. The development of flexible labour markets has also led to the casualization of work. For the winners, particularly those with portable skills in growing sectors like the information-related industries, these changes herald 'new times' – offering opportunities for greater individual freedom and self-realization and a more democratic, decentralized, less hierarchical workplace and society. The losers see only 'hard times' – dominated by fragmenting businesses, labour redundancies and part-time and poorly paid jobs. The crisis induced by the 'financialization' of the global economy since the 1980s is also considered.

The nation-state is a relatively recent political organization, dating in its complete form from the French Revolution. Nation-states replaced multinational kingdoms, principalities, religious domains and empires. In Chapter 5, we consider whether globalization inevitably means that there will be a decline in the power and influence of the nation-state. We look at the changing role of the state, in particular at the transition from the Bush to the Obama presidencies and what this implies for future state relations.

DIVISIONS AND INEQUALITIES

Global changes are overlaid on prior inequalities between people and serve also to introduce new lines of dominance and subordination. Sociologists have always given much thought to the problem of how to conceptualize and explain the forms of inequality found in all societies and the ways in which these vary both between societies and over time. The unequal distribution of power, wealth, income and social status between individuals and groups is not random but is patterned or structured. Some groups are marginalized; others enter the charmed circle of privilege and security. In Chapters 6 and 7, we provide an account for the extremes of poverty and wealth, power and powerlessness in today's world. According to some theorists, whose views are examined in Chapter 8, the system is rigged to protect the interests of the leading players. Can those who lose out ever alter their place in the pecking order? Could it be to the ultimate benefit of the powerful that the poor achieve some upward social mobility and raise their standards of living? Can social uplift be induced from the top, for example through the actions of benign social democratic politicians? Alternatively, will the only redress come from oppositional social and political movements emanating from the grassroots level?

Those who die from famine, natural disasters or in civil wars are the ultimate global losers, but other groups are also highly vulnerable. As the race gets faster, those at the back – groups such as the unskilled, the unemployed, those who experience discrimination and the urban poor – appear to be trailing even further behind. We probe the condition and possible trajectories of some of the victims of recent global changes, probing the ways sociologists have grappled with various schemes to understand how these forms of inequality and disadvantage arise and how global change perpetuates, modifies or enhances them. In Chapter 7, we concentrate on class, noting the development of an unprotected working class, dubbed a 'precariat'. In Chapter 8, we consider forms of hierarchy based on gender and the various ways in which women's networks have moved to a global scale of activity. Next, in Chapter 9, we examine the origins and manifestations of race and racism from a biological, historical and sociological perspective. The interaction of inequalities based on class, gender and race is discussed using the idea of 'intersectionality'.

Chapter 10, the final chapter in Part 2, centres on corporate power. We show how TNCs have become dominant players in global affairs. They profit from the increased level of economic globalization and indeed can be said partially to cause this outcome. Are these ubiquitous organizations the Trojan horses, or perhaps the battering rams, of international capital? Such is their power and influence that they are often accused of dictating to rich and powerful states, while completely overwhelming poor states. What is their economic role in integrating the global economy? What are the social consequences, positive and negative, of TNCs' activities?

EXPERIENCES

As we have explained, one of the great strengths of sociology is its focus on the behaviour of people, whose lives are increasingly meshed in global flows. For example, the flows of tourists, international communications, new forms of transnational urban, cultural and sporting life, and the more intense globalization of many religions create unsettling experiences for people in all nation-states and across national frontiers. Part 3 analyses these experiences. In Chapter 11, we look at how global crime and particularly the drugs trade impact on the lives on consumers and producers. Those who principally profit from the trade are the 'drug barons', the smugglers and the dealers. But it is difficult to eliminate the trade while it forms so vital a part of the cash income gained by poor farmers in countries like Afghanistan, Nepal and Jamaica and while the demand for recreational and addictive drugs in rich countries seems insatiable. Also in Chapter 9, we provide a wider context in which to understand the origins and character of terror and terrorism and how violence has affected the welfare of many women.

To both popular opinion and concerned policy-makers, population growth is one of the most critical problems facing the world. Under intense pressure, politicians have sanctioned or encouraged extreme measures to control population. But, as we argue in Chapter 12, we need to distinguish evidence about population growth from prediction, projection and prejudice, and we need to question whether measures to control migration and population growth are appropriate and effective. Only a small proportion of the world's population consists of international migrants, but numbers alone are not the major driving force to control and restrict global migration. International migrants can bring highly motivated labour, economic skills and cultural renewal to many countries. They fill gaps in the labour market, particularly in affluent Western countries where the population is ageing and fertility is low. Nonetheless, they have managed to inflame public sentiments in many countries and politicians have consequently sought to control and restrict their movement.

In Chapter 13, we adopt a global approach to the study of family and intimacy and ask what happens to family relationships under conditions of globalization. Looking particularly at the UK and Japan, we examine how family structures and everyday family life differ across the globe. What are the rituals of intimacy? How do we negotiate our rights and responsibilities towards our families? We start by examining early sociological analyses of the family and consider the contribution that feminist scholars have made to family sociology. We then assess whether individualization theories are an accurate characterization of what has been happening to family relationships lately.

Drink a cup of coffee or tea and you instantly connect to the global marketplace. The list of world goods that arrives in this way is formidable and grows all the time. World goods are products that in whole or part are grown, processed, packed, manufactured, recorded, filmed or staged in a multiplicity of locations often far from the place where we finally purchase and experience them. In Chapter 14, we look at the effect of multiple sourcing. In particular, we ask whether we have become easy targets to those who wish to sell us consumer goods or whether consumers have been empowered by the choice available in the global marketplace.

We are increasingly aware that our purchases and possessions also carry various meanings, from the discreet logos of an exclusive brand to the 'in your face' messages that many consumers emblazon on their T-shirts.

In Chapter 15, we show how forms of identity based on lifestyle and leisure have replaced or augmented earlier bonds of loyalty and association based on family, community, nation and work. With increased affluence and the fragmentation of class loyalties, many people in affluent and poorer countries alike are constructing a life narrative around their participation in leisure activities like sport and tourism. We discuss both these activities. The rise of mass international tourism necessarily involves the mobility of people who have an opportunity to engage in direct social exchanges with hosts and who experience other societies at first hand. This creates at least the possibility of shared cross-cultural experiences.

Girding the globe are lines of communication that snake along the seabed, stretch across the terrain and bounce from satellites to earth. As we look at the ubiquitous television screens, our sense of distance from other places and other societies suddenly shrinks into insignificance. We live, in a famous phrase, in a 'global village'. As is made clear in Chapter 16, who controls the media and channels of communications and for what purposes provide important sociological data. We also discuss the significance of the telephone, particularly the mobile phone, along with the arrival of linked computer networks, as a mass consumer good. These have rocketed information – its processing, storage, creation and distribution – to a central place in the national and global economy. We also consider the newly important role of the social media.

For sociologists, the key issue is not whether religion is 'true' or 'false', but why it manifests itself in all societies, what meanings are invested in it, and what social functions it provides. Other pertinent questions raised in Chapter 17 include whether there is a long-term tendency towards secularization (the normal finding that is still accepted by many sociologists), or whether we are experiencing a significant and long-term revival of religious sentiment. We review what sociologists have contributed to the study of religion, consider why religion has claimed so powerful a place in contemporary life, examine how the global claims of religion are advanced, and ask whether the practice of religion provides a threat to social cohesion or is a means of attaining that condition.

For much of human history, life was rural. In the year 1800, 97% of the world's population lived in rural areas. Fast forward to the year 2000 and we find that 254 cities each contained over 1 million people. The forms of settlement and the ways people lived in cities became the sites of study by some of the world's most eminent sociologists. Durkheim described the transition from 'mechanical' to 'organic' forms of solidarity; Simmel saw large cities as inducing anonymity, loneliness and the sense of being a stranger, while Park and Burgess at the University of Chicago looked at the 'ecological patterning' and spatial distribution of urban groups. As we explain in Chapter 18, in the current era, certain cities, called 'global cities', are emerging, with residents sharing conditions of life, attitudes, behaviour patterns and tastes with equivalent residents of other global cities rather more than with their co-citizens living in the hinterlands. They might lose their national culture or downgrade it in favour of an international and cosmopolitan culture.

DYNAMICS AND CHALLENGES

All too often, the literature of globalization assumes that people are mere chaff in the wind, unable to influence the nature and direction of social change. In Part 4, we question this assumption and show how global social movements have emerged or been re-energized. These movements connect struggles at different levels, attempt to reshape the emerging world order and seek to create democratic and participatory possibilities. In Chapter 19, we show how the public sphere is gradually widening as an informed citizenry uses access to information and the growing possibility for mobilization to develop organizations that are both free from state interference and able to challenge its authority. Having such a civil society is properly regarded as a sign that people are, at least potentially, capable of taking on state power and globalization, both often depicted as inanimate forces, playing out their logic without human intervention. When social organizations are involved in creating links and networks to advance their particular causes they are called 'social movements', and when they operate transnationally, 'global social movements'.

One of the most influential and visible global social movements is the environmental or green movement, discussed in Chapter 20. The development of an environmental movement is a major reversal of the prevailing nineteenth-century idea of unquestioned progress and civilization. The increased consciousness of the threat of global warming has finally mobilized the leaders of some powerful nation-states into effecting international agreements to control carbon dioxide emissions and making largely rhetorical commitments to protect the environment. However, the power of the energy lobby in the USA and the massive use of non-sustainable energy by China in its breakneck thrust to industrialization are both important constraints in developing a viable global environmental strategy to protect our vulnerable world.

The creation of strong social bonds is one of the most powerful of human impulses and, as we have seen, is an abiding concern for sociologists. Paradoxically, for some the threat of globalization often reinforces family and kinship and other local attachments, ethnic sentiments and religious beliefs. Many people seem to need to belong to closely knit groups that protect their sense of self and provide a feeling of wellbeing and security. As we explain in Chapter 21, this tendency is usefully understood as 'identity formation', a process that happens at a number of levels. Often identity formation can be benign, for example in looking after the welfare of one's family, including infants or vulnerable seniors. However, the subnational level where ethnic groups, sharing a common descent, religion or language, are mobilized often generates enormous tensions. The global age has thus produced an unexpected and even perverse outcome. Despite, or perhaps because of, the pressures to come together, fierce struggles have ensued to keep people apart. Although we lay emphasis on 'localism' – to encompass movements based on religion, race, ethnicity and subnational sentiments – we also reflect the possibility of people creating ties between themselves that foretoken the development of transnational and cosmopolitan consciousness.

In Chapter 22, we conclude by considering the continuing controversies and emerging debates in global sociology. One debate revolves around the extent of globalization and the differing reactions to it. We use some convincing empirical research to show that globalization is indeed a powerful and growing force in the contemporary world. There are those who support, decry or wish to reform aspects of globalization. While the reformers have made some progress in the attempts to change the global order, there has been little headway made at the level of constructing an ideological alternative to neoliberalism, which has occasioned such a massive shock to the functioning of the world economy and society. The collapse of cherished ideologies (like communism) and the near collapse of the certainties of neoliberalism have allowed some space for alternative, even utopian, thinking. Hopefully, this will give us some new conceptions and new ways forward. In particular, we argue that global public policy needs to develop in five areas – reviving mutuality, managing difference, creating greater equality, promoting a more pervasive democracy, and developing a sustainable economic and environmental model.

PART 1
Interpretations

1
The making of global sociology

In this chapter we shall look first at some of the key starting points for sociologists and some milestones in the discipline's development. The founders of the discipline made ambitious and universal claims, positioning the discipline as a general science of humankind. However, for a long time the primary concern was to construct sociologies that made sense of particular nations and their societies. To an extent this inhibited or delayed the move towards a more transnational outlook. Accordingly, we also examine the more recent theoretical and substantive changes that have prompted some sociologists to develop concepts, theories and approaches that make sense of the more complex and interconnected world we now see around us – a global sociology. Although seeing the discipline through a global perspective is becoming more and more common, not all sociologists would agree that this should henceforth be the sole preoccupation of the profession. Nonetheless, we hope to convince you that further developing a global sociology is, indeed, a vital and necessary goal that gives crucial insights into our evolving world.

KEY STARTING POINTS IN SOCIOLOGY

Sociology developed in nineteenth-century Europe by positioning itself against prior bodies of knowledge, notably philosophy, history and theology. All three were seen as unable to capture the import and drama of industrialization, urbanization and revolution, processes that were rapidly transforming the modern world.

SOCIOLOGY AS SCIENCE

Like economists and political scientists, sociologists aligned themselves to an emerging body of secular scientific thought known as the Enlightenment (see Chapter 3). Auguste Comte (1798–1857), who coined the term 'sociology', argued that the gradual understanding of scientific laws would make sociology the governing science that glued all other forms of science together. For this to happen, observation, experiment, comparison and history would be utilized to enhance the scientific claims of the discipline (Kreis 2000).

Comte's influence eventually gave rise to an approach called 'positivism'. This can briefly be defined as the attempt to discover, measure and analyse regularities and patterns in social behaviour in an attempt to minimize the influence of the sociologist's own (value-laden) interpretations. Of course, unlike the natural sciences, sociologists cannot ethically conduct controlled experiments on people in the same way that laboratory scientists can manipulate or dissect living, non-human creatures to conduct and test their research, although the latter are also subject to growing ethical scrutiny and regulation. Nonetheless, using large data sets, for example from censuses and aggregate data on income and expenditure, through complicated statistical calculations (such as multivariate analyses), and by comparisons across space and time, sociologists have been able to offset, although not completely obviate, some of their initial scientific disadvantages.

SOCIOLOGY AS THE COMPARATIVE STUDY OF SOCIAL LIFE AND SOCIETY

Perhaps the most obvious and crucial characteristic of humankind is that practically everybody lives collectively in what is generally termed 'society'. Hermits throughout history constitute an interesting exception, although even they often re-enter social life after undergoing a period of spiritual renewal (France 1996: Ch. 1). In any case, we need to make the obvious point that if we all dispersed to live by ourselves, humankind would disappear.

Thus, we are social creatures, so share certain attributes and behave in certain common ways that do not rely on our individual beliefs, nationalities, ages, gender, statuses or wealth, important as these and other factors are in describing how we differ. At the same time, we do not have to experience biological modification (understood in the Darwinian sense of evolution) to adjust to large-scale changes, for example in the move from preindustrial to industrial society, or in the phenomenon that interests us, the move towards a more global society. We can record our actions, recall our history, reflect backwards and project forwards. We can stick to old ways or adopt new ideas. This makes the tasks of sociologists different from and more complicated than those of biologists, who can assume that inherited characteristics largely control animal behaviour (Elias 1978: 108). To investigate our more complex subject matter, we therefore have to look at how particular societies have evolved, compare them with others, and consider which social changes and behavioural patterns seem to be universal or, by contrast, which seem to be particular to one society or cluster of societies.

SOCIOLOGY AS IMAGINATIVE UNDERSTANDING

Any consideration of variations in social conduct between societies raises the question of whether scientific sociologists can really understand all the fine grains of human behaviour and social interaction through formal methods and statistical techniques. We must recognize that positivist sociologists have achieved much in accumulating reliable information, developing testable concepts (called 'hypotheses'), refining research techniques to ensure greater reliability, and producing a body of social policy. In the case of the latter, their work has informed governments on everything from the causes of crime and football hooliganism to social mobility (how people move up and down the class and occupational structure) and the value of educational attainment. Nevertheless, other approaches have emerged and flourish alongside positivism, complementing its insights.

Especially important here is the interest in the 'the self' or the 'subjective' in social life, a crucial dimension that is largely missing in statistically led sociology. This takes us into the meaning of a particular act – the meaning, that is, to the social actor, to other social actors or to an outside observer, who may or may not be a sociologist. To address this issue, the great German sociologist Max Weber (in Coser and Rosenberg 1976: 213–14, 219) called for *Verstehen* – loosely translated as 'understanding', but in one sense better thought of as 'insight' or even 'empathy'. *Aktuelles Verstehen* is a form of superficial, immediate understanding, while *erklärendes Verstehen* probes motivations, intentions and context to give a deeper meaning or possible interpretation.

Subjective or interpretative sociology gained its most powerful expression in what is known as 'symbolic interactionism', a label applied to a group of sociologists working in Chicago who followed Weber's emphasis on *Verstehen*. As Rock (1996a: 859) explains, symbolic interactionists argue that knowledge is not a simple mirror of an object. Rather, 'people actively create, shape and select their response to what is around them. Knowledge is then presented as an active process in which people, their understanding and [external] phenomena are bound together.' Sociologists working in this tradition seek to get inside people's skins, as it were, to see how social actors (as well as others around them) understand situations symbolically and literally. This is particularly important when the subjects are not respectable or conventional citizens and are the objects of all manner of prejudices and stereotypes. Sociologists working in this tradition often explore the social worlds of criminals, prostitutes, drug users, HIV sufferers, sexual deviants and gang members.

SOCIOLOGY AND THE SEARCH FOR KNOWLEDGE

Honesty and integrity are at the heart of any genuine search for knowledge. This means that sociologists, like other scientists (*scientia* is the Latin word for 'knowledge', so there is no reason to be diffident about using the expression), cannot start by assuming the answer. We have to let the facts speak for themselves, honestly report the answers our respondents give, faithfully record our observations and not twist arguments to suit our private purposes or political positions. For positivist sociologists this is so self-evident it is barely worth mentioning. Those working on comparative and historical sociology and those in the interpretative tradition also seek to follow scientific procedures and methodologies.

A PAUSE TO REFLECT

Some sociologists suggest that, despite showing honesty and integrity in conducting their research, it is difficult to exclude the values and beliefs they hold. Precisely because we are human and engaged in research on the human condition, we may find ourselves 'taking sides'. Is there bound to be bias in sociological research? Can this be minimized by insisting that sociologists openly declare their values before they report their findings?

The search for sociological knowledge may, however, mean that the inadequacies of public policy become all too evident. Sociologists often uncover policies that are ineffective, destructive, produce unintended consequences, or are ethically indefensible. The subjects of their research often may challenge official characterizations, but may also throw the sociologist off guard. In revealing findings that contradict their own assumptions and beliefs, sociologists are expected to be even more meticulous in their research reports. Taking two examples may make the argument clearer. Let us suppose you are a researcher with strong feminist views and most of the people you question say they love to look glamorous and depend greatly on the attentions of enraptured males to make them feel good about themselves. Suppose again you are a sociologist with Marxist views and your working-class respondents say that they have no sympathy with their fellow workers. In fact, many cannot wait to make enough money to send their children to posh schools so they can escape their class background. You may not like these answers, but you have faithfully to report them. Nor should you at any point prompt or suggest an answer. To do so may mean receiving the answer you want to hear (many people will effect a friendly consensus with interviewers or perhaps just want to get rid of them), but you would thereby be engaged in an ideological, not a sociological, exercise. Because we are human and dealing with human behaviour (not something like carbon dioxide emissions, atomic matter or molecules), it is even more important that we do not cheat.

SOCIOLOGY AS CRITIQUE AND ITS PUBLIC RESPONSIBILITY

Being careful to ensure that our evidence and research methods reach a standard above reproach does not prevent us from commenting on the great moral issues of our time, such as war, poverty, financial crises or inequality. In addressing these issues, sociologists are divided. Some centre their work on professional recognition and remain within academia, while others work with policy-makers. Others again feel the need to engage with the public and see that as a legitimate extension of their roles as sociologists. Burawoy (2005) avers that although there are some overlaps between these categories and some of us move between them, we now, in effect, practise four kinds of sociology – professional, critical, policy and public (Table 1.1).

TABLE 1.1 Burawoy's four types of sociology		
Type of sociology	Common cognitive practices	Target audience
Professional sociology	Advanced theoretical and empirical work, using explicit scientific norms	Peers, those who read professional journals
Critical sociology	Foundational and normative, driven by moral vision	Critical intellectuals, those who engage in internal debates about sociology
Policy sociology	Empirical, concrete, applied and pragmatic	Policy-makers in government, business and the media
Public sociology	More accessible/relevant theoretical and empirical work, lectures and media appearances	Designated publics including students, the local community and religious groups

Source: Adapted from Burawoy (2005).

SOME MILESTONES IN THE HISTORY OF SOCIOLOGY

THE FRENCH REVOLUTION

A series of social upheavals that began in 1789 with peasant revolt, monarchical collapse and moderate middle-class leadership. From 1793 to 1795, the urban poor of Paris and other cities, led by radicals such as Robespierre, pushed the revolution in a more violent and nationalist direction. An increasing involvement in European wars also led to the successful mass mobilization of citizen armies and the centralization of power.

As we have mentioned, the discipline of sociology is much older than many of its students believe. It has its roots in the period after the French Revolution when political conflict, rapid urbanization and social turmoil convulsed European societies.

Intellectuals sought to explain both the bewildering chaos and the new possibilities around them. Karl Marx, for example, saw the French Revolution and the European revolutions of 1830 and 1848 as harbingers of a new revolutionary order that a class-conscious and politically motivated working class (he called workers the 'proletariat' after the dispossessed class of ancient Rome) would usher in. Box 1.1 is a summary of some of the most important developments in sociological thought from the mid-nineteenth century to the present day. It indicates how involvement in the discipline spread beyond the first industrial societies.

BOX 1.1 Timeline in sociology

1842 The publication of *Positive Philosophy* (1853) by **Auguste Comte** (1798–1857). Comte wanted to find regularities, even laws, in social life that resembled Newtonian physics. He allied sociology to the scientific models of the Enlightenment. His ideas were linked to those of scholars in the other two major social sciences – economics and political science. They dismissed philosophy as too speculative, theology as the rationalization of superstition, and history as too subjective and superficial. These writers saw themselves as champions of a new way of understanding reality. They wanted to establish general laws of human behaviour, to formulate hypotheses that could be tested, and to develop strict scientific methods (Wallerstein 1996: 31).

1848   The publication of *The Communist Manifesto* by **Karl Marx** and **Friedrich Engels** ([1848]1967), who argued in this influential pamphlet that: 'The history of all hitherto existing society is the history of class struggles.' They saw an increasing impoverishment of the workers, whom, they thought, would become class-conscious and throw off the yoke of capitalism. Karl Marx (1818–83), who worked in Germany, France and Britain, saw the waves of rebellion in 1830 and 1848 as ushering in a new era of social revolution. He was consequently interested in class conflict and the dynamics of large-scale social change. He sought to be international in his outlook. Marx wrote on India and the USA and, as his socialist ideas caught hold, he found himself in dialogue with revolutionaries from Russia to Cuba. **Eleanor Marx**, his daughter, became a pioneer feminist thinker and agitator.

1874   The publication of **Herbert Spencer**'s (1820–1903) *Principles of Sociology* (1902). He proposed an organic theory of society (likening it to a living organism) and was preoccupied with slow, long-term evolutionary change. His work paralleled Charles Darwin's writings on the animal and plant worlds. Incidentally, it was he, not Darwin, who coined the expression 'the survival of the fittest', a notion that resonated well with the unregulated capitalism of the period.

1892   The foundation of the first department of sociology in the USA. Three years later, the *American Journal of Sociology*, still the leading journal in the field, was established. The discipline was often concerned with the adaptation of new immigrants to their new settings, urban settlement patterns (the 'Chicago School' produced celebrated studies in this field), industrial relations and community studies.

1898   In France, the renowned French sociologist **Emile Durkheim** (1858–1917) founded *L'Année sociologique*. This journal contained material on law, customs, religion and social statistics. Durkheim concentrated on the elements that bind societies together, an issue close to the heart of a society that had experienced the disintegrating effects of revolution and an invasion (in 1871) by Prussia. Durkheim understood that his discussion of how social order and consensus were to be reached necessarily involved comparison with other groups. He tried to understand the religious practices of the Australian Aborigines and systematically collected statistics from a number of European countries to undertake his famous study of suicide.

1905   The publication in German of **Max Weber**'s (1864–1920) most famous book *The Protestant Ethic and the Spirit of Capitalism* (1977). In addition to work on his native Germany, Weber wrote on Spain, Italy and ancient Rome and was fascinated by the different ways in which religious belief facilitated or inhibited the development of capitalism. He was the first sociologist of comparative religion, having examined Hinduism, Confucianism, Buddhism and Judaism, in addition to his well-known studies of Protestantism. He also sketched out an ambitious study of Islam. In his engagement with Marxism, he sought to develop a holistic sociology that added to the issue of class identities, questions of status, political power and values, which together would define the opportunity structure available to people.

1907   Britain's first chair in sociology was endowed by Martin White, a Scottish businessman. It was held jointly at the London School of Economics by **Edvard Westermarck** (1862–1939) and **Leonard Trelawny Hobhouse** (1864–1929). They made pioneering contributions to methodology, the study of social justice and family life.

1959   **Mysore Narasimhachar Srinivas** (1916–99) was invited to Delhi University to establish and head the Department of Sociology at the Delhi School of Economics, founded in emulation of the London School of Economics (see Figure 1.1). In his *Religion and Society among the Coorgs of South India* (1952), Srinivas showed that the caste system was much more porous than Western scholars had assumed. Lower castes facilitated social mobility by adopting the language and social habits of higher castes – a process Srinivas described as 'Sanskritization'. Srinivas made an important start in establishing and promoting the discipline in the world's second most populated country.

1979   The foundation of the Chinese Sociological Association in the largest country in the world after years when the Communist Party of China was suspicious of the discipline. Professor **Fei Xiaotong** (1910–2005) was elected as its first and second chairperson. According to its website (http://219.141.235.75/

english/Associations/CSA/t20050105_4298.htm), the association aims to 'undertake sociological research in light of China's practices with a view to develop the academic cause of sociology and serve the socialism-building of a prosperous, democratic and modernized China'.

1994   Sociologist **Fernando Henrique Cardoso** (1931–) was elected in a landslide victory to the presidency of Brazil (see Figure 1.2). (Cardoso was previously the president of the International Sociological Association.) Although re-elected to a historical second term, he lost to Luiz Inácio Lula da Silva (the left-wing candidate) in 2004.

1999   **Anthony Giddens** (1938–), well-known British sociologist, then director of the London School of Economics, took 'The Runaway World' (what is commonly called globalization) as the theme of his Reith lectures, the BBC's prestigious annual series of lectures.

2001   The number of current serving UK university vice-chancellors (equivalent to presidents of US universities) included seven established sociologists.

2006   The International Sociological Association held its periodic conference on the continent of Africa for the first time ever. The theme of the ISA World Congress of Sociology was 'The Quality of Social Existence in a Globalising World'.

2011   The death of the Harvard sociologist Daniel Bell (1919–2011), whose book *The End of Ideology* (1960) was chosen by the *Times Literary Supplement* in 1995 as one of the 100 most influential books since the Second World War. He argued that meta-ideologies, such as communism, liberalism or socialism, were no longer credible and that social change was better effected by small technical fixes and social policy adjustments.

FIGURE 1.1 Mysore Narasimhachar Srinivas (1916–99)
One of India's most distinguished sociologists, his work on how lower castes emulated higher castes and on village life in India has helped to explain this complex society to non-Indians and Indians alike.

FIGURE 1.2 Fernando Henrique Cardoso (1931–)
Former president of Brazil and earlier of the International Sociological Association. He undertook major research on Brazil's poorer regions and on dependency theory. He speaks English, French, Portuguese and Spanish fluently.

THE GLOBAL TURN IN SOCIOLOGICAL THINKING

Two main processes mark sociology's move towards developing a global perspective. First, many scholars associated with the sociology of advanced Western countries have looked outwards towards societies very different from their own. Simultaneously, scholars from an ever widening range of societies have been adding their insights to the discipline. An emerging concern has been that a changing world of growing interconnectivities requires a different, much broader kind of sociological analysis (explored in detail in Chapter 2). Here we examine how these broadening processes gradually took shape through the work of various sociologists. Second, the reality of a more dangerous world in which crises, dilemmas and puzzling opportunities – some new – press in on us in multiple ways also drives the need for a global sociology. Thus, like other disciplines, sociology must expand its geographical and intellectual horizons – recognizing that profound changes at the global level are challenging the nature of local communities and national societies. We outline some of these transformations later in the chapter.

TRYING TO BREAK AWAY FROM NATIONAL ORIENTATIONS

An important limitation of sociology is that, despite the universalizing ambitions of a number of its founding figures, it has taken a long while to expand beyond its heartland in Western industrial societies. This was partly because the study of non-Western societies was, at first, left to anthropologists who, in describing the unusual and exotic, failed to develop general laws applicable to all humanity. Their preoccupations more or less propelled them to find difference rather than commonality.

Looking back at the period of colonialism, one can see that anthropologists were often constrained by their professional preoccupations and close links to colonial governments (Asad 1974; Lewis 1973). However, social and cultural anthropologists also defended the integrity of the people among whom they worked against what they considered the corrupting influences of colonial administrators, traders and missionaries. Canadian fur traders bribing Hurons with whisky or the spreading of fatal venereal disease to the Polynesians were hardly edifying moments in the history of encounters between European and non-European people. It is too late, however, to wrap people in cellophane and freeze them in a time warp. Our increasing interconnectivities make it impossible to preserve tribal iceboxes or human zoos. In the wake of the 1948 Universal Declaration of Human Rights, we live in an interdependent, globalizing world. We cannot explain differences between peoples simply by giving each of them a different voice. We need to find ways of comprehending and comparing societies and peoples that apply from Afghanistan to Zimbabwe, from the Aborigine to the Zulu. In short, a sociology that specifically sets out to encompass a global dimension has become both urgent and necessary.

Another factor explaining sociologists' relatively late interest in understanding societies outside Europe, North America and Australasia was the strong national loyalties many sociologists felt, especially in the first half of the twentieth century. Interestingly, as we have seen, some of the trailblazers of sociology – particularly Auguste Comte, Herbert Spencer, Karl Marx, Max Weber and Emile Durkheim – were interested in countries outside their own. But, despite this promising beginning, from about the beginning of the First World War (1914) to the end of the Second World War (1945), comparative and holistic sociology went into decline in Europe and North America. This probably had something to do with the growth of intense nationalist feelings and the attempt to fabricate exclusive, powerful, modern nation-states.

As the First World War approached and inter-European rivalry raged remorselessly, imperialist and nationalist sentiments were easily inflamed. The big events and large-scale forces at play in the early decades of the twentieth century can often be tellingly illustrated by small examples, such as the stoning of humble dachshunds, the German 'sausage dog', in London's streets despite the famed British love of animals. In this frantic atmosphere, those

XENOPHOBIA

The hatred and fear of foreigners.

espousing international causes were derided. Even the international labour movement found itself at the mercy of **xenophobic** passions. Instead of accepting the Marxist message that 'workers have no country', young men lined up to fight for their emperors, tsars, kings and kaisers and many perished for their deference.

Sociologists were inevitably caught up or caught out by this nationalist fervour. In Russia, for example, sociologists (like many other academics) became little more than servants of the state. Others, the dissenters or members of victimized minority groups, left their countries of birth. Prominent Italian, Austrian and German scholars had to flee from fascism and Nazism to other European countries or to the USA. After the Second World War, these scholars made major contributions to the intellectual life of their adopted countries.

A PAUSE TO REFLECT

The social construction of who is 'in' and 'out' (or who is included or excluded) is a primary concern for sociologists. Is there a biological or instinctual basis for such behaviour? Why are some groups particularly targeted and excluded?

THE GREAT DEPRESSION (1929–39)

The most severe capitalist downturn ever known, although some have compared the global economic crisis beginning in 2007/8 with it. By late 1932, in the USA alone, around 15 million workers were unemployed. The crisis began in October 1929 when company share values on New York's Wall Street stock exchange crashed. A number of stockbrokers and investors jumped to their deaths from their skyscraper offices. A series of escalating bank and currency collapses soon turned the crisis into a global one. German Nazism and Japanese fascism were partly caused by the world economic collapse.

In the period up to 1945, sociologists in the USA and the UK remained intelligent observers and critics of their own societies, but they rarely lifted their heads above the concerns immediately around them. In front of their eyes were the mass unemployment caused by the **Great Depression**, the mobilization of men for the front, and the deployment of women on the 'home front'. Discussions of social problems and social realities were focused almost entirely on local community, urban or national contexts.

POST-1945: WIDENING WINDOWS ON A MORE COMPLEX WORLD

The end of the Second World War heralded a new balance of international forces. Japan was one of the defeated countries. Yet, as a late industrializing and non-Western country it had proved a formidable enemy. It had brought the USA into the war. The Second World War also shifted the locus of political and economic power from Europe to the USA. For its part, the Soviet Union made enormous strides in technological development, including sending the first cosmonaut to space in 1961, but such achievements concealed underlying weaknesses in the economy. The French, British, Dutch and Portuguese empires rapidly began to unravel under the impact of nationalist pressures. This shifting balance of power prompted four sets of concerns for sociologists and other social scientists:

1. Sociologists asked what explained Japan's sudden emergence as a leading industrial power. Were there certain elements in Japanese culture that generated appropriate forms of work and military discipline? Was there some connection between the revival of Shintoism and Japan's interest in European science, akin perhaps to the Enlightenment or even to Max Weber's idea that particular kinds of religion were linked to the development of capitalism? Was the restoration of the emperor the crucial historical event (1867/68), or the end of feudalism in 1869? The basic dynamic of the Japanese spurt to industrial, political and military prominence was inexplicable to all but a few non-Japanese social scientists, the sociologist Ronald Dore (Box 1.2) being one honourable exception.

2. Was the USA able to stabilize the world through a mutual threat of annihilation with the Soviet Union? The very acronym MAD (mutually assured destruction) suggested a sort of crazy logic of threat and counterthreat depicted brilliantly in the classic 1964 film *Dr Strangelove Or: How I Learned to Stop Worrying and Love the Bomb*. The 'iron curtain' separated East from West, but there were intense and often dangerous rivalries in the space race and even in sporting contests. Passionate debates arose over the virtues and drawbacks of planning or the market, an assured basic standard of living or individual freedom. These debates were played out in the countries in what was then called 'the Third World', whose allegiance the rival superpowers eagerly sought.

3. The old empires were clearly on the way out. Reluctantly, the British left India, which became independent in 1947. This was the prelude to the decolonization of the rest of Asia, Africa, the Middle East and the Caribbean. The Dutch evacuated Indonesia in 1949 and later the French and Portuguese were also forced to abandon their colonial possessions in Asia and Africa, often retreating in the face of armed rebellion. Amid much conflict, the French yielded to the force of Algerian nationalism in 1962, while former Portuguese Mozambique became independent in 1975.

4. There were new actors on the world stage. People of all colours and backgrounds, not just white people, were 'making history'. It had been arrogant and even absurd for dominant ethnic groups to believe that they were the only ones who counted. All convictions of racial and cultural superiority were shaken to the roots after 1945.

Of course, some people continued to live in the past. Nonetheless, far-sighted thinkers and politicians realized that the post-1945 period required a change in public consciousness. One example of the new openness was the foundation in Paris of the United Nations Educational, Scientific and Cultural Organization (UNESCO) in 1946. Three decades later, Article 1 of UNESCO's General Conference of 1978 reinforced the universalizing spirit, proclaiming that: 'All human beings belong to a single species and are descended from a common stock. They are born equal in dignity and rights and all form part of humanity' (Banton 1994: 336–7).

Not only was there a shift in mood towards universalism but there was also a legion of societies 'out there' whose conditions of life were largely unknown to Western scholars. Led by the USA, but soon followed by Japan and the European countries, 'area studies' programmes at universities were announced or augmented. Scholars were encouraged to find out anything they could about the former colonies as well as about the communist countries behind 'the iron curtain'. Moreover, significant bodies of writers and academics, sociologists included, from outside Europe and North America began to make their mark.

Latin America was decolonized in the nineteenth century so it was not surprising that Chilean, Brazilian and Mexican sociologists had time to develop sophisticated theories to explain why their societies remained economically and culturally dependent on 'the centre' (the rich, industrialized North), despite decades of political autonomy. One important Latin American sociologist addressing this issue was Fernando Henrique Cardoso (see Cardoso and Faletto 1969), later the president of Brazil (Figure 1.2). Other influential contributions to the understanding of the developing world came from political economist Samir Amin (1974) from Egypt, the Martinique-born psychiatrist and political activist Franz Fanon (1967), or sociologists such as Hamza Alavi (1972) from Pakistan and Jamaican-born Orlando Patterson (1982), who wrote key works on the peasantry and on the evolution of slavery and freedom.

Gradually, sociologists working in Europe and North America began to appreciate that they needed to widen their comparative perspectives. In so doing, they found themselves returning to some of the concerns of the pioneer sociologists, finding fresh possibilities of understanding other societies and helping to illuminate their own cultures and contexts. Their theories were many and diverse but Box 2.1 outlines a few of these new ideas.

- **Barrington Moore** (1967, 1972) thought that a comparative historical sociology was needed to understand why some societies prospered while others languished, and why some turned into democracies and others dictatorships. In his ambitious comparative study of Britain, America, Japan, India and China, he considered how the cultural foundations, historical trajectories and socioeconomic origins – through different kinds of peasantry and aristocratic systems of land ownership and farming – had interacted in constraining and/or shaping the direction, speed and character of their transitions to industrial societies.

- Other US sociologists like **Talcott Parsons** (1971) tended to talk in terms of a wider notion of 'modernization', which involved the 'non-Western' world 'catching up' with the achievements of the 'Western' world and Japan.

- German scholar **André Gunder Frank** (1967, 1969), who worked in Chile for a number of years, was influenced by the theories of 'dependency' and 'underdevelopment' current in Latin American circles. He popularized their work by writing in English and extended it in new directions.

- Although the term 'Third World' originated with a French journalist, English sociologist **Peter Worsley** (1967) also drew from writings by Latin Americans, Asians and Africans to define the distinctive characteristics of the Third World, one that was relatively poor, neither capitalist nor communist, neither Western nor non-Western.

- **Ronald Dore** learned his Japanese during the Second World War and he is one of the few Western sociologists who have been acclaimed in Japan for his understanding of Japanese society. His major books were *City Life in Japan* (1958), *Land Reform in Japan* (1959) and *Education in Tokugawa Japan* (1965), when he was largely concerned with describing and analysing the remarkable process of Japanese industrialization and modernization. He has worked on Japan for about 60 years and was elected to the Japan Academy in 1986 as an honorary foreign member.

- **Ulrich Beck** updated his *The Risk Society* (1992) with *World Risk Society* (1999a), now arguing that we are increasingly intermeshed with other societies by virtue of 'manufactured risks' that cross boundaries. Unlike the earthquakes and floods of old, our main risks now arise from human action and operate on a global level – including nuclear energy, carbon consumption, genetic engineering and deforestation.

GROSS NATIONAL PRODUCT

A common measurement economists use to assess a country's wealth. In recent years, this has been challenged as a poor instrument because it conceals vast discrepancies of wealth inside a country and fails to measure welfare or contentment. The government of Bhutan has pioneered an alternative key to measure these rather important aspects of life, which it calls the 'index of gross national happiness'.

What emerged from the disparate contributions of Western sociologists was the realization that the paths of development or underdevelopment of individual countries could not easily be predicted. Within what was formerly called the 'Third World', some countries 'took off' and succeeded in economic terms, while others bumped along at the bottom. We can contrast, for example, the case of Ghana (by no means the poorest country in West Africa) with South Korea. Crow (1997: 130) cites data showing that whereas the two countries shared a similar **gross national product** (GNP) per capita in the 1960s (about US$230), three decades later South Korea was 10–12 times more prosperous.

Again, there were strong social and cultural contrasts between countries. Some, like Singapore and Japan, appeared seamlessly to develop a creative synthesis between local and imported Western cultures. Others, including some societies in the Middle East, found that the religious convictions of their populations jarred with the largely secular, consumerist culture of the West. Many societies historically characterized by large rural populations and agrarian pursuits now suddenly had bloated urban concentrations with massive levels of unemployment.

The term THIRD WORLD was used mainly during the Cold War period to distinguish the nonaligned poor countries from the First World (the rich capitalist democracies of the West) and from the Second World (the communist-led countries of the Soviet bloc). Increased differentiation between the rich and poor countries of Asia, Africa, Latin America and the Middle East, together with the political collapse of nearly all the communist countries, has meant that the term is of less and less value. Although countries are still highly unequal in their wealth and power, they do not fit neatly into three groups.

If we take into account the diversity of the societies previously classified under the rubric THIRD WORLD, it becomes apparent that classifying countries into different subsections of the globe is a perilous and inexact business. Moreover, as we argue later in Chapters 12 and 14, there is a high level of interpenetration between countries, through travel, migration, financial flows and cultural borrowings, to name a few factors. It is increasingly difficult to isolate a country and to declare that all people living there comprise a single society. In effect, we cannot always be sure of the difference between the 'internal' and the 'external'.

Immanuel Wallerstein made perhaps the most daring and important response to this problem (see Global Thinkers 1). In the opening book of a series of works, he advanced the notion of 'the modern world system'. Having considered the difficulties of arranging the world into neat hierarchies and isolating the nation-state as the primary unit of sociological analysis, Wallerstein (1974: 51) decided he would

abandon the idea altogether of taking either the sovereign state or that vaguer concept, the national society, as the unit of analysis. I decided that neither one was a social system and that one could only speak of social change in social systems. The only social system in this scheme was the world system.

This declaration symbolizes what an increasing number of sociologists have come to realize. We have to try to think globally, recognizing that while social changes may vary considerably in each setting, there are overarching processes and transformations that operate at a global level and impact to one degree or another on everybody.

GLOBAL THINKERS 1 IMMANUEL M. WALLERSTEIN (1930–)

Immanuel Wallerstein pioneered 'world system theory', one of the most important accounts of large-scale social change since the 1970s. At the beginning of *The Modern World-System* (1974: 15), Wallerstein boldly announced that

> in the late fifteenth and early sixteenth century, there came into existence what we may call a European trade economy . . . it was different, and new. It was a kind of social system the world has not really known before and which is the distinctive feature of the modern world-system.

What was hidden behind Wallerstein's apparently simple declaration was a challenge to conventional understandings of the world:

- For Wallerstein, political structures (like empires and states) were given undue importance. Instead, he laid emphasis on interpenetrating trade networks that crossed state boundaries. Transnational competition for labour, market share and raw materials drove the world system forward and linked it together. This emphasis on trade led many scholars to accuse Wallerstein of being 'an economic determinist', that is, someone who overemphasizes the causal role of economic factors. Despite writing extensively on culture, social movements and politics, he has never entirely shaken off this charge.

- In line with his demotion of formal political ideologies, he rejected the division of the world into 'First' (rich capitalist), 'Second' (communist state-planned) and 'Third' (poor Southern) worlds. Instead, he proposed an alternative trichotomy – core, semi-peripheral and peripheral. There is a resemblance to the theory of three worlds, but Wallerstein injected an important causal relationship. The core societies draw profit from the peripheral societies, while the peripheral societies are underdeveloped because they are locked in a subordinate relationship to the core. However, ascending peripheral and declining core societies can move to the semi-periphery. The great virtue of this model was to insist that all societies were locked into one world system and that there could be movement within the system. (Clearly, the rise of China and India is better explained by world system theory than by three worlds theory.)

Wallerstein's commanding synthesis was nevertheless attacked. For example, Abu-Lughod (1989) suggested that Wallerstein had totally missed prior non-European world systems. Others argued that world systems alone could not explain the collapse of state communism in 1989. Again, a number of commentators have maintained that Wallerstein does not allow a sufficient place for politics and cultural analysis in his arguments, a charge he denied (Wallerstein 1989, 1991). His theory remains an influential and powerful current in global sociology.

Sources: Abu-Lughod (1989); Hall (1996); Wallerstein (1974, 1989, 1991).

THEORIES OF UNEVEN DEVELOPMENT

Through the construction of his influential world system theory, Wallerstein (1974, 1979) argued that capitalism and not nation-states created the world order. This is because, in its drive to spill outwards in search of profits, capital has always disregarded national borders. A set of stable structured relationships between three types of country – the dominant core, the semi-periphery and the dependent periphery – eventually resulted. The semi-periphery, characteristically neither as technically advanced nor as rich as the core countries, nor as lacking in autonomy and condemned to dependence as the periphery, serves as a buffer between the other two, in that it divides the potential opposition to the continuing domination of core capital.

Because the designation of a particular country to a position in this hierarchy is not fixed, some movement between them is possible – as in the case of Japan's remarkable rise from the periphery before the 1870s to second position in the core bloc by the 1970s. Movement from the periphery to the core is, however, normally difficult because, having once assured their hold over other countries, the dominant players use their control to perpetuate various unequal exchanges. Put simply, the core countries, which are in a position to manipulate their control over technology and markets, underpay other countries and producers for their goods and services and overcharge them for their purchases. We discuss specific examples of this in Chapters 4 and 5, for example the imposition of international trade regimes that allow rich countries to subsidize their own agriculture but constrain poor countries from protecting their weak manufacturing sectors. Or, in another example, compelling poor countries to open their economies and markets to incoming Western investment flows.

Gradually, and working on a global scale, capitalism has created an increasingly integrated world economy dominated by the logic of profit and the market. Conversely, it has generated excluded, marginal, dispossessed and poor people. This outcome was consequent on an often complex and ever shifting world division of labour based on two closely related processes:

1. Progressively tying more and more countries into the global market through their status as the buyers and sellers of various commodities, for example minerals, tropical raw produce, manufactured goods or advanced technology.
2. The tendency of capital to maximize whatever kinds of economic advantage a given country can provide through its prevailing organization of labour and class relations. For example, capitalism is able to adapt to or perpetuate numerous forms of social exploitation whether of slaves, serfs, sharecroppers, tenant farmers, landless labourers or semi-free migrants (see Cohen 1987).

Accordingly, the logic of accumulation dominates the world capitalist system. At all times, it works to safeguard and expand the capitalist nature of the overall system and, in particular, to protect the interests of its leading players. At the economic level, it forms one unified system. At the political level it is pluralistic, while at a social level it generates extremes of poverty and prosperity, along with a wide range of intermediate positions.

Many criticisms have been levelled at world system theory, but one of the most persistent focuses on Wallerstein's relative lack of interest in the political dimensions of power. Bergesen (1990: 70–5), for example, argues that the role of political power was crucial in explaining the origins and spread of capitalism. In Chapter 3, we explore this idea in the European context, suggesting that the possibility and actuality of interstate conflicts inclined rulers to introduce top-down reforms that intentionally or unwittingly fostered technological and commercial development. Bergesen argues that conquest and the introduction of state structures were what enabled colonial countries to impose various forms of forced labour and unequal trading terms on their dependencies, and not their ability to slot already established local market relations into a world division of labour.

KEY CONCEPT
The **NEW INTERNATIONAL DIVISION OF LABOUR** divides production into different skills and tasks spread across regions and countries rather than within a single company. From the 1970s onwards, as key production functions shifted away from the old industrial zones, hitherto agricultural countries, particularly in the Asia-Pacific region, rapidly joined the ranks of the new international division of labour.

THE NEW INTERNATIONAL DIVISION OF LABOUR

Partly in response to the perceived deficiencies of world system theory, a team of German researchers (Fröbel et al. 1980) propounded the idea that a NEW INTERNATIONAL DIVISION OF LABOUR (NIDL) had emerged. They were reacting particularly to the rapid industrialization of East Asian and other newly industrializing countries (NICs) and to the partial deindustrialization of the old heartlands of capitalist production. As we observe in Chapters 4 and 7, from the 1960s and 70s there was a growing tendency for some transnational corporations (TNCs) to locate the more labour-intensive parts of their overall operations in developing countries, so creating 'world market factories'.

Advocates of the NIDL idea argued that locating some manufacturing processes in cheap labour havens did little to improve the living standards and development prospects in the poor countries in question. By contrast, the export of capital increased the growing ranks of unemployed people in the West. The only winners, they argue, are the TNCs. While these theorists suggest that the NIDL has not fundamentally altered the core countries' ability to dominate the world capitalist system, they are alert to the existence of 'global losers' in all countries. Like world system theorists, they are sceptical about the periphery being able to overcome its relative economic backwardness despite its recent, partial shift from dependence on raw material exports to the export of cheap manufactured goods.

One can also direct some of the criticisms levelled against world system theory at the NIDL (Cohen 1987: Ch. 7). Certainly, it seems to undervalue the capacity of some states in developing countries to use political power to create conditions for a successful transition to at least semi-peripheral status, and sometimes core status, in the world order. The leaders of some successful NICs, such as Singapore and Malaysia, are acutely aware of the danger of being trapped in a cheap labour, low-tech, industrial future. To counter this, Malaysia, for example, founded 11 universities and developed a ten-mile deep 'Cybercity'. For its part, Singapore has turned itself into a major educational hub. By 2002 it had recruited 50,000 international students to its highly ranked universities, a number that is projected to grow to 150,000 by 2015. The theory also seriously undervalued the likelihood of large countries such as India and China using exported manufactures as a means of supercharging their own economies, lifting considerable numbers of their own people out of poverty and even racking up numerous trade credits with the USA. It is doubtful that the theorists of the NIDL would have predicted that the changes they noticed would have resulted in the USA running a large trade deficit with China from 2005 onwards.

AN AGE OF UNCERTAINTIES BUT ALSO OPPORTUNITIES

The development of some sectors and countries and the continuing underdevelopment of other activities and areas trigger competition for labour, resources, technology and capital. This phenomenon is sometimes described as 'uneven development' and can be seen as the

POSTMODERNISM According to postmodernists, in contrast to the previous era of modernity, family, class, community and national loyalties are becoming increasingly less important in determining our lives, as are social expectations linked to things such as gender or race. Instead, these structures, along with the moral and political certainties about the nature of truth and destiny with which they are associated, have largely disintegrated. Simultaneously, our increasing exposure to huge amounts of information through the mass media and information technology and their association with a battery of swirling signs and images have caused a communications overload. We no longer know what 'realities' signs represent, so everything becomes a simulation. Like truth and morality, reality and authenticity become less believable. We are left free to forge our own identities out of an increasingly diverse cultural repertoire, but this may cause us some anxiety.

underlying cause of the financial crisis, which began in 2007. In this sense, the immediate economic crisis revealed a more deep-rooted malaise, as the instabilities and uncertainties arising from uneven development have led to what looks likely to become an unprecedented and prolonged condition of chronic uncertainty and insecurity permeating virtually all geographical regions and dimensions of human life. The practices, relationships, rules and values we once took for granted no longer seem reliable or valid. Similarly, boundaries between inside and outside, between 'us' and 'them', truth and lies, or reality and fantasy break down to be replaced with complexities we cannot easily comprehend. Indeed, since the late 1980s, the social sciences, and not just sociology, have been grappling with the theme of uncertainty and the disintegration of social as well as philosophical boundaries through the discourse of POSTMODERNISM, a concept that is now going out of fashion but that held sway for 30 years.

Globalization has intensified the impact of postmodernism by increasing the fragments of meaning and cultural references that flow through our lives. Hall (1992: 302) aptly referred to this marriage of the postmodern and global when he talked about the maelstrom of the 'global post-modern'. We expand this theme in Chapter 2. Globalization has not only broken down every kind of boundary in the economic sphere, but for many people it has also reduced access to stable employment and jeopardized any prospect of a lifetime career – once the basis on which people planned and built their future lives (certainly in the industrialized West). In a global economy characterized by relentless competition for employment, most people encounter the casualization of work, the likely prospect of stagnant or falling real incomes, and jobs that lack meaning or provide little or no chances of comradeship.

UNCERTAINTY AS A SPACE TO SHAPE THE FUTURE

On a more positive note, pervasive insecurity and boundless complexity, coupled with a stream of constant, interconnected dangers, also create possibilities – a potential for ordinary people to exercise a little or even a great deal of influence in shaping the future lives of humanity (Hardt and Negri 2000). There are several reasons why this seems likely and we discuss some of them (especially the rise of a global consciousness and its implications) in Chapter 2. However, here we point to several additional elements at work that are perhaps entirely new and may take us in the same direction:

1. The uncertainties already outlined suggest that it is more difficult than ever before to predict future events. Expressed in a metaphorical sense, we are experiencing a situation in which – as two pioneer sociologists of global change, Robertson (1992) and Albrow (1996) suggested – all the balls of human existence are currently in the air and we cannot be certain where, when and how they might fall. This, in turn, leads to a condition of openness, a new prospect in human affairs in which everyone might demand their say.

2. The breadth of problems accompanying globalization creates an urgent need for people and governments to shape the direction of global forces in ways that are safe for everyone. Since governments acting alone cannot realistically resolve most of these problems and risks, there are opportunities for more cooperation and mutual understanding. Because the alternative may be disastrous for all, we must dare to hope for constructive action in the pursuit of human betterment.

3. Unlike earlier times, the rich and powerful will find it more difficult to escape the impact of the crises associated with uncontrolled globalization. Although economic power can

buy considerable immunity, the elites will still partly share with the poor and powerless some common problems, such as:

- collapsing market values and uncertain property prices linked to financial crises
- destabilizing social unrest created by growing inequalities when hundreds of millions, perhaps billions, of people cannot afford the rising price of food, water, urban space and healthcare
- demands for political representation and freedom, which, at least for some periods, cause deleterious and disturbing breakdowns in law and order
- mutating viruses rippling across the world
- the risk of skin cancer from ozone depletion
- the effects of increased hurricanes and floods
- food shortages, crime waves and spreading violence aggravated by genocidal wars or environmental devastation.

A PAUSE TO REFLECT

In February 2011, a devastating tsunami and earthquake hit Japan, damaging a number of nuclear reactors at the Fukushima plant. In trying to cool down the impaired nuclear reactors, firefighters from the region allowed themselves to be radiated. Why are some people prepared to take serious risks for their friends, family, community or nation?

To cope with the gravity and complexity of global problems, politicians and bureaucrats will need to co-opt and win the support of a wider public. They must provide a space in which an active citizenry can shape the future, in which democratic movements can work together across national and cultural boundaries. Attempts by old autocracies to resist this change are likely to fail, as indicated by the uprisings in the Middle East and North Africa in 2011.

The impact of the recent global recession appeared for a while to generate openness to change. Its severity threw into stark relief the dangers and self-defeating consequences of allowing unregulated financial institutions and markets to dominate economic policy. Under pressure from their disgruntled, insecure citizens and failing businesses, some governments have devised policies to regulate destructive banking practices and promote market reforms. The continuing power of the banks to resist reform suggests that these changes have not gone far enough.

REVIEW

That sociology drew on Enlightenment thought was a crucial factor in endowing the discipline with its strong positivist tradition. Sociology also evolved as a diverse and plural discipline with several important streams. One of these consists of interpretive sociology, which explores how subjective elements shape people's actions and meanings. Because we are dealing with human nature and social conduct, we need to identify commonalities and differences. Sociology therefore requires a historical and comparative perspective. It also needs and has developed methodologies that are designed to gather knowledge, including highly intimate data, but in ways that minimize the influence of the researcher's ideological inclinations. Nevertheless, stringent attempts to expose our work both to self-criticism and to the critiques of others do not preclude suggesting alternative policies or arguing for a different political, social, economic and moral order.

In this book, we are particularly concerned to show how the guiding principles of the discipline can be used to develop a global sociology. Sociology must also adapt to the changing world even as it seeks to explain it. Global changes, problems and even current and likely future crises demand that we extend our state-centric theories, define new research agendas and develop an agreed comparative method. In short, the interdependence of the local, national and international demands a global outlook. In this book we try to mark this shift in the moorings of the discipline, although of course sociology will be transformed by the work of hundreds of theorists and thousands of those engaged in more factually based studies. Following in the footsteps of innovative sociologists before us, we try to show how some aspects of global social change impact on and are influenced by changes at local, national or regional levels.

Visit the companion website at www.palgrave.com/sociology/cohen3e for extra materials to check and expand your learning, including interactive self-test questions, mind maps making links between key themes, annotated web links to sociological research, data and key sociological thinkers, a searchable glossary and much more.

FURTHER READING

If you would like to explore the theory and concepts that inform the discipline (on which we have little space to expand), a reliable account is J. Scott's *Social Theory: Central Issues in Sociology* (2004), in which there are 'focus boxes' to aid comprehension.

G. Crow's *Comparative Sociology and Social Theory* (1997) gives a good account of how sociologists of development came to understand societies other than their own. Chapters 6 and 7 are particularly helpful.

L. Sklair's *Globalization: Capitalism and its Alternatives* (2002) is a substantial revision of an earlier pioneering introductory text. Although it particularly stresses the economic aspects of globalization, it provides a wide-ranging and thoughtful analysis of global life.

Another good text, with a global orientation, is J. J. Macionis and K. Plummer's *Sociology: A Global Introduction* (2008).

QUESTIONS AND ASSIGNMENTS

1. Is Burawoy's distinction between professional, critical, policy and public sociology an adequate characterization of the discipline?

2. Why did sociology take a 'national turn' in the period 1914–45 and is the discipline still marked by national preoccupations?

3. Provide a sociological account of why Japan has been so successful in the post-1945 period.

4. Using a web search or following up on the names provided in this chapter, find the principal work of an African, Asian, Latin American or Caribbean sociologist. Summarize their main work, with the particular task of finding out what you did not know before and what helps you understand the human condition.

2
Thinking globally

Sociologists have always studied societies other than their own. The discipline contains a rich comparative tradition clearly traceable through the work of leading figures like Auguste Comte, Karl Marx, Emile Durkheim, Max Weber and Talcott Parsons. Nevertheless, these pioneers and subsequent sociologists often treated societies as if they were separate entities, each with its own clear boundaries. The goal was to acquire an understanding of a society's internal dynamics and structures, its distinctive historical and cultural traditions, and its particular directions of social change. Until recently, this was perfectly valid and insightful. The growing significance of global changes for all societies, however, has rendered this approach and the national traditions it generated less meaningful.

In this chapter, we explore the meaning of 'globalization' and 'globality' and ask what is distinctive about the processes so described. Are globalization and globality new phenomena and, if so, to what extent and in what senses? It will become clear that globalization has developed from earlier processes such as modernization, industrialization and imperialism and that sometimes these earlier changes carry their own momentum. However, this does not mean that globalization is beyond the control of human agencies. On the contrary, human actors and social organizations have been intimately involved (sometimes unwittingly) in shaping the nature and direction of global forces in the past and there is a need and an opportunity to take up the challenge of doing so in the future. Indeed, never has there been a greater urgency to make decisions or resolve conflicts to secure humanity's future than now.

GLOBALIZATION: KEY CONCEPTS

According to Albrow (1990: 9), globalization refers 'to all those processes by which the peoples of the world are incorporated into a single society, global society'. These changes are incomplete. They are long in the making and impact on different locations, countries and individuals in a highly uneven manner. Nevertheless, the processes of globalization have increased in scope and intensity and this has been happening at an accelerating rate. We suggest that globalization is best understood as a set of mutually reinforcing transformations that occur more or less simultaneously. No single one of these is necessarily more significant than the others. Here, we can make a useful analogy with the plethora of threads that are woven into a length of multicoloured fabric. Once woven together it is impossible to assign a special role to each thread – each only has value or significance as part of the whole.

While thinking about the cloth of globalization in this way, we now utilize some key concepts developed by social scientists in the attempt to identify the core processes, practices and consequences associated with globalization. These will provide us with an organizing pivot around which we can conduct our exploration of globalization. The key concepts are:

- the deterritorialization of social life and new experiences of time and space
- increased cultural 'scapes' and flows
- the 'glocalization' of cultural experiences
- intensifying worldwide networking across all activities
- the growing influence of global mobilities and complexities.

DETERRITORIALIZATION: CHANGING CONCEPTS OF TIME AND SPACE

There is a powerful sense in which the core experience of globalization amounts to the DETERRITORIALIZATION of social life. It has become possible – through international laws and agreements, the worldwide extension of capitalism, and information technology (IT) – and sometimes necessary for social actors to spread their activities far outside the immediate localities to which, throughout most of history, they were usually confined. Robertson (1992: 8, 27), a leading globalization theorist, has argued that it is as if cultures and societies are being squeezed together – along with their members and participants – and that this increases their mutual interaction. He describes this as 'the compression of the world'. Of course, modernization also increased the possibility of conducting social activities outside the immediate local environment (Giddens 1990: 51–7), but globalization has provided a giant, additional impetus.

Numerous human activities now regularly cross borders, defy vast distances and sometimes breach ethnic/national cultural barriers. These include business deals between giant corporations and their many suppliers, and political protests and transnational criminal gangs smuggling people, drugs or other illegal goods across continents. Migrants are another crucial example, with ethnic groups transplanting some of their members to host societies across the world where they might construct imitative cultures drawn from being in continuous contact with people at home through business, family and political or ceremonial ties. Not only have relationships become less dependent on being embedded in particular localities but a growing number of more generalized, impersonal phenomena have also broken free of specific territories and may impact on everyone irrespective of nationality (Scholte 2005). Included among these are climate change, the spread of new diseases, the worldwide effects of inflation and perhaps social unrest deriving from oil, food and water shortages, and of course the rise of integrated, computerized financial markets, which trigger crises that cannot easily be contained – as was evident in 2008.

Exchanges related to deterritorialization powerfully restructure our lives and, in a sense, they are turning the world into one place and one system. This creates a radical shift in how we understand and experience space and time. In this respect, Harvey's work (1989: 240–54) has been particularly pioneering. He argues that, in premodern societies, space was understood in terms of concrete localities. With movement dangerous and social life unpredictable during periods of war, pestilence and famine, most individuals felt safer remaining where they and their families enjoyed fixed, unchanging rights and obligations. Memories of past disasters, the passing of the seasons and the cycle of agricultural work determined how people understood time and space, but at least seven important changes gradually altered their perceptions:

> **KEY CONCEPT**
>
> DETERRITORIALIZATION With globalization it becomes increasingly possible and probably necessary for individuals, groups and organizations to shift some of their activities away from their own areas and familiar relationships and to pursue agendas and relationships with actors situated across national borders.

> **RENAISSANCE**
>
> The word derives from the French for 'rebirth' and refers to the revival of classical philosophy, literature and art in early modern and modern Europe. Over a period of 800 years, starting in the eighth century, artistic and scientific thinking flowered in Europe. This was accompanied by the rise of intellectual life, including the founding of universities, secular states and rational values.

1. The beginnings of Arab, Chinese, Pacific Islander and European exploration and navigation of the world.
2. Copernicus's theory, published in 1543, which established that the sun, not the earth, was the centre of our planetary system.
3. The discovery of the rules of perspective in visual art.
4. The rise of humanist, people-centred ways of thinking about human life during the Renaissance, which tried to escape from a solely religious preoccupation with the divine as the source of all meaning and truth.

5. The increasing use of the mechanical printing press.
6. The advent of the mechanical clock.
7. The unfolding revolution in transport technology associated with industrialization.

Let us consider transport technology in more detail. Until the advent of the steamship in the 1850s, the movement of all goods was slow, expensive and unreliable. By the mid-twentieth century, however, commercial aircraft and large ocean-going vessels (super-freighters) were rapidly shrinking 'real' distances and vastly accelerating – and cheapening – the movement of people and goods (Table 2.1).

TABLE 2.1 Changes in the speed of transport, 1500–1960s (kilometres per hour)			
1500–1840	1850–1930	1950s	1960s
Horse-drawn coaches/sailing ships	Steamships and locomotives	Propeller aircraft	Jet aircraft
16 kph	56–104 kph	480–640 kph	800–1120 kph

Source: Dicken (1992: 104).

Step by step, often through quite sudden bursts in technical knowledge, it became possible to measure, divide and so map the physical and temporal dimensions of the world into universal, standardized and predictable units. For example, without the geographical coordinates of longitude and latitude, travel by ship or aeroplane would be considerably more difficult. Harvey (1989: 240) calls the outcome of these ideas and discoveries 'time–space compression'.

A PAUSE TO REFLECT

Time and distance have dwindled in significance in shaping human actions. We may be less bound by ties to specific places and events, but does this mean that space and time become freely available for us to manipulate and control? Do you concur in the view that with life becoming faster, distance has been conquered or, at the least, rendered less weighty? Can you think of ways in which this differs between your parents' generation and your own?

What are the implications of this shift? We can accomplish far more things in any given unit of time and events crowd in on us at an ever greater speed. Increasingly, we judge distance in terms of the time required to complete a journey rather than by the number of kilometres between two points. As Harvey (1989: 293) pointed out, since the 1950s, mass television ownership, coupled with satellite communications, made it 'possible to experience a rush of images from different spaces almost simultaneously, collapsing the world's spaces into a series of images on a television screen'. These experiences have now become customized, democratized and more pervasive with the diffusion of the internet.

Thus, time–space compression has put many of the world's inhabitants on the same stage and has brought their lives together for the first time. There is scope, even for people who do not know one another, to interact through internet chat rooms, blogging, Facebook and other forms of virtual relations in cyberspace. For example, the various worldwide Manchester United fanzines or followers of punk rock groups are globally linked (O'Connor 2002). As early as 2001, radical activists used the internet to expose the sweatshop conditions experienced by many workers or to fight for 'fair' rather than simply 'free' trade (Klein 2001). Few predicted, a decade on, the remarkable capacity of the internet to mobilize opinion. A notable example is the Occupy Wall Street movement, protesting against the greed of global financiers, which started with an appeal in *Adbusters*, a Canadian magazine, in July 2011. The

KEY CONCEPT

Most sociologists see CULTURE as the repertoire of learned ideas, values, knowledge, aesthetic preferences, rules and customs shared by a particular collectivity of social actors. Drawing on this common stock of meanings enables them to participate in a unique way of life. In this usage, the human world consists of a plurality of valuable cultures. Each can only be fully interpreted by its participants. With migration, travel and much greater knowledge of other societies, the boundaries between cultures have become increasingly blurred. In contemporary discussions, therefore, more emphasis is placed on the overlapping or permeability of cultures.

occupation of Zuccotti Park, near Wall Street, began on 17 September 2011. Less than a month later similar occupations took place in 80 countries. Of course, we must remember that the world's inhabitants do not hook into these networks equally, especially those who inhabit poor, remote regions of the world.

INCREASED CULTURAL INTERACTION: FLOWS AND SCAPES

A second component of globalization concerns the increase in cultural flows propelled around the world in unprecedented quantities and with great speed and intensity. The term CULTURE has a multiplicity of meanings.

For many sociologists, culture is used broadly to depict all the modes of thought, behaviour and artefacts that are transmitted from generation to generation by example, education or the public record. In an everyday context, however, it refers to specific intellectual, artistic and aesthetic attainments in music, painting, literature, film and other forms of expression. Culture in this sense is particularly rich in imagery, metaphors, signs and symbols. The magnificent stone sculptures (called moai) that the Neolithic peoples of Easter Island executed are just one illustration (Figure 2.1). With respect to this second depiction of culture, in Western societies the earlier distinctions between 'highbrow' and 'lowbrow' (popular) culture enjoyed by ordinary people are eroding. Nevertheless, it is clear that most such cultural experiences, from art galleries to pop music and blockbuster films, are now thoroughly commercialized and only available by paying money. Contemporary commercialized culture is linked especially to the rise of the mass media and the widespread dissemination of consumerist lifestyles.

A PAUSE TO REFLECT

Sociologists and cultural studies theorists have argued that culture is an embracing concept that includes how ordinary people live, work, pray, engage in recreation and create everyday objects. How are cultures reproduced, subordinated or exploited? Are you a producer or consumer of culture? Can you and your friends live without it and, if so, with what consequences?

COLUMBUS

He 'discovered' the 'New World' in 1492. (Of course those who were 'discovered' already knew they were there.) This opened the way for Portugal and Spain to begin colonizing the ancient Aztec, Inca and other civilizations of South America. It also gave momentum to the circumnavigation of the oceans, encouraged other European powers to establish plantation economies based on African slave labour in the Americas, and led to the establishment of the USA.

While closely linked to culture, we also need to consider the growing importance of knowledge pertaining to abstract systems of understanding. Unlike culture as a way of life or as expressed in artistic forms – where meanings are rooted in particular societies or social groups – knowledge remains applicable in any context. This is because it refers to impersonal, largely autonomous and universal (scientific) truths. The elaboration of the binary codes that drive the language of computers provides a good example.

Throughout most of human history, culture and knowledge were acquired and reinforced mainly in informal, everyday learning situations associated with close relationships in family, church and community life. Their diffusion to other social contexts took place slowly, for example through sea voyages, trade, conquest and religious proselytization. Perhaps the most far-reaching of such voyages was that undertaken by Christopher Columbus who, with the support of King Ferdi-

FIGURE 2.1 Moai at Ahu Akivi ceremonial site, Easter Island
Travellers and scholars have been mystified by the purpose of these sculptures. Archaeologists now believe they were fashioned for religious reasons. The sculptures were moved about 20 km and averaged 14 t in weight. It is thought they were pushed along tree logs lubricated by oil from palm trees. So devoted were the islanders to appeasing the gods by making massive sculptures that they cut down all the trees and then died out because they had destroyed their environment. This experience may tell us something about the depths of unchecked human folly.

nand and Queen Isabella of Spain, set sail in 1492 across the Atlantic to reach the Indies. Instead, he reached the Bahamas, the Caribbean and South America.

The cultural interactions arising from increased contact between peoples have transformed our experience of meanings and knowledge. Ultimately, this led to an immense expansion in the scope and spread of abstract knowledge linked to science and the growing availability of mass, formal education. Moreover, the humble letter was augmented by the telephone and the fax, which in turn have been superseded by instant messaging, email and mobile communication, rendering interactions faster and faster. A number of important consequences have followed from increased cultural interaction:

1. It is increasingly possible (and sometimes necessary to our very survival) to know about other people's cultures. If we do not, we run the risk of being excluded from many potential benefits.
2. The electronic mass media of communication, along with fast transport, have the capacity to affect all those exposed to them and to incorporate them into a single experience. Accordingly, we live in what McLuhan (1962: 102) called a 'global village'. This is especially evident in the case of global mega-events such as the Olympic Games of 2008 in Beijing or the football World Cup held in South Africa in 2010.
3. We are made conscious that we live in a pluralist, multicultural world and are invited to participate in its many different aspects embodied, for example, in cuisine, religious practices and marriage customs. Of course, Western and especially US influences still appear to dominate the world cultural and knowledge flows, but this is likely to change as Brazil, China, India and other emerging economies add their unique contributions to global cultural flows.

However, because it has become increasingly possible to lift cultural meanings out of their original societal contexts and transplant them to other societies, there is a further consequence. Thus:

4. More often than not, these incoming cultural experiences, and the meanings they bring, arrive as fragments. This idea was vividly developed by Appadurai (1990, 1991) through his concept of 'scapes'. Here, the various cultural items flowing round the world invariably arrive as partial, disjointed elements that do not usually impact on us with equal force. One source consists of the multiple 'ethnoscapes' – social customs, religious ideas, culinary, musical or fashion items – diffused through many host societies by millions of migrants as they seek work or refuge across many countries. The 'mediascape', a second especially powerful scape, spreads not only through the information, images and narratives that the commercial mass media disseminate via television, film, magazines, advertising and the internet (Szerszynski and Urry 2006), but also through the branded, seductive lifestyle identities fashioned by huge companies. Kenway et al. (2006: 107) call them 'consumption scapes' and argue that these exercise an especially powerful influence over global youth. Then there are 'ideoscapes' transmitting elements of various discourses and value systems such as human rights or democratization, 'technoscapes', in the form of various innovations in production systems, and 'financescapes', which include currency flows and the products designed to share business risk or personal, household or company debt.

Appadurai draws attention to several interesting consequences of these various scapes. One is that, although their lack of coherence does not always allow us easily to make sense of globalization, they can furnish us with a rich repertoire with which to construct our own imagined individual world from the kaleidoscope of the fragments we select. Because incoming cultural items can sometimes provide visions of alternative ways of conducting social life, they may offer hope of greater personal autonomy to those suffering the injustices and inequalities of local poverty or oppression. As Appadurai (1991: 192) argues, 'fantasy' may become 'social practice'. Finally, insofar as some cultural fragments disseminate widely, for example those brought by advertising and branded goods, they may help some individuals begin to think of 'themselves as global', not just local or national social actors (Urry 2000: 185).

GLOCALIZATION PROCESSES

Continuing with the theme of cultural interaction, the concept of GLOCALIZATION has also become central to the way scholars make sense of certain global changes. Borrowing from a marketing term employed by Japanese companies that modified their global products to match and blend with each country's cultural requirements, Robertson (1992: 173–4, 1995) developed the concept of glocalization as a theoretical device for analysing how all kinds of local and global forms mutually engage with each other under the influence of different social actors, especially those 'from below'. Rather than assuming some inanimate force of homogenization, he showed how the global becomes modified by its contact with the local.

Quite often, local professionals, especially cultural entrepreneurs such as musicians, actors, journalists or media people, play leading roles in selecting and merging local, national and global cultural elements, although in the end the reactions of ordinary consumers are also crucial in deciding what changes enter the 'local' cultural repertoire. Of course, glocalization occurs in numerous other fields including sport, fashion, health, religion, commerce and the development of abstract knowledge by epistemic communities sharing each other's ideas and research. Indeed, there is endless and constantly increasing scope for growing

> **KEY CONCEPT**
>
> GLOCALIZATION is a term used to describe how global pressures and demands are made to conform to local conditions. Whereas powerful companies might 'customize' their products to local markets, glocalization operates in the opposite direction. Local actors select and modify elements from an array of global possibilities, thereby initiating some democratic and creative engagement between the local and the global.

complexity and choice in local and global life associated with borrowing, absorbing, rebor-rowing and reabsorbing cultural elements (Urry 2003: 84–7).

THE POWER OF WORLDWIDE NETWORKING

Sociologists and others have been interested in networks for some decades and have studied them alongside groups and social institutions such as the family and community. Certainly, networks became more significant with modernization and industrialization as economic activity became more specialized, contractual and dependent on new skills and dispersed operations. Social networks link a greater or lesser number of participants whose relations to each other vary between being highly dense and close-knit – with most members knowing each other – and loose-knit with interaction revolving around a few key individuals or hubs. Granovetter (1983) provided a prescient analysis of the dynamics of networks. As he observed, most citizens remain locked into quite dense networks clustering around particular localities, although they will probably also participate in others that are more widely dispersed, for example national business or leisure organizations. Because most social networks remain relatively localized, the information circulating within them tends to be repetitious, unexciting and non-innovative. Often, new stimuli occur when particular members forge connections with people who are mere acquaintances whom they meet fortuitously, perhaps on a business trip, at a conference or on holiday. Thus, supposedly weak ties such as these are functional in that they spread and infuse new information into largely separate localized networks that would otherwise become rather stale. There is, consequently, strength in weak networks.

Globalization massively deepens the significance of social networking in human life. This is partly because the essentially open, non-hierarchical, decentralized, borderless and relatively informal character of networks endow them with an intrinsic capacity to spread beyond the confines of particular localities. Increasing global cooperation also calls for new and practical ways of managing spatiality. As Amin (2002: 395) argues, global networks allow innumerable business, cultural, migrant, political, criminal and other agents to 'make space' work for them by connecting and energizing their previously separate practices. In addition, the market power and technologies that globalization helps to generate and spread provide the resources on which its effectiveness depends, especially given that globalization reduces the constraints of distance on every form of social activity. IT is especially crucial in this respect, for by reinforcing the key dynamic of all networks, it strengthens weak ties. In other words, the physical distance between members is far less important than the reality of being connected in the first instance. Indeed, according to Castells (1996: 470), by the 1990s networks dependent on IT become the most dynamic and appropriate vehicles through which to deal with virtually all kinds of global activity, although face-to-face inter-actions are far from becoming redundant. A network logic and mode of organizing global life has increasingly come to the fore. One example is Facebook, the social networking site, which had 845 million users worldwide by December 2011, with over 50% logging in every day (Facebook n.d.).

INCREASING GLOBAL MOBILITIES AND COMPLEXITIES

We have seen that globalization strongly tilts the balance of human activity away from fixed, permanent and stable experiences that occur within predominantly containerized places or nations and rather more towards a dynamic of continuous and inescapable movement. Thus, globalization fundamentally involves a vast increase in mobilities of all kinds, whether we are talking about:

- conveying material goods by sea, rail and air
- individuals crossing borders as tourists, businesspeople, students or migrants

- the movement of various political, business or scholarly elites between global cities as they meet to share knowledge or organize world events and policies
- the constant flows of 'disembodied' images, signs, money, credit, debts and competitive pressures circulating through the world's stock, currency, commodity and other markets via various silent signals (James 2005: 201).

Urry (2003), however, argues that these mobilities inevitably bring greater complexity to human experience. This is partly because some organizations operating across the globe, such as investment banks, the International Monetary Fund (IMF), Oxfam or Toyota, provide the core around which a vast assortment of other units, policies and pressures revolve. Unravelling these globally integrated networks (Urry 2003: 56–7) or attempting to regulate them is difficult. Also, the sheer quantity of mobile elements – including waste products, diseases, advertising slogans and website messages – and the speed at which they tend to move bring an element of fluidity to global life (Urry 2000: 38–42). But fluids are often uncontainable and it is hard to predict their influence or direction. Thus, given their liquid nature, they can and frequently do penetrate, percolate or infiltrate in unforeseen directions. This, he suggests, is certainly true of many consumer brand images. Urry (2003: 56) also suggests that social life is now inconceivable without our dependence on technologies of all kinds, including the internet, mobile phones, satellite TV, cars or aircraft. Accordingly, although humans have always depended on different technologies, it has become much more difficult than in the past to determine where the will and intention of social actors begins and ends compared with the needs and possibilities of the machines with which they are 'intricately' entwined.

KEY AGENTS OF GLOBALIZATION: TRANSNATIONAL ACTORS

Who or what are these leading non-state transnational agents whose actions have done so much to extend and intensify the interconnections across national borders since the Second World War?

TRANSNATIONAL CORPORATIONS (TNCs)

In many ways TNCs are the most powerful of such agents. There is a much longer discussion of TNCs in Chapter 10, but here we record their most important features:

- their global power and reach – half the largest economies in the world are TNCs and not countries
- their key role in creating an interdependent world economy as each TNC superimposes its own global grid of integrated production lines and investment activities dictated by its own, not national, needs
- their connections to the world financial system, including the instantaneous, computerized markets for foreign currencies, which in September 2010 reached the equivalent of $4 trillion (4 million million) of stateless money bought and sold every single day (Lauricella and Kansas 2010).

INTERNATIONAL GOVERNMENTAL ORGANIZATIONS (IGOs)

Like TNCs, IGOs constitute an important case of a wider phenomenon – the rising ability of supra-state actors to shape world affairs. Indeed, it is precisely because states cannot solve global problems alone that they have established a large number of IGOs to function at their bidding. However, sometimes, as you might expect, these organizations take on lives of their own. Such bodies first began to be effective in the nineteenth century with the growing need for rules and procedures to standardize cross-border transactions. The most important IGOs historically are probably the League of Nations, established in the wake of the First World War, and the United Nations (UN) founded after the Second World War. While in 1900 there were 37 IGOs, by 2011 the number had risen to 137. The UN alone has 17 subsidiary bodies and 26 specialized and related agencies (www.intergovernmental.org).

INTERNATIONAL NONGOVERNMENTAL ORGANIZATIONS (INGOs)

Like their national counterparts, INGOs are autonomous organizations and not accountable to governments, although they may work with them at times. Some INGOs have been powerful forces in world affairs. For example, peace, anti-slavery and labour organizations collaborated extensively across national borders in the nineteenth century. The number of INGOs has grown at a remarkable rate, especially since the 1950s. Today, their range of activities is vast, encompassing religious, business, professional, labour, political, green, women's, and sporting and leisure interests, among many others. You have probably heard of some of the most famous INGOs, such as Greenpeace, the Red Cross, Oxfam and Amnesty International, but there are literally thousands of others operating transnationally, and many more that mainly confine their operations within nation-states. According to Held and McGrew (2002: 18), there were more than 47,000 INGOs by 2000, although not all were equally global in scope.

GLOBAL SOCIAL MOVEMENTS (GSMs)

Although there is a great deal of overlap between these two descriptions, we can consider that particular INGOs are nested within more general GLOBAL SOCIAL MOVEMENTS (see Chapter 19).

> **KEY CONCEPT**
>
> GLOBAL SOCIAL MOVEMENTS are informal organizations working for change on an international scale, but galvanized around a single unifying issue. Examples of global social movements include the human rights, peace, environmental and women's movements.

Because the more activist INGOs mobilize world opinion on political and moral issues, their campaigns sometimes mesh with the activities of GSMs. An example of this convergence was demonstrated at the UN's Earth Summit held at Rio de Janeiro, Brazil, in the summer of 1992. Then, an estimated 20,000 representatives from environmental and other INGOs held an alternative 'green festival' in alliance with people associated with the world's stateless and aboriginal peoples. The annual World Social Forums, which started in 2001 at Porto Alegre, Brazil, also provide a space for INGOs to meet, develop critiques of neoliberal forms of globalization, and provide alternative global solutions.

DIASPORAS AND STATELESS PEOPLE

A number of DIASPORAS (such as the Greek, Jewish and Parsi ones) long predate the nation-state. Other diasporas, however, arose because of religious, ethnic or political disputes with national ruling classes over the demand for full citizen rights, the recognition of semi-autonomy, or the granting of independent national status. Their experience of persecution or neglect compelled some to leave voluntarily or seek asylum in other countries, thereby forming global diasporas of linked, displaced peoples (Cohen 2008). Among such groups are Africans (within which there are often distinct national diasporas), Kashmiris, Tamils, Sikhs, Armenians and Palestinians.

> **KEY CONCEPT**
>
> DIASPORAS are formed by the forcible or voluntary dispersion of peoples to a number of countries. They constitute a diaspora if they continue to evince a common concern for their 'homeland' (sometimes an imagined homeland) and come to share a common fate with their own people, wherever they happen to be.

Distinct from diasporas in that they have not been dispersed internationally, there are said to be around 5,000 indigenous or aboriginal peoples whose societies lack state structures. Their total numbers are more than 350 million and together they constitute 5–6% of the world's population (Hall and Fenelon 2008: 6). They demand the return of their tribal homelands and proper recognition of their cultural identities. These aboriginal groups, stretching across Canada, the USA, Australasia and South America, have worked with the United Nations Centre for Human Rights in an attempt to establish a universal declaration of rights for non-state peoples worldwide. They also formed the International World Group for Indigenous Peoples (www.iwgia.org).

Like the INGOs, such groups need no convincing that in today's world the expression of local identities is only viable in a global forum and context. To this end they coordinate their struggles at the global level and try to harness media opportunities to bring attention to their plight. According to Friberg and Hettne (1988), their political activities and intentions are captured exactly in the catch phrase, 'act locally but think globally'.

BOX 2.1 Acting locally and thinking globally: the runners of Tarahumara

The Tarahumara Indians live in Chihuahua state, a remote region, high up in the mountains of northern Mexico. Here they have earned a reputation for extraordinary feats of endurance, with their champion runners sometimes racing continuously for two days and nights at very high altitudes. Life for the approximately 60,000 Tarahumara people is arduous. Over time, the pressures of commercial development dominated by white Mexicans have forced them to move from their original homelands and have pushed them onto higher lands where cultivation is unrewarding. Temperatures often fall to −20°C in winter.

In the early 1990s, several years of drought – probably linked to heavy deforestation in the area – meant that their 'normal' condition of hunger turned to famine. Most children suffer from malnutrition to some extent and among the poorest communities infant mortality may exceed 50%. Sadly, these pressures have compelled more and more Tarahumara people to migrate to Mexico's largest cities.

In a bid to gain the world's attention, the leaders of an organization dedicated to alleviating the Tarahumara's conditions – Wilderness Research Expeditions – encouraged their best runners to visit the USA and participate in important athletic events. Running to win international publicity and to raise money for food aid began in 1993.

In late September 1996, six Tarahumara champions spent a weekend running the equivalent of four 26-mile marathon races through the Angeles national forest in California, much of it above the snow line. In doing so they were not equipped with the high-tech, designer sports gear deemed essential by Western athletic personalities. Instead, they wore leather sandals made at home. They are said to be rather bemused by all the fuss Westerners make about the rules of competition, timetabling and accurate measurements of fixed racing distances. Moreover, they find the experience of running in major US events rather boring since back home their races combine long-distance racing with kicking a ball up and down the mountains. Nevertheless, the willingness of these runners to 'go global' generated the funds to distribute 60 tons of food to the Tarahumara people.

In 2009, a number of scientists challenged the US$20bn global sports footwear industry, led by Nike. Daniel Lieberman, professor of biological anthropology at Harvard University, concluded that: 'A lot of foot and knee injuries currently plaguing us are caused by people running with shoes that actually make our feet weak, cause us to overpronate (ankle rotation) and give us knee problems' (cited in McDougall 2009). It seems that all along the runners of Tarahumara have been ahead of the game. Nike marketers set to work and developed a new shoe, called 'Nike Free', with its slogan 'Run Barefoot'. Sold at £65.00 a pair, users are advised to change the shoes every few months.

Sources: Gunson (1996); McDougall (2009).

OTHER TRANSNATIONAL ACTORS

Daily, huge numbers of ordinary citizens are engaged in forging transnational connections as they travel across national boundaries. At their destinations, they may reside as temporary visitors or seek long-term settlement. Whatever their circumstances and motives, they transport their cultures and lifestyles with them while becoming exposed, to various degrees, to the host societies' cultures. Among the many categories of individual or small-group travellers, we can identify the following six types:

1. Migrants in search of income opportunities in the growth poles of the world economy, such as Chinese family tycoons stretching their business interests from Hong Kong to Toronto or Los Angeles (Mitchell 1995; Zhou and Tseng 2001) or poor Mexicans constructing family, religious, political and entrepreneurial linkages between their new homes in New York City and their home villages (Smith 1998).
2. According to the World Tourism Organization based in Madrid, the numbers of international tourists crossing the world's borders reached around 880 million in 2009, despite the decline of tourism from 2008 because of the most severe world recession since the 1930s. By way of comparison, there were 159 million tourists in 1970 (http://www.unwto.org/index.php).
3. Professionals, such as lawyers, journalists, architects and scientists, many of whom feel 'at home' anywhere in the world (Hannerz 1990: 237–51) and contribute to the formation of a transnational culture. Sometimes, their experience of being strangers working together on the same project away from their countries of origin may bind them into enduring multinational friendship networks (Kennedy 2004).
4. Media, rock/pop and sports personalities.
5. Corporation personnel, business consultants and private entrepreneurs whose multifarious activities knit together the strands of the global economy and who increasingly share a common outlook as world economic elites (Carroll and Carson 2003; Millar and Salt 2008; Sklair 2001).
6. A miscellaneous group including students, airline pilots, drug dealers, diplomats, au pairs and many more besides.

THE IMPACT OF GLOBALIZATION

Globalization impacts on us in myriad ways, but two weighty consequences are especially evident. These are the rapidity with which the lives of all humans are becoming ever more interconnected, and the reality that societies and nations face a growing number of similar problems they cannot solve alone.

ALL ROADS LEAD TO INCREASING INTERCONNECTIVITIES

Everything we have said so far points to the inescapable reality of a world in which the range and intensity of interconnectivities existing between social actors continues to increase whatever their geographical and/or cultural distance. These ties bind localities, countries, companies, professionals and other groups as well as individuals into ever denser networks of transnational exchanges. Thus, we live in a 'network society' (Castells 1996) in which a network rather than a societal logic drives social relations. Moreover, Urry (2000, 2003) suggests that words like 'networks', 'fluids', 'flows' and 'mobilities' provide far more revealing metaphors for understanding the less predictable and decentralized character of contemporary life than words like 'society', 'structures' and 'institutions', which conjure up images of territorial fixity and the detailed regulation of life within social containers.

The cumulative impact of these interconnections has meant that societies, and their cities and regions, have tended to spread outwards so as to merge and become coextensive with other societies (see the discussion on global cities in Chapter 18). At the same time, the once clear-cut separation between the sphere of national life and the international sphere has largely broken down. For example, until quite recently, most social scientists, especially political theorists, regarded nation-states as by far the most dominant, if not the only, players in world affairs. Nonetheless, the swelling number of transnational actors pursuing their own interests through networks of ties now parallels purely interstate relations. Ultimately, as Waters (1995: 28) observed, we can expect a situation in which 'the entire world is linked together by networks that are as dense as the ones which are available in local contexts'.

THE COMMONALITY OF PROBLEMS

The growing commonality of problems facing all nations and peoples interlaces the fabric of globalization. Beck (1992, 1999a, 2000a), for example, argues that we all are compelled to live in a world risk society (see Global Thinkers 20) and certainly it is a common perception that the world is constantly under assault. The media have long brought the events and crises taking place in near and distant locations into our living rooms on a daily and hourly basis. Thus, many can recall the following events over the past decade:

- the destruction of the twin towers in New York on 11 September 2001
- the second invasion of Iraq in March 2003 – preceded on 15 February by at least 300 anti-Iraq war marches taking place in more than 60 cities across the world
- the earthquake and subsequent tsunami on 26 December 2004 when the seabed of the Indian Ocean was ripped apart leading to the loss of 200,000 lives from 13 countries, including Sumatra, Thailand, India and Sri Lanka
- the global financial crisis that escalated almost out of control in October 2008. But for the massive intervention by the US and other governments, which virtually nationalized many leading banks, the worldwide recession that continued into 2009 might have been much worse (see Chapter 4)
- the Haiti earthquake in January 2010 when at least 250,000 people died and a million were rendered homeless. It led to massive worldwide rescue operations by governments, charities, INGOs and private individuals with huge global media support
- the displacement of millions of Pakistanis when the Indus river flooded in August 2010
- the dramatic rescue of 38 Chilean miners in October 2010 after being trapped underground for 68 days
- the earthquake, tsunami and nuclear leaks in Japan in March 2011 that killed about 20,000 people, displaced many more and threatened (and continue to threaten) the health of millions of Japanese.

Such events graphically remind us of our common humanity – our vulnerability to accidents and misfortunes – and the existential truth that we all inhabit the same small planet.

While startling visual images are experienced as collective shocks, there are more material reasons for our sense of empathy with other human beings. On our compressed and integrated globe, our choices not only rebound on our own lives, but also directly affect the lives of others far away. We are often unaware of this and do not intend our actions directly to harm distant strangers. For example, figures provided by the World Bank in 2005 suggested that people living in the industrialized countries on incomes above US$30,000 constitute about 15% of the world's population, yet between them they earned four-fifths of the 'world product'. In stark contrast, the poorest billion individuals living on less than $100 a year, who formed approximately 17% of the world's population, had at their disposal less than 0.3% of the world's product (Pogge 2007: 132). In 2008, the three richest people in the world – Microsoft chairman Bill Gates, investor Warren Buffett and Mexican telecom mogul Carlos Slim Helú – held combined assets of US$174bn (www.therichest.org) and were wealthier than the poorest 48 nations combined. Because their global economic clout is so great, the decisions the wealthiest groups and individuals make about what to produce and consume, or how to invest their money, may cause unemployment, falling export prices, and the loss of livelihood for workers and peasants in distant lands.

GLOBAL THINKERS 2   ROLAND ROBERTSON (1938–)

Robertson's contribution to globalization studies has been highly significant and goes back to the late 1960s. His central interest in culture, particularly religion, provided one entry point through which he gradually developed his theoretical work on globalization. We draw heavily on some of his ideas throughout the book, so here we elaborate themes not discussed fully or at all in the main text.

Thematization of the world as a single space

Robertson argues that, even though most individuals retain strong affiliations to localities, nations and peoples, it is vital to place the world as a whole and the global human condition at the centre of our thinking. Thus, despite continuing conflicts and divisions within and between societies, the world exists in its own right as an increasingly autonomous and integrated entity with its own unfolding logic, dynamics and integrity. Analysing it requires new conceptual tools.

The history of globalization

He suggests that globalization has continued for a long time and is not simply a product of modernity. He identifies five phases. For example, the first began in the late medieval period from around 1400 and the most recent commenced in the late 1960s (the 'uncertainty phase'). The latter has been characterized not only by accelerating technological change, increasingly numerous global actors and social movements and a much increased sense of global consciousness but also by growing crises associated, for example, with environmental problems, multiculturalism and the rise of groups resistant to globalization, such as religious fundamentalists.

The local and the global

Robertson often reminds us that globalization does not mean the destruction of localities and their identities. Rather, exposure to the former compels the local to reinvent itself in the light of the incoming global by selecting and absorbing those elements it finds conducive. This is precisely what modernizing countries like Japan did in the nineteenth century; it reinvented its unique national particularity in relation to the universal models flowing in from other modernizing nations by imitating and then rendering them 'Japanese'. Indeed, the very existence of the local or the particular has always presupposed a framework of self-understanding that involves knowledge of the universal – other peoples, countries or cultures. As with individuals or societal collectivities, identity construction always requires an 'other' against which difference can be measured.

Source: Robertson (1992, 1995, 2001).

Another reason for sharing concerns is that certain global problems require global solutions. Acting alone, governments cannot protect their borders, territories or the lives and wellbeing of their citizens from a number of situations. The cross-border fallout of radioactive material following the 1986 nuclear accident at Chernobyl, the growing risks of future water and food shortages, the nearly unstoppable dissemination of new diseases through air traffic, international drug trafficking and global terrorism are all examples of the limits of purely national interventions. Only collaboration between governments and global regulation can provide genuine solutions. Whether or not this will be forthcoming is open to doubt. We are uncertain how far citizens will exercise pressure on governments and agencies at both national and transnational levels.

The impact of global industrialization on the planet's **biosphere** perhaps provides the most obvious and compelling example of the shared, global nature of many problems. According to Yearley (1996: 28): 'the world's growing environmental problems are connecting the lives of people in very different societies … it is ultimately impossible to hide oneself away from these phenomena altogether.'

It is not solely the materialistic lifestyles of the world's rich minority

THE BIOSPHERE

Comprises the atmosphere, the oceans, lakes and rivers, together with the varied and complex systems of plant life and living organisms from bacteria to fish, animals and humans.

that are responsible for global environmental devastation. In many developing countries, even the poorest and most marginalized people have been driven to abuse their own environ-ments because of rapid population growth and the pressure on poor people to cultivate steep hillsides and semi-desert.

GLOBALITY: A NEW PHENOMENON

In Chapter 3, we will be reminded that some of the processes involved in globalization have long historical roots although they have recently accelerated in their impact. What is distinc-tive and new in the world today is the emergence of 'globality'. Robertson (1992: 132) defines this as the 'consciousness of the (problem of) the world as a single space'. In similar vein, Albrow (1990: 8) referred to those 'values which take the real world of 5 billion people as the object of concern … with a common interest in collective action to solve global problems'. (The sentiment still applies although we now have 2 billion more people.) In short, whereas globalization refers mainly to a series of objective changes that are partly outside us, globality refers to the subjective realm. How have we internalized the changes associated with globali-zation so that they are now incorporated into our emotions and our ways of thinking? These are the four major aspects of globality that we discuss:

- thinking about ourselves collectively while identifying with all humanity
- the end to one-way flows and the growth of multicultural awareness
- the empowerment of self-aware social actors
- the broadening of identities and the move towards cosmopolitanism.

THINKING ABOUT OURSELVES COLLECTIVELY

Humankind, and not just a small coterie of intellectuals, has begun to be capable of thinking about itself collectively as one entity. At times, our shared concern with the category 'human-ity' is beginning to extend beyond our affiliation solely to people of the same ethnic, national or religious identities. Robertson (1992: 183) argues that while we are still a long way from the world being capable of acting 'for itself', the idea of this is becoming more and more significant and pressing. For example, many people, particularly young and educated people, articulate a strong conviction that everyone has certain rights as a human being. They express moral outrage when these rights are violated and demand that human rights are universally protected by interna-tional conventions and laws.

This involves a clear break with even the recent past. A poignant illustration of this capacity to empathize across old divides was the successful worldwide campaign demanding the release of Nelson Mandela (Figure 2.2),

© LOUISE GUBB/CORBIS SABA

FIGURE 2.2 Nelson Mandela in March 1990 on his release from 25 years in prison
Mandela went on to lead the African National Congress to victory four years later, when he became state president of South Africa. Apartheid was formally ended and full citizenship granted to all South Africans. His extraordinary dignity, wisdom and other human qualities crossed many barriers of caste, class, ethnicity, nationality and religion.

KEY CONCEPT

APARTHEID was not simply the informal practice of racial discrimination, but an elaborated ideology of state-sanctioned and legalized 'separateness', based on racial groups. The whole population was classified into four main groups – whites, Bantus (Africans), coloureds (people of mixed heritage) and Asians – who were provided with separate schools, universities, social facilities (even down to park benches) and housing. In practice, whites got the best deal.

KEY CONCEPT

The year 1492, when Columbus reached the Americas, can be taken as a convenient symbolic marker opening the modern era. However, the orientations towards MODERNITY only began to crystallize from the seventeenth century. They involved the growth of a questing spirit, a powerful leaning towards rationality – the search for verifiable knowledge – and a belief in the possibility of transforming the material world in the pursuit of social 'progress'. The project of modernity eventually boosted science and culminated in industrialization and urbanization.

KEY CONCEPT

All humans reflect on the consequences of their own and others' actions and perhaps alter their behaviour in response to new information. This quality of self-awareness is of great interest to sociologists because it speaks to the motives, understandings and intentions of social actors. In contemporary societies, REFLEXIVITY is said to intensify as every aspect of social life becomes subject to endless revision in the face of constantly accumulating knowledge.

who had come to symbolize the fight against APARTHEID and the denial of human rights in South Africa.

GROWTH OF MULTICULTURAL AND TRANSNATIONAL AWARENESS

Perlmutter (1991: 898) argues that previous attempts to impose 'civilization' on the rest of humanity by expanding imperial powers normally involved conquest. Similarly, access to the 'benefits' of the victor's civilizing values required a willingness to submit to its 'superior' laws and institutions. Now, however, for the first time in history, 'we have in our possession the technology to support the choice of sharing the governance of our planet rather than fighting with one another to see who will be in charge' (Perlmutter 1991: 901). In this view, the long era of one-sided cultural and political flows is over. At last, nations and cultures are more willing to recognize and accept cultural diversity. Increasingly, too, they regard cooperation around a set of shared values and structures as necessary and desirable.

Giddens (1990: 51–7) makes a similar point when he observes that although most of the features we associate with MODERNITY originated in the West, these forces have now spread and flourish autonomously across the world. Each country is capable of determining its own version of modernity and projecting this onto the global order. By dissolving the West's former ability to monopolize modern forms of power, the globalization of modernity is simultaneously bringing the period of Western dominance to an end (see Chapter 3).

REFLEXIVE SOCIAL ACTORS AND MODERNITY

Globality contains a further important subjective component. Several writers (Beck 1992; Beck et al. 1994; Giddens 1990, 1991) have pointed to the growing number of social actors who are empowered to exercise REFLEXIVITY in their daily lives (see also Global Thinkers 5 and 20).

Reflexive, self-conscious individuals seek to shape their own lives while redefining the world around them. In many contemporary societies, the growing number of such individuals has begun to form a critical mass of those willing and able to activate and seize control of the dough of social life through the yeast generated by their own capacities for critical self-determination.

This widening exercise of reflexivity is partly linked to the development of mass education and the wide dissemination of the principle of doubt on which the scientific method is built. These have empowered citizens to gain access to specialized expertise, professional training and the means to acquire various kinds of lay expertise. Suitably armed, reflexive citizens may challenge the truth of claims put forward by governments, corporations and the scientific community itself.

Beck (1992, 1999a, 2000a) and Beck and Beck-Gernsheim (2002) articulate this idea with particular force. They argue that modernity and its consequences – relentless economic growth, the unchecked powers of military, technological and scientific institutions – now seem to threaten the viability of the planetary biosphere. Having been liberated from the risks once endemic to an era of economic scarcity (at least in the rich countries), we are now surrounded with vast new, all-pervasive and possibly uncontainable risks. These are directly caused by the very institutions of science and industry that modernity itself engendered. The once powerful identities provided by class, family, patriarchal gender relations, community or church have largely been destroyed. This, in turn, has helped to enlarge the scope for exercising individual freedom, especially for women.

However, such gains come with costs. Greater personal freedom to define who we are and how we wish to live also compels us to assume full responsibility for determining our own life paths, including our mistakes. Thus, we are on our own; our lives have become more insecure. We have greater freedom but more personal responsibility for managing our own lives. In a sense, we have no choice now but to engage in harsh reflexive activities involving 'self-confrontation' (Beck et al. 1994: 5), while engaging in the critical appraisal of established institutions because our survival and that of the planet depends on this. The discipline of sociology is itself both a product and an outcome of our greater capacity for reflexivity. According to Rosenau (1990: 13): 'today's persons-in-the-street are no longer as uninvolved, ignorant, and manipulable with respect of world affairs as were their forbears'. They have also widened their emotional loyalties far beyond immediate family and community.

A PAUSE TO REFLECT

Giddens (1994: 95) asserts that the sphere of the global is no longer remote to most humans; it has become 'in here', rooted in our consciousness. Do you agree that globalization has brought knowledge and awareness of other cultures into the heart of our daily lives? Does this lead to a collective easing of social barriers, or has globality become yet another major force that fosters increasing reflexivity and individualization?

A burgeoning, transnational power base of non-state organizations and increasingly connected global citizens' networks is taking shape. Many of those involved are also highly critical of the established order. This offers a potential for the formation of effective global alliances from below as the World Social Forums (WSFs) comprising worldwide representatives from a kaleidoscope of people's associations and INGOs have demonstrated. Starting in 2001, there have been 10 WSFs, the first three and the fifth held in Brazil. Among the many groups represented at WSF4, held in Mumbai, India, for example, were trade unionists from 40 different worldwide labour organizations. Among other events, they organized a rally, two conferences and eight workshops. Included in the trade union section were representatives of the Dalit Handloom Weavers Welfare Group – an Indian labour rights association that especially protects the interests of workers from the untouchable castes (Waterman and Timms 2004). WSF8 took the form of a global day of action and mobilization at hundreds of local sites around the world. A central concern of those involved in these WSFs has been the struggles of ordinary people to resist the neoliberal capitalism (Chapters 4, 6 and 7) pushed on the world by the G7 nations, the World Bank and the IMF since the early 1980s (Vargas 2009).

THE BROADENING OF IDENTITIES: TOWARDS COSMOPOLITANISM

A final component of globality concerns what Robertson (1992: 29) calls 'relativization' and we shall call 'broadening'. Today, no person or institution can avoid contact with, and some knowledge of, other cultures. Moreover, our comparisons with and understandings of other cultures alter our allegiance to our own particular local culture, which is less likely than formerly to provide the only resources we need for deciding where we belong. The reverse process also, however, becomes important to us; we need to judge and reach some decision on how we feel about other cultures. As Robertson (1992: 100) suggests, there is a steady increase in the interpenetration of the local and the global by each other.

Such encounters may encourage a growing number of individuals to develop cosmopolitan orientations or at least to move further in that direction. The discourse on cosmopolitanism has a long history and many different types have been identified (see the readings in Cheah and Robbins 1998; Holton 2009; Novicka and Rovisco 2009; Vertovec and Cohen 2002).

Scholars hold many different views on what forms cosmopolitan behaviour may take and on the various fields – whether political, philosophical, ethical, cultural, economic, or social – in which it may be played out. Nevertheless, it is useful to identify two main perspectives (Kennedy 2010: 16–18). The first, derived from Hannerz's (1990) influential work, points to the willingness of certain people to be open to and knowledgeable about ethnic or national cultures different from their own, as well as actively to seek encounters with representatives of these cultural 'others' in everyday situations. This desire to acquire and exercise cultural or aesthetic expertise has, however, been criticized on the grounds that only highly educated wealthy individuals enjoy the necessary resources required for such explorations, such as a proficiency in foreign languages, leisure and money (Calhoun 2002; Cheah and Robbins 1998: 254–5). A second perspective, with clear relevance to the possibility of globality, is provided by Tomlinson's (1999: 183–6) notion of 'ethical glocalism'. This refers to the practical willingness of individuals to take responsibility for the condition of the world as a whole and/or for the plight of people living in societies other than their own whom they almost certainly do not know. Such actions could involve anything from buying fair trade products (Holton 2009: 21) to joining a public demonstration against human rights abuses in Zimbabwe, or lobbying governments to adopt a much tougher stance at G20 conferences with respect to action against global warming or curbing the powers of international banks.

REVIEW

In this chapter we have made a crucial distinction between globalization, consisting of a series of objective, external elements that are profoundly changing our world, and globality as a subjective and reflexive awareness of these changes. We have argued that the various processes of globalization are inseparable and synchronous. In identifying the four aspects of globality, we have suggested that people can draw on their own capacities for critical self-examination to make a contribution to social life. This emphasis contrasts markedly with much of the literature you will read in which individuals are often represented as helpless chaff, victims of the tornado of globalization. We explicitly recognize awareness, agency and organization. We are keen to show that individuals, groups and movements can use the opportunities that global changes provide to advance the common cause of humanity.

Visit the companion website at www.palgrave.com/sociology/cohen3e for extra materials to check and expand your learning, including interactive self-test questions, mind maps making links between key themes, annotated web links to sociological research, data and key sociological thinkers, a searchable glossary and much more.

FURTHER READING

R. Robertson blazed the trail that others now follow. Although his book, *Globalization: Social Theory and Global Culture* (1992), is quite advanced, you should sample some chapters, especially 1, 3, 5, 6 and 12.

D. Harvey's *The Condition of Postmodernity* (1989) is wide-ranging and raises many issues we discuss later on. Parts II and III are particularly relevant.

J. Urry's *Sociology Beyond Societies* (2000) is a quite difficult but useful book that expands and builds on many themes relating to the sociology of globalization developed by earlier writers.

P. Kennedy's *Local Lives and Global Transformations: Towards World Society* (2010) explores the issues in this chapter at greater length (see especially pp. 1–80).

QUESTIONS AND ASSIGNMENTS

1. To what extent does the distinction made between globalization as a set of objective processes and globality as subjective awareness hold true?

2. Explain the concepts of 'time-space compression', 'deterritorialization' and 'global networks'. What implications arise from these concepts?

3. Identify the main forms of transnational activity in which non-state organizations, movements and individuals engage, and evaluate the different ways in which they may contribute to globalization and globality.

4. Why is 'reflexivity' necessary to the appreciation of globalization?

3

Modernity and the evolution of world society

When did humankind first become capable of understanding itself collectively? All early societies fabricated mythologies to explain their origins and to separate themselves from others. For the Sioux, the creator was the 'Great Spirit', for the Yoruba 'Olodumare', for the Jews 'Yahweh' and for the Polynesians 'Maui'. Their human followers would gain protection by the fervour and constancy of their devotion. It was but a short step for scattered peoples to understand themselves as distinct 'humans' protected by their own god or gods. Other people with whom they came into contact were thought of as potentially dangerous 'barbarians' or 'subhuman'. Through trade, religious conversion, travel and conquest, diverse and separated societies across the globe slowly began to relate to each other, although past fears were often not far from the surface.

From about the seventeenth century, the European powers began to outstrip the rest of the world in the sophistication of their ideas and military technology, the strength of their navies, and the organization of economic production. This astonishing transformation eventually enabled Europe to spread its new institutions across the globe and triggered the phenomenon we call 'modernity', the logical precursor to the current era of globalization.

In this chapter we examine five successive phases of modernity and global integration:

- the development of forms of premodern globalizations
- the emergence of capitalist modernity in Europe and its rise to global dominance in the eighteenth and nineteenth centuries
- the colonial and racial domination European powers effected in various parts of the world
- transformations in the world economy after the Second World War and the leading role played by the USA
- the move towards worldwide capitalism after 1989 and the growing economic and political challenges to the USA as the world's sole hegemonic power.

PREMODERN FORMS OF GLOBALIZATION

A number of the threads making up the garment of globalization described in Chapter 2 were already present in the world long before the rise of modern nation-states. As empires evolved and religious domains spread, early forms of **premodern globalization** developed. Historians of the premodern world (McNeill 1971; Needham 1969; Roberts 1992) show how many ancient societies were connected in important ways and how cultural legacies were bequeathed by declining or conquered civilizations. The ancient civilizations of the Middle East, China, Greece and Rome unified large areas. Even from the ninth to the thirteenth century, when Europe consisted of a patchwork of separate, fragile kingdoms and aristocratic fiefdoms, the overarching framework of Christianity held it together in relative tranquillity. Christianity provided the following features:

> ### PREMODERN GLOBALIZATIONS
>
> These comprised early aspirations to universalism that nonetheless failed to embrace all humanity or attain global reach.

1. The cultural universalism of shared religious belief and ritual.
2. The use of Latin as a common language of interstate communication in addition to its use in church liturgy.
3. The power and status of the papacy as a mediator between states and a restraining influence on political rulers.
4. The organizational structure of the Latin Church built around various monastic orders and straddling territorial boundaries.

In short, for centuries the Church functioned as a powerful and unifying trans-European body (Wight 1977: 26–9, 130–4). Other structures assisted it, especially interstate links based on dynastic marriages, the alliances between Christian royal houses, and the system of diplomacy involving rules of mutual recognition concerning emissaries and ambassadors (Bergeson 1990: 67–81).

Europe was also involved in multiple relations with other civilizations during this period. The rise and expansion of the Islamic states in the seventh century eventually extended Muslim influence to North Africa and over much of southern Europe. Muslim rulers were finally expelled from their last stronghold in Granada, southern Spain, in 1492. The long struggle to push back the frontiers of Islam helps account for the earlier emergence of powerful monarchies in Portugal and Spain compared with the rest of Europe. The formation of the Holy Roman Empire in AD 962 – an alliance between Christian states – was also linked to the desire to protect Christendom from external attack (Smith 1991: 59, 62).

The authority of the Holy Roman Empire was never uncontested. In particular, Islamic power, especially in southern Europe, was considerable. Islam made important contributions to the arts and sciences, the establishment of centralized forms of government and innovations in agriculture – particularly the introduction of irrigation systems. These agricultural changes later proved highly beneficial to the semi-arid countries of Spain and Portugal. The expansion of Islam to North Africa and Spain, which began in 711, was finally halted by the expulsion of the last Muslim rulers in 1492, the culmination of over 700 years of the *Reconquista* (reconquest) by Christian monarchs. Between the eleventh and thirteenth centuries, the Pope and the Catholic Church sanctioned the Crusades, which were designed to liberate the 'Holy Land' from Islamic control. The long saga of Christian–Muslim antagonism has created a legacy of mutual misunderstanding of each other's cultures and intentions, a legacy that still endures and that has recently escalated dangerously.

Europe's economy and trading relations also depended on links with other civilizations. Gold, brought across the Sahara by Arab camel caravans from the mines of West Africa, was Europe's most important source of bullion from Roman times until the sixteenth century. The Spanish conquest of South America opened up silver imports (Hopkins 1973: 46). With European traders tending to run a more or less permanent trade deficit with the Orient, bullion flowed east to pay for Indian textiles of unrivalled quality – silk, indigo and spices. Indeed, this trade provided the principal motivation for the first explorations of the globe by Portugal and Spain starting in the fifteenth century. Colonial conquests followed (Smith 1991: 70).

However, there was no certainty that Christianized Europe would take the lead. The Islamicized countries had provided important sources of knowledge, for example in mathematics, as had India and Persia. Indeed, other civilizations had long been far ahead of Europe in many spheres. This is especially true of China, from where many inventions, ideas and much technological knowledge flowed to Europe during the fourteenth and fifteenth centuries. According to Jones (1988: 73–84), even before this time, the Song (Sung) dynasty (960–1279) in China had attained hitherto unsurpassed levels of economic development, including terracing and manuring in agriculture, the manufacture of iron using coke in blast furnaces, harnessing water power for spinning cloth, and state investment in canals and other public assets. Some of these innovations were not widely adopted in Europe until the early eighteenth century.

A PAUSE TO REFLECT

Taking a protracted view, one could argue that China was dominant for 17 out of the last 20 centuries and will re-emerge as a co-hegemon with the USA in this century. In general terms, why do you think that countries, regions and cities gain or lose political and economic power?

Despite the significance of the early exchanges between civilizations and the expansionist ambitions of ancient empires like Rome, there are important differences between these premodern globalizations and the contemporary situation. This also holds for the universalizing religions of former times, including Islam and Christianity. They were universalizing in the sense that they aspired to reach all people. However, they never attained the influence that globalization and globality have achieved in today's world. There are several reasons for this:

1. The globalizing missions of ancient empires and religions only incorporated a minority of people outside their heartlands.
2. People everywhere lacked detailed knowledge of other cultures. The knowledge possessed by tiny educated minorities was fragmentary and often relied on travellers' hearsay.
3. Most of these ancient empires and religions viewed the world in terms of a clear division between the 'civilized' and the 'barbarian'.
4. Thus, their mission was to civilize nonbelievers or foreign barbarians and this involved a one-way transmission of 'culture' from the superior to the subordinate group. Mutual acceptance and interaction on equal terms was either inconceivable or very unusual.

CAPITALIST MODERNITY: EUROPEAN FOUNDATIONS

Significant changes took place in Western Europe between the sixteenth and nineteenth centuries. 'Modernity' is the term used to describe this 'nexus of features'. As Albrow (1996: 55) maintains, modernity 'included the combination of rationality, territoriality, expansion, innovation, applied science, the state, citizenship, bureaucratic organization and many other elements'. Here, we want to concentrate on five of these elements:

• the emergence of the nation-state
• the rise of a body of universal secular thought – 'the Enlightenment'
• the emergence of modern capitalism and Marx's analysis of this process

- the growth of rationality
- the outward spread of European societies, leading to colonialism.

Each of these developments was mutually reinforcing. Each helped create an environment hospitable to the eventual emergence of industrial CAPITALISM and the process of modernity. Drawing on important contributions to historical sociology by writers such as Tilly (1975) and Skocpol (1979), Giddens (1985) argues that the emergence of the European nation-state was probably the single most crucial force accounting for the rise of successful capitalism in Western Europe.

THE NATION-STATE SYSTEM

Unlike other world civilizations, Europe consisted of a number of autonomous countries in close proximity to one another, each of more or less equal power. Their survival as independent entities in a climate of nearly continuous war required a long process of internal state building. This culminated in the rise of a succession of powerful rulers. The state's bureaucratic reach and control over its population was progressively strengthened and deepened through measures such as:

- increasing tax revenues
- improving communications
- partially taming the nobility by making it more dependent on the perks derived from state office
- centralizing the nation by suppressing regional identities
- monopolizing the most efficient means of violence for conducting wars
- encouraging and subsidizing technological and craft development
- investing in naval and army strength
- nurturing local trading classes whose wealth could be taxed or borrowed to help finance state expansion.

Alongside all this, many governments pursued a policy of national economic aggrandizement, called MERCANTILISM. European states engaged in naval warfare, amassed gold and silver, gave preference to domestic business and, wherever possible, insisted that goods be carried in nationally owned ships.

The key role of actual and potential interstate violence and competition in stimulating these changes seems clear. What resulted was a fragile balance of power between the various European states and an elaborate system of alliances. No state was sufficiently ascendant to crush its rivals permanently and to create an empire. Had one giant European empire emerged, along the lines of the Russian or Ottoman Empires, internal reform would probably have been stifled as there would have been little external pressure on rulers to tolerate such things as the growth of a vibrant CIVIL SOCIETY of independent entrepreneurs, craftsmen, scientists and intellectuals. Again, in a large empire, high-ranking officials would have been recruited on the basis of aristocratic privilege rather than merit. (Chapter 19 explores civil society in contemporary settings.)

By the end of the eighteenth century, the much strengthened European states were better equipped than states elsewhere to impose institutional reforms from above. They abolished feudalism, imported and/or encouraged advanced technologies and science, or removed the obstacles to market freedom – necessary measures for a leap into large-scale production and a turning away from crafts and farming. Of course, these absolutist monarchs and governmental elites did not intend this to pave the way for a subsequent drive to industrialization and modernity. As Elias (1994) argued, the complex networks of inter-dependent social interactions in which humans constantly and consciously engage often lead to unanticipated consequences.

Industrialization was, of course, also driven by the rise of populist nationalism based on the notion of equal citizenship (an idea we discuss in Chapter 5) generated by the 1789 French Revolution. Other factors were the dramatic emergence of an industrial bourgeoisie in Britain and the non-state directed and slow onset of the world's first major Industrial Revolution beginning around 1780. From this date we can notice the increasingly wide-spread deployment of machinery – driven by non-animal sources of power – and full-time wage workers in permanent factories. In Britain it took about another 70 years for factory production to spread from cotton textiles to most other industries.

The technological and economic lead provided by the Industrial Revolution also gave Britain military opportunities. Not surprisingly, the British example was soon followed by other imitative, modernizing governments in Europe and the newly independent American states, largely driven by the interstate tensions and rivalries we have described.

EUROPEAN ENLIGHTENMENT THOUGHT

We have already referred to the Enlightenment, and it is explained in more detail in Box 3.1. This was a body of influential ideas that gradually spread across Europe during the eighteenth century. The scientific discoveries and advances that people like Copernicus (Figure 3.1), Bacon and Newton (Badham 1986: 10–20) achieved in the previous two centuries fostered an optimistic view of the potential for human progress through the power of reason. Such ideas, in turn, contributed to the continuing development of science while boosting the orientations towards modernity. Enlightenment thinkers included philosophers and writers such as Hume, Diderot, Montesquieu, Condorcet, Voltaire, Kant and Goethe.

© BETTMANN/CORBIS

FIGURE 3.1 Cleric and astronomer Nicolas Copernicus (1473–1543) (after a painting in the Historical Museum, Kraków)
Copernicus boldly claimed that the earth rotated on its axis every 24 hours and that it went round the sun once a year. German philosopher Goethe maintained:

> Of all discoveries and opinions, none may have exerted a greater effect on the human spirit than the doctrine of Copernicus. The world had scarcely become known as round and complete in itself when it was asked to waive the tremendous privilege of being the centre of the universe. Never, perhaps, was a greater demand made on mankind – for by this admission so many things vanished in mist and smoke! What became of our Eden, our world of innocence, piety and poetry; the testimony of the senses; the conviction of a poetic religious faith? No wonder his contemporaries did not wish to let all this go and offered every possible resistance to a doctrine which in its converts authorized and demanded a freedom of view and greatness of thought so far unknown, indeed not even dreamed of.

Source: http://www.blupete.com/Literature/Biographies/Science/Copernicus.htm.

BOX 3.1 The central ideas of the Enlightenment

1. Humans are social animals whose cultures and individual capacities for good or evil are not innate or fixed but originate in social relationships and so can be modified and improved.

2. A belief in the importance of critical reason, scepticism and doubt.

3. The human capacity to utilize these resources through observation, empirical testing and the acceptance of the fallibility of all knowledge.

4. A consequent rejection of the intolerant, closed ways of thinking associated with blind religious faith and metaphysical speculation.

5. All humans have a right to self-direction and development – best achieved where governments became constitutional or accountable.

6. The possibility of attaining self-realization through practical involvement in, and attempts to transform, the material world.

Source: Seidman (1983: Ch. 1).

Together, Enlightenment ideas added up to a virtual revolution. The modern person was a unique individual with enormous potential for learning and improvement and deserving of the inalienable right to freedom. Implicit, too, was the promise of a tolerant, pluralist and secular society engaged in the pursuit of human progress through scientific endeavour and free from unaccountable government, religious bigotry and superstition.

A PAUSE TO REFLECT

For some, the grand universalizing claims of the Enlightenment are no longer relevant or are seen merely as culturally specific forms of reasoning and political project. Different civilizations and cultures, it is argued, have equally valid forms of thought. For others, separating peoples in this way is a dangerous mistake and they argue that we need to reaffirm Enlightenment values. How can this debate be resolved?

Those who wrote the US Declaration of Independence (approved on 4 July 1776) in the wake of the **American Revolution** exemplified the practical possibilities of the Enlightenment ideals. The second sentence of the Declaration of Independence is: 'We hold these truths to be self-evident, that all men are created equal, that they are endowed by their Creator with certain unalienable Rights, that among these are Life, Liberty and the pursuit of Happiness.' At the time, it did not occur to the founders of the US state that these rights should also be granted to women, or to Native Americans and African Americans. However, that the declaration was proclaimed in universal terms at all meant that representatives of the excluded 'others' could eventually use its provisions in their struggles to join the included. This would ultimately allow them to mitigate some of the many injustices perpetrated against them.

AMERICAN REVOLUTION

Following a war with the British starting in 1775, the USA became the first modern country to win independence from colonial rule. Representatives of the individual states finally agreed at the Philadelphia Convention in 1787 to establish a federal government with limited powers enshrined in a written constitution.

MARX'S ANALYSIS OF CAPITALISM

The Enlightenment provided a powerful intellectual critique of the highly regulated forms of feudal life but, as Marx understood more than his contemporaries, feudalism was also a spent force in economic terms.

MODE OF PRODUCTION
Marx developed the concept to describe the characteristic social relations that marked particular ways of organizing production. Slavery, feudalism and capitalism are all modes of production in this sense.

Its successor **mode of production**, industrial capitalism, was a highly dynamic and indeed unstoppable force for generating social transformation. Many preceding changes had paved the way for the emergence of capitalism, but especially significant were:

- the creation of a fully commoditized economy in which everything, including land and labour, had a price and so could be bought and sold in a market

- the exercise of, often violent, measures to dislodge self-sufficient peasants and craft producers from their farms and workshops – so forcing them in ever greater numbers to live by selling their labour to capitalist entrepreneurs as wage workers.

This separation of direct producers from their means of production (their land, animals and tools) was a crucial precondition for the rise of industrial capitalism. Once self-sufficient producers were brought under the domination of capital, the way was open for three crucial changes that had never been realized before on such a scale:

1. Labourers could be organized more efficiently for they had contracted to sell their labour at an agreed price. The employer, who owned the means of production, was therefore free to decide how equipment and workers should be utilized.
2. Having become dependent, wage workers could no longer live through self-employment. Thus they were transformed into consumers who spent their incomes in the markets created by the growing capitalist system.
3. Capitalism contained internal motors that drove it relentlessly towards outcompeting the remnants of pre-capitalist craft and peasant production. It was also constantly compelled to transform its own system of business organization.

These built-in mechanisms included the compulsions of profit and expansion, interfirm competition and the inevitability of conflict between wage labourers and entrepreneurs over working conditions and the distribution of profits. Together, these factors impelled capitalists to cheapen and improve their products in order to capture new markets or displace their rivals. With increased maturity and organizational strength, workers compelled employers to raise the productivity of labour by investing in more advanced plant and machinery and adopting more streamlined systems of business organization and marketing. Consequently, capitalism expanded the productive forces by developing ever more advanced technology, harnessing the power of science, increasing the scale of production, and developing joint stock companies and markets to facilitate greater capital pooling. Thus, as Marx observed, capitalism is never static for long. Rather, constant change at all levels of society is inevitable and capitalism was driven to expand globally (see Box 3.2).

BOX 3.2 Marx and Engels argue that capitalism must expand globally

Marx and Engels vividly anticipated most of the globalizing consequences we have since come to associate with capitalism. These are:

1. The Western drive to incorporate the non-Western world into the global economy through imperialist conquest.
2. The necessity for independent but backward countries to adopt their own local capitalist projects.
3. The potentially universalizing power of materialism and rising consumerist aspirations in fostering the desire for change.
4. The tendency for capitalism to transform societies in rather similar ways.

These are some key extracts from *The Communist Manifesto,* first published in 1848:

> The need for a constantly expanding market for its products chases the bourgeoisie over the whole surface of the globe. It must nestle everywhere, settle everywhere, establish connections everywhere.

The bourgeoisie has through its exploitation of the world-market given a cosmopolitan character to production and consumption in every country. . . . All old-established industries have been destroyed or are daily being destroyed. They are dislodged by new industries, whose introduction becomes a life and death question for all civilized nations, by industries that no longer work up indigenous raw material, but raw material drawn from the remotest zones; industries whose products are consumed, not only at home, but in every quarter of the globe. In place of the old wants, satisfied by the products of the country, we find new wants, requiring for their satisfaction the products of distant lands and climes. In place of the old local and national seclusion and self-sufficiency, we have intercourse in every direction, universal interdependence of nations. And as in material, so also in intellectual production. . . . National one-sidedness and narrow-mindedness become more and more impossible.

The bourgeoisie . . . draws all, even the most barbarian, nations into civilization. The cheap prices of its commodities are the heavy artillery with which it batters down all Chinese walls, with which it forces the barbarians' intensely obstinate hatred of foreigners to capitulate. It compels all nations, on pain of extinction, to adopt the bourgeois mode of production. . . . In one word, it creates a world after its own image.

Source: Marx and Engels ([1848]1967: 83–4).

THE GROWTH OF RATIONALITY

When thinking about modernity, contemporary sociologists lay more emphasis on cultural and intellectual changes than on Marx's economic arguments. In this view, the belief in progress through rationality was a major factor in transforming societies. This idea lies deep in European cultural and political history but was particularly associated with the gradual extension of literacy, the development of science, the pressures for more democracy and the heritage of the Enlightenment. Also, once established, capitalist rationality and modernity were mutually supportive, each creating scope for the other.

Another extremely influential line of thought concerning the historical development of rationalization comes from Weber, whose ideas we summarize in Global Thinkers 3 below. Although Weber believed that all humans reflect on their actions and actively interpret and explore the implicit 'logic' attached to the cultural meanings occurring in their societies, he also thought that over time a particularly powerful kind of rationality had emerged uniquely in Europe. He called this 'formal rationality' and he believed that ultimately this had overshadowed other kinds (Brubaker 1991; Weber 1978). Several causal processes fed its rise. Among these were the quasi-equalitarian and cross-ethnic civil society that had emerged in the medieval city, the legacies of Roman law, and the fact that in Christianity, kinship relations (as opposed to the worshipping individual) have no special ritual significance. Europe also drew on the resources provided by colonial exploitation and saw the gradual emergence of free labour – no longer bound by social, locational or religious obligations to serve particular interests. Weber further argued that, from the sixteenth century, Protestantism also played a key role in helping to transform the character of Western rationality, since it emphasized the importance of a lifelong, disciplined, self-denying, not to say perfectionist approach to whatever vocation or position God had called one to as a necessary path to achieving salvation in the next world (Chapter 17).

As these rationalization processes gradually merged, Weber argued that something very crucial took place. The rise of formal rationality partly smothered the pull of tradition, affective bonds to friends or family, and selfless goals such as duty to God or the desire for justice, equity or fraternity. Increasingly, individuals, groups or institutions sought the least costly way of matching means to ends in a systematic, calculative way by applying scientific and empirical knowledge. This deliberate process could, in principle, be applied to most kinds of activities but it is in the modern governmental, professional and organizational bureaucracies (where officials are engaged in achieving consistent, standardized and coherent rules and systems of administration) and in the ruthless competitive and profit-driven struggles among capitalist businesses that formal rationality becomes most appropriate and most dominant. However, Weber eventually became pessimistic about the prognosis for modernizing societies.

GLOBAL THINKERS 3   MAX WEBER (1854–1920)

Max Weber's groundbreaking contributions to sociology included the following interventions.

Defining social action

The idea that 'society' is constructed around the meanings interpreted by and shared between individuals whose actions then partly express these meanings and are motivated by them. Sociologists can also use this same empathizing capacity and process as a pathway towards 'understanding' social actions – a methodological approach Weber called *Verstehen*, perhaps usefully translated as 'empathy'.

Power versus authority

Power can only endure if it is incorporated into our everyday beliefs, thereby becoming accepted as legitimate (modernists believe that rule-making processes are based on abstract principles of equity and impersonality that they can help determine through democracy).

Formal rationality

As we have seen with modernity, actions were more purposive and oriented towards calculability; they were pursued more systematically, with clear goals in mind, and incoming knowledge, often highly technical, became crucial. Formal rationality brings greater impersonality, predictability and control to factory, office, army, hospital or law court, leading to greater efficiency, economic growth and control of nature. However, Weber was also disturbed by three consequences:

1. *Disenchantment of the world:* science, technology and material improvement lead to disenchantment – religion and magic become less believable. Religion provides ethics – concerning how we should live – but formal rationality is only concerned with facts and the most efficient means for achieving goals.

2. *The iron cage:* once established, the logic of formal rationality – whether through the capitalist market or bureaucratization processes – remorselessly dominates modern life. 'Rationalized' bureaucracy stifles us in red tape.

3. *Substantive rationality withers:* historically, people have attached the highest value not to self-satisfaction or economic gain but to goals such as serving God, fraternity, equality and justice, that is, doing what is 'right'. But formal rationality undermines and replaces these with a narrow materialism.

Weber and globalization today

Because capitalism is now global, the iron cage of market compulsion encompasses consumers and workers worldwide. It also compels pharmaceutical companies to invest in drugs that will sell rather than those that are needed by the world's poor who lack purchasing power. Yet, simultaneously, we also see global social movements such as Jubilee 2000 and the Global Justice Movement (Chapter 19) struggling to reform world capitalism so as to make it fairer, less unequal, that is, to replace formal with substantive rationality globally.

Sources: Brubacker (1991); Gerth and Mills (1946); Weber (1978).

Turning to a more recent and optimistic view of the links between rationality and modernity, Giddens (1990) sees the latter as consisting of three kinds of mutually reinforcing orientations – the capacity to diminish time and space, the development of abstract forms of knowledge, and the capacity for reflexivity. There is no doubt that with vastly improved, cheaper and safer means of travel and communication and the ever more precise measurement of space and time, people experienced 'time–space distanciation' (Giddens 1991: 21). It became possible for social exchanges to flourish independently of place and time, across vast distances and time zones. Thrift (2004: 583) adds that new forms of spatial awareness can generate new qualities of existence. Boundaries are subverted by 'fluid forces which have no beginning or end and which are generating new cultural conventions, techniques, forms, genres, concepts, even … senses'.

The second orientation Giddens identified is a diminishing dependence on face-to-face ties to particular people and specific social contexts. These 'disembedding' processes meant that social life became more dependent on abstract systems of knowledge and impersonal forms of communication such as education and literacy and a generalized use of symbolic tokens, especially money and credit. This included the proliferation of expert systems, or professional services, for example in healthcare, banking or legal advice, in which clients were required to place their trust.

Finally, as we saw in Chapter 2, Giddens (1990: 36–45) considers self-monitoring or 'reflexivity' as fundamental to modernity. He claims that whereas 'all forms of social life are partly constituted by actor's knowledge of them', what is 'characteristic of modernity is … the presumption of wholesale reflexivity – which of course includes reflection upon the nature of reflection itself' (Giddens 1990: 38, 39). In modern societies, self-monitoring is applied to all aspects of life; it takes place constantly and is undertaken as much by organizations and governments as by individuals.

Giddens (1990: 63, 177) further argues that these three orientations facilitate the 'stretch-ing' of social relationships across the world and sustain complex interactions between people situated far apart. Indeed, he explicitly states that modernity is an 'inherently globalizing' force. It also helps to create what he calls a 'runaway world' where nothing is certain and every aspect of life seems to be in constant flux (Giddens 2002). Nevertheless, his argument implies that globalization is simply modernity (plus capitalism and the nation-state) writ large. This seems rather a limited view because, as we saw in Chapter 2, globalization and globality have generated certain unique properties, especially the emergence of a global consciousness. This could not necessarily have been inferred solely from a familiarity with the structures and orientations of modernity. As Robertson (1992: 60) insists, globalization has acquired a 'general autonomy' and 'logic' of its own.

THE ONSET OF EUROPEAN COLONIALISM

European countries were able to spread out of their continent precisely because of their economic, military and intellectual lead, often borrowed from other civilizations. The decisive advances were in seafaring and navigational techniques – improvements in the compass, navigational charts, astrolabe and rudder – and the use of gunpowder and firearms, cannons and guns (Smith 1991: 56). The Portuguese, who led the field in navigational exploration, reached the tip of southern Africa in 1489. Vasco da Gama finally entered the Indian Ocean in 1497. Brazen exploits, including the defeat of the Muslim fleet in the Indian Ocean in 1509 and the creation of a whole series of forts and trading stations across Asia, soon followed. Thus began the long period of European trading domination over much of the non-Western world and the extension of colonial rule that was eventually to follow (Smith 1991: 77–8). We continue this theme in Chapter 9, where we examine the link between colonialism and racism.

FROM 1945 TO THE 1980s: THE ERA OF US DOMINANCE

The three decades following the end of the Second World War saw dramatic economic and political changes worldwide. Moreover, the strong hand of the USA was clearly evident in all of them. Indeed, partly because of US influence, each change became entangled with the others and served to enlarge and deepen the extent to which a world society was evolving.

The USA was economically very powerful at the close of the First World War, but periods of isolation and economic protectionism restricted its global role. However, after 1945, its economy emerged undamaged with stronger, re-equipped industries. This time it assumed the burden of managing world capitalism, including playing the central role in the Bretton Woods system (see below for a description of this system). Generously, it kept its own huge economy open to imports while tolerating some protectionist measures by weaker countries

while they recovered from war. It also freely permitted the purchase of
its technology. The USA became the world's leading creditor nation,
supplying grants to Europe (through the Marshall Plan) and Japan. It
supplied loans on favourable terms to other countries, although this was
something of a Trojan horse, allowing US-located TNCs to penetrate
new markets.

Together, these actions by the USA helped the capitalist economies
recover from the devastation and huge economic expense of the Second
World War. The willingness of the USA to help its Western allies shoulder the military costs accompanying the onset of the Cold War in 1947
also helped.

The most obvious areas in which US political and economic influence was paramount were in:

- the establishment of the Bretton Woods world financial system under US leadership
- the decolonization of most Third World countries
- the emergence and then consolidation of the Cold War era of East–West rivalry
- the 'golden age' of economic growth and Keynesian economic policies.

THE BRETTON WOODS FINANCIAL SYSTEM

Bretton Woods is the name of a small town in New Hampshire where 44 countries, mainly
allies of the USA, met in July 1944 to formulate policies for global economic cooperation.
The conference played a major role in stabilizing the postwar financial situation (Brett 1985:
62–79). Here, it was agreed that Western countries would operate a system of semi-fixed
exchange rates in managing their currencies, while minimizing their use of trade-inhibiting
policies such as currency devaluation, tariffs and import controls.
Meanwhile, the USA agreed to stabilize the dollar – already by far the
world's strongest currency – tying its value to gold reserves and permitting its currency to be used freely as world money.

The Bretton Woods system also involved establishing several key
economic international governmental organizations (IGOs). The most
important were:

- the World Bank, designed to help individual countries finance long-term infrastructure
  projects through providing loans at favourable rates
- the International Monetary Fund (IMF), which provided short-term financial assistance
- the General Agreement on Trade and Tariffs, a world forum to facilitate regular discussions between member countries on these issues. In 1995 it became the World Trade
  Organization (WTO).

THIRD WORLD DECOLONIZATION

Even before the end of the Second World War, there were stirrings of protest against the colonial domination of so many parts of the world by France, Britain, the Netherlands and Portugal. After 1945, however, the phalanx of anticolonial forces became much more apparent and
more effective. Among other things, the challenge to Western colonial power threatened
notions of racial superiority. Japan had successfully attacked British colonialism in the Far
East, although it was later defeated mainly by US military power. Mass protest led by the
remarkable leader Mahatma Gandhi eventually persuaded the British to leave India, which
became independent in 1947. This was the prelude to the decolonization of the rest of Asia,
Africa, the Middle East and the Caribbean. European expansion and colonialism had drawn
far-flung parts of the world into a relationship with the global economy. Nonetheless, it had

often done so with great cruelty and without the consent of the colonized peoples who, after 1945, were ready to enter a new era.

Successive US administrations also played a role in encouraging further decolonization by France, Britain and the Netherlands. There were political and economic motives for doing so. The USA wished to prevent the spread of communist movements and regimes, especially in the war-torn Asian countries, although it failed to do so in North Korea, China and Vietnam. It also wanted to penetrate the previously closed colonial markets. The European powers had used these markets as captive outlets for their home industries and as key sources of raw materials. The USA now wanted 'a share of the action'.

THE ONSET OF THE COLD WAR

The East–West Cold War dominated global politics from 1947 to 1989. In Europe, the 'iron curtain' – an expression British wartime Prime Minister Winston Churchill coined – divided the communist Warsaw Pact countries from the Western NATO (North Atlantic Treaty Organization) allies. It created a bipolar system with each side managed and ruled by its dominant power – the communist bloc by the Soviet Union and the capitalist democracies by the USA. Each side tried to gain the technical lead in a race to acquire supremacy in nuclear arms and space age technology.

With the success of the Chinese communist revolution in 1949, the Cold War became more complicated because it spread the conflict across much of Southeast Asia. A key test of both side's determination to continue the struggle came in 1950 when the communists of North Korea invaded South Korea with Chinese support. The USA promised military protection for East Asia. In fact, quite early in this period of crisis and rivalry, President Truman (1945–52) persuaded the US Congress to pour money into the national and world economy through arms expenditure and military aid. There were large deployments of troops in Europe and Asia and this long period of military spending, particularly on the Korean War, helped encourage the long postwar boom (Arrighi 1994: 273–98).

A 'GOLDEN AGE' OF ECONOMIC GROWTH AND KEYNESIAN ECONOMIC POLICIES

Although estimates vary, during the long boom from 1950 to 1975, the world's economic output is said to have expanded by an unprecedented 2.25 times (Harris 1983: 30). Using slightly different dates, Hobsbawm (1994: 288) claimed that the 'golden years' of economic growth and technological development from 1950 to 1973 meant that, for '80 per cent of humanity, the Middle Ages ended suddenly in the 1950s'. Although most remained poor by Western standards, even people living in the colonial and ex-colonial countries were caught up in this economic transformation.

By the mid-1950s, Europe and Japan had recovered from the devastation of war and were achieving new levels of prosperity. In 1959, Harold Macmillan was re-elected as the British prime minister, with the famous slogan, 'You've never had it so good', attributed to him. Even the poor developing countries had a good decade, with commodity prices for their agricultural produce and minerals attaining heights never achieved before or since. During the 1960s, Japanese economic might and the rising power of the newly industrializing countries (NICs) became evident, along with rapid rates of industrialization and urbanization in countries like Brazil and Taiwan.

Another key factor in underpinning the post-1945 economic boom was the widespread adoption of Keynesian national economic management policies. John Maynard Keynes was a major twentieth-century economist. In the 1930s, when unemployment brought on by the Great Depression was causing widespread distress, his theories challenged orthodox views on how best to explain and deal with the booms and slumps characteristic of capitalism. The

BOX 3.3 Global peace and war: key moments (1945–2011)

1945   End of Second World War but the onset of the nuclear age when, in August, the USA exploded two atomic bombs in Japan. The UN was established and in December it issued the Universal Declaration of Human Rights.

1947   Cold War 'officially' began with President Truman's declaration that the USA would protect democracies from the threat presented by totalitarian (communist) regimes.

1949   China went communist under the leadership of Mao Zedong and drove the nationalist and pro-capitalist forces into exile in Taiwan. The USSR exploded an atomic bomb.

1950–53   The period of the Korean War, which hardened Cold War lines.

1957   The USSR launched *Sputnik*, the first human-piloted spacecraft. The space race began in earnest.

1962   Cuban missile crisis; Soviet nuclear missiles placed in communist Cuba led to a confrontation with the USA. The world was poised for nuclear war but this was narrowly averted when Soviet Premier Khrushchev agreed to remove the missiles.

1963–75   American military involvement against North Vietnam's largely peasant army. After years of heavy US bombing and escalating conflict, US forces were pushed into a stalemate and withdrew.

1969   Moon landing by US team; the majesty of planet earth became fully apparent to everyone with access to the media.

1972   Rapprochement between the USA and China following President Nixon's visit.

1980s   President Reagan initiated his 'Star Wars' nuclear 'defence' programme.

1989   Soviet Premier Gorbachev relinquished further claims to 'defend' Warsaw Pact countries; collapse of Eastern Europe communist regimes as popular revolutions broke out. Cold War ended.

1992   End of communism in the Soviet Union, which dissolved into independent republics. First Gulf War to reverse Iraqi invasion of Kuwait and 'safeguard' world oil reserves. Sanctioned by UN, but demonstrated US leadership and power.

1992–99   In many regions, years of bloody civil wars, episodes of ethnic cleansing, mass genocide and sometimes disintegration into warlordism, partly as the aftermath of the Cold War and requiring a huge increase in UN peacekeeping operations and/or NATO or US interventions legitimized by the UN. Examples include Bosnia (1992–96), Kosovo (1999), Somalia (1993), Rwanda (1993–94), Democratic Republic of Congo (1999–2000) and East Timor (1999).

2000   George Bush became US president and soon blocked or revoked several weapons treaties such as the Comprehensive Test Ban Treaty, refused to sign up for the Kyoto Protocol in 2002, saying that the US economy would be harmed by measures to reduce its greenhouse gas emissions, and refused to recognize the International Criminal Court, designed to deter political leaders from permitting extreme human rights abuses in their countries.

2001   Al-Qaeda, Osama bin Laden's Islamic terrorist group, destroyed the twin towers in New York, killing 3,000 people and provoking mass world revulsion. Bush declared a 'war on terror'.

2001–10   US bombing campaign and then invasion of Afghanistan as part of a concerted strategy to eliminate global terrorism.

2003   After much opposition within the UN, the EU and from worldwide anti-war movements, coalition forces (mostly US and UK ones) invaded Iraq, ostensibly to rid the world of Saddam Hussein's weapons of mass destruction.

2009   Barak Obama was sworn in as the 44th president of the USA, with a promise of fostering greater international cooperation.

2011   Air power directed by NATO was used to target Gaddafi's regime in Libya in support of insurgents claiming democratic rights.

Sources: Castells (1998); Chomsky (2003); Pugh (2002).

uncertainties and diverging expectations of consumers, savers and investors often worked against each other and made rational economic decision-making difficult. He saw that, left unregulated, market forces tended to generate widening inequalities of income and wealth, making it impossible for mass demand to reach levels sufficient to keep consumption, investment and therefore employment at politically acceptable levels. He suggested that governments should play a more proactive role in spending on public resources and stimulating demand – so creating jobs and investment. He also advocated using the tax system to redistribute income from the rich to the poor (called 'progressive taxation'), because the poor would normally spend rather than save their additional income, thereby fuelling demand. His arguments and policies became widely accepted by Western governments in the 1940s and gave capitalism a new lease of life. They also strengthened the long boom and so contributed to globalization. (As we shall see in Chapter 4, Keynesian policies also underlie the attempts to recover from the post-2007 global economic crisis.)

Prosperity helped fuel important changes especially in the advanced countries. Life expectancy rose and many people were better educated than ever before, even in the developing countries. The consequences of such changes first became widely evident in the 1950s. However, they almost certainly generated cumulative effects, which by the late 1960s were giving rise to the demand for, and higher expectation of, greater personal freedom of choice in all spheres of life. Meanwhile, globalization meant that such powerful influences could not be contained within the rich countries but spread to the communist and developing world through education, the mass media, tourism and TNCs. Box 3.4 provides a timeline of these changes.

BOX 3.4   The desire for more personal freedom

Private leisure and consumption

1950s   The invention of the 'teenager'. Youth cultures became ever more evident and generated their own markets, musical and other cultural concerns.

1954   Dawn of the TV age: 30% of households in the UK had TV. This rose to 89% by 1963.

1956   The new genre of 'rock music' emerged. Elvis Presley achieved international fame with 'Heartbreak Hotel' and the film *Jailhouse Rock*. Adolescent rebellion became fashionable. Popular culture became big business.

1960s   Age of mass ownership of the motorcar began. Suburbanization increased while inner-city zones declined. Spread of supermarket shopping. Rapid expansion of systems of higher education across the world and international tourist travel took off.

1970s   The sexual revolution characterized by greater freedom to experiment and have multiple partners became stronger and was allied to the feminist and gay rights movements. In the West, rising divorce rates and fewer children suggested the retreat of the family.

1980s   Rock/pop music, with its emphasis on electric technologies, loud, continuous rhythms and self-expression, was absorbed into and hybridized by non-Western musical forms, everywhere helped by the spreading use of cassettes, videos and TVs across the world.

2000s   Ushered in a period of freedom 'on the move', with downloads and connectivity to mobile devices and tablets allowing instant communication and consumption of music, films and other popular entertainment and services.

Action for greater personal freedom and justice

1954   Beginning of the civil rights movement in the USA by African Americans. Reached its heyday in the mid-1960s.

Mid-1960s Anti-war movement in the USA against involvement in Vietnam began and spread to Europe. It coalesced with the drug culture and the 'hippie' revolt against continuing bureaucratic restraints on sexual/personal freedom.

1968	May 'revolution' by workers and students in France against the materialist pressures of capitalism.
Late 1960s	Feminist movement for gender equality took off in the USA and soon spread.
1969	Birth of the gay rights movement in the USA.
2005	Civil partnerships between same-sex partners, allowing similar rights and responsibilities to marriage, were recognized in the UK.
2011	The Arab Spring commenced, with popular demands for democracy and freedom in Tunisia, Egypt, Libya, Bahrain, Syria, Yemen and the Palestine territories.

KEY CHANGES SINCE 1989

Since the 1980s, several important transformations have been taking place both within and between nations. Their combined and cumulative impact has once again begun to shift the locus of world power in new directions. By the dawn of the new millennium in 2000, some observers suggested that these transformations pointed to a coming era of relative US economic decline, even though the country's military power continued to be unassailable. It is also interesting that these changes all furthered and indeed accelerated the evolution of a world society, albeit in rather different ways. Taking these in turn – although of course they overlapped – we can chart the following:

- the end of the Cold War and collapse of the USSR between 1989 and 1992, which opened the way for a much broader based world capitalism
- a growing tendency for the USA to shore up its declining manufacturing industries by pushing open market policies onto the developing countries while strengthening its already world-class financial industries
- the rise of the BRIC countries, especially China, and their growing demand to wield international influence, giving rise to a more multipolar world order.

THE COLLAPSE OF THE USSR: AN ERA OF WORLDWIDE CAPITALISM

During Ronald Reagan's presidency (1981–89), neoconservative strategists encouraged the US government to pursue a relentless and expensive weapons policy designed to end the supposed military and weapons threat from the Soviet Union. This was called the 'Star Wars' nuclear defence policy. Reagan was also persuaded to put pressure on developing and other countries to adopt radical, open market polices of economic liberalization. Later presidents continued this strategy.

The huge costs of responding to the US Star Wars programme helped to bankrupt the USSR and encourage its government to end the Cold War. This move was finally triggered in 1989 when Premier Gorbachev decided against providing Soviet military backing to Eastern European countries plagued by huge demonstrations against their communist regimes. The sheer expense involved also highlighted Soviet technological deficiencies, especially in computerization and its declining ability to fund the arms race. (By the early 1990s the costs incurred in this venture had shackled the USA with a national debt of $3 trillion.) Moreover, the Soviet Union's weakening internal grip reflected its inability to insulate its citizens – mainly through restricting incoming cultural traffic and travel – from Western influences. This was especially evident in the spheres of shopping and leisure where the seductive attractions and choices available in the West contrasted sharply with the meagre possibilities available to people living behind the iron curtain (Urry 2000: 42).

The end of the Cold War also saw the emergence of 15 new states in 1991, formerly part of the USSR, thus allowing the Soviet Union's former East European Warsaw Pact 'allies' to assert their political autonomy. A huge parallel change in the world economy, particularly with respect to the supply of potential workers available to global capital, accompanied and helped to generate this transformation. According to some estimates, this doubled in the decades after 1980 (Freeman 2007) to reach around 3 billion prospective workers by 2000.

US ECONOMIC AND FINANCIAL POLICIES: SHORING UP ITS HEGEMONIC POWER

Two overlapping policies were pursued during the Reagan (1981–89), Bush Sr (1989–93), Clinton (1993–2001) and Bush Jr (2001–09) presidencies. While both policies were primarily designed to protect US economic interests and underpin its continued hegemonic role in world affairs, they unintentionally stepped up the momentum towards creating a world society. One, which became known as the 'Washington Consensus' (Bello 1994, 2001), concerned the USA's ability to impose a set of global economic priorities on the world, while the other involved furthering the reach and profitability of the US financial sector.

While claiming to help poor countries solve the huge debt problems they had built up between 1970 and 1982 and encouraging them to adopt more sensible market-oriented development policies, the USA used its control of the IMF and World Bank and its influence over the G7 governments to compel many weak states to accept economic reforms called 'structural adjustment programmes'. In exchange for debt relief and continued access to US and G7 markets, these neoliberal policies required governments to open their economies to overseas trade (led by Western corporations) and capital flows (almost entirely G7 investment, often involving short-term 'hot' money inflows), while demanding the privatization of state assets and the abolition of subsidies and price controls designed to foster local businesses and protect poorer citizens.

A PAUSE TO REFLECT

It may be useful to distinguish between 'hard' power (military might, economic power and political coercion) and 'soft' power (the power to persuade through the instruments of popular culture, diplomacy and emulation) (Nye 2004). Thinking only about the soft power of the USA, what elements, for example its films, music or democratic traditions, do you find seductive and why?

By the end of the 1990s, even the highly conservative IMF conceded that these policies may actually have increased poverty in the poorest countries and inequality in the world as a whole. Many commentators (for example Bello 2001; Harvey 2003; Stiglitz 2002) have criticized these policies and their worldwide imposition for this very reason. Yet, it is also important to note that the worldwide dissemination of neoliberal economic policies played a huge role in accelerating and intensifying the processes of economic globalization through greater market and investment interconnectedness. At the same time these policies eventually generated opposition movements across many countries, which eventually fed into the formation of a global civil society (Chapter 19).

Turning to the US domestic economy, it was apparent by the 1970s that many of its core industries were increasingly subject to import penetration. In particular, Japanese, then South Korean and, more recently, Chinese manufacturers, among others, have exposed the USA to a long period of deindustrialization of its older industries. Partly because of this, the real incomes of many US citizens have either declined or remained stagnant since the 1980s. This brings us to the second government strategy, designed to slow down or prevent relative economic decline.

Since 1980, successive US governments have acted to further the interests of those economic sectors in which they retain a world competitive advantage. These include, among others, the biogenetic, pharmaceutical, aeronautical, IT, cultural and media industries. Here, interestingly, we should note that the continuing dominance of the US dollar as a world currency accords the US financial sector – epitomized by Wall Street's investment banks, stock market brokers, insurance and other financial interests – a strong global advantage. In addition, successive US governments have sought to enhance Wall Street's existing advantages (Bello 2001; Gowan 2009) by creating high-earning financial products for world markets (see Chapter 4 for more detail) and by pushing more open market, capitalist policies onto the world in accordance with the Washington Consensus. Together, these policies have underpinned each other and, in the process, buttressed US global economic power.

A BIPOLAR OR MULTIPOLAR WORLD

At the end of the Cold War, the USA emerged as the world's sole superpower, although its continuing dominance is already in question. By the late 1990s it had become apparent that the USA's long-term strategy of trying to preserve its hegemonic leadership in the economic sphere was threatened. In addition, the global strength and earning power of Wall Street finance proved to be a double-edged sword. For decades the Asian central and private banks have been stockpiling the dollar earnings accumulated by their domestic manufacturing exports to the USA (Brenner 2002; Gowan 2009). Much of this had been reinvested in the USA through the purchase of US treasury bills or government securities. For example, China alone held US government treasury bonds to the value of US$541bn in 2008 (Wearden and Stanway 2008). This has helped to keep US interest rates low and the dollar artificially strong. Equally significant for global politics, the US government has also been able to use this money to fund its huge budget deficit for domestic spending and overseas military activity. This left US businesses and households much freer than they might otherwise have been (for example, if the government had been forced to impose austerity measures) to borrow, spend and consume at low rates of interest – including increasing their mortgage debt.

This process causes turbulence in the delicate balance of debt and spending between the Pacific and American economies. For one thing, the massive trade imbalances clearly demonstrate the reality of rapidly growing BRIC and especially Asian economic power. One indication of this is that in 2000 only 27 of the world's top 100 TNCs were wholly or partly US owned (Dicken 2003: 222–4). There is also the issue of whether and for how long Asia will tolerate US indebtedness and its role in helping to perpetuate US military dominance worldwide and higher living standards than are justified by US domestic efficiency. Could China at some point call a halt to dollar stockpiles and constant trade imbalances and decide to invest these surpluses in its own economy rather than the USA? This, in turn, might mean the dollar's collapse with perhaps serious repercussions for the global economy.

Another challenge to US political superordination is that a multipolar world consisting of a growing number of economically powerful countries will massively increase the competition for world raw materials, especially oil, thereby leading to price increases, scarcities and perhaps future military struggles for control of strategic resources. We examine the military implications of recent US policies in Chapter 5.

REVIEW

A world society has been emerging in a halting way ever since the world religions first questioned the inhibitions induced by local beliefs and mythology – particularly through the spread of Buddhism, Islam and Christianity. The rise of modernity in Europe more fundamentally challenged a narrow ethnocentric outlook.

The formation of powerful, well-armed nation-states provided a basis for capitalist industrialization while the Enlightenment led to new cultural and scientific outlooks that fed into modernizing impulses. Empowered by new wealth and technology and energized by capitalist competition for markets and raw materials as well as by national rivalry, the European powers subjected other peoples to their rule, particularly in the eighteenth and nineteenth centuries. This widened markets and spread European languages and social and political institutions.

The emergence of the USA during the first three-quarters of the twentieth century as first a giant economic engine and then as a superpower gave globalization a further massive boost. In recent decades, other trends have become apparent in the moves towards a world society. Globalizing forces have become largely autonomous and self-sustaining and their survival or expansion depends less and less on the actions of particular nation-states. For example, despite its continuing military and economic superiority since the 1970s, the USA has been unable to arrest the rapid industrialization of China and India and their growing share of world trade. US policies designed to contain global terrorism have also proved unsuccessful so far and, indeed, its 2003 Iraq invasion may have increased the likelihood of terrorism.

In short, a more complex, polycentric world of competing powers, each with its own version of modernity and particular cultural legacy, has replaced the bipolar one of the superpowers. We live in a world of many robust players, transnational and national, state and non-state, and each is determined to influence local and global events. We shall encounter these two themes many times in the chapters that follow.

Visit the companion website at www.palgrave.com/sociology/cohen3e for extra materials to check and expand your learning, including interactive self-test questions, mind maps making links between key themes, annotated web links to sociological research, data and key sociological thinkers, a searchable glossary and much more.

FURTHER READING

Formations of Modernity (1992), edited by S. Hall and B. Gieben, offers a highly accessible discussion of the nature and causes of modernity. You may find Chapters 1, 2 and 6 especially helpful.

A. Giddens' *The Nation-state and Violence* (1985) provides a readable account of the rise of the European absolutist states.

K. Marx and F. Engels' short pamphlet, *The Communist Manifesto*, first published in 1848, the year of revolutions across Europe, offers a passionate and clear introduction to their conception of capitalism and why it needed to be superseded.

W. Hutton's *The Writing on the Wall: China and the West in the 21st Century* (2007) offers a clear, excellent dissection of both China and America's strengths and weaknesses in a complex world situation.

QUESTIONS AND ASSIGNMENTS

1. What were the main historical antecedents to the evolution of a world society and why were they limited in their effects?

2. Which one or more of the historical causes discussed do you think exercised the strongest influence in intensifying the process of globalization? Give your reasons.

3. Outline the main ways in which the USA played a leading role in reshaping the postwar world, and list the reasons for its recent period of relative economic decline.

4. Can you explain the rise of India and China, particularly in the twenty-first century?

4

Work, production and finance

How people experience work is a central theme in sociology, although more recently the discipline has been equally concerned with consumerism, leisure, personal lifestyles, popular culture and the media. Despite this new emphasis, our earnings from paid employment are what give most of us access to the pleasures of contemporary non-work life. In this chapter we examine the changing nature of work in the global age and consider how the transformations associated with it affect our lives.

We look first at the so-called golden age of mid-twentieth century 'Fordist' prosperity and examine the national and global basis for its success and its impact on work and social life. We then examine the explanations for its partial decline and outline some of the coincidental transformations that were gathering pace at the same time. More recently, additional changes have further shaped the world of work, often in ways that impose new burdens and risks. In particular, chronic job insecurity and the casualization of employment have become uncomfortable realities for all but a small minority of workers. This is partly linked to the rise of the BRIC economies, especially China and India, and the emergence of a more complex and competitive world economy. The increased power of the financial industries since the 1980s, however, has further complicated the nature of world capitalism while rendering everyone's life more susceptible to prolonged economic crises.

THE FORDIST REGIME OF ACCUMULATION

According to Aglietta (1979) and Lipietz (1987), so-called 'regulation theorists', despite competition between firms and inner conflicts between workers and capital, capitalism often passes through long periods of relatively uninterrupted economic growth. This depends, however, on the existence of two stable systems – a balance within individual companies between employees' rewards and capitalists' profits, and a societal-wide acceptance of a cluster of regulations, procedures and cultural expectations that set appropriate standards and establish supportive political policies. This regulatory climate appears to have worked well between 1948 and the early 1970s. When one or other system becomes unstable, however, then a radical restructuring has to take place before economic growth can resume and signs of social conflict disappear. We now examine both scenarios with

KEY CONCEPT

Named after its pioneer, the car maker Henry Ford, FORDISM is an industrial system involving the mass production of standardized goods by large, integrated companies. Each company was composed of many different, specialized departments, each producing components and parts that were eventually channelled towards the moving line for final assembly.

KEY CONCEPT

ALIENATION Marx believed that it is mainly through creative, self-directed work in the satisfaction of our own needs that we fully realize our inner selves and potential. However, under capitalism, workers become estranged or alienated from their skills and their potential, since now they are compelled to work for capitalists to survive and the product of their labour no longer belongs to them. Sociologists have employed this term more generally to describe the powerlessness and lack of creativity believed to be endemic in many aspects of contemporary life.

respect to the era of FORDISM. We shall look first at the national and worldwide management systems that facilitated its spectacular rise and success before going on, in the next main section, to examine the fault lines that appeared during the 1970s and that began to undermine its former success.

THE RISE OF MASS PRODUCTION AND CONSUMPTION

From the end of the nineteenth century until the early 1970s, Fordism, which was accompanied by highly effective systems of regulation both at the national and world levels, increasingly dominated the world economy. Henry Ford developed 'Fordism' between 1908 and 1916 while manufacturing the Model T car at his Highland Park and River Rouge plants in Detroit (Figure 4.1). He is generally credited with pioneering the mass production techniques that were eventually applied to the industries, packing processes, and even agricultural practices of many countries. You will gain some idea of what it was like to work under Fordist conditions from Box 4.1.

The Fordist production regime involved a number of difficult and ALIENATING experiences. Work was fragmented into many different activities, for example welding a particular bolt onto the corner of a toy or operating a specialized machine for pressing out one of the metal pieces used to assemble a refrigerator door. Each worker carried out one of these highly specialized tasks repeatedly, often remaining on the same job for long periods of time. This made work tedious and unsatisfying, but it simultaneously made for overall speed and efficiency.

BOX 4.1 Work experience in a Ford motor plant in the 1960s

Huw Beynon's (1973) classic study of the Ford motor plant at Halewood in Liverpool offers a fascinating account of working life at a typical mass production plant in the late 1960s. Ford established its three Halewood plants between 1958 and 1963, although its largest UK investment remained at Dagenham. At Halewood, the moving assembly line – which came to symbolize the essentially disempowering nature of twentieth-century machine-dominated Fordist manufacturing – was situated in the same factory where the car bodies were painted and fitted with their final trimmings (lights, seats and so on). Over 80% of the manual workers employed in a car assembly plant supplied backup support for those working on the line.

About 16,000 different components had to be 'screwed, stuck or spot-welded' (Beynon 1973: 105) to the moving car bodies as they slipped down the line. Each worker was tied to his station and repeated the same fixed tasks. On average, the line workers were allocated two minutes to complete each job. When market demand was expanding, the management might decide to speed up the line or reduce the manning levels. This meant frequent changes to work schedules and a need for intensified output. Six minutes out of the 480-minute working day were allowed for visits to the toilet and other natural functions. Those on the moving assembly line were rarely able to increase their output by a burst of effort to create a brief space for smoking or chatting with workmates. Moreover, the noise levels made talking virtually impossible (workers resorted to hand signals) and they could not disrupt the operations by leaving the line or failing to complete a task in the allocated time.

All this rendered socializing with workmates very difficult, while the work itself led to loneliness, tedium and relentless pressures that often generated disputes and work stoppages. Employees coped by thinking about the relatively high wages they would spend at the weekends (better money than could be obtained by semi-skilled workers elsewhere), joked with their workmates or played tricks on the foremen. Some dreamed of moving to a more 'worthwhile' job.

Source: Beynon (1973).

GLOBAL THINKERS 4 KARL MARX (1818–83)

© BETTMANN/CORBIS

Karl Marx was a social scientist as well as a revolutionary, the two roles being fused in his famous statement: 'The philosophers have only interpreted the world differently; the point is, to change it.' Marx tried to do both. His social theory generated a rich vein of ideas and arguments that have preoccupied scholars for 150 years. His political interventions gave rise to 'Marxism', an ideology that informed radical social thinkers, movements for international labour solidarity and revolutionary parties in many parts of the world. The great revolutions in Russia and China were underpinned by his thinking. Here we evoke his key starting points and ideas:

1. *Marx was a materialist.* He drew on previous German philosophers like Hegel who saw the world moving forward through a relentless competition of ideas – as one idea emerged another contradicted it. The resulting thesis in turn generated opposition. This dialectic attracted Marx but he rejected Hegel's idealism (in the sense of spirit, ideas and consciousness) in favour of materialism. What people ate, how they lived and how they produced goods and commodities needed to be placed at the centre of any analysis, thereby extracting, as he put it, 'the rational kernel from its mystical shell'.

2. *Marx was a historian.* He placed the movement of the dialectic within successive historical 'modes of production'. Primitive communism was replaced by slavery. The dialectic conflict between masters and slaves led to feudalism, the internal contradictions of which led in turn to capitalism. There the workers and capitalists (Marx called them the 'proletariat' and 'bourgeoisie') would engage in a massive social conflict leading to socialism and thence (in its higher stage) to communism. Only then would human conflict end.

3. *As a sociologist,* Marx had many insights into how the 'forces of production' linked to the 'relations of production'. This is sometimes called the 'base-superstructure' question. For Marx, forms of consciousness derived from a particular relationship to the means of production. Thus, when 'great masses of men are suddenly and forcibly torn from their means of subsistence and hurled onto the labour market' (Marx 1976: 876), they become conscious as a class. Working together in difficult factory conditions led to trade unionism and, Marx supposed, a commitment ultimately to overthrow capitalism by revolutionary means. In this prediction Marx was clearly wrong, although why he was wrong still provokes passionate debate.

Sources: Avineri (1968); Cohen (1978); Marx (1976).

A precondition for efficient production was the adoption of the principles of 'scientific management', or TAYLORIZATION, a term derived from the American engineer Frederick Taylor. From the 1890s he played a leading role in encouraging US industrialists to measure work activity precisely while establishing the optimum time required for each task. It has been widely argued that Taylorist techniques were ultimately designed to capture the shop-floor knowledge and skills once possessed by workers and to incorporate these into machinery and management practices. This progressively deskilled the workforce and increased management's ability to control the labour process.

At the plant level, a technostructure of scientists, engineers and others became necessary, supported by a hierarchy of managers striving to coordinate the multiple activities. The result was that both the creative design processes involved in production and the actual control of the latter shifted decisively from workbench to laboratory and office. These changes in work organization normally enabled management to obtain much higher and perhaps continuously rising levels of worker productivity for each given level of investment in plant and machinery.

KEY CONCEPT

TAYLORIZATION is the name given to the process accompanying Fordism, whereby managers scientifically studied work tasks with a view to finding ways of breaking them down into highly specialized and efficient components, which removed most of the skill and responsibility that workers had formerly exercised.

FIGURE 4.1 Ford's Highland Park plant in 1913

History was made as the flywheel magneto was the first manufactured part to be built on a moving assembly line. Mass production was born. By breaking up jobs into simple repetitive tasks, the power of craftsmen was broken.

FIGURE 4.2 Chiquita banana plantation, Cahuita, Costa Rica, 1996

Central American bananas are generally cut and packed on Fordist principles. The idea of a moving assembly line was copied from Chicago meat packers, who in the 1900s adopted the practice of hanging hog carcasses from a moving overhead rail, a technique used now in banana packing and many food-packing and industrial processes.

Unsurprisingly, Fordist plants required heavy and long-term investment in plant, capital-intensive equipment and research facilities. Thus, plants contained numerous departments, each specializing in a different activity, and the outputs of all these departments were then brought together for final assembly. This meant that large complex corporations became the dominant forms of business enterprise. In the late 1960s, for example, the Ford factory in Detroit employed 40,000 workers on one site, while Ford factories at Birmingham and Dagenham in the UK each had more than 25,000 workers. Indeed, in 1963, one-third of the British labour force employed in private industry worked in companies of 10,000 or more (Webster 2002: 64). Three additional features of the Fordist era can be noted:

1. It was assumed that the labour force would be predominantly male with women providing a 'stable' mother-centred family life. Since the beginning of the industrial era, the majority of women had always worked before marriage and often returned once their children were older. However, only a minority had worked full time. For example, the proportion of UK women who did this between the 1950s and the 1980s remained more or less constant at one-third (Edgell 2005: Ch. 4).

2. In all countries the Fordist economy rested mostly on national foundations. Again, this is demonstrated by the British case, in which even by the late 1960s UK firms supplied nearly 90% of the domestic market for manufactured goods (Webster 2002: 67).

3. Despite its negative features, mass production led to increased productivity and therefore the possibility of higher wages and gradually improving work conditions. In addition to rising wages, the sheer scale and relatively standardized nature of the output drastically reduced the costs of producing each item. For example, the average price of Ford's Model T car fell from $850 to $300 between 1908 and 1923 (Edgell 2005: Ch. 5). Gradually, therefore, the increased flow of cheaper, standardized commodities meant that mass production created an era of mass consumption. This was accompanied by the expansion of advertising, credit facilities and marketing services, an expanding public sector, and the growth of science and administration. Meanwhile, a leisure society evolved in which workers spent their rising wages on cars, holidays, improving their

homes and a restricted range of consumer goods. In short, Fordism enabled capitalism to resolve one of its previously recurring problems, namely a tendency towards under-consumption, or a limited market.

THE MANAGEMENT OF FORDIST INDUSTRY

In the USA, much of the prosperity that Fordism generated began in the 1920s, but the Great Depression and Second World War delayed it. Elsewhere, the era of mass consumption, along with the widespread diffusion of US management techniques and the re-equipping of postwar industries, arrived in the 1950s. Fordism in the factories helped lay the foundations for postwar prosperity. The successful Fordist formula relied on governments pursuing favourable policies, like Keynesianism, in the period after 1945.

In Chapter 3 we outlined the main ways in which global forces boosted prosperity after the Second World War. At the national level, too, we can identify a cluster of policies that provided a supportive environment for Fordist expansion. These measures were partly prompted by the fear of communism (Hobsbawm 1994), together with the spectres of the Great Depression and fascism. The key plank of these measures was an accommodation between labour and capital, including full union recognition, accepting skill demarcations demanded by workers, linking wages to gains in productivity, and improving wages, working conditions and pensions. In some companies jobs were traded in exchange for workers' acceptance of Fordist production methods, while other firms, especially in Germany and Scandinavia, adopted more conciliatory worker–manager consultation schemes.

Issues of social cohesion and social justice were also given much more attention by the state. This state intervention strove to achieve a social democratic accord whereby everyone had a right to a minimum of lifetime protection and security. In Europe – and to a lesser extent in Japan and the USA – governments improved the welfare state and adopted Keynesian spending policies through increased investment in publicly owned services and enterprises. Full employment became the top priority and some governments attempted income redistribution through progressive taxation.

THE CRISIS OF FORDISM AND DECLINE OF THE 'GOLDEN AGE'

The 'golden age' of high production and consumption and secure employment began to disintegrate from the late 1960s onwards. We now examine the forces that led to a decline in the Fordist system.

WORKER DISSATISFACTION AND MORE DISCERNING POSTMODERN CONSUMERS

The Fordist system depended on full employment and rising prosperity. This increased union power and made it difficult for employers to resist wage demands. High wages contributed to the build-up of inflationary pressures and some firms became uncompetitive. Moreover, many unions began to resist the 'Fordist bargain', in which workers dropped radical demands in exchange for recognition at work and greater material prosperity. Worker disillusionment set in when profits began to fall in the late 1960s and economic growth slowed, a process exacerbated by the oil price rises of the 1970s and increasing worldwide competition, especially from Japan (see below) and some NICs such as Brazil and South Korea. Indeed, the 1970s saw a major profits crisis for Western capitalism and several years of economic recession.

NEOLIBERALISM is an economic ideology that celebrates the free market, the minimalist state and individual enterprise. British Prime Minister Margaret Thatcher and US President Ronald Reagan embraced it so readily that 'Thatcherism' or 'Reaganism' are now seen as synonyms for, or variants of, neoliberalism. The doctrine was dominant in the period when failing and unattractive forms of communism prevailed as the major ideological contrast. However, with visible social inequalities and the incapacity of the state to act effectively to ameliorate them, increasing concern surrounds the domination of neoliberal ideologies.

By the 1950s a consumer youth culture had emerged with no memory of prewar poverty. Again, from the 1970s, postmodern sensibilities meant that consumers became interested in the creation of personal identity and individual lifestyles through the possession of fashion and designer goods (Featherstone 1992). This led to growing market pressures for more customized goods – designed to meet the individual's personal requirements – and helped to cut a giant swathe through the rather rigid Fordist mass production system. In its place, a more adaptable system gradually emerged based on a greater ability to cope with rapid changes in demand and more direct interactions between producers and their market outlets.

THE TURN TO NEOLIBERAL ECONOMICS

In the early 1970s all the wider forces supporting Fordist production more or less concurrently lost their former momentum. Depending on which interpretation one uses, worker–employer relations entered either a new era of greater flexibility, or an era of relative disorder and uncertainty characteristic of global capitalism today. The latter interpretation implies that the current system now lacks the kind of regulatory regime that sustained the golden years.

A key change undermining Fordist production was the adoption of NEOLIBERALISM by more and more governments from the early 1980s onwards. Neoliberal economic policies involve deregulating economic life, attempting to reduce the role of the state, and opening up capital and trade to global market flows. As we explained in Chapter 3, through the Washington Consensus, the USA and G7 nations advocated neoliberal economics for both their own and weaker economies. Overall, the consequence has been an increase in the openness of countries to global economic pressures and competitive forces, which are difficult to resist or control.

JAPANIZATION: A MORE COMPETITIVE WORLD ECONOMY AND FLEXIBLE LABOUR

The success of Fordism spread industrialization worldwide and intensified international competition. Thus, by the 1960s the war-torn economies of Europe and Japan had recovered. Soon they were exporting to the USA. These exports enabled them to generate the dollars required to repay US loans and purchase US machinery. As the economic recovery gathered pace during the 1960s, US TNCs tried to capture a share of the growing European markets by engaging in foreign direct investment. Quite soon, however, a parallel drive by European firms to invest directly in the US market matched this accelerated 'Americanization' of European economic life.

This rapid increase in international competition – the leading TNCs had offices, sales networks, advertisements and neon signs in all the major cities of the world – placed further pressure on companies to increase the distinctiveness of their products. Cut-throat competition also underlined the importance of price as a factor in competitiveness and highlighted the problem of rising domestic wage levels. Higher wages were now an obstacle to business success.

Japan played a particularly crucial role in spearheading a change towards more flexible practices for organizing labour and production. With approval from the USA, it successfully pursued a policy of export-led growth from the mid-1950s onwards. By the 1970s its companies had made massive inroads into the home markets of all its competitors while keeping its own domestic economy relatively closed. At the same time, growing manufactured exports from the NICs, initially of low-value goods, also increased the penetration of imports into the North American and European markets.

So successful was foreign, especially Japanese, competition by the 1970s that many European and US companies began to imitate Japanese management practices, a process known as JAPANIZATION and, from the following data, we can see why. In automobile production – a core part of the structure of developed economies – Japanese output rose rapidly, reaching 11 million vehicles in 1980 compared with 8 million in the USA in the same year (Dohse et al. 1985: 117). Also in 1980, Japanese home production accounted for 28% of total world output and captured 25% of the US market. By 2006, Toyota had outstripped General Motors as the world's number one motorcar manufacturer.

'FLEXIBLE' LABOUR AND WESTERN DEINDUSTRIALIZATION

With flexibility the hallmark of Japanese production, one can view the Japanization of work and business organization as a significant factor in the worldwide shift towards an era of greater flexibility and insecurity in work conditions. Indeed, considered overall, since the 1970s a major shift – more evident in the advanced countries – has occurred in how work and employment are experienced. The main features of this shift are continued deindustrialization and the increasing insecurity and casualization of work. We now summarize its central trends:

1. Many manufacturers, supermarkets and department stores have cut costs by downsizing their labour forces. In other words, they shrink their in-house operations to a core of activities in which they enjoy special advantages and concentrate on cultivating their market brand (Klein 2001). This normally involves subcontracting, often on a worldwide basis. In the 1980s, by franchising most of its production to more than 3,000 operators in 57 countries, the clothing retailer Benetton shrank its labour force to 1,500 (Webster 2002: 76–7). By 2004, for example, Bangladesh had become a haven for outsourced garment production, with 3,280 factories employing around 1.8 million, mainly women, workers (Wills and Hale 2005: 10–11).
2. From the late 1960s, many TNCs also cut labour costs by relocating plants to export-processing zones, where wages were low, workers non-unionized and governments repressive, or to areas in their own country with weak unions, for example the 'sun-belt' southern states of the USA.
3. Firms reduced the proportion of their workforce eligible for permanent employment, pensions and sickness and unemployment benefits. The remainder formed a growing army of casualized workers – part time, temporary, seasonal or homeworkers. Labour became bifurcated (McMichael 2000: 191) between a permanent core and a casualized majority performing 'McJobs'. By the 1980s part-time work had risen to 30–40% of total employment in the advanced countries (cited in Beck 2000b: 56).

There have been several attempts to provide an overarching label with which to characterize the current era. These include 'disorganized capitalism' (Lash and Urry 1987), 'flexible accumulation' (Harvey 1989) or 'post-Fordism' (Lipietz 1987). However, some writers see more underlying continuities than discontinuities between the eras preceding and following the 1970s, although they concede this was a watershed in many respects. They therefore prefer to use the label 'neo-Fordist' (Webster 2002).

PARALLEL TRANSFORMATIONS

By the 1970s Fordism had been beset by the certain transformations that had been working their way through the world economy. These were the increased importance of the service industries and the knowledge economy, the revolution in information and communication technologies (ICTs), and the growing role of women in the workforce.

THE SHIFT TO SERVICE JOBS AND THE SYMBOLIC OR KNOWLEDGE ECONOMY

In the 1960s the shift of employment towards the service industries, which characterized all modernizing societies, became much more important. Just after the Second World War services accounted for 49% of jobs in the USA (Bell 1973: 132), but by the 1990s this proportion had risen to between 70% (Webster 2002: 45) and 75% (Dicken 2003: 525) in the USA and most advanced countries. The decline in manufacturing jobs was particularly acute in the UK from the mid-1960s, but accelerated during the 1970s across most European countries (Dicken 2003: 525). From its postwar peak in 1979 at 20% of the workforce, manufacturing employment in the USA is just over 10% of the total workforce.

The term 'services' is an inclusive category covering different levels of job satisfaction, job security and income opportunities and, as such, it obscures the distinction that exists between the broad swathe of low-skilled, poorly paid, often casualized and insecure jobs and highly skilled professional work in what are increasingly referred to as the 'symbolic knowledge or creative industries'. Using examples, we now explore some of this variation below.

A PAUSE TO REFLECT

While alienated and exploited labour marked the Fordist era, it often provided job security and acceptable wages. The neoliberal era has produced casualized, poorly paid and mobile labour, at least in the unskilled sector, although welfare systems in the rich countries have cushioned the worst effects of unemployment. How would you assess the virtues and disadvantages of both Fordism and neoliberalism?

By 1990 'professionals' made up nearly one-third of the workforces of advanced countries. Professionals work in medicine, research, science, law, engineering, the 'caring' occupations, ICTs, the media and education. Although many scholars have pointed to the growing contribution of the knowledge industry in promoting exports and creating wealth in advanced economies, some (for example Elliot and Atkinson 2008: 178–83) are sceptical about its potential to replace older industries in terms of employment or earnings. Hutton (2007: 334–7) suggests that the knowledge industry encompasses 'hard' and 'soft' forms of knowledge and creativity. The former include the technical and scientific skills required to build machinery or transport systems, to devise new forms of credit and loans in banking, or to design distinctive media or IT products. Soft knowledge is 'less tangible' (Hutton 2007: 335). It includes the creativity, leadership, communication, empathy, emotional intelligence and ability to generate a social arena and cultural milieu in which the skills and aptitudes of others can be harnessed. Soft knowledge is thus important in advertising, web design, the social media, healthcare, education and investment banking. Hutton also argues that people in the knowledge economy are equipped to cope with the increasingly sophisticated demands of consumers and that this is an area in which the advanced economies tend to be way ahead of their rapidly industrializing rivals in the developing world. Since 1990, the proportion of the working population employed in the knowledge industry in Britain has risen to more than 40% (Hutton 2007: 336).

The lower level jobs in the service sector tend to be in catering, tourism, domestic work, some aspects of healthcare, transport, the retail trade, the leisure and entertainment industry, and the various fast-food outlets. Food chains like Pizza Hut, Taco Bell and Starbucks have spread throughout the world since McDonald's first opened in the USA in 1955. By March 2011 McDonald's had 32,737 restaurants across the world – over half of which were outside the USA – with total sales of US$24bn in 2002 (*Wall Street Journal*, 8 March 2011). Interestingly, the fast-food industry has developed some key organizational features that are generally acknowledged to be strongly Fordist in character. Other businesses in the service sector have adopted some of the organizational features of the Fordist-leaning fast-food industry. These include retail outlets such as the Body Shop, Ikea, Walmart, H&M Clothing, Gap, and Subway, the main food rival of McDonald's. These features also developed in certain tourism, sports, healthcare and education providers.

Ritzer (1993, 1998, 2004a, 2004b) has applied Weber's insight into the dominant tendency towards formal rationality in modern capitalist economies (see Global Thinkers 3) to the fast-food and other service sectors. He argues that these sectors are successful because they have maximized the market and profitable potential provided by four operating principles – efficiency, calculability, predictability and control through technology. Predictability involves the assurance 'that products and services will be the same over time and in all locales' (Ritzer 2004a: 14), as well as the need for employees to adopt certain 'scripted' behaviours when dealing with customers, including ritualized 'pseudo interactions' such as wishing everyone a 'nice day' and being dressed in familiar company uniforms (Ritzer 2004a: 91). Work arrangements – limited menus, timed and programmed operations, technologies that standardize food mixtures and an assembly-line system – and time-saving equipment like microwave ovens and automatic drink dispensers combine to control and deskill workers (Ritzer 2004a: 15, 189). Accordingly, homogenized and interchangeable employees mass produce standardized products for highly rationalized and profitable companies.

A PAUSE TO REFLECT

To some extent Fordist or 'neo-Fordist' (Edgell 2012) principles have now taken over the service sector – ordering food and serving it in fast-food outlets are good examples. Is there scope for such intense rationalization in organizations such as schools, nursing homes or health centres? Alternatively, will increased sophistication in consumer choice limit the extent to which services can become standardized or 'industrialized'?

THE REVOLUTION IN ICTs

Another impact on work and leisure has been the revolution taking place in ICTs – much of it emanating from the innovative mix of young and experimental technologists working in numerous tiny firms and often linked to universities, initially based in and around California's Silicon Valley (Castells 1996: 53–60). This revolution, which gathered pace during the 1970s, was boosted in 1971 by the invention of the microprocessor or chip, which hugely increased the amount of information that could be stored. This heralded an 'information society', whereby knowledge – whether in the form of scientific research, design, the media, or creating new products, formula or symbols – became the key component in wealth creation, reducing the significance of other inputs like manual labour, raw materials or energy.

The emergence of the knowledge or symbolic economy has in turn made possible the rise of what Castells and other writers (Urry 2003; Webster 2002) call the 'network society'. Here, businesses and other organizations can now spread much more easily across borders, and may become less centralized and hierarchical while transferring power much more into the hands of the knowledge makers and disseminators. Castells (1996: 240) also avers that the transition to post-Fordism was partly rooted in technological change. The reverberating implications of ICTs are discussed further in Chapter 16.

THE DRAMATIC MOVEMENT OF WOMEN INTO THE WORKFORCE

The proportion of women in paid work increased from 49 to 69% between 1970 and 1990 (Beck 2000b) and reached 70.5% by 1994 (Castells 1997: 159). Similar rises have been recorded for other countries over the same period: from 33.5 to 43.3% in Italy, 47.4 to 59% in France and 48.1 to 65.3% in Germany (Castells 1996: 253). The scale of this increase is not confined to the developed countries but also occurred in countries such as Egypt and Brazil. Overall, the International Labour Office estimated that, by 2007, 1.2 billion women were economically active – most outside their homes – compared with 1.8 billion men (ILO 2008).

Linked to this massive and more or less worldwide increase in female paid employment has been not only the improved educational participation rate for girls but also greater economic independence from kin and husbands. Beck and Beck-Gernsheim (2002: 23) regard these changes as a 'global gender revolution', since it has paved the way, albeit unequally across countries, for women to exercise more choice over whether or who to marry (or divorce), when and whether to have children and how to balance career and family identities. Whereas for nineteenth-century middle-class women 'everyday life was nearly always a fenced-off preserve of family and neighbours', now women can 'display expectations and wishes that extend beyond the family' (Beck and Beck-Gernsheim 2002: 64) and begin to 'make a life of their own'. Similarly, Castells (1997: 135) talks of the 'challenge' to the patriarchal family and the 'transformation of women's consciousness'. We discuss these changes and their implications more thoroughly in Chapter 8.

GROWING WORLD COMPETITION AND THE RISE OF THE BRIC COUNTRIES

KEY CONCEPT

BRIC COUNTRIES is a term (or acronym) coined in 2001 that is now often used to group Brazil, Russia, India and China, although other increasingly wealthy nations such as Mexico and South Korea are sometimes added to them. Each included country enjoys increased leverage in the global economy because it possesses oil and/or other mineral wealth, an advanced industrial base, a strong growth rate, high-tech agriculture or a combination of these. Their growing political influence is demonstrated by inclusion in the G20 leading group of nations at major world meetings in place of the former G7 group. At the end of 2011 Brazil's economy overtook the UK's as it moved into sixth position globally. India, currently at number 20, is projected to be the fifth biggest economy by 2020.

In the 1950s a growing number of NICs began to manufacture and export a widening range of products. Between 1953 and the late 1990s, the share of world manufacturing output coming from NICs rose sharply from around 5 to 23%, while that of the developed countries correspondingly shrank from 95 to 77% (Dicken 2003: 37). In the late 1950s Southeast Asia's four 'tiger' economies of South Korea, Taiwan, Singapore and Hong Kong spearheaded this competition, although other countries, including Brazil, India, Malaysia, Thailand and Mexico, also became increasingly important players. By 2000 Hong Kong, South Korea, Mexico, Taiwan and Singapore were ranking tenth, twelfth, thirteenth, fourteenth and fifteenth respectively among the leading world exporters of manufactured goods, with their share falling between 2.2 and 3.2% compared, for example, with Canada's share of 4.3%, Italy's of 3.7% or France's of 4.7% (Dicken 2003: 40).

CHINESE MANUFACTURED EXPORTS

By the beginning of the twenty-first century, China and India, two previously slumbering giants, were rapidly recovering the share of world economic output they had held for centuries prior to the West's industrial leap forward in the eighteenth and nineteenth centuries. Their rapid catching up exercise was based not on exotic craft goods and scarce raw materials, as before, but on their ability to compete on the same high-tech terms as the advanced economies. Rather different processes, however, are fuelling their growing importance in the global economy.

China's rise from a poor agricultural country in the 1940s to second place in the world economy by 2010 is remarkable. Within the space of 29 years, from 1978 to 2007, and fuelled by growth rates of 9–10%, China's economy grew ninefold. Similarly, between 1978 and 2003, its average per capita income increased six times while city dwellers almost doubled to around 400 million (Hutton 2007: 4). Many factors account for this expansion, including the investment in education and agriculture by the communist government of Mao Zedong up to 1976, before market reforms were introduced. However, the most important of these factors has been that China decided to focus strongly on the rapid expansion of its manufacturing base, as well as to encourage vast inward private investment and to accelerate industrial growth by constantly searching for new export markets. Since its admission to the WTO in December 2001, China's dominance in textiles, shoes and computer parts has been steadily growing. In the first four months of 2005, Chinese shoes exported to the European Union (EU) rose by 700%, threatening shoe manufacturing in Spain and Italy. Likewise, 237 million T-shirts were imported into the EU. Manufacturers in China have perfected the art of the niche market. Look down at the fly on your trousers or the zipper on your skirt. It is 80% certain that it was produced in a dusty town called Qiaotou in Zhejiang province. There, in 1980, three brothers started a button and zip factory by picking up buttons on the street. By 2005 the town was exporting two million zips a day (*The Guardian*, 25 May 2005).

It is hardly surprising that China has increasingly been labelled as the 'workshop of the world'. In terms of its overall position in the global economy, estimates again vary. Measured in terms of US dollar equivalent values, the World Bank's development indicators in 2010 placed China third, coming only just behind Japan, with a gross domestic product (GDP) of $4.33 trillion compared with the USA's $14 trillion and Japan's $4.9 trillion. Using another measure that takes account of comparative differences in real living costs between countries, however, the World Bank places China second with a GDP of $7.9 trillion – a spectacular result, although still only half that of the USA (World Bank 2010). In terms of exports, China moved to the number one slot in 2010 (Table 4.1).

A number of projections suggest that China will probably become the largest economy and will overtake the USA by 2025. Indeed, PricewaterhouseCoopers (2008) – an influential global management consultant group – suggests that, given current rates of economic growth and taking the US economy as the base line of 100, by 2050 it is likely that China's economic weighting will be around 129 compared with India's 88. On the other hand, China faces some huge internal obstacles to continued economic growth. These include:

- deepening inequality within the urban population and between the countryside and cities
- demands from migrants in the coastal export zones who lack job security and work up to 80 hours a week for very low wages
- low labour productivity compared with the West
- extensive political corruption
- restricted freedom of speech, which may inhibit creativity and innovation
- limited welfare provision, which compels the population to rely on savings, so limiting the development of a home market (see Hutton 2007; Kwan Lee 2007).

TABLE 4.1 Top 10 countries by value of exports (US$), 2010		
1	China	1,506,000,000,000
2	Germany	1,337,000,000,000
3	USA	1,270,000,000,000
4	Japan	765,200,000,000
5	France	508,700,000,000
6	South Korea	466,300,000,000
7	Italy	458,400,000,000
8	Netherlands	451,300,000,000
9	Canada	406,800,000,000
10	UK	405,600,000,000

Source: CIA (2011).

Aware of these challenges, recent governments are trying to introduce appropriate reforms. Meanwhile, the rest of the world looks on with a mixture of awe and anxiety as we anticipate the many ramifications of living with a new superpower.

INDIA'S WORLD-CLASS SERVICE ECONOMY

In 1991 India further opened its economy to overseas investment and competition and expanded its already substantial industrial base. Since then its rate of economic growth has risen substantially. Moreover, as a nation, India's self-confidence and increased global cultural and economic influence have been clearly evident, for example in its export of literature, music, Bollywood films and not least because of the worldwide success of its highly trained and much sought after migrant professionals in medicine, scientific research, IT, the social sciences and humanities. While India's technical achievements, research and exports in steel, chemicals and pharmaceuticals are impressive, its home-grown service industries also fuel economic growth. Again, India's huge, highly educated middle class of more than 250 million people, swelled by decades of government and family investment, has proved an invaluable economic asset.

Relatively low wages compared with those of comparable workers in advanced countries, the ability of IT to offset the constraints of distance, and the growing importance of symbolic knowledge worldwide have endowed India's educated middle class with a competitive advantage in establishing a niche in the world market for middle-level services. The latter include call centres and processing legal, medical, commercial, bank and insurance information, which are areas that are in increasing demand from consumers, private businesses and governments. India's export of IT-related services expanded more than 10 times between 2000 and 2006, rising from US$565m to US$6.2bn over the period (Paus 2007: 13). Many comparisons are made between China and India, but perhaps the most intriguing difference is that India has been able to combine economic growth with political freedom, whereas China has achieved its spectacular economic growth while remaining a one-party state.

THE FINANCIALIZATION OF THE GLOBAL ECONOMY SINCE THE 1990s

Since the 1980s, the significant empowerment and expansion of the world's financial services have transformed the lives and employment prospects of countless millions of people. Demands from this sector have led to changes in political and government policies, in particular the deregulation of markets and businesses. This same process of FINANCIALIZATION has also allowed the finance sector to siphon off much of the wealth that the non-financial professions generate in the 'real' productive economy and produce in factories, on farms, or through construction, mining or the creative industries.

> **KEY CONCEPT**
>
> FINANCIALIZATION describes the increased relative importance of financial products, such as government bonds, stocks, shares and derivatives (products that insure against the future risk of loss or price changes), and of the institutions that deal in them, including commercial and investment banks, brokers, hedge funds, and pension and investment fund managers. Financialization also refers to the capacity of this sector to suck economic resources out of the productive industries.

In doing so, the financial services industry has made little direct contribution to the productiveness of the rest of the economy (Elliot and Atkinson 2008: 195). For example, investment banks, private equity companies and other agents have taken over perfectly viable companies, cherry-picking their most profitable assets for short-term profit rather than attempting to improve their operations. Losing productive workers often accompanies this process. In the USA alone, takeover deals between 1995 and 2005 were valued at $9 trillion, with no obvious gains in productivity (Hutton 2007).

We need to make two caveats to this depiction of the financial sector as parasitic. First, it provides a growing share of tax revenues and this partly explains why governments are reluctant to intervene to reregulate it, despite the risks to the wider economy that its activities pose. Second, the established retail or commercial banks continue to perform their traditional roles as havens for savings and as a source of overdrafts and loans without which businesses or consumers could not function. For example, in 2008 the UK government bailed out two big banks, the Royal Bank of Scotland (RBS) and Lloyds TSB, because of their key role in facilitating loans to the productive economy. This happened in a number of other countries as well. Despite a common belief to the contrary, the retail commercial banks form only part of the financial sector and were not the main drivers of the financialization process defined above.

As the recent global recession has demonstrated, the financial sector has the capacity to distort massively how the remainder of the economy functions, while contributing to inequality and further intensifying the employment insecurity that many workers have already experienced. The Occupy Wall Street movement crystallized the opposition to this skewing of the economy and, in particular, the shrinking opportunities available to younger people, even if they have secured a good education. The dominance of the financial sector is shown by the increased proportion of corporate profits that now come from banking, insurance and trading in various countries, especially the USA and the UK. In 2005 this reached almost 35% compared with only 10% in the 1960s (Ford 2008). While the financial services industries flourish in the advanced established economies, they are also gaining ground in developing countries. In both cases, a combination of five factors has ensured that finance has become truly global and interconnected:

1. The tendency for US governments since the 1980s to promote Wall Street as a way of helping to counter the relative economic decline of its national economy in the face of growing international competition (Gowan 1999, 2009).
2. The adoption of open market and liberalization policies worldwide. This enabled long-term and short-term investment capital (hot money) to flow freely into many developing countries and then, sometimes just as quickly, to exit. Where these sudden outflows of capital occurred – as in 1997 from some Asian economies, but also from Mexico in 1994 and Russia in 1998 – entire economies were left in a state of collapse, their currencies and property prices fell, and local businesses and banks were bankrupted.
3. Huge trade imbalances between the USA and Asia have been partly recycled into the US economy, either through the purchase of government bonds or via Wall Street's financial dealings. This encouraged businesses and households to borrow large amounts of money and led to further imports. The extended credit then fuelled demand, which allowed the Chinese and other Asian economies to grow much faster than they would otherwise have done.
4. Since the mid-1990s, many investors and banks across the world, not just in the North, have been prepared to invest in what have proved to be largely false promises of high returns from the new financial products invented by Wall Street's financial wizards.
5. These investment packages often involved a type of security (collateral debt obligations) that included so-called 'subprime' or 'toxic debts' consisting of highly risky mortgage borrowing, which later collapsed in value in 2007 as house prices fell in the USA, thereby triggering a worldwide banking crisis.

THE TRAJECTORY OF FINANCIALIZATION: RISK

The deregulation of banks and other financial institutions in the 1980s, which was particularly notable in the UK and USA, coincided with:

- the abolition of most controls on capital flows between countries – so opening up the world to Wall Street trading activity
- the rapid growth of various saving schemes and pension funds as employees sought to provide for their retirement.

Consequently, increasing supplies of money searching for profitable investment outlets flowed towards investment banks and other financial institutions just at the time that finance was being deregulated nationally and globally. How these financial agents responded to these opportunities tells us how the financial crisis both began and accelerated.

Investment banks and fund managers increasingly looked for avenues that would yield higher returns than either government bonds or comparatively safe corporate shares held on a long-term basis. This hunt for higher earnings required new, innovative financial products and practices that could earn higher returns but carried a higher risk (Elliot and Atkinson 2008: 196). Financial houses increasingly engaged in the secondary trading of securities on their own account rather than simply performing as brokers acting on the instructions of their client investors. For many traders this became their most important source of profit (Gowan 2009: 8–10). Maximizing returns both for the client and the banks often took precedence over the need for long-term security.

As traders bought and sold increasing volumes of securities, there was a huge increase in the turnover value of shares and other securities. The agent's charges in fees and commissions rose with the frequency of sales. As Ford (2008: 24) noted: 'Whatever way you look at it, agents have somehow managed to get their hands on between 40 and 80% of the return that would otherwise have accrued to investors.' Those who engage in these secondary trading practices on behalf of clients earn approximately $500bn worldwide each year in management fees and commissions. In effect, the croupiers have taken over the stock markets. Over the lifetime of a share, the leakage to agents probably amounts to one-quarter of its value and reduces the final value of pensions for lifetime savers. Taking their cue from sociologists, behavioural economists have also shown that markets do not necessarily enable investors to make rational choices. Frequently, investors act on imperfect information and make guesses, take risks or act as lemmings, especially when prices rise.

The market therefore tends to generate speculative bubbles with little relationship to real economic trends. Moreover, because most investors – including pension fund managers and charities – have little knowledge of how financial markets operate, they hire financial 'experts' to invest on their behalf. As we have seen, however, the latter are driven by the urge to maximize their own financial returns and frequently this involves the pursuit of short-term profits and switching clients' resources between different assets to permit charging commissions and fees. This leads to a misallocation of economic resources and allows financial agents to capture a disproportionately large share of any gains from capital investment and wider economic growth. Gowan (2009: 7) argues that much of this 'speculative arbitrage' (buying and selling on the expectation of price changes) amounts to a kind of gambling. Gowan (2009: 7) further suggests that speculative arbitrage has frequently spilled over into what he calls 'asset-price bubble-blowing'. Here, traders actively generate price differences by deliberately entering a chosen market in strength thereby pushing up prices. This may tempt less wary investors to follow suit in an atmosphere of rising values. Once the asset price attains a certain level, the traders then sell their share of the assets – recouping large speculative profits in the process – but burst the bubble through these same actions, leaving prices to tumble for other investors. He cites several likely examples of this process, including the doubling of oil prices in 2007/08. This, he claims, was due less to world shortages than to the pouring of investment funds into the speculative purchase of oil and various other commodities.

Financial deregulation also allowed banks to expand massively the volume of profitable assets they could lend to borrowers. Banks have always re-lent a safe fraction of the deposits savers place in their safekeeping. By retaining approximately one-eighth or one-tenth of these deposits, banks were able to guarantee they had the reserves needed to respond to the demands of savers as and when they wished to make withdrawals. Recycling their capital base to businesses or consumers creates credit and generates spending and investment throughout the economy. Also, those who borrow and then spend and invest bring much of this cash back into the banking system where a proportion of it can again be recycled into the economy. All this constitutes established practice. Since the 1970s, however, banks have expanded their fractional capital base by a multiple, in some instances, of up to 40 times their actual deposits. This huge increase in lending has resulted in an unprecedented rise in credit creation. Much of this lending was unsafe, especially the extensive mortgage lending in the USA to low-income borrowers in insecure employment.

Financial agents also created new products or diversified others. J. P. Morgan, one of the USA's largest investment banks, developed much of this widely applauded financial innovation in the mid-1990s (Tett 2009). In particular, it devised various kinds of credit derivatives. In fact, derivatives have long existed as a financial product. They operate as a kind of insurance for farmers, miners and other businesses wishing to reduce the risk of future price changes for their products – or hedge their bets – by agreeing to sell their product at a fixed price before it is ready for sale. Then, whatever the final price, their returns are guaranteed at the earlier arranged price. The market for many other kinds of derivatives developed rapidly from the late 1980s onwards. According to David Chapman (2005), the director of a Canadian mutual trust fund called Bullion Management Services, by 2005 international interest rate and currency derivatives had reached a value equal to more than $200 trillion.

A PAUSE TO REFLECT

For many people, what happened in the banking and financial sector was 'out there' and nothing to do with them. However, the recession, which began in 2007, alerted us that our pensions, mortgages, savings, jobs, homes and welfare entitlements are at risk from banks collapsing and countries defaulting anywhere in the world. What ways can politicians devise to insulate individual societies and the world at large against such risk? Is there anything we, as citizens, can do to reduce our dependence on unstable financial institutions and those taking large risks with the savings we place in their care?

The J. P. Morgan team elaborated this process even further by devising credit derivatives for outstanding loans or debts. These entail banks turning their own and other companies' liabilities into products and then parcelling them into bundles for sale as securities, or securitization (Elliot and Atkinson 2008: Ch. 7). Examples of such debts include mortgage loans to house buyers, loans to students through special loan companies, and hire purchase agreements for motorcars or other consumer goods. In effect, the financial agents engaged in creating these profitable securities out of debts or loans were able to make profits from their own and other investors' outstanding loan obligations by selling these on to yet other investors (such as pension funds) as income-earning securities.

Reputable rating agencies assisted them in the task. In exchange for fees, the rating agencies used sophisticated mathematical models to 'prove' that the risks associated with these financial products were minimal, particularly if the debts were mixed in such a way that tranches of high-risk, high-yield debts were bundled together with low-risk, low-yield ones. This is what happened in the years leading up to the financial crisis of 2007/08, which hinged fatally around the subprime mortgage debts (theoretically high yielding but also high risk) taken out by many poor citizens across the USA in the preceding years. Indeed, around $6 trillion worth of US mortgage debts were incorporated into various securities (Elliot and Atkinson 2008: 244).

ENDGAME 2007–10: THE BURSTING FINANCIAL BUBBLE AND ITS IMPACT

From summer 2007 to autumn 2008, a series of financial crises erupted and spread through the global banking system, but struck most forcibly in the USA and the UK. The most serious rupture to the mask of public confidence occurred when Lehman Brothers filed for bankruptcy in September 2008 – the largest such move in American history. Despite having assets to the tune of $600bn, Lehman had borrowed so much money, largely to invest in housing-related assets, that its liabilities had reached 31 times the value of its capital base. As the US subprime mortgage crisis escalated, with falling property values and millions of householders defaulting on their mortgage payments, Lehman Brothers eventually collapsed (Figure 4.3). Panic hit other leading banks because most were also holding vast liabilities involving securities that contained toxic debts. In addition, the interconnections associated with mutual lending, borrowing and funding between the leading banks were so intense that the collapse of one was likely to pull down others in a kind of domino effect.

In the wake of Lehman's collapse, a number of leading banks in the USA and UK rapidly faltered. Merrill Lynch, Citibank and the insurance group AIG in the USA and the Lloyds Banking Group and RBS in the UK were especially notable cases. For example, early in 2007 Citibank's shares were valued at $55, but by June 2009 they had fallen to $3. Eventually, its directors had to write off capital losses to the value of $105bn – mostly guaranteed by the US government and taxpayers. Citibank probably only survived because the government partly nationalized it by taking a 34% stake (Ford and Larsen 2009). The British government took similar action to prop up Lloyds TSB and Northern Rock building society. In fact, between April and October 2008, the three central government banks – America's Federal Reserve, the Bank of England and the European Central Bank – between them pumped in $5 trillion of government and taxpayers' money, equivalent to approximately 14% of global GDP (Gowan 2009: 19).

Why did governments act on this gigantic scale when most had previously argued that interfering with capitalist markets was politically unacceptable or counterproductive? Their actions are partly explicable because it was widely feared that allowing the banks to collapse would have paralysed the usual economic flows, with catastrophic consequences for jobs and incomes. As it was, the volume of lending to ordinary borrowers and investors in the main economy fell dramatically. Meanwhile, panic and mistrust between the banks was widespread. Many had acquired securities carrying toxic debts and had lent and borrowed money that might never be repaid to investors and other financial institutions. Moreover, the latter might also be liable to insolvency as the weight of bad debts they carried also unravelled. Consequently, for a long time banks drastically reduced or froze their mutual lending operations and reduced the supply of credit and loans to the wider economy. To counter this, governments believed they needed to inject huge funds into the financial system.

Of course, these government actions left a deep legacy. Governments faced a double squeeze. On the one hand, as the recession bit hard, their incomes from tax revenues fell. On the other hand, their spending rose massively as they bailed out the banks, pumped money

© ANDY RAIN/EPA/CORBIS

FIGURE 4.3 A departing Lehman Brothers employee

A Lehman Brothers employee departing with his personal effects as the company goes into liquidation. The collapse of the company, seen as one of Wall Street's safest and most reputable, was the most visible symbol of the depth of the 2008 recession.

into the wider economy, and met higher welfare demands from the growing numbers of unemployed. Sooner or later the citizens ultimately have to pay for the government's spending, either in the form of higher taxes or through cuts in public expenditure, and most governments enacted severe policies along these lines in 2010. For years to come, ordinary citizens across the world will be paying for the excesses of financial deregulation through higher taxes, massive cuts in public services and, probably, higher unemployment.

REVIEW

The era of high productivity, high consumption and secure employment is now over. Instead, we have moved to a period of economic globalization, rapid technological change, post-Fordism and the increased power of financial industries in an age of largely unregulated free markets. The combined effect has been to weaken labour's bargaining power and to expose a growing proportion of employees everywhere to the risk of unemployment, the reality of casualized work, and conditions of work and pay that reduce workplace autonomy and employment rights while increasing economic and lifestyle insecurity. At the same time, a growing proportion of the global population has been sucked into, and become dependent on, the capitalist, profit-oriented market system for their livelihoods. Although globalization tends to be blamed for these and other problems, they also need to be seen as a consequence of the widespread adoption of free-market economic policies. Indeed, as one commentator complains, many governments have 'become convinced' that only private markets and those that juggle money between them should be permitted to determine the shape and direction of the world – not states, political leaders or, presumably, the citizens who elect them (Hutton 1998: 13).

Visit the companion website at www.palgrave.com/sociology/cohen3e for extra materials to check and expand your learning, including interactive self-test questions, mind maps making links between key themes, annotated web links to sociological research, data and key sociological thinkers, a searchable glossary and much more.

FURTHER READING

S. Edgell's *The Sociology of Work* (2012) offers an up-to-date, thorough and accessible examination of most themes relating to work, including Fordism and post-Fordism.

F. Webster's analysis in *Theories of the Information Society* (2002) explores many issues and debates pertaining to the ways in which ICTs are changing our experience of work and leisure.

The readers by A. Amin (ed.) *Post-Fordism* (1994) and T. Elger and C. Smith (eds) *Global Japanization?* (1994) contain summaries of the main debates in these areas. They are really aimed at advanced students and academic specialists; nevertheless, most of the readings are reasonably accessible and will amply reward those who persevere.

Written in simple but lively prose, L. Elliott and D. Atkinson's *The Gods that Failed: How Blind Faith in Markets has Cost Us Our Future* (2008) provides a layperson's account of the rise of the financial industries and explores the impact this has had on everyone's economic life.

QUESTIONS AND ASSIGNMENTS

1. Summarize the main differences between Fordist and post-Fordist production either (a) as systems for organizing production and dealing with market demand or (b) in terms of their effects on employees' work experiences and lifestyles.

2. How did changing global factors contribute to the decline of Fordism?

3. In different ways, first postwar Japan and then, more recently, China and India have carved out national paths to economic success. Examine these briefly and show in what ways each has affected work and employment in the advanced economies.

4. What do you understand by the process of financialization, and what policies operating at the international or global level, and introduced by some governments nationally, contributed to the rise of the financial industries?

5
Political sociology: changing nation-states

In the nineteenth and early twentieth centuries, modernizing governments were largely successful in persuading individual citizens to submerge their personal passions and identities into those of the NATION-STATE. Three entities, society/people/country, came to be regarded as virtually synonymous with, or perhaps subordinated to, the idea of the nation. In this chapter we look at sociology's contribution to the study of nationalism, the nation-state and the idea of citizenship, and how this is changing in the face of globalization.

We also assess the power and role of nation-states in a global era. Many observers have suggested that in a globalizing world, the capacity of nation-states to shape domestic and world change has already declined and may do so further. This has given rise to such concepts as the 'hollow state' (Hoggart 1996) or the 'borderless world' (Ohmae 1994). Some commentators suggest that the era of the nation-state may be ending. Most submit this conclusion is much too premature and that the functions of the nation-state are merely changing in the face of globalizing forces. We assess this debate and argue that, despite the global changes undermining the exclusive primacy of the nation-state system, there is currently no prospect in the near future of a world government emerging that is able to assume the equivalent role at the global level that governments still play nationally. We might not consider this to be a desirable outcome anyway. Moreover, securing recognition as a nation-state is still an urgent goal for many currently stateless people.

SOCIOLOGY, NATION-STATES AND THE INTERNATIONAL SYSTEM

We argued in Chapter 3 that the nation-state, particularly in Europe, predated and accompanied the rise of modernity and industrial capitalism. It acted as a centralizing agency, steadily acquiring control over traders, aristocrats, towns and religious bodies. Driving this process of state building was military and economic rivalry between several European nations.

Both the French and Industrial Revolutions gave a new and forceful momentum to the processes of state and nation building in the context of international rivalry. The first of these revolutions proclaimed the universal rights of humanity, further centralized the French state and, by unleashing citizen armies, propelled nationalist fervour across Europe's territories. This galvanized the birth and spread of modern popular nationalism. Britain's Industrial Revolution compelled other countries to recognize the potential military threat to their national security posed by a more technologically advanced economy.

One by one the nineteenth-century nation-states – in Europe, America and later Japan – began to push towards the goal of state-led industrialization. They strengthened the structures of the state and imposed reforms designed to remove any remaining obstacles that might impede the release of enterprise, market incentives or scientific and technological learning. More recently, many other states have followed a similar course. Indeed, those faced with even greater external military threats to national survival after 1945, including several Southeast Asian states such as South Korea, responded in even more determined ways to external threats, seeing state-led industrialization as the main path to national survival.

In short, the forces most responsible for promoting modernization came not just from social pressures created by civil society; rather, they originated within and among the elites who controlled the nation-state itself. Thus, as Albrow (1996: 7) succinctly explains:

> the story of modernity was of a project to extend human control over space, time, nature and society. The main agent of the project was the nation-state working with and through capitalist and military organization.

BOX 5.1 European nation-states in the twenty-first century: towards the past?

Medieval Europe consisted of numerous political units with local identities that were often far stronger than any national loyalties. Those units also held multiple affiliations to cities, to the Catholic Church based in Rome and to monastic orders. Today, economic integration among the member states of the European Union (EU) continues to deepen, although this is threatened by the fiscal crisis facing the euro. In 2007 the number of EU member states rose from 25 to 27, but there is concern that this may slow down future integration, as reaching policy consensus becomes more difficult with growing diversity. The crisis facing the euro in 2011 has also affected the confidence of the EU. In 2005 both the French and Dutch electorates voted decisively against ratifying the EU constitution, which was designed to intensify and streamline EU integration. In 2009 voting levels for the EU parliamentary elections fell to historically low levels. Meanwhile, the EU states are subject to the same globalizing forces as nation-states everywhere. Is Europe, therefore, returning to its medieval past? Perhaps, 'yes', if the German situation is any indication.

German politics today

Like many countries, for example the USA, Australia and India, Germany forms a federation with 16 *Länder*, units of provincial government, each enjoying considerable political autonomy from central government. It appears the *Länder* are trying to extend their 'independence' even further. Thus:

- Each *Länder* has established its own offices at, and relationships with, the EU in Brussels in attempts to obtain resources.

- The *Länder* have altered the federal constitution so that they can resist any further ties developing between central government and the EU of which they might disapprove.

- Some *Länder* are trying to establish their own special trading relations with nation-states outside the EU such as China.

The wider European picture

The German *Länder* are not especially unusual. For example:

- Other EU countries exhibit strong regional loyalties and even antipathy to central governments. Catalonia in Spain is one notable example, but Belgium, Italy and France also have regional governments and deep local identities.

- In 1999, even centralized Britain devolved power to newly elected governments in the 'Celtic' regions of Scotland, Wales and Northern Ireland and later re-established London as a city region with substantial autonomy. The electoral victory of the Scottish National Party in 2011 is likely to accelerate the prospects of a higher level of independence for Scotland.

- Across Europe, cities as different as Barcelona, Manchester and Lyon are establishing special ties to the EU and to cities in other European countries (and outside the EU) to obtain grant aid, attract investment and encourage cooperation in sport and education as well as cultural and other exchanges.

- Universities, schools, town councils and professional associations are also making cross-boundary links, therefore bypassing the national government.

Source: Freedland (1999).

CLASSICAL SOCIOLOGY AND SOCIAL CHANGE

By the mid-nineteenth century many observers were becoming increasingly alarmed by the consequences of industrial capitalism. Not surprisingly, early European sociologists struggled to understand these changes and their dangers. At the core of much of their thinking was the attempt to conceptualize the essential features of what they saw as traditional compared with modernizing societies and to come to terms with the assault the latter was having on the imagined virtues of the former. These are just three examples of such thinking:

1. *The loss of community:* The German sociologist Tönnies ([1887]1971) distinguished between societies characterized by *Gemeinschaft* (community) and those marked by *Gesellschaft* (contractual relations). Contemporary sociologists still generally use the German words. Tönnies mourned the demise of the warm, all-embracing *Gemeinschaft*-type communities of medieval times based on unquestioned friendship and shared beliefs and their replacement by the impersonal, even anonymous, structures found in modern, urban *Gesellschaft* societies. The latter are built primarily around loose, often impermanent, essentially contrived and non-overlapping associations. The relationships they contain are driven primarily by the demand for achievement and legitimized by contract and mutual interests.

2. *Declining social cohesion and moral order:* Another concern theorized by sociologists was the impact of industrialism, urbanism and SECULARIZATION on societal cohesion. Modern societies seemed to be marked by growing materialism, class conflict, egotism and individualism. These changes, which accompanied rapid urbanization and economic crises, combined with the declining hold of Christianity, threatened to push individuals towards social isolation or moral confusion. Modern economic life raised people's expectations to unrealizable levels and confronted them with collapsing certainties previously guaranteed by community and religion (see Chapter 17).

3. *The conscience collective:* Durkheim thought that alongside the integration produced by the division of labour, modern societies must evolve a much more flexible and abstract value system based on the conscience collective – 'a new set of universally significant moral bonds' (Turner 1994: 135) at the national level. This would champion mutual respect for human rights and the sanctity of the individual. This resembles the idea of globality – humans share an intensifying consciousness of themselves as forming one single collectivity – discussed in Chapter 2.

KEY CONCEPT

SECULARIZATION refers to the declining hold of religious belief and practice over most people's lives during the industrialization process. Growing exposure to scientific knowledge and new ideas, combined with a more materially secure environment, render most individuals less reliant on the moral and spiritual certainties provided by religion in preindustrial societies.

UNIVERSALISM AND NATIONALISM

Interest in universal themes and human progress can be traced back to the 1830s via the social theory of Saint-Simon (Turner 1994: 133–5). Saint-Simon greatly influenced the great French sociologist Emile Durkheim (1858–1917), especially on the question of how to find a 'new set of universally significant moral bonds' to replace the religious convictions threatened by secularization, while cementing together the more complex national and world orders created by industrialism. Political events also strongly influenced Durkheim (see Global Thinker 17), especially France's humiliating defeat in the short war with Prussia in 1871 and the powerful patriotic sentiments this generated.

Durkheim thought that the heady unifying passions that French nationalism generated might provide a substitute for declining moral certainties and societal incoherence. Thus Durkheim's thinking largely, although not entirely, displaced universalist themes. The spectre of socialism accentuated the urgency with which modern nation-states sought to deepen their control over industrial societies in the last decades of the nineteenth century. Marx had predicted that capitalist exploitation would ultimately foster a revolution, introducing socialism by means of an increasingly organized and militant working class. Indeed, growing evidence of working-class strength and the internationalist aspirations of socialism 'sent shudders through nation-state society' and pushed it 'into overdrive to find an alternative and better theories' (Albrow 1996: 45). Another crucial event that reinforced the national leanings of many intellectuals, at least initially, was the outbreak of the First World War in August 1914. Much to the astonishment and deep regret of many, especially those on the left, this was met by surges of patriotic sentiment right across Europe.

A PAUSE TO REFLECT

It seems easier to achieve moral and social cohesion on a smaller scale. However, if families are often more cohesive than large nation-states, are they also more oppressive, threatening individual freedom and self-expression? Is there an ideal unit size in which friendliness, mutual support and a sense of community can be combined with recognition of individuality and creative dissent? How would you describe the ideal size and characteristics of a social unit?

Sociologists have often been involved in research helping states trying to head off social conflict. The classic studies of London by Henry Mayhew (1864) and Charles Booth (1889–91) comprised sympathetic accounts of the life and conditions of the poor, but were also motivated by the desire to arrest any revolutionary tendencies they might cultivate. After the Second World War, social investigators conducted research into social welfare, often with state funding. They established specialized teaching programmes and contributed to policies designed to ameliorate adverse social conditions. Their thinking was increasingly built around the nation-state and its needs. Many governments also began to create or further develop a welfare state. This was designed to offer some degree of economic security from the inherent uncertainties of market economies in the form of unemployment, old age, sickness and other benefits. The extension of the state into everyday life cemented a powerful form of social bond, CITIZENSHIP. Indeed, it can be argued that state/political elites deliberately used citizenship as a nation-building strategy (O'Byrne 2003: 64). This linked citizenship to territorial affiliations, legal/administrative institutions and a state-centred discourse.

KEY CONCEPT

CITIZENSHIP entails membership of and inclusion in a national community. It confers a set of entitlements – to legal equality and justice, the right to be consulted on political matters, and access to a minimum of protection against economic insecurity – but simultaneously requires the fulfilment of certain obligations to state and society.

CITIZENSHIP: ENTITLEMENTS AND OBLIGATIONS

Citizenship is basically a modern Western invention. It involves the idea that there should be a bundle of uniform rights to which everyone in a nation-state is equally entitled. This would have been unthinkable in premodern societies. It also implies an inherent bargain or contract whereby, in return for a set of rights or entitlements, citizens are expected to demonstrate loyalty to the nation-state and its objectives, while accepting certain obligations or duties. These include the willingness to accept military conscription, pay taxes, seek employment and obey the law. Thus, historically, rulers were able to provide citizens with a stake in nationhood and industrialization. This also meant democratization by providing 'an equality of membership status and ability to participate in a society' (Roche 1992: 19).

T. H. Marshall's (1950) ideas about citizenship influenced a generation of thinkers. He observed that citizenship involved three sets of rights, which, he claimed, had emerged in a sequence as a result of events taking place approximately in the eighteenth, nineteenth and twentieth centuries:

1. *Civil rights* were attained first. They include the right to own property and arrange contracts, to free assembly, speech and thought, and the right to expect justice from an impartial legal system based on laws that apply equally to everyone. Where civil rights do not exist, neither personal freedom nor market enterprise is fully realizable.
2. *Political rights* confer the ability to participate in national decision-making through voting for the political party of your choice at elections. However, political citizenship also implies the right to establish one's own movement or to seek direct access to positions of leadership in party, government or some other power-exercising forum.
3. *Social rights* involve access to welfare provisions that provide a protective floor below which individual and family incomes are not supposed to fall. Normally, social rights include old age, disability, family and unemployment benefits and the right to decent housing, education and health. Such minimum security, it is hoped, gives everyone a chance to enjoy personal autonomy and the benefits of economic growth. Also, without social rights, the inequalities and insecurities of capitalism might push some people to levels of permanent poverty where they are too weak to exercise their civil or political rights.

Over the past 20 or so years, there has been a strong revival of interest in citizenship, as well as a development of Marshall's original ideas and a concern for related issues such as universal human rights. For example, while citizenship presumes national inclusiveness, it also raises the possibility of the internal exclusion of, for example, disabled people, women or children (Lister 1997: Ch. 2). Women, in particular, were until recently 'banished to the private realm of the household and family' (Lister: 1997: 71), because they were assumed to be predominantly carers who neither required nor deserved financial reward or independence since their 'breadwinning' husbands met their needs. In a globalizing world, where disadvantaged migrants increasingly seek work or political asylum in the prosperous countries, many 'external' groups encounter racism and discrimination from officials or host members and become 'non- or partial citizens' (Lister 1997: 42, 45).

Further complicating this situation are the numerous contemporary migrants moving to North America, Japan and Western Europe, who, unlike their nineteenth-century counterparts, seek only (or are allowed only) partial assimilation into their host societies and retain strong and enduring transnational family, cultural, political and business connections with their home country (see, for example, Faist 2000; Jordan and Düvell 2003). The existence of ethnic groups in multicultural societies with limited loyalties to each other and dual or overlapping affiliations to their host and home societies raises complicated ethical, political and practical issues over whether, acting mutually, states need to make access to citizenship more flexible. Citizens living in a global world of constant mobility will also need to accept changes and this may include learning to become cosmopolitan citizens (Delanty 2000; Held and McGrew 2002; Holton 2009: 94–5, 142–7).

© AFP/GETTY IMAGES

FIGURE 5.1 A rally in Vilnius, Lithuania on 11 March 2012
Nationalism continues to have a strong hold on sections on the population. This rally was organized by the National Centre of Lithuanians and the Lithuanian Nationalist Youth Union. Independence Day marches with people, including skinheads, chanting 'Lithuania for Lithuanians' have taken place in central Vilnius for the past couple of years.

Clearly, the sociology of citizenship is being radically rethought. One of the biggest challenges it now faces, as we have seen, is the idea of 'global citizenship' as national economies become increasingly integrated, governments are compelled to cooperate, and numerous transnational agents collaborate across national borders (Delanty 2000; Holton 2009: 40–7).

SOCIOLOGY, NATION-STATES AND INTERSTATE RELATIONS

As we have seen, until the 1960s sociologists tended to focus on single societies and showed a more limited interest in the emerging relationships and connections that were being formed between different societies or states. The study of international or interstate relations was mostly left to a branch of political science called 'international relations'. Until recently, this relied on a particular model of interstate relations called 'the realist perspective'. In this model, world society is largely synonymous with the relationships that exist between sovereign nation-states, but since states are driven to enlarge their spheres of interest at the expense of other nation-states, they are inherently liable to conflict. States also differ in their capacity to shape events. The more militarily powerful tend either to dominate weaker states through various kinds of coercion or lead by forming alliances and seeking a balance of power. Such leading states are hegemonic.

Irrespective of whether or not states are dominated, statehood never seems to go out of fashion. Since the Treaty of Westphalia in 1648, which recognized the nation-state system legally, the idea has, at first slowly, then more rapidly, gathered pace. The growth of nation-states can be seen in Table 5.1. However, Table 5.1 needs some explanation and qualification. The last row correctly lists 208 states, but in 2011 the number of UN states was 193. This is because not all sovereign states automatically choose to join the UN; for example, the Vatican, Tonga and Montenegro are not members. Again, a number of countries are caught in anomalous situations, for example:

- Taiwan is not recognized because of a dispute with China
- Palestine is still in the process of achieving formal autonomy from Israel

- Tibet is not recognized as independent by China
- North and South Korea may eventually unite
- Many countries and territories are still dependencies of some kind.

Civil wars and disputes in some countries, for example Iraq, mean that the founding of new states – including Kurdistan – cannot be discounted. Others see a future in which vastly populous city regions in effect become more powerful than states. Some states recognized as sovereign and independent have very small populations. If those with fewer than 100,000 citizens were to be excluded, the number of states would fall from 208 to around 165.

TABLE 5.1 The age of the nation-state system

Date	No. of recognized states	Cumulative totals	Comments
Before 1800	14	14	Not including the Ottoman, Russian, Chinese and Austro-Hungarian Empires
1800–1914	37	51	South American countries gained independence from Spain and Portugal plus UK dominions
1915–39	11	62	For example, Ireland, Poland, Finland
1940–59	22	84	Surge of independence for former colonies especially in Asia and the Middle East
1960–89	72	156	Veritable flood of developing countries gaining independence in Africa (41), the Caribbean (11), Asia (14) and elsewhere
1990–2011	52	208	Dissolution of the USSR and Yugoslavia (22 new states), plus Namibia, Eritrea (following war with Ethiopia), Yemen, East Timor (2003) and others. South Sudan became independent in July 2011

Sources: Anheier et al. (2001); Kegley and Wittkopf (2004); Kidron and Segal (1995).

SOVEREIGNTY

The ability of a state to make and enforce its own policies and laws in its own territory and over the people living within its borders.

KEY CONCEPT

The nation is an IMAGINED COMMUNITY in four senses. It is imagined because the member of even the smallest nation will never know most of its members. The nation is imagined as limited because even the largest of nations has a finite boundary beyond which there are other nations. It is imagined as sovereign in that is displaces or undermines the legitimacy of organized religion or the monarchy. Finally, it is imagined as community because regardless of actual inequality, the nation is conceived of as a deep, horizontal comradeship.

PUTTING 'SOCIETY' BACK INTO NATIONAL AND GLOBAL POLITICS

Since the 1960s, sociologists have led the way in generating interest in global matters and rediscovering transnational exchanges. Indeed, observers have been increasingly struck by the rapid growth of powerful non-state, transnational bodies, especially TNCs and the growing interdependence between nations. All this requires growing interstate collaboration and calls into question the meaning of national **sovereignty** and territorial autonomy. A solely state-centric view of world politics no longer makes sense. We now explore one recent sociological critique of international relations theory and then discuss the development of a feminist approach to the study of nationalism and global relations.

Shaw (1994) suggests that international relations theory has largely ignored the state's embeddedness in the many dense networks of class and other interests and identities that make up society. These same entities are often locked in conflict over ethnic, regional, religious, gender and class differences and affiliations. This makes it all the more remarkable that during the nineteenth century in many Western societies a strong populist sense of national community and identity became established (Shaw 1994: 89, 92). During the era of early modernization, the intervention of intellectuals, artists, political leaders and others helped this process along by creating the idea of nationhood (or national community) and bringing it sharply into focus. Here, Anderson's (1983: 15–16) concept of IMAGINED COMMUNITIES identifies what was involved.

GLOBAL THINKERS 5 ANTHONY GIDDENS (1938–)

Globalization and modernity

Much of Giddens's work has been concerned with globalization (see Chapter 3) and the ways in which modernity operates as a globalizing force. Premodern societies provided certainties that neither permitted nor required validation from individual actors. In modern societies, nothing remains certain for long because human reflexivity and the self-monitoring of conduct rely instead on continuous incoming knowledge. In other words, we redefine our actions rather than accept traditional guidelines. Globalization further heightens this transformational tendency. We live in a 'runaway world' in which everything 'seems out of our control', including influences such as scientific and technological developments that were supposed to make life more predictable. Globalization also becomes part of our subjectivity so that our personal lives are constantly being revolutionized and reinvented. Giddens suggests that:

1. *Traditional routines* wither and actors lose former certainties, while class, locality and kinship no longer provide clear social directions. 'Moderns' are compelled to take charge of constructing their own self-identities and life biographies.

2. *Lifestyle* becomes highly significant. This is not just about 'superficial consumerism' but requires an integrated set of practices that facilitate self-actualization through a coherent life narrative and personal identity.

3. *Risks* no longer result primarily from natural events. Rather they abound and occur because of the dangers unleashed by modern industrial and scientific activities, for example chemical spills, global warming and climate change.

4. *Intimacy:* modernity leads to a 'democracy of the emotions', with family relationships and friendships built on openness, trust, equality and mutual respect. This compensates for the anxieties and personal risks associated with declining tradition, although therapists, counsellors and self-help manuals may also be helpful.

5. *Family:* modern birth control and education separate sexuality and love from reproduction. Thus, women now enjoy or demand more choice regarding marriage. This liberation from kinship pressures and constant childbirth is leading to 'coupledom' rather than lifelong marriage in many societies. Children are likely to be treated as individuals.

6. *Rising fundamentalisms:* much of this is resisted by various religious, national and ethnic fundamentalisms. Adherents try to restore the one all-encompassing truth and life path that believers are duty bound to obey on pain of divine or secular punishment. The changes promised to women by the globalization of modernity are seen as especially dangerous.

Thus, Giddens sees a global struggle not between civilizations but between those who desire cosmopolitan openness in a world of cultural complexity versus those who seek refuge in 'renewed and purified tradition'.

Sources: Giddens (1990, 1991, 1992, 2002); O'Brien et al. (1999).

Similar tendencies have appeared more recently in some developing countries. In fact, in most Western nations, and in many others, society preceded the state and the nation, as did individual loyalties to social groups (Shaw 1994: 94). Shaw also shows how the notion of a civil society – social groups with shared interests operating in the political arena existing between the individual and the state – has increasingly been applied to the global and not just the national sphere (see also Anheier et al. 2001, 2002; Keane 2003). We discuss global civil society in Chapter 19.

THE FEMINIST REASSESSMENT

In Chapter 8 we examine feminist theory and its considerable importance in compelling all academic disciplines to rethink many of their theories about gender relations. However, some feminist theory has also been central in contributing to sociologists' interest in nation-states and global affairs. We now summarize three examples of such contributions, all of which concern not only women, society and the nation-state but also war and violence.

Women and the state

Far from being gender neutral, the state not only 'treats women unequally in relation to men … it [also] constructs men and women differently' (Yuval-Davis and Anthias 1989: 6). State power has been used to enforce control over women in many ways. A key example is shown by government policies during the two world wars. At first, women were pressed into factories, offices and other forms of war work as men were mobilized for military service. Later, when the men were demobilized, governments conducted campaigns to persuade women to return to domestic life for fear of social unrest caused by male unemployment. Welfare policy is also important, especially the decision to withhold certain child benefits from single mothers. Thus, governments wishing to discourage such families could decide to make such rights conditional on women responding to certain compulsory training or work schemes.

Women and nationalism

The very way in which women's contribution to nationhood is envisaged and understood – whether by established traditions or state officials – reveals the hold of certain deep-rooted assumptions about the 'proper' role of women in national life (Halliday 1994: 160–4). In particular, in most countries, women have been regarded as the main carriers of their country's unique cultural heritage, which it is their duty as mothers to transfer to the nation's children (Yuval-Davis and Anthias 1989). This is also linked to their childbearing capacity to produce the next generation of male warriors for future wars. Here, population policies – what Foucault (2008) referred to as the exercise of biopower (see Global Thinkers 11) by states – have been crucial in either encouraging women to have more children, as in nineteenth-century France and the Soviet Union after the 1917 revolution, or in discouraging certain 'undesirable' minorities from doing so.

Women, violence and contemporary warfare

In wartime, women were usually either kept away from the main zones of conflict or served in an auxiliary capacity, for example in field hospitals or as drivers. However, with the resurgence of recent nationalisms, genocidal wars and the collapse of many states, especially in Africa, since the end of the Cold War, much of this appears to have changed:

1. There has been a 'wide-scale retreat from even a qualified observance of those historic rules of war which had offered protection to non-combatants' (Jacobson et al. 2000: 4), so that civilian women and even children have often been deliberately targeted as war victims.
2. Although there are historical precedents, in certain recent wars, for example following the collapse of Yugoslavia, in Liberia and Sierra Leone during the 1990s, and more recently in the Sudan and the Democratic Republic of the Congo, we have seen a systematic sexualization of violence and 'the use of rape as a war strategy' (Jacobson et al. 2000: 12).
3. In countries such as China and the USA, increasing numbers of women have actively sought to become frontline warriors. In the USA, women comprised 13.4% of the active forces, 23.7% of the reserve and 14.0% of the national guard in 2009 (www.army.mil/women/today.html).

BUSH AND OBAMA: FROM IMPERIALISM TO MULTILATERALISM?

According to Nye (2002), all hegemonic powers deploy a combination of hard and soft power – namely military and economic clout versus a moral/political example through persuasion and inducements. Wielding soft power means that other nations look upon a hegemon's ability to influence international regimes, laws, norms and institutions as mostly legitimate. Soft power is also gaining ground because the information age brings all kinds of ideas, images and information across borders and into every home. We saw in Chapter 3 how after the Second World War the USA mostly wielded soft power, at least in respect of its allies. In fact, partly through the global influence of its commercial cultural interests – Hollywood, TV networks such as CNN, the music industry, and its technical lead in developing IT – this continued until recently. How did this situation change during the second Bush presidency and why?

THE ASSERTION OF HEGEMONIC POWER, 2001–09

The USA emerged from the end of the Cold War as the sole superpower, which enhanced its power over its allies and potential freedom for manoeuvre. Although less evident during the Clinton presidency, at least militarily, after President Bush's accession to power in January 2001, the world was left in no doubt that the USA was intent on exercising its hegemonic position. While its assertion of national power was partly grounded in narrow self-interest, underlying anxieties about its uncertain future and possible long-term weakness were also gnawing away at some political leaders' sense of assurance. The events of 11 September 2001, when al-Qaeda destroyed the twin towers, fuelled these fears and legitimized the further application of global power. We now unravel the potent mix of events and perceptions that propelled the USA into an era of overseas aggression.

Several scholars (for example Bello 2001; Brenner 2002; Chomsky 2003; Harvey 2003) argue that since January 2001, but in accentuated form after 9/11, there was a clear policy shift in the USA's involvement in world affairs from multilateralism to unilateralism. Chomsky (2003) goes further and states that the Bush presidency led to the assertion of a blatant 'imperial grand strategy', although he acknowledged that this merely crystallized traits long present in US politics and foreign policy. Through the operations of the Central Intelligence Agency, the USA had a history of covert intervention in the affairs of a number of countries involving bribery, threats and coups. There were also cases of direct military action, often with the declared intent of promoting democracy. This, however, has been largely unsuccessful. Meernik (1996: 395–6) shows that of the 27 US interventions between 1950 and 1990, in over half the cases there was no change with respect to democracy, while in more than half of the remainder, the states became somewhat less democratic. The USA also has a record of pulling strings in the UN, holding back on its financial support for the UN, or sidestepping rules or agreements it disliked. Chomsky's view, however, is that this exercise of blatant national interest was substantially ratcheted upwards at the end of the Clinton presidency.

A PAUSE TO REFLECT

The USA remains the most powerful country in military and economic terms, so its foreign policy is of great importance not only to US citizens but to the rest of the world. Taking a long, say, 100-year view, US foreign policy seems to swing from periods of isolation to those of engagement and intervention. What accounts for this vacillation? Does the US government intervene to keep the peace, promote democracy and human rights, or because of its own economic interest?

In practical terms, its go-it-alone posture meant that the US government felt free both to withhold its support from widely supported initiatives and to undertake preventive wars in the pursuance of what it considered to be its interests. One early example of this unilateralist stance came in 2002 when the US repudiated the Kyoto Protocol on greenhouse gas emissions, which was signed in 1997 and became effective in 2005. More seriously, the US government opted to take unilateral military action both in Afghanistan in 2001 and Iraq in 2003 without the majority agreement of the UN and supported only by a handful of coalition partners. Pressure to secure votes in the UN even led to the US threatening certain countries with the loss of aid or economic tariffs levied against their exports.

During the Bush Jr presidency, the USA also repeatedly claimed to speak on behalf of all nations and demanded the right to take any action it deemed appropriate in pursuing that goal. Fuelling the US government's assertion of global power was its view that all other nations and peoples subscribed to its interests, morality, culture and political and economic system: its model was universal (Harvey 2003: 191–2). Accordingly, nothing could be permitted to restrain or threaten its power. In a speech to the UN on the anniversary of 9/11 in 2002, Bush asserted:

> We will use our position of unparalleled strength and influence to build an atmosphere of international order and openness in which progress and liberty can flourish in all nations. ... The United States welcomes its responsibility to lead in this great mission. (cited in Harvey 2003: 4–5)

How can this move towards unilateralism be explained? Clearly, as already suggested, the end of the Cold War and the terrorist attack on New York in 2001 go some way towards providing an explanation, but Harvey (2003) suggests that at least four additional factors were at work:

1. After 2001 neoconservatism took precedence over neoliberalism as the USA's most potent means of asserting global power (Harvey 2003: 184–5, 190–3). Neoconservatives such as Rumsfeld, Cheney and Wolfowitz date back to the Reagan years (1981–89), when they acted as Cold War warriors and had strong connections with the US industries that produced the hardware and technologies with which the Pentagon could fight its wars and keep ahead of the USSR.
2. There was a longstanding fear that materialist and hedonistic values had corrupted US society. For example, the 1990s experienced race riots, massacres of school children by their peers, and the destruction of the Oklahoma state building in 1996 when nearly 200 people died. One somewhat conspiratorial view is that the ruling class was intent on constructing a global threat sufficiently strong to reactivate patriotism, civic virtues, religious values and a sense of collective responsibility. Accordingly, the government utilized the national solidarity engendered by 9/11 and then the 'war on terror' to divert attention from internal divisions.
3. Many neoconservatives wondered whether the USA could guarantee its own domestic oil and other economic interests, especially given the industrialization of the BRIC countries. Even more critical was the concern over the USA's ability to retain its global hegemonic supremacy and keep other rising powers at bay, especially the increasingly unified EU, the Asia-Pacific region and, in particular, China. Harvey (2003: 195–9) suggests that this critical context of world power rivalry and future uncertainties provides the most credible explanation for the US invasion of Iraq.
4. Given the critical role of oil for the foreseeable future, the Iraq War fits into this larger picture because, by controlling Iraq's oil stocks and, even more importantly, turning Iraq into a client state, the USA acquired the opportunity to take control of the entire Middle Eastern 'global oil spigot' (Harvey 2003: 19), the region in which world stocks are the largest, around 50%, and most likely to last the longest.

While this argument emphasizes elite perceptions of how to overcome threats to US dominance, it is also important to understand George Bush's appeal to the electorate and, in particular, his re-election in 2004. In an analysis of the rhetorical and narrative style of his campaigns, two communications analysts suggest that Bush was able to harness the fears of a significant group of Americans 'who do not quite know who they are, where they are going or how to get there'. Describing him as a 'postmodern president', they see Bush as 'operating in the interstitial zone separating the symbolic from the material world' (Hart and Childers 2005: 195). Because they wanted certainty in the wake of 9/11 and other fears, many Americans saw Bush's determined and folksy style as more reassuring than the more subtle analyses of US problems that other candidates provided.

OBAMA'S USA: A RETURN TO MULTILATERALISM?

For most of the world, seeing a black person attain the most powerful office in the USA was a truly remarkable occurrence and many people across the world seemed to breathe a sigh of relief when Barack Obama was elected US president in November 2009, following a campaign centred on hope for the future. The expectations for his presidency and for the difference he might make to the USA's future role in the world were extremely high. By 2010 it was clear that Obama had chosen to follow a more multilateralist path than his predecessor as he sought dialogues based on mutual respect and shared interests with the EU, China, the Middle East, South America and Russia. In the latter case, for example, in spring 2010 his government signed a major treaty to reduce nuclear arms. In addition, his tone when engaging with foreign governments, including Iran, was much less strident and dominating than in the previous era.

Several points can be made about the actual practice of exercising global leadership. First, it is notable that Obama supported the decision to ensure that the London conference on dealing with the global financial crisis in April 2009 was organized around the G20 rather than the G8 group of countries, which indicated that he recognized the advent of a multipolar world. Obama has often been more radical than other leaders in dealing with the financial crisis. He called for collective global action to clamp down on tax havens and to improve the IMF's monitoring of the financial system. Within the USA, he has also advocated tougher rules to ensure banks are more restrained in their future capacity to lend freely and focus more on lending for long-term growth rather than risky, short-term speculation.

By contrast, a fresh American approach to climate change was less evident at the Copenhagen environmental conference in December 2009. With others, the USA also baulked at the provision of technical and financial assistance to developing countries to enable them to cope with environmental measures without jeopardizing their struggle to overcome poverty. In any case, the US Senate's reluctance to sanction more rigorous caps on greenhouse gas emissions constrains Obama's scope for changing his government's stance on environmental issues, bearing in mind the pivotal role of senators who represent the interests of miners in the coal states. Moreover, much of the US public remains sceptical about global warming and/or resents the idea of the government relinquishing its sovereignty by complying with the demands of global institutions (Freedland 2009; Munck 2007; Southern Poverty Law Center 2001). We examine this issue more thoroughly in Chapter 20.

With his period in office incomplete at the time of writing, it is premature to attempt a rounded evaluation of Obama's record and global impact, although some observers have struck a notably critical note (Ali 2010). Many as yet unknowable events and contingencies, such as the unfolding economic crisis and rapidly changing events in the Middle East, are likely to intervene and alter current policy intentions and priorities.

DOES GLOBALIZATION MEAN THE DECLINE OF THE NATION-STATE?

In this section we consider the suggestion that, in some ways, nation-states have declined, albeit rather less than some observers have claimed. Then, in the final main section we try to balance the argument by offering some alternative viewpoints.

CLARIFYING THE TERMS OF THE DISCUSSION

Shaw (1997: 497) suggests that it makes more sense to say that state powers are undergoing various transformations than to say that they are declining. Such changes are both a precondition for and a consequence of further globalization. Shaw also reminds us that confusion over what exactly we mean by the 'nation-state' has hindered the debate, because people usually refer to it in its 'classic' nineteenth- and early twentieth-century form when there were far fewer autonomous states than there are now (see Table 5.1 above). Moreover, most countries relied on their independent military capacity to protect their sovereign territories and monopolized the legal control of the right to use violence over their territories and citizens, which was how Max Weber defined a modern state.

Seen from this perspective, it is clear that most nation-states, especially those that recognize international law or belong to powerful regional blocs such as the EU, have lost some of their former powers. The EU requires its member states to hand over some decision-making to the Brussels-based European Commission and the Council of Ministers and to accept certain common directives and regulations. However, if we adopt Held's (1989) distinction between sovereignty (a state's ability to make and enforce its own policies and laws) and autonomy (a state's capacity to achieve its policy goals), we can clarify our discussion considerably. Held (1989) identifies five areas in which most states have progressively lost some of their national autonomy in recent decades:

1. States requiring external financial assistance have to adhere to the demands of IGOs such as the IMF and World Bank.
2. The majority of states have a declining capacity to determine their own military strategies and foreign policies. This is because security agreements, weaponry and national defence are organized in joint alliances and because unified command structures such as NATO control the power blocs.
3. Following the disintegration of the former Soviet Union, with its vast arsenal of weaponry, and increased mobility across borders of criminals, terrorists and others (Thachuk 2007), it is now relatively easy for individuals and groups to obtain lethal arms, small explosives and even certain types of nuclear weaponry. This privatization and democratization of the means of destruction signify a further dimension of declining state control (Hobsbawm 1994: Ch. 19).
4. A growing body of international law is increasingly infringing on state autonomy. In general, compliance rests on the interests and goodwill of the states themselves. There are, however, significant exceptions to this, including several rulings of the European Court of Human Rights concerning questions of equal pay and sexual discrimination in the workplace, which have forced member states to amend their national laws (Held 1989: 199–200). In addition, in 1997 a permanent world criminal court, the International Criminal Court at The Hague in the Netherlands, finally obtained the capacity to charge heads of states and other leading figures with genocidal crimes against humanity, which, although the USA withdrew from the agreement in 2002, a number of governments ratified. Several world leaders, including Milošević of Serbia and Pinochet of Chile, have since been indicted for crimes against humanity (Kegley and Wittkopf 2004: 584). The Bosnian Serb General Mladić was indicted in June 2011, after 16 years in hiding.
5. The ability of states to determine effective national economic policies is declining in the face of globalization. We now discuss this aspect in more detail.

ECONOMIC AUTONOMY

Excluding the special restrictions on members of regional economic groupings, such as the EU and the North American Free Trade Agreement, and the rules governing membership of IGOs such as the IMF and the WTO, a loss of economic autonomy has at least four aspects:

1.   The key role played by TNCs has made some capital much more mobile, even footloose. TNCs can decide where to deploy their various plants most profitably, what forms of employment policy they prefer, and where to deposit their liquid assets (see Chapter 10).
2.   Through the TNCs, Sklair (2001) sees the formation of a transnational capitalist class that is linked to the rise of global corporate power. Its members share several things in common: they seek to exercise control over the workplace, over domestic and international politics, and over the effects of consumer culture on everyday life. They also adopt global rather than local perspectives, think of themselves as citizens of the world, and often share similar luxury lifestyles (Calhoun 2002).
3.   The value of a country's currency and its government's ability to determine interest rates were once important economic weapons. Now, with the growth of 24-hour currency markets, the deregulation of banks, the growth of a vast financial system, developments in communications technology, and huge volumes of debt and credit moving around the world, uncontrollable money flows often dominate the transnational economy (Lauricella and Kansas 2010; Stiglitz 2002). Moreover, as we saw in Chapter 4, their endlessly speculative nature has produced a kind of 'casino capitalism' (Strange 1986). This sucks wealth out of the 'real' economy, while exposing everyone to the risk of financial bubbles and crashes. All this renders the key tools of government economic management decreasingly effective – especially when governments fear the lobbying power of big banks and financial markets and desist from imposing regulatory control over the latter.
4.   Governments confront a 'borderless world', but not only with respect to flows of technology, investment and money. According to Ohmae (1994: 18–19), of 'all the forces eating them [territorial boundaries] away, perhaps the most persistent is the flow of information'. Although governments could once monopolize information and perhaps manipulate it to influence national populations, this has become much more problematic with ICTs (Nye 2002).

THE CONTINUING NEED FOR EFFECTIVE NATION-STATES

Can the nation-state really be in terminal decline when its longstanding preoccupation with military security, autonomy and national identity continues to shape world politics? To deal with this question, and drawing on concrete examples, we now explore three themes:

*   the continuing saliency of national concerns in human affairs
*   the huge imbalance between different states in their capacity to exercise either their sovereignty or their autonomy
*   the fact that nation-states and their priorities are undergoing change rather than diminishing in scope.

INTRASTATE AND INTERSTATE CONFLICTS

There have been numerous recent crises to remind us of the continuing saliency of unresolved or new military, nationalist, interstate or ethnic conflicts in many parts of the world and of their capacity to ignite tensions. According to Smith and Bræin (2003: 70–1), there were more than 125 wars across the world between late 1989 and early 2003 and the great majority – around 90% – involved civil rather than interstate wars. Together, these wars killed around 7 million people, most of them civilians. The ending of the Cold War and the collapse of the Soviet Union have given impetus to the resurgence of national and ethnic demands and rivalries. Here are some of the many examples:

1.   The crisis in the Balkans, which began with the dissolution of Yugoslavia in 1989 and led to the genocide and civil war in Bosnia that lasted until 1995. The rekindling of the crisis in Kosovo led to NATO bomb attacks on Serbia from March 1999.

2. The first Iraqi invasion of Kuwait in 1990, followed by the Gulf War of 1991, and then the second Iraq War led by US forces in 2003, ostensibly to prevent the spread of Iraq's supposed weapons of mass destruction and the country being used as a terrorist base.

3. The continuing dispute between China and Taiwan, which briefly escalated into armed conflict in 1995 and was perhaps a foretaste of future conflicts in the Pacific region. It was also striking that in 2008, the year China hosted the Olympic Games and espoused its message of a global sports society, the Chinese government sent troops into Tibet and used violence to quell an uprising among people who were demanding greater autonomy.

4. Uncertainties over long-established ethnic, linguistic, religious or regional demands for autonomy in Northern Ireland, Canada, Spain, Palestine and several African countries. Sometimes, too, questions of unresolved identity result in prolonged violence and large-scale bloodshed, as when the Tamil Tigers' failed insurrection against the Sri Lankan government came to a head in 2010.

5. Uncertainties surrounding the UN's interventions, especially its failure to undertake effective global peacekeeping operations in Somalia, Bosnia, Rwanda, and multistate involvement in the war originating in the Democratic Republic of Congo.

6. The proliferation of chemical and nuclear weaponry as a rising number of countries (India, Pakistan, Israel and South Africa) acquired the capability to produce their own weaponry or seem likely to do so in the near future (Brazil, Iran and Argentina).

A PAUSE TO REFLECT

There are strong indications that most nation-states are losing some of their sovereignty and autonomy, yet many people around the world still passionately want and are prepared to fight for a state of their own. What accounts for the continuing attractions of statehood? Will states be able to enforce their initial preference that people be required to be citizens of one, and only one, nation-state, or will they increasingly have to accept many residents holding dual or multiple citizenships/nationalities?

NATION-STATES: VARIATIONS IN GLOBAL INFLUENCE

In their capacity to exercise influence, there is a huge practical difference between the few large, powerful nation-states and the very large number of quite small ones, although this discrepancy tends to be overlooked. The former – which includes EU countries like France and the UK, the USA, the BRIC group and Mexico – tend to do well in international negotiations. They also have more chance of successfully imposing legal or policy constraints on global capitalism and market forces. We encountered these huge power imbalances in our discussion of the USA as a hegemonic power.

The poorer, smaller nations, however, with tiny populations and relatively undeveloped economies that rely on a few raw materials, normally have limited scope for action. Many were also once colonies, so only emerged on the world stage relatively recently. We explore this further in Chapter 20 when we discuss the international negotiations on climate change. For example, even when acting together, the poor countries usually produce very meagre results at international WTO forums like Doha in their attempts to redress imbalances such as subsidies for farmers in the rich countries or the import restrictions the EU and the USA impose on some of their manufactured goods. By contrast, countries with vast oil wealth, such as China, India, Russia and Saudi Arabia, have increasingly been able to assert their national interests on the world stage. An example of this is in the increasing extent to which these and other nations are able to accumulate wealth and key assets as diverse as African farmlands or valuable inner-city properties through special investment vehicles called 'sovereign wealth funds' (Vidal 2010a). This demonstrates the continuing desire to preserve and augment nation-state power in a world context.

STATES IN TRANSFORMATION: AN URGENT NEED FOR COLLABORATION

It seems that states are neither disappearing nor losing power but starting to exercise different sorts of power. This is particularly evident in the fostering of national competitiveness – the rise of the 'competition state' (Teschke and Heine 2002: 176) to replace the welfare state. Accordingly, as capitalism is transformed and breaks free of the nation, so the political institutions of the state change and become increasingly internationalized to serve the interests of transnational capitalism. Together, they form what Robinson calls a 'transnational state'. This includes a transnational network of politicians and officials sympathetic to global capitalism, and elites linked to various supranational economic and political forums. These 'transnational state cadres act as midwives of capitalist globalization' (Robinson 2002: 216).

Recent events – particularly the financial crisis of 2008/9 – were a stark reminder that some nation-states remain powerful players in shaping global and local affairs. Nonetheless, the situation is complex and full of contradictions. That governments had to grapple with collapsing international banks, the freezing of credit and loans, the spectre of businesses of all kinds going bankrupt, and a frightening increase in global unemployment are clear indications of how far economic globalization has proceeded and how it now threatens the autonomy of even the most powerful states. Yet, during this crisis, governments discovered that they were the only bodies with the will, policy instruments and authority to act effectively to prevent a far worse world recession. Incidentally, while nationalizing banks, increasing regulatory powers and embarking on vast spending programmes, these same governments found themselves having to reverse years of opposition to the idea of interfering in free markets.

REVIEW

In examining sociology's contribution to our understanding of the links between society and the nation-state, we have tried to explain why its interest in global relations has been limited until recent decades. We then explored both sides of the debate on the supposed decline of the nation-state in the face of globalizing tendencies and have suggested the need to exercise caution when considering such arguments. Certainly, it seems as if some aspects of the debate about the nation-state versus globalization are dated and simplistic and need a drastic rethink.

In this regard we end the chapter with a final idea. As we saw in Chapter 4, the recent global financial crisis has brought many key issues to the fore. It is particularly notable and interesting how quickly governments realized that their moves to stem national economic disintegration, if they were to have any hope of working at all, required virtually unprecedented intergovernmental collaboration at the global level. To some extent this realization was demonstrated at the G20 meeting in London in April 2009. Although the full potential of, and necessity for, interstate collaboration has yet to be more generally acknowledged, the way forward for the world's nation-states now seems much clearer than it did prior to this crisis.

Visit the companion website at www.palgrave.com/sociology/cohen3e for extra materials to check and expand your learning, including interactive self-test questions, mind maps making links between key themes, annotated web links to sociological research, data and key sociological thinkers, a searchable glossary and much more.

FURTHER READING

C. W. Kegley Jr and E. R. Wittkopf's *World Politics: Trend and Transformation* (2004) provides a wide-ranging discussion of changing approaches to the study of international relations and the volatile nature of world politics in an age of rapid globalization. It is regularly revised and includes pictures, maps, tables and other accessible material.

D. Held and A. McGrew have written a number of leading works on politics and globalization. Their short book, *Globalization/Anti-globalization* (2002), includes an immense amount of relevant information and many carefully summarized assessments of the debates on the changing nature of power.

G. Delanty's *Citizenship in a Global Age: Society, Culture, Politics* (2000) offers a comprehensive review of theories of citizenship and shows how they need to change with globalization.

Chapter 1 on democracy by P. Lewis and Chapter 4 on citizenship and welfare by D. Riley in *Political and Economic Formations of Modernity* (1992), edited by J. Allen et al., would be useful accompaniments to the first part of this chapter.

R. J. Holton's *Globalization and the Nation-state* (2011) goes beyond the 'either/or' arguments that characterized the early debate about globalization and the nation-state and instead assumes coexisting global and national processes that intersect, connect, conflict and mutually influence each other.

QUESTIONS AND ASSIGNMENTS

1. Explain how and why mainstream sociology paid little attention to states and global relations until relatively recently.

2. Critically assess the contribution of the realist perspective to our understanding of the world order.

3. Are Marshall's three kinds of 'rights' adequate to an understanding of contemporary forms of citizenship?

4. 'The nation-state is in terminal decline, but there is no alternative structure capable of picking up its former functions.' Discuss.

5. What are the chief difficulties involved in considering the debate about globalization and the nation-state?

PART 2
Divisions and inequalities

6
Global inequalities: debates and case studies

We have seen earlier how the expansion of capitalism created an increasingly integrated world economy dominated by the logic of profit and the market. While some grew richer and many escaped poverty, the benefits of capitalism are, by the very nature of the ideology and system, conferred unevenly. Capitalism thus has a dual impact, generating wealth and lifting more and more people out of destitution, while also creating excluded, marginal, dispossessed and poor people. Different regions of the world experience the impact of an expanding capitalism very differently. In this chapter, we see how four social groups – famine victims, workers in deindustrializing areas, peasants, and the urban poor – are disadvantaged. Many people accept this outcome as natural or inevitable, and look upon those who have lost out in the race to prosperity as lazy or perhaps even biologically inferior. The poor and disadvantaged sometimes even blame themselves for their condition. Although sociologists are interested in how blame is assigned and what people believe about how they got to where they are, they also seek more complex explanations for the growth and perpetuation of poverty and other forms of disadvantage.

GLOBALIZATION AND POVERTY

The multiple effects of economic globalization, which became even more evident from 1990 onwards, brought with them a continuing debate focused on the central issue of world inequality and, more particularly, poverty. Who was winning and who was losing and to what degree, if at all, was economic globalization helping to reduce the incidence of poverty, particularly in the developing world?

These questions require us to consider how to characterize poverty, or even whether it is necessary to do so. Poverty is essentially a contested concept. This is partly because, in a diverse and changing social world, people perceive it differently in different contexts and partly because it is a political concept, implying and requiring remedial action (Alcock 1997: 6).

Sociologists have distinguished between the concepts of 'absolute poverty', where people live below subsistence level, and 'relative poverty', which is 'based on a comparison between the standard of living of other members of society who are not poor' (Alcock 1997: 89). In other words, relative poverty is defined according to social needs rather than basic material needs, but it can be devastatingly marginalizing in its effects, impacting significantly on people's opportunities in terms of educational achievement, health and employment chances. As a loose description, the Copenhagen Summit (UN 1995: 57) proposed that:

> [Poverty is] lack of income and productive resources to ensure sustainable livelihoods; hunger and malnutrition; ill health; limited or lack of access to education and other basic services; increased morbidity and mortality from illness; homelessness and inadequate housing; unsafe environments and social discrimination and exclusion. It is also characterized by lack of participation in decision-making and in civil, social and cultural life. It occurs in all countries: as mass poverty in many developing societies, pockets of poverty amid wealth in developed countries, loss of livelihoods as a result of economic recession, sudden poverty as a result of disaster or conflict, the poverty of low-wage workers, and the utter destitution of people who fall outside family support systems, social institutions and safety nets.

Despite the admirable breadth of this definition and its drafters' wisdom in observing that poverty is by no means confined to developing countries – a theme to which we return later in the chapter – since the 1997 conference, the UN has tended to focus its concern and actions on trying to deal with poverty in the poorer countries. The Millennium Development Goals (MDGs) it adopted in 2000 clearly demonstrate this point. In adopting these goals, the UN also spelled out in detail the specific targets we need to achieve to overcome poverty in the near future. Box 6.1 provides an outline of the UN's main programme and concerns.

A PAUSE TO REFLECT

In *Globalization: The Human Consequences*, Bauman (1998: 99) refers to a group affected 'by fate rather than choice'. What locks many people into poverty? Do you know anyone who can be described as 'trapped in poverty' and, if so, what could they do to improve their life chances?

Before examining the key moments in the evolving debate on poverty in the developing world, it is necessary to point out that scholars hold different and opposing views on its presence, severity, the direction in which it is moving, and how best to ameliorate it. Those who argue that it is gradually falling also tend to link this 'success' to the worldwide adoption of neoliberal economic policies and more open trade and capital movements, which we discussed in Chapter 3. The World Bank and most of its officials, particularly in the last quarter of the twentieth century, are probably the most influential upholders of this position. Ranged against them is a group of scholars who became increasingly critical of the World Bank position in particular and of neoliberal economics in general (for example Bello 2001, 2002; Pogge 2007; Wade 2004, 2007, to name but a few). A few World Bank officials, including the Nobel laureate Joseph Stiglitz (the bank's former chief economist and senior vice president for development policy), have joined the dissenters (Stiglitz 2002).

IS GLOBAL POVERTY IN RETREAT?

In its publication, *World Development Indicators* (2004a), the World Bank pointed to a spectacular reduction in poverty over the 20-year period from 1981 to 2001 when measured by the number of people living on less than US$1 a day. Thus, according to these figures, 350 million people escaped absolute poverty during these years, which translated into a reduction in the percentage of the world's population living in poverty from 39.5% to 21.3%, a remarkable improvement of 18.2%. The promoters of neoliberalism also observed that GDP per capita in all developing countries rose by 30% over the same period. The gains in the wealthy countries were even more spectacular.

BOX 6.1 Forging a global momentum: the Millennium Development Goals

The United Nations established the MDGs in 2000 when Kofi Annan was secretary-general. Leaders from 189 countries attended the founding meeting, which 'embraced a vision of the world in which developed and developing countries would work in partnership for the betterment of all' (UN 2009: 54).

The goals
Among its eight MDGs, due to be achieved by 2015, were the attainment of universal education, the empowerment of women, better conditions for women, and the pursuit of development in an environmentally sustainable way. The years 1990 and 2000, particularly 1990, served as baselines for measuring changes and achievements.

Targets and indicators
To bolster the eight goals and monitor progress were 18 clear operational targets and 48 indicators. The 2009 report summarized successes and failures and pointed to areas where it might be impossible to meet goals by 2015.

Overcoming world poverty
The first goal, which is to 'eradicate extreme poverty and hunger', contains three clear targets:

1. 'Halve, between 1990 and 2015, the proportion of people whose income is less than $1 a day'
2. 'Achieve full and productive employment and decent work for all, including women and young people'
3. 'Halve, between 1990 and 2015, the proportion of people who suffer from hunger' (UN 2009: 6-12).

On target for poverty reduction: some conclusions from the 2009 report
1. In 2008, higher world food prices halted the progress made on eradicating hunger since the early 1990s. Some 90 million more people may have experienced extreme poverty in 2009 than before the recession.

2. The advance in reducing child malnutrition from 1990 to 2007 will not be enough to meet the 2015 target. Thus, more than a quarter of children in the developing world remain underweight for their age. Again, higher food prices and the recession will derail further progress.

3. The goal of moving towards gender equality and women's empowerment has made substantial progress, but rising female unemployment for paid work, reduced funding for maternal health, for example prenatal care and safe childbirth, and family planning programmes are likely to stall future progress.

Source: UN (2009).

On closer examination, this image of a cornucopia of wealth cascading down to the world's poor melts away in the face of 'uneven development', the theme of this chapter. A World Bank (2004b) press release noted that while India and China had reduced poverty, many other countries are either bumping along in much the same way or going into further relative and absolute decline. The World Bank (2004b) further noted that:

> the number of people living on less than two US dollars a day in eastern Europe and Central Asia rose from eight million (2 per cent) in 1981 to over 100 million (24 per cent) in 1999, dropping back to slightly more than 90 million (20 per cent) in 2001.

Further, if we remove China from the equation, the number of people living on less than a dollar a day actually increased slightly over the measured period. All this raises the question of whether we should attribute this economic success to 'neoliberal globalization' or to some special features obtaining in the high-growth countries of the former 'Third World'.

In China's case, a number of factors played a role. These include, for example:

- the return of the powerhouse of Hong Kong to the mainland
- the mass mobilization of labour possible in a nominally communist country
- the input and importance of the Chinese diaspora
- the country's relatively high levels of education
- an international balance of political forces that allowed China open access to Western markets.

At any rate, although China's ability to export to Western markets partly propelled its economic success, there is a strong case for arguing that its internal policies, involving a 'form of state-led capitalism very different from that enjoined by the liberal argument' (Wade 2007: 114; see also Hutton 2007), were equally or even more crucial factors. This, in turn, meant that the government could retain control of its national banking system, promote state and national enterprises alongside foreign investment, and, above all, keep a firm watch over the flows of capital in and out of the economy. This is exactly what Japan, South Korea and other East Asian governments had done until US pressure in the 1980s compelled them to open up their economies to global capital flows.

China's internal policies are, of course, the opposite of those the West has pushed and the World Bank has applauded since the 1980s. Indeed, China's strategy closely resembles the historical stance of much of the developed world, which adopted protectionist policies as it industrialized, thus allowing domestic industries and local capitalism to flourish. It now looks hypocritical or perhaps self-interested for Western countries and Japan – together with institutions such as the IMF and the World Bank – to foist on China a global order extolling the virtues of free trade (Chang 2008; Wade 2004).

RECENT RE-EVALUATIONS

In 2008, Chen and Ravallion, two prominent World Bank experts, undertook a major reassessment of world poverty. While the World Bank had derived its earlier findings from national price surveys taken from 117 countries using 1993 as the baseline, in the revised analysis they used 2005 figures with data from 146 countries. They based these more recent price surveys on much larger samples of households and the research was conducted more rigorously under the supervision of national government officials. Consequently, the 'internationally comparable' standards they attained to compare the prices of everyday commodities between countries were more accurate. Moreover, it is likely that the 1993 price comparisons valued the government services available to poor people too highly and underestimated the effects of inflation (Chen and Ravallion 2008: 6).

With the improved World Bank methodology and taking $1.25 rather than $1 as the main poverty line, Chen and Ravallion (2008) reach the following conclusions (see also Table 6.1):

- The proportion of the world's population living on less than $1.25 a day halved between 1981 and 2005, falling from 52 to 26%. In absolute terms, more than 500 million people moved out of extreme poverty (Table 6.1).
- Using 2005 as the baseline and the more reliable poverty line of $1.25 a day, their revised analysis indicated that one-quarter of the world's population remained in poverty, considerably more than previous estimates based on the lower poverty line. Thus, they observed that 'the developing world is poorer than we thought' (Chen and Ravallion 2008: 34).
- As previously indicated, China's success in reducing poverty accounted for the greater part of world poverty reduction. In fact, 600 million fewer people were living on less than $1.25 a day in China in 2005 than in 1981 (Chen and Ravallion 2008: 25). If China is taken out of the analysis, the annual average rate of reduction in world poverty over the period 1981–2005 falls from 0.8% to 0.3% (Chen and Ravallion 2008: 24). This strongly suggests that if China is excluded from the 2005 figures, the developing world is unlikely

to attain the MDG of halving poverty by 2015 unless substantial and rapid changes are made to the current measures (see also Box 6.1). The persistence of deep poverty in sub-Saharan Africa and parts of South Asia is particularly notable.

A PAUSE TO REFLECT

In 24 years, between 1981 and 2005, 600 million people moved out of poverty (defined as US$1.25 a day) in China. The figures elsewhere are much less impressive. What did the Chinese do to achieve such results and why, by contrast, have many developing countries not managed to replicate such progress? Do the poverty reduction strategies in China come at a price, and how would you define that price?

- Of those living on daily incomes of just over $1.25, or between $1.25 and $2, between 1981 and 2005 the numbers living in poverty rose from just over 600 million to nearly 1.2 billion (Chen and Ravallion 2008: 24; Table 6.1). The same authors assert that rising world prices for food and other essentials – as happened between 2006 and 2008 – will worsen the extent and degree of poverty. Although the world recession largely reduced this threat during 2009, as prices for many commodities fell, by 2010 alarm was being raised once again over world food prices.
- In a later paper, Chen and Ravallion (2009) explored the likely impact of the world recession from 2007 onwards and predicted that this, too, will slow down the rate at which poverty will decline, irrespective of whether we adopt a poverty line of $1.25 or $2 per day.

TABLE 6.1 Number of poor people in the developing world (in millions)	1981	1990	1999	2005
1. 1993 estimate: living on less than $1.08 per day				
World total	1489	1248	1067	931
Excluding China	855	873	897	858
2. 2005 estimate: living on less than $1.25 per day				
World total	1896	1813	1696	1377
Excluding China	1016	1130	1250	1169
3. 2005 estimate: living on less than $2 per day				
World total	2535	2756	2872	2561
Excluding China	1563	1795	2102	2088
4. 2005 estimate: living on $1.25–$2 per day				
World total	639			1184
Excluding China	525			919

Note: Figures are rounded up.
Source: Chen and Ravallion (2008).

MULTIDIMENSIONAL POVERTY INDEX

In 2010, Alkire and Santos, two researchers working in collaboration with the UN Development Programme on the Oxford Poverty and Human Development Initiative, published the details of an alternative approach to measuring world poverty. Some of their initial findings suggest that poverty normally involves several overlapping and often mutually reinforcing variables. Incomes or living standards constitute only one contributor, albeit a powerful one. Arguably, a multidimensional approach provides a broader picture of the incidence of real poverty and the different ways it can entrap households in a spiral of misery from which it is difficult to escape. Taking households as their unit of analysis, they outline three dimensions – health, education and standard of living – with each given an equal weighting and measured using 10 indicators. The indicators utilized with respect to living standards are a household's access to electricity, its own sanitation, clean drinking water nearby, clean cooking fuel, non-dirt flooring, and ownership of resources such as a bicycle, radio or refrigerator that allow household members to function more effectively in their environment.

Alkire and Santos (2010: 22) suggest that a household is poor if it suffers an overall weighted deprivation of more than 30%, either through the effects of poverty within any one dimension or some combination of indicators across two or more dimensions. Their data came from 104 countries, which together made up around 78% of the world's population, or 5.2 billion people, and pertained to the year 2007. The following are among the many salient conclusions of their research:

1. In 2007, an estimated 32% of the population in the 104 countries in question were living in poverty. This is 1.7 billion people, which is a considerably higher figure than the one Chen and Ravallion provide.
2. Their analysis (2010: 43–9) reveals huge national, ethnic, urban–rural (poverty rates are invariably higher in rural areas), local and regional variations. For example, whereas only 10.4% of the populations of Latin America and the Caribbean (51 million people) are poor, 13.7% of the people of East Asia and the Pacific (255 million people) are 'multidimensionally poor'. This means that nearly two-thirds of the population of sub-Saharan Africa (458 million people) and more than half (54.7%) the population living in South Asia exists in a state of poverty.
3. This chronic deprivation in South Asia includes India, despite its recent high growth rate. It also exposes the extent of the continuing inequality in India and other countries. Thus, eight Indian states, including Bihar, Orissa and West Bengal, alone contain 421 million poor people on the new index – a higher number than for Africa's 26 poorest states (Alkire and Santos 2010: 32).

Having described the overall character of global poverty and its disputed trajectory since 1990, we now need to observe which particular social groups in various countries and regions are being notably affected by social fragmentation and marginalization.

GLOBAL THINKERS 6   WALDEN BELLO (1945–)

Bello is a political economist from Thailand. He is a widely respected analyst and critic of neoliberal globalization, as well as a campaigner for international justice.

Twenty-five years of failed policies

Since 1980, neoliberal economics has produced some winners but many more losers, particularly among 'Third World' countries and their poor majorities. The winners are the already rich business elites, international banks and TNCs, now free to relocate their capital wherever they can earn the highest returns. They are also now empowered to maximize profits for shareholders without needing to exercise the environmental or social accountability that workers and/or governments once demanded in the national interest.

Behind this shift towards economic globalization and neoliberalism, Bello sees three additional forces.

US global power

Since the early 1980s, the US government has used its power to protect the interests of its corporations and those economic sectors, for example biogenetics, pharmaceuticals, ITC, the media/cultural industries, banking and finance, in which (for the time being) it retains a world lead. It has used its control as the single largest contributor to the IMF and World Bank and as the world's largest market to force nations to open up their economies to the competitive superiority of its companies.

Inequality

Since the 1970s, growing inequality has resulted in massive underconsumption. Thus, worldwide car output in 2002 reached 80 million but demand was barely three-quarters of that. This applies as much to countries like South Korea or Brazil, where elites resist attempts to redistribute income, as it does to Europe or the USA. In the latter, wages for most workers remained static for 20 years prior to 1997, while income and wealth distribution became much more unequal. The vast majority have to rely on growing debts to increase their spending.

Democratic political stagnation and crisis

Governments are frightened to tackle this inequality. The resultant underconsumption and falling profits explain why corporations require an open world economy, for it makes it easier for them to move their plants in search of lower wages. Bello's reforms for fairer, more stable world economic governance call for:

- reimposing controls on capital flows across borders, including taxing these – the suggested 'Tobin tax'

- making the IMF, the World Bank and the WTO more transparent and amenable to the needs of the South

- where sensible, deglobalizing by encouraging more nationally owned activities that create local jobs and investment

- organizing and exposing governments, IGOs and TNCs to much more political pressure, with a view to demanding policies that reduce inequality both nationally and globally.

Source: Bello (2001, 2002).

FAMINE VICTIMS: HOW FAMINE ARISES

Ray Bush (1996: 169) observed that by the mid-1990s hunger was causing between 13 and 18 million deaths a year worldwide, or 35,000 a day. In developing countries, hunger caused 60% of deaths among the under fours. In Africa, he continued: 'the most vulnerable groups are agriculturalists and pastoralists [and] the poor, the elderly and women are the first to suffer'. A 1994 report for the World Bank (cited in Bush 1996: 173) depicted an equally bleak picture of population growth outstripping the growth in agricultural production in most countries in sub-Saharan Africa. The resulting 'food gap' meant that, between 1974 and 1980, the import of cereals increased by nearly 4% each year while food aid rose by 7% a year. This food crisis in Africa has continued until today, although in 2009 the UN reported that the incidence of hunger – measured in terms of the proportion of the population defined as undernourished – declined from 32 to 28% between the early 1990s and 2007. Similarly, over the same period, the proportion of underweight children under five in Africa fell from 31 to 28% (UN 2009: 11–12). Nevertheless, this same UN report also indicated a slight reverse during 2008 with respect to both these improvements. It linked this to rising world food prices from 2007 and expressed concern that world food shortages might again hinder further improvement in the future.

FOOD INSECURITY

At a global level, there is a surplus of food. Why, then, are there so many starving people in the midst of plenty? In the USA and Europe, producers often destroy or store food to sustain the market price. Each year thousands of tonnes of vegetables end up in landfill sites or are bulldozed into the sea. The process of hoarding to sustain farm prices has yielded bizarre phrases like 'butter mountains', 'wine lakes' and 'meat banks'. Why do we not simply send surplus food to poor countries? The answer is not as easy as it might appear. Sending food abroad as aid can sometimes distort and damage local economies. For example, the export of wheat to Nigeria, which started as free aid during the period of that country's civil war (1967–69), altered tastes, undermined local staple crops, and ultimately resulted in the displacement of farmers from their land. Nigeria became enmeshed in what Andrae and Beckman (1985) called 'the wheat trap', whereby the government used precious foreign exchange to buy US wheat, which Nigerian consumers now demanded, while attempts to start domestic production failed to provide more than 10% of the total needed.

Attempts to work within the logic of the world food system can force small farmers to the wall. Many farmers in poor countries can neither produce at globally competitive rates nor ward off cheap imports. One reason for this is that they have to compete with the vast agri-businesses that form integrated 'global food chain clusters' (Hendrickson and Heffernan 2002: 347), which can, at a very low cost, bind the tiny individual outputs of millions of farmers worldwide into factory food systems. The world trade regime, which the World Trade Organization (WTO) and rich countries dominate (Reitan 2007: 109–11, 120–1), also works against their interests. Despite the developing countries' efforts at various WTO conferences in Doha over several years to reach a fairer global agreement, the rich countries continue to subsidize their own farmers and to dump their excess products – whether as aid or as below-cost food – onto poor countries.

While it is reasonable to assume that changes in public policy in both rich and famine-prone countries should be able to address the problem of food insecurity, we need first to understand the fundamental causes of famine. Food insecurity turns into famine for three reasons: natural disasters; lack of entitlement (or access) to food; and policy failings, which we discuss in turn.

Natural disasters

Natural disasters such as droughts, hurricanes, floods, earthquakes and tsunamis can easily disrupt a precarious agricultural system. When these strike, the threat of famine comes from the shortage in the supply of food arising from what insurance companies call 'an act of God'. People, either through the media or in popular discussions, rarely question such an obvious explanation for famine. Yet, such a view has some real limitations:

- Why are some societies afflicted with similar disasters able to avoid famine or to recover more rapidly?
- Do established agricultural policies and practices contribute to the likelihood of famine arising in the wake of a natural disaster? For example, deforestation, burning wood for fuel, and soil erosion through overgrazing might all massively amplify the threat of famine.
- Are there enough roads and airstrips to provide easy access to the sites of a likely famine?
- Are there adequate storage facilities for grain, edible tubers or rice?
- Are there enough pipes laid and pumping stations installed to safeguard water supplies?
- Are there adequately organized and trained civil defence and emergency services?
- Has a failure to promote land reform forced poor people onto marginal land where they are most vulnerable to sudden climatic or political changes?

Such questions seek to explore sociological explanations for famine, namely those that critically assess commonsense assumptions and focus on the social and political dimensions of the problem.

Entitlement theory

The most important alternative approach to famine is through 'entitlement theory', which Sen (1981; see Figure 6.1) developed and later extended in his joint work with Dreze. There, Dreze and Sen (1989: 9) define the concept of entitlement as follows:

What we can eat depends on what food we are able to acquire. The mere presence of food in the economy, or in the market, does not *entitle* a person to consume it. In each social structure, given the prevailing legal, political, and economic arrangements, a person can establish command over alternative commodity bundles (any one bundle of which he or she can choose to consume). These bundles could be extensive, or very limited, and what a person can consume will be directly dependent on what these bundles are.

It is often far from clear precisely what these 'commodity bundles' are. Certainly, purchasing power, although potentially important, is not the only kind of entitlement. For example, in parts of India, Central Asia and most of Africa, rural dwellers have either very modest cash incomes or none at all. Under these circumstances, other kinds of entitlement intervene:

- Can the rural dweller go into a local forest and trap or hunt game to supplement the family diet, or has that land been designated a wilderness area and is protected by armed rangers hired by, for example, the World Wildlife Fund?
- Can small farmers collect fruit, berries or edible flora and fungi? Or have the big farmers destroyed all these pickings (a last remnant of the hunter-gatherer society) through the private registration of land, the use of herbicides and pesticides, and the production of (often inedible) crops for the world market?
- Can peasants call on their landlord for a loan, or will this engender yet another turn of the screw of **debt peonage**?
- Can peasants turn to kin or clan, or are they so far down the road of private capital accumulation that they choose not to help a relative?
- Can women assert their entitlement to equal treatment when historically they have been victims of patriarchal family structures?

> **DEBT PEONAGE**
>
> A system whereby loans in cash or kind are made to poor peasants by rich farmers, and paid back by a share of crops or income gained by the debtor or the debtor's descendants.

In short, it is not obvious what 'entitlement' means and the very poor are facing increasingly acute dilemmas:

- Is it worth starving to preserve one's assets, at least to give one's children a chance to survive?
- Alternatively, must one place oneself at the mercy of a local political dignitary and swear an oath of permanent fealty and obeisance in exchange for immediate relief (and thus, incidentally, reinvent something akin to feudalism)?
- Can any individual solution be successful or enduring, or does one have to organize to defend collective rights?
- If that is unsuccessful, is there nothing else to do but to trudge in a pitiful line towards the feeding stations where earnest white volunteers dispense handouts flown in from all over the world?

Policy failings

Sen's entitlement theory has provided a radical alternative to the 'natural' explanation for the reason for famine and, since the early 1980s, has held centre stage for in-depth discussions about the problem of food insecurity. Although not intending to supersede Sen's theory, other authors such as Bush (1996) and Keen (1994) place more emphasis on the political factors and failings that trigger famine. It is evident that adverse effects on agricultural production can result from civil war as farmers flee the land in fear of their lives. Could some political actors be using famine as a crucial part of their means of prosecuting a civil war, rather like some retreating armies pursue a 'scorched earth' policy to deny food and materials to their enemies? This raises the question of whether famine serves the interests of some parties, for example:

- merchants, who may be hoarding staples or buying livestock at knock-down prices
- suppliers of grain from other sources

FIGURE 6.1 Amartya Sen (1933–)
Sen developed entitlement theory, and is a Nobel laureate in economics, but has made notable contributions to general social science issues.

FIGURE 6.2 A starving Dinka child
A food bowl covers the face of a starving Dinka child on his way to a famine relief station at Thiet in southern Sudan. Accusations that the politicians in the Muslim-dominated north of the country deliberately deepened the periodic famines in the Christian south exacerbated a civil war between the regions, which finally ended in 2005. South Sudan became independent in July 2011.

- politicians whose desire for power and territory or hatred of other ethnic groups might incline them either to be phlegmatic about famine in a particular area or to do little to help
- local elites who use their access to global aid flows to feather their own nests rather than send the supplies to areas where they are needed.

Keen (1994) takes this logic even further. He argues that there was a high level of intentionality in the famines in Sudan (Figure 6.2). According to him, the Islamic Sudanese ruling class used famine as a stick with which to beat the heads of its opponents, particularly the southern Christians. This is a chilling conclusion to reach and, although developed only in relation to one country, it challenges some of the rival theories used to explain famine. Facing a loss of popularity with its own supporters in the north and an environmental crisis, the regime saw the creation of famine in the south as a way out of its dilemmas. Alluding to Sen's theory, Keen (1994: 13, 14) writes:

> Notwithstanding Sen's emphasis on poverty as the root of famine, it was, in a sense, precisely the wealth of victim groups that exposed them to famine. Processes of famine involved the forcible transfer of assets from victim to beneficiary groups in a context of acute political powerlessness on the part of the victims. … The 1985–89 famine was the creation of a diverse coalition of interests that were themselves under intense political and economic pressures in the context of a shrinking resource base and significant environmental crisis in the north.

In 1998, when famine again loomed in the Sudan, the country divided into religious factions. Christian charities poured aid into the south, while several Islamic countries supported the government in Khartoum. In short, cruel as this is, one can consider famine as an instrument of politics.

WORKERS IN THE DEINDUSTRIALIZING COUNTRIES

It is important to recognize that globalization is only one interlude in a long and continuing process of disruptive economic change. Capitalism has always been highly uneven and unequal in its impact within and between societies. Perpetual technological and market upheavals drive it internally and whole industries, regions and skill structures rise and fall with relentless regularity. Think, for example, about the cotton industry in northwest Britain that gave the Industrial Revolution in the early nineteenth century its leading worldwide edge. Yet, by the 1920s it had waned in the face of growing competition from rival textile industries in America, Europe, Japan, India and Egypt.

DECLINING PERMANENT JOBS AND STARK ALTERNATIVES

As we saw in Chapter 4, since the late 1970s the globalization of industrial production, the widespread adoption of free-market economics, and the trend towards post-Fordism have together led to the deindustrialization of many once established and prosperous regions across the advanced countries, although so far this has been less marked in Germany and Japan. The main casualties of these rust-belt zones have been blue-collar manual workers. Overall, by the mid-1980s well over two-thirds of the labour force in advanced countries had left manufacturing and were classified as service workers, while the wages of manual workers in the USA, and several other countries, have not risen in real terms for more than 20 years. To take one example, France's GNP grew by 80% in the 20 years after 1973, yet in the same period unemployment increased twelvefold to reach over 5 million in 1993 (McMichael 2000: 191). Australia, one of the few developed countries to have weathered the post-2007 recession successfully, has also seen a massive shift from mining, agriculture and manufacturing to the services sector, which accounted for 70.6% of GDP in 2010 (CIA 2011). Directly linked to this transformation, working-class people in traditional industries have experienced a parallel decline in welfare benefits in many countries, stagnant or falling real incomes, and often long periods of unemployment.

Furthermore, where new jobs have emerged to replace the permanent well-paid ones that have been lost, the former normally involve non-contractual, insecure forms of casualized work or 'McJobs', namely part-time, temporary or seasonal work without prospects or social benefits. In addition, they tend to arise in low-grade services, many of which were once largely the preserve of women and that include such jobs as cleaning, catering, domestic service and retail work. With the pay for such work often barely, if at all, above the minimum wage, and hours of work frequently long, unsociable and in poor working conditions, it is hardly surprising that the established populations of many cities are averse to seeking such employment. Instead, first-generation migrants are increasingly occupying these jobs. In London, in 2005, foreign-born migrants made up 35% of the working age population and this group is increasingly filling the majority of McJob vacancies (May et al. 2007). May et al. (2007: 155) state that nearly half of all domestic workers, cleaners, labourers, refuse collectors, caretakers and porters are foreign born, but the figure is 60% in hotels and restaurants.

Because of the low wages, many workers, especially those who belong to migrant communities, can only support their families by undertaking several casualized jobs at the same time. Thus, in Germany, the ratio of people in regular or standard, full-time, permanent and secure employment compared with those in casual or part-time employment had fallen from 5:1 in the early 1970s to 2:1 by the mid-1990s (Edgell 2005: Ch. 4). Similarly, by 2008, the proportion of Japanese employees in mini-jobs – 'temporaries' – constituted nearly 33% of the workforce compared with 23% in 1997 (Hayashi 2008). Given that such trends have long been common within many developing countries but have now spread to the older industrial zones of advanced countries, many commentators have argued that we are now seeing the 'peripheralization' (Hoogvelt 1997) or 'Brazilianization' (Beck 2000b) of the North.

POTENTIAL REACTIONS: SINK ESTATES AND RIGHT-WING POPULISM

These massive declines in traditional factory employment have generated wider consequences. They have subjected whole communities to poverty, mental illness, rising crime and other problems because of the downward spiral created by a huge reduction in worker spending power on local taxes, leisure facilities and the social fabric. Moreover, the combination of long periods of high individual unemployment within families, especially among older workers, the concentration of disadvantaged people in particular locales, and the declining socioeconomic vitality of entire communities has sometimes given rise to a near collapse of employment seen as a realistic life alternative or a valid culture towards which young people can aspire. Indeed, high levels of youth unemployment are often evident in the deprived areas of these cities; for example, the figures for Paris in 1997 and Naples in 1991 were 22 and 73% respectively (Murie and Musterd 2004: 1448). The result, in many cities such as Pittsburgh, London, Brussels, Berlin and Paris, has been the rise in some urban areas of so-called 'sink estates' dominated by a drug culture, low-grade criminality, violent behaviour, and family disintegration among some groups of individuals, as in parts of London (Watt 2006). While the wholesale adoption of post-Fordist, free-market practices in the former communist countries after 1992 had variable results, in Russia, in the years immediately following the demise of communism, the experience seems to have been wholly deleterious. One Russian worker in four, which amounted to more than 20 million people, was not paid regularly and the delays were often for up to six or even twelve months.

A PAUSE TO REFLECT

In August 2011 there was widespread rioting in London and other UK cities. More than 3,000 people were arrested and only 8.6% of the first 1,000 defendants charged either had jobs or were full-time students. Does this indicate that alienated and deprived youth are striking back against being excluded from the fruits of global economic progress? Given the absence of political slogans or clearly articulated demands, were the rioters simply illegal consumers rather than rebels? Can we expect more unrest of this kind?

We refer here to the rise of populist right-wing groups and political parties. According to Mudde (2007), the members of such groups uphold a cluster of core values. These are a belief in nativism – the nation should be exclusively occupied by its long-established inhabitants – a desire to live in a highly ordered if not authoritarian society, and a marked preference for the patriotic commonsense knowledge of 'ordinary' people rather than the abstract thinking of intellectuals. Adherents also tend to be suspicious of, if not hostile to, the minorities they fear threaten the nation from within, especially migrants who dilute native values, but also gays, feminists and established ethnic minorities. Such reactions have been particularly notable in Europe, where it has contributed to growing electoral support for radical right populist parties, which, on average, gained 8% of votes during the 1990s (Liang 2007).

PEASANTS AND LANDLESS LABOURERS

As capitalist social relations spread unevenly across the globe, one of the most notable 'losers' is the peasantry. In the nineteenth century, social theorists like Marx assumed the inevitable decline and even disappearance of the peasantry. People thought that modernization and industrialization would signal the end of rural pursuits and, at the beginning of the twenty-first century, there are indeed indications that urbanization is increasingly the norm, with just over half of the global population living in cities by 2009. Yet, the process is much delayed and is less fully advanced than earlier expected; in fact, large numbers of people still live in rural areas. Of course, not all are 'peasants', an ambiguous term we have used casually, although not yet defined. To do so, we need to provide some sense of the nature of rural social differentiation. The class structure of the rural world is every bit as complex as that of urban areas, although this is often overlooked. In Table 6.2 we depict an elementary approximation of a typical rural class structure in Asia, where most rural dwellers live.

TABLE 6.2 A simple rural class structure	
Landlords	Live off rented land cultivated by tenants
Rich peasants	Live off own produce and surplus produced by hired hands
Middle peasants	Live off own produce generated mainly by family labour
Poor peasants	Own or rent some land but also have to work for others for their subsistence
Landless labourers	Own no land and have to sell their labour power

Source: Adapted from Bagchi (1982: 149–50).

Religious, gender, ethnic and (in India and some other places) caste overlay these class distinctions. For example, scavengers, butchers, leatherworkers and night-soil workers (collectors of excrement) are at the bottom of the caste hierarchy and, despite the attempts of the inspirational leader Mahatma Gandhi and successive governments of India to abolish the notion of untouchability, it is often difficult for people to escape their occupationally defined and inherited castes.

THE PEASANTRY AND THE DISRUPTION OF THE RURAL WORLD

What has all this to do with uneven development? The answer is that the processes of industrialization, urbanization and commercialization have profoundly disrupted the rural world. We need to see 'the peasantry', therefore, not so much as a residual category (Marx's position), or an unchanging 'traditional' category, but as a differentiated group subjected to, and evolving with, the new international division of labour. There are now very few peasants who produce entirely for subsistence or even for consumption in the local market. Instead, most rural pursuits now tie into the global marketplace and there are at least four ways in which this has happened.

First, since the 1950s, the Green Revolution, which distributes high-yielding seeds to farmers, has integrated the rural world into the global marketplace. Governments and research workers saw the Green Revolution as a means of abolishing famine forever. At first, sociologists like Pearse (1980) argued that the unintended consequences of this innovation were highly adverse. Only the richer farmers could afford the pesticides, fertilizers and water necessary to make the seeds productive. The seeds also worked better on a larger scale, so the richer peasantry often bought out smaller farmers. Later, social scientists reported a more benign outcome, particularly in Asia. As the cost of the technology fell, often with the help of government subsidies, poor and middle peasants were able to deploy the new seeds.

GREEN REVOLUTION

The diffusion of high-yielding varieties of seeds, particularly wheat, maize and rice. (Not to be confused with the green/environmental movement.)

Second, huge corporations subcontract farm production to vast numbers of worldwide small producers. However, many are also direct owners of land and employers of labour in their own right. At the top of the tree are vast agricultural TNCs like Monsanto, which provide chemical fertilizers, pesticides, herbicides and genetically engineered crops, or Del Monte, whose cans of fruit are available on just about every major supermarket shelf. Such firms are correctly described as being involved in 'agribusiness'. They have bought vast areas of land in many countries, previously held as common land or owned by the middle peasantry, and turned this into a series of 'field factories' – using hired labour to plant, weed, pick and pack the produce. Small and middle farmers have been driven to the wall, or can only survive by working part time for the big companies. As we see in Chapter 10, when peasants become dependent on global agricultural supply chains, this often leads to a radically changed rural workforce whose members could not survive without a contract to produce flowers, food and juices for the rich North. Supermarkets such as Walmart, Tesco, Asda and Carrefour are especially powerful in shaping the fate of small farmers everywhere. This is because their concentrated market share allows them to demand lower prices from their farm suppliers and to squeeze some small producers, those who cannot cope with ever more demanding regulations and lower costs, out of production altogether. Moreover, supermarkets are often less concerned with quality than with ensuring the steady supply of a 'big volume of some generic, anonymous, bottom-of-the-range, own-label' product (Blythman 2007: 238). Again, this benefits the large farmers while often hurting the smaller ones.

A third source of pressure on peasants, although it often equally threatens tribal and indigenous people, comes from huge government development projects such as road or dam building. Frequently, these projects require the privatization of land or natural resources such as forests and lakes and this in turn leads to the displacement of rural people in massive numbers. As of June 2008, the Three Gorges dam on the River Yangtze in China had displaced 1.2 million people. The 3,000 large dams built in India since 1947 have so far displaced 21.6 million people. These are mainly women, tribal and other marginalized people, and small farmers who are pushed off the land and out of their communities because their established patterns of usage conflict with the needs of 'national and global capital' (Kothari and Harcourt 2005: 121). More recently, there have been alarmist newspaper reports that China is buying vast tracts of land in Latin America and Africa to feed its immense population, although one scholar (Brautigam 2010) provides a more sympathetic assessment of China's ambitions. It remains unclear whether the local inhabitants will end up as tenant farmers, agricultural workers or the victims of mass evictions from their traditional sources of livelihood (Vidal 2010a).

Finally, continuing developments in biotechnology financed by governments and large corporations often exacerbate the difficulties that peasants already face. Particularly important here is the purchase of various genetic plant materials that then become the basis for company claims to patent rights or trade-related intellectual property rights. These confer the monopoly right to own whatever future products anyone develops from such genetic materials. From the perspective of numerous small farmers, this attempt to privatize the genetic content of plants that previously belonged to everyone and were part of the common, shared stock of 'earth's water, forest, air, land and seeds' (Reitan 2007: 150) seems tantamount to hijacking their future livelihoods.

Considered overall, these relentless pressures have driven many peasants into penury or landless desperation. They eke out a miserable existence on more and more marginal land or are forced to become landless labourers, drift to the slums around the big urban areas, or accept work with such a level of exploitation that it amounts to near slavery.

THE URBAN POOR: MEGACITIES AND SLUM DWELLERS

The rural areas in many poor countries are incapable of sustaining a self-sufficient life. Dim as the prospects are for obtaining permanent urban employment, the chances of gaining access to some kind of livelihood and to better services are usually greater there than in the countryside. Harrison (1981: 145) described the resultant migration, which continues across the developing world, as 'of epic, historic proportions' (see Chapter 18). Drawing on UN-commissioned research conducted by University College London in 2002/3, Davis (2006: 15–16) explains how, given current urban growth rates, by 2015 there will be approximately 550 cities in the world that contain at least 1 million people. This compares with only 86 in 1950. China alone had 166 cities of this size by 2005. Because most urban growth occurs in the developing world, the majority of future urban dwellers will live in its cities. Many will be megacities – defined as containing a minimum of 8 million inhabitants (Davis 2006: 1–2). Moreover, much of the rapid urbanization occurring across the South involves the 'reproduction of poverty, not the supply of jobs' (Davis 2006: 16).

Several stark consequences directly result from this situation. One is that most urban dwellers have to rely on finding micro-niches in the informal economy for their livelihoods and frequently these are low in skill, lack legal or official recognition, and are overcrowded and therefore intensely competitive. This obviously leads to chronic insecurity and even danger. This sector encompasses a diverse range of occupations and activities (Figure 6.3). They include religious ascetics, the insane, the physically disabled, huge numbers of micro-traders (selling items like matches or nuts), touts for taxis and buses, pickpockets, thieves, fresh-food preparers, prostitutes, handcart or rickshaw pullers, beggars, day labourers, homeworkers operating at the extreme lower end of global subcontracting networks, as well as apprentices and their 'masters'. All these are part of the rich social landscape in the cities of the poor countries. At times, many of these activities involve criminality and/or disregard official regulations. Further, since family survival requires that every member find an income-earning opportunity, child labour of one kind or another, for example carpet or toy manufacturing in India and Pakistan, is often endemic.

Overall, according to research conducted under the auspices of the UN-HABITAT (2003) project, it is highly probable that around two-fifths of the economically active population in the South and their families depend on the informal economy for their livelihoods and most live in cities. Because their lives are so precarious, so fraught with the tensions that stem from poverty and intense competition over a tiny patch of urban economic space, and given that their activities mostly occur outside the expanding modern sector of the economy, some observers view the Southern urban poor as structurally irrelevant to, and excluded from, mainstream global capitalism. One expert on global inequality, for example, refers to 'the detached', namely those who are in effect 'cut off from the "mainstream" of economic life' (Standing 2009: 115). At the same time, the cities they inhabit function, up to a point, as containers for the world's 'surplus humanity' (Davis 2006: 174).

A second consequence is that roughly three-quarters of the fast-growing urban population in the South live in slums. Indeed, in Davis's (2006) terminology, we inhabit a *Planet of Slums*. Looking at this figure another way, approximately one-third of the world's urban population lives this way and this constitutes roughly one-sixth of humanity, or a billion people. The word 'slum' embraces several possible types of habitation and their occupants are either illegal squatters in shantytowns at the edge of the city, the inhabitants of overcrowded inner-city private tenement buildings, or simply the shifting residents of urban spaces such as stations or pavements (Davis 2006: 16–18). Shantytowns, also known as 'favelas', 'barrios' or 'cardboard cities', are temporary settlements characterized by inadequate shelter, poor roads and no sewerage, electricity or piped drinking water. Inner-city habitations, however, invariably reveal the same paucity of utilities. Wider provisions like sports fields, libraries, schools, health centres or parks are undreamed-of luxuries.

A few examples will illustrate the sheer magnitude and ubiquity of this phenomenon across the South:

1. In São Paulo, Brazil's largest city, the proportion of the population living in favelas grew from just over 1% in 1973 to nearly 20% in 1993.
2. In the 1990s, India's slums expanded 2.5 times faster than its overall population, while, according to estimates, by 2015 Delhi, the capital city, will have a slum population of

© FERNANDO MOLERES/PANOS

FIGURE 6.3 Waste pickers in Guatemala City, Guatemala
Many children engage in sorting and scavenging for recyclable materials to sell on, and are often injured by glass, sharp metal and discarded chemicals.

around 10 million. This is hardly surprising, given that approximately 400,000 of the half million new arrivals in Delhi each year end up living in slums.
3. Official figures from just one of China's numerous cities, Beijing, show that around 200,000 unregistered migrants, or 'floaters', arrive in the city each year from the rural areas and many end up living in illegal slums (Davis 2006: 17–18).

Many newly arrived migrants to the urban areas seek to maintain some kind of link with the countryside, for practical as well as emotional reasons. Some describe this as 'circular migration' or a 'dual system'. As Gugler (1995: 544) succinctly described it:

> The 'dual-system' strategy is sustained by kinship groups that control rural resources, in particular access to the ancestral lands. The village assures a refuge in a political economy that fails to provide economic security to many of the urban population and that often threatens an uncertain political future. For many urban dwellers, the solidarity of rural kin provides their only social security, meagre but reliable. Often they look forward to coming 'home'.

The living conditions of people in many cities of the global South are so bad that most writers – including Marx in the mid-nineteenth century – believe that the urban poor have little or no capacity to engage in revolutionary political action. Yet, some writers (for example Flusty 2004) have noted the presence of a reforming, self-improving zeal behind certain community actions to improve the slum dwellers' environments and standards of living. This more positive outcome often occurs alongside the involvement of professionals, students and NGOs who work with the urban poor to obtain basic goods and resources. In addition, their position seems to improve dramatically if there is a strong civil society and some reasonable degree of political democracy. Such improvements arise for an obvious reason – politicians competing for office need votes. If the urban poor can cohere for political action, gradually roads, subsidized building materials, waterborne sewerage and piped drinking water arrive. International action to increase aid, reduce national debt burdens and so on can also play a key role in reducing the extent and intensity of urban poverty. In fact, according to the UN (2009: 47), such efforts linked to the MDGs have begun to have some impact. By 2005 the numbers living in slums had fallen since 1990, while across most world regions conditions had improved – more had clean water, better sanitation, durable housing and adequate living space.

REVIEW

There have been a number of macroscopic attempts to explain why uneven development, or global inequality, arises. World system theorists, scholars interested in the new international division of labour, and authors who write about the social marginality that arises from economic globalization have all provided valuable insights. All three agree on one central insight, namely that the spread of capitalist social relations can wipe out entire agricultural populations and labour forces in many countries, regions and cities. This negative outcome is likely to arise when the introduction of neoliberal economic policies challenges the nature of society and the form of its political governance. This situation was particularly evident in post-communist Russia, where speculative capital and incompetent government triggered a near disintegration of society for at least a decade.

In this chapter, we have sought to make these general theories 'come alive' by discussing four adversely affected groups – famine victims, workers in deindustrializing areas, peasants and landless labourers, and the urban poor. Considered overall, we can say that the significant differences between the global winners and global losers may turn on the kinds of basic amenities set out as goals and targets established by the UN in 2000 – such things as the provision of clean water, access to shelter and healthcare, and the chances of surviving infancy. The cost of providing these amenities is not particularly high when measured against the vast amounts disbursed, for example, on global military spending. Rather, what is most needed is the political determination to engage in interstate and intersocietal collaboration designed, in the words of Ban Ki-moon, the current secretary-general of the UN, to 'free a major portion of humanity from the shackles of extreme poverty, hunger and disease' (UN 2009: 3).

Visit the companion website at www.palgrave.com/sociology/cohen3e for extra materials to check and expand your learning, including interactive self-test questions, mind maps making links between key themes, annotated web links to sociological research, data and key sociological thinkers, a searchable glossary and much more.

FURTHER READING

M. Davis's *Planet of Slums* (2006) provides an excellent overview of urban problems and the experiences of different groups across the world.

In *American Apartheid: Segregation and the Making of the Underclass* (1993), D. S. Massey and N. A. Denton consider the consequences of deindustrialization in the USA, especially for black workers.

A. Sen's *Poverty and Famine: An Essay on Entitlement and Deprivation* (1981) has been contested in detail, but it remains a classic work that is challenging and stimulating if you give it a little time. (You can ignore some of the more technical economics and still grasp the essence of the argument.)

R. Wilkinson and K. Pickett's *The Spirit Level: Why Equality is Better for Everyone* (2010) is a remarkable achievement. Using international data and comparisons between states within the USA, they show that greater equality benefits everyone, both poor and rich. Note that this is a statistical exercise, not a political tract, but it has important political implications.

QUESTIONS AND ASSIGNMENTS

1. Will the poor always be with us, as the saying has it?
2. How does famine start and how is it continued, deepened and ameliorated?
3. According to the 2001 census, India has 638,365 villages. Can migration to the cities be contained by bringing electricity, education and small enterprises to rural India?
4. Assess the extent to which workers in industrialized countries have been victims of economic globalization.

7
Class, income and wealth

Sociologists have always sought to conceptualize and explain the social inequalities present in all societies and to monitor how these vary both between societies and over time. The unequal distribution of power, wealth, income opportunity and social status between individuals and groups is not randomly distributed, but patterned and structured. Particular social groups find themselves persistently denied the same access to social rewards and resources as other groups. Through the various forms of discrimination, as well as the ideologies and culturally dominant values to which disadvantaged groups are exposed, they learn to accept their 'proper' place in society, one example of what sociologists call SOCIALIZATION. This is particularly evident in the case of women, as we shall see in Chapter 8, where we explain how, from birth onwards, infants of both sexes across virtually all societies in the world absorb notions of innate biological and cultural inferiority and female subordination. Customary beliefs, political ideologies and organized religion have often played central roles in instilling convictions that a given social order is normal, necessary or divinely sanctioned.

In general, we can say that structured forms of inequality often operate along three main axes of gender, race/ethnicity or class. Each of these in turn generates its own structure of unequal practices, giving rise to institutionalized sexism, racism or class divisions/conflict. Gender and sexual orientation, race and class also crosscut each other in various complex ways, sometimes reinforcing and at other times weakening the impact of existing inequalities.

We also need to remember that the relative significance of different kinds of inequality can change. In fact, the particular manifestation of these axes of disadvantage varies quite markedly between different societies and over time. Moreover, as we discuss briefly in Chapter 9, other sources of inequality, such as religious affiliation, disability, civic status and age, also operate to create social inequalities. Sexual orientation constitutes yet another source of inequality and we say something about this alongside the main discussion of gender in Chapter 8. We examine the issues particularly associated with race in Chapter 9.

In this chapter, we concentrate on the structured distribution of wealth and income and how these find expression in class stratification and patterns of inequality. We have already explored some aspects of this in Chapter 6. There, we looked in detail at current debates on poverty. We saw that, depending on what poverty line we adopt and/or how many dimensions we include in the definition, poverty remains deeply implicated in the lives of perhaps one-third, or more, of humanity, or somewhere between 1.7 and 2.5 billion people (see Table 6.1). In the first section of this chapter, we explore sociological definitions of, and explanations for, social class differences in income and wealth, with particular emphasis on nationally based societies. We then turn to patterns of global inequality. Although inequalities within nations remain highly significant and extremely divisive, there is evidence to suggest that the worldwide spread of a capitalist market economy is deepening global inequalities. In the final section, we examine the idea that we need increasingly to think in terms of an emerging global class system. Here, arguably, we can already discern the emergence of two central agents – a world proletariat, most of whose members face the chronic insecurity that stems from needing to compete for work on a global stage, and a mobile transnational capitalist class.

CLASS IN THE ERA OF NATIONALLY BASED CAPITALISM

One of the richest people on earth is Bill Gates, the owner of Microsoft. On 1 April 1999, a surge in the stock market price for his company meant that Bill Gates's fortune was estimated at the headline figure of US$100bn. At that time his personal fortune was greater than the GNPs of all but the richest 18 nations, and worth more than twice all the US dollar bills in circulation. If Gates stacked his bills on top of each other, he would have had to climb 16 miles to get to the top (*Daily Telegraph*, 8 April 1999). On the same night, 1 April 1999, there were 3 million people in the USA sleeping in hostels, shelters or on the streets. Amazingly, a decade later, he and his wife joined forces with Warren Buffett, another super-rich investor, to persuade billionaires to gift half their wealth to philanthropic causes. While the three have been remarkably generous with their money, for example giving US$3bn a year for world health, the tax authorities in the USA indicate that the wealthiest 18,000 individuals in the country gift not half but only 5–6% of their income (Loomis 2010). It should be added that philanthropy is much more evident in the USA than in most other countries. Clearly, philanthropy alone, however munificent, will not fundamentally change income discrepancies.

The very large discrepancies between countries, which we discussed in relation to poverty in Chapter 6, parallel the massive economic inequalities within any one country. Sociologists use the terms 'social stratification' or 'class' to discuss these and similar differences. Strictly speaking, class differences are but one form of stratification. Others include slavery and caste.

SLAVERY

Many ancient societies practised slavery, with slaves worked to death either in mining or in building pyramids, religious monuments, irrigation systems and public works. In some settings like northern Nigeria, household slaves were treated more benignly, sometimes as favoured servants. The plantation slaves of the New World, however, were firmly put in their place and, until emancipation (1834 in the British Caribbean and 1865 in the USA), were treated as goods and chattels that could be owned, bequeathed or inherited. Sadly, as we demonstrate in Box 7.1 on contemporary forms of slavery in Brazil, there are still many slaves in the world.

BOX 7.1 Contemporary slavery

It is often thought that slavery was abolished in the nineteenth century and that only residual examples of it remain. By contrast, Bales (1999: 9) argued that there were 27 million slaves in the 1990s: 'There are more slaves alive today than all the people stolen from Africa in the time of the transatlantic slave trade.' This claim, reasserted in Bales et al. (2009), rests on a particular definition of slavery, namely controlling people with violence (or the threat of violence) and exploiting them for financial gain. On this broad definition, Bales et al. include 15–20 million bonded labourers in India, Pakistan, Bangladesh and Nepal, child soldiers, child labourers, trafficked sex workers and those sold as brides.

A more restrictive legal definition would insist on the idea that a slave is a form of property that can be bought and sold in the marketplace, bequeathed to one's beneficiaries in a will or inherited. A slave's servile status, in this more legalistic definition, does not end on their death, but is passed to their children who remain the property of a slave owner. This more limited definition of slavery brings down the estimated numbers considerably, but we are still talking of millions of slaves.

Brazil and India are now much better known as two highly successful growing economies, but they have been beset by continuing legacies of unfree labour. After many complaints and reports by human rights NGOs and the Catholic Church about unfree labour being used in the interior of the country, particularly in Amazonia, the government set up an anti-slavery team. In July 2007, they freed 1,000 coerced labourers living in appalling conditions on a sugar cane plantation in the Amazon. According to a BBC report (3 July 2007): 'human rights and labour organisations believe that between 25,000 to 40,000 people could be working in conditions akin to slavery in Brazil'.

The numbers of bonded labourers in India are much greater, perhaps about 10 million. Under a system of debt bondage, a labourer (usually a very poor agricultural worker) pledges their labour in exchange for a loan. When it becomes clear that there is no realistic prospect of paying off the loan, debt bondage arises, the debt often being passed intergenerationally. The continuing oppression of the very poor in rural India serves to perpetuate the caste system (see below).

Sources: Bales (1999); Bales et al. (2009).

CASTE

Associated principally with Hindu India, the members of a caste system inherit a status that assigns them to their occupation in one of four theoretically impermeable groups. The priests (Brahmins), regarded as the closest group to religious purity, have the highest status. Then follow the warriors, merchants and labourers. The 'untouchables' fall beneath this hierarchy and historically had to undertake 'unclean' tasks such as collecting human excrement from cesspools. Mahatma Gandhi, the great Indian leader, sought to liberate the 'untouchables' by renaming them *Harijan* – people of God – and insisted on them having full rights of social citizenship.

Although some limited social mobility is sometimes possible in slave and caste societies (see Srinivas 1952), slavery and caste are essentially closed social systems. A system of class stratification, by contrast, allows somewhat more, or very much more, movement between classes, although one must always remember that movement can be 'downward' as well as 'upward'.

CLASS AND NATIONAL CAPITALISMS

Until recently, most attempts to analyse inequality and social stratification in terms of class rested on the assumption that capitalism functioned within the nation-state. Each capitalist society would emerge from a particular synergy between its unique state-led modernization project and the outcome of the political struggles, if any, designed to push through or resist the radical reforms necessary to create an educated, mobile population and free market. Examples of such political struggles might include abolishing the monopoly privileges of the nobility with respect to land ownership and access to high state office, or freeing the peasantry from customary ties to agricultural work and place (Gershenkron 1966; Skocpol 1979).

Of course, as each urban industrial society gradually formed, national scholars intended that, to a greater or lesser extent, the concepts they designed for analysing the social classes present in their societies would, given their overall structural similarities, have wider applicability for all advanced capitalist industrial societies. Moreover, capitalism had never been narrowly restricted to one geographical area. Large trading companies had a long history of carving out markets overseas long before the industrial era. In addition, the industrial corporations emerging in the late nineteenth century fiercely competed for overseas markets and quickly sought captive sources of raw material for their factories and safe avenues for long-term investment. Early twentieth-century thinkers such as Lenin (1988) and Luxemburg (1972) explained that the impetus for colonialism, empire building and, ultimately, world wars largely originated from this competition between nationally based businesses.

Even during the twentieth-century spread of Fordist industry (Chapter 4), capitalism remained fundamentally grounded within each national economy until as late as the 1970s. Recall, for example, Britain where, as late as the late 1960s, UK firms supplied nearly 90% of the domestic market for manufactured goods (Webster 2002: 67). You should bear this underlying argument in mind while we proceed through the next subsections where we examine the different ways in which people usually define class, how classes form, and how their power is perpetuated or undermined. While (as in gender or racial inequality) pre-Enlightenment thinkers tended to assume that class differences were natural or divinely sanctioned, sociologists have tended to position themselves around four major perspectives, which overlap to some degree. These are:

- Marxist and neo-Marxist notions of class
- Weberian views of class
- class models based on work and occupation
- the argument that cultural practices also define class and shape life opportunities.

MARXIST AND NEO-MARXIST NOTIONS OF CLASS

Marx's considerable body of writing included intermittent and sometimes inconsistent attention to the issue of class. When he was writing for a popular audience, as he and Engels did in the 1848 *Communist Manifesto*, he tended to simplify his scheme into two 'great' classes, the bourgeoisie and the proletariat. On other occasions, he talked of six different classes in Germany and seven in Britain; he also wrote about the peasantry and the 'lumpen-proletariat' (the urban poor, without regular employment) in considerable detail. Neo-Marxists later revived discussions of the intermediate and adjunct classes surrounding his two 'great' classes.

The basic schema rested on a distinction between 'a class *in* itself' and a 'class *for* itself', the first drawn from the external and objective description of an observer (like Marx). Marx thought that one could define classes according to the particular relationship they held to the means of production, distribution and exchange. Did they own property, capital or factory premises? Had they inherited money? Did they buy or sell goods or their labour, and at what level? Marx defined the proletariat principally by arguing that they had nothing to sell other than their labour power and nothing to lose other than the 'chains' that oppressed them.

Marx was clear that the presence of a common objective situation was a necessary but insufficient definition of class. Members of a particular class also had to feel part of that class subjectively and to seek to defend, advance or maintain their class interests. He described peasants in France as a 'sack of potatoes', artificially bundled together but unable to act on their own behalf. They could not represent themselves and were not a class because they lacked class-consciousness.

LABOUR POWER

The capacity to work for a given time, a given rate of pay and at a particular level of skill and effort.

Scholars have criticized Marx's model on a number of levels. Nowadays, with a family car, house and some capital (typically in a pension), many workers have a lot more to lose than their chains. A significant number of middle-class clerical, professional, service and information-related occupations have also developed, which makes the idea of a bipolar class structure too simple. Managers, small employers and the self-employed also have contradic-

A PAUSE TO REFLECT

With the increased recognition of inequalities within and between societies, sociologists have been re-examining class-based models of societies. Are the ideas of Marx and Weber fundamental to our understanding, or are they now largely out of date? What factors – including income, wealth, prestige, political power, appearance, accent, or consumption and cultural dispositions – are decisive in defining a class?

tory class positions, which makes them neither workers nor owners of capital. A number of neo-Marxist sociologists like Wright (1985) have sought to accommodate these changes in revised versions of Marx's class structure. Braverman (1974) has shown how office work – hitherto regarded as an escape from a proletarian blue-collar status – is becoming proletarianized because it forces workers in such settings to lose their autonomy.

WEBERIAN VIEWS OF CLASS

Max Weber, who with Karl Marx and Emile Durkheim is one of the most important founders of sociology, was interested in how class played out in social interactions. He thought that Marx structured his views on stratification too narrowly around economic factors, so added social and political aspects to round out the picture. Weber thus developed three intersecting aspects of stratification:

1. *class*, which at a descriptive level, is similar to Marx's scheme
2. *status groups*, which define the 'social honour' accorded to a particular group or occupation
3. *political power* (Weber confusingly calls this 'party'), which determines how people mobilize to secure their advantage in competitive settings.

KEY CONCEPT

CULTURAL CAPITAL Despite the marked tendencies towards social levelling associated with mass education, affluence, consumerism and highly accessible forms of popular culture, Bourdieu (1984) argues that a dominant 'high' culture continues to flourish. Those whose education or other experiences have enabled them to acquire taste and distinction by investing in various kinds of discerning, detailed, cultural knowledge may be able to gain advantage in the competitive struggle for wealth and power.

Weber's scheme has generated some important new lines of sociological reflection and inquiry. Following Weber, we need to accept that a multiplicity of class positions arise when his three aspects of stratification – economic class, social status and political power – fail to coincide. Thus, an aristocratic family might exclude a ruthless, wealthy capitalist with bad manners and unrefined cultural tastes from its social circle, yet accept a penniless parson, colonial officer, or poet as a respected and valued member of the community. In effect, a stock of CULTURAL CAPITAL may offset a person's meagre financial capital. Finally, a trade union leader or police chief of a US city may routinely exercise considerable influence, yet have neither money nor high status.

Before leaving this discussion on cultural capital, we shall expand a little on Bourdieu's use of the term and his wider understanding of class. His work draws quite strongly on Weberian insights into the multiple and potentially overlapping character of the different resources for which social actors compete to improve their life chances. Like Weber, he argues that there are different kinds of capital:

*   *economic* – wealth, income
*   *social* – membership of clubs, networks, acquaintanceships
*   *cultural* – artistic knowledge, educational credentials, technical/professional qualifications
*   *symbolic* – the ability to legitimize privileges by persuading others that you have a right to them.

Further, he suggests that several processes occur in late-capitalist industrial societies:

- with the relative shift to a service and knowledge-based economy, cultural capital gains more importance than previously; as we explained above, many people with little economic capital are now able to succeed
- the type, source and level of education available to individuals more critically affect their class position
- consumer practices and preferences, along with lifestyle, become much more significant in enabling social actors to compete for social position.

The media attention and celebrity status accorded to people in the sports, entertainment, fashion and popular music industries provide a powerful example of the last phenomenon. It also attests to the power of lifestyles and consumerism, as media attention seems to have more to do with high earning power than the possession of actual talent. Moreover, the celebrities who gather around a powerful, seductive culture serve as role models for many people. We yearn to know the details of their romantic and sexual proclivities, fashion priorities, latest health and body-improving fads and designer tastes. We believe, perhaps, that with a little luck we can realistically aspire to reach their dizzy heights.

Because culture in all its forms – taste, distinction, qualifications, symbolic knowledge, changing fashion and consumer desires – becomes central to the reproduction of class and society, the struggles to control the codes, dominant meanings and systems of representation caught up in these assume greater significance than previously (Bourdieu 1984; Bourdieu and Wacquant 1992; Schwartz 1997).

CLASS MODELS BASED ON WORK AND OCCUPATION

Schema and typologies of class are of practical importance in developing social and employment policy, conducting censuses, marketing goods and services, and predicting social and demographic trends. Occupational stratification is the most commonly applied determinant of class, mostly because the reward system (how much you are paid), the status system (how much you are valued) and the conditions you encounter at work follow occupational lines. We compare three such models in Table 7.1 (Goldthorpe and Runciman are well-known UK sociologists).

TABLE 7.1 Class schema in the UK		
UK registrar-general's scale	Goldthorpe's scheme (simplified)	Runciman's classes (percentages in 1990)
Professional occupations	Professionals/administrators/managers	Upper class (<1%)
Intermediate occupations	Non-manual employees/sales personnel	Upper middle class (<10%)
	Small proprietors/self-employed artisans	Middle middle class (15%)
	Farmers/smallholders	Lower middle class (20%)
Skilled occupations	Technicians/supervisors/skilled manual workers	Skilled working class (20%)
Partly skilled occupations	Semi-skilled/unskilled	Unskilled working class (30%)
Unskilled occupations	Agricultural workers	Underclass (5%)

Note: The registrar-general is responsible for conducting the decennial census in the UK.

Sources: Marsh et al. (1996: 237–9), citing Goldthorpe et al. (1980) and Runciman (1990). Reproduced with permission from *Making Sense of Society: An Introduction to Sociology*, Marsh, I., Keating, M., Eyre, A., Campbell, R. and McKenzie, J. (eds), Pearson Education Limited.

While there is by no means a perfect match between the three schemata provided in Table 7.1, there is nonetheless a broad consensus that the class hierarchy matched an occupational scale. This sort of neo-Weberian view of class was virtually unassailable until the early 1990s when academics questioned it on a number of grounds. A fundamental critique was that prioritizing employment as the 'key axis of inequality' had marginalized the other determinants, especially gender, race, ethnicity and age (Devine and Savage 2005: 1). Absolutely central to this argument was the contribution of feminist scholars who were concerned not only that occupational scales tended to favour those in formal employment and miss those in part-time and domestic household work – disproportionately women – but that the focus on employment and jobs had often neglected the overall massive increase in the numbers of female workers, especially from the 1970s onwards (Chapter 4). With two household earners, the question then arose as to whose occupation or income would be used to assess class position (see Crompton 2008: 20–1). Indeed, the occupation of a woman's husband or father was often used rather unproblematically to infer her class situation. A further difficulty, as we argued in Chapter 4, is that the nature of work has itself changed, and individuals are increasingly likely to have multiple occupations, at different points on the scale, over their life spans – as well as periods of unemployment. Many become small entrepreneurs, but only for limited periods. Models of the class structure based on occupation and employment also need to take account of these developments.

CULTURAL PRACTICES AND CLASS IDENTITIES, POSITIONS AND OPPORTUNITIES

From the 1980s, many sociologists began to insist that the role of cultural practices and dispositions in defining class identities and situations had been neglected while recent social changes rendered this unsatisfactory. In part, sociologists were responding to the growing influence of Bourdieu's ideas about cultural capital as explained earlier in this chapter. But additional factors were at work:

1. All the transformations discussed in Chapter 4 – the partial demise of Fordist production, the substantial deindustrialization of the advanced economies, and the parallel, huge expansion of a wide range of service industries – led to a massive decline in the number of industrial manual workers. Most had regarded themselves as working class and had been so designated by scholars.

2. A key component in the rapidly expanding services sector consisted of cultural industries in the mass media, fashion, music, popular entertainment, heritage, advertising and so on. Much of this commercial activity involved creating an abundance of signs and images and attaching these to commodities, celebrities, businesses, media products and so on. Indeed, as we shall see in Chapter 14, some sociologists suggested that this proliferation – or hyperinflation – of signs meant that many products were increasingly purchased more for the attractive meanings attached to them by advertising and media manipulation than for their intrinsic usefulness as goods.

3. Alongside the growing economic importance of commercial cultural products, another major social transformation was also taking place, namely the rise of consumerism. This, in turn, was closely linked to the possibility of constructing personal identities through individual lifestyle practices – including one's personal tastes in bodily adornment and clothes, music, holidays, furniture and decorating, and health and food preferences. It was suggested that such choices and personal expressions were becoming at least as important to many citizens, as a way of saying who they were, as their job, income or occupational prestige. Perhaps for some they were more important.

4. One likely outcome was that, especially among young people, the once clear boundaries between middle- and working-class lifestyles could, and did, break down. Thus, irrespective of class background, many individuals came to share and purchase the same cultural preferences for particular styles of music, clothing or other items as part of their project for projecting a particular persona into social life (Chapter 16).

This increasing sociological focus on the supposed cultural influences shaping class identities appears to suggest that class membership is, at least in part, a voluntary choice because it is the result of a series of individual moral and cultural choices. But if class is understood in this way, we are each largely responsible for our own fate, including our income level, job security and exposure to poverty. However, this line of argument raises certain difficulties, as several sociologists have noted. Looking at the case of Britain, for example, Skeggs (2005: 50–5) argues that some working-class attributes are evaluated negatively in moral and cultural terms. Thus, people designated by politicians, the media or middle-class citizens as being members of the working class are frequently regarded as lacking in taste in their cultural choices. Allegedly, they are seen as wasting money on vulgar, glitzy products, engaging in excessive consumption (including unhealthy foods and beverages), and watching too many trashy TV programmes – as supposedly indicated by the abundance of satellite dishes found in working-class localities. Skeggs (2005: 56) also discusses how the Labour government of the late 1990s described some members of Britain's white working class as welfare scroungers, noisy yobs and people who had avoided acquiring productive knowledge through educational achievement. As such, their lifestyles were presented as blocking Britain's ability to function successfully on the global stage, while impeding their own greater social inclusion in national society.

The supposed behaviour of working-class women is especially likely to be subjected to negative moral evaluations. Here, a major accusation is that they show excessive attention to their appearance and engage in irresponsible sexual activities. In Skeggs's (2005: 63) words, the 'display of sexuality' is 'pathologised when attached to working class women's bodies'. Yet, when this attention to personal appearance and sexual behaviour is 'reworked' and becomes associated with the bodies of middle-class women who presumably enjoy high cultural capital – as in the American TV series, *Sex and the City* – such behaviour becomes remoralized and 'recoded as glamorous'.

In short, there is a danger with this emphasis on the link between culture and class that economic deprivation and poverty become much more the result of 'cultural deficiency' on the part of the individual (Skeggs 2005: 64) than the consequence of stark structural and often worldwide inequalities that are only a tiny number of people have much hope of surmounting. Similarly, and drawing on other researchers, Crompton (2008: 112) observes that: 'economic inequalities are effectively subsumed within (displaced onto) cultural resources'. Thus, the victims get most of the blame for their own lowly class situation.

RECENT EVIDENCE OF RISING GLOBAL INEQUALITY

Scholars, governments, some IGOs such as the ILO and World Bank, and all the OECD (Organisation for Economic Co-operation and Development) countries have noted a marked tendency over the last 30 or so years for inequalities of income and wealth across the world to increase. As with poverty, there is disagreement over the extent to which this is occurring, how to interpret the phenomenon, what might be the main factors involved and other issues. If inequality is indeed rising across much of the world – and the data discussed below seem to suggest that it is – then economic globalization undoubtedly provides a part of the explanation. Yet, other factors such as the rise of Asia, financialization and the shift towards a more predatory form of capitalism (outlined below) are also important and by no means reducible to globalization. Whatever the explanation for rising inequality, most observers agree that an excess of inequality – however judged – both within and between countries is a cause for concern. Not only might swamping markets with goods that people cannot afford to buy destabilize capitalism, but also rising poverty alongside affluence is likely to provoke major unrest, including perhaps violence and crime. We begin this section by briefly outlining some of the data on inequality within countries before turning to the theme of global inequality.

INEQUALITY WITHIN NATIONS

Since the 1970s, inequality within nations has become increasingly evident in many countries, including Japan and a number of EU countries such as Germany and Sweden (Atkinson 2005), and the process is not confined to advanced countries. Despite China's much noted and widely applauded success in massively reducing poverty since around 1980, while pulling down world poverty levels in its wake by the sheer force of the numbers involved (see Chapter 6), a widening income gap between rich and poor has become equally apparent. This growing inequality, strongly entwined with rapid economic growth, became especially evident after 1989. Then, the Chinese government switched the bulk of its provision of credit and other economic benefits from peasants and rural entrepreneurs to urban areas – particularly towards foreign businesses, the rebuilt state enterprises and through funding for urban facilities (Huang 2008). Following the same theme, Pogge (2007: 142–3) refers to data that demonstrate how, between 1990 and 2001, the income share accruing to the top 10% rose from one-quarter to one-third, while that of the bottom 80% fell. This decline was particularly marked among the bottom 30%, whose relative share of income decreased from nearly 13 to only 8.5%, and the decline was even more marked in the case of the bottom decile. Set against the historical record of other countries, this rising inequality has occurred extremely rapidly. A steep and widening income gap is appearing between the fast-growing urban areas and the western, mainly rural, provinces, where virtually half of China's population lives on incomes that are often only one-tenth of those found in prosperous cites such as Shanghai. Income gaps are also widening alarmingly within the cities, particularly the discrepancy of incomes between the rising middle class and migrant workers (Hutton 2007: 30–1; Kwan Lee 2007).

Growing income inequality among the richer countries is especially marked in the USA and the UK, where it may even be intensifying. In Britain, for example, a government-commissioned report published in early 2010 demonstrated that inequality levels had virtually returned to those existing at the end of the Second World War, before the welfare and tax reforms of the late 1940s were implemented. The report showed that the household wealth of the top 10% of the population was more than 100 times higher than that of the bottom 10% – and the latter's wealth, which averaged less than £8,800, included possessions such as cars (cited by Gentleman 2010: 4). Standing (2009: 99) states that the richest 5% in the USA saw their incomes rise by 60% between the late 1980s and 2006, while the richest quintile (20%) enjoyed a rise of 36%: the incomes of the poorest quintile, by contrast, increased by only 11% over the same period. Even more startling, Standing (2009: 99) describes how the real incomes of the top 0.1% of the US population rose by more than half (51%) between 2003 and 2005, suggesting that the rate of increase was accelerating – at least prior to the advent of the recession in 2008. Overall, this means that a tiny number of individuals 'earned' 5% of the total US national income and pulled in a minimum of $10m each year (Standing 2009: 102).

A PAUSE TO REFLECT

The question of inequality within societies and between societies is at the heart of much sociological inquiry. Does the crux of the matter still revolve around differences in incomes and the nature of employment? How successful have feminist and other scholars been in challenging this view? To what extent has class become a cultural 'football', being kicked around to score points against negatively evaluated lifestyles?

Standing embellishes this argument with some additional points:

1. Much of the rising income of this tiny elite poised at the pinnacle of the business class invariably comes from its involvement in the world of corporate business and/or finance where profits also increased dramatically in the early years of the new millennium.
2. By 2005, the degree of inequality in the USA was at the same high level as in the 1920s – just prior to the Wall Street crash of 1929 and the onset of 10 years of savage world recession (Standing 2009: 99).
3. The tax cuts introduced during the second Bush presidency between 2005 and 2009 particularly benefited the better off, especially the so-called entrepreneurial wealth creators. Thus, the average tax rates for the richest 1% dropped to 23% between 2000 and 2006 (Standing 2009: 99). Extremely high salaries, bonus payments, large guaranteed 'exit' payments, relatively low taxes and other perks mean that, unlike virtually all the other income groups in the population, the members of this elite are 'immunized against the risks of the market society' (Standing 2009: 104). They can afford to pay for their healthcare, schooling and pensions without being dependent on whatever state welfare system remains. In effect, they can decouple from mainstream society.

GROWING GLOBAL INEQUALITY SINCE 1980

Measuring inequality on a global scale is fraught with methodological difficulties, not least the need to decide which of several possible measures to adopt. One, designed to yield an international measure of inequality between countries, is gross domestic income (GDI), which measures and compares mean incomes for a range of different countries. To make international comparisons, statisticians weight the GDI measure to take account of differences in population. For example, approximately one-fifth of the world's population lives in China, which is significant. Neither the GDI nor the weighted GDI, however, takes account of income differences within countries. Another measure, which focuses on individual household differences, is much more difficult to undertake. This not only relies on detailed, reliable household surveys from many countries but also provides a more complete picture of actual world inequality (Milanovic 2007) both within and between countries. The Gini coefficient index is used to measure all kinds of inequality along a mathematical continuum ranging from 0 to 1 – the higher the figure, the greater the degree of inequality.

If we utilize Milanovic's data and take China out of the equation, we find that both weighted and non-weighted international inequality has risen since 1950 and the increase is particularly sharp and noticeable from 1980 (Milanovic 2007: 31–2). The third measure of world inequality, based on individual household surveys, also indicates that global inequality measured by the Gini coefficient was extremely high during the last decade of the twentieth century (between 0.62 and 0.66 depending on the year) if China is excluded. The figure was even higher than the Gini coefficient for countries such as Brazil and South Africa, which are renowned for their extremely high levels of in-country inequality. Milanovic (2007: 32) claims that this level of world inequality is 'unparalleled in world history'. However, because it exists at a global level – where there is no overall government and many constraints inhibit cross-country reaction – it fails to generate the kinds of instability and protest that can destabilize nations and compel their governments to take some kind of remedial action.

Another way of viewing this shift towards a more unequal world is to compare the percentile shares of national income the different population groups receive within each country. Using World Bank data for 2005 taken from 167 countries, Sutcliffe (2007: 66–9) compared the incomes of the richest 20% with those of the poorest 20%. By 2003 they were 32 times richer, almost certainly due to the rising incomes linked to rapid economic growth across much of Asia. The richest 5% were 121 times richer than the poorest 5% in 1980 and 130 times richer by 2003. The sharpest increase has been between the very richest 1% compared with the poorest 1% and here the ratio rose from 216 in 1980 to an astonishing 564 by 2003.

THE SUPER-RICH AND AVERAGE WAGE EARNERS: COMPARISONS

The calculations and estimates of a number of additional experts confirm a tendency, repeated across many countries, that a tiny minority of individuals is accruing an increasingly large share of global income, while that of other sections of the population is falling. For example:

- In 2008, just before the financial crash, the richest 1,100 people had almost twice the value in assets as the poorest 2.5 billion people (Rothkopf 2008).
- Many of the world's richest people now live in the developing world and this includes some of the poorest countries. In Mexico, 6% of GNP accrues to 20 people (Standing 2009: 102). In these cases, links with international finance are usually responsible for driving up the immense wealth of such individuals.
- The steepest rise in earnings is among corporate executives and people working for the large financial institutions. This is hardly surprising, given that the top 50 finance companies control a third of the world's total wealth, approximately US$50 trillion (Standing 2009: 103).
- According to the ILO (2008: 18), US executives received 140 times the average earnings in 1990 but this had risen to 500 times the average in 2007.
- Each of the top 25 corporate directors of Britain's leading companies received an average of more than £10m in remuneration for the year 2007/8 (the total sum was £315m). This was 484 times larger than the average national wage of £20,800 and in the same year when the share value of the top 100 companies listed on the London Stock Exchange fell by almost one-third (Finch and Bowers 2009).

THE SHIFT FROM NATIONAL TO GLOBAL CLASSES

We clearly have to approach with circumspection any assertion that we are currently moving towards a world in which global rather than national classes function in their own interests, as we certainly need a lot more evidence to substantiate any such claim. Moreover, even if classes 'in themselves'– whose members share similar chances of access to global resources – already exist, most scholars agree that this is a long way from the situation in which classes recognize their common situation irrespective of national differences, forge a consciousness of themselves as a class, and begin to advance their global claims collectively. Bearing these provisos in mind, we now describe the several transformations that, at least from an observer's perspective, seem to point to the emergence of various objective class groupings. This is particularly evident in the case of a possible world proletariat and a transnational capitalist class.

A WORLD PROLETARIAT COMPETING FOR JOBS

In the nineteenth century, Marx and Engels predicted that a worldwide industrial working class would emerge, that it would develop a common revolutionary consciousness and that, finally, it would usher in a political struggle to establish socialism. While the first part of this process can, arguably, be said to have arrived, such are the levels of unevenness and sectional (national and subnational) sentiments that many workers are pitched against one another rather than linked to a common cause.

As we have shown in Chapter 4, several economic and technological transformations combined to create a situation in which capitalist economic activity moved beyond national borders. These include the rise of a powerful global financial sector, 24-hour integrated currency and security markets, and a revolution in ICTs. Since the early 1980s, we have also seen the dismantling of previous constraints on capital flows and commodities across borders and a parallel increase in international trade. This, in turn, has fuelled the tendency for many huge TNCs to establish diversified networks of affiliate and subsidiary companies across many markets and countries. We say more about the latter in Chapter 10. If we wish to investigate whether and in what sense an embryonic global working class is emerging, however, we also need to take into account the following developments:

- the parallel effects of two massive recent geopolitical transformations, the end of the Cold War between 1989 and 1992, and the capacity of some developing countries to achieve industrialization, not least China and India
- the possibility that, on a world scale, capitalism has become much more predatory
- the linking together of national economies through global supply chains, involving every kind of commodity (including human care), together with a significant increase in the outsourcing of manufactured goods and services to offshore sites.

We explore the third of these factors in Chapter 10, but here we examine the first two of these themes and their wider implications in some detail.

GEOPOLITICAL TRANSFORMATIONS

The ending of the Cold War had a number of momentous consequences:

1. It largely removed the spectre of communism as a possible military threat to world capitalism – in the form of an aggressive USSR – and as a credible and viable economic system and way of life to which people could aspire.
2. It removed the incentive to seek or retain the kinds of reforms that, to some extent, Western governments and capitalist interests had previously accepted as a way of avoiding the prospect of massive working-class discontent and perhaps the possibility of revolution (Hobsbawm 1994). Thus, as we have seen, during the first half of the twentieth century and especially following the Second World War, in many countries democratic social legislation either legalized or bolstered the trade unions. Workers' rights to social insurance, sickness pay, unemployment rights and pensions improved, governments designed more progressive taxation regimes to redistribute income from rich to poor, and there was an acceptance of Keynesian full-employment economics.
3. It exposed the new states that emerged from the collapse of the Soviet Union to market competition and inflows of capitalist investment. Similarly, it created new and alternative venues where Western companies could find not only cheap but also highly skilled workers, thus increasing the world competition for jobs.

The rise of the NICs from the 1960s and, more recently, the rapid industrialization of China have hugely increased the size, complexity and degree of competition – and therefore uncertainty – evident in what is increasingly a global economy rather than one consisting merely of a series of largely separate national ones. To this scenario we need, of course, to add India, with its vast middle class of perhaps 300 million highly educated professionals and semi-professionals, who are increasingly capturing a share of world servicing work, with the aid of ICTs. Similarly, its leading industrialists in, for example, steel, engineering, chemicals and pharmaceuticals are beginning to capture large chunks of production and investment in Western economies (see the discussion in Chapter 4). One expert writer on world employment refers to all this as the 'Chindia' factor in the global economy (Standing 2009: 63).

Together, the geopolitical transformations outlined in the above two points brought a further momentous change to the world's working population. We refer here to the doubling in the supply of potential workers available and exposed to capitalism that has occurred over the past 20 or so years (Freeman 2007: 25–6). Accordingly, the numbers grew from nearly 1500 million in the years prior to 2000 (one-third of these based in advanced economies and the remainder in the non-communist developing world) to approximately 3 billion by 2000. The IMF has also arrived at estimates similar to those Freeman suggested and argues that the global labour supply available to capitalism has in fact grown approximately fourfold since 1980 (*The Economist*, 4 April 2007).

PRECARIOUS WORKERS

Given that globalization means that capital is mobile and no longer has 'an address' (Bien-efeld 2007: 20), it would be surprising if businesses did not find ways to exploit the situation and the parallel possibilities that the huge increase in the supply of workers has opened up. This is pertinent because, unlike capital, which can move easily, poverty, family ties and cultural pressure to remain tied to their locales and nations constrain all but the most highly skilled workers. Economic migrants are, of course, notable exceptions. Consequently, accord-ing to Robinson (2002: 217), compared with nation-states, global corporate business has gained considerably more control over labour. This means that, in relation to capital, labour has become a 'naked commodity' no longer able to rely on local community or family rela-tions for support. Put another way, economic globalization subjects working people – espe-cially those who inhabit the advanced economies – to a process of turning hard-won benefits back into commodities. Thus it largely strips them of the rewards they once received from both their state and private employers, such as inflation-proof pensions, sick pay and unem-ployment schemes. Instead, workers in the advanced economies now have to rely on money wages or, if they can afford it, private insurance for many of their needs (Standing 2009: 57–8). At the same time, a new 'global labour–capital relation' has gelled in which – as we have seen in earlier chapters – a 'global casualization or informalization of labour' has occurred and, along with it, all kinds of problems and chronic insecurities over jobs, incomes, careers and long-term employment (Standing 2007).

More recently, Standing (2009: 109–14) developed this last argument by identifying two overlapping class fragments that together can perhaps be seen as constituting a global prole-tariat. One consists of 'the core: a withering working class' (Standing 2009: 109), while the increasingly dominant second group is what he refers to as the 'precariat'. The economic condition of these individuals is inherently unstable and insecure, irrespective of whether they work in low-grade services, parts of the knowledge industry, as labourers, or in the remnants of manufacturing. The first group consists of either male manual workers or females in service occupations. Once, both enjoyed stable, full-time employment and identi-fied themselves as belonging to a particular occupation. The men, at least, earned relatively high wages, tended to belong to trade unions, and benefited from a welfare state established to 'serve their needs' (Standing 2009: 109). With the decline of this class since the 1970s, though, its members have lost most of their previous advantages and tend to collapse into the second group below this core. In other words, this class is in complete 'disarray'. As Standing (2009: 110) explains, we now see:

> the new legions of the precariat flitting between jobs, unsure of their occupational title, with little security, few enterprise benefits and tenuous access to state benefits. They include the more fortunate of the vast informal economy. ... The precariat is the group that has grown most, and its role in the recommodification process is pivotal, since its existence pressures those above to make concessions to make themselves more market-able. ... The precariat is a global phenomenon.

In such a situation, nation-states prioritize policies designed to protect and foster their econ-omy's competitive edge or niche in the global market. Governments try to do this not by protecting national workers from foreign competition but rather by inducing them to gain more skills and become flexible, multitasking employees who are prepared to work longer hours, often for lower wages, and tolerate deteriorating working conditions, smaller pensions and ever more limited welfare protection. Teschke and Heine (2002: 176) refer to this situa-tion as the demise of the 'welfare state' and in its place the rise of the 'competition state'. According to Standing (2009: 79), this intensifying pressure on workers everywhere to compete in a vastly expanded and increasingly worldwide labour market results in 'down-ward pressure' on wages and working conditions.

PREDATORY CAPITAL

As if capital's greater mobility and need to survive in an era of significantly intensified trade rivalry did not create enough pressure on workers, there is a further suggestion that capital has also become more predatory since the 1980s than it had been during the mid-twentieth-century decades of Fordist production. Atkinson (2005) argues that, until recently, most companies did not automatically push wages down in response to market pressures, because they valued company loyalty and rewarded seniority. Theirs was a gentler kind of capitalism. Now, however, in the era of investor capitalism, maximizing profits and 'returns to shareholders and share values' has become the 'overriding' if not the only goal (Atkinson 2005: 59). As we saw in Chapter 4, much of this has to do with the increased involvement of finance in the ownership and running of business. Other writers have reached similar conclusions. Hutton (2007: 26) claims that 'a business culture has developed where the share price is the be-all and end-all'. One consequence has been the 'world's biggest takeover boom' in the years between 1995 and 2005 (see Chapter 4). Here, profits and share values are driven up not by increasing the productivity of the company taken over or expanding its operations by investing in better technology and skills, but by stripping the latter of its most lucrative assets, downsizing its operations, and imposing extensive job cuts (see also Gowan 2009: 24–5; Harvey 2003: 145–69). A further consequence is that, through such actions, company directors and financiers are able to reward themselves with higher salaries and bonus deals as well as improve their shareholders' gains (Elliot and Atkinson 2008: 215–16).

A PAUSE TO REFLECT

Let us suppose that capitalists have always sought to expand their markets, squeeze as much output from their workers as possible and drive up profits. They have, after all, to survive under competitive conditions. Do we then require additional explanations for the recent turn towards a more predatory, ruthless and greedy version of capitalism? Is there a greater tolerance among voters and governments of extreme inequality and a growing ethos of self-interest and individualism?

According to Atkinson (2005: 59), predatory capital is due not only to financialization and the greater mobility of capital but also to cultural and political changes in advanced societies, particularly the dilution of social goals in favour of individual self-aggrandizement. This attitudinal change distracts citizens from noticing wider structural changes, persuades them that they too can aspire to getting rich, and prompts the thought that it would be potentially disadvantageous for them to challenge the growing discrepancies in income and wealth. As we saw in Chapter 2, the work of Beck and Beck-Gernsheim (2002) contains strong echoes of this argument on individualism. Added to this is the claim that a range of checks and balances once embedded capital firmly within political and social institutions, compelling it to take some account of the needs and demands of ordinary people and their political representatives (Hutton 2007); however, these are now much weaker or have virtually disappeared. Strong trade unions, powerful media pressure to ensure that companies serve the wider national interest, the company loyalty of shareholders, directors and employees, pride in the long-term survival of businesses, and a greater government willingness to regulate business and prevent unfair competition are now just things of the past.

A MOBILE TRANSNATIONAL CAPITALIST CLASS

At the top level of the class structure, elites have always been transnational. The European royal houses intermarried and held land and political titles in several countries, while aristocrats were frequently multilingual, with dispersed residences and a cosmopolitan conscious-

GLOBAL THINKER 7 LESLIE SKLAIR (1940–)

Leslie Sklair's early work was concerned with the meaning and manifestations of 'progress', linking the concerns of a sociologist and a moral philosopher. He thought that 'progress consists in the satisfactory solution of problems of men in society and the satisfaction of needs, both individual and social' (Sklair 1970: 207). Of course, the use of the word 'men' in this sense in now archaic. It was clear that Sklair was concerned with the aspirations of all people, in the industrialized and developing countries.

While his discussions on progress were confined to a theoretical exegesis of Enlightenment and post-Enlightenment thinkers (including Comte, Marx, Weber, Toynbee, Sorokin and Spengler), he soon revealed his capacity for undertaking detailed empirical work. He worked successively on patterns of development in Ireland, free-trade zones in Egypt, the opening up of China (in particular Shenzhen) to capitalist development, the *maquiladoras* (assembly plants) in northern Mexico, and the growth of a consumer culture in Shanghai.

These experiences of Asia, North Africa and Mexico provided real-life training grounds for a reconnection to his synoptic, theoretical work, manifested notably in his *Sociology of the Global System* (1991, rev. edn 1995, 3rd retitled edn *Globalization, Capitalism and its Alternatives*, 2002). Although the title suggested a close connection to Wallerstein's world system (see Global Thinkers 1), he is in fact quite dismissive of Wallerstein, suggesting that 'there are signs that the paradigm is approaching exhaustion' and that Wallerstein was having difficulty in dealing with the industrialization of 'non-hegemon countries' (Sklair 1995: 38). Both charges are difficult to sustain, but there is no doubt that Sklair made significant advances in delineating what he called 'transnational practices'. These practices centred on the analysis of four social actors –TNCs, consumers in all countries, governments in developing countries, and emerging transnational classes. By focusing on these practices, Sklair (1995: 88) breathes life into the global system. For example, the managers of corporations pursue profit-maximizing strategies and tax avoidance schemes, while consumers buy products, ideas and values to create a 'consumerist world-view'.

Sklair's most ambitious claim is that a transnational capitalist class has emerged, comprising four overlapping fractions: those who own and control TNCs, politicians and bureaucrats, professionals, and consumerist elites (Sklair 1997). Sklair recognizes that to fulfil his definitional criteria, a transnational class would have to show evidence not only of social formation, but also consciousness, reproduction and social action to defend its emerging interests. Although his book-length account of a transnational class is generally persuasive, it could be argued that each of the criteria he advances is not met in full.

Source: Sklair (1970, 1991, 1995, 1997, 2001, 2002, 2005).

ness. The control wrested from such elites in transformations like the French Revolution concentrated power in the hands of national bourgeoisies, which used state power to consolidate their grip on wealth and social position. Nevertheless, some scholars believe that globalization and the increased mobility of capital have combined to undermine some of the powers that nation-states once exercised over their national capitalist classes and local economies. Sklair (2001: 2), for example, argues that as state power has diminished so

> transnational forces, processes and institutions, not based on the state, might be taking its place. The prime candidates for this role as we enter the twenty-first century are the transnational corporations. The power and authority of the transnational capitalist class derives from the corporations they own and control.

Robinson and Harris (2000: 12) agree that TNCs and financial institutions now drive contemporary capitalism. As they put it: 'organic class formation is no longer tied to territory and to the political jurisdiction of nation-states'.

In Chapter 10, we examine the respective powers that TNCs and nation-states exercise in more detail. In the meantime, some case studies and a host of aggregate economic data support the idea that a new global ruling class has emerged. Included among the evidence are the increasing relocation of production to multiple sites, the growth and mounting mobility of financial capital, the global marketing of key brands, the globalization of legal, architectural and accounting firms, the enormous rise of cross-border mergers and acquisitions, and the equally spectacular growth of foreign direct investment flows. Such data would satisfy some Marxist sociologists who support the argument that economic forces determine social relations. However, Robinson and Harris (2000) and Sklair (2001) are careful to add that members of the transnational capitalist class tend to:

- occupy key positions in government ministries and the central banks
- staff organizations that support globalization like the WTO
- attend certain prestigious universities and business schools
- sit on the boards of key foundations, for example Ford and Carnegie
- dominate bodies like the World Economic Forum, business round tables and chambers of commerce.

Interestingly, Carroll and Carson (2003) provide strong evidence, based on rigorous research, of a powerful group of individuals who move easily back and forth between political and economic roles, commercial and public positions and across national borders, while exercising exactly this kind of coincidence of shared privilege, influence and power. Their research involved mapping the overlapping networks in which the five leading IGOs engage in formulating world economic policy – such as the Paris-based International Chamber of Commerce – and their links to the top interlocking company directors drawn from the leading 350 corporations. They then identified a core of around 620 individuals within this already powerful group (Carroll and Carson 2003: 39). They also found that many move between corporate positions and elite policy-making IGOs while cementing ties and reinforcing each other's ideas. Similarly, they liaise with governments, global think tanks, corporations, and with each other. Together, the authors suggest, these individuals form a 'global corporate elite'.

We are not interested only in the capacity of the members of this emerging transnational, mobile elite to accumulate personal wealth and prestige while collectively exercising enormous influence over global events and institutions. We also need to look at their social relations, values and lifestyles. Sassen (2007: 173–83) notes that the members of this emergent global class of corporate business leaders who engage in 'global circulation' often retain their ties to both their nations and their transnational interests. She observes that although the influence this class wields derives from its managerial control functions rather than any strictly Marxist idea of the actual ownership of the means of global production, the 'basic agenda for this class remains profit-making … a rather narrow utility logic: the drive for profits' (Sassen 2007: 176). Nevertheless, the transnational character of this class, with its cross-border transactions and movements, generates two consequences.

One is that its members require physical locations in which to work, meet their colleagues, competitors, politicians and bankers, and conduct deals and negotiations. In other words, they require a 'hyperspace' of office buildings, hotels, residential districts, schools for their children, abundant sources of entertainment and, of course, airports. A transurban network, comprising around 40 global cities, provides these locations (Sassen 2007). We discuss global cities in more detail in Chapter 18. Based in these cities are not only the global or regional headquarters of leading banks and TNCs but also a gamut of leading producer service companies, in the fields of insurance, management consultancy, accountancy and law, which provide supportive functions for the corporate giants, as well as a wide range of additional facilities. From these global cities, the transnational business class constructs 'cross-border corporate economic space' (Sassen 2007: 176).

The second consequence is that members of the transnational class also need to express their emotional, aesthetic, family and other personal identities both as individuals and as a collectivity; they feel the need to display their high levels of economic, social and cultural capital through their patterns of leisure, consumption and choice of residence. One likely claim here is that the combination of mixing with people from diverse cultures, their high levels of education, and exposure to a wide range of aesthetic experiences through travel turns them into cosmopolitans. Among other things, this class 'may open up to diverse cuisines and urban landscapes' (Sassen 2007: 176). The members of this class may see themselves as belonging to a 'global community' (Rofe 2003: 2519) of like-minded people who, as Rofe noted among his elite respondents living in Sydney and Newcastle in Australia, believe they are exempt from the waves of xenophobia that engulf the parochial locals who protest about immigrants.

Butler's study of elite professionals living in a gentrified neighbourhood in Islington, north London came up with similar findings. His respondents believed that they demonstrated many aspects of a cosmopolitan lifestyle and values, which included a strong preference for cultural diversity and exotic tastes in consumer choices. They had constructed a 'bubble' (Butler 2003: 2474) existence separate from the less well-off people living around them, including a social milieu that was exclusively white in a city with a high migrant population, while making sure that their children only attended exclusive schools where they would meet others from exactly the same privileged backgrounds. Claiming to live a global, cosmopolitan lifestyle was little more than an attempt to legitimize their wealth, prestige and influence (Butler 2003). Calhoun (2002: 105) calls it a fake 'consumerist cosmopolitanism', and sees it as divisive, exclusive and largely the product of a particular era of neoliberal globalization. In place of a group of individuals whose cosmopolitanism is expressed through leading the struggle to reform global inequities and spread social justice and democracy, we find a class dedicated to its own narrow career interests and to furthering the wealth that global capital has accumulated (Calhoun 2002: 108).

REVIEW

Most of the discussion in this chapter has focused on theoretical attempts to understand differences of wealth, income and status, and on how, in practice, these factors shape societies and people's lives over time. Until now, and with good reason, scholars have concentrated primarily on delineating concepts and developing theories designed to understand social class structures within nationally based capitalist systems. A fundamental source of contention, and with a long history dating back to the early twentieth century, has been whether and to what extent the economic dimension of patterned inequality – based on ownership or non-ownership of the means of production – is the dominant factor in determining people's life chances. The obverse position is that other resources, particularly claims to status, occupational prestige, social connections, lifestyle and education, can have an equally important, if not more important, effect on shaping people's lives.

Gradually, however, the character of industrial societies became more complex and diverse. New occupations proliferated, education became more crucial as a determinant of social position, house ownership and pension funds gave people a stake as owners of capital, and consumerism offered alternative aspirations, diversions and sources of difference even to those on low incomes. Consequently, during the later decades of the twentieth century, most sociologists interested in class recognized the increasingly multiple, overlapping and fluid nature of social inequality and, therefore, the often contradictory class locations in which many people found themselves.

More recently, globalization raised the spectre of an emerging global class structure in which, despite different national loyalties, members face similar experiences and conditions with respect to how the income, wealth and jobs they are able to command determine their life chances. We suggested that if we can indeed discern the outlines of such global classes, then they are most readily applicable to a transnational capitalist class and an emerging world proletariat. Considered objectively against the backdrop of rising income inequality, the financialization of all aspects of life, the global orientation of large corporations, the increased mobility of capital in a world economy riven by growing trade rivalries, and a massive expansion of workers urgently seeking employment worldwide, it is difficult to deny the existence of these two global classes.

Yet, their capacities to express and/or act on some kind of global class-consciousness are subject to very different possibilities. We can probably make a case for suggesting that a tiny transnational capitalist class, exhibiting an awareness of its shared, narrow interests and laying claim to a lifestyle based on weak or nonexistent cosmopolitanism, is clearly emerging. Moreover, its members are increasingly seeking to protect their privileges by acting as a class in numerous ways. For example, they take advantage of tax avoidance schemes, send their children to exclusive schools, move in carefully constructed, narrow social milieux, help one another gain access to jobs, live in expensive gentrified locations, and join powerful international associations as an extension of their work. The situation is more problematic for the far more localized proletariat, divided, as its vast membership is, by language, nationality, religion, limited access to resources, and continuing North–South income differences. In any case, whatever models scholars create in the future as they attempt to make sense of global class structures, they will need to embrace fluidity, multi-positioning and the reality of contradictory class locations.

Visit the companion website at www.palgrave.com/sociology/cohen3e for extra materials to check and expand your learning, including interactive self-test questions, mind maps making links between key themes, annotated web links to sociological research, data and key sociological thinkers, a searchable glossary and much more.

FURTHER READING

Class analysis remains a central concern in sociology, although the focus has passed through several stages. In the 1960s and 70s, Marxist theory was particularly influential, before interest shifted more to questions relating to culture and lifestyle. There is a neo-Marxist account of class in E. O. Wright's book, simply titled *Classes* (1985), while R. Crompton's *Class and Stratification* (2008) reflects a post-feminist and cultural analysis.

Another influential non-Marxist account on Britain's class structure is J. H. Goldthorpe et al.'s *Social Mobility and Class Structure in Modern Britain* (1980).

G. Standing's *Work after Globalization: Building Occupational Citizenship* (2009) is quite challenging, but Chapters 3 and 4 examine material relating to global classes in an accessible but expert manner.

Although not concerned exclusively with the themes of global inequality and class differences, Chapters 3, 4, 7 and 8 of P. Kennedy's *Local Lives and Global Transformation: Towards World Society* (2010) examine a number of case studies that explore in detail many of the issues covered here in a world context.

QUESTIONS AND ASSIGNMENTS

1. Compare, contrast and critique occupational versus cultural analyses of class within national societies.

2. Is class analysis still important in understanding nationally based social inequalities?

3. Summarize and then, giving your reasons, prioritize the list of factors that are objectively creating a world proletariat. How might one subject this kind of analysis and scenario to critical scrutiny?

4. Evaluate the case for arguing that a transnational business and professional class has emerged that has shared objective and subjective characteristics.

8 Gender and sexualities

Issues concerning gender and sexuality have moved centre stage in the contemporary world. The discourses surrounding them and the struggles to contest oppression on the grounds of gender or sexual preferences have become truly global in their geographical reach and ability to provoke controversy in all cultural situations.

In this chapter, we first examine the various theoretical arguments about the social construction of gender and the number of ways in which women have experienced multiple forms of inequality and oppression throughout history. We look at women's exploitation, both as workers and as women, in various global workplaces. We note how their huge and often unique contribution to the global economy is scarcely recognized and poorly rewarded. Women have been fighting against their subordination for centuries and an organized international feminist movement became a key political player at many levels from the late nineteenth century onwards. Since then, feminism has broadened and radicalized its agenda over time, united women from many countries, and intervened effectively in the political life of more and more countries. Accordingly, we chart some of the key moments in this process.

Since the 1960s, gay people have increasingly mobilized politically and culturally. We examine some of their concerns and growing willingness to organize across borders. Their goal, like that of some radical feminists, has been to question the hitherto dominant worldwide ethos of heterosexuality – or what has been called 'hegemonic heteronormativity' (Klesse 2007) – as the only 'normal' and legitimate form of sexuality. Gay, lesbian, bisexual and transgender people have also challenged the sociocultural structures that force them to choose between either denying their sexuality or accepting life as a socially disenfranchised outsider.

GENDER HIERARCHIES, PATRIARCHY AND WOMEN'S SUBORDINATION

Throughout most of this century, and especially from the late 1960s, there has been growing awareness of women's oppression historically. Numerous scholars, who are often women, have undertaken a fundamental re-evaluation of most existing theories in the humanities and social sciences because these mostly ignored, or misunderstood, women's historical and

SUFFRAGE MOVEMENT

This movement demanded votes for women as a first principle of equality and liberation. It was at its height in the USA and the UK in the late nineteenth and early twentieth centuries, but it was not until women were used 'on the home front' in factories during the First World War that their cause was won. Even then, when the UK conceded the vote in 1918, only women over 30 were eligible (women over 21 were given the vote in 1928). In the USA, women's suffrage was granted in 1920.

contemporary roles (see Box 8.1). Consequently, especially in sociology, an influential and distinctive perspective has emerged.

Despite their greater visibility since the 1960s, women's struggles have a long history and we outline some of these later. In the 20 or so years before the First World War, the suffrage movement became a highly significant form of mass collective protest in many advanced countries (see Figure 8.1). The demand for voting rights normally went hand in hand with demands that women should enjoy the same educational and job opportunities as men and the same freedom of access to social and public life.

We can distinguish two waves of feminism:

- *First-wave feminism*: This liberal feminist determination to attain individual freedoms formed the first wave of the women's movement in the nineteenth and early twentieth centuries. It involved what Zalewski (1993: 116) called the 'add women and stir' variety of feminist thought. This is the idea that women's liberation required the extension of the Enlightenment principles of equal dignity, respect and rights for all citizens. Everyone, including men, would benefit from the new abilities unleashed once women – the other half of humanity – were free to seek personal fulfilment. Liberal feminism remains influential today, but it is largely the preserve of white, middle-class, Western women.
- *Second-wave feminism*: A second wave of feminism, which burst onto the world scene in the late 1960s, spread outwards from the USA. A common idea was that women possessed certain distinctive characteristics such as a greater capacity for nurturing than men and a stronger inclination to seek harmonious relationships. It followed that if women could project their more highly developed moral priorities through the attainment of political power, the world might be more peaceful (Stienstra 1994: 52).

© MANCHESTER DAILY EXPRESS/SCIENCE AND SOCIETY PICTURE LIBRARY

FIGURE 8.1 A woman suffragette *c.* 1910
A woman suffragette campaigning for the vote in the UK is restrained by policemen. The important role British women fulfilled in replacing male workers sent to the front during the First World War accelerated demands for the vote, but they did not win full voting rights until 1928.

Three central propositions emerged from the post-1960s second wave of feminist thinking:

1. Male and female roles and characteristics are mostly learned and/or imposed on individuals and this results in a process of societal engendering.
2. Women's contributions to social life are invariably regarded as less significant than those of men and give rise to a condition of gender inequality.
3. A long-held cultural acceptance of gender inequalities characterizes relationships in virtually all societies.

These are now explored in more detail.

THE ENGENDERING OF FEMININITY AND MASCULINITY

People in virtually all societies have traditionally assumed that maleness and femaleness are natural and unalterable conditions. While men supposedly find it easy to be brave, women tend towards caring roles and homemaking. Societies have always used these supposed natural, biological differences to justify a clear division of labour in male–female task allocation.

Second-wave feminists disagreed profoundly with these characterizations. They argued that, unlike those biological differences that are anatomical and genetic in character, gender is an acquired identity. As Peterson and Runyan (1993: 5) bluntly put it: 'we *learn*, through culturally specific socialization, how to be masculine and feminine and to assume the identities of men and women'. It is not biology but differing cultural expectations and social treatments that make us into 'males' or 'females'. Consequently, cultural processes mostly determine whether a person assumes child-rearing and homemaking roles along with economic activities linked to domesticity (cooking, cleaning or caring for others), rather than occupations such as hunting, herding animals, working with machines or exercising political leadership.

THE GENDER HIERARCHY AND FEMALE SUBORDINATION

Are gendered identities innate, or do social actors evaluate them differently, with real-life consequences? Overall, masculine roles are regarded as socially more 'useful' and technically more 'difficult' to perform than feminine ones. Feminists argue that, in most societies, this creates a hierarchically structured system in which gender relations are highly unequal and women's contributions attract less social standing than those of men. Consequently, fewer rewards accrue to them and they enjoy less power. Even the equal attainment of civil or political rights is unlikely to remove all oppression, since these rights usually refer to public life, not to the private realms of household and family. There, women may remain subject to forms of domination from husbands, sons and male relatives that cultural values may legitimize and economic dependency may underpin.

> ### KEY CONCEPT
>
> PATRIARCHY is a form of oppression that elevates men to positions of power and authority. Feminist writers argue that patriarchy is so deeply embedded that it appears in early societies as well as in feudal, capitalist and self-proclaimed socialist societies. Marxist feminists stress that sexual divisions of labour are functional and relate to the evolving class structure. Other writers have pointed to the role of religion or the structuring and labelling of female and male roles. Whatever the origin of this role differentiation, it has now become culturally and even psychoanalytically inscribed. This makes patriarchy difficult to dislodge.

PATRIARCHAL SOCIETIES AND PATRIARCHAL RELATIONS

Discussion among feminists regarding the nature, extent and causes of PATRIARCHY has generated an important debate and some disagreement. Box 8.1 outlines the main divisions within recent feminist thinking with regard to the nature, causes and significance of patriarchal relations.

Early sociologists such as Maine, Engels and Weber defined patriarchy as a system of preindustrial, usually nomadic or pastoral, socio-economic relations in which the eldest males exercised more or less unconstrained power over younger males and women and where production was based almost entirely in the household. Social life was organized mainly through allegiances to extended systems of kinship (or lineage) based on descent from a common blood ancestor. Those who belonged to the same lineage shared property and owed powerful loyalties and responsibilities to each other.

While women normally bear all the direct responsibility for childcare and domestic life – including preparing food and fetching water and fuel – their burden of biological and social reproduction usually extends to playing a key role in food production through agriculture. Such women grow the food with which to feed their husbands, children and perhaps some of their extended kin. The role of women in food production is particularly important in Africa.

Compared with Africa, the people living in most parts of Asia and some of the Middle East practised a much more intensive and efficient form of agriculture, which involved permanent settlements and customary land rights. Because the farmers customarily fertilized, irrigated and deep ploughed the fields, they needed access to heavy animals such as oxen, and, according to Boserup (1970), this intensive, plough-based agriculture created a sexual division of labour in which men played a more central role in crop cultivation than their counterparts in pastoral and stateless societies. In particular, men assumed the main responsibility for the heavy physical work associated with harnessing animal power to field management and staple cereal production. The women undertook the lighter agricultural tasks such as weeding and winnowing grain, assumed responsibility for dairy production, and reared smaller animals.

Religious beliefs and customary arrangements that largely confined women to the home or domestic sphere, while subjecting them to the control of husbands or male kinsmen, were superimposed on this division of labour. One extreme form of this was the demand for purdah in Islamic societies, although the degree to which such practices were strictly enforced varied a good deal. They were invariably less evident – and less possible – in poorer households. Thus, wealth and social rank also influenced the position of women in such societies. In the more prosperous families of traders, government officials or larger landowners, it was a mark of social status that women could withdraw from all but the least onerous economic tasks while their exclusion from public life might be quite strictly enforced. Kandiyoti (1997: 91) argued that women living in such societies could negotiate with their husbands and male kin over the 'patriarchal bargain – protection (from males) in exchange for submissiveness and propriety'. They could also resist changes that men introduced if these threatened female security. Thus, we should not necessarily regard women in patriarchal societies as passive victims.

> ### PURDAH
>
> The practice of secluding women by covering their bodies from the male gaze, or virtually keeping them behind screens and away from all forms of public life.

The idea of Muslim women spending much of their lives in purdah also takes no account of their increasing role in theological discourse and leading religious services. As van Doorn-Harder (2006) shows, in Indonesia, women interpret sacred texts and exercise a notable religious influence. They also use Islam as a mobilizing force for improving women's access to education and furthering their political and social rights. In China, there are many women imams and women-only congregations. In 2006 Morocco allowed the training of female imams. Even in Iran, still a redoubt of patriarchal Islamic control, a ban on women leading ritual services has been reversed.

A PAUSE TO REFLECT

Religious belief and cultural practices vary a good deal across societies. Should we be relaxed in simply accepting difference or are there some social practices that should be opposed in defence of human rights, or perhaps because some of us judge that they are oppressive? If you are a woman, would you wear a wig, as some ultra-Orthodox Jewish women do, on the grounds that the sight of hair is unduly sexually arousing? If you are relaxed about this practice, what you do think about honour killings or female circumcision? Should governments or INGOs intervene to constrain certain social practices and how should they do that?

BOX 8.1 Feminist debates on patriarchal relations

Radical feminists

Millet (1977: 25) defined patriarchy as the 'institution whereby that half of the populace which is female is controlled by that half which is male'. For radical feminists, male supremacy derives from men's ability to control women's bodies, for example in sexual relations, childbirth and the tendency for a predominantly male expertise to dominate modern health practices and technology. The latter systematically stigmatized and excluded the knowledge that women herbalists and health practitioners accumulated in the preindustrial era. The prevailing ethos of heterosexuality as the supposedly 'normal' form of sexual relations reinforces male dominance. Male violence, especially in domestic life, which the authorities often tolerate, also makes it possible. The need for women to separate their lives as much as possible from those of men offered one obvious solution. Another remedy required a concerted programme to empower women to challenge male rules and assumptions. For all its faults, radical feminism has been enormously influential.

Critique of radical feminism

From the late 1970s, however, people have increasingly contested these radical interpretations. Thus:

1. If the roots of male domination lie primarily in women's sexuality and their childbearing/rearing roles, then feminist analysis and aspirations seem to bring back the conventional view from which they have tried to escape, namely that women's subordination is biologically determined.

2. Radical feminists employ these views of patriarchy indiscriminately and without regard for its distinctive relevance to specific historical periods and cultures (see Kandiyoti 1997).

3. Given its many forms, it is unclear what is so systematic about patriarchy that it continues to persist across all societies.

Marxist feminists

For Marxist feminists, women's oppression derives mainly from the logic of capital accumulation. Capitalists need to cheapen the cost of producing each generation of workers. Women's unpaid domestic family labour and child rearing enables capital to achieve this aim, albeit with the help of the social welfare and educational provisions the state supplies. In addition, capital can use women's domestic responsibilities as an excuse to pay them lower wages. For similar reasons, they can also conveniently slot women workers into part-time and temporary employment without having to pay social benefits or provide job security. However, many Marxist feminists have increasingly recognized that certain aspects of patriarchal relations, for example the widespread resort to male violence, are not always reducible to the needs of capital. Patriarchy interacts with capitalist oppression.

The ethnic/race critique of white feminists

Feminists living in the South have argued that colonial exploitation, the need for male–female unity in the struggle against Western imperialism, and the repression to which NICs subject women have often been much more harmful to Southern women than the way their family life is organized or their men control their sexuality. Similarly, non-white women living in Western countries often encounter forms of discrimination that affect their lives much more dramatically than any tensions that may emanate from 'traditional' cultural family values. For example, African Caribbean women in Britain are much more likely to be the family's main breadwinner than their white British counterparts (Bruegel 1988), yet poverty compels many to seek full-time jobs that often yield very low wages.

Postmodern feminism

Postmodernists emphasize that no 'fixed' structures or absolute values shape human behaviour. They celebrate cultural differences and insist on individuals' increasing capacity to construct (or deconstruct) lifestyles. Postmodernists have been sceptical of other feminist views. Thus, the argument that we can clearly delineate the social category of 'women' and that all women share a common unity of interests smacks of essentialism – a belief in the innate and irreducible nature of things or social entities. Such an argument overlooks the increasing number of choices women can make about how to present themselves as feminine and how to organize their lives. From a study of women's magazines, Coward (1978) argued that whereas the magazine *Good Housekeeping* expressed femininity in terms of family and household roles, *Cosmopolitan* encouraged women to seek sexual expression through glamour and bodily beauty.

Sources: Bruegel (1988); Coward (1978); Kandiyoti (1997); Millet (1977).

FROM PRIVATE TO PUBLIC FORMS OF PATRIARCHY

Walby (1990) believes that a major shift has taken place in the forms of patriarchal domination characteristic of both the private and public spheres of industrial societies:

1. *Working but still low paid:* Western countries no longer exclude women from formal paid employment and, by the late 1980s, they made up virtually half the official labour force of most such countries. Nearly half of them, however, are in part-time employment. In addition, despite legislation designed to ensure wage equality, they continue to earn roughly three-quarters of male wages for the same work. Also, in the UK, women's average earnings decline after the age of 30 while those of men go on rising into their forties (Elliot 2010). Moreover, they tend to congregate in specifically female-designated employment enclaves such as the caring professions (in health, social work and education) or in low-paid industries and services, including catering, garment manufacturing and clerical work.

2. *More choice, but still the child carers:* Access to paid employment, the attainment by girls of educational levels similar if not superior to those obtained by boys, the right to divorce and birth control, and the assignment of formally equal citizen rights have all helped to give women much greater freedom of personal choice and control over their bodies. Yet, while they can break free from unhappy marriages and even rear children as single mothers, such options leave them dependent on state welfare and legislation, highly susceptible to a life of poverty, for example after divorce, and still faced with the primary responsibility for childcare.

3. *Sexually free but still in danger:* Women still face the real possibility of male violence in domestic and public life, and are exposed to a double standard of personal morality that tends to label them as 'slags' or 'sluts' if they choose multiple sexual partners, even though such freedoms clearly benefit men as well while not exposing them to the same stigma. At the same time, pornography has now become a vast industry and most of this trade degrades women and exposes them to increased risks of personal exploitation and physical danger.

4. *New models, old realities:* While media representations of women seem to respect the goals of independence, freedom and equal opportunity, beneath the glossy surface the message points in a different direction, with personal fulfilment still thought to depend on motherhood, heterosexual love and a lifelong marriage. The media usually portray divorced women as returning to the safe fold of male protection through a 'happier' second marriage. Meanwhile, all aspects of popular culture strongly emphasize the need to cultivate sexual attractiveness as the key to winning male approval.

GLOBAL THINKER 8 SYLVIA CHANT

Sylvia Chant has made an important contribution to our understanding of the complex links between gender and poverty through her empirical research in a wide range of developing countries, including studies of urban youth in the Gambia, female-headed households in Mexico, single mothers in the Philippines, and changes in family life in Costa Rica.

Chant's major theoretical contribution to development has been the rethinking of the 'feminization of poverty thesis'. She argues that we need to reconceptualize gendered poverty as multidimensional, encompassing many contributing factors such as:

- Gender divisions of labour within the home, gender differences in decision-making, and women's vulnerability to gender violence.

- Women's exposure to time poverty as a result of multiple labour burdens, much of which is unpaid, affecting their ability to exit poverty.

- How gender closely interacts with other axes of social differentiation, such as age, 'race' and 'migrant status', to produce complex experiences of gendered poverty.

- The need for men as well as women to be involved in poverty reduction initiatives, as women's unpaid labour will continue to be used as the solution to the lack of state welfare support.

Chant argues that it is problematic and dangerous if women are the ones held responsible for tackling and overcoming poverty in their communities and suggests that we need 'a shift in focus from the "feminization of poverty"' to a "feminization of responsibility"'. Chant has attempted to refine poverty measurement tools such as the Gendered Inequality Index, developed by the United Nations Development Programme (UNDP), but she combines this quantitative approach with an interest in how our ideas about gendered subjectivities shape how women's poverty is tackled.

Katherine Brickell and Sylvia Chant (2010) argue that gender and development policies often capitalize on women's altruistic practices in poor communities but that this ends up reinforcing gender stereotypes of women as naturally selfless. This includes women's tendency to put their children before themselves and to spend the money they earn on their family rather than themselves. Although development agencies acknowledge women's role in economic development, they often exploit women's altruistic tendencies and their social capital. They suggest that women's altruism should be seen as a response to both processes of gendering and economically restricted options and not a 'natural' female trait that can be converted into economic capital.

Chant's work on gender and poverty is truly global in that she has done empirical research in a wide variety of societies, which allows her to compare how women's disadvantage differs across the globe. She is also a rare example of a global thinker who has used her research to effect change at the policy level for development agencies such as UNDP, ILO, UNICEF and the World Bank.

Sources: Brickell and Chant (2010); Chant (2008, 2009).

WOMEN AND ECONOMIC GLOBALIZATION

As we saw in Chapters 4 , 6 and 7, economic globalization means that capital has become increasingly footloose. TNCs, for example, have become much freer to move plant, technology and goods across the globe while fragmenting production operations between sites located in different countries. Because states are often anxious to attract investment from TNCs, the corporations have remained relatively unencumbered by global or state regulation. In addition, since the mid-1980s, the IMF and the World Bank have imposed neoliberal reforms on many Southern countries as a condition for helping to arrange debt rescheduling and further loans. Such policies have forced governments to reduce their spending and abolish subsidies. This, in turn, has led to higher food prices, increased unemployment, and widespread cuts in welfare spending on things such as rural clinics. Much of this has hit the poorer groups hardest and a large proportion of the most disadvantaged consists of single-parent households headed by women.

WOMEN'S MOVE INTO THE GLOBAL WORKFORCE

Neoliberal policies have tended to drive women to seek work in the global economy. Moreover, global supply chains now characterize much of the global economy (see Chapter 10), especially in garment making, electronics and fresh produce like grapes, tomatoes and flowers. In general, foreign companies and their overseas partners draw on pre-existing gender practices and inequalities, especially in the garment industry, but also actively build them into their recruitment procedures as a strategy for acquiring low-cost labour and enhancing their competitiveness (Elias 2004). Thus, in the garment industries of Morocco, Bangladesh and Cambodia, they make up 70, 85 and 90% of the employees respectively (Figure 8.2). The corresponding percentages in fresh foods in Colombia, Kenya and Zimbabwe are 65, 75 and 87% respectively (cited in Raworth 2005: 16–17).

FIGURE 8.2 Women machinists in a Cambodian garment factory
Women entered the global labour force in large numbers from the 1980s.

It is important to note that for many women employed in the rural or urban global work-force, exposed to the uncertainties of neoliberal economic policies, it is impossible to disentangled the situation they face as workers from the gender inequalities and patriarchal power structures they equally face as women. Thus, in addition to low wages, long working hours that often make no concessions to family responsibilities, unpaid overtime, job insecurity, and unhealthy workplace conditions, women everywhere, but especially in the global South, often have to contend with abuses relating directly to their gender. An obvious example here occurs where abuse stems from sexual harassment from male employees, supervisors or bosses. Alternatively, they may face violent and/or threatening behaviour – again, sometimes linked to resisting male demands for sexual favours. Such incidents are more likely to affect very young women living away from home, or women who lack the support and protection of a husband or male relative – the unmarried, widows or the elderly. The employers and/or families of some very young women sent from their parental home in the countryside to the cities in search of work often compel them to live in dormitories under close supervision. However, the human rights standards and health and safety provisions in such establishments are often lamentable by their absence. Moreover, in many situations, women workers find it difficult if not impossible to obtain the support of male-dominated trade unions and they may lose their jobs if they complain (Hale 2004).

Ultimately, it is only possible to solve these dilemmas if local women's movements struggle to confront them in their own way and on their own terms, particularly where elements of gender subordination and patriarchal pressures coincide with workplace conflicts over wages and conditions. At the same time, whether as workers or self-employed producers, for example of farm produce such as cocoa or cashew nuts (Carr 2004), resistance is more possible and efficacious if women can forge links with a growing number of overseas agencies committed to providing various kinds of assistance. Among these agencies are global women's networks, INGOs such as Oxfam, fair and ethical trade organizations, certain Western government departments, or an array of UN organizations. Here, alongside the undoubted difficulties it confers on women, globalization does at least provide a framework in which communications take place, markets open up, networks form and institutional links become accessible. These can offer women new economic opportunities that they may be able to harness to their advantage (Carr 2004). We return to this theme below.

PROTECTING HOMEWORKERS

Historically, women have always made a significant contribution to manufacturing, but much of it was hidden from view because they worked in tiny unregulated enterprises or at home. The 'sweatshop' conditions typical of these activities are highly unsatisfactory. Homeworkers earn very low rates of pay, work under poor and sometimes dangerous conditions, need to meet employer deadlines, and have no legal rights. Because of their isolation, they find it difficult to organize and, even if they did, their employers could easily shift the work elsewhere. In common with the armies of urban women in the South who eke out a living in overcrowded service occupations – often as street traders, domestic servants or sex workers – the livelihoods of homeworkers exist outside and beyond the reach of regulation. Similarly, the insecurities and problems they face involve much more than meagre, unreliable earnings. They include such things as the high costs of everyday necessities like rent and food, the limited availability of clinics and basic health facilities, and the unsympathetic attitudes of the police and local officials towards the inhabitants of squatter settlements (Rowbotham and Linkogle 2001). Employers are also able to reduce the costs of training the workforce because in industries like garment manufacturing, the teenage girls have usually already acquired the skills they need from within their families.

The most pronounced growth of homeworking is in garment making, where many women operate at the very lowest rungs of the global system in which production is divided into numerous specialized tasks and then distributed across different countries and levels of production. Moreover, homeworking is not confined to the developing world. In fact, it has spread widely across the cities of the North and is often a source of employment for illegal immigrants (Ross 1997: 13). It has also spread to other industries, including the manufacturers of carpets, shoes, toys, consumer electronics and automobile parts (Rowbotham 1993: 9–24). The ability to attain greater producer flexibility and to cheapen costs partly through homeworking enables retailers to earn very high profits by placing huge mark-ups on the imported price of the final products.

However, the business strategy of these powerful retailers carries several risks. Probably the most serious arises because these goods mostly carry designer labels, which consumers value greatly and so they command high prices. By the same token, this exposes companies to 'potentially embarrassing ... human rights violations'. They 'cannot afford to have the names of their designers, endorsers, or merchandizing labels publicly sullied [or be] embarrassed by revelations about the exploited labour behind their labels' (Ross 1997: 25). Thus, the public esteem in which a brand name is held is worth a great deal of money. Increasingly, the various feminist groups campaigning on behalf of women employed as homeworkers have sought to educate consumers in the principles of ethical or fair trading (Boris and Prugl 1996: 6).

Remarkably, and despite the enormous obstacles they face, homeworkers have also formed effective organizations in several countries. For example, HomeNet (www.homenet-southasia.org) is a South Asian network with strong links to the UN and similar organizations; it represents 50 million homeworkers in Pakistan, Nepal, India, Sri Lanka and Bangladesh. It also has strong links to another influential network based in India and founded in 1972 called the Self Employed Women's Association (www.sewa.org). This has many achievements to its credit in building campaigns and empowering poor women to develop paths to self-reliance. At the same time, the Geneva-based International Labour Organization (ILO), an arm of the UN, tries to establish worldwide standards for the treatment of workers and monitors the conditions that pertain in different countries. At a conference under ILO auspices in June 1996, an international coalition of feminists, trade unions, homeworker associations, NGOs and fair trade organizations was successful in obtaining a new ILO convention for home-based workers, although much more work still needs to be done in this area.

KEY CONCEPT

GLOBAL CARE CHAINS are made up of women who cross boundaries from poorer to richer countries to work as nannies, nurses and domestic workers. The care chain involves interconnected nodes of migration between rural and urban areas and between poor and rich countries. The links tend to reinforce, rather than obviate, existing global inequalities. An unpaid family member at the bottom of the chain tends ultimately to replace the emotional labour expended.

WOMEN AND GLOBAL CARE CHAINS

Until recently, researchers have concentrated on studying global supply chains in manufacturing and agriculture and have ignored GLOBAL CARE CHAINS, a phenomenon considered in a number of innovative studies, notably Chang (2000), Hochschild (2000), Sontag (1993) and Yeates (2004). (See Hochschild (2000), who is credited with developing the concept.)

Instead of producing finished goods, millions of women are involved in 'producing' services. They supply physical labour, such as cleaning, cooking, nursing and washing, and emotional care, which involves showing affection and concern for others. Increasingly, various service intermediaries are managing the shipping of migrant care workers from the South to the rich countries, where they mostly find employment. These include:

- governments, such as the Philippines, which see the export of Filipino service workers to Western or other Asian countries as a major source of export revenue
- national public institutions like the British National Health Service
- thousands of legal or illegal recruitment agencies for nannies, nurses, cleaners and others, sometimes linked to international criminal gangs
- corporate recruitment companies, such as Kelly Services, which are mostly based in North America.

As indicated in our definition, care workers are engaged in a number of different occupations, including:

- *nurses* or *paramedics* working in hospitals or residential nursing homes. In the Philippines, for example, there are around 100,000 registered nurses but most work overseas in European, Middle Eastern, Japanese or North American hospitals and homes
- *carers* who nurse sick or elderly people in their own homes as part of local, state or federal health systems. In the USA, home healthcare workers look after 4 million people and are organized by 10,000 home health agencies
- *housemaids* and *nannies* working in middle-class private households, whether with legal visas/permits or as illegal workers
- *cleaners*, working in hospitals, government offices or company buildings.

Although a relatively new concept, the notion of a global care chain has given impetus to at least four new lines of enquiry:

1. Most care workers remit part of their earnings to support their children or other family members at home. The quantity of these remittances now vastly exceeds foreign aid programmes.
2. Rich countries benefit hugely from the supply of cheap and often skilled care workers without the necessity – as in the case of their own nationals – of having to pay towards the reproductive cost of rearing and educating them, for these were borne by governments and families far away. Are these clear economic advantages going to overcome the xenophobic fears of the host populations?
3. It is paradoxical that middle-class Western women can hire Southern nannies to look after their children so that they can continue their high-paid careers, while the latter have to forgo the experience of caring for their own children left behind at home. Can gender solidarity exist between women when social class as well as North–South inequalities are so large?
4. Foreign care workers are often deprived of equal welfare rights, face uncertainties over whether or not their visas and/or work permits will be renewed, and are required to work long hours for poor pay. A large proportion, however, are illegal and so they face added

difficulties. A survey of 18 New York agencies in 1993 found that illegal care workers averaged around US$175 a week, whereas legal employees could earn as much as US$600. What are the relations between care workers in the legal and illegal sectors?

A WORLDWIDE FEMINIST MOVEMENT: CONFRONTING PATRIARCHY

We now chart the course of some of the struggles in which women have engaged to improve their situation, giving special emphasis to those that have assumed a global dimension. There is a growing literature on the far more numerous local actions by women's groups in ever more countries and you can read about these in books edited by Asfah (1996), Basu (1995), Moghadam (2007) and Molyneux (2001).

A PAUSE TO REFLECT

It is not always easy to decide what is, or is not, women's liberation. Many French feminists regard the wearing of a burqa by Muslim women as a sign that these women are oppressed. Do you agree and do you support governments in France, Belgium and the Netherlands who have banned the wearing of the burqa in public places? What do you think of the argument, sometimes advanced by Muslim women, that modest dress allows them to act with dignity, and that some Western women display an excessive regard for men's opinions of sexual allure in choosing their attire, thus making them more oppressed?

Women were involved in political campaigns in the nineteenth and first half of the twentieth centuries, including attempts to secure international peace. Certainly, from the late eighteenth century onwards, women increasingly made important and sometimes initiating contributions to revolutionary protest – as in the moves against the monarchy in the summer and autumn of 1789 in France. They also resisted slavery in the USA, reacted against colonialism and joined or led strikes. Women agitated for better working conditions in factories and textile mills across the world, including Lancashire in the UK, and cities in North America and tsarist Russia (Carroll 1989: 4–9). For the most part, we can regard this first wave of feminist struggle as an attempt to secure for women the same liberal freedoms and opportunities that were available to men. Second-wave feminism from the late 1960s was more radical and led many women to conclude that they had every right to challenge and reconstruct the patriarchal world. As Enloe (1989: 17) suggested: 'the world is something that has been made; therefore, it can be remade'.

THE CONSTRAINTS ON WOMEN'S MOVEMENTS

In many situations, women face more constraints than men when they engage in social movements. Moreover, involvement in social protests often becomes progressively more difficult for women as actions move away from specific contexts. There are several reasons for this:

1. In many societies, women are less likely to have easy access to money and land; they are more likely to live in poverty and tend to be less well educated than men. Customary obligations and daily routines that bind them to a host of domestic and productive services of an intrinsically local and fixed kind are also more likely to tie them down (Harcourt and Escobar 2005).

2. Patriarchal social relations frequently render women vulnerable and dependent. This is especially likely in rural areas. In some societies, a woman may only participate in public life, including voting or engaging in outside employment, if she has her husband's permission, a situation that can virtually confine her to the domestic compound (Harcourt 2005).

3. All these eventualities curtail freedom of movement. Unless protests are local in orientation and do not seem to threaten established male rights, women's participation may be difficult and dangerous.

4. Where women in the South join protests, these are rarely concerned solely with feminist issues. Rather, their actions are likely to be intertwined either with wider struggles against oppression, such as a demand for democratization (Basu 1995: 9–11), or with environmental threats, for example dam projects that remove access to land or forests on which local people, particularly women, depend for their livelihoods (Kothari and Harcourt 2005).

A further constraint on women's capacity to participate in protests worldwide was the emergence, or intensification, of various racial, historical and North–South differences (Jacobs 2004). Of course, one can also regard these differences as a rich source of diversity offering opportunities to exchange ideas and experiences. Nevertheless, there is general agreement that they inhibited progress towards world unity, particularly in the decade from 1975 to 1985 and probably beyond. Thus, while feminists in the USA and Europe might have sound reasons to demand abortion rights or to campaign against the sexual exploitation of women through media trivialization, beauty shows or pornography, Southern feminists may have quite different priorities. Combating repressive forms of state birth control that bear down most heavily on the poorest groups constitutes one such problem. Others include rapes committed by police and other state officials against those within their jurisdiction (Radford 2000), or, as in India, the widespread so-called 'dowry deaths' (Kumar 1995), when young wives become the victims of pressure from in-laws for dowry payments after marriage. Women in poor countries differ most from their Northern counterparts in that they recognize that they need to tackle all forms of inequality, including patriarchy, simultaneously as part of the same struggle. In any case, numerous Southern groups were soon finding ways to express their concerns both at national and regional levels.

By the early 1990s, women's global struggles were becoming stronger and more diverse. Southern women found it easier to join global as well as local struggles because they had previously carved out their own areas of independence (Miles 1996: 57–60). Increased personal familiarity through contacts established at conferences and other venues and greater humility by Western feminists about their assumed right to define the terms of the global struggle against patriarchy also helped to heal earlier wounds.

GROWTH OF THE WORLDWIDE MOVEMENT

Four significant changes and tendencies boosted women's movements from the 1970s and contributed to greater unity and mutual understanding:

1. The UN and the older generation of liberal feminists who worked within its institutions helped to create a framework for increased networking.

2. The rise of second-wave radical feminism, mainly in the North, invigorated the women's movement worldwide and women's groups emerging in the South.

3. Women worked to create their own autonomous facilities for representing women's views and achieving effective communications.

4. Women increasingly are realizing that they face common problems in private and public life and are seeking various forms of collaboration.

The first two are now explored in more detail.

The UN framework for networking

Under the influence of an older generation of liberal feminists and international women's groups, the 1945 foundational Charter of the United Nations specifically referred to the equal eligibility of women to participate in all UN debates and organizations and granted consultative status to the representatives of several international women's organizations. Further, it set up the Commission on the Status of Women to consider the special needs of women worldwide (Stienstra 1994: 75–86). In addition, the 1948 UN Universal Declaration of Human Rights clearly stated nobody could deny such rights on any grounds, including sex. While radical feminists found these gains insufficient to meet women's real needs, they at least provided a platform from which to launch their more radical arguments. Eventually, with its 1975–85 UN Decade for Women built around three conferences, the UN created a powerful momentum for further change (see Box 8.2).

The first two conferences exposed divisions. Nevertheless, the UN decade was a 'watershed' because it pushed women's concerns onto the agendas of IGOs and facilitated cooperation (Friedman 1995: 23). Gradually, too, women from different cultures and regions learned how to network more effectively – often empowered by the internet – and to gain and share new knowledge. Working together across cultural and regional divides has been especially successful in the area of women's human rights (Bunch et al. 2001: 228). The involvement of the UN in promoting gender equality was given a significant boost in July 2010 by the formation of UN Women, a body set up to promote women's empowerment and to eliminate discrimination directed against women and girls (www.unwomen. org). The incoming director of the new body is Michelle Bachelot, Chile's first female president (2006–10).

BOX 8.2 The global women's movement: key events and selected achievements

The UN decade of women, 1975–85, key UN-sponsored conferences
- 1st World Conference on Women, 1975, Mexico City, which 6,000 delegates attended.
- 2nd World Conference on Women, 1980, Copenhagen, 7,000 delegates.
- 3rd World Conference on Women, 1985, Nairobi, 15,000 delegates from 150 countries, holding 2,000 workshops.
- 4th World Conference on Women, 1995, Beijing, 8,000 delegates.

Key consequences of Nairobi conference (1985)
1. Many more representatives came from developing countries and they were more inclined to declare their own aims. The animosity evident between delegates from the North and South at the previous two conferences diminished.
2. Several new regional and international networks resulted from this conference. These included the Latin American Committee for the Defence of Women's Rights, the Asia-Pacific Forum on Women, Law and Development, and Women Living Under Muslim Laws, which representatives from eight Muslim countries formed. All sought to facilitate exchanges of information on legal matters pertaining to human and legal rights.
3. The International Women's Rights Action Watch, launched after the Nairobi conference in 1986, also focused on women and human rights. While promoting and monitoring the progress of the UN's work, it lobbied governments and international bodies, including NGOs, on the issue of human rights and women.

Other important conferences and events
1. The UN General Assembly 1979, when worldwide pressure from groups demanding change to protect women from discrimination contributed to the General Assembly's decision to support the Convention on the Elimination of All Forms of Discrimination against Women (CEDAW). States accepting the convention have to take whatever steps are needed to prevent discrimination. By 2010, 186 countries had ratified

CEDAW, although some had introduced reservations, mostly on religious or cultural grounds. Those refusing to ratify the convention so far are the USA, Iran, Sudan, Somalia and three Pacific Island states.

2. The UN Second International Conference on Human Rights took place in Vienna in 1993. Building on earlier dialogues about women and human rights, the women's groups were well organized and successfully lobbied 160 governments present at the conference. They also called for an end to gender bias brought about by religious extremism.

Sources: Miles (1996); Peters and Wolper (1995); Stienstra (1994); www.cedaw2010.org.

Second-wave and Southern feminism

The critique of patriarchy and all pretension to male superiority by second-wave feminism was much more comprehensive than anything the earlier feminists had offered. It created a sense of intellectual and moral coherence that few could ignore and explored new avenues with energy and confidence. This included invading or seeking alliances with all previously male-dominated organizations, including NGOs, trade unions, churches and religious bodies, sports and arts organizations, local and national politics, the professions (especially health, medicine and law), and all knowledge-creating centres such as universities.

Women's groups in developing countries increasingly joined the second-wave feminists. Among the issues included in this widening agenda were:

*   sex tourism and prostitution across the world
*   all forms of public and private violence against women
*   the need to persuade governments and the UN to accept that women's rights must be firmly incorporated into the human rights agenda
*   the often adverse working conditions that a growing number of women worldwide experience in the export processing manufacturing industries outlined later
*   the urgent need to rethink the development aims and priorities that states in developing countries and powerful IGOs like the IMF and World Bank have promoted.

India's case starkly illustrates some of the dilemmas that women's movements face. Despite a resurgence of Hindu fundamentalism, India rightfully commands respect as a tolerant country with a cherished regard for the pursuit of democracy and a long history of social reform and modernization. However, even before the recent rise of religious fundamentalism, governments found it difficult to tolerate or encourage the extension of some constitutional freedoms to women and family life. Thus, while the Indian constitution allows government to intervene to prevent discrimination against members of certain lower castes, it does not permit such state interference in customary law where this relates to family life and the domestic position of women (Jaising 1995; Kumar 1995; Radford 2000). Women's movements in India have consequently found it necessary to politicize the private realm of husband–wife relations, marriage and family life.

Throughout the global South, women's movements are realizing continuous changes to their lives, focusing particularly on women in precarious economic situations and those badly affected by patriarchal practices. Initial suspicions of feminists from rich countries have been gradually allayed. United by their common problems, women's groups across the world increasingly collaborate in their attempts to influence governments, IGOs and other powerful elite institutions. We have already discussed one problem they have in common, namely the difficulties that economic globalization and neoliberal policies have created for numerous women across the world. Another concerns the resurgence over the past 20 years of various forms of religious orthodoxy and right-wing thinking, with the two often being synchronous. This has presented a threat to some women, especially in the USA, India, various Muslim countries in the Middle East, Israel and parts of the former Soviet Union.

THE GLOBAL GAY MOVEMENT: CHALLENGING HOMOPHOBIA

This chapter covers the theme of gender and sexualities and it is important to remember that this topic is not only confined to women or conventional forms of sexual relations. A core ingredient in the prejudice and discrimination homosexuals experience is the widespread assumption that only heterosexual activity is acceptable in religious and cultural terms and/ or is 'normal' to human behaviour. Klesse (2007) calls this 'hegemonic heteronormativity'. For this reason, gay groups have tried to contest this dominant, orthodox view of human sexuality, which, incidentally, some radical feminists also believe helps to legitimize male dominance of and violence towards women.

Challenges to heteronormativity are particularly difficult to put into effect in certain countries of the global South. Some 80 countries worldwide criminalize acts of consensual homosexuality, but the authorities in Malawi, Zimbabwe and Uganda, in particular, have shown themselves to be highly intolerant of gays and ruthlessly punish gay activists. Over half the countries concerned evoke the 'sodomy' laws still on the statue book from British colonial times, but a number are making these laws even harsher (*The Economist*, 21 May 2010). Even in relatively tolerant societies, gay people of both sexes may feel uncomfortable unless they conceal their sexuality from mainstream society. In any case, the 'opposites' of male and female, the distinction between sex (as biologically defined) and gender (as socially constructed) has become blurred, which discussions about gay, lesbian, bisexual and transsexual identities and the development of androgynous musical and dress styles clearly reinforce.

Gay people who remain in their original localities close to their immediate family, school friends and neighbours are especially likely to acquire the status of an outsider. Indeed, gay people may find it difficult to feel at home anywhere. Unlike other 'migrants', they have no 'homeland' to which they can dream of returning. Nevertheless, migration – perhaps in search of the relative anonymity of a city or another country – is often necessary and at least allows them to acknowledge their gay identity by finding and joining others in the same position. In the words of one scholar, migration makes it possible to be yourself and provides the means of becoming 'full citizens in a queer world' (Binnie 2004: 85). Such actions may help to compensate for the reality that the gay person nevertheless remains an 'outsider' who shares with others a sense of 'disenfranchisement rather than entitlement' (Binnie 2004: 105).

Although their common plight worldwide seems to predispose many gay people to cross cultural as well as national frontiers, propelling many towards cosmopolitanism, most writers on gay cultures point to the need for extreme caution before jumping to conclusions about the existence of such a thing as 'the global gay' (Altman 1996: 77). Wide local, ethnic, national and religious differences in the practice of gayness in everyday life are evident between societies, while the ease with which people can travel and migrate is 'gendered, classed and racialized' (Binnie 2004: 84). Moreover, stark income differences can lead to as many divisions among gays as in the heterosexual world (Binnie 2004: 62–6).

A PAUSE TO REFLECT

How tolerant are people on questions of sexual orientation? Perhaps surprisingly, an ABC News/ *Washington Post* poll conducted in 2010 found that 83% of American adults support lesbians, gays and bisexuals serving in the US military if they do not publicly disclose their sexual orientation. This is the so-called 'don't ask, don't tell' practice that has been accepted in the military for some time. The support falls by 10% if they do disclose their sexual orientation. There is much lower support for same-sex marriage in the USA. What are the dynamics in accounting for this variation in attitude and, in particular, is hypocrisy a natural ally of tolerance?

Nevertheless, globalization has made it easier to communicate within, as well as across, ethnic or national cultures and borders, whether through information technology, co-present relations, or both. Among the various sites and milieux that are available for fostering gay social relationships are businesses catering for the 'pink pound', international gay festivals, newspapers and other media forums dedicated to gay concerns, and cheap tourist travel. Within cities, too, particular sites, especially certain bars and restaurants, serve as gay venues. The international pandemic of AIDS created a new and greater urgency for sharing information and resources across different nationalities and cultures (Nardi 1998). Moreover, gay political and cultural movements that began originally in countries such as the USA, Australia and Germany in the 1960s soon united in international political protest and culminated in the formation of the International Lesbian and Gay Association in 1978.

Indeed, despite the continuing vitality of local gay movements, in recent decades we have seen the emergence of a 'globalizing … gay community and political identity struggling for equality' (Nardi 1998: 571). Altman (2001: 86–7) concurs with this suggestion. He argues that globalization 'has helped create an international gay/lesbian identity … by no means confined to the western world'. At the same time, this 'gay world' provides a key example of an emergent global subculture 'where members of particular groups have more in common across national and continental boundaries' than with those from their own countries. We need further research before we can establish whether their experiences have led some gay people to express their sense of belonging to a wider global community of oppressed or marginalized groups whose members are not gay.

REVIEW

Women's struggles have made important contributions to the growth of an emergent global society from below. The women's movement satisfies the primary criterion of a global social movement, namely 'global reach'. There is hardly a country in the world where its impact has not profoundly altered gender relations. Moreover, the timescale for this transformation is impressively short, with most of the force of the movement only evident since the 1970s. The movement spread so fast partly because it adopted participatory forms of grassroots organization but also because the speed and density of communications facilitated the global transmission of positive images of women.

Like other social movements, the women's movement has been partly borne along by its universal appeal. However, the compulsion to respond to vast and sometimes threatening forces for change has also propelled its expansion. These global changes appear to affect many people, including gay people, but perhaps they challenge women more than others. This is partly because the patriarchal oppression and economic disadvantages most women face create an almost unprecedented potential for unity of thought and action. However, the resources associated with globalization – communications technologies, faster and easier travel, and the ever more rapid dissemination of all kinds of knowledge – offer women exciting opportunities to benefit from shared experiences and pooling their acquired knowledge.

Visit the companion website at www.palgrave.com/sociology/cohen3e for extra materials to check and expand your learning, including interactive self-test questions, mind maps making links between key themes, annotated web links to sociological research, data and key sociological thinkers, a searchable glossary and much more.

FURTHER READING

C. Enloe's *Bananas, Beaches and Bases: Making Feminist Sense of International Politics* (1989) is not intended to provide an especially sociological analysis. However, it is witty, accessible and offers a useful way into theorizing about gender.

From Patriarchy to Empowerment (2007), edited by V. M. Moghadam, contains 20 chapters by scholars from across the world on women contesting different kinds of oppression, and contains material from the Middle East, North Africa and South Asia.

S. Rowbotham is a central figure in the development of feminist thought. In *Homeworkers Worldwide* (1993), she gives a lively and simple introduction to this topic.

J. Binnie's *The Globalization of Sexuality* (2004) is highly readable and provides a lively and thoughtful exploration of the links between globalization and gay cultures.

QUESTIONS AND ASSIGNMENTS

1. What constraints have there been on women's actions, and to what extent has globalization provided opportunities to overcome them?
2. Assess the relative significance of the UN and its associated institutions in strengthening the world feminist movement compared with other factors.
3. Drawing on case study material, assess the impact of recent worldwide economic changes in encouraging women to collaborate transnationally.
4. What are the similarities and differences between the women's and gay movements with respect to their links to globalization?

9
Race, ethnicity and intersectionality

Race and ethnicity form one of the three main axes around which social inequality has most often been structured throughout history, the others being class and gender. Unequal practices associated with race and ethnicity may include a range of possible activities that diminish the life chances of those deemed to belong to certain designated racial groups. These include individual interpersonal misunderstandings and prejudices, institutionalized racism embedded in major public services such as the police or education, or – in extreme cases – slavery. All arise from the supposed phenotypical (observed) characteristics and appearance of certain 'races', which, allegedly, constitute indications of their 'inferior' dispositions and abilities.

We first examine how European involvement in the developing world through trade and imperialist ventures left a legacy of racist thinking that nourished stereotypical notions about the supposed inferiority of conquered or dominated peoples. We next consider the ways in which biologists and sociologists have approached the study of race. At the same time, we expose some of the origins of racist thinking in various misconceptions and myths underpinned by a paucity of scientific data and the absence, until recently, of rigorous methodology. We then explore a key contemporary context – struggles over scarce resources in today's cities – in which race relations, especially among the young, are often raw and conflictual. We follow this with a discussion of intersectionality, in which class, gender and race, as well as the experiences they provoke, rarely operate in isolation. Rather, they frequently interact and so forge complex synergies of practices, disadvantages and opportunities. This section will, therefore, forge links with some of the discussion in Chapters 7 and 8. Finally, we explore briefly some additional forms of social inequality that some sociologists insist are important in shaping people's life chances and daily experiences.

RACE AND COLONIALISM

Many of the encounters between colonizing European powers and the indigenous peoples they came to dominate across the non-Western world contributed to the growth of racist beliefs, stereotypes and sentiments not only among those who actually ruled the native population but also among their home compatriots. The story, however, is not a straightforward one. For one thing, the encounters between Europeans from the sixteenth century onwards involved a host of different situations. For example, the European explorers and traders met small, scattered societies, such as the Khoi and San in South Africa and the Aborigines in Australia. However, they also encountered civilizations, like that of the Aztecs, who inhabited current-day central Mexico, and large empires in India and China. In China, the emperor and his court believed that theirs was the 'central kingdom' around which all others were scattered. Strange stories abounded. As late as the First Opium War (1839–42), which the European powers waged to control the profitable drugs trade, English sailors were depicted in drawings with tails behind their legs. Such depictions were the mirror images of the racial bigotry that was eventually to characterize much of European colonial expansion.

We should note that attitudes towards non-Western societies hardened over time, turning from curiosity and even admiration to contempt and denigration. Thus, the disdainful manifestations of nineteenth-century European power contrasted markedly with earlier European travellers' awed wonder and astonishment at seeing the Taj Mahal, the delicacy of the Benin bronzes, the palaces of Iztapalapa and the massive pyramids of Egypt. At the time of the encounter with European explorers, these buildings and artefacts showed that other advanced civilizations had often surpassed any equivalent achievements in Europe. Interestingly, in the eighteenth century, prior to the formal advent of colonial political control, the relationships of British traders and administrators with their Indian business and administrative colleagues were often characterized by mutual interest and understanding of each other's cultures. It was common for British men to have liaisons, marry and establish families with Indian women – the Anglo-Indian population numbered 500,000 in 1947.

ETHNOCENTRISM

Derives from the Greek word for people, *ethnos*. Ethnocentrists see their ethnic group or nation as the model against which all others have to be judged.

Enlightenment thinkers also exhibited generous attitudes in that they regarded humanity as a single species on a gradual path to self-improvement. Irrespective of cultural differences, all were capable of reaching the end state of 'civilization'. On the other hand, there was a certain ethnocentrism at the core of these views because they implied that what obtained in eighteenth-century France and Germany was the preferred destination of all humanity.

Even before the formal colonial takeover of power, manifestly racist feelings and practices became all too evident in relations between Europeans and non-Western people. Eric Williams (1972) developed a powerful explanation for this in the 1960s. His analysis provides a starting point for any attempt to understand the link between racist attitudes and encounters across the North–South divide, even though his primary concern was with the causes and impact of the Atlantic slave trade. This was a particularly vicious, sustained case of racist beliefs and practices, which continues to scar black–white relations in many countries.

Williams argued that the slave trade expanded when the compulsions of profit and competition, which are intrinsic to a budding commercial capitalism, were being established across Europe and the settlements in the Americas. This, and the increasing economic advantages of producing tropical materials such as sugar, tobacco and cotton for export to Europe and elsewhere, placed a premium on the availability of cheap, disciplined labour that would survive hard tropical conditions. The indigenous peoples of the Caribbean were limited in number and did not flourish under harsh plantation conditions. Moreover, most white people had no need to accept the arduous working conditions and very low wages that were characteristic of tropical plantation labour unless they were indentured servants who were forced to submit to a long period of labour in the colonies. The 'solution' that evolved was to ship captive Africans across the Atlantic as slaves. Estimates differ, but the first major quantitative study by Curtin (1969) indicated that 9,566,000 Africans landed in the Americas between 1500 and 1870, although many did not survive the arduous conditions of the sea passage. If they arrived alive, they were sold like animals and turned into lifelong unpaid labourers lacking any legal rights or even, in many instances, the chance to establish some kind of family life.

Williams (1972) asked how, despite their Christian religious beliefs and the influence of Enlightenment thought, those involved in this trade, especially plantation owners in Brazil, Jamaica and the southern states of the USA, could justify brutally capturing, selling and enslaving other human beings on such a massive scale over several centuries. For a long time, even the Christian churches, priests and congregations at home and in the colonies failed to condemn a hideously cruel practice driven entirely by profit and manifestly contradicting the basic teachings of the New Testament, which taught that God had created all humans as equal and as deserving to be judged solely by their behaviour and actions, not by their physical appearance or worldly position. According to Williams, those involved in the slave trade and most people at that time resolved this most obvious contradiction by persuading themselves that black Africans and many other non-Western peoples were subhuman. Accordingly, they neither deserved nor needed the same rights and opportunities as those associated with the biologically and culturally superior white race. Indeed, exposure to the discipline, order and culture of white people, even through slavery, might exercise a civilizing influence that was unavailable in their own societies. In one form or another, such pernicious and dangerous beliefs were widely diffused across European societies of origin and settlement and they left a legacy of muddled, dangerous thinking. In different ways, too, such views almost certainly infected the approach towards political rule in the colonies that European rulers later pursued.

A PAUSE TO REFLECT

European colonialism commenced roughly in the 1870s and was largely concluded by the 1960s. During the imperial period, it is probably right to suggest that social Darwinian ideas (see definition below) underlay attitudes to difference. What accounts for the partial endurance of attitudes celebrating the innate superiority of one group over another? Are there more contemporary and perhaps more subtle forms of racial discrimination in the twenty-first century and how do we recognize them?

The Enlightenment bypassed most European colonialists of the late nineteenth century. Rather, the *Lords of Human Kind* (Kiernan 1995) annexed territories in the name of their monarchs, sent out governors in plumed hats and announced they had assumed 'the white man's burden' in civilizing the rest of earth. The so-called 'scramble for Africa' (1881–1914) was particularly arrogant – as European powers competed in annexing, invading and settling large chunks of Africa. At the Berlin Conference of 1884–5, some semblance of order was given to this process, as boundaries were drawn on the map of Africa, but the opinions of Africans counted for nothing. Once they realized that they could make massive fortunes by subordinating the rest of humanity, these imperialists swept aside any Enlightenment or Arcadian notions they might have harboured. Instead, they stole rubber trees from Brazil, mined gold and diamonds in South Africa, logged lumber from the equatorial forests, and extracted opium from China. With cheap or coerced labour and speculative capital, they established sugar, cocoa, tobacco and sisal plantations. These imperialist adventurers, the plantations they started and the financiers who propped them up were the early precursors of the transnational corporations (TNCs) discussed in Chapter 10.

The cruelty of many colonial occupying forces was legendary. Take the case of German South West Africa, now Namibia. In October 1904, after several uprisings against German rule, General von Trotha, the military head of the occupying forces, issued an extermination order directed at the local population, declaring that:

> inside German territory every Herero tribesman, armed or unarmed, with or without cattle, will be shot. No women or children will be allowed in the territory: they will be driven back to their people or fired upon. ... I believe that the Herero must be destroyed as a nation.

Within a year, that is virtually what happened. The Herero population dwindled from around 60,000–80,000 people to just 16,000 – a loss of some 75–80% (Figure 9.1).

© ROBERT HUNT LIBRARY/MARY EVANS

FIGURE 9.1 Seven native Herero men chained together in German South West Africa (now Namibia)
A rebellion by the Hereros against the German colonists took place between 1904 and 1907, leading to the death of thousands of Herero by means of starvation and thirst, when they were driven into the Namib Desert. Survivors were held in concentration camps where they were used as slave labour, many dying of disease, overwork and malnutrition. This virtual genocide prefigured other ghastly genocides of the twentieth century.

SOCIAL DARWINISM

Social Darwinists appropriated Darwin's idea of natural selection to justify inequality between individuals and groups, with the implication that inherited and biological differences were innate and more important than social interventions. Colonialism, for example, was justified in terms of the inherent superiority of Europeans.

Although many people put up spirited fights for their independence, the superiority of European guns and military tactics usually won through. The very ease of these brutal victories promoted ideas of **social Darwinism**, which European imperialists supposed lent support to the idea that they were inherently superior to the people they colonized. The legacy of the Atlantic slave trade and the colonial subjugation of all sub-Saharan Africa (other than Ethiopia) have contributed to contemporary discrimination and prejudice against people of African descent.

RACE AND ETHNICITY: CHALLENGING MYTHS

The word 'race' is now inextricably associated with the idea of 'racism' – discrimination on the grounds of observable difference. This was not always the case. We once took the expression, 'the human race', as a unifying notion, suggesting more commonality than difference. It laid emphasis on a single species, the implication being that we share more common features – physical, biological and social – than the characteristics that divide us. To avoid the confusion of using race in the sense of the total human race, it is probably sensible nowadays to talk of 'humanity' or 'humankind'.

'Race' can also refer to a group of people connected by a common origin who share common features because of their supposedly common descent. This also often meant having social and historical features in common, such as a shared language, a single place of settlement and a political community – what we would nowadays think of as a 'nation'. Before the Second World War, people frequently spoke of the 'French race', the 'German race' or the 'British race' in this way, although such notions now seem either quaint or perhaps even sinister.

In general, the expression 'race' continues to have two senses – a supposedly scientific sense that some biologists and physical anthropologists use, and a sociological means of understanding how popular forms of heterophobia (fear of difference) are expressed, diffused and acted on.

APARTHEID

The Afrikaans word for the systematic, legalized discrimination that existed in South Africa between 1948 and 1994. The Population Registration Act of 1950 classified the population in different racial categories, with education, residence and marriage only permitted within each category. Although the system technically supported difference rather than hierarchy, in practice the good jobs, the best housing, the vote and other favourable opportunities and resources were reserved for the whites. With the election of Nelson Mandela as president in 1994, the system was legally dismantled, although class differences have replaced race differences and many black people remain poor and marginalized.

EVALUATING BIOLOGICAL NOTIONS OF 'RACE'

The idea of classifying people into racial categories started in the sixteenth century and remained an important concern for biologists and physical anthropologists until the 1950s. As Stephan (1982: 171) argues:

> For more than a hundred years, the division of the human species into biological races had seemed of cardinal significance to scientists. Race explained individual character and temperament, the structure of social communities, and the fate of human societies. … At times this commitment to race subtly modified the reception and interpretation put upon new biological theories. At the very least, belief in the fixity, reality and hierarchy of human races – in the chain of superior and inferior human types – had shaped the activities of scientists for decades.

In the wake of the Second World War, the scientific credibility of the idea of a racial hierarchy in humankind was fundamentally questioned. Once Nazi racism and anti-Semitism had been defeated on the battlefield, their horrific consequences became apparent when the starving remnants of the *Undermenschen* (the Nazi word for 'subhumans') stumbled from the concentration and death camps established by Hitler's regime. Although their intentions were not genocidal, the ideologists of the apartheid regime in South Africa also used racial categories for discriminatory social practices, suggesting, for example, that only certain races were fit to perform certain tasks.

The association between 'racial science' and political repression all but abolished the word 'race' from polite scientific discourse. However, a small but determined group of biologists and physical anthropologists still insists that it is important to study subspecies (of the human species) that have developed distinguishing characteristics through segregation or relative isolation. Generally, such biologists do not stress phenotypes (appearance) but rather more complex and less visible biological characteristics (called genotypes). For example, biologists will refer to blood types and their distribution, to particularities of 'gene pools', to differences found by the human genome project, and to the chromosomes of different populations.

Some of this is valid science, but it can have dangerous social and political implications. Occasionally, we must concede, such studies can serve socially responsible ends, for example in the testing and treatment of a disease like sickle-cell anaemia, which is more common among people of African descent. More dubiously, however, some scientists have linked genotype to the distribution of intelligence across populations (see Box 9.1).

FIGURE 9.2 The Martin Luther King Memorial, Washington

Martin Luther King has become the iconic figure for nonviolent civil rights activism in the USA and many other places. He was assassinated on 4 April 1968, aged 39.

Steve Jones (1993), a leading geneticist, has warned against the tendency to dress prejudice up as science and points out that a human being has about 50,000 genes (only about 10 of which affect skin colour) that act in complex and unexplored ways. Much of the existing material on heredity and race is simply bad science. The most damaging refutation of biological notions of race lies in the extensive history of the migration and mixing of peoples – and the breakdown of all reputed 'pure' types.

BOX 9.1   Race and intelligence: US experiences

Elementary intelligence quotient (IQ) tests were first applied on Ellis Island, near New York, where the applications of 12 million immigrants entering the USA were being processed. The fear of allowing immigrants from Eastern and southern Europe, who were perceived to be simple-minded and 'inferior', prompted this development. In the First World War, army recruits and school pupils were given IQ tests. The lower scores of African American and Americans of Eastern and southern European descent were held to be attributable to their inferiority, but served only to indicate the cultural and linguistic biases of the tests. In these tests, Jews were held to be inferior; this is difficult to square with the fact that 37% of US Nobel laureates are Jewish, some 19 times their percentage in the population.

In the 1960s, the controversy erupted again around the work of Arthur Jenson (1969), a Harvard educational psychologist, who argued that 80% of variance in IQ performance was attributable to heredity and that African Americans were inherently inferior in certain intellectual abilities. These 'findings' were explosive, in that conservative and reactionary politicians used them to block remedial educational and social programmes, such as the 'Head Start program', which was designed to provide early educational support to deprived communities. If, these politicians reasoned, African Americans were incapable through their genetic inheritance of changing their situation, why waste taxpayers' money? There are many problems with this analysis, not least that other groups, unrelated to African Americans, showed a similar gap of 10–15 points in IQ tests, other African origin groups (such as those from the West Indies) did not manifest a gap, and, in any case, 'to make statements of heritability concerning such a polygenic trait [as intelligence] goes well beyond the scope of modern genetics' (van den Berghe 1994: 151).

Like a bad tune that will not go away but floats back in a slightly different key, Herrnstein and Murray (1994) argued in *The Bell Curve: Intelligence and Class Structure in American Life*, their 845-page tome, that inequality is at the heart of the human condition and that difference is in the nature of things. Their racial thinking is only thinly disguised. Instead of 'races', their world is made up of 'clans' (a complete violation of the meaning of this word), each possessing different qualities – all of which, we are told, we should value. Rather than bemoaning the fact that blacks are intellectually inferior to whites (a claim they virtually take for granted), the authors suggest we should celebrate their values of spirituality, movement, dance, rhythm and music. By including a discussion of the low IQ of the white 'underclass', they hoped to dilute the exclusive concentration on black failures in other similar literature. Yet these devices are by way of a mask beneath which are still visible the old, discredited claims of biological inferiority and superiority.

Sources: http://en.wikipedia.org/wiki/Jewish_American; Malik (1996: 205–9); van den Berghe (1994).

SOCIOLOGICAL NOTIONS OF RACE

Sociologists fully accept that race categories are commonly, but normally ignorantly, used in popular discourse and in social and political life. However, they point out that these common categories relate imperfectly to physical attributes such as skin, hair or eye colour. For sociologists, phenotype is important, but only as one social marker – one among many – that serves to generate the categories that regulate the distribution of advantage and disadvantage. The loose use of the expressions 'black', 'Asian', or 'white' provides a good example of how contingent and temporary are these popular racial expressions and labels (Box 9.2).

BOX 9.2 The strange story of race labels

1. In apartheid South Africa, 'black' meant the totality of non-whites, including Indians, coloureds (people of mixed descent), San and Khoikhoi as well as those of dark-skinned African descent.

2. In Australia, 'black' means of Aboriginal descent. (Incidentally, indigenous Australians have only a very remote genetic connection to Africans.)

3. In Brazil, 'black' means somebody who is self-evidently thought to be of African descent. (Many Africans were brought to Brazil as a result of the slave trade.) Indigenous people and those who have mixed ancestry are excluded. According to popular Brazilian folk wisdom, 'money whitens the skin', so rich black Brazilians are 'white'.

4. In the USA, by contrast, people who are only barely discernibly of African descent will be considered 'black' (often legally so in the southern states before the 1960s and now socially). They also may well describe themselves as 'black', although this label has been discarded in favour of 'African American'.

5. If we turn to Britain after the 1950s, some immigrants from the Caribbean and the Indian subcontinent (together with the radical intelligentsia) used the category 'black' to suggest that they were experiencing hostility or indifference. They saw themselves as forming an underclass, or poor section of the working class, and being denied access to the most favoured goods and resources.

6. Later, in the UK, people of Indian, Pakistani and Bangladeshi backgrounds became more generally known as, and used the self-description, 'Asian'. However, 'Asian' excluded Chinese, Japanese and Malaysian people.

7. These last exclusions are received with particular puzzlement in the USA, where the category 'Asian American' definitely includes Chinese and Japanese.

8. Finally, by way of a concluding absurdity, we might note that in apartheid South Africa, because the Japanese did not fit the local categories and the government was anxious not to offend such a powerful investing and manufacturing nation, the regime regarded the Japanese as 'honorary whites'. Thus, they were allowed, for example, to inhabit 'white' areas and stay in 'white' hotels.

One after another, racial labels are found to be socially and politically constructed and reconstructed in particular settings. This has led some sociologists to argue that the category 'race' is too insubstantial to consider in a sociological sense. Some, like Miles (1989), would like to abolish 'race' (or always keep it in inverted commas), although they are certain there is a phenomenon called 'racism'. This position is not as bizarre as it may seem. The fact that 'races' are socially constructed does not mean that they are fictional or unimportant. Sociologists draw inspiration from William Isaac Thomas's remark (the 'Thomas theorem', formulated in 1928) that: 'If men define situations as real, they are real in their consequences.' In other words, people think in racial terms, therefore their conduct and behaviour and the wider structure of social action will reflect those beliefs.

John Rex (1986), another prominent race relations theorist, suggests that we can delineate what he calls 'race relations situations'. If, he argues, intergroup interaction is marked by severe conflict, hostility, oppression and discrimination (all these going beyond what the competition of a free labour market permits), we have a 'race relations situation'. There are clear practical advantages to this idea. It is both sociological and contextual. It can be used to account for the variety of labels and situations that apply to different groups. For example, the Jews in the context of Nazi Germany were a 'race', while in the context of, say, contemporary USA they are 'only' an ethnic group. Again, because there is often an element of biological determination in the justifications proffered for discrimination, it may be valid to consider that all intergroup hostility of the severity described above can be considered a 'race relations situation'.

KEY CONCEPT

Sociologists who work in the tradition of SOCIAL CONSTRUCTIONISM lay very little emphasis on an objective reality that has to be discovered, or subjective perceptions and experiences of reality. Instead, they focus on how continuous social interactions create shared meanings. In the cases of 'race' and 'ethnicity', for example, social constructionists look at how the 'other' is constructed, defined and characterized, notions that might then become simplified through stereotypes.

KEY CONCEPT

SITUATIONAL IDENTITY arises when an individual constructs and presents any one of a number of possible social identities, depending on the situation. In the most individualistic versions of this phenomenon, an actor deploys an aspect of their identity – a religion, an ethnicity, or lifestyle – as the context deems a particular choice desirable or appropriate.

ETHNICITY

As the extent of intergroup conflict has proliferated in the late twentieth and early twenty-first century – in Lebanon, Northern Ireland, Sri Lanka, the former Soviet Union, the former Yugoslavia and many African countries – it has become difficult to contain all cases of conflict-ridden interaction between similar looking groups under the heading 'racial'. This leads to a suggestion that we might distinguish between race and ethnicity in one simple and obvious way. In the case of 'race', SOCIAL CONSTRUCTION is based on physical difference, while the social construction of ethnicity is based on less obvious differences, or social markers, for example culture, nationality, language or religion.

However, the contemporary use of the notion of 'ethnicity', or what some writers like Hall (1992) call 'new ethnicity', goes well beyond a further movement away from biological categorization. Sociologists have sought to find out how 'otherness' and 'difference' are constructed through discourse, imagery, representation and language, as well as through behaviour. Despite their allusive, metaphorical and literary quality, discussions of otherness in this mould are inherently more subtle and often more optimistic than many discussions of racism. They easily admit more liberating possibilities of self-examination and autocritique, while an appeal to conscience, common humanity or self-interest can, Sampson (1993) suggests, be used to reduce perceived difference.

This more open view of identity construction starts from the assumption that, in a postmodern world, identity is more fragmented and the phenomenon of multiple social identities is much more common than previously assumed. Individuals may attach themselves to, or withdraw from, any one identity or category in a more fluid way, depending on the context. This is called SITUATIONAL IDENTITY.

There are obvious limits to the manipulative use of situational identity. It is relatively easy to change a religion or one's clothes. It is more difficult to alter one's physical appearance, although the large sales of skin-whitening and hair-altering products signify a successful strategy of 'passing', even in such racially divided societies as the USA and South Africa. The idea of 'new ethnicities' has proved liberating for many sociologists, despite its real-world limitations. Diversity and difference can be celebrated, while those who have been traditionally regarded as enduring victims can be more positively seen as evincing but one flexible cultural possibility and social persona among many.

GLOBAL THINKERS 9 PATRICIA HILL COLLINS (1948–)

Patricia Hill Collins is a distinguished professor of sociology at the University of Maryland and a former president of the American Sociological Association. She has made important contributions to intersectionality and 'the matrix of domination'.

Intersectionality and black women's experience

Black women's experiences, particularly in the USA, are seen to lie at the intersection of three dominant axes of inequality – race, gender and class. Focusing on them offers fruitful insights into structures of domination and inequality. However, Hill Collins argues that, in order to challenge inequality, all people need to learn how to transcend their group situation and understand others. We need to:

- bring other sources of oppression into our analysis, such as sexual orientation, religion, age and ethnicity

- recognize that nearly all social groups experience some oppression (most people are simultaneously oppressed and oppressors in different contexts)
- understand that, despite the shared systems of oppression affecting people in the same social category, every individual's situation is unique.

Grappling with the 'matrix of domination'

For Hill Collins, intricate relationships evolve within 'the matrix of domination', the contexts being:

- *structural:* the systems of law, politics and economics set the parameters to people's life chances, and these are slow to change
- *disciplinary:* various bureaucracies organize and control social behaviour through setting rules and routines, managing surveillance, and working to define what counts as 'knowledge'
- *hegemonic:* the cultural realm through, for example, language, imagery, school syllabuses and the mass media, which shape consciousness and persuade people to accept the prevailing distribution of power and rewards as legitimate
- *interpersonal:* the distribution of authority within, and reinforced by, the everyday interpersonal relations of family, community and workplace.

Resistance within any specific matrix of domination – particularly the hegemonic and interpersonal structures – can occur when individuals pursue self-determining possibilities. Individuals can:

- interrogate themselves to understand their predicament, including how their actions oppress others
- deconstruct and deny the dominant values that define some people as inferior and less worthy than others
- reconstruct knowledge in dialogue with others embroiled in the same
- reflect on shared personal experiences and moral responsibilities towards both the self and others whom the same or different kinds of inequality oppress.

This alternative interpersonal knowledge is built on an ethics of caring. It rejects the impersonal, value-free kind of scientific knowledge that objectifies the subject of study and denies the political implications that are always present in human relationships – leaving the oppressed without hope or assistance.

Source: Hill Collins (2000, 2005).

URBAN NIGHTMARES AND RACIAL DIVISIONS

The academic debates about situational ethnicity, where identities are negotiated through 'ethnic choice' and negotiations about identity, are often a million miles away from what happens on the street where violent crime usually involves poor people attacking other poor people. There, the massive divisions that result from urban social inequalities create a lethal cocktail of fear among those who have money, property and employment, and resentment among those who lack such goods and resources. The siege mentality that results has implications for public and private responses to both anticipated and actual crime. By the mid-1990s, in California, expenditure on prisons had overtaken the education budget, while in Los Angeles alone there was an average of 35 crimes reported every hour, 10 of which were listed as violent crimes, such as murder, rape or aggravated assault (Burbach et al. 1997: 28–9). US citizens spent twice as much money on private guards as the government did on police (Martin and Schuman 1997: 9). This 'internal measure' of the decay of the nation-state is every bit as telling as the argument that nation-states may be losing the battle to control global capital (see Chapter 5).

When the prism of 'race' overlays social inequalities, an explosive situation can result: in post-apartheid South Africa, for example, property crimes involving violence were rife for eight years following the collapse of the repressive white-dominated state, although they now seem to be abating. Rural–urban migrants previously excluded from the cities under the notorious 'pass laws' have now joined immigrants from even poorer countries in the formerly 'white cities'. With little change in white economic power, massive black unemployment, and the growth of shantytowns, it is hardly surprising that many people turned to crime. The long campaign of armed resistance to apartheid and the civil wars in neighbouring countries fomented a market in weapons and a gun culture. Wealthier South African citizens, including many blacks who have 'made it', are uneasy about travelling at night and many have turned their homes into fortresses, with alarm systems, burglar-proof bars, high walls, guards, dogs and weapons. Armed response units operated by private security firms provide backup.

A similar scenario unfolds in Brazil, where one property developer has created a 'safe city' west of São Paulo, called Alphaville. He boasts that he is 'creating the conditions for heaven on earth' and that he knows nothing about the famous French film made by Jean-Luc Godard in 1965 called *Alphaville*, which predicted a technological nightmare of total surveillance and social control (see Box 11.1). Life has truly imitated art. High walls, sensors and spotlights surround the Brazilian Alphaville. Private security guards, often police officers trying to augment their regular salaries, cruise around the periphery. Every visitor must show an identity card and be authorized by the residents. Nannies, kitchen helps and chauffeurs have their police records checked. No residents with criminal records are accepted (Martin and Schuman 1997: 171–2). Alphaville now comprises 20,000 residences, protected by 1,000 private security officers.

YOUNG SECOND-GENERATION URBAN MIGRANTS: COPING THROUGH MUSIC

It is simplistic to believe that all young second-generation migrants feel trapped between their parents' homeland culture and the culture of the host society in which they grew up, or that they respond to their predicament in similar ways (Lithman and Andersson 2005). Andersson's (2005: 42) research in Oslo, Norway shows that while some migrant youths form gangs based on neighbourhood territory and their ethnic enclave, others pursue education, identify with a broader youth community, and reject identity politics grounded in ethnicity. They are also aware that a permanent return to their parents' country is unrealistic since that way of life has also changed. Nevertheless, the real difficulties that most young migrants confront relate less to their cultural marginality than to what place they are able to occupy in the economic and political life of their host country. Their lack of economic opportunity is probably their most pressing problem. The story is familiar more or less everywhere, including Germany, Sweden, Norway, France and Britain – high rates of unemployment, a scarcity of jobs, even insecure and low-paid ones, alienation from school, educational failure, and living in heterogeneous, rundown metropolitan areas where there is little community solidarity (Sernhede 2005).

Sometimes, local ethnic organizations emerge with the specific aim of countering these difficulties. For example, the Young Muslim Organization formed in London in the late 1970s was an attempt to increase the self-esteem of young Bangladeshis, despite unemployment and discrimination, by offering a comprehensive and authentic religious ethos that took account of their daily lives (Eade and Garbin 2006). Perhaps equally as harmful is the way in which the police, certain politicians and a sensationalist mass media tend to represent them, especially their young, as dangerous criminals, thereby diverting public attention away from society's failure to address its social problems. Covert racist undertones, or even overt sentiments, lurk behind or within these representations. In a space between their ethnic background and the othering practices of the host society, many young migrants forge an identity and create strategies for coping with their situation.

A PAUSE TO REFLECT

Labelling and stereotyping are common reactions to unfamiliar social groups or those that have acquired a reputation of some sort, for good or ill. When you walk down the street, are you aware of visible differences between people? Do you classify them into different 'types' and assign labels to these types – 'Latino', 'white', 'black', 'Asian', 'mixed', 'Arab' or whatever? How did you acquire these labels and do you think they are accurate? Do you assign certain characteristics to certain groups?

One way of doing this is through music (Andersson 2005: 31–2; Sernhede 2005) and here rap has been especially significant. Originating in the Bronx in New York in the early 1970s, early rap – like previous black musical forms such as jazz, rock and soul music – expressed the dissatisfactions of young, inner-city African American men. Lipsitz (1997: 26) noted that rap and hip hop appealed to young, urban African Americans 'who found themselves unwanted as students ... as citizens or users of city services ... and even unwanted as consumers by merchants increasingly reliant on surveillance and police power to keep urban "have-nots" away from affluent buyers'. Since that time, rap and hip hop have evolved in various ways. What began as an expression of political unrest and ethnic grievance eventually became a musical form that in the hands of some rap artists – such as 50 Cents and Busta Rhymes (Doward 2003: 8) – became one avenue through which corporations sold merchandise in exchange for paying large sums to the relevant musicians. Like earlier kinds of popular music originating in black culture, the appeal of rap music soon spread far beyond young African Americans. It not only attracted middle-class youth but also became increasingly popular among young people across the cities of the world who felt oppressed by the dominant majorities – in France, New Zealand, Algeria, Morocco, South Africa, Italy, South Korea and Japan, to name but a few (Mitchell 2001: 12–33). Because Sernhede's research, carried out in an immigrant suburb called Angered in Gothenburg, Sweden, demonstrates the intertwining of these themes so well, we finish this section with an account of his work.

TERRITORY, BELONGING AND MUSIC IN SWEDEN: A CASE STUDY

Sernhede (2005) addresses not only the existence of alienation among young migrants but also the importance to them of carving out a definite territorial urban space. Swedish surveys indicate that around 40% of young people under the age of 18 live in relatively deprived metropolitan districts, are mostly from foreign backgrounds, and have very low incomes. In some urban locations, more than half the children under the age of seven have migrant parents who are unemployed (Sernhede 2005: 273). Most migrants are also concentrated in well-defined ghettos or neighbourhoods, which the media portray as riven with criminality and racial or religious divisions. Because these areas tend to be highly heterogeneous ethnically and nationally, first-generation migrants find it difficult to form wider, cross-ethnic ties (Sernhede 2005: 274). Sernhede found that most young, second-generation migrants shared a strong sense of alienation from Swedish society. They argued that neither native Swedes nor Swedish institutions showed any interest in interacting with them, and they felt excluded from both Sweden and their parental homeland. The young men, especially, identified strongly with their neighbourhood, from which they derived a sense of security, protection, identity and sociality; it constituted their homeland and for them existed separately from Sweden (Sernhede 2005: 178).

This sense of 'non-belonging' led some to believe that their common identity as immigrants defined who they were and brought them together irrespective of their origins. As one youngster graphically suggested, 'alienation is our nation' (Sernhede 2005: 277). Moreover, migrants often find it easier to forge cross-ethnic friendships with others living on the same street of their urban ghetto, whom the host society and media equally stigmatize, or with oppressed people in distant locations, than with members of the mainstream society. Such feelings of commonality were particularly strong among an active hip hop group of around 50 young musicians with Middle Eastern, African and Latin American backgrounds in one of the ghetto areas of Angered. They believed that, through their music, they spoke not only to all immigrant youth living in Sweden's city suburbs but also to the entire emergent migrant underclass across Europe. They saw their music as a form of aesthetic protest as well as an explicitly political weapon in the struggle against racism, police brutality and marginalization. Some of their lyrics expressed their historical resentment of white European aggression in Africa and Latin America, while others celebrated the Indian tribes' erstwhile cultural achievements and political resistance to the Spanish in the Andes (Sernhede 2005: 281–2). This group, despite its strong 'ghetto identity' (Sernhede 2005: 283), felt connected to people living in cities across the world and was relatively informed about the conditions under which people lived in far-flung cities, for example the Chicanos in Los Angeles. These musicians bought CDs and videos from other countries and exchanged musical ideas on the internet. As one young musician suggested: 'hip-hop people all over the world have the same language so it is easy to live with them. Hip-hop is a language for those that live in ghettos' (Sernhede 2005: 283).

INTERSECTIONALITY: GENDER/RACE/CLASS INTERACTIONS

This chapter together with Chapters 7 and 8 on class and gender explore different axes of social inequality. However, it is important to note that the complexity of social reality is such that if one disconnects the axes, one runs the risk of oversimplifying what actually occurs or imposing more ideological significance to one axis than to another. For example, many feminists insist we subordinate the categories of class and race to patriarchy. Some Marxists, by contrast, often dismiss race as an epiphenomenon by suggesting that the capitalist class fosters racism in order to separate sections of the working class into hostile warring elements and distract them from taking a unified stand for better conditions. Orthodox Marxists, who think that the key issue about gender equality is to encourage women to join the labour force, also often treat the liberation of women rather narrowly. Just as ideological are those who start from the assumption that one can understand everything through the prism of race. Race is held to be 'primordial', fundamental and logically preceding other forms of inequality.

> **KEY CONCEPT**
>
> All social actors cope with and perhaps contest the often conflicting but also mutually reinforcing demands and sometimes injustices they confront during their lives and that emanate from their simultaneous positioning along a combination of criss-crossing or transverse axes of inequality. These may include not just class, gender and race but also sexual orientation, age, religion, disability and ethnicity. INTERSECTIONALITY therefore means that while part of each actor's multiple experiences of domination and/or subordination may change over time, large minorities often face a much heavier and more intransigent cluster of oppressions constraining their actions for long periods or even permanently.

This privileging of one index of social inequality over another is a form of ideological overclaiming. However, during the past 20 years, feminist sociologists have led the way in developing alternative analyses that provide some escape from this dilemma based around the concept of INTERSECTIONALITY. This idea has been developed in a numbers of ways.

First, a major impetus for the early development of intersectionality theory came from sociologists such as Patricia Hill Collins (see Global Thinkers 9) in the USA. They partly broke with white middle-class feminists because they argued that the latter were neglecting the reality that most African American women were exposed to racist and not just patriarchal and economic forms of oppression and these combined to create multiple forms of domination that drastically limited their life chances.

Second, scholars such as Yuval-Davis (2009) and Anthias (2005) have argued that intersectionality applies to everyone, not only those who suffer multiple disadvantages. Indeed, we all have multiple identities depending on the particular context (so-called 'situational identity') and the way our experiences change over time and are historically driven throughout our life course. As scholars, we are interested in exploring the different categories and weightings of inequality that may shape an individual's life at any one time. But from the perspective of each actor's own subjectivity, a person experiences their situation as a whole rather than as a series of fragmentary influences and segments coming at them from various 'outsides' (Anthias 2005). Actors may also respond and contest these inequalities in very different ways.

Third, a number of intersectionality theorists argue that for this and other reasons it is crucial to avoid an additive approach where we simply note the inequities that result from one category such as class and then go on to list those that are shaped by yet other forms of inequality, say, racism, gender and homophobia or disability. The danger here is that when we separate out each category of inequality, we simply revert back to the very kinds of analysis we were trying to avoid, whereby one institutional form of inequality – perhaps weak bargaining power in the labour market or a family life marred by patriarchy – emerges as apparently dominant. In any case, such an analysis ignores the actor's own subjectivity: how do they experience and deal with these complex, converging and interacting forms of oppression (Yeon Choo and Marx Ferree 2010).

One example of a genuinely intersectional but non-additive approach can be seen in Hale's (2004) work on young women working in factories in the countries of the global South, discussed in Chapter 8. Sent by their parents from rural areas in many cases, so vulnerable to domination from male workers, employers, landlords or the men who supervise the dormitories where they stay, many face a complicated mixture of oppressions. As employees who are often refused protection from male-dominated trade unions, they may endure particularly harsh forms of workplace exploitation, including low wages, long hours of work, unpaid overtime and unhealthy if not dangerous workplace conditions. It is almost impossible for them – or for us as scholars observing from the outside – to disentangle this economic oppression from the physical abuse, mental abuse and sexual harassment they simultaneously experience at the workplace and perhaps outside factory hours from male workers, supervisors or employers, abuses closely linked to deep-seated local cultural dispositions rooted in family life and community traditions. Perhaps, too, racial discrimination is sometimes implicated where, as migrants to the city, the women belong to national or ethnic groups different from those of their various oppressors.

Yeon Choo and Marx Ferree (2010: 140–1) offer another interesting example of the advantages of pursuing a non-additive analysis of intersectionality. They discuss the case of middle-class black and white parents in the USA and the dilemmas they face over enhancing their children's educational advantages. One of the studies they interrogated found that both sets of middle-class parents demonstrated equal and intense concern about their children's school and learning experiences compared with working-class parents. It appears, therefore, that social class is the dominant factor at work in shaping children's likely educational attainment and this overrides differences in racial background. However, Yeon Choo and Marx Ferree suggest that additional research reveals how black middle-class parents also tend to monitor their children's experiences constantly to ensure that teachers do not impose racial stereotypes by harbouring lower expectations of their children. They also try hard to insulate their children from the possibility of racist abuse coming either from other white children or from employees attached to the school such as bus drivers or indeed teachers. Such parental 'care work' intrinsically encompasses class and racial concerns simultaneously and it is misleading to try to separate these or to assign more significance to one or the other.

A PAUSE TO REFLECT

The proponents of 'intersectionality' hold that racism, sexism, homophobia and discrimination on other grounds (such as age, civic status, disability and religious affiliation) are mutually compounding and cumulative. However, do we often need to know which index causes most discrimination to any particular group at any particular time? How could we set about operationalizing the theory of intersectionality?

Despite its powerful insights, intersectionality theory raises concerns. For one thing there is a danger of overburdening the analysis of a particular situation with too many dimensions and intersecting experiences of inequality. Thus, if we wished to examine the oppressions to which recent immigrants are exposed, it might be sensible to explore their gender, age (perhaps whether under or over 30), class (upper, middle or lower) background and nationality (say, Pakistani, Indian, Ukrainian or Chinese). This gives about 48 possible categories to examine and that is before we try to take account of their length of stay, legal status as a migrant, marital situation, sexual orientation, rural or urban background or other salient factors likely to shape their experience of inequality. Indeed, pursued too far, intersectionality theory may require us to engage in a vast number of case studies and perhaps, given that everyone's situation is unique, as many as there are humans in the world. This would render comparative analysis extremely difficult, if not well-nigh impossible. At a time when we increasingly need to take account of the shared ways globalizing forces are shaping our world and common futures – and not just our individual everyday lives – an intersectionality approach might lead us into an unnecessarily complex mode of analysis.

SOME UNDEREXPOSED FORMS OF SOCIAL INEQUALITY

While we do not dissent from the argument that class, gender and race/ethnicity are the origins of the main forms of inequality, we want to give at least some brief consideration to a few additional sources of discrimination and social inequality.

RELIGIOUS AFFILIATION

Many of the world's 193 recognized nation-states have constitutions that protect the rights of their citizens to worship freely and to choose their own religious affiliation. However, there are notable exceptions. Here are just two. The Bahá'í Faith, founded in the mid-nineteenth century, has experienced continuous persecution in Iran, where many thousands of its adherents have been martyred and executed. Bahá'ís are accused of apostasy, which makes them liable to death, lifetime imprisonment and persecution. Their houses are plundered, their property confiscated and they are denied legal and employment rights (Cooper 1985). In China, the Communist Party of China (CPC) still declares the country atheist and discriminates against openly practising members of the five religious faiths it recognizes – Buddhism, Taoism, Islam, Catholicism and Protestantism. However, the CPC has been especially intolerant of the Falun Gong, founded in 1992, which it denounces as 'an evil cult' (see Box 17.1). Its followers may number as many as 70 million, which rivals the membership of the CPC itself. By the turn of the century, there were reports of 2,786 deaths of Falun Gong members in police custody and more than 100,000 had been sent to labour camps (Schechter 2000). Suppression of the Falun Gong continues. In 2010, the Chinese government launched a three-year campaign to persuade members to abandon their faith.

DISABILITY AND 'MOBILITY RIGHTS'

Discrimination on the grounds of impaired mobility, for example people who are wheelchair users, has been brought to many people's attention where disabled groups are well organized and lifts, ramps, parking spaces and toilets have been adapted and designated for their use. Lobby groups, such as the US Disability Rights Education and Defense Fund (www.dredf. org), have notably expanded the category 'disabled' to include in their memberships those suffering from cancer, epilepsy and diabetes as well as those who experience impaired mobility. Some 49 million people in the USA therefore belong to the 'disabled' category and they constitute a powerful constituency. In most of the poorer countries, there is very little self-organization among disabled groups and their protection and welfare tend to be left to episodic acts of charity.

Cass et al. (2005) advocate adding spatial or mobility rights to the normally accepted categories of civil, political and social rights. They argue that disabled people are not the only ones affected. Restricted physical access to goods, values and commodities is, they insist, a more general phenomenon. As social networks in work, family life and leisure become more extensive, geographical isolation, the cost of transport and information deficiencies lead to isolation and social exclusion. Mobility, in terms of the availability and price of transport, and access to information, goods and services, shows wide global and regional discrepancies and a basic difference between rural and urban areas, as well as between the rich and poor. (Recall the poor, mostly black, residents of New Orleans without their own transport trying to evacuate the city during hurricane Katrina in 2005.)

CIVIC STATUS

In ancient Greece, the Spartans relied on the Messenian helots, a subordinated foreign labour force, who had to give part of their produce to their masters, could not serve in the army and had no legal or civic rights. Many contemporary societies also show an increasing tendency to create new helots – people tolerated because they work or provide services, but for whom the longstanding population has little sympathy and does not wish to include in its body of citizens. The question of who should have access to the vote, a passport, free or subsidized healthcare, free or subsidized education, unemployment and disability benefits, a pension and a host of other entitlements is increasingly becoming contested as host populations confront the newcomers in their midst. The proliferation of temporary statuses that governments have invented to assign to new helots is illustrative. They give newcomers 'exceptional leave to remain'; they call them 'temporary workers', 'guest workers', 'resident aliens', 'protected persons' or 'undocumented persons', that is, anything short of full citizens with a complete suite of benefits and entitlements.

AGE

There are many wealthy senior citizens; nonetheless, as the demographic profile changes, age will become an increasingly important axis of social inequality in all societies, but particularly in rich Western societies and Japan (Table 9.1). Poverty is often concentrated in the elderly, although social intervention can help. For example, in the UK the number of elderly people needing social assistance fell from 1.8 million in 1974 to 1.4 million 17 years later. Longer life spans, more pressure on health services, numerically more elderly people and fewer people of working age taxed to sustain increases in pension payments easily reverse these gains. In addition to poverty, the elderly are more prone to sickness, more likely to be disabled and more likely to experience mental health problems. Mental health problems may arise because of dementia (affecting about 5% of the UK population), isolation (as friends and families die or move away), bereavement (when spouses and family die) and overreliance on other elderly carers, who are themselves vulnerable to the trials and tribulations of increasing age (Spicker 2005).

That older people have a greater likelihood of becoming marginalized and excluded is a demonstration of how the different axes of social inequality can increase and become mutually reinforcing. For example, an older person in an insecure, low-paid job (the class axis) is more likely than their

TABLE 9.1 Percentage of people aged 60 plus in the population		
	Year 2000	Year 2050 (projected)
More developed regions	19	32
Less developed regions	8	20
World	13.5	26

Source: UN (2004).

younger, more secure and better paid counterpart to retire to a poorly ventilated or inadequately heated house, experience health problems, and have an inadequate retirement income (the age axis). Again, women generally outlive men (the age axis), but because they are more likely to be in poorer paid jobs, often take time out to raise their families, and are less likely to be paying into an occupational or state insurance fund (the gender axis), they are more likely to spend long years of their advancing age in poverty.

The greater durability of the extended family in poorer countries and among rural populations protected the elderly and accorded them abundant respect and affection. However, with the urbanization of many countries in the South and the nuclear family rapidly becoming the norm, families are now sometimes discarding their elderly relatives. This was virtually unknown in Africa, say, 50 years ago. Even more frighteningly, many are having to become parents again. In 2001, the International Federation of Red Cross and Red Crescent Societies announced that at least 5 million grandparents were looking after children who had lost their parents to HIV/AIDS. The statement continued: 'the psychological strain of caring for terminally ill children and coping with their death can be devastating. The stress of taking on the burden of responsibility for orphaned grandchildren is also huge. It is not unusual for grandmothers to be caring for 20 children' (Medilinks 2001).

REVIEW

Biologists and geneticists can now identify gene clusters quite precisely. However, with so much genetic overlap between different social groups and actual behaviour and appearance varying so widely within any chosen social category, scientists find it impossible to imbue the category 'race' with much, if any, explanatory significance. On investigation, sociologists find that people construct racial labels for social and political reasons that often serve to legitimize the actions or interests of dominant classes. Alternatively, such labels reflect the fears – such as competition for jobs – and difficulties that most ordinary people have in dealing with cultural difference. Consequently, most sociologists see little explanatory or analytical value in the category 'race', although they are aware that racial thinking is ubiquitous and may engender real and harmful social practices. In this chapter, we explored two enduring situations in which racist behaviour and institutions either created new, or reinforced existing, inequalities and had a profound effect on the lives of denigrated social groups. First, we considered the historical evolution of European racist thinking and linked it partly to the rise of tropical plantation agriculture and later to the colonial conquest of the non-Western world. Then, we explored the contemporary experiences of second-generation urban migrants whom sections of the mass media and some politicians often vilify and blame unfairly for wider socioeconomic problems. This marginalized situation and, for many, prospect of only the most insecure employment encourage some young migrants to turn to music or other artistic pursuits as a way of asserting new identities and forging alliances across ethnic and national boundaries.

We also argued that, as sociologists, we cannot decide in advance of our research which axis – gender, race or class – might best explain the social reality we face, for they intersect in complex ways, which may not only reinforce or overlay one another but may also generate unpredictable and intertwined situations and dynamics with which social actors have to cope either singly or through collective responses. For example, it is not immediately obvious which condition most blights the life of a poor, uneducated woman in rural India – the prevalence of an entrenched patriarchal culture, or her family's landlessness in a region where employment is highly precarious for everyone, her caste, ethnic or tribal membership, or the stage she has reached in her life span. Moreover, the constraints imposed by all or any of these conditions will almost certainly hold back any attempt she might make to escape her situation of inequality. Age – an underexposed form of inequality – exhibits the same features. The meagre pension that follows a working life in low-paid employment (probably worse for a woman) is likely to go hand in hand with inadequate health insurance, substandard accommodation and the statistical likelihood of dying at a relatively early age.

Visit the companion website at www.palgrave.com/sociology/cohen3e for extra materials to check and expand your learning, including interactive self-test questions, mind maps making links between key themes, annotated web links to sociological research, data and key sociological thinkers, a searchable glossary and much more.

FURTHER READING

K. Malik's *The Meaning of Race* (1996) is a lively and interesting account, while E. Cashmore's *Encyclopedia of Race and Ethnic Studies* (2004), which should be available in most university libraries, contains excellent short entries by leading world scholars.

Black Feminist Thought: Knowledge, Consciousness and the Politics of Empowerment ([1990]2000) is a key text from P. Hill Collins. It has been widely praised because, among other qualities, it deals with the intersecting oppressions of gender and race.

P. Hill Collins co-edited a volume of readings on race and inequality with J. Solomos, one of the UK's leading scholars on race issues, called *The Handbook of Race and Ethnic Studies* (2010).

H. Yeon Choo and M. Marx Ferree's article 'Practising intersectionality in social research: a critical analysis of inclusions, interactions, and institutions in the study of inequalities' (2010) is a useful and relatively rare attempt to apply intersectionality theory, in this case, to middle-class parents from white and black backgrounds who are trying to negotiate the educational options open to their children.

QUESTIONS AND ASSIGNMENTS

1. How important are forms of exclusion and inequality that are not specific to ethnicity/race, class or gender?

2. What is the difference between ethnicity and race?

3. Provide examples of the ways in which gender, class and racial inequalities (a) reinforce each other and (b) contradict each other.

10

Corporate power and social responsibility

Some writers argue that the globalization of economic life has already proceeded to unprecedented levels and is set to intensify. At the heart of these claims is an assessment of the activities of the transnational corporations (TNCs). These ubiquitous entities can be seen as the Trojan horses, or perhaps the battering rams, of global capital. Have they escaped their national origins? What is their economic role in integrating the global economy? What are the social consequences, positive and negative, of TNCs' activities?

To assess their impact, we need to see their activities in the round. We summarize the views of advocates and detractors of TNCs in Table 10.1, but explore their arguments in more detail later. Past academic literature concentrated on TNCs in the manufacturing, extractive and financial sectors but we focus on the financial sector, building on the discussion in Chapter 4. We look at supermarkets and consider how their immense buying power affects farmers and others in their GLOBAL SUPPLY CHAINS.

We shall consider the issue of corporate social responsibility. Is this a positive sign of TNCs' commitment to think of people as well as profit, or a fig leaf designed more for public relations purposes?

ORIGINS AND CHARACTERISTICS OF TNCs

Conquest and trade were at the heart of the European powers' expansion and often provided the raison d'être for the creation of TNCs. Many companies resulted from the British imperialists' motto of 'trade follows the flag'. Take the case of the British traders who penetrated the mouth of the River Niger in West Africa. They began by trading with local chiefs, then succeeded in persuading the British Crown to grant them a charter to legitimate their activi-

TABLE 10.1 TNCs and their social consequences: contested views

Process	Positive social consequences	Negative social consequences
The expansion of TNCs	Provides consumer goods, skills and new technology	Allows power to be exercised anonymously and without social responsibility
The forging of alliances between powerful nation-states and TNCs	Allows states and TNCs jointly to develop research and technology at little cost to taxpayers	Diminishes the state's sovereignty and responsibility to its citizenry
The spread of TNCs to the NICs, especially to export-processing zones	Provides jobs, raises standards of health and safety, and pays taxes	Exploits workers and places too much power in the hands of local elites

ties and eventually founded the Royal Niger Company. W. H. Lever, a soap manufacturer in Britain, bought the company and then amalgamated it with another trading company, the United Africa Company. Thus, the giant Unilever, one of the biggest UK-based TNCs, was born and the names of some of its products reflect the company's tropical origins; 'Palmolive' soap referred to the West African palm oil that went into its manufacture, while 'Port Sunlight', close to Liverpool, was where the tropical products were unloaded and processed.

Overseas expansion was not only a European phenomenon. The trading networks of Chinese, Japanese and Indian merchants across South and East Asia were less visible, but profoundly important, for they often ultimately resulted in the formation of very large international enterprises. One big international Chinese trading clan – the long-established Teochew – illustrates this well. In 1939, the clan advanced a loan to Li Ka-shing, one of its penniless but ambitious relatives who had arrived in Hong Kong as a refugee. He began to make his fortune from a transnational chain of factories making high-quality plastic flowers, buckets, toys and other household items (Seagrave 1995). He bought the sprawling 1986 Expo site in Vancouver for a massive expansion of his international property empire, and is now the richest person of Asian descent in the world.

Some Japanese TNCs also started out as giant trading companies (sogo shosha). Although they have now turned into enormous, integrated, commercial, financial and industrial conglomerates (nine in total), trade was their initial purpose. The six major sogo shosha operating in Japan today not only deal with around half the Japanese exports but also function as major investment banks and have developed enterprises in a range of different fields. In 2010, the investments of Mitsui & Co., one of the largest sogo shosha, included Chilean copper mining, steel processing in Thailand, solar batteries in the USA and a 24-hour shopping channel in Japan (Hoenig 2010). The sogo shosa provide a range of services for other small companies, not just their own, including, for example, credit loans, guarantees, venture capital and legal assistance.

CHARACTERISTICS

Many of the world's leading TNCs are engaged in exploiting petroleum, with Shell, BP, Exxon Mobil, Total and Chevron the most notable among them. Even if a brand name marked on the forecourt of a filling station differs, one of these TNCs is still likely to own the company or supply the petrol from its refineries. As the volume of easily exploitable oil diminishes, these companies are moving robustly into other energy sectors. TNCs in manufacturing are often involved in producing the ubiquitous motorcar. Then there are banks, insurance companies and a number of IT companies (Table 10.2).

By definition, TNCs operate in two or more countries. Branch plants and subsidiaries, sales, research and development take place on a number of sites. Why do TNCs wish to locate abroad? For the extractive industries or agriculture, the answer is obvious; they have to be on the spot to extract the oil, strip the timber, mine the gold or grow the pineapples. Other reasons to decentralize, however, are to secure new markets or stop their rivals getting there first. The lower profits and better organized labour forces that characterize industrialized countries partly account for the movement of capital away from the USA and Western Europe after the 1970s.

Many developing countries, by contrast, had abundant supplies of cheap, non-unionized labour. Newly industrializing countries were also prepared to offer attractive incentives such as an absence of planning and environmental controls, low health and safety standards, and tax-free holidays. With dramatic improvements in international transport and communications facilities in the form of containerized shipping, cheap air cargo, computer, telex and fax links, it was not necessary to locate the site of production near the end market, especially for low-bulk, high-value goods. Moreover, young women who were likely to remain non-unionized were available to staff the world market factories (Cohen 1987: 220–53; Fröbel et al. 1980).

When TNCs open up new markets, the consumer booms they create can massively fuel their profits. In fact, by the 1990s, the biggest consumer and manufacturing boom in world history had begun throughout the great new frontier of China. Certainly, in 2007 it was second and only just behind Germany in terms of export values. It probably moved into the number one position during the recession, notching up around $1.2 trillion in 2009, with Germany slipping to second place due to the recession and the USA in third place (Bradsher and Dempsey 2010). Seagrave (1995: 279), a seasoned observer of the Chinese scene, described how, in the 1990s, residents in Beijing started to throw off its image as the drab capital of a communist country:

> Chinese yuppies were washing their hair in Procter & Gamble shampoo, starting their day with Nescafé instant coffee, driving to work in new Toyotas with electronic pagers clipped to their shirt pockets, then heading for the karaoke bars where they can sing along with music videos and mix Hennessey brandy in Coca-Cola. … As average earnings passed the US$1400 a year mark, the majority of people in China for the first time were able to buy such basic consumer items as refrigerators.

As we can infer from the famous brands mentioned, TNCs are a symbolic and practical demonstration of Western affluence and 'freedom', even if that freedom is sometimes individualistic and consumer led (see Chapter 14). The former communist regimes were particularly vulnerable to the naive notion that political freedom equates with consumer choice. On the day after the Berlin Wall came down (9 November 1989), East Berlin youths celebrated their release from communist tyranny by swaggering down the main streets with tins of Coca-Cola in their hands.

DEFINITION

Having described the origins and some characteristics of TNCs, we are now in a position to give a more formal definition. In extending Dicken's argument (1992: 47), we arrive at a sixfold definition. TNCs:

1. Control economic activities in two or more countries.
2. Maximize the comparative advantage between countries, profiting from the differences in factor endowments, wage rates, market conditions, and the political and fiscal regimes.
3. Enjoy the capacity to shift resources and operations between different locations on a global scale.
4. Operate with a level of financial, component and operational flows between different segments of the TNC greater than the flows within a particular country.
5. Spread individualism and consumerism to the far corners of the world (see also Sklair 2001).
6. Enjoy significant economic and social power, which can be exercised to 'good' or 'bad' effect.

TNCs AS GLOBALIZING AND INTERNATIONALIZING AGENTS

There are two contrasting views on the economic power of TNCs. The first emphasizes their globalizing capacities, a position we associate particularly with the work of Dicken (1992, 2007), Sklair (2001) and others and with which we largely concur. The second, more sceptical view, advanced notably by Hirst and Thompson (1996), suggests that TNCs have not established a global economy and have not superseded the nation-state.

TNCs AS GLOBALIZING AGENTS

Dicken (1992, 2007) argues that TNCs are the single most important force in creating global shifts in economic activity. Ever since the 1950s, world trade – the sum of all the imports and exports bought and sold by all the world's countries – has grown significantly faster than world production. Dicken (1992: 16) sees this as 'a clear indicator of the increased internationalization of economic activities and of the greater interconnectedness which have come to characterize the world economy'. This, in turn, points to the role that TNCs play in binding together national economies. Foreigners own an increasing share of the value of many countries' 'national' assets in part or in whole. For the same reason, a growing portion of each country's productive capacity, technological knowledge and skills is an organized extension of the capacities located in other countries. TNC decisions about whether or not to invest in particular locations dominate much of the world's economic system. The resulting flows of raw materials, components and finished products, technological and organizational expertise, as well as skilled personnel constitute the basic building blocks of the global economy.

In fact, empirical evidence strongly bears out Dicken's case:

1. In 1970, there were about 7,000 TNCs. As early as 1992, TNCs accounted for one-third of total global economic output (UNRISD 1995: 53). This share was considerably greater than the total value of all the goods and services entering world trade through exports by national firms selling directly from their country of origin to a market in another country. According to Dunning (1993: 14), TNCs also accounted for about three-quarters of world trade.
2. However, according to the *World Investment Report 2009* (UNCTAD 2009), and despite the adverse impact of the global recession on most companies, by 2009 the number of TNCs had increased to 82,000 and together these owned around 810,000 foreign affiliates.
3. We can measure the extent of a company's globalization by looking at its transnationality index (TNI), which calculates the average of each company's three ratios – foreign assets to total assets, foreign sales to total sales, and foreign employment to total employment. Data suggest that the average TNI for the largest TNCs increased from 57 in 2004 to 67 by 2008 (UNCTAD 2009: 19). The largest 100 TNCs started in developing countries had attained a high TNI, of between 51 and 55 by 2008.
4. Other data point in the same direction. For example, whereas total foreign direct investment amounted to $58bn in 1982, by 2008 it had reached almost $1.7 trillion (UNCTAD 2009). Similarly, the exports of goods and services by the foreign affiliates of TNCs rose in value from $2,396bn to nearly $20 trillion between 1982 and 2008. The number of workers employed in foreign affiliates also rose dramatically in this 20-year period from nearly 20 million to more than 77 million.
5. By 2007, seven TNCs from developing countries were included in the top 100 global companies compared with none in 1993. If we turn to the listing of top companies provided by CNNMoney (n.d.), we find that nearly one-fifth of the top 500 TNCs (91 companies) were based in developing countries, including 49 in China, 10 in Latin America (especially Brazil and Mexico) and 8 in India.

INTERNATIONAL, BUT NOT GLOBAL, AGENTS

Hirst and Thompson (1996: Ch. 4) examined data on more than 500 TNCs from five countries in 1987 and compared these data with similar material on more than 5,000 TNCs from six countries (France, Japan, the UK, the USA, Germany and the Netherlands) for the period 1992/3. What stood out clearly for these authors was the extent to which TNCs 'still relied upon their "home base" as the centre of their economic activities, despite all the speculation about globalization' (Hirst and Thompson 1996: 95). Thus, they argued that the world economy may have become 'international' but it certainly was not yet a 'globalized economy' (Hirst and Thompson 1996: 8–13). They also suggested that the world's economy might indeed be hardly more 'international' than it was before the First World War.

Hirst and Thompson (1996) also stressed the political limitations to the mobility of capital. Businesses normally prefer to operate where they feel secure and enjoy a comfortable rapport with a supportive local culture and market situation. Similarly, the sphere of the economic often consists in large part of relatively immovable plant, equipment and infrastructure as well as employees 'trapped' at any given time in particular locations by community and family responsibilities, job availability, skill and language capacities, and the legal restrictions of citizenship.

Hirst and Thompson's analysis presents a theoretical difficulty. Following the insight offered by Lash and Urry (1994: 61–2), we must distinguish between two aspects of economic life – the cultural, symbolic and knowledge-based component, and the more material or physical one. While the first is inherently mobile and capable of rapid emulation and transference between places and organizations, the second is necessarily rooted in specific locations at any one moment in time. As Castree et al. (2004: 17) suggest:

> uneven geographical development and local specificity persist. In short, the world economy demonstrates a paradoxical, rather skewed character; in some respects, it has become highly globalized while in others there are, and may remain, certain finite limits to this process.

In this sense, Hirst and Thompson's position is perfectly correct although perhaps misleading.

Moreover, the empirical evidence outlined above suggests strongly that we have reached a critical point where we can safely assert that a global economy exists and that it revolves in large part around TNCs. Even the recent economic recession has failed so far to dent that situation. In any case, we cannot establish the true extent to which TNCs dominate economic decision-making merely by calculating their overall direct ownership of assets or amount of foreign investment, for none of that takes account of the massive amount of subcontracting and outsourcing to millions of smaller firms worldwide in which they continuously engage. There is also the issue of the crucial role that large banks and other financial businesses play as motors of the global economy and their increasingly transnational character.

THE INCREASED POWER OF FINANCIAL CORPORATIONS

In Chapter 4, we analysed how and why financial corporations have come to exercise such a dominating influence over the fates of nations since 1980. This process of financialization involves the capacity of companies operating in finance to suck resources out of the productive industries, including much of their contribution to wider economic growth. One indication of this is the rising proportion of corporate profits derived from banking, insurance and trading in various securities (broking) especially in the USA and the UK. In 2005, this reached almost 35% compared with only 10% in the 1960s (Ford 2008). We can also ascertain this by considering the total assets available to the world's top 10 financial TNCs. In 2009, their combined assets were equal to $23 trillion (UNCTAD 2010), more than 1.5 times the USA's GDP. Yet, often the financial industries make little, if any, direct contribution to the productiveness of the main economy (Elliot and Atkinson 2008: 195). Indeed, there is wide agreement that the financial industries were responsible for leading the global economy towards near collapse in 2008.

Yet, so crucial is finance to economic life in general that the EU, UK and US governments felt obliged to offer $14 trillion to prevent a widespread collapse of the banking system (Cassidy 2009). The public in the advanced countries deeply resents the burden that has fallen on them to bail out the banks and deal with the wider consequences of the crisis, particularly since many observers believe that the leading financiers knew that they were taking huge risks with other people's money (Hutton 2010). Even more galling is the realization that the people who ran the financial system seem to have evaded any damage to themselves personally. Thus, by late 2009 the game of paying themselves vast bonuses had resumed since declining bank competition combined with government support had pushed up bank profits substantially. For example, less than a year after a massive global bailout of banks by governments, and given its daily profits of around $35m, Goldman Sachs had established a bonus fund for its employees of at least $10bn and was preparing to pay higher bonuses to each of its employees than ever before (Cassidy 2009; Clark 2009). In addition, Goldman Sachs was not alone in continuing to operate a bonus culture of such proportions.

TNCs AND NATION-STATES: COMPARATIVE ECONOMIC WEIGHTING

Having considered some aspects of the relationship between TNCs and nation-states in Chapter 5, we focus here on their relative economic power. We can do this by treating corporate revenues as equivalents to countries' GDPs and ranking them by their economic size. Table 10.2 provides a measurement of the 120 most important economic units in the world today using data from 2009 for countries and from 2010 for TNCs. This reveals that there are 59 nation-states and 61 TNCs on the list, although the TNCs are concentrated in the lower half. Nonetheless, this means that some 137 states (of the 191 the UN recognized in 2009) had smaller economies than the 61 largest TNCs.

TABLE 10.2 Economic power of countries and TNCs, 2009/10					
Rank	Country/corporation	GDP/sales ($m)	Rank	Country/corporation	GDP/sales ($m)
01	United States	14,256,300	16	Netherlands	792,128
02	Japan	5,067,526	17	Turkey	617,099
03	China	4,984,731	18	Indonesia	540,277
04	Germany	3,346,702	19	Switzerland	500,260
05	France	2,649,390	20	Belgium	468,522
06	United Kingdom	2,174,530	21	Poland	430,079
07	Italy	2,112,780	22	Walmart	408,214
08	Brazil	1,571,979	23	Sweden	406,072
09	Spain	1,460,250	24	Austria	384,908
10	Canada	1,330,067	25	Norway	381,766
11	India	1,310,171	26	Saudi Arabia	369,179
12	Russian Federation	1,230,726	27	Iran	331,015
13	Australia	924,843	28	Greece	329,924
14	Mexico	874,902	29	Venezuela	326,498
15	South Korea	832,512	30	Denmark	309,590

TABLE 10.2 (cont'd)

Rank	Country/corporation	GDP/sales ($m)	Rank	Country/corporation	GDP/sales ($m)
31	Argentina	308,741	69	Peru	126,734
32	South Africa	285,983	70	Assicurazioni Generali	126,012
33	Royal Dutch Shell	285,129	71	Allianz	125,999
34	Exxon	284,650	72	New Zealand	125,160
35	Thailand	263,856	73	AT&T	123,018
36	United Arab Emirates	261,348	74	Carrefour	121,452
37	Finland	237,512	75	Ford Motor	118,308
38	Colombia	230,844	76	ENI	117,235
39	Portugal	227,676	77	J.P. Morgan Chase	115,632
40	Ireland	227,193	78	Hewlett-Packard	114,552
41	Hong Kong, China	215,355	79	EON	113,849
42	Toyota Motor	204,106	80	Ukraine	113,545
43	Japan Post Holdings	202,196	81	Berkshire Hathaway	112,493
44	Israel	194,790	82	GDF Suez	111,069
45	Malaysia	191,601	83	Daimler	109,700
46	Czech Republic	190,274	84	Kazakhstan	109,115
47	Egypt	188,3346	85	Samsung Electronics	108,927
48	Sinopec	187,5187	86	Citigroup	108,785
49	State Grid	184,496	87	McKessen	108,7012
50	Singapore	182,232	88	Verizon Communications	107,808
51	AXA	175,257	89	Crédit Agricole	106,530
52	Nigeria	168,994	90	Banco Santander	106,345
53	Pakistan	166,545	91	General Motors	104,589
54	China National Petroleum	165,496	92	HSBC	103,730
55	Chevron	163,527	93	Siemens	103,6055
56	Chile	163,370	94	America International Group	103,989
57	ING Group	163,204	95	Lloyds Banking Group	102,967
58	Romania	161,610	96	Cardinal Health	99,613
59	Philippines	160,476	97	Nestlé	99,114
60	General Electric	156,779	98	CVS Carework	98,7298
61	Total	155,887	99	Wells Fargo	98,636
62	Bank of America	150,450	100	Hitachi	96,593
63	Kuwait	148,024	101	International Business Machines	95,758
64	Volkswagen	146,205	102	Dexia	95,144
65	Algeria	140,577	103	Gazprom	94,482
66	Conoco Phillips	139,515	104	Honda Group	92,400
67	BNP Paribas	130,708	105	Aviva	92,140
68	Hungary	128,964	106	Petrobras	91,869

TABLE 10.2 (cont'd)

Rank	Country/corporation	GDP/sales ($m)	Rank	Country/corporation	GDP/sales ($m)
107	Vietnam	91,854	115	Bangladesh	89,378
108	Royal Bank of Scotland	91,767	116	Enel	89,329
109	PDVSA	91,182	117	Slovakia	87,642
110	Metro	91,152	118	UnitedHealth Group	87,138
112	Morocco	90,859	119	Société Générale	84,157
113	Tesco	90,234	120	Nissan Motor	80, 993
114	Deutsche Telekom	89,794			

Sources: Fortune 500 (2010); World Bank (2009).

TNCs may not necessarily exercise their economic power in a negative way, but it is clear that in certain circumstances they can cause serious disruption to national economic and social plans. Here are some of the ways in which this might happen:

1. Local capital has difficulty competing. TNCs usually pay higher wages and, to compete, local employers have to lower wage costs, worsen employment conditions and sacrifice quality.
2. TNCs have disproportionately more marketing power than local economies, even for an inferior product. When one of the present authors lived in the Caribbean, locally owned shacks served wonderfully succulent and spicy portions of chicken. They were then undercut by a certain US 'brand leader', which subsidized imported chickens and took losses over a two-year period until it could drive the local firms out of business. Not surprisingly, the prices of its inferior, less healthy, product soon rose.
3. Local politicians are anxious to encourage inward investment and are often willing to accept corrupt payments in exchange for accepting the company's plans, facilitating its operations, and allowing it to send its profits out of the country with minimal tax. Often these plans conflict with national plans. Consequently, the poor countries are sucked into a cycle of further dependence.
4. TNCs are often in a position to influence tastes and consumption patterns in a nega-tive way. We have already alluded to a fast-food outlet, but below we provide a case study of tobacco, in which we show that some corporations use glam-orous adverts to promote cigarettes in developing countries to offset their reducing profits elsewhere. In this and other cases, TNCs have the capacity to subvert and under-mine the power of even quite large nation-states.

© HERVE COLLART/SYGMA/CORBIS

FIGURE 10.1 TNC marketing
Marketing by a TNC reaches an indigenous family in the remote Brazil/Colombia border area. The statuette of the Eiffel Tower has been given as a promotional gift by a representative of Avon Cosmetics.

EXPORTING LIFESTYLES: THE CASE OF TOBACCO

The health implications arising from the way some TNCs are able to diffuse Western lifestyles are a cause for some concern. While we focus on the tobacco industry, similar critiques apply to the sugar, fast-food, pharmaceutical and several other industries (see Box 10.1 on pharmaceutical companies). We can relate the growth in tobacco consumption in Western countries between 1900 and 1975 to urbanism, modernity and the increase in leisure and consumption. Smoking among friends at work as well as at play was a way of expressing group affiliation. In 1956, the British Doctors Survey (led by Richard Doll) first provided convincing statistical evidence of the link between smoking and lung cancer. As evidence emerged that smoking hugely increased the likelihood of high blood pressure and hardening of the arteries, Western governments gradually started to impose restrictions on smoking. A ban on smoking in public places came into force in England in 2007. Meanwhile, the climate of opinion hardened against smoking.

Faced with falling sales, the large cigarette TNCs turned increasingly to the consumers and workers of the South and especially the huge Asian market. This shift meant that, by 1997, only 14% of smokers lived in North America or Western Europe, whereas 55% lived in Asia, 12% in Africa or the Middle East, and 9% in South America. The predictions are that, by 2030, 70% of tobacco-related deaths are likely to occur in the developing countries compared with 50% today (www.tobaccofreekids.org/campaign). In China, the world's most populous country, around 70% of men currently smoke compared with only 35% of men in the West.

Many countries manufacture their own tobacco products. Today, China's state tobacco company is the largest producer in the world. It produced 1.7 trillion cigarettes and employed half a million workers in 2005 (Hu 2008). The Chinese government also raises 10% of its tax from cigarette sales, although half is then spent on the health costs this incurs plus lost work time (Godrej 2004: 12). From the mid-1980s, US manufacturers – led by market leader Philip Morris and its famous Marlborough brand – followed by the other big world companies, placed pressure on China and other Asian governments to remove trade restrictions on Western tobacco products or risk incurring Western import sanctions (Godrej 2004). The second biggest tobacco TNC, British American Tobacco, evaded this blockage by establishing a secret factory in a joint partnership with the government of North Korea, one of the last remaining nominally communist countries. Smuggling by criminal gangs is one major avenue through which cheap tobacco products enter countries. In 2010, an estimated 12% of global consumption was thought to be illegal (www.tobaccofreekids.org/campaign).

Extensive advertising offering access to an American or Western lifestyle accompanied the entry of Western tobacco products to Asian and other markets. Adults of all income groups in the poorer countries engage in smoking, especially in urban areas. Among the poor, tobacco consumption is not just a perceived passport to a more exciting lifestyle but it also provides relief from the stresses caused by a life of relative poverty in crowded, dangerous cities (McMurray and Smith 2001). However, according to Klein (2001), since the early 1990s, the promotion not just of cigarettes but also of a whole range of products has been directed especially towards young middle-class people. She argues that vast and growing markets 'are the great global hope' for corporate capital involved in selling and advertising products that represent Western lifestyles. Teenagers are even more significant because, 'more than anything else or anyone else, logo-decorated middle-class teenagers, intent on pouring themselves into a media-fabricated mould, have become globalization's most powerful symbols' (Klein 2001: 118).

GLOBAL THINKERS 10   DAVID HARVEY (1935–)

We discussed Harvey's work on American imperialism in Chapter 5. He is a social geographer interested in spatial analysis and his work reminds us that social relationships and human behaviour take place in particular spaces and periods. We need to avoid 'spatial fetishism' (Harvey 1982: 374), which endows properties of space with a power they do not possess.

Capitalism and place

Nevertheless, Harvey (1985) sees time and space as providing the enabling and constraining conditions of social conduct, although they can also, to a degree, be 'socially constructed'. In traditional societies, space and time were naturalized phenomena, but industrial capitalism altered that fundamentally. The proletariat needed to be concentrated in urban centres with 'the reserve army' of unemployed people who were 'a necessary condition to sustained accumulation', for the 'accumulation of capital and misery go hand in hand, concentrated in space' (Harvey 1982: 418).

Postmodenity

Later, Harvey argued that postmodernity (see online glossary) 'compressed' and speeded up space and time (Harvey 1989), with better communications, virtual contact, cheaper travel and digitalization perhaps the most obvious factors. Harvey suggests that while Fordism involved standardization and mass production, the 'more flexible motion of capital' that followed made life less predictable. It also brought contingency, 'the fleeting, the ephemeral, the fugitive' to the fore (Harvey 1989: 171), with simulacra (images or representations of reality) replacing reality and being turned into commodities that occupy ever more of our leisure. Consequently, for some, postmodern life becomes mimicry or even artifice. Others seek to reaffirm their identity in what seems a meaningless world: they are looking for a 'place'.

Source: Harvey (1982, 1985, 1989).

WORKING FOR TNCs

TNCs, by definition, are spatially dispersed and employ workers in many countries. We can use the number of employees outside the country in which a TNC's headquarters are located as a first gauge of the degree to which it has decentralized its operations. A spectacular 96% of Nestlé's 253,000 employees work outside its Swiss headquarters. General Motors, by contrast, 'continues to employ far more people in the US than in any other single country' (Kiely 2005a: 109). Some commentators have used the continued concentration of employment and assets in the country in which the TNC originated to argue that 'the image of foot-loose capital dispersing investment throughout the globe is a fallacy' (Kiely 2005a: 109). This view fails, however, to recognize that direct employment by TNCs is only part of the story. As we indicated in our discussion of 'flexible labour' in Chapter 4, the more common contemporary model is the use of subcontracting, both in manufacturing and agriculture, to deliver the products that TNCs wish to market and sell. Because subcontractors and farmers are often almost entirely dependent on the goodwill of a small number of TNCs – or even just one – they become, in effect, indirect employees. One can observe a mix of indirect and direct employment in two important examples – workers in export-processing zones and growers and farmers supplying supermarkets.

WORKING IN EXPORT-PROCESSING ZONES

Since the 1960s, TNCs have been engaging in 'offshore' production through both direct employment and the use of subcontracting in **export-processing zones** (EPZs), mostly in developing countries. Governments offer special inducements – tax privileges, duty-free imports, the promise of cheap labour, limited or nonexistent health, safety and environmental regulations, and perhaps free or subsidized plant and infrastructure – to encourage foreign firms to establish their labour-intensive assembly operations in a given country. In the 1970s and 80s, most of the labourers – over 90% in some EPZs – were young women, although the gender balance is now less skewed. Some employers say that women have 'nimble fingers', which makes them suitable for work on electronic circuit boards, while others pointed to their industrial discipline. In these characterizations, one has to distinguish between convenient stereotypes and the reality facing many female workers in poor countries – namely, an adverse labour market and the desire to escape from the patriarchy characteristic of many rural societies.

> **EXPORT-PROCESSING ZONE**
>
> A free-trade enclave in which foreign firms, or subcontracted local firms that produce goods for export, are encouraged to locate.

The industries most likely to locate in low-wage regions, including EPZs, whether owned locally, internationally or jointly, tend to be those that manufacture garments, shoes, soft furnishings, toys or other low-value consumer goods. Those that manufacture domestic electrical goods or engage in the assembly stage of the production of semiconductors – when the individual microchips are wired together to form integrated circuits and incorporated into various final products – are also prone to locate there. The common factor is that the goods produced are destined for export. Industrial production in such sites grew rapidly, as did its export potential. For example, between 1966 and 1972, US imports of manufactured goods from EPZs located in developing countries increased by an annual average of 60% (Harris 1983: 147). EPZs now flourish widely across the developing world. They have long been prominent in Asia, including China, which established four 'special economic zones', similar to EPZs, as part of its economic reforms in the late 1970s, with Shenzhen, adjacent to Hong Kong, being the largest. Caribbean and African countries have also encouraged offshore development.

In Mexico, the Border Industrialization Program created a gigantic EPZ, near the US border, consisting of thousands of labour-intensive assembly plants (called *maquiladoras*). The venture, which started in 1965, was the result of a deliberate government decision to create local employment in the depressed regions of northern Mexico by manufacturing low-value goods for export to the US market. The US authorities hoped that the provision of work in Mexico would reduce the flow of undocumented migrants north of the border. However, this part of the scheme failed because the jobs mainly went to young women (not to males, who were the most numerous migrants), while unemployed people from other depressed regions of Mexico flooded into the area in a desperate attempt to find work. The attempt to create a barrier to stop migrants effectively created a 'honey pot' that attracted them (Cohen 1987). Current reports by trade union representatives and researchers continue to talk of low wages, long hours, non-unionized workers, and the generation of huge amounts of human and chemical waste with inadequate disposal facilities. Despite its negative features, the Border Industrialization Program is officially a success. In 2004, it employed approximately 1 million people in its more than 3,000 plants (Villabos et al. 2004) and, in 2005, 45% of all Mexico's export earnings came from the *maquiladoras* (http://www.dallasfed.org/data/data/maq-charts.pdf).

GLOBAL SUPPLY CHAINS: THE ROLE OF THE SUPERMARKETS

Three of the top 120 TNCs are supermarkets (Table 10.2). All three – Walmart, Tesco and Carrefour – are primarily food outlets. When you fill your shopping trolley with groceries, it is impossible not to notice the amazing variety of countries from which fresh, frozen, processed, canned and bottled food and drink arrives. The retailers are clearly responding to consumer demands for fresh, exotic, high-quality, cheap and out-of-season produce. Are strawberries on your Christmas menu in northern Europe? No problem – growers in the southern hemisphere will oblige.

A PAUSE TO REFLECT

Looking at the labels on the goods in the big supermarket is where we can readily see how closely the world is interconnected and how global supply chains have developed. The long distances that many items have 'travelled' have led to a concept of 'food miles' and to various campaigns to reduce food miles, mainly on environmental grounds. But are consumers prepared to accept a reduced choice in order to source locally? What will happen to the producers of vegetables, fruit, cut flowers and other produce from poor countries?

Social scientists have undertaken some revealing research on global supply chains by carefully examining the 'trail' of particular products. Freidberg (2001), for example, followed 'the trail of the global green bean' from French and British outlets to their suppliers in Burkina Faso and Zambia, former colonies of France and Britain respectively. The two supplying countries had similar populations and per capita incomes (10 million and US$320 each), and continued to have close relationships with their former colonial powers, the UK and France. Thereafter, the stories diverged. The French wholesalers imported most of the African green beans to the 'Marché internationale de Rungis' (Rungis international market, the largest wholesale food market in the world), a sprawling set of packing sheds, warehouses and loading bays near Orly airport on the outskirts of Paris. The supply chain telescoped down to many small producers and, in the packing sheds in Ouagadougou (the capital city), hundreds of women separated good beans from the rejects. The British used Zambia as a source, but the suppliers were two giant farms, financed by foreign capital with expatriate managers in charge and agricultural workers paid on a piecework basis. By following the trail of the green bean, this study has revealed a significant contrast – in the first case the global supply chain has sustained peasant agriculture, in the second it has undermined, perhaps destroyed, it.

OPPOSING TNC POWER

The primary criticism of TNCs is that they exercise power without responsibility. Examples of TNCs acting without regard to the social or environmental needs of local people or the planet are legion but here are three:

1. Shell in Nigeria has continued to exploit natural resources with considerable ruthlessness and indifference towards the local communities near which the company works and whose land it has appropriated or bought for a song. Under the leadership of Ken Saro-Wiwa, an organized opposition group in the Ogoni area sought to get Shell to recognize its social responsibilities, for the oil and waste from the plants had been polluting the fishing grounds and villages. According to the federal authorities, Saro-Wiwa had played a role in the deaths of four Ogoni chiefs who were purportedly Shell supporters. Although the prosecution knew that he had been away at the time, he was charged with conspiracy and, despite many calls for clemency from all over the world, he was executed on 10 November 1995. On 14 December 1995, against the background of much opposition, Shell announced the continuation of a £2.5m plant in Nigeria.

2. In December 1984, a major industrial disaster took place at Bhopal in central India when poisonous gas leaked from a US plant owned by the Union Carbide Corporation

(Figure 10.2). More than 2,800 workers, their families and others in the surrounding community died in the days following the leak, and at least 20,000 were injured. Union Carbide has consistently stalled legal proceedings instituted to gain compensation and claimed that it was not responsible for the wrongdoings of its subsidiary.

3.   In April 2010, BP's Deepwater Horizon oil rig, based off Louisiana's coastline, exploded, killing 11 people and injuring 17 others and, over a period of months, spilled around 170 million gallons of oil into the Gulf of Mexico. The oil then contaminated the beaches of Louisiana and Florida, harming wildlife and the coastal livelihoods of thousands of local people. There are additional issues besides the environmental and social problems that this event caused. These include the continued thirst of modern citizens for oil as world stocks decline, as well as the question of how governments and electorates can ensure that corporations like BP adequately test their cutting-edge technologies prior to utilizing them. They also need to set up proper systems to manage the impact of any accident that might occur. During the mid-term Congressional elections, it was noticeable that Louisiana politicians – who receive election donations from oil companies and whose constituencies need the jobs generated by the oil industry – were reluctant to challenge the power of the oil giants (Deslatte 2010).

Shareholders are supposed to constrain TNCs, but they usually comprise large anonymous blocks of shares that pension funds, insurance companies and banks have bought with little regard for a company's affairs beyond its profit capabilities. Arguably, the TNCs' acquisition of new rights under international law in the early 1990s to enforce patents, trademarks and copyrights significantly enhanced their freedoms, for these rights restricted the ability of national governments to insist on the TNC training local labour or to impose other strong conditions on inward investment (UNRISD 1995). In any case, their greater mobility due to globalization allows TNCs to choose the most favourable tax and regulatory environment for their investments. Meanwhile, governments compete to attract TNCs to their shores (Cragg 2005) and tend to be relatively quiescent in their dealings with these giants. For example, when Royal Dutch Shell proposed dismantling an oil rig at sea, which opponents claimed would result in extensive pollution, it was not the UK or any government that persuaded Shell to dismantle its rig but extensive protests – including a widespread consumer boycott of Shell petrol stations – by Greenpeace and INGOs collaborating transnationally. Equally, in its operations in Ogoniland, the opposition to Shell did not come from the Nigerian government, but from a small local protest group with support from Amnesty International, Greenpeace, PEN (the international writers' lobby) and various other human rights groups.

Several strategies have come into play in the last 25 or so years to counter

FIGURE 10.2 Corporate irresponsibility
The Union Carbide explosion at Bhopal, India in December 1984 resulted in many deaths, injuries and genetic mutations.

some TNCs' irresponsible exercise of power. Together, they help fill the 'vacuum' between 'waning government capacity and interest to regulate the parameters of acceptable business behaviour' (Hirschland 2006: viii) and the reluctance of corporate management to restrain their predominant 'paradigm' of profit maximization. Of these, the following four have been the most prominent.

First, IGOs such as the OECD and IMF put pressure on TNCs to adopt effective policies of self-regulation involving the adoption of corporate codes of conduct. These set out the obligations of TNCs to their stakeholders, which include employees, the public and developing countries. However, these self-imposed codes of conduct tended to run aground over key issues such as deciding who should determine what constitutes a decent wage in particular countries and, indeed, how to compel governments to permit trade unions or empower local workers. To some observers this approach seemed little more than a 'smokescreen' for covering up the real intentions of TNCs, namely competing for profit (Cragg 2005: 14). Other observers are more optimistic and believe that an increasing number of businesses are adopting serious internal strategies of corporate social responsibility (CSR) (Smith et al. 2010). Key spokespersons in the global economy – for example business leaders in 2009 meeting at the annual World Economic Forum in Davos (cited in Craig Smith et al. 2010a: 8) – have also made this case very strongly, especially following the clear evidence of corporate financial complicity in the world recession commencing in 2007.

Second, as Hirschland (2006) held, the evident limitations of corporate self-regulation prompted or intensified the actions of many IGOs and INGOs – such as Greenpeace, Oxfam and the World Wildlife Fund – to develop global networks that would focus specifically on encouraging TNCs to exercise greater CSR. This meant not only placing pressure on governments and the public but also targeting particular companies and industries with poor records and exposing their deficiencies through the media – as we saw in the case of Shell's North Sea oil rig. Quite quickly, these networks of cooperating pressure groups became more effective and contributed to the thickening webs of activities that make up global civil society (see Chapter 19). According to Hirschland (2006: 8), by 2006 more than half the Fortune 250 leading US companies were providing regular reports of their ongoing environmental and social performances. One of many strategies that emerged from the activities of these global social networks was the Ethical Trading Initiative. With other INGOs, such as the Clean Clothes Campaign and Women Working Worldwide, the Ethical Trading Initiative sought to improve conditions for women garment workers across the South. The idea was to mount public campaigns to raise popular awareness and understanding among consumers targeted at large corporations such as Nike that subcontract their production to numerous firms in long global supply chains (Hale 2004: 161).

Third, we should not forget that a growing number of individuals across the world, through making ethical investments – whether as consumers or investors/savers – participate in bottom-up micro-actions designed specifically to challenge corporate behaviour. Such individuals choose to direct all or part of their savings into pension or investment funds that deliberately channel their money into companies with accredited ethical and/or environmental strategies. By 2007, ethical investment funds had reached $1 trillion in Europe and $2 trillion in the USA, with Asia now following suit (Ethical Investment Research Service 2009). Ethical consumerism is, of course, the other direction from which individuals seek to shape TNC actions directly. In the UK, for example, approximately 5.3% of all consumer spending in 2006, or £32.3bn, was on ethical goods and services. This was equivalent to £664 for every UK household compared with £366 in 2002 (Ethical Consumer Research Association 2007). Interestingly, recent research across six countries (the USA, Germany, Spain, Turkey, India and South Korea) examined the notion of 'socially conscious consumers' in an effort to identify whether those who demonstrate this quality do so with respect to most commodities and for a number of social and ethical causes. They concluded that, irrespective of nationality, there are 'large differences in the knowledge that consumers possess about the social attributes of the products they purchase' (Auger et al. 2010: 158). In general, too, consumers know and care more about environmental issues than labour conditions.

A PAUSE TO REFLECT

By scaling up, large supermarkets can force food prices down for most consumers. Similarly, large factories can also reduce unit costs and deliver affordable cars, electronics and many other goods. Given this, can small-scale producer or consumer cooperatives compete with the giants? Are there ways of cooperating outside the money economy that have not fully been explored or utilized?

Fourth, political campaigns of active protest targeted against particular TNCs obviously constitute another crucial example of grassroots attempts to resist corporate onslaughts on people's livelihoods and ways of life. One of many such instances occurred in Plachimada, a little village in Kerala, India. Local people complained that a new bottling plant established by Coca-Cola in 2001 – one of 27 in the country – was drying up its wells. The company tried to disarm its critics by distributing waste sludge, discarded after water treatment, as 'free fertilizer' to the villagers. As Rajeev (2005) remarks, this act of 'generosity' turned out to be the undoing of the company. The sludge had no value as a fertilizer and, as an independent scientific report confirmed, it contained cadmium, a known carcinogen that causes mental retardation. The company's operations were drying up the fields and wells, and the water in those that remained was unfit for drinking. As Paru Amma, a village woman who lives in this once verdant area, explained: 'one way or another, this plant should be shut down and the management made to pay compensation for destroying our paddy fields, fooling us with fake fertilizer and drying out our wells' (quoted in Rajeev 2005). Finally, in August 2005, the Kerala State Pollution Control Board ordered the closure of the plant, and in 2011 Coca-Cola was declared liable for up to $48m for damages and the clean up of the plant.

BOX 10.1 Breaking the stranglehold of the big pharmaceutical companies

Under the rules governing TRIPS (Trade-Related Aspects of Intellectual Property Rights) adopted by the WTO in 1995, countries are permitted to issue a 'compulsory licence' designed to limit the international restrictions on patent protection if they face a national health emergency or monopoly practices that push up prices abnormally. Evoking this rule is difficult in practice.

The case of HIV/AIDs
South Africa has the highest number of HIV/AIDS victims in Africa. In 1997, it amended its legislation and ordered the issue of a fast-track compulsory licence permitting the Department of Health to import cheaper medicines, including antiretroviral drugs. In 1998, 42 pharmaceutical companies instigated a lawsuit against the South African government because of the action it had taken. American companies lobbied the US government to take action against countries they saw as challenging TRIPS rules on drug products while Swiss and German companies also weighed in.

The global campaign
A vigorous global campaign ensued in support of South Africa's actions. It called for the lifting of restrictions on the export and import of cheap generic drugs and the withdrawal of threats to trade and other penalties against such countries. It brought together pressure groups in South Africa, scientists in the USA and elsewhere, INGOs such as Médecins Sans Frontières and Oxfam, as well as a host of activists in many countries.

The result
The campaign lobbied governments, the WTO, the UN and various companies. In March 2001, demonstrations took place in 30 world cities. In November 2001, the WTO Doha conference simplified and extended the system allowing countries to relax drug patenting laws in cases of extreme public health threats, which made it easier to import generic drugs. By 2003, the WTO had consolidated this agreement, and President Bush supported moves to ensure that Africa received cheaper drugs without incurring trade penalties.

Yet, the circumstances under which compliance with TRIPS rules can be revoked remain unclear. Poor countries have also held back from importing generic drugs despite the WTO's concessions because they still fear trade and other retaliation from the rich countries.

Sources: Kumaranayake and Lake (2002); Seckinelgin (2002).

REVIEW

As we have shown, there is a lively debate about whether TNCs have indeed superseded the nation-state in both political independence and global economic reach. In their social role, some argue that TNCs do both good and harm, or do more good than harm. They are a source of jobs for local people; they also pay taxes that the host country can use for socially beneficial programmes, transfer technology, help industrialize agricultural countries, and manufacture products that people want at prices they can afford. The TNCs' new interest in CSR has resulted in many schemes to improve the welfare of their employees and the communities in which they work.

Against this rosy view has to be set the evidence that CSR is by no means characteristic of all TNCs. Communities, consumers, the environment and the company's workers often need protection from corporate unaccountability and irresponsibility. Sometimes the power of consumer boycotts is effective, sometimes bad publicity leads the company to mend its ways, while, in many cases, public authorities ultimately have to be involved in legal or other constraints if protests against TNCs are to succeed.

Visit the companion website at www.palgrave.com/sociology/cohen3e for extra materials to check and expand your learning, including interactive self-test questions, mind maps making links between key themes, annotated web links to sociological research, data and key sociological thinkers, a searchable glossary and much more.

FURTHER READING

Easily the most accessible book on this topic is P. Dicken's *Global Shift* (2007). It contains useful information on TNCs, world trade and investment and key industries looked at in a global context.

M. Wolf's *Why Globalization Works: The Case for the Global Market Economy* (2005) offers a sturdy defence of corporations which, he says, do not dominate the world through their brands.

Although an advanced book on TNCs, *Global Challenges in Responsible Business* (2010b), edited by N. Craig Smith et al., explores some recent and accessible research on issues around CSR. The three chapters in Part II are especially interesting.

QUESTIONS AND ASSIGNMENTS

1. What reasons could be given to support the proposition that the world economy is much more internationalized and integrated than it was before the First World War?
2. Describe the major characteristics of an EPZ. Why do corporations wish to locate there?
3. Evaluate the positive and negative social effects of TNCs in the developing countries.
4. Evaluate the power of consumers to change the conduct of TNCs.

11

Crime, terrorism and violence

As we argued in Chapter 5, the leaders of nation-states find it exceedingly difficult to deal with some of the social, economic, political and security problems that exist at a global level. Whether it is trying to stop civil war in Rwanda, Kosovo, Liberia, Somalia, Sudan or Syria, contain expansionist military leaders like Saddam Hussein, or develop a regulatory framework to police flows of capital, bilateral agreements between nations appear to be inadequate. The development of regional blocs, military alliances like NATO (North Atlantic Treaty Organization) and even the UN system have not always worked effectively at the global level. While all these issues are of major concern, probably the most important failures of global control that come within our purview as sociologists are crime, where we focus particularly on the transnational drugs trade, terrorism, and the infliction of violence on women, both by states and in domestic situations. In this chapter, we examine these afflictions of global society and consider their extent and likely causes.

CRIME WATCH

In this section, we consider how sociologists think about crime and its relationship to deviance and social control, examine some of the methodological difficulties associated with defining and measuring criminal behaviour, and discuss the crime of murder as a vehicle for exploring these questions in more detail.

DEFINING AND MEASURING CRIME AND DEVIANCE

'Crime' covers a multitude of activities, some extremely violent and injurious to third parties, others much less so. Activities on the 'softer' end of the criminal spectrum include forms of conduct that many people would find unobjectionable. From around the 1970s sociologists in the USA and the UK began to use the word 'deviance' to describe 'behaviour that is banned, censured, stigmatized or penalized' (Rock 1996b: 182). While deviant conduct can include criminal behaviour, it also includes behaviour that attracts disapproval although it is legal, as well as activities that are on the fuzzy boundaries between the two, smoking cannabis being one such example. The very indeterminacy of the boundary between crime and deviance, which varies historically and geographically, creates difficulties in measuring crime rates. Statistics on crime are notoriously difficult to interpret: indeed, the cynical expression (attributed to former British Prime Minister Benjamin Disraeli) 'lies, damned lies and statistics' seemed almost to have been invented to cover the case of crime. In addition to the problem of definition, there are other difficulties:

- There is often a large difference between the incidence of crime and the incidence of reported crime. Some crimes might be undeclared to protect an insurance premium, because of distrust and fear of authority, or other reasons.
- In many countries, while people might report crimes to a local police station, data collection might be inefficient and statistical services nominal.
- Where law enforcement is effective, reported crimes will go up, but where low rates are recorded, this might indicate indifference to law enforcement, a collapse into gang rule or even warlordism, rather than provide evidence of a low crime rate.
- Victim surveys and police figures characteristically show different incidences of crime.
- It might be in the interests of the police to show they are more effective than they are (where funding depends on meeting targets), or less effective than they are (where this can be used to leverage more resources).

> ## KEY CONCEPT
>
> Deviance theory suggests that being deviant has less to do with actually being different than being judged and treated as different by others. Stanley Cohen (1972) pointed to a process involved in labelling individuals or groups as 'deviant' where the mass media, politicians or other spokespersons (perhaps priests, magistrates or the police) identify particular groups as socially dangerous and undermining social norms. By exaggerating, distorting and sometimes even inventing narratives about these groups, and then using their access to popular opinion to publicize their views, these influential individuals play on public fears and prejudices and thereby – sometimes unintentionally – release and/or aggravate widespread unease (a MORAL PANIC) concerning the alleged threat to public morality.

SOCIAL CONTROL IN SOCIOLOGICAL THEORY

Sociologists have generally believed that social control is necessary to modern societies, given that older forms of customary and communal authority broke down with industrialization. For example, early industrial labourers had to be taught the habits of punctuality, hard work and thrift at the workplace. In the early factories, employers often complained that workers would arrive drunk, take off feast days and often not turn up at all on Monday mornings. 'Clocking on' (inserting clock cards into a machine), penalties for lateness and other forms of surveillance were instituted to overcome these 'bad habits'. In Box 11.1, we pinpoint some key moments in the evolution of sociological thinking concerning social control.

BOX 11.1 Social control: an evolving discourse

Societal-wide systems of social control

Social welfare, prisons, asylums, children's homes, mass schooling and even the extension of voting rights are all vehicles through which those with power, wealth and authority can control dissent and potential rebellion. This need not mean that there is some giant conspiracy at work; the 'exigencies of capitalism' cannot explain everything. The professional and upper classes may harbour and seek to reproduce their nostalgic image of a peaceful, rural community. In addition, the poor, and not the rich, are the principal targets of violence and crime. Their greater exposure often predisposes them to favour more extreme measures of social control, such as hanging, public executions and beatings.

Deviance and its amplification

Since the 1970s, sociologists have used the notion of social control more imaginatively to describe general pressures to induce conformity. Stanley Cohen (1972) referred to the moments when the official agents of social control, such as the police or courts, swing into action against drug takers or youth gangs as MORAL PANICS. The negative labels the media use to depict groups that have become 'folk devils' in the public imagination to some extent condition their interventions. In a complicated feedback loop, some of these groups actually relish their public notoriety – so a process of 'deviancy amplification' develops as each side plays to the gallery.

Michel Foucault's key contribution

Foucault made further conceptual breakthroughs (see Global Thinkers 11). In *Discipline and Punish* (1977), he echoes some Marxist views in seeing the 'Great Incarcerations' of the nineteenth century as part of a common design. As Cohen (1985: 25–6) argued, for Foucault: 'thieves into prisons, workers into factories, lunatics into asylums, conscripts into barracks and children into schools were all corralled in the service of capital'. However, Foucault also pointed to more subtle forms of surveillance and discipline. Instead of brutal spectacles like the guillotine, the panopticon (an all-seeing tower in a prison) designed by Bentham engaged in unobtrusive but unremitting surveillance. Discipline was not merely external but good for you. Psychiatrists, teachers and social workers became unwitting agents of social control.

Social control today

In wealthy contemporary societies, technology has considerably enhanced the capacity for surveillance. Closed-circuit TV (CCTV) systems are placed in many shopping malls and busy streets, while computerized databases and the internet have generated a new set of 'footprints' that can be followed by a determined investigator. On average, adults in the developed world have their details recorded on 300 databases. Lett et al. (2010) have examined how the public reacted to the installation of a CCTV system in the streets of a Canadian town.

Sources: Cohen (1972, 1985: 25–6); Foucault (1977); Lett et al. (2010); Mayer (1983: 17–38).

MURDER MOST FOUL

Earlier we outlined some key methodological difficulties in thinking about crime. Nonetheless, it is doubtful whether misreporting, statistical anomalies and definitions alone can explain the vast differences in certain recorded crime rates between countries. Take the case of the murder (or 'intentional homicide') rate in the 15 worst affected countries (Figure 11.1).

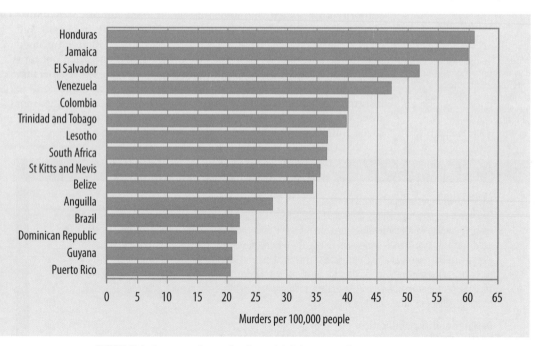

FIGURE 11.1 Reported murder (homicide) rate in the 15 worst countries, 2007/8, per 100,000 people

Notes: Anguilla, Colombia and the Dominican Republic figures are for 2007, all others for 2008. International crime statistics take time to collect and are usually three or four years out of date. Where there are multiple sources available, we have consistently cited the higher rather than the lower figure, and the internationally recognized, rather than national, statistic.

Source: UNODC (2011).

Although we must be cautious because of the statistical problems already outlined, there appear to be some patterns in the data presented over the years. In the early part of this millennium, many of the highest ranking homicide countries had recently experienced rapid social change as political circumstances altered dramatically. On the list of high scorers were Russia, Estonia, Lithuania, Latvia, Belarus, Ukraine, Kyrgyzstan, Moldova, Poland, Georgia and Armenia, which, as we can see from Figure 11.1, have disappeared a decade later. Before 1989, repressive communist parties had controlled and provided the citizens of these countries with welfare systems (however grim and uniform). Highly competitive forms of capitalism (sometimes called 'mafia capitalism') then suddenly replaced the party and welfare systems, with dramatic effects on the murder rate. The authorities now seemed to have tamed the worst excesses of this period. Countries that still appear on the list include South Africa, which experienced a massive shift from rigid apartheid control on the movement of Africans to free labour mobility. Colombia and Jamaica, which also appear again, are marked by the presence of strong drug cartels that have seized state authority in some areas. In such circumstances, political uncertainty, social distress, a breakdown of routine policing, and a loss of community cohesion may well provide the underlying conditions in which murder rates go up. Small countries with weak state structures are also prominent in the list.

To these particular observations, we add the general point that recent major transformations – especially the growing inequalities associated with marketization and globalization – have played some role in increasing the incidence and character of certain kinds of crime at the global level. In the next section, after a brief examination of recent estimates of these, we discuss the main likely causes of increasing transnational criminality.

GLOBALIZATION AND CRIME

For many years, international tourism has been the largest legitimate sector of the global economy. The largest without the qualifying adjective, however, is global crime, the five most profitable forms of which bring in profits of US$591bn (The Allegiant.org 2011). International criminal activity can include anything from people trafficking (smuggling immigrants or illegal workers), trade in forbidden goods (such as medicines or artefacts from ancient civilizations), computer fraud, violating patent, licence or copyright agreements, illegal arms dealing, smuggling cigarettes, alcohol and stolen cars, and the trade in drugs.

Indeed, the drug trade remains the most lucrative criminal activity and its consequences are highly corrosive. The turnover in the world heroin market went up more than twentyfold from 1970 to 1990, while the cocaine trade increased more than fiftyfold over the same period (Strange 1996: 114). The UN Office on Drugs and Crime (UNODC 2011: 8) estimated that, in 2010, the cocaine market was worth US$37bn in North America and US$33bn in Europe. This served to sustain the habit of 210 million people who used illicit drugs each day, 200,000 of whom die daily. Nevertheless, some other activities are beginning to compete with illegal drugs as key sources of income from international crime. People trafficking across borders, thought to be the fastest growing criminal activity, is particularly notable among these. Estimates vary, but the US Federal Bureau of Investigation claims that this was equal in value to $9.5bn in 2005 (cited in Shelley 2007: 198). The US government estimates that 600,000–800,000 people are smuggled worldwide annually, while the ILO argues that if those forced into migration are included in the figures, the number at any one time could be as high as 12 million (Miko 2007: 40). Most of these are women who end up in forced prostitution or sexual slavery, not to mention children who all too often are used for child labour, pornography or sexual activity. Ebbe (2008: 18) cites data from the International Organization for Migration claiming that each year more than 500,000 women and children are trafficked into Western Europe alone, mostly from the new states that emerged after the collapse of the USSR.

It is possible to gain an overall view of the extent of global crime by trying to estimate the extent of global money laundering. This is an essential activity both for local and transnational criminals, since they need to find ways of concealing the cash they 'earn' while attempting to 'clean' it by transferring it into legal businesses. This provides them with the same opportunities as lawful businesses to gain the advantages of safe, long-term capital accumulation as opposed to juggling money between different spending activities and risky venues (Palan 2009). Casinos, hotels, housing estates or building companies are typical legal investment outlets for transnational organized criminals.

The IMF and World Bank estimated the value of illegal global money laundering in 2002 at around US$1 trillion (Thachuk 2007: 17, 20). However, in 1999, an Australian scholar (Walker 1999) suggested that this figure was probably nearer US$2.8 trillion, although some of this comes from the tax evasion activities in which many legal businesses engage. There are several avenues through which to launder criminal money. These include mingling dirty money with the legal earnings of businesses such as nightclubs or restaurants, purchasing businesses or the items they produce before selling them on to lawful companies (Lilley 2006: 72–8), or siphoning dirty money through the 70 or more tax havens (offshore banking services) that currently exist. With organized crime and offshore banking closely interdependent, it is no accident that they have developed conjointly as cash from the drug trade in the USA flows into the various tax havens (Palan 2009: 35).

EXPLAINING THE GROWTH OF GLOBAL CRIME

While no single factor can explain the upsurge in transnational crime, certain key causes stand out. In what follows you will notice how entangled these are. First, the more open borders and increased international trade accompanying globalization and the deregulation of finance and economic activity have given legitimate individual investors, tourists, banks and TNCs new opportunities to prosper and earn higher profits. These same opportunities, however, have also enabled cross-border crime to blossom. Two examples will illustrate this well. First, Palan (2009: 47) claims that many legal businesses set up subsidiary companies and arrange some of their contracts in tax havens to lower their tax burden and evade restrictive regulations. In addition, the tax havens guarantee opacity, which includes the promise that the true ownership of assets will remain difficult to determine. This also provides 'great opportunities' for criminal businesses to route their dirty money through, and establish their own businesses in, tax havens. They are then able to channel their earnings into lawful businesses via legal banks and other companies. Second, the greater flows of transport across the now more open borders have also increased the opportunities for smuggling, especially in the EU and North America. Thus, partly in anticipation of the North American Free Trade Agreement (NAFTA) in 1994, Mexico deregulated its trucking industry in 1989 so that by 1996 around 220,000 vehicles were crossing the US border each day (Andreas 2000: 134).

Second, the widespread adoption of neoliberal economic policies, often under G7 and especially US pressure, has also exercised a powerful influence. Those who profit from the drug trade are primarily 'drug barons', smugglers and dealers. However, increased poverty, especially among peasants, linked to, among other pressures, land loss, reduction of government subsidies, increased competition from foreign companies and falling farm prices, has driven many poor farmers to become suppliers. Switching to more competitive and lucrative crops seems a rational, not to say enterprising, strategy compared with coping with the falling incomes from growing legal crops. It is hardly surprising, therefore, that farmers in countries like Afghanistan, Bolivia, Nepal and Jamaica have chosen this option. In fact, in some places, growing coca, opium poppies or marijuana allows farmers to ride the tiger of the global neoliberal economy without it ripping them apart.

Third, the same technological revolutions in ICTs and transportation that have enabled legal businesses to benefit from economic globalization have also underpinned a proliferation of transnational criminal activities. Clearly, internet facilities, mobile phones and laptops enhance the ability of criminal gangs to coordinate their activities over distances, but they also enable them to send information and warnings to their own or other gangs. These might concern risks such as impending police raids or the need to alter supply routes (Castells

1998: 198). Computerization and electronic banking further facilitate the laundering of dirty money, as they enable gangs to move money secretly and rapidly through a variety of national banks and/or into offshore banking havens such as the Cayman Islands or Luxembourg (Williams and Baudin-O'Hayon 2002: 132). Technological innovations in the transport of commercial cargo by rail, sea and air have also cut the costs of moving goods and speeded up trade flows. For example, the carrying capacity of tankers and ships has risen massively in recent decades, while containerization has simultaneously become standard practice. By the mid-1990s, some ships could carry up to 6,000 containers but, with growing international trade, it becomes impossible, even for armies of customs officials, to search every ship, which has thousands of containers, to look for illicit substances (Andreas 2002: 41).

Fourth, geopolitical changes have also contributed to rising transnational crime. China's reunification with Hong Kong in 1997 is one example. Ahead of this event, some Hong Kong Triad criminal gangs migrated to various countries in the world, especially to those with established Chinese ethnic communities such as the North American Pacific and east coast seaboards (Chu 2002). Another was the establishment of the EU single market. The collapse of the USSR and ending of the Cold War proved especially critical, for these transformations resulted in the rise of many new states, the reunification of Germany, and the widespread removal, or easing, of previous barriers to the movement of people, money and goods. This, in turn, made it possible for illegal, as well as legal, commodities to flow in and out of former Soviet Union countries and across Europe on a vast scale – currencies, foreign and IMF loans, cigarettes, stolen cars, women trafficked for illegal sex, weapons, nuclear material and other commodities (Castells 1998: 193).

Fifth, the role of nation-states and IGOs in criminalizing certain activities by enforcing the prohibition of particular substances and activities is also extremely important, as it reduces the supply of certain commodities that consumers desire, pushes up their price and creates opportunities for making huge illegal profits (Andreas and Nadelmann 2009; Castells 1998). In effect, 'prohibition is at the nub of organized crime' (Serrano 2002: 16).

Finally, there is a sense, too, in which the worlds of lawful and illicit economic activity 'coexist … merge and interpenetrate' (Mittelman 2009: 171). It is not always easy to see where their borders begin and end. They are both empowered by all the changes outlined and driven by the impulsions of profit, competition and enterprise. This has several consequences. One is that the overlap between lawful and illicit economic activity and their co-dependence on the same global processes mean that crime is 'tunnelling deeply to the roots of civil society' (Mittelman 2009: 173). The 'social disintegration' of some societies, which is associated with globalization, unemployment, declining welfare and governments' insistence on pushing for ever more neoliberal market reforms while separating these from social policy considerations, does not help. Burbach et al. (1997: 22) offered a similar analysis when they suggested that increased inequality, which the media exacerbate, 'make[s] people more and more cynical as they see that the rich take what they want, and then taunt the rest of society through the media, the movies and advertising with the "good life" of consumerism'. The result, according to Mittelman (2009: 172), is a 'growing culture of crime disembedded from the structures of society and resistant to eradication'. All this makes it extremely difficult for governments to control transnational criminal activity, especially when they are reluctant to cooperate with other countries.

A PAUSE TO REFLECT

Punishment for serious crimes varies a good deal. For example, the death penalty has been retained in 22% of the 193 UN-recognized countries and territories, while in the USA, 34 of the 50 states permit the death penalty. How do we account for the different legal responses to murder (unlawful homicide)? In the countries or states where convicted perpetrators are jailed, rather than hanged, gassed or electrocuted, what evidence is there of successful rehabilitation?

DRUGS: DEMAND AND SUPPLY

The trade in drugs crucially depends on two things. First, there is a massive demand for illegal substances, especially, although not solely, in Europe and the USA. The UN Office on Drugs and Crime (UNODC 2005) has estimated that the industry caters for the needs of around 5% of all adults aged over 15 in the world, although this figure includes cannabis. Second, the trade depends on the pitiful need of farmers in a number of supplier countries to continue to grow drugs – a dependence that links the poorest in the poor countries to the most desperate in the rich countries. As Hargreaves (1992: 3) commented on the extent of the demand in the USA in the late 1980s and early 1990s:

> In 1990, one in five people arrested for any crime were said to be hooked on cocaine or crack. Americans spend a staggering US$110,000 million a year on drugs (US$28,000 million on cocaine), more than double the profits of all the Fortune 500 companies put together and the equivalent of America's entire gross agricultural income.

Around 5–6 million US residents casually, or habitually, use illegal drugs. If demand is virtually insatiable, what happens on the supply side of the transaction? Take the case of Bolivia. This poor Latin American country was already the largest producer of raw coca leaf in the world, but it tripled its production of refined cocaine between 1989 and 1991, placing it in the number two slot worldwide. (Coca is 'refined' by mixing the leaves with sulphuric acid, paraffin and lime, before being dried for export. We do not invite you to try this recipe!)

Hargreaves (1992: 34–6) recounts the story of a Bolivian coca farmer called 'Paredes', who had previously raised pigs and sheep and grown maize. When drought struck in 1983, his animals died one by one and his crops failed. The ground was so hard that he could not even bury the animals. He left for the coca-growing area where, after many misadventures, he managed to obtain title to five hectares of land. He worked on another farmer's plot in exchange for a promise of seeds and seedlings, but when the farmer refused to honour his promise, Paredes stole some seeds. He had his first full harvest 18 months later; he was in the coca-growing business. He, like thousands of other farmers, resorted to coca growing because virtually any other economic endeavour was fraught with insecurity. Between 1980 and 1985, Bolivia's economy nose-dived; GNP dropped by 20%, unemployment increased from 6 to 20%, and inflation rose to an amazing 24,000% a year. It is hardly surprising that coca offered such an attractive alternative. Evo Morales, a former coca farmer and now Bolivia's president, has strongly supported coca growers.

A PAUSE TO REFLECT

The 'war on drugs' (President Nixon coined the phrase) cost a great deal of money and is widely seen as ineffective. Suppressing the demand for drugs is less popular than suppressing the supply, even though the former might yield better results. Is this 'war' simply a way of assuaging popular opinion? Is it time to legalize drugs, or perhaps certain drugs, license their sale, and tax the suppliers and customers? What difficulties would such a strategy cause?

Given its social and economic importance to some countries, the drug trade also tends to erode political life, with no firm distinction made between illegal and legal businesses in Russia, Somalia, Jamaica, Afghanistan, Colombia and Indonesia. The connections between crime, politics and business are often so seamless that the players can barely tell the difference. Even where there have been determined efforts to crack down on the drug trade, sometimes with the help of foreign aid, success has been limited. Let us take three examples:

1. In the 1980s, the George Bush Sr administration provided Colombia with financial aid and military personnel to crack the power of the notorious Medellín drug cartel, which had effectively acted as a state within a state. After a year on the run, Pablo Escobar, the world's biggest cocaine boss, was finally cornered. Despite his capture, he was still influential enough to dictate the terms of his imprisonment. He wanted, and got, a 10-acre site, with its own football field and luxurious furnishings. The authorities had effectively become a free security squad to protect him from his many enemies (Hargreaves 1992: xi). Meanwhile, drug money fuelled the spread of weapons and this led to kidnapping, extortion and increased attempts to intimidate officials such as judges and the police while inter-gang violence intensified (Serrano and Toro 2002: 170–7).

2. The attempt to eradicate the drug industry in Colombia, which eventually produced some results, merely encouraged its spread to other areas of Latin America (Campbell and Bowcott 2008: 19). For example, peasant distress, associated with Mexico's adoption of structural adjustment programmes in the 1980s and its increased integration into the US economy following the inception of NAFTA in 1994, played a key role in propelling Mexico into becoming a major drug-producing country (see Figure 11.2). However, the US attempt to control Colombian drug trafficking in the 1980s drove the Mexican/Colombian cartels into finding an alternative route. This resulted in Mexico becoming one of the world's main suppliers of cocaine (20–30%) and marijuana to the USA. Serrano and Toro (2002: 162) estimated that, during the 1980s, up to 300,000 Mexican peasants were earning money through illegal drug cultivation.

3. The 'war on terror', initiated by George Bush Jr, started with an invasion of Afghanistan (2001) and the displacement of the Taliban regime. Although dedicated to a radical and confrontational style of Islam, the Taliban at least had some commitment to uprooting opium production. The American invasion and the unsettled conditions that followed gave poppy growers a renewed lease of life, with the proportion of world heroin sourced in Afghanistan moving from 76% in 2003 to 83% in 2009 (Figure 11.2).

Before leaving this account of the global drug trade, we should remember that it has consequences other than fostering violence and political and civil unrest in supplier countries. The most obvious is that, as its victims struggle to feed their addiction and rival local gangs fight to secure commercial drug territories, the industry vastly increases the levels of national, domestic and violent crime. This then endangers the health and even lives of those involved, whether through violent struggles or simply the impact of drug abuse on users and the risk of contracting HIV/AIDS through needles. These cumulative health risks, along with the loss of income for users and their families as their capacity for employment declines, contribute to the health and welfare bills that governments and taxpayers must endure. Finally, drug abuse has also penetrated international sports. Before 1989, Cold War rivalry fuelled abuse because governments behind the iron curtain, which were intent on demonstrating the strength of the Soviet bloc and its allies, encouraged athletes to take performance-enhancing drugs. Since then, the causes are mostly the increasing pressure to commercialize sport and illegal betting. Thus, gold medallists or sports professionals like golfers or tennis players stand to make fortunes

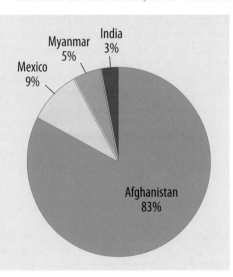

FIGURE 11.2 Shares (percentage) of world heroin production, 2009
Source: UNODC (2011: 71).

in product endorsements, appearance fees, or TV commercials. With ever more sophisticated and difficult-to-detect performance-enhancing drugs, and with large rewards in the offing, it has become extremely difficult to regulate international sports.

WHITE-COLLAR CRIME

White-collar crimes, which involve fraud or deception, are those that the more respectable members of society perpetrate. Easier access across borders, computer link-ups, improved means of transport, and modern forms of communication all make these crimes easier to commit. Mostly, they require either the complicity of reputable officials or professionals working for the police, customs, a law firm, bank or business, or the capacity to deceive such officials. Frequently, smuggling of some kind is the main intent. The EU is a case in point, since there is no overall authority yet there are open borders between countries. Where sales tax rates differ, as they do for alcohol and cigarettes, smuggling takes place on a massive scale. Although often carried out as a family enterprise by tourists and visitors, cigarette smuggling is big business. Thachuk (2007: 15) thinks that it is likely that around one-third of cigarettes consumed in Britain are smuggled into the country. Moving away from Europe, Desroches (2003) believes that criminal gangs are heavily involved in the illegal transport of cigarettes into Canada from the USA. The production and sale of pirated or counterfeit goods, such as luxury watches, handbags and fake medicines, have also increased rapidly in recent years and may form around 7% of world commerce (Thachuk 2007: 17).

Smuggling is often so large in volume that it threatens legitimate trade and can be used to corrupt state officials. Massive 'turf wars' result as criminal gangs carve up exclusive territories the better to suborn bureaucrats, set up extortion rackets and gain access to illegal goods. The murder rate in Moscow went up by 50% between 1992 and 1995, much of it explained by the attempts by 3,000 organized gangs to drive out their competitors (UNRISD 1995: 72). There was so little distinction between criminal and state activities in Russia that people plundered state arsenals of weapons for private profit. They fed submachine guns to terrorist organizations and even some of Russia's nuclear arsenal was for sale on the international market. In *Russia in the Abyss*, Nobel prize-winning writer Alexander Solzhenitsyn (1998), a former arch enemy of the Communist Party, excoriated Russia's post-Soviet rulers, claiming that 'Russia is ruled by a band of selfish people who are indifferent to the fate of the people and do not even care whether they live or die' (*Daily Telegraph*, 2 June 1998).

Outright criminal activity also took hold in the respectable corridors of Wall Street and the City of London. In 1989, Michael Milken, a respectable bonds dealer, was indicted on 98 charges of fraud and racketeering, although he was only convicted of six lesser charges and sentenced to 10 years. Known as the 'junk bond king', he was released in less than two years. ('Junk bonds' offered a high yield but had an even higher rate of default.) Also common was 'insider trading', which refers to confidential information that is misused to inflate or collapse a share price. In 1994, changes in the share price that only insider information could explain preceded one-third of the 100 largest merger deals in the USA (Burbach et al. 1997: 71).

CORPORATE CRIME

As indicated earlier, because jurisdictions and definitions differ, it is sometimes difficult to decide quite what constitutes a crime. The cases of Enron, Union Carbide and Goldman Sachs, however, provide three examples of 'corporate crime'.

Reckless speculation in the US stock market in the 1990s brought a dramatic collapse and bankruptcies. By early 2002, the value of US shares had dropped by US$4 trillion. Enron, energy supplier and one of the 50 biggest public companies in the USA, which recorded more than US$100bn in sales and US$1bn in earnings in 2001, was the most dramatic example of the crash. Within six months, the company was bankrupt, having lost $90bn in market value.

The shocking thing about this was not so much that this massive company had collapsed, but that its managers and auditors were aware of the company's financial position and had sought illegally to conceal it from investors and employees. Company executives and board members quietly unloaded shares, while Arthur Andersen, the previously respectable global accountancy firm, shredded evidence that demonstrated its awareness or complicity in these transactions. About 25,000 employees lost most of their savings.

Enron shocked not only radical critics of corporate power but also people who were heavily involved in the world of finance, such as Felix Rohatyn, a former governor of the New York Stock Exchange, managing director of the financiers Lazard Frères & Company and, from 1997 to 2000, the US ambassador to France. Rohatyn (2002: 6) held that 'a large proportion of the stock market was becoming a branch of show business and it was driving the economy instead of the other way around'. Beyond the 'sordid situation of Enron itself' lay the integrity of financial markets in general where deregulation and a lack of ethical conduct might ultimately undermine capitalism per se. Certainly, his remarks seem prescient in the light of the financial collapse of 2008 described in Chapter 4. At the end of January 2006, Ken Lay, Enron's founder and former chair, and Jeffrey Skilling, the company's former CEO, were finally tried in Houston for fraud and conspiracy.

Our second case is about the horrific leak of lethal gases from the Union Carbide plant in Bhopal, India, in December 1984 (see Chapter 10). Pearce and Tombs (1993: 187–211) describe the dire consequences of the event. It exposed more than 200,000 local people to fumes, seriously affected 60,000, more than 20,000 were injured, and about 10,000 may have died since as a direct result of the leak. Babies are still being born with birth defects. The parent company in the USA denied it had a bad safety record, claimed its Indian subsidiary was to blame, and sought to deflect attention by claiming that sabotage was involved. The company managed to twist the arm of the Indian government into accepting a very low settlement of US$470m for all victims. This deal was in exchange for a guarantee that Union Carbide would escape prosecution. The company's lawyers deflected an attempt to try the case in the USA, where they would probably have been awarded substantial damages. They were able to override the parent company's central role in the design and installation of the plant and 'finger' the Indian government for its poor regulatory apparatus and inadequate inspectorate.

As we have seen, fraud by major international financial institutions is not new, but against the backdrop of the global financial meltdown of 2008, the alleged actions of Goldman Sachs, a major US investment bank, are particularly notable. In April 2010, America's Securities and Exchange Commission (SEC) took out a lawsuit against Goldman Sachs. The SEC accused the bank of collaborating with Paulson & Company, a major hedge fund, which duped investors such as the Royal Bank of Scotland into buying a package of securities based on a special selection of subprime mortgages that those involved allegedly knew were likely to fail. The investors asked that ACA Management, an independent mortgage security expert, examine the securities. Persuaded that Paulson also intended to invest in these same securities, the latter agreed to validate them. However, Paulson apparently took steps to profit handsomely by betting through a credit derivative that the more the securities collapsed in value, the greater would be its own financial return (Clark 2010; Hutton 2010). Thus, Goldman Sachs deliberately set up one client/partner to lose while another apparently benefited at its expense. Similar cases of fraud – making balance sheets look stronger than they are to bid up share values and bonus payments and tax evasions – may have been widespread in the financial industries.

UNDERSTANDING TERRORISM TODAY

The challenges posed by terrorism were never more visible than on 11 September 2001, when two commercial aeroplanes flew into the World Trade Center in New York and another targeted the Pentagon. The death toll was large – 2,889 people died in the World

ISLAMIC JIHADISTS

In the contemporary context, they are radical, fundamentalist followers of Islam who are prepared to take up arms or commit acts of terrorism in defence or pursuit of their religious beliefs. Many scholars of Islam insist that 'jihad' means 'struggle' or 'striving', with no necessary assumption of violence. However, in political rhetoric and current contemporary use, there is definitely a connotation of the use of violence.

Trade Center and at least 189 in Washington – and included hundreds of foreigners from 60 countries. The loss of 343 firefighters and 78 police officers, who had rushed to help, gave the 9/11 tragedy particular poignancy. As Alexander (2002: 1) says, these outrages were 'unprecedented in scale, coordination and timing'. That they happened in one of the world's most important cities at the heart of its financial and media districts, which was, of course, intentional, meant that the story was broadcast to the far corners of the world in graphic and explicit detail.

As we now know, Islamic jihadists perpetrated the atrocity and followed up their attack against the 'West' with others in Madrid and London. In London, on 7 July 2005, suicide bombers operating simultaneously on the underground train system and a bus killed 52 people and injured more than 770. Although not all terrorist incidents are driven by or connected with Islam, many of them are. In 2010 alone, there were nearly 5,000 victims of terrorism worldwide (Table 11.1).

TABLE 11.1 Worldwide terrorism incidents, 2010

Country	Attacks	Dead	Wounded	Hostage	Victims
Somalia	33	437	896	0	1,333
Iraq	19	265	927	0	1,192
Pakistan	15	214	520	26	760
Afghanistan	20	255	214	1	470
Russia	3	41	202	0	243
Burma	1	10	170	0	180
India	3	39	80	12	131
Iran	2	24	83	0	107
Congo, Democratic Republic	6	84	3	16	103
Sudan	1	10	4	80	94
Yemen	4	48	31	0	79
Nigeria	1	12	38	0	50
Algeria	2	22	20	1	43
Philippines	1	10	30	0	40
Turkey	1	10	14	0	24
Colombia	1	11	0	0	11
Ecuador	1	10	0	0	10
Total	**114**	**1,502**	**3,232**	**136**	**4,870**

Note: The data cover only incidents involving between 10–19 casualties.
Source: US National Counterterrorism Center (2010).

In our discussion of global religion in Chapter 17, we consider whether there is doctrinal support for violent jihad, why a minority of Muslims have turned to terrorism, and what opportunities exist for peaceful coexistence between people of many faiths and those with none. By contrast, here we want to gain some deeper understanding of the origins and nature of terror and terrorism. Indeed, the very horror of these events demands that we ask difficult questions to try to explain the phenomenon.

ORIGINS AND DEFINITIONS

According to Tilly (2004: 8–9), the word 'terror' entered the Western political vocabulary as a description of the French revolutionaries' actions against their domestic enemies. The Reign of Terror (1793/4), over which revolutionaries like Robespierre (Figure 11.3) presided, was meant to strike fear into the hearts and minds of those who opposed the new regime. About 17,000 legal executions took place, many of them in public using the newly invented guillotine, with another 23,000 illegal ones. The revolutionary armies also brutally repressed the counter-revolutionary uprising in the Vendée (1793–9). Revolutionary governments have frequently used state-supported terror to eliminate their enemies and intimidate those who might sympathize with them. Think of the purges Joseph Stalin ordered (1936–8), which, together with deportations to labour camps and state-induced famines, probably resulted in the deaths of more than 10 million Soviet citizens. Think also of the madcap deurbanization policies of Pol Pot in Kampuchea, together with his attacks on unpopular ethnic minorities and Buddhist monks, which resulted in the deaths of between 1.5 and 2.3 million people – one in eight of the population – over the period 1975–79.

The problem with seeing state-induced terror merely as a property of revolutionary fervour getting out of hand is that there are many examples of governments without any revolutionary credentials perpetrating state terror. We can think of the Argentine junta after 1976 when between 20,000 and 30,000 people 'disappeared' in a 'dirty war' conducted by sections of the police and military. General Pinochet in Chile ordered the kidnapping, torture and disappearance of opponents to his right-wing regime. Apartheid South Africa, Mobutu's Zaire, Idi Amin's Uganda, Stroessner's Paraguay, 'Papa Doc' Duvalier's Haiti, and many other regimes show that holding onto power through terror can arise in a number of circumstances. Sometimes states justify their use of terror by arguing that they need to use such means because their opponents are terrorists.

© STEFANO BIANCHETTI/CORBIS

FIGURE 11.3 Maximilien de Robespierre (1758–94)

In a speech of 5 February 1794, French revolutionary leader Robespierre coupled terror with virtue, declaring:

> If the spring of popular government in time of peace is virtue, the springs of popular government in revolution are at once virtue and terror: virtue, without which terror is fatal; terror, without which virtue is powerless. Terror is nothing other than justice, prompt, severe, inflexible; it is therefore an emanation of virtue; it is not so much a special principle as it is a consequence of the general principle of democracy applied to our country's most urgent needs.

Robespierre fell victim to the terror he had helped to unleash, dying on the guillotine a few months after making this extraordinary speech.

Source: www.fordham.edu/halsall/mod/robespierre-terror.html.

CHARACTERISTICS AND WIDER IMPLICATIONS OF NONGOVERNMENT TERRORISM

The US State Department defines terrorism as: 'politically motivated violence perpetrated against non-combatant targets by subnational groups or clandestine agents, usually intended to influence an audience' (cited by Tilly 2004: 7). This is similar to Bergesen and Lizardo's

(2004: 38) definition of subnational/transnational terrorism as: 'the premeditated use of violence by a non-state group to obtain a political, religious, or social objective through fear or intimidation directed at a large audience'. Since the 9/11 attacks on America, much attention has been directed at understanding the phenomenon of non-state or subnational terrorism while thinking through its wider implications. There are many reasons for this but the following stand out:

1. The US and other governments used these events as a pretext for embarking on wars in Afghanistan and Iraq, and for intensifying security and surveillance measures including reducing some civil liberties.
2. Islamic terrorism demonstrated that while deploying easily accessible destructive technologies and hidden worldwide networks linked by ICT, a handful of individuals could breach highly sophisticated security systems and wreak havoc and fear even in the world's most powerful military state. This highlighted the vulnerability and weakness of states, international institutions and the global economy (Thachuk 2007).
3. Unlike guerrilla movements, which normally attack military targets from their secret bases in remote rural areas, contemporary terrorists use concealment and disguise to attack civilians en masse in urban areas. This makes them not only highly dangerous but also extremely difficult to track or counter. Their hidden presence partly explains why governments adopt extreme measures to regain control.
4. The purpose of such acts of violent aggression is to harm groups of people who happen to be in the wrong place at the wrong time and whom the terrorists believe are jointly responsible for the wrongs they are trying to put right. The huge improvements in travel and communication that accompany globalization have reduced the constraints of distance and time that previously made it extremely difficult to reach and attack unknown people living far away. As Black (2004: 22) argues, technology 'both globalizes the possibility of terrorism and magnifies its destructive capability'.
5. Black (2004: 17–18) further suggests that these actions are designed to frighten governments and societies into restoring something the terrorists believe they have lost, such as a traditional culture, territory or political independence. The Palestinian demand for the return of land from Israel is an obvious example but there are many others.

GLOBALIZATION, STATES AND NONGOVERNMENT TERRORISM

Bergesen and Lizardo (2004: 43) argue that, like so much else, terrorism has itself become globalized. Its shifting character makes it more difficult to control and understand, thus some explanations fail to capture certain key structural dimensions. Bergesen and Lizardo (2004: 42–3) list six contemporary features:

1. Terrorist organizations have moved to a network form. Instead of a hierarchical cell with a single command structure, the organization has become more fluid, with many centres.
2. The identity of the organization is more difficult to pinpoint. For example, more than one organization or none will quite often claim responsibility for an attack.
3. Terrorist demands become hazier, vaguer or even nonexistent. There were, for instance, no specific demands made at the time of 11 September 2001.
4. There is movement towards more religious ideologies. This includes the Islamic jihadists, but also others like Aum Shinrikyo, a group that released the nerve gas sarin in the Tokyo underground in 1995, killing 12 and injuring thousands (see Juergensmeyer 2003). Earlier waves of terrorism focused on class demands, as with the Japanese Red Army or the German Red Army Faction (Baader-Meinhof gang) of the 1960s and 70s.
5. Terrorists disperse their targets globally rather than confine them to Europe and the Middle East. In recent years, there have been transnational terrorist attacks in Indonesia (Bali), Argentina, Kenya, Tanzania and the USA to name but five countries.

6. Terrorist violence is becoming more indiscriminate, with innocent citizens, 'noncombatants' or even passers-by being victims.

Bergesen and Lizardo (2004) also discuss some possible explanations for contemporary nongovernmental terrorism. Their bold suggestion, based on a comparative and historical analysis, runs as follows. Perhaps there are causal links between terrorism and successive phases of globalization. Could terrorism be a defensive reaction to the changes that hegemonic empires, now the USA, but earlier the Ottoman, Austro-Hungarian and British Empires, unleash? The historical precedents also suggest that terrorism arises and increases as the empire/hegemonic power is declining. This is because the empire is no longer able to enforce its will by economic power and consent alone. Instead, it uses military force, or the threat of military force, merely to maintain its position. This provokes the terrorists, who are further encouraged when the empire shows signs of being overstretched militarily.

A PAUSE TO REFLECT

The 'war on terror' was declared by President George W. Bush in 2001, some 30 years after the 'war on drugs' was declared. Will the fate of the war on terror be equally unsuccessful? What strategies and tactics can be deployed to discourage terrorism and how can these be promoted internationally?

Bergesen and Lizardo (2004) note that terrorists seem to come from organizations in autocratic, semi-peripheral states (see Global Thinkers 1). Others argue that some states provide an environment where terrorists can flourish, although this often applies equally to transnational criminals. 'Weak' states that lack legitimacy because their rulers place their own interests or those of their kin, ethnic group, region of origin or political faction above those of the public interest are one key example. In addition, such states are unable to police their borders effectively and fail to implement policies and regulations that might empower their citizens. As such, they provide 'excellent sanctuaries' (Williams and Baudin-O'Hayon 2002) where terrorists – and criminals – can hide and plan their various activities.

In certain cases, the capacity of terrorists to gain control of sections of the government through threat, extortion, deceit, shared ideological concerns and monetary inducements may culminate in a situation in which terrorist cells effectively 'mould' these states and their institutions to meet their own needs. To do so, they plan their future moves, recruit and train activists, and maintain active communications and networks with groups in other countries (Thachuk 2007: 9–11). Recent examples of such weak states are Afghanistan, Pakistan, Colombia, Sudan, Liberia, Sierra Leone, Angola and some Balkan states.

Another type of state that may operate to bolster global terrorism is highly authoritarian and oppressive, also perhaps internally divided and/or penetrated by foreign conspiratorial groups (Lilley 2006; Napoleoni 2004). Such states have been particularly useful for al-Qaeda, for they enable it to survive as a world network of quasi-autonomous cells, each able to plan its own conspiracies (Napoleoni 2004: 196–9). Obvious examples are Saudi Arabia and the Gulf Emirates, with Syria, Iran and Egypt following close behind.

WOMEN, VIOLENCE AND HEALTH

Many forms of violence against women – by the state, during wars or ethnic conflicts, or in domestic life – as well as more general forms of abuse continue to leave deep scars on contemporary global life. At times, they may even be life-threatening, but they always affect their physical and mental health.

GLOBAL THINKERS 11 MICHEL FOUCAULT (1926–84)

© BETTMANN/CORBIS

Discourses and knowledge

Foucault argued that no one can understand the world outside a given language and the concepts and assumptions it contains. Therefore, knowledge is the product of discourses. These are systems of metaphors, narratives and unwritten and unconscious conventions about what constitutes 'knowledge' and how it is to be obtained in any one era.

Power, knowledge and the regulation of bodies

Foucault suggested that specialized discourses associated with modernity – such as penology/criminology, psychiatry and medicine – increasingly confer power on those professional groups and government administrators who claim a monopoly of such knowledge. Power therefore has the following characteristics:

1. It is synonymous with knowledge, which generates the right and means to demand obedience to various disciplines.

2. It is double-edged because the disciplines demanded by modernity are simultaneously internalized by citizens – they believe these serve their interests – and externally enforced by regulations and sanctions.

3. Consequently, power diffuses everywhere in modern society, through all social relationships and wherever knowledge and professionalism are found. It is not necessarily concentrated in particular institutions or individuals.

4. In the extreme case of externally imposed regimes of control, citizens experience a high degree of panopticism, which means that aspects of their lives are subject to intense observation and regulation through the factory, the army, policing, the judicial system, the prison, the hospital/clinic/asylum and the school/college.

Biopower

The economic and military priorities of modernizing states require huge amounts of information and biopower – the need to control the productive and reproductive, and therefore the sexual, activities of the entire domestic population. Again, this involves a combination of individual self-discipline based on acquired knowledge, such as birth control techniques, and on external surveillance by professionals and institutions.

Power–knowledge under globalizing conditions

Foucault was concerned with national-based societies. However, we can adapt his ideas to a globalizing world society/economy. Thus, we could argue that global corporate capitalism exercises control over our consuming, leisured, hedonistic bodies through constant advertising, media exposure and peer group pressure. We also internalize consumerist orientations. We become knowledgeable, fashion-conscious and responsive spenders. With regard to health, we – and not the state – become exercise taking, dieting citizens who believe we must be morally responsible for our bodies, thus buying the commercialized diet regimes, private health plans, jogging kits and so on that the market provides.

Sources: Foucault (1973, 1977); Lee and Jackson (2002); Sheridan (1980).

STATES, WAR AND VIOLENCE AGAINST WOMEN

In this section, we consider institutionalized or 'public sector' male violence and its consequences. Historically, women and children have always tended to become the victims of violence through war (Mittelman 2009), but recent changes, sometimes linked to globalization, have increased the likelihood of this happening. These include:

*   the declining control that states now exert over their borders
*   the escalation of regional conflicts and civil wars, as in the Balkans in the aftermath of the Cold War

- the declining capacity of states to control or prevent armed conflict, as in Somalia, Liberia, the Democratic Republic of the Congo, and the drug-fuelled wars between the army and various gangs in Colombia
- the changing nature of warfare itself. Thus, certain types of weaponry, such as rocket-propelled grenades, landmines, mortars and small arms, have become more easily accessible and widely dispersed.

All this, in turn, seems to have altered the rules governing warfare, because previous codes of conduct that at least tried to minimize harm to noncombatants, especially women and children, have been abandoned (Jacobson et al. 2000). One consequence of this has been that women and children now make up 70–80% of the world's refugees (Kelly 2000: 53).

The highly gendered nature of state institutions and the way in which militarized masculinity creates a basis for organized violence have often placed women in difficult and subordinate situations (see Enloe 1989, 2000). One of the most appalling ways in which this set of circumstances has been played out has been the deployment of sexual violence against women, by state or other armed forces, as a deliberate strategy of war. Many feminists (for example Kelly 2000; Radford 2000) believe that this is partly because women are seen as the carriers of a nation's or tribe's culture. When combined with the persistence of deeply patriarchal cultures and some men's contempt for or even hatred of women, which the tensions of war intensify, there is a danger that 'women's bodies and women as a group' (Kelly 2000: 50) will be seen as targets of military aggression.

In war, the hatred of the enemy is 'expressed through and transformed into the hatred and violation of women' (Radford 2000: 177). Rape and other forms of violence against women in war become ways of humiliating the enemy, of capturing and dominating its territory, for 'women's bodies are constructed as ... territory to be conquered' (Kelly 2000: 50). Because of the children that may result from multiple rapes, however, they are also a means of destroying the enemy's culture and replacing it with that of the victor. All this was clearly and terribly manifested in Bosnia in the early 1990s and, according to Radford (2000), distressingly similar reasoning has been evident at times in the communal violence Hindu extremists pursued against Muslims.

WOMEN, HEALTH AND DOMESTIC VIOLENCE: COMPARISONS

We tend to assume that people are safest when at home but this turns out to be far from the case, especially for women. We explore this theme by considering the results of a recent world study by the World Health Organization (WHO). This covered urban and rural areas in 10 countries – Bangladesh, Brazil, Ethiopia, Japan, Peru, Namibia, Samoa, Serbia, Thailand and Tanzania. The WHO (2005) study showed that the greatest risk to women from violence occurs in their intimate relationships with husbands and, to a lesser degree, other male relatives. The WHO research identified four forms of risk:

1. Between 13 and 61% of women experience physical violence from their intimate partners in the course of a lifetime, while between 4 and 49% experience severe violence. The incidence was often higher in rural rather than urban areas and was especially pronounced in parts of Peru, Ethiopia, Tanzania and Bangladesh. It was lowest in Japan.
2. Husbands or partners committed between 6 and 59% of the acts of sexual violence. Sometimes, the victims of these attacks were very young women forced into early marriages.
3. The violence frequently began during a pregnancy and would then continue on a regular basis.
4. Between 20 and 75% of the women in the sample reported emotional or psychological abuse; between 12 and 58% reported it having occurred within 12 months prior to the survey. Examples of such controlling behaviour included restricting the woman's contact with her family and friends, demanding permission to seek healthcare, or consistently ignoring her.

Unfortunately, the reluctance of governments and official organizations to interfere in domestic/family life or to challenge patriarchal cultures amplifies the forms and effects of physical, emotional and sexual violence in the home. Consequently, much domestic and sexual violence against women and children goes unreported, so is rarely tackled: in effect, it is state sanctioned, as the perpetuation of so-called 'honour crimes' in India and Pakistan starkly demonstrates (Baxi et al. 2006). For example, transgressions of family codes of honour are considered so serious that it is not unusual for a family member to kidnap, torture and murder a woman – and sometimes her male partner – who wishes to marry or have sexual relations with someone from a different caste, culture or class. At times, revenge rapes also take place. During a 10-week period in the summer of 2010, for example, the police in India's northern states recorded 19 'honour killings'. However, many were listed as 'suicides', and for this and other reasons, the real figure is almost certainly at least 10 times higher (Chamberlain 2010). The violence that families inflict – with the collusion of police, tribal councils and local communities – contravenes constitutional law. Nevertheless, state and federal governments seem powerless to intervene, particularly during periods of rapid social change.

Domestic violence is also directly associated with ill health, especially permanent physical damage, reproductive problems (including miscarriages), memory loss, mental illness, dizziness and AIDS. Indeed, one of the most common ways women contract HIV/AIDS is from their husbands demanding unprotected sex after contracting the disease when working away from home.

REVIEW

All the issues addressed here – crime, drugs, terrorism and the violent abuse of women – testify to the need for a much more radical break with the international, regional and bilateral agreements of the post-1945 period. A series of interstate agreements cannot control cross-border crime, and until resources and alternative development initiatives are forthcoming to help people whose livelihoods depend on producing narcotics, it will be impossible to reduce the supply of drugs. Too little effort has been made to control the demand for illicit drugs. Similarly, the range of activities defined as 'terror' or 'terrorism' require a much greater understanding and a more sophisticated response than unilateral interventions – even by the world's superpower. Indeed, ineffective military intervention against terrorism or state-sponsored terrorism may actually signify the relative decline of a hegemonic power and provoke further acts of terrorism. In the case of violence against and abuse of women, much stronger globally enforceable moral codes coupled with constant exposure of injustice seem to be absolute preconditions for change. Certainly, the failure to control these continuing scourges of social life – intensifying partly because of globalization – point to the need for more effective bilateral agreements, much stronger transnational agencies, a deepening global consciousness and, perhaps ultimately, something like a world government.

Visit the companion website at www.palgrave.com/sociology/cohen3e for extra materials to check and expand your learning, including interactive self-test questions, mind maps making links between key themes, annotated web links to sociological research, data and key sociological thinkers, a searchable glossary and much more.

FURTHER READING

Transnational Threats: Smuggling and Trafficking in Arms, Drugs and Human Life (2007), edited by K. L. Thachuk, contains detailed material on all the forms of crime examined here.

L. Napoleoni's *Terror Inc: Tracing the Money behind Global Terrorism* (2004) provides a highly accessible discussion of the fascinating links between crime, governments, social institutions and terrorism, replete with numerous examples.

Many chapters in *States of Conflict: Gender, Violence and Resistance* (2000), edited by S. Jacobs et al., provide vivid case studies, coupled with careful analysis that helps to unravel this complex subject.

QUESTIONS AND ASSIGNMENTS

1. How useful are official statistics to the sociological study of crime? If there is so great a demand and so limitless a supply, is it possible to stop the trade in cocaine and heroin?

2. Show how patterns of social control have changed in contemporary societies.

3. What are the new features of contemporary terrorism?

4. Using specific examples, examine how and why many women's experiences of health and family life reflect the realities of gender oppression and political change.

PART 3
Experiences

12 Population and migration

The number of people living on earth has increased dramatically. Although estimates vary, in about 8000 BC there were 4.5 million people. In AD 1, there were 170 million. Two thousand years later, at the end of the twentieth century, there were about 6000 million (6 billion). Moreover, despite high infant mortality rates in poor countries, disease, poverty, famine and the spread of the HIV virus, their numbers are rising steeply, depending on certain assumptions (see Figure 12.3 below). On 30 October 2011, the UN chose Danica Camacho, a baby born in Manila, the Philippines, to symbolize the 7 billion mark. A number of projections suggest that the global population will peak at 9.3 billion in 2050. In this chapter, we explain how we measure population growth and ask whether the anxiety about overpopulation is exaggerated. We also consider how it might be possible to reduce population growth.

Steep rises in birth rates are normally most prevalent in agricultural societies and rural areas. The spectacular growth of urban populations is as much the result of migration to cities as of increasing family sizes. Increases in international migration often follow high levels of internal migration. Although the number of global migrants is small in relation to national migrants, their presence often provokes frenzied bursts of xenophobia in receiving countries. What new forms has international migration taken and what have been the reactions to this supposed 'threat'?

THE FEAR OF OVERPOPULATION

The fear of overpopulation is often the most prevalent concern of ordinary citizens. The rapid growth in the world's population has been a matter of fierce debate at least since Thomas Malthus (Figure 12.1) anonymously published his *Essay on the Principle of Population* in 1798, when the world's population was less than one-ninth its current size. The book was highly influential in the nineteenth century – perhaps as important as the writings of the French revolutionaries. It strongly informed the thoughts of Herbert Spencer (a major early British sociologist) and influenced Charles Darwin (Figure 12.2) and the social Darwinists. In the twentieth century, Malthusian ideas ramified through the work of the eugenicists (who wanted to produce a better class of person through selective breeding) and eventually into contemporary discussions of overpopulation in the light of the earth's fragile ecological balance.

Malthus attracted as many enemies as friends and followers. Karl Marx attacked his avocation of population restraint, sarcastically noting that Malthus had an indecent number of children himself. Here Marx was repeating a common misconception. Malthus did not have 11 children, as reputed, but three, only one of whom survived to adulthood. Marx (cited in Nicholls 1995: 324) wrote: 'Since [as Malthus argues] population is constantly tending to overtake the means of subsistence, charity is folly, a public encouragement of poverty. The state can therefore do nothing but leave the poor to their fate and, at the most, make death easy for them.' Nicholls' (1995) view is more sympathetic, but he does not dispute that Malthus was part of the conservative reaction to the French Revolution and was responding to the threat to family and property that certain revolutionary ideas foretokened.

Malthus thought that a breakdown of the old social order would accelerate a natural tendency for population to grow faster than food supply. His statistical calculations were simple. He assumed that while food supplies grow arithmetically (as in $1\rightarrow2\rightarrow3\rightarrow4$), population grows geometrically (as in $1\rightarrow2\rightarrow4\rightarrow8$). He thought the desire for sexual intercourse and the level of human fertility were likely to be constant. We now know that considerable variations in fertility can be caused, for example, by shifts in cultural norms, patterns of disease, birth control measures and increased affluence, but his thinking was reasonable at the end of the eighteenth century. Because of his assumption of constancy, Malthus reasoned that the only way population growth could be halted was through the painful sanction of famine.

FIGURE 12.1 Thomas Malthus (1766–1834), prophet of doom?
Would famine finally halt a population too large for the world's resources?

FIGURE 12.2 Charles Darwin (1809–82)
His work on natural selection was used by the social Darwinists to justify eugenic ideas.

Nicholls (1995) shows that in several important respects Malthus's contribution was subtler than Marx and his other detractors allowed:

- In later editions of his *Essay*, Malthus accepted that moral restraint (abstinence) and later marriage would impose additional constraints on overpopulation, short of famine.
- He was not a 'zero-growth' theorist and believed it was a religious duty to populate the world. He even lamented 'the present scanty population of the earth' at large.

- He thought emigration could help match population to resources.
- He was not, as Marx averred, against all forms of state intervention or the enemy of the working class. Indeed, he supported the early socialist Robert Owen in his attempts to promote legislation to limit the use of child labour in the cotton industry.

Nevertheless, there is no doubt that the expression 'Malthusian' is now back in fashion and is being used to signify concern about the imbalance between population and resources. Given the moderate pace of economic development and the limited take-up of birth control measures, some modern-day Malthusians argue that famine or other forms of severe social breakdown will act as Malthus suggested. So was Malthus right? In three areas, he was not:

1. His crude statistical calculations assumed the doubling of the European population every 25 years. In fact, as historical demographers have pointed out, the population has doubled every 50 years (approximately) since 1800.
2. War and disease proved more effective means of birth control than famine. For example, the heavy losses of young men in the First World War seriously slowed down population growth in France and the UK and led to pro-natalist policies in France, while the influenza pandemic of 1918/19 killed somewhere between 20 million and 40 million people.
3. The growth in European agriculture has more than kept pace with the growth in population. This is also true of much of Asia, with the partial exception of India.

Despite these major flaws in his analysis, Malthusian ideas have a nasty way of resurfacing. Let us take a few examples. A crude, discriminatory version of the Malthusian message was demonstrated by the eugenics movement, which promoted procreation among a favoured few. A similar logic, in more extreme versions, justified the Aryan breeding programme of the Nazis and the policies of the apartheid regime: covert sterilization for blacks, pro-natalism for whites. Another related example is the realization, long after the Second World War had ended, that the odious practices of Nazi Germany had spread to countries with a much more benign reputation. Following a newspaper exposé in 1997, it was revealed that between 1934 and 1976, more than 40,000 Norwegians, 6,000 Danes and 60,000 Swedes, mainly women, were sterilized. As late as 1953, the Swedish National Board of Health decided to sterilize 16-year-old 'Nils' against his wishes on the grounds that he was 'a sexually precocious mixed type', meaning that, according to the wall charts supplied by the State Institute of Racial Biology, he was not racially pure (*The Guardian*, 3 September 1997).

The population question is also now being coupled with ecological issues. This is an important aspect of global thinking best represented by the idea of 'Spaceship Earth'. Our planet is seen as an integrated living system dependent on the biosphere (a thin skin of earth, water and atmosphere). It has a limited and precarious life. Overpopulation may disrupt this system and cause destruction. In this kind of thinking, the sanctity of human life, which is at the heart of so much religious and ethical thought, is subordinated to the greater good of the planet.

UNDERSTANDING POPULATION GROWTH

Malthusian arguments are based on a complex mixture of science (perhaps 'perverted science'), surmise and prejudice. To oppose speculation and uninformed opinion, sociologists need to be aware of the basic toolkit of demographers, who deal with the size, composition, distribution of, and changes to, populations. Utilizing the *CIA World Factbook* and based on estimates for 2010, we now mention just a few of the elements that go into the calculations:

1. *The crude birth rate:* measures the number of live births per 1,000 members of a population in a given year. The US (2010) figure was 13.83 (down by 12.67 since 1947). The Kenyan rate was 53.8 in the mid-1980s but had fallen to 35.14 by 2010. Sharp drops have been generally evident in the advanced countries; for example the German rate is 8.21 (2010).

2. *The fertility rate:* computes the number of live births per woman over her lifetime and is another, perhaps more intuitive, way to measure population. It takes a fertility rate of at least 2.0 for a population in a developed country to replace itself. The fertility rate dropped from 3.8 in 1947 to 1.8 in the mid-1980s in the USA, and more dramatically in Western Europe. France and Italy (1.2) showed very low fertility rates in the 1990s. Singapore, interestingly, was also at 1.2 in the mid-1990s.

3. *The crude death rate:* an important way of correcting growth assumptions derived from the other two calculations above. In the USA it was 8.38 per 1,000 of the population in 2010. By comparison, Chad, a poor country in West Africa, had a death rate of 44.1 per 1,000 in the late 1980s, a situation made worse by famine and civil war. This had fallen to 15.79 by 2010. However, Haiti's was 32.31 in mid-2010, undoubtedly a reflection of the earthquake and the poor coordination of relief and resettlement efforts.

4. Closely related to the death rate is the *infant mortality rate (IMR):* the number of deaths among infants aged below one year per 1,000 of the infant population. Finland, Japan and France had low IMRs (less than 3.5) in 2010, while the USA was 6.14, well down on 2005. In the worst years of famine in Ethiopia, it was 229. The IMR and subsequent child deaths are particularly significant in determining fertility behaviour. If there is a good chance that your child will die, it is perfectly reasonable that you will seek to have more children to ensure against that contingency.

It is important to be cautious in utilizing statistical research because demographers can produce data, or interpretations of data, that can be misleading. If we measure and project long-term changes in healthcare, income, social behaviour, fertility choices, personal security, levels of pollution and many other factors, we can infer complex, perhaps dangerous, but also sometimes contradictory outcomes.

Returning to population growth, it would be foolish to deny that the current projections provide cause for concern. As Figure 12.3 shows, the world's population is due to grow to at

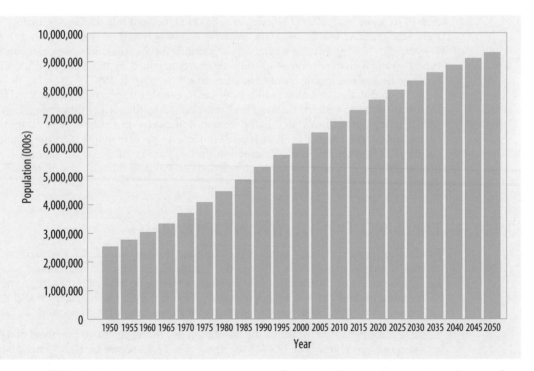

FIGURE 12.3 Projected global population growth, 1950–2050 (medium variant, thousands)
Source: UNDESA (2011).

least 9.3 billion by the year 2050 on a medium variant. If population growth occurs at the highest variant rate, it is likely to have severe effects on food supply, sound urban management, crime, security, health and social support for the poor.

Of course, projections are not certainties, but rather act as credible warnings of what might happen. Present trend projections are often wrong, sometimes because people change their conduct in response to earlier plausible warnings. For example, the most crucial counter-argument to that of the neo-Malthusians is that the annual growth rate of the world's population slowed from 2.2% in 1963, reached 1.5% in 1992 and then 1.13% in 2009 (CIA 2010). It is projected to drop to 0.4% in 2060, a rapid downward trend in demographic terms. Fertility rates are also projected to drop in all regions, bar Europe, where a very modest increase is projected to take place between 2045 and 2050 (Royal Commission on Environmental Pollution 2011: 27). Similar projections of the annual growth rate appear in Figure 12.4.

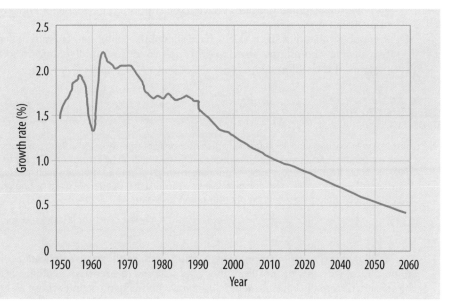

FIGURE 12.4 Projected global population growth rate (percentage)
Sources: MoD (2005), drawing on US Census Bureau, 2002 data.

Country studies also provide support for the view that with the lower growth rate, the world's population is likely to level off at about 9.3 billion people by 2050 (MoD 2005: 27; Figure 12.3). We can add that the successful NICs (like Singapore) show a rapidly diminishing birth rate in conformity with those of the wealthy Western countries. There also seems no reason to suppose that religion interferes unduly with this pattern, as the cases of Catholic Italy and urban Latin America show.

THE WORLD'S POPULATION: CAUSE FOR CONCERN?

There are a number of principal findings by demographers and sociologists in respect of population growth:

1. A consistent result is that economic prosperity is the most powerful predictor of a reducing birth rate in all countries. With better health facilities, the IMR and child deaths decline, so there is less need for 'insurance children'. With adequate benefit systems, pensions and welfare, parents are less dependent on children in their old age

(although this will cause other problems), so they do not need to have so many. For individuals and families, prosperity rises with fewer children. Acquisitions of clothing, leisure, travel and holidays are enhanced and there is a cultural shift away from children towards consumption.

2. Increased prosperity is usually marked by an increased number of women entering the labour market, often in their childbearing years. If women have careers or hold jobs, the span of years where the greatest fertility arises is reduced. The improvement of women's status, including greater opportunities in education, also reduces family size.

3. In developed countries, the main demographic problem is the low birth rate, which in the absence of high rates of immigration can have a marked effect on the social pyramid. It moves from its normal shape, through a Christmas tree shape, oak tree shape and finally to an inverted pyramid over the course of about 120 years. Young people predominate at the beginning of the period but gradually elderly people (with their greater health needs and often inadequate pensions) have to be supported by a smaller and smaller number of people of working age.

4. A number of studies in the USA have shown that within a generation, certainly within two, people who migrate from poor to rich countries rapidly conform to the birth rate patterns of their adopted homes.

A PAUSE TO REFLECT

Birth control measures work less efficiently than economic prosperity in controlling population. However, pending wealth and good healthcare programmes for all (which will not be easy to deliver), should INGOs and governments promote methods of birth control? Are such measures constrained by the so-called 'technological fallacy' – the idea that people will use a technology if they are properly informed when, simply, they may not wish to?

While unbridled population growth could damage the earth's delicate ecology, we need to be careful with this proposition. First, the scientific evidence of ecological fragility has to be separated from the commitment to doomsday thinking by people whose fear and emotions are stronger than their reason. Second, as in many areas where science and politics overlap, there are disturbing signs of the development of a fanatical minority of pro-ecologists. In the 1980s and 90s in particular, so-called 'ecoterrorists' were responsible for tree spiking (hammering metal into trees to foul chain saws and mill blades), blocking wastepipes and chimneys, and sabotaging heavy machinery. Later, attacks were made on university laboratories researching genetically modified crops (*The Guardian*, 3 April 2008). Wimberley (2009) warns against the tendency among some ecologists to treat humans as mere functional units subordinate to the overall interests of 'planet earth', and suggests instead that humans find their place in a complex, nested hierarchy – individual, familial, social, environmental, cosmic and spiritual.

There are also clear ethical limits to population control measures. Most people would agree that civil war, ethnic cleansing, compulsory sterilization and gas chambers are morally unacceptable. A couple of other practices that have been widely used are, at the very least, morally dubious. Doctors used the first in the 1970s and 80s in a number of countries (including Sweden, South Africa and the UK). They sought to persuade mothers at the vulnerable moment when they gave birth that sterilization was medically necessary or desirable. The second, used by the government of India in the 1970s, but now abandoned, was to promote sterilization by bribing people with goods (like a radio) or money. Not only are these practices ethically questionable, but there is also considerable evidence that they work, if at all, only in a fragmentary way. Questions of population growth have to be seen in context – environmental degradation, political conflict, land reform and food security (see Chapter 6). Food producers and urban workers need adequate security (where is my next meal coming from?), political stability (will my family have a future?) and healthcare (are my children likely to survive?). With these elements guaranteed, sometimes at quite low levels of income or service provision, birth rates are likely to continue to decline.

WHERE DO THEY ALL GO? URBANIZATION AND INTERNAL MIGRATION

Despite good grounds for assuming that population growth can be contained, the sheer weight of numbers in some countries creates concern. If there is little or no food for the rural population, where do they all go? The bulk of population growth is absorbed by the burgeoning cities in the developing world. On 23 May 2007, a symbolic moment was reached. There were, on that date, more urban than rural people worldwide. The speed of this development has been dramatic:

- in 1850, no country could be described as 'urban' (with over 50% living in cities)
- in 1900, only one could, Great Britain
- in 1970, nearly all advanced nations were urbanized
- in 1970, 50 cities had more than 1 million inhabitants
- in 2000, 254 cities had populations of more than 1 million people
- by 2015, given current urban growth rates, this number may rise to around 550 cities. China alone had 166 cities of this size by 2005 (Davis 2006: 15–16).

Perhaps the most dramatic discussion of this movement to the burgeoning cities across all continents is Doug Saunders' *Arrival City* (2011), where, he argues, about 2 billion people are on the move and seeking to establish a precarious toehold in residence, employment and the exercise of their social and political rights. We examined some of the consequences of this rapid urbanization in Chapter 6, mentioning, for example, crowded living quarters and shantytowns that may deteriorate into unhealthy, crime-ridden urban slums. Fortunately, sociologists and planners have observed more positive outcomes, particularly in Latin America, where residents have improved their dwellings and succeeded in persuading the municipal authorities to provide electricity, rubbish collections, schools and health clinics (Box 12.1). Other migrants maintain links with their old villages. What this adds up to is urbanization without industrialization and urbanization without adequate employment.

BOX 12.1 Slums and marginality in Brazil

The idea that poor slum dwellers were forever condemned to poverty and despair was decisively challenged in a powerful book, *The Myth of Marginality* (1976), by Janice Perlman, which focused on the favelas (shantytowns) around Rio de Janeiro. She showed that, in many cases, aspirations were high, residents often worked in the formal economy, and the informal (unregulated) economy was vibrant and productive. Self-help leading to the improvement of housing, living and social conditions was taking place and could be enhanced. The book became a classic of social research and urban planning and was subsequently praised by the president of Brazil.

Perlman and others suggested that the gradual incorporation of the slums into the city – through creating streets, providing electricity, and voting for certain politicians who were committed to delivering services – would eventually enhance the life of the residents, but they stressed that official help was no substitute for community action. While many thought that the recognition of legal tenure (title) to slum properties was to be a prelude to self-improvement, Handzic (2010) suggests that even that measure can follow, rather than precede, economic betterment. As Handzic (2010: 16–17) writes: 'the informal sector has proven to be very productive and resilient outside of, and complementary to, Brazil's heavily regulated formal economy'.

The favelas of Brazil have also generated a considerable cultural industry around them. Michael Jackson's video

They Don't Care About Us (1996) was partly filmed in Rio de Janeiro's Zona Sul, and was intended to condemn elite attitudes to the poor. Later, the full-length feature film *City of God* (2002) reinforced the message. The exposure these films gave to the slums has generated a considerable tourist industry, with some 3,000 visitors coming each month to Rio's slums. The government and tourist offices are now actively engaged in promoting, even producing, what Freire-Medeiros (2009: 581, 584) calls a 'touristic favela', a 'safari among the poor', or 'favela chic'.

In 2010 Janice Perlman updated her classic 1976 book under the title *Favela: Four Decades of Living on the Edge of Rio de Janeiro*, and interviewed some of her original respondents.

Sources: Freire-Medeiros (2009); Handzic (2010); Perlman (1976, 2010).

Historically, internal migration to urban areas was driven not only by population growth but also by land enclosures and the need for industrial labour. While these factors still operate, nowadays we must add the demand for energy (especially hydroelectric power), the Green Revolution and genetically modified crops, the provision of wildlife parks and conservation areas, and the commercialization of planting, logging, cropping and packing ('field factories'). All these factors have led to the massive displacement of rural populations from the land. India and China, where one-third of the world's inhabitants are found, are the key countries involved, but others include Nigeria, Brazil, Indonesia, South Africa and Mexico. (Chapters 6 and 10 examine these themes in China and Mexico.)

THE GLOBALIZATION OF MIGRATION

As we have said, the bulk of all migration is internal. Jordan and Düvell (2003: 66) put the figure at 2%, but more recent estimates place this at around 3.3%. Cohen (2011: 17), citing 2010 data from the International Organization of Migration, suggests that there are 214 million migrants and 15.2 million refugees. These numbers exclude internally displaced people (27.1 million in 2010), and undocumented or illegal migrants, the numbers of whom are inherently impossible to calculate precisely. Despite these relatively low percentages indicated (remembering that the global population was nearly 6.9 billion in 2010), international migration is a highly sensitive political issue. Many politicians and political groups, some of the mass media and others across the advanced countries have frequently fostered moral panics (Chapter 11) over the numbers of migrants entering their countries. Similarly, they have exaggerated or distorted issues relating to the impact migrants may have on housing, welfare and other resources (Mudde 2007).

These reactions turn not only on absolute numbers, but also on the rate of increase of migration, the rise of asylum seekers and undocumented migrants, their concentration in particular cities and regions, and the sheer variety of places and cultures from which they have emanated. In the UK, London's experience is particularly revealing. By 2005, the foreign-born population constituted more than one-third of that city's working population (May et al. 2007). For Britain as a whole, first-generation migrants made up approximately 13% of the entire workforce compared with around 7% in 1997 (Travis 2007). The highly visible increase in the number of sending and receiving countries leads to what Vertovec (2007) calls the 'super-diversity' of contemporary migration flows. This is partly linked to the end of the Cold War and the huge increase in the numbers moving between and outside the territories that were once part of the Soviet Union. For example, since the early 1990s, the numbers of people moving within, between and from Eastern Europe and Central Asia have grown hugely, particularly into the Russian Federation, Germany and other EU countries (around 38 million), but also further afield to North America and Israel (perhaps another 20 million) (Mansoor and Quillan 2006: 35). Another factor has been the inflow to EU countries of people from Africa, often arriving after dangerous sea voyages – such as from Libya to Italy or from West Africa to Spain via the Canary Islands (Rice 2008). The driving forces for this mass exodus of illegal African migrants include lack of opportunity for young people (often young men) for gainful employment as well as civil wars and genocide, for example in Liberia, Somalia, Sudan and the Democratic Republic of the Congo. Countries now contain a huge diversity of migrant groups from many countries.

What we are seeing, therefore, is the globalization of migration flows, in that people are both coming from, and seeking a haven in, far more countries than ever before. This is in marked contrast to the pattern of labour migration that occurred after the Second World War. Then, most flows were from the former colonial territories to their old metropolises, or from adjacent poorer countries to their richer neighbours. Indian, Pakistani and West Indian workers went to the UK, Algerians went to France, Turks and Yugoslavs went to West Germany, while Mexicans went to the USA in even greater numbers. This was at a time when economic growth was strong in Europe and North America and certain kinds of labour were in short supply. However, in the early 1970s, labour immigration for permanent settlement in the more powerful industrialized countries of Europe and North America virtually stopped. In their place, other kinds of migrants became much more evident and the character of migration changed substantially. We discuss these realities in the next section.

Returning to the issue of the increasing diversity of migration flows, we can say that this creates a situation where migrants find themselves living in close proximity not only to the host population but also to great numbers of other migrants with backgrounds very different from their own. About 40% of today's migrants are South–South migrants, but we hear a great deal more about those who have migrated to rich societies. Unlike in the nineteenth century, there they find host countries with relatively large, and already diverse, populations. These complexities help to explain why contemporary migration flows to the North are often associated with tensions and conflicts as well a great number of policy debates.

THE CHANGING CHARACTER OF INTERNATIONAL MIGRATION SINCE THE 1980s

Whatever the exact numbers involved at any one time, international migration undeniably plays a hugely significant role in shaping globalization and creating a more interdependent world. It also has the inherent capacity to evolve continuously and adopt new dominant forms and features. We now examine this second point in more detail by exploring four aspects of migration that have been increasingly evident since the 1980s:

- the centrality of refugees in contemporary migration flows
- the significant growth in undocumented workers
- the significance of women in migration flows, mostly moving under their own steam
- the increasingly transnational character of contemporary migration and its causes and implications.

REFUGEES: CHANGING PRESSURES

The twentieth century can be characterized as a century of the refugee. Yet it is difficult to gain an exact estimate of the scale of the global refugee population. The commonsense view might suggest that the term refers loosely to those who have been forced to abandon their homes because of natural disasters, wars or civil wars or who are victims of religious or ethnic persecution. In short, the emphasis is on events for which the individual cannot be held responsible. Humanitarian and pro-refugee lobbies typically deploy a wide definition and seek to persuade governments to offer support to all those in distress.

By contrast, the legal definition of a refugee arose from a 1950 UN Resolution, later incorporated into the 1951 Convention relating to the Status of Refugees (Geneva Convention) and the 1967 Protocol relating to the Status of Refugees; some 144 states (out of a total

UN membership of 192) have now ratified either one or both of these instruments (as of August 2008). In effect, protection was extended to people outside their country of nationality because of a well-founded fear of persecution by reason of race, religion, nationality and political opinion or membership of a particular social group. Despite its generosity of spirit, the determination of who was, and who was not, a refugee was left very much in the hands of the receiving state. Unfortunately, this gave virtual carte blanche to government officials, politicians and whoever sought to narrow the grounds for admission and recognition.

The global scale of refugee flows in the twentieth century can be indicated in this quick historical overview, summarized in five points (cf. Zolberg et al. 1989):

1. About 9.5 million refugees were created as a result of the unsettled conditions of the First World War, followed by the revolutionary upsurges in Germany and Russia.
2. The Nazi threat to the Jews and Gypsies generated another wave. The historical evidence is now convincing that Hitler's initial plan was expulsion, not annihilation. However, when it became clear that most countries were refusing entry to the refugees, Hitler moved to the final solution – eradication. At the end of the Second World War, there were 11 million people outside their countries and in need of assistance.
3. State formation often generates large numbers of refugees. The independence of India in 1947 was followed by the creation of Pakistan. Large numbers of Hindus and Muslims crossed to their respective 'sides'. In 1948, the formation of the state of Israel produced the Palestinian refugee problem. A special agency, the UN Relief and Works Agency for Palestine Refugees, supervised the creation of camps, especially in Gaza, where the refugees and their descendants (2.2. million people) still struggle for their dignity, independence and a decent standard of living.
4. Refugees fleeing from communist regimes during the Cold War were often welcomed in the West, as they provided useful opportunities for scoring propaganda victories. East Germans, Czechs, Hungarians, Russian dissidents and Cubans all fled to the West.
5. Beginning in the late 1970s and early 1980s, but accelerating thereafter, the number of refugees increased dramatically. The total number of 'persons of concern' recorded by the United Nations High Commission for Refugees (UNHCR) rose from about 10 million in the 1970s to 17 million in 1991, then to 27 million in 1995, and to a record 36 million in 2010 (see Table 12.1). To understand Table 12.1, we need to remember that 'others of concern' include not just recognized refugees but also asylum seekers whose claims for recognition under the 1951 Geneva Convention have not yet been recognized, refugees returned to their countries of origin or third countries but who have not yet been integrated, and internally displaced persons (IDPs). IDPs are persons who do not cross recognized state boundaries, and their number rocketed in 2010 due to famine, civil wars and inter-ethnic violence.

TABLE 12.1 Asylum seekers, refugees and others of concern to the UNHCR, selected years							
End of year	Refugees	Asylum seekers	Returned refugees	IDPs	Returned IDPs	Various	Total population of concern
1997	12,015,400	776,000	926,600	4,573,100	100,300	1,404,100	19,795,400
2002	10,594,100	979,500	2,426,000	4,646,600	1,179,000	953,300	20,778,600
2010	8,806,880	983,440	251,460	15,628,060	2,229,540	411,710	36,460,330

Source: UNHCR (2005: 91, 2011).

Several changes help to account for the rising numbers of worldwide refugees during the past 20 years (outlined in point 5 above):

1. The end of the Cold War (1989) and the switch by the former Soviet Union and its allies to a policy of open borders meant that Western countries were confronted with a large

number of unwelcome migrants. Where there was a policy of welcoming co-ethnic immigrants – in Israel, Greece and Germany – no great problem arose. Elsewhere, immigration laws designed to keep people out replaced the Berlin Wall designed to keep people in. With the end of the Cold War, the political refugees of yesteryear became the economic migrants of today.

2. As noted earlier, the countries of Africa and Asia, and not just the European nations, increasingly generated large numbers of refugees. This was especially the case with the poorest countries in these regions where war, famine and ethnic conflict commonly triggered forced migration.

3. The Balkanization of the former eastern bloc – which followed the collapse of the Soviet Union – also became a key factor, especially in the former Yugoslavia. Our TV screens were filled with images of lines of pathetic people fleeing brutality and civil war in Bosnia, Croatia and Kosovo, victims of 'ethnic cleansing'. In the early months of 1999, over half a million refugees fled from Kosovo to nearby Macedonia and Albania as NATO forces sought to halt the ethnic cleansing carried out by Serbian forces. The NATO intervention may have been morally justified, yet it served also to accelerate the flight from Kosovo.

4. The political violence perpetrated by the ruling classes against democracy campaigners in Arab countries during 2011, the so-called 'Arab Spring', has led to further waves of refugees to neighbouring countries (Figure 12.5).

© BRASIL2

FIGURE 12.5 A tent city in Turkey, June 2011
A tent city erected by the Turkish Red Crescent in Turkey's Hatay province to receive refugees fleeing from political violence in Syria. State violence conducted on behalf of President Assad's regime has energized the opposition movement, but the government enjoys considerable public support and it seems inevitable that the flow of refugees will continue.

A PAUSE TO REFLECT

Large waves of refugees seem to follow break-ups of empires and the formation of new states. How has the international community ameliorated this problem in the past? Examine the alternatives of (a) stable countries admitting more refugees, (b) encouraging or accepting the formation of more and more nation-states, or (c) intervening militarily to secure the peace and avoid civil war. Which of these options has worked in particular places and why?

UNDOCUMENTED WORKERS

The term 'undocumented' refers to people often defined as 'illegals' but the category is wider than that. The use of passports only became worldwide around 1914. Consequently, illegal residence was a vague concept and in many regions, particularly Africa, it remains so. When many of Africa's national boundaries were decided at a conference of colonial powers in Berlin in 1885 (Chapter 9) by drawing lines on a map, little account was taken of the fact that ethnic groups were thereby split between countries while seasonal and pastoral migratory flows continued. In the early twenty-first century, the unreality of many African boundaries remains a problem. This is not unique to Africa since similarly permeable boundaries exist between northern Spain and France and between Mexico and the USA. Sometimes, states give up the business of trying to police the border – so, in effect, tolerating undocumented migration.

Undocumented labour now takes two predominant forms: overstaying and deliberate illegal entry. The first phenomenon reflects the increasingly practical difficulties of managing the turnstiles that turn ever faster as more and more people file through. Take London's Heathrow airport, which in 2010 was the world's largest airport hub in terms of the number of international travellers it handled. It serves over 90 airlines and more than 170 destinations. In 2010, 65.8 million international flyers passed through (some of them repeat passengers). With such numbers and complexity, it would be astounding if a minority did not manage to violate the terms of their entry or work rights; for example, a student who works in a fast-food outlet, violating the terms of their student visa. Others stay on after their entry visas have expired and enter the shadowy world of illegal work and residence.

However, there is also increased evidence of organization behind illegal entrants but this takes different forms. Large sums of money change hands, entry certificates and visas are forged, and border guards are bribed. Often, travel and shipping agents are involved. A second dimension to illegal immigration is the frequent complicity of employers. The most obvious example here concerns Mexican labour in the USA, particularly before 1986. Up to that point, it was illegal to be an undocumented worker, but not illegal to employ one. 'Coyotes' (the local name for labour recruiters) commonly supplied gangs of workers to order. There is often a contradiction between employers, who need cheap or compliant workers, or labour with particular skills and qualities, and the government, which needs to be responsive to public opinion. The unions organizing indigenous workers are also usually on the side of the state.

A third dimension of illegal migration is linked to the fastest growing form of organized transnational crime, namely people smuggling (see Miko 2007: 39; Shelley 2007: 198). Using 2004 figures, Passel (2005) estimated that there were 10.3 million unauthorized foreigners in the USA in March 2004, many of them Mexicans. This was a rise of nearly 2 million on the 2000 figure, a net increase (after deducting departures and the number legalized) of nearly 500,000 a year. Moreover, it is estimated that approximately 70% of illegal migrants from Mexico employ the services of professional smugglers to help them move and this may involve up to 120 smuggling rings (Shelley 2007: 201–6). Worldwide, the ILO in Geneva suggests that, at any one time, more than 12 million people have probably been trafficked across borders if we include those forced into migration (cited in Miko 2007: 40).

If the pressures to migrate are strong and employers are complicit and offer work, it seems that border controls will never be fully effective. Governments respond in at least three ways (sometimes simultaneously). They turn a blind eye to placate public opinion, pretend that borders are securely policed, and, occasionally, they recognize reality by legitimating the status of illegal workers by allowing an amnesty.

WOMEN MIGRANTS

Feminists in the 1960s declared that women were 'hidden from history'. Generally, this is an accurate observation, but particularly so in the migration field. Many earlier studies of migration only dealt with 'the women left behind' in the rural areas. Alternatively, women were considered as dependent or family members, being seen essentially as the baggage of male workers. Some of this may have been justified, in that males were often the pioneer migrants. However, even historically, we are discovering evidence that women were more independent actors than had previously been assumed. In the case of early British immigration to the USA, being attached to a settler family, usually as a family servant, often involved a later escape to some kind of independence. Immigration law had the same effect. Another example is that of Caribbean women coming to the USA or the UK in the post-1945 period. Much of the legislation during periods of restrictions forbade labour migration but permitted family reunification – on humanitarian grounds or to conform to international law. So women made opportunistic marriages or faked relationships.

Despite these historical examples of women operating independently of men, it is clear that, numerically and sociologically, we have entered a new phase of female migration. Women now constitute around half of all international migrants and increasingly they move in search of employment rather than for family reasons. Some take up work in sweatshop manufacturing in cities such as Los Angeles, having already become familiar with such work and the commercial world of huge cities before leaving their countries of origin (Sassen 1991). Most of this independent movement in response to a demand for women, however, involves entering the global service economy. Some of this involves the sex industry, particularly in Southeast Asia. Hostesses, sex workers and entertainers are required in significant numbers in countries like Japan – and are generally supplied from China and Thailand. A more respectable version of the trade is in the 'mail order bride' trade – dominated by the Philippines. The Philippines is also the market leader for domestic labour, exporting tens of thousands of maids, nannies and domestic workers each year to the Middle East and many other countries.

These markets are driven from both ends. On the supply side, the Philippine and other governments regard labour exports much like any other export – a foreign currency earner. This is primarily because of the significant remittance income returned by Filipinas abroad. Foreign exchange is also earned on the substantial agency and recruiting fees paid from foreign sources. On the demand side, changes in gender power in Western countries have had a significant impact. Young women in the West tend to be more reluctant to be confined to the kitchen and the home. Also, as late as the 1920s, hundreds of thousands of British women were in domestic service but now there are hardly any. The gap is filled from abroad. To brides and domestic workers, add the many waitresses, casual staff in fast-food outlets, cleaners, nurses and other kinds of care workers (see the discussion of global care chains in Chapter 8), but also secretaries, hotel reception staff and stewardesses supplied from outside the country of work.

GLOBAL THINKERS 12 NINA GLICK SCHILLER

Interestingly, as a researcher on migrants from all over the world, Nina Glick Schiller was herself the grandchild of immigrants to New York. She has held leading university posts as a professor, research director and senior research associate in Germany, New Hampshire, USA and Manchester, UK. In 1992 she was a founding editor of the journal *Identities: Global Studies in Culture*.

After first formulating a transnational paradigm for the study of migration, she developed a critique of methodological nationalism – a perspective that views nation-states as the primary containers of human activity, encompassing society, territory, economy and nation, all located within fixed frontiers. Methodological nationalists tend to regard migrants as dangerous outsiders who disrupt the racial/cultural purity and inherent social order of national societies. They therefore presume it is imperative that migrants become assimilated – just like 'us' – so that social cohesion is not disturbed. For Glick Schiller, the equivalent of methodological nationalism for early anthropologists involved assuming that the small-scale societies they studied formed unitary, cohesive, self-sufficient cultures operating within fixed territories – 'tribes without modern states' (Wimmer and Glick Schiller 2002: 305).

Even today, some researchers look at those who migrate from such societies to the cities of the North through an 'ethnic lens'. This regards their practices as largely an expression of their transplanted ethnic cultures rather than something they have constructed partly in response to the experiences of discrimination they have encountered along with the 'politicization' (Wimmer and Glick Schiller 2002: 305) of their ethnicity by the media, politicians and other host agents. Among Glick Schiller's key counter theorizations – ones she developed collaboratively with other migration scholars – are the following:

1. Based largely on pioneering research shared with Linda Basch and Cristina Szanton Blanc (Basch et al. 1994), Glick Schiller (2007) recorded that migrants to the USA from Haiti and other countries had constructed multifaceted transnational social fields (networks of networks) that tied them simultaneously to their home villages, families, regions and nations and to the life available to them in USA cities. Understanding such migrant networks was only possible if scholars moved beyond methodological nationalism.

2. Although transnational processes and relations flourished through religious, artistic, trade, intellectual, financial and many other practices long before the current era of globalization, they have become much more widespread and evident in recent years.

3. It is crucial for migration scholars and others to assert that threats to social cohesion do not come from migrants and their external connections but from 'the forces of globalization and capitalist power relations that are restructuring all our lives' (Glick Schiller 2007: 65) – irrespective of whether we remain sedentary or migrate.

Sources: Basch et al. (1994); Glick Schiller (2007); Wimmer and Glick Schiller (2002).

We need to add one caveat to this discussion. At least insofar as the global sex trade is concerned, criminal gangs are also involved in women's 'migration', whether for illegal sex tourism and prostitution – in countries such as Thailand or Japan – or for purposes of forced prostitution in Europe where young women from Eastern Europe, the Balkans and Ukraine provide the largest numbers (Miko 2007: 40–1). In fact, four-fifths of those trafficked and forced into becoming illegal migrants are women (Miko 2007: 40). Irrespective of region, this particular form of female migration is a cause for deep concern. Despite this frightening example, the majority of migrating women are nonetheless moving from being invisible dependants to independent social actors.

TRANSNATIONAL MIGRATION AND 'SALAD BOWL' HOST SOCIETIES

Despite assumptions to the contrary, many Europeans caught up in the waves of migrations to the Americas in the nineteenth and early twentieth centuries moved back and forth several times before finally deciding whether to return to their original homeland or settle in the New World. Moreover, most remained in contact with relatives and friends at home, sent money when they could, and some did not wish to lose their cultural affiliation with their original homeland. There is, however, wide agreement among scholars of migration that whereas a large proportion of those from the earlier waves did finally opt to become fully assimilated national citizens in their adopted countries, today the majority of migrants from the global South operate with rather different motives and intentions. They hope eventually to obtain full citizenship in the host society and enjoy the rights and advantages this confers, but most do not wish to relinquish their sense of identity with and attachment to their homeland or their economic, cultural or even political involvement in its events and social life. And, given the opportunities provided by cheap travel, instantaneous communication and international finance compared with the recent past, they have no need to do so.

Thus, replacing the 'melting pot' metaphor, in which migrant cultures eventually became mixed and merged to form a dominant US, Australian or Canadian national culture, today, in France or Britain and elsewhere, we find cultural pluralism or a 'salad bowl' society of many ethnic groups maintaining much of their culture yet all somewhat affected by living in the host society. Alternatively, we might refer to 'switching board' societies (Zhou and Tseng 2001), in which each host society operates rather like an aircraft carrier onto which different ethnic/national groups land and put down some roots – usually involving the construction of a replica home society or cultural enclave within the host nation. They continue to use the host country as a base from which to conduct a range of ongoing activities and to maintain multiple connections with people in their sending society and/or with diasporic members around the world. Because second and further generations are exposed to the host society's educational and media influences in addition to the cultures transplanted by their parents' generation, these connectivities may partly diminish over time.

Insofar as today's migrants from the South act in this way, they are said to be engaged in a form of transnationalism (Jordan and Düvell 2003; Pries 2001; Vertovec 2009). Transnational migrants do not merely cross territorial borders but simultaneously construct 'multistranded social relations … that link together their societies of origin and settlement' (Basch et al. 1994: 7), which may encompass not just familial and economic interactions but also religious, cultural and political ties and projects. Consequently, they are said to live bifocal or multifocal lives, with no complete affiliation to either their host or home country. This generates new dynamics, which may produce 'bricolage' or 'creolization' in music (Chapter 14), fashion and other fields of culture, the playing out of multiple and sometimes divided loyalties and much else besides.

SOME REASONS FOR TRANSNATIONALISM

Several recent changes occurring in host and home societies help to explain the causes of transnational migration. First, the revolution in communications has altered everyone's experience of time–space compression (see Chapter 2). It has made it easier than ever before for migrants to keep in touch with their immediate families, wider kinsfolk and others, irrespective of physical distance.

Second, with development stalling in many countries, or in particular regions within countries, the more adventurous or relatively better-off members of such societies face a range of choices. They can migrate to the overcrowded megacities in their own country, but they are often confronted with high unemployment and slum housing (see Chapter 6). Some utilize the SOCIAL CAPITAL (Faist 2000) in the form of remittances and contacts available to them from fellow villagers who had already migrated. A significant minority, however, travel abroad to pursue the promise of future work and to take advantage of whatever help earlier migrants can offer them in terms of housing, family work or credit in starting a future business. With globalization, it becomes increasingly possible and probably necessary for individuals, groups and organizations to shift some of their activities away from their own areas and familiar relationships.

Third, when not working for the family, migrants from the South tend to find employment in the low-skilled service sector, including catering, cleaning and shelf-stacking. As we saw in Chapters 4, 6 and 7, such jobs tend to be casualized and chronically insecure, poorly paid and, in many instances, with few prospects for long-term economic improvement. Faced with this precarious situation, Portes (1997) suggested that it makes sense for today's migrants to build reliable ethnic socioeconomic enclaves of mutual support and protection within the host nation while retaining an escape route back to their homelands. This means keeping up strong transnational links.

KEY CONCEPT

SOCIAL CAPITAL refers to the use of networks and social relationships to secure jobs, economic advantage or social prestige. Social capital can also be seen as creating a latticework of reciprocity that facilitates democracy and trust. Putnam (1995) suggests that a lack of social capital can result in a deficit of democratic participation. More controversially, Putnam (2007) also argued that, in the short run, high rates of immigration and diversity reduce social capital, leading to lower levels of altruism and community solidarity.

Fourth, according to Waldinger and Fitzgerald (2004), the actions of both sending and receiving states contribute to the transnational character of contemporary migration. For example, some governments in the South actively encourage their citizens overseas to maintain links with their home country because they value the financial remittances the latter send home and the wider opportunities they offer for exporting home-produced commodities – foodstuffs, crafts and other goods – to overseas citizen communities and others. Also important are the host government's shifting migration policies, fluctuating criteria of citizenship, and the changing terms under which these may occur as the host society tries to control the flows of foreign nationals across its borders (Massey 2005).

Finally, notwithstanding the strong currents of anti-immigration feeling that often flourish in host societies, today the tolerance of ethnic diversity and dual identities is generally much greater than in the past. Political priorities fluctuate and there is currently a strong push in many Western nations towards cultural conformity and a single political loyalty. Nonetheless, national, religious and ethnic subcultures often thrive, thus allowing multiple forms of identity fed by new migrants and old affinities to persist.

THE COMPLEX CHARACTER OF TRANSNATIONALISM

Before leaving this discussion, we need to emphasize that the scenario we have just sketched is highly generalized. Each particular example of transnationalism demonstrates its own peculiarities. In addition, the experiences and actions of migrants normally evolve as circumstances change over time in the global economy, in the host society, and in their home nation and government.

For example, transnational connections sometimes lead to social divisions because the financial remittances that migrant parents, for example Hondurans in the USA, send home to their children enable the latter to benefit from better educational and other opportunities than those available to the other young people in their vicinity. Often, these young people remain unaware of the struggles and relative poverty that their absent parents might have to endure overseas (Schmalzbauer 2008). Similarly, Mercer et al. (2009) show how in African countries such as Tanzania, Cameroon and Ghana, overseas migrant networks in the North exert less influence on development projects in their home towns or regions than those that local elites or fellow nationals who migrated to other African countries are able to exercise. Thus, they suggest that proximity remains a key factor in understanding how development is managed and controlled. Moreover, some transnational migrants eventually return to their homeland but their individual circumstances, reasons for doing so and ability to benefit from this can vary widely. In their study of Moroccan migrants in the Netherlands, de Bree et al. (2010: 506) show that while some were able to prepare their return partly by utilizing networks they had built over time, and felt 'personally satisfied' and quite comfortable about becoming reintegrated into Moroccan society, others returned reluctantly and found re-engagement difficult. Also, women were not usually able to exert much if any influence one way or another over their husbands' decision to stay or return and in fact some second-generation women who returned felt 'uprooted' from the Netherlands and 'longed to return' (de Bree et al. 2010: 506).

A PAUSE TO REFLECT

Advocates of transnational migration sometimes argue that it can provide a win–win–win scenario. Host governments can use migrants when needed and ask them to return home when they are not. Migrants can acquire skills and enhanced income, while home societies can profit from remittances, investment and the diffusion of expertise acquired abroad. Is this too optimistic a picture and what flaws are evident, or might emerge?

We should also emphasize that this discussion has focused on relatively poor migrants from rural settings. An increasing number of economic migrants, however, have skills and educational qualifications that render them attractive to Northern employers and governments. In addition, their likely access to greater reservoirs of cultural capital and familiarity with middle-class urban institutions and cultural life may make them much less reliant than their poor migrant cousins are likely to be on their fellow nationals. They may well be equipped to cross cultural as well as national boundaries and follow a more explicitly cosmopolitan trajectory in their work and/or private social lives (Kennedy 2004).

REVIEW

Since the days of Malthus, commentators and scholars have made grand pronouncements about the world's population. Politicians have sanctioned or encouraged extreme measures to control population in general or, more usually, control sections of the population stigmatized on racial, national, class or religious grounds. Precisely because of its controversial nature, it is important to differentiate between evidence about population growth and prediction, projection or prejudice. In this chapter we have provided some basic tools with which to undertake this task. Again, we have summarized some of the most important findings relevant to the population debate, showing, for example, that population growth rates are falling dramatically.

Surplus population is absorbed into the growing cities. Historically, it has been absorbed at such a rate that in many of the developed countries, those who live in the countryside and depend on it for their livelihood are a small minority of the population (in Britain about 3%). In other countries, particularly China and India and, to a lesser extent, Nigeria, Brazil and Mexico, a considerable proportion of the population still lives in rural areas. However, the urbanizing tendency is universal and most migrants are absorbed, usually with great difficulty, into the cities of the developing world.

Yet, a small but crucial group become international migrants and we have examined some of the key groups, changes and causal influences associated with this. The transnational character of contemporary migration may generate tensions and potential conflicts partly because many are not especially interested in seeking full cultural assimilation. However, transnational migration also creates crucial interdependencies binding North and South together – filling the employment gap in the care industry created by ageing populations in the North, or undertaking badly paid and unpleasant but essential work that local people prefer to avoid. From a Southern perspective, the financial remittances that many migrants send home to their kinsfolk and villages are of immense significance. The World Bank estimated that remittances worldwide reached around US$350bn in 2004 (Ratha 2009), falling slightly as the 2008 recession kicked in to US$316bn (Cohen 2011: 17). In many countries remittance income is more important in generating economic growth and job opportunities than overseas aid, tourist income and foreign investment combined.

Visit the companion website at www.palgrave.com/sociology/cohen3e for extra materials to check and expand your learning, including interactive self-test questions, mind maps making links between key themes, annotated web links to sociological research, data and key sociological thinkers, a searchable glossary and much more.

FURTHER READING

W. T. Gould's *Population and Development* (2008) is written by a population geographer who has considerable awareness of social issues, including, notably, the effects of HIV infections.

M. Livi-Bacci's *A Concise History of World Population* (4th edn, 2006) is balanced and thoughtful (a 5th edition is expected in 2012).

S. Castles and M. Miller's *The Age of Migration: International Population Movements in the Modern World* (4th edn, 2009) provides an accessible introduction to many of the topics on migration covered in the second half of this chapter.

R. Cohen's *Migration and its Enemies: Global Capital, Migrant Labour and the Nation-state* (2006) covers many of the themes on migration discussed here, including an appraisal of how al-Qaeda's attack on New York in 2001 has affected migration flows and policies.

QUESTIONS AND ASSIGNMENTS

1. Was Malthus essentially right?
2. What reasons would lead you to the view that population growth might stabilize, without famine?
3. Are 'underpopulation' or ageing populations significant problems?
4. Why is international migration such a sensitive issue?
5. What is different about transnational migration today compared with previous forms of migration and how can this be explained?

13

Globalization, families and social change

Families not only provide a key form of social cohesion but they also act as an important site for the reproduction of social inequalities. In other words, they shape what kinds of individuals we become and therefore 'who' makes up society. There is much evidence that the family and other key personal relationships established in childhood play a significant part in producing socially competent and happy adults. At the same time, personal relationships play an important role in maintaining social divisions, that is, 'they can provide training in [hate] as well as love and in dominance and submission as well as cooperative efforts' (Jamieson 1998: 166). Personal relationships are not driven purely by pleasure; they are also shaped by material and economic circumstances that can, in turn, often reinforce gender, class and ethnic divisions. Families are simultaneously sites of pleasure, togetherness and intimacy, and of exploitation, oppression and inequality. In this chapter, we take this contradiction as a starting point for our discussion of families in a global age.

We adopt a global approach to the study of family and intimacy and ask what happens to family relationships under conditions of globalization. Throughout this chapter we examine the extent to which families are being transformed in late modernity and consider the extent and speed of this change in diverse families across the globe. How do family structures and everyday family life differ across the globe? What are the rituals of intimacy? How do we negotiate our rights and responsibilities towards our families? A second concern is with the extent to which globalization is affecting families and relationships. We start by examining early sociological analyses of the family and consider the contribution that feminist scholars have made to family sociology. We then assess whether individualization theories are an accurate characterization of what has been happening to family relationships lately. We follow this with a comparative discussion of family relationships in two regions and an exploration of the impact of globalization on intimacy and family relationships.

THE SOCIOLOGY OF THE FAMILY

Sociological research on the family did not become established until the second half of the twentieth century; early studies drew on a functionalist logic and sought to examine what the role of the family is within society. The work of American sociologist Talcott Parsons in the 1950s is a key milestone in this type of family analysis.

Parsons and Bales (2003: 16) saw the nuclear family as a bounded unit of intimates characterized by mother–father and child–parent relations. They described the function of the family as twofold – the socialization of children into society and the stabilization of adult personalities. Men were designed to provide for the instrumental needs of the family unit – food, shelter and other material necessities – whereas the housewife was supposed to satisfy the family's expressive needs, such as affection, emotional support and socialization. As long as individuals performed their instrumental or expressive roles, the family worked as a functional unit and contributed to the stability of the society as a whole. A gendered division of labour was therefore seen as vital for the harmonious and orderly functioning of society. Such functionalist analyses of family relations relied on seeing men and women as having fundamentally different capacities; this explains their different roles in the family, a fact that feminist scholars later sought to contest. It is important to note that this so-called 'traditional' family defined by the male breadwinner model was an exceptional occurrence in the Western world lasting only a few decades after the Second World War, suggesting that this is an ideological view of the family, an issue to which we return later.

Second-wave feminists argued that the traditional allocation of roles within the family reflects not the instrumental characteristics of males and females respectively but the existence of patriarchal power within the family. Their analyses highlighted how the heterosexual institution of marriage has played a key role in the oppression of women, since it locked them into a position of economic dependency on men and confined them to domestic and childcare work. Even today, much contemporary research suggests that marriage is rarely an equal partnership and that gender inequalities permeate even our most private relationships. For example, it is not just the division of labour between husband and wife that is inequitable but also their access to economic resources. Jan Pahl's (1989) research on money and marriage shows that women generally contribute a larger proportion of their income to the household budget and spend less on themselves than their male counterparts.

THE TRANSFORMATION OF INTIMACY

Important changes in the patterns of family life that have taken place over the past 40 years form a backdrop to the theoretical debates about the transformation of intimacy: the sociology of the family has changed both to reflect and explain these changes. Significant trends include the increase in divorce rates and cohabitation before marriage, the diversification of family forms, including stepfamilies and same-sex families, and the postponement of marriage and parenthood. How have sociologists explained these changes?

The publication of *The Transformation of Intimacy* by British sociologist Anthony Giddens (1992) led to a number of heated debates in sociology about the nature of contemporary changes in family relationships and to what extent individualization was affecting them. He writes that 'marriage becomes more and more a relationship initiated for and kept going for as long as it delivers emotional satisfaction to be derived from close contact with another' (Giddens 1991: 89). According to Giddens (1992), a key feature of the late modern PURE RELATIONSHIP is 'opening up to someone', namely disclosing intimacy through sharing one's inner thoughts and feelings. Because this kind of intimacy involves constant self-examination, it requires high levels of reflexivity from social actors. Also, it depends on a certain amount of privacy, which only becomes possible in late modern societies when households are organized in such a way that members of the same family unit are not always in close proximity with one another.

Anthony Giddens (1992) describes couple relationships in late modern industrialized societies as characterized by what he calls the PURE RELATIONSHIP, whereas in modern societies 'romantic love' was the ideal. Pure relationships are based on trust, intimacy and egalitarianism rather than on the obligation and duty previously seen to anchor modern societies. The rise of therapy is closely tied to the emergence of the pure relationship, ideally requiring opening up to someone's inner world and communicating one's emotions. The pure relationship is also risky since it relies on a voluntary commitment and is sought only for what the relationship can bring to the partners involved, and terminated at will if it is no longer satisfactory to either partner.

Another significant feature of late modern society for Giddens (1992) was that intimate social relationships have become 'democratized'. Consequently, the bond between partners – even within a marriage – has little to do with external laws, regulations or social expectations, but is based solely on the relationship between two people – a trusting bond based on emotional communication. Where such a bond ceases to exist, modern society is generally happy for the relationship to be dissolved. This is what Giddens (2002: 63) calls 'a democracy of the emotions in everyday life'. He claims that the democratization of interpersonal relationships is what has transformed intimacy. In turn, he suggests that a more profound equality between men and women is emerging through this transformation.

The arguments that Giddens developed in *The Transformation of Intimacy* (1992), however, continue to provoke debate. For one, it has been argued that personal relationships are actually not as free-floating from social structures as he suggests. His optimistic account of what is happening to personal relationships downplays the material conditions and social inequalities that affect them. Another weakness of the book is that he bases his grand theoretical account of the changes in personal relationships on insufficient empirical evidence. In *Intimacy: Personal Relationships in Modern Societies*, Lynn Jamieson (1998) argues that a closer look at empirical research reveals a much messier and less equal picture of intimate relationships.

One of her main contentions is that, contrary to Giddens's propositions, a desire for mutually disclosing intimacy does not necessarily drive friendships and family interactions. She suggests that there are many different ways of being close to someone that do not involve self-disclosing intimacy. Jamieson challenges Giddens's account of contemporary intimate life on the grounds that reciprocity does not actually characterize most intimate relationships. She finds Giddens's argument that families have become increasingly democratic and that relationships between infants and parents are more equal unconvincing. She holds that democratic principles do not necessarily underpin child–parent relationships and that even if an ethos of mutuality between parents and children is invoked, it might actually mask the traditional imposition of parental control through authority. Jamieson thus raises the question of whether the idea of a pure relationship is applicable to other personal relationships beyond the heterosexual couple.

Jamieson also argues that we need to focus more on exploring the power differentials in family relationships and on the ways in which class, gender and ethnic inequalities affect family life, an area Giddens neglects despite empirical evidence that these divisions still matter. Jamieson thinks we can have a sense of being equal and intimate despite inequalities, and feels that families put a great deal of energy into sustaining a sense of intimacy despite inequality. Giddens and Jamieson offer different estimations on what is happening to intimacy in modern Western societies. However, while they disagree about how we should characterize this change, they agree that there are huge changes in intimate relationships.

Moreover, Giddens's thesis that we are freer than we ever were to conduct our intimate relationships outside the constraints of tradition seems inappropriate for understanding family relationships in non-Western countries, where individualization and tradition intermesh in complex ways. If 'disclosing intimacy' – sharing one's inner thoughts and feelings with a loved one – is not the sole organizing principle of personal lives in Western societies, this is even less the case in some non-Western societies such as Japan, where talking about yourself and sharing your feelings are unlikely to be seen as necessary components of a good relationship.

Individualization in the context of the family does not mean that people are becoming more selfish at the expense of socially indispensable so-called 'traditional family values'. It means that the traditional (mostly religious and legal) external constraints on marriage and family have progressively disappeared and left people having to find individual solutions to structural social problems. For example, the so-called traditional 'breadwinner' and 'home-maker' family roles have been individualized: in the current economic climate, a single male breadwinner often earns too little to support his family financially; similarly, in a context in which relationships are not expected to last forever, taking on the homemaker role becomes a risky strategy.

A PAUSE TO REFLECT

Do you think that the recent changes to family life, including trends like the rising rates of cohabitation and divorce and the postponement of marriage, mean we are more or less close to our families than we were 50 years ago? Are these changes starker in some regions of the globe than others? In which societies do you think individuals are able to strike a balance between maintaining responsibilities for their families and for themselves?

Having discussed the flaws of Giddens's attempt to understand the impact of individualization on the family, we shall see in the remainder of this chapter that measuring and capturing the extent of social change in intimate life is a challenging task for all sociologists.

THE MEANINGS OF 'FAMILY'

KEY CONCEPT

According to David Morgan (1996: 186), 'family represents a quality rather than a thing' so that sociologists can and should use the word 'family' as an adjective rather than a noun. Looking at FAMILY PRACTICES means being concerned with the diversity of families and how they are created through everyday interactions by social actors, recognizing that being part of a family is not just to do with blood ties. The term 'family practices' also implies an attunement to the fluidity of family life and a move away from being concerned with the structure of the family; it enables sociologists to look at how family is performed in the everyday setting by social actors and what family means to people in context. Morgan's concept has been widely used in recent scholarship on family life and relationships, especially in the UK.

The word 'family' is becoming an increasingly contested term for sociologists because it fails to capture the diversity and complexity of intimate ties in late modern societies. This has led to a move away from definitions of families purely in terms of household and kin and towards acknowledging the different ways in which they extend beyond that parameter. As a result, some sociologists of the family have started to pay more attention to how people incorporate intimacy and family into their everyday lives. A focus on everyday practices of intimacy, and on what family means to people, allows sociologists to refrain from imposing their own definition on the participants and to capture the diverse ways of behaving in a family-like way, which go beyond formal family structures and blood ties. David Morgan, a sociologist of families, coined the phrase FAMILY PRACTICES, thus directing attention to the fact that families are not static but created through everyday interactions by social actors. A further trend in sociological scholarship on families and relationships is a concern with studying the emotions that social actors experience when falling in love, becoming a parent, or experiencing bereavement, and seeing those feelings as the products of social interaction.

COMPARATIVE FAMILY STUDIES

A comprehensive comparative mapping of family relationships across the globe is a large-scale endeavour and to date few scholars have attempted to provide an international perspective on the study of families. Not only are family structures diverse, but also there are huge variations across human societies in the ways people express intimacy. Below, we consider studies of family life in the UK and Japan and what constitutes a family in these different settings to assess the extent of change in the meanings given to family and the family practices in which individuals engage.

Roopnarine and Gielen (2005) suggest that family structures across the globe fall along a continuum. While some remain anchored in traditional patriarchal mores, with heterosexual marriage as the cornerstone of family life, in most developed societies there is a greater variety of family forms – including cohabitation, single-parent families and gay/lesbian families – and a greater redefinition of traditional gender roles. Goran Therborn (2004) identifies seven family systems, each with its specific regional, social and cultural characteristics (Table 13.1). According to Therborn, these different family systems change according to external factors, such as modernization and globalization. Although it may be useful to have this typology in mind, it seems to us that these categories fail to capture the complexity of changes happening to families everywhere and a classification is not our aim here. Instead, we focus on examining how families manage the tensions between tradition and responsibilities to one's kin on the one hand and democratic structures that allow for more individualistic orientations on the other.

TABLE 13.1 Therborn's world family systems typology	
Family systems	Characteristics
Sub-Saharan Africa	• Patriarchy with some gender autonomy • Mass polygyny • High fertility • Authority centred on local chiefs
European + New World Settlements	• Least patriarchal • Based on marriage by consent • Neolocal pattern of household formation • Monogamous • Fertility controlled by couples
East Asia	• Most explicitly patriarchal • Confucian filial piety – deference to fathers and male ancestors • Fertility geared toward reproducing the male bloodline • Central role of the family as collective structure in decision-making • Low religious influence
South Asia	• Strict patriarchy • Fertility controlled by patrilineal household • High Islamic influence
West Asia/North Africa	• Patriarchy centred on controlling the sexuality of women, through seclusion or veiling • Patrilocal norms • Detailed Islamic control of family matters stated in legal codes (Sharia law)
Southeast Asia	• Less patriarchal • Less sexually controlled • Strong parental involvement in marriage formation • Bilateral kinship • Bhuddist relaxed norms
Creole America	• Patriarchal white ruling class • Phallocratic culture of informal sexuality, frequent non-marriage • Matrifocal household • Authority based on racism, and class-based poverty

Sources: Adapted from Therborn (2004); Monnier (2010).

UNITED KINGDOM

One view of families in Western Europe conjures up a picture of equality, choice, plurality and a general weakening of the influence of tradition on family life. It emphasizes the declining rates of marriage and rising rates of cohabitation and divorce (see Figure 13.1), sees love-based egalitarian heterosexual partnerships as forming the centre of family life, and tolerates diverse family forms, including single-parent and, to some extent, same-sex families. Alongside Jamieson et al. (2002), we want to tell a different story, one we think provides a more nuanced and accurate picture of family formation in Britain. The studies discussed below show that gender inequalities continue to shape intimate partner relationships and that marriage and the nuclear family continue to hold normative power despite the increasing diversity of family forms.

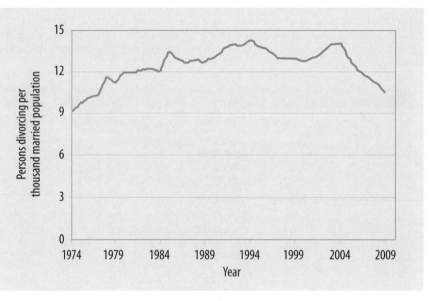

FIGURE 13.1 Divorces in England and Wales, 1974–2009
Source: ONS (2011).

It has been argued that higher rates of cohabitation before marriage signal the decline of the institution of marriage. However, there is evidence that the symbolic meaning of marriage remains strong and that tradition continues to shape how people formalize their intimate ties. Research on cohabitation shows that couples choose it for a variety of reasons, whether as a trial before marriage, or as a long-term alternative to marriage; it is clear, however, that the decrease in marriage rates and increase in cohabitation do not signify a lack of lifelong commitment in partnerships. For example, Jamieson's research on the partnership plans of young men and women in the late 1990s suggests that cohabitation does not mean there is a weakened sense of commitment in relationships, but rather a weakening sense of any added value to marriage, as most participants assumed that marriage would make no difference to their relationship. At the same time, participants emphasized the symbolic significance of marriage through the social event of the wedding.

Andrew Cherlin (2004) has argued that although marriage as an institution may be in trouble, its symbolic standing has never been higher. He suggests that this is precisely because it has undergone a process of deinstitutionalization, so it is now an individual choice. Cherlin believes that although the practical importance of marriage has declined, its symbolic significance has increased. Since marriage is now rarer, it has become a marker of the quality of the relationship and a form of social bragging, whereas previously it was simply seen as a passport to adulthood. Weddings continue to be important rituals in the UK, although focused on consumption and personal achievement rather than the bringing together of two families.

Intimate relationships are often regarded as partnerships based on love between people who share their resources equally, but several studies suggest that the way resources are allocated in a household mirrors the unequal power relationships between men and women. There is an association between controlling the household finances and who holds power in the household. This also occurs in the context of a gendered labour market, where women are segregated in lower paid jobs and experience the effects of the continuing pay gap, which means that, on average, they earn 17% less than men in the UK (Fawcett Society/UNISON 2007). Although there is a trend for couples to have separate bank accounts, Caroline Vogler's (2005) study of cohabiting couples found that while they explicitly claimed to organize their finances on the basis of equality, this often had highly unequal outcomes. So long as couples earned similar amounts, then separate accounts and equal contributions to mortgages were likely to result in egalitarian outcomes, but when one partner (usually the man) earned more than the other, the higher earner tended to have more control over money as well as greater access to it for his or her own use. Vogler (2005) suggests that one of the main reasons couples find it so difficult to talk about money may be precisely because inequalities over access to it threaten to reveal the myth of egalitarian partnerships. This draws our attention to how discourses of equality in marriage often fail to match up with actual practices.

Gender inequalities also come to the fore when we consider who does the emotional work required to sustain relationships. Duncombe and Marsden's (1993) qualitative research with couples found that many women expressed unhappiness about men's unwillingness or incapacity 'to do' emotional intimacy, which they saw as necessary to a successful partnership. Duncombe and Marsden (1993) describe this as the gendered division of emotion work, whereby it is assumed that women will take responsibility for the management of emotions inside their relationships. To cope with their partners' reluctance to do emotional work, they found that women were either forced to build emotional relationships elsewhere (either with children or their women friends) or to accommodate to men's emotional distance over time. This is a far cry from Giddens' depiction of a pure relationship in which reciprocity between partners is achieved. The asymmetrical expression of emotional needs can partly be explained by men and women's different susceptibility to discourses of romantic love. Women continue to be represented as the more emotionally expressive and nurturing gender. Dominant discourses of masculinity, by contrast, send the signal that being overtly emotional is antithetical to masculinity. As Duncombe and Marsden (1993) argue, women's demands for emotional reciprocity in relationships may be the next frontier of the battle for gender equality.

NEW FATHERHOOD

The ideal of new fatherhood is a good example of how gender inequalities adapt to social change. There is widespread agreement among sociologists that the breadwinner model of fatherhood, in which the father takes the main responsibility for the family's financial provision, is being abandoned and replaced by an expectation that men should now be involved emotional carers. Although the breadwinning model of fatherhood has no doubt weakened, with many men and women rejecting statements suggesting that fathers should concentrate on the economic role while the mother's job is to take care of the home and children, there is little agreement about exactly what this new type of fatherhood entails. Dermott (2008) argues that there is a gap between a culture and conduct of fathering, so that although ideas about fatherhood have changed, the actual practices have changed much less.

Various studies of fathering have shown a significant gap between alternative discourses of fatherhood and actual fathering practices. There is an expectation of a good father–child relationship based on an emotional connection, but that relationship exists independently of an increased time commitment for fathers. Dermott (2003: 10) provides evidence that intimate fathering is compatible with a restricted investment in caring labour: 'the extent of fathers' practical involvement in childcare should not simply be assumed from statements of a desire for intimacy'. Although fathers may only spend a few hours with their children each day, key symbolic activities like reading them a bedtime story and going to their school play are seen as sufficient markers of intimacy. Therefore, having an emotional connection between father and child does not necessarily entail a fundamental transformation of fatherhood; it can still be centred on and incorporate aspects of the breadwinning model.

JAPAN

Japanese families have been undergoing rapid changes since the latter decades of the twentieth century. These rapid social transformations include a fall in marriage rates, an increase in divorce rates (although remaining lower than in other industrialized countries), an increase in the number of single women, a rise in the average age of marriage, low fertility rates, and a decrease in traditional three-generation households, especially in urban areas. For example, the fertility rate in Japan was 1.34 in 2000, which is lower than the USA but comparable to that of many European countries. The average age of first marriage in Japan has risen from 25.8 in 1980 to 29.4 in 2005 (Kamano and Khor 2008: 161). More than half of all Japanese women are still single at the age of 30 (Naito and Gielen 2005). There are also higher numbers of married women working outside the home, although the rate of working mothers with young children remains low at only 23.4%.

These changes are coupled with other trends, such as the tendency for children to live with their families until marriage and the very low rates of births outside marriage, which reflect considerable continuity in family formation. Changes in gender relations in Japan appear relatively slow, with fathers' roles still being seen mainly as breadwinning and men contributing little to family and household labour. The Japanese family remains a more stable and cohesive unit than the Euro-American equivalent. Japan, by comparison, remains a highly integrated society, which, partly because of the strong influence of Confucianism, privileges group harmony over individual autonomy. Naito and Gielen (2005) argue that, although the demographic trends and changes to the family that Japan is experiencing are

FIGURE 13.2 Japanese family-centred values
A young Japanese woman lovingly helps her grandmother eat an ice cream, but will strong family-centred values sustain into the future? Population projections suggest that Japanese aged 65 years and older will constitute 40% of the population by 2055, the result of lower fertility and increasing life spans.

similar to those occurring in other Western countries, the psychosocial interior of Japanese family life is still best captured by the concept of 'symbiotic harmony', with values such as loyalty and commitment being held in high regard. Much of the scholarship in this area says family continues to be absolutely central to Japanese people's lives, while actual ideals and practices of family are in the midst of quite radical transformation.

The studies discussed so far favour a cultural explanation for the specificity of the changes occurring in Japanese family life. Rebick and Takenaka (2006), however, suggest that the ways in which the Japanese family is changing are not unique, as Italy shares similar demographic features with Japan, including high rates of marriage, low rates of births outside wedlock, and a tendency for children to live with their parents rather than with their future partners until they get married. Despite these important similarities, Trifiletti (2006) points out that, given the different histories of their familial welfare regimes, there are no simple parallels between the Italian and Japanese cases. This suggests that, in understanding changes in families globally, we need to be alert to both the cultural specificity and the similarities in patterns of family formations across the globe.

In what follows we further examine this tension between change and continuity in gender relations in Japanese society by considering the changing meaning of marriage from the perspective of single women and the extent to which fatherhood is being renegotiated.

JAPANESE FATHERS

With very few male employees taking their entitled paternity leave and Japanese fathers reportedly spending as little as 16 minutes a day nurturing their child, the Japanese Ministry of Health, Labour and Welfare launched a campaign in 1999 entitled 'the joy of childcare' to sensitize fathers to the importance of their responsibility as parents. Although government campaigns praise and encourage involved fathering, in reality fathers are indirectly discouraged from becoming primary carers. Nakatani's (2006) research on nurturing fathers in Japan suggests that, since most childcare facilities are designed for mothers, fathers who are involved in their children's daily care often face barriers and criticism from their seniors and colleagues. Their belief in gender parity as well as what kind of social and institutional support they receive influence these men's decision to become involved in their children's care. Nakatani (2006) thus rightly points out that unless there is a revision in work patterns to cut long working hours and introduce flexible timekeeping, nurturing fatherhood can only become a reality for the privileged few. Nonetheless, fathers working in non-mainstream occupations, such as farmers in rural areas, may be able to see more of their family than salaried men, so economic conditions coupled with changes in attitudes will inevitably have an impact on family life.

The contradictory discourses about fathering in contemporary Japan create a decided contrast between the traditional breadwinning disciplinarian father who is seen as receding and the new caring and emotionally involved father. Quantitative research by Ishii-Kuntz et al. (2004) suggests that a change in attitudes alone may have little effect on Japanese men's involvement in childcare, and the authors recommend that the government should focus on reducing men's working hours and creating family-friendly policies in the workplace. This suggests that, in Japan as in the UK, attitudes towards fathering are changing faster than actual practices.

BOX 13.1 Marriage, heterosexuality and 'parasite singles' in Japan

Nemoto (2008) suggests that Japanese professional women's postponement of marriage is an individual solution to structural problems of gender inequality. Her study found that women experienced emotional ambivalence about getting married: they envied the higher social status and financial stability that married women enjoyed, but also viewed their financial independence as a form of resistance to traditional femininity. She argues that the deinstitutionalization of marriage apparent in Western countries, whereby individuals seek less traditional living arrangements and an emotionally intimate relationship, cannot fully explain the decline of marriage rates in Japan, given that Japan has low rates of cohabitation and births outside marriage. Japanese sociologist Yamada (1999) has disparagingly described the growing number of women who avoid marriage and motherhood and remain economically dependent on their parents as 'parasite singles'. Nemoto, however, provides a more complex analysis based on women's accounts of their lives:

- She found that these women had avoided marriage because it would inhibit their autonomy. Marriage was synonymous with self-sacrifice and having the task of running a household alone was a responsibility that was incompatible with their chosen career.

- Women's postponement of marriage was also linked to their desire to avoid sexist men and compounded by their inability to find Japanese men who held egalitarian beliefs about gender.

- The participants also reported that, as career women, they were perceived as unfeminine, threatening to men and therefore unsuitable 'marriage material'. Paradoxically, given that the participants complained about men's unrealistic ideas about femininity, these women nevertheless expected to marry highly educated 'masculine' men earning higher salaries than their own.

Nemoto's analysis highlights the difficult choices these women face and captures how they were simultaneously complying with some gendered discourses while also transgressing norms about femininity. Paradoxically, the tendency for more women to postpone or forego marriage has allowed sexual minorities to challenge the norms of a heterosexist society. Kamano and Khor's (2008) study of lesbian women's relationships in the Kanto area suggests that the increasing acceptability of postponing marriage, combined with the nonexistence of a heterosexual dating culture in Japan, has made it easier for lesbians to 'pass' as single women who do not intend to marry. A less positive consequence is that the apparent similarities between heterosexual single women and lesbians render lesbian lives invisible, making it difficult for them to be open about their relationships to their friends and families.

Sources: Kamano and Khor (2008); Nemoto (2008); Yamada (1999).

COMPARATIVE FAMILY STUDIES AND GLOBAL SOCIOLOGY

These snapshots of family life in two countries suggest that gender inequality, partly resulting from the differential links between motherhood and femininity and fatherhood and masculinity, is a key constant shaping family structures and relationships across cultures.

When assessing the extent of change in gender relations initially, Japan appeared more static, with stricter gender roles than in the UK; however, when comparing studies of fatherhood in both places, we find a common pattern. Although public discourses of fatherhood celebrate involvement and fathers say they want to be more involved in raising their children, the actual practices of fathers seem slower to change. We hope that this small comparative endeavour has alerted you to the difficulty of locating data sets that allow for meaningful comparisons. Although demographic data are more easily available, there is a relative lack of sociological qualitative studies in non-Western countries, making comparisons less balanced for capturing a vivid picture of family life. However, the difficulty of developing a comparative method should not mean we give up on it: in fact, we argue it continues to be a necessary project for a global sociology. As we saw in Chapter 1, a significant aspect of sociology is its concern with the comparative study of social life, so we need to consider which social changes and behavioural patterns seem to be universal or, by contrast, which seem to be particular to one part of the globe. Here we have seen that although there are important similarities across our two case studies in terms of gender inequalities in the family, the impact of individualization on family life is greater in the UK than in Japan. This approach has allowed us to gain insight into the differential extent of social change across societies and suggests that comparisons of qualitative studies can provide significant resources for developing a global approach to the sociology of families.

GLOBALIZATION AND INTIMACY

Here we consider how and the extent to which globalization is affecting family and intimate relationships. The families most critically affected are those living far apart from one another through migration and, in this context, we shall see that IT plays a crucial part in enabling 'transnational families' to maintain long-distance relationships. Moreover, we argue that globalization affects intimate relationships in ways that both reproduce existing inequalities and create new patterns of global inequality. This is not to say that globalization weakens family ties and threatens intimacy; instead, we would suggest that as more families are increasingly dispersed throughout the globe, it is creating new possibilities and new challenges for people maintaining and creating new family ties.

In their excellent volume on *Love and Globalization*, Padilla et al. (2007) suggest that because theoretical discussions of globalization have usually been concerned with political, economic and technological transformations on a macro-level, they have not captured how these processes are experienced at the subjective and local level and how they influence the most intimate parts of people's lives. They argue that love as a unique cultural domain is particularly sensitive to globalizing processes and that insights from local ethnographic studies can considerably deepen our understanding of the intersection between globalization and love. This is an approach we share and adopt in the discussion that follows.

TECHNOLOGY AS FACILITATOR OF GLOBAL INTIMACY

In Chapter 2 we discussed how electronic media have facilitated the compression of time and space and how this has important implications for those who live far away from their loved ones and their sense of togetherness. Such technologies bring with them a range of new problems and possibilities for developing and maintaining personal relationships. Conventionally, intimacy is assumed to involve the physical proximity of bodies – in fact, the adjective 'close' is a synonym of 'intimate'. Following this logic, distance from loved ones as a result of globalization could be presumed to threaten intimacy. Research suggests that communication technology, especially the internet, facilitates emotional closeness between family members over distance. This technology offers the opportunity for meaningful daily contact between loved ones, but it should not be assumed that the internet is intrinsically either beneficial or detrimental to families. To what extent technology facilitates relationships that are closer to Giddens' version of the pure relationship as democratic is also up for debate.

Gill Valentine (2006) holds that the internet enhances intimacy among family members living far from each other and describes it as the glue that binds family members together. It not only allows family members to exchange information and news more easily and to meet caring responsibilities over long distances, for example internet shopping for a grandparent or online banking for a child, but it can also be especially important for transnational families in which parent and child are separated but maintain close contact. Email allows absent parents to provide emotional care and children to negotiate autonomy from their parents and to seek their permission to do things. Valentine proposes that online and offline intimacies are bound in complex ways and that life around the screen and life on screen are mutually constituted, meaning that there is no straightforward way in which ICT impacts on families as this will depend on the context.

BOX 13.2 Information technology and transnational caring

Wilding's (2006) research into the role of ICT in transnational caring in Australia, Ireland, Italy, the Netherlands, Iran, Singapore and New Zealand shows that although information technologies have transformed the ways in which families can exchange support across long distances, there are also limitations to them. Here we highlight the main findings of the study:

- As new communication technologies develop and the costs of using them drop, they are incorporated into existing communication practices. Each new technology that comes along adds a layer of interaction, thus increasing the overall frequency of communication between families. This means that families are in touch much more regularly than before.

- More than the actual words exchanged, which participants reported usually comprised meaningless jokes, statements about the weather, or comments on sporting events, it is the moment of interaction that is important for the sense of closeness between family members.

- This disjuncture between imagined proximity and physical separation was particularly problematic at times of illness or crisis. ICTs may be described as 'sunny day' technologies, as the loss of sight, hearing or keyboard competence can impair our capacity to communicate with loved ones, and they provide few opportunities for involvement in the practical care of ageing parents.

- Wilding also suggests that virtual communications often reflect continuity with the past. For example, sibling relationships that were strained prior to migration continued to be strained despite the availability of ICTs. Moreover, the availability of ICT could also increase pressure on migrants to communicate with kin they would rather avoid and provided opportunities for family members to demand financial help.

- There was evidence of a gendered division of labour, with women having most of the responsibility for keeping in touch with kin abroad. However, this division was gradually becoming less demarcated with the introduction of emailing, which seemed to facilitate men's participation.

Source: Wilding (2006).

In the case of one of Wilding's participants (Box 13.2) whose mother suffered from dementia, communication technologies were no longer able to keep him connected with her. This draws our attention to the assumption that we enjoy healthy bodies and minds in caring for our families across distance. Moreover, although internet technology does not necessarily impoverish family and personal relationships, it does limit the experience of intimacy because of its disembodied nature. To what extent can we have a full sense of intimacy with our loved ones if we are not physically together? Elspeth Probyn (1995) has argued that, ironically, desire can be frustrated by distance as spatial segregation accentuates longing. Although communication technologies can facilitate loving, caring and even sexual relations, this is not always an adequate substitute for a parental hug or a lover's caress; the absence of touch can serve to accentuate the longing for another body. Thus, it seems that rather than making the body redundant for intimate relationships, communication technologies reassert the significance of bodily contact.

It has been suggested that email is the technology that most influences family relationships because it is cheaper, faster and more informal, allowing a private form of contact between individual family members and overcoming the difficulty of communicating across time zones. However, other studies draw attention to telephony as significant for maintaining transnational family ties. Vertovec (2004) was one of the first to notice and discuss this trend. His research pointed to the significant role of phone cards in non-elite migrants' lives as they facilitate cheap calls, which he describes as a kind of social glue connecting small-scale social formations across the globe. Uy-Tioco's (2007) research on Filipina migrant workers on the east coast of the USA suggests that mobile phone technology has empowered Filipina migrant mothers to continue their mothering across time and space and to maintain relationships with their children. Through text messaging, mothers in faraway countries are able to ask their children about their day at school, remind them to do their homework, bid them good night and momentarily suspend their physical separation. Although the costs of this are high, many participants sent more than 30 texts a day to their families. Uy-Tioco argues that, although empowering, mobile phone technology has also reinstated the idea that caring and nurturing are solely the mother's role. While being the breadwinner for the family has to some extent masculinized the role of these migrant mothers, this has not led to a renegotiation of parenting gender roles in Filipino households, for even when mothers are far away, they are still seen as the ones responsible for nurturing their children. This study aptly captures the complex ways in which technologies simultaneously provide solutions for maintaining relationships as well as reinforcing existing inequalities within families.

Horst's (2006) research on the integration of mobile phones in Jamaican transnational communication suggests that although most Jamaicans interviewed saw mobile phones as an unadulterated blessing, in that they made communication with family abroad cheaper and created a sense of involvement in their daily lives, they also increased obligations to kin and could be used as a form of surveillance by partners or family members. The relatively high availability of mobile phones in the country places Jamaicans at the forefront of mobile phone usage and also makes up for their lack of access to internet technologies. While mobile phones facilitated an increased ability to communicate outside Jamaica, they did not dramatically change the dynamics of power and inequality within these transnational fields: those outside Jamaica were still perceived as having more income and mobility and were expected to send money to kin back home. But the mobile phone made it much easier to receive money for a specific purpose, such as school fees or uniforms, and made it easier to collect money in an emergency.

Moreover, Holmes's (2006) research on Australian couples 'living apart together' found that phone contact was still the most important medium of communication, with daily conversations often covering what their loved one had had for dinner or how their day at work had gone. A sense of being close was facilitated by maintaining familiarity with each other's daily routines rather than sharing inner thoughts and feelings, suggesting that intimacy is often grounded in the everyday and the material, rather than in opening up one's soul, which is at the core of Giddens' thesis. Research into the ways transnational families use communication technology suggests that it can facilitate increased closeness and intimacy, yet simultaneously become burdensome because it creates new responsibilities and obligations for kin. As we suggest in Chapter 16, the internet and telephony have both positive and negative effects on people's everyday lives. This tension, which has been evident throughout the chapter, is reconfigured here in transnational space and complicated by inequalities between members of a family living in more or less affluent parts of the globe.

GLOBALIZATION AND NEW RELATIONSHIPS

Here we look at how increased mobility through migratory and tourist flows produces particular kinds of sexual and romantic relationships and what this tell us about the intermeshing of globalization and intimacy. Much of the research in this area suggests that globality supports specific forms of intimacy, thus creating new kinds of romance, courtship, sexual relations and marriage across borders. Some studies characterize these relationships as a blurring of the distinction between love, obligation and transaction, while others depict them as marked by inequality and oppression. People in cross-border marriages, migrant domestic workers, care workers and migrant sex workers all experience these new types of intimate relations; and drawing on ethnographic case studies, we consider two of these groups.

Bloch's (2010) study of post-Soviet women migrants to Turkey suggests that love forms a key part of transnational mobility. She found that although women migrated initially for work, their intimate relationships with Turkish men also shaped their migration. Female migrants could turn these relationships to their economic advantage. They helped them sustain contacts with their families back home through sending remittances, sponsoring relatives' visits to Turkey, or gaining longer term visas and/or residency status. Their ties with Turkish men, who were often married, brought them stability, financial support and emotional sustenance. Such relationships blurred the divide between emotional and instrumental ties and suggest that the forms of intimacy migrants forge in their adopted countries are relationships in which love, romance and material benefit merge together. Thus, a complex interweaving of motivations and emotional attachments defines these women's migratory experience. At the same time, troubling power imbalances also define these relationships, which the stereotyping of post-Soviet women as sexually available increases. Women resisted the power imbalance by avoiding marriage as it would have curtailed their freedom and meant providing unpaid domestic labour. Bloch's study draws attention to how shifting configurations of global capital shape personal and intimate lives, and how women migrants' emotional entanglements mesh with their economic need.

Sex tourism and the sexual relationships between locals and tourists provide an attention-grabbing example of how globalization creates different and new forms of intimacy. Recently, a number of studies have examined sexual relationships between hosts and guests in the Caribbean's international tourism industry, but authors disagree about how we should characterize these relationships and even whether they can be described as 'intimate'. Drawing on fieldwork with sex trade workers in Cuba and the Dominican Republic, Cabezas (2004) argues that it is worth distinguishing the motivations and experiences of different erotic travellers involved in this new form of sexual commerce. She describes the sexual activity between tourists and locals as 'blurry', with elements of romance, leisure, consumption, travel and marriage intertwined. While many trade their sexual services for cash, many others who participate in the sexual economy do not. Therefore, not all sex tourism should be classified as sex work; it is best understood as a continuum along multiple gradations of erotic, affectional and economic practices. Cabezas attributes agency to Cubans and Dominicans, whom she sees as challenging their subordination within the global economy, whereby love, friendship, companionship, or sex with tourists offers them the possibility of escaping brutal poverty. Again, this challenges the assumption that love, romance, work and money are separate notions, an issue to which we return below.

Other sociological studies of global sex tourism, by contrast, have argued that relationships between tourists and their hosts are deeply unequal and exploitative. They draw attention to 'othering processes' as characteristic of relationships that eroticize racial and cultural difference. For example, O'Connell Davidson and Sanchez Taylor's (1999) research on Western male sex tourists in the Caribbean emphasizes Western tourists' economic power and the racist dimensions of these transactions. Combining Marxist and postcolonial approaches, they argue that the demand for sex tourism in the Caribbean can primarily be explained because it gives men the opportunity to indulge in racialized sexual fantasies and to access the kind of gendered power they lack in the West. Their economic and race privileges explain why these men engage in prostitution in developing countries and not back home. They found that male sex tourists demonstrated different kinds of sexualized racism to justify their sexual transactions, such as invoking that Jamaicans are more uninhibited about sex and are naturally sexually promiscuous. Ultimately, O'Connell Davidson and Sanchez Taylor (1999: 42) would see romances that others describe as combining emotional connection with economic transactions as 'fantasies of mutuality', which merely cover up the commercial basis of the sexual interaction and obscure the inequalities between the two parties.

THE COMMODIFICATION OF INTIMACY

COMMODIFICATION

This refers to the ways in which goods, services and even relationships are turned into commodities, to be bought or sold in the marketplace. The Marxist notion of 'commodity fetishism' (Chapter 14) further suggests that we have come to overvalue or even 'worship' possessions and goods.

The idea that real love and affection cannot be bought with money and that economic transactions corrupt personal relationships are central to our ideas about intimacy. We consider whether economic activity on a global scale should be seen as creating and sustaining intimate ties or as destroying them. We also consider to what extent the concept of commodification can usefully further our understanding of relationships between intimacy and economics in the context of global capitalism.

In *The Purchase of Intimacy*, Zelizer (2005) analyses the ways in which the boundaries between commercial and loving relationships are policed and challenges the idea that money corrupts intimacy. She argues that the idea that money devalues intimacy is based on moral judgements that deem exchanges as appropriate in certain relationships but not in others. The taboo associated with mixing money and intimacy comes from the doctrine of separate spheres and hostile worlds. In other words, there are sharply separated arenas for economic activity (the public sphere) and intimate relations (the private sphere) and contact between the two leads to disorder and contamination. The problem with this doctrine is that it views the domestic sphere as protected from the harsh world of market capitalism and fails to recognize the all-encompassing nature of the market. Different stakeholders, including families and governments, defend their 'authentic' versions of intimacy when they are being transgressed. Zelizer analyses breach of promise lawsuits in the USA, which illustrate that economic transactions constantly mingle with intimate life. While the courts saw some gifts exchanged between courting couples as appropriate, anything too expensive or ostentatious was seen as inappropriate because it could be misconstrued as something a man would give to a mistress or prostitute. Money became the basis of courtship from the 1930s and was used to determine the status of a relationship. In return, this was legislated by courts by matching intimate relationships with appropriate economic transactions as a way of policing the boundary between proper and improper forms of intimacy.

A PAUSE TO REFLECT

We have seen that economic exchanges between loved ones often create and sustain intimate ties rather than threatening them. Do you think that we can avoid mixing money with our intimate relationships? Does money necessarily corrupt intimacy? Does this differ in relationships between individuals coming from unequal parts of the globe? Is it true to say that intimacy is becoming increasingly commodified in contemporary societies?

Other scholars have drawn attention to the ways in which aspects of intimate and personal relations – especially those associated with reproductive labour – are increasingly commodified and implicated in broader global capitalist processes. Studies on transnational intimacies illustrate that relationships assumed to be based primarily on paid work also involve complex forms of intimacy and emotion, and those assumed to be based on love are linked in new ways to commercial practices. For example, Illouz's (2007) analysis of internet dating suggests that romantic encounters are being turned into economic transactions – writing a profile on a dating website is really marketing oneself to potential partners. For Illouz, internet dating combines the logic of psychology and consumerism and demands a rationalized mode of partner selection in which speed and efficiency are privileged and everything is dictated by the market.

In her essay 'Love and gold', Arlie Hochschild (2003) (Global Thinkers 13) considers how intimacy and economics are connected on a global scale. As we saw in Chapter 8, the term 'global care chains' describes the large flow of nannies, nurses and care workers from poorer developing countries who come to work in the West, an example of emotional and economic inequalities between the North and the South. Hochschild argues that, in caring for Western children, these women are engaging not only in an economic transaction but also in an intimate exchange because, separated as they are from their own families, they often come to love these children as their own. These migrant mothers give the love they would otherwise have given to their children back home to their employer's children, resulting, Hochschild argues, in a 'global heart transplant'. The nanny's love is commodified under capitalist conditions, resulting in a new emotional imperialism between North and South and an unequal distribution of love across the globe. Hochschild draws attention to emotions as an increasingly important dimension of globalization and provides a powerful political critique of how these resources are unevenly distributed across the globe, but her analysis leaves very little space for the complex and contradictory feelings that migrant nannies are likely to experience.

GLOBAL THINKERS 13 ARLIE HOCHSCHILD (1940–)

Arlie Hochschild is a professor of sociology at the University of California, Berkeley. She has made an important contribution to research on the gendered division of labour at home and in the workplace and more widely to debates about work and family life in the contemporary USA. She is also widely known as one of the founders of the sociology of emotions, combining insights from symbolic interactionism with a Marxist approach to studying inequalities. In her first book, *The Managed Heart* (1983), Hochschild deployed the concept of 'emotional labour' to analyse the display of socially desired emotions of air hostesses and debt collectors. She posits that employees experience emotional labour when their organization dictates how they are to feel and express emotions in return for a wage. She argues that the commodification of feelings as customer service is harmful as it leads to the alienation of workers.

In *The Second Shift*, Hochschild and Machung (1989) studied the ways in which couples negotiate housework. They found that women continued to assume the primary responsibility for these tasks – 'the second shift' – even when their hours of paid work, earning power and theoretical commitments to altered gender roles had increased. They conclude from this that couples are made up of faster changing women and slower changing men who are caught in a 'stalled gender revolution', as women have absorbed the greater part of the extra work that the changes in gender relations have generated. In 'Love and gold' (2003), Hochschild analyses the way emotional labour has gone global by looking at the transnational provision of motherly care and love. She describes a South-to-North 'heart transplant' as immigrant care workers from countries such as the Philippines and Sri Lanka leave their young, their elderly and their communities in the poor South to take up paid jobs caring for the young and elderly in families of the affluent North such as the USA. Such jobs call on workers to displace their longing for their own long-separated children, spouses and elderly parents onto the children and elders for whom they care in the North. These global care chains then reinforce global inequalities by redistributing emotional care labour from those in poorer countries for consumption by those in richer ones.

Hochschild's more recent work on the commercialization of intimate life draws attention to human emotion as an important feature of how global capitalism functions, a dimension of globalization not considered until recently.

Sources: Hochschild (1983, 2003); Hochschild and Machung (1989).

It is interesting to note that the Marxist concept of commodification (Chapter 14) is widely used in much of the scholarship on intimacy and globalization and manages to provide powerful, up-to-date sociological analyses of these fairly new processes. This illustrates both Marx's enduring relevance as an early global thinker and the creativity of sociologists who have adapted his concepts. Marx never fully considered intimate and family relationships in his work, although in 1848 he and Engels made this telling comment in *The Communist Manifesto* ([1848]1967): 'The bourgeoisie has torn away from the family its sentimental veil, and has reduced the family relation into a mere money relation.' Nonetheless, as Constable (2009) points out, commodification should not be the end point of the analysis and future research should not lament the decline of authentic relations outside the realm of capital; it should attend to the multiple, complex and transformative ways in which emotional ties and relationships are developing across local and global spaces and accommodate the conditions of late modern capitalism.

A PAUSE TO REFLECT

According to Arlie Hochschild, the care deficit created by women's mass entry into the labour market in the North is being filled by migrant nannies from the South, suggesting that instead of a redistribution of care labour between men and women, we are witnessing widening inequalities between poorer and richer women across the globe. What are the implications of this phenomenon for the global women's movement? How might this 'care deficit' be resolved differently?

REVIEW

In this chapter we have illustrated that despite huge social changes, including individualization and globalization, there is little evidence that they are leading to the weakening of family ties and that families and personal relationships continue to be central to people's lives across the globe. Although the extent of changes in the structure of families varies enormously across countries, there does seem to be a general trend towards greater freedom from strictly defined gender roles and a desire for a renegotiation of family responsibilities, even if little has changed in practice, as the scholarship on fatherhood demonstrates. Sometimes, these changes in gender relations have been the result of feminism and women's entry into the labour market, but in other parts of the globe women have always been engaged in both child rearing and providing economically for their families. However, it is also important not to overestimate the extent of these changes in family life because much of the research suggests that there are important continuities in family life and that often, as in the case of Japanese 'parasite' singles, old scripts reinvent themselves under new guises. Overall, we have seen that the ways in which we study the social world matter. For example, by attending to the subjective experiences of people captured by ethnographic research, we can attain a more complex and vivid picture of globalization that reflects how social actors are both affected by and shape global processes. Similarly, by focusing on the practices and emotions of families rather than just their formal structures, we can go beyond seeing families as primarily the sites for the negotiation and reproduction of inequalities.

We started this chapter by saying that families are simultaneously sites of togetherness and intimacy, and exploitation and oppression. Perhaps in reaction to Giddens' overly optimistic account of the democratization of intimate life, we have drawn more attention to how family relationships remain deeply unequal, especially those between men and women but also, under conditions of globalization, between family members within and across continents. Hochschild's discussion of migrant nannies and love as a global commodity illustrated this point. We have also seen that the economic conditions of social actors deeply affect family and intimate relationships. Nevertheless, our discussion of how technology is allowing transnational families to sustain intimate ties over long distances provided a predominantly positive consequence of globalization. Finally, we drew attention to the increasing significance of the market in shaping intimate relationships everywhere. However, this is not all bad news because globalization does not just result in greater commodification of intimate relationships but also offers opportunities for defining new sorts of relationships that can challenge social norms.

Visit the companion website at www.palgrave.com/sociology/cohen3e for extra materials to check and expand your learning, including interactive self-test questions, mind maps making links between key themes, annotated web links to sociological research, data and key sociological thinkers, a searchable glossary and much more.

FURTHER READING

Love and Globalization: Transformations of Intimacy in the Contemporary World (2007), M. Padilla et al.'s excellent edited volume, is well worth having a look at; it features ethnographic case studies from diverse parts of the world, including Egypt, Brazil and Greece.

D. Brennan's *What's Love Got to Do with It? Transnational Desires and Sex Tourism in the Dominican Republic* (2004) does not just have a catchy title, it is also an excellent study of sex tourism in the Dominican Republic.

Global Woman: Nannies, Maids and Sex Workers in the New Economy (2003), edited by B. Ehrenreich and A. Hochschild, is a pioneering collection of essays in this field.

N. Constable has written an excellent review essay, 'The commodification of intimacy: marriage, sex, and reproductive labor' (2009). This is great if you want an overview of the field or are interested in commodification.

The Handbook of World Families (2005), edited by B. Adam and J. Frost, provides a comparative perspective, with chapters on family life in 25 countries worldwide.

QUESTIONS AND ASSIGNMENTS

1. Why should sociologists of intimacy be concerned with economics?
2. Describe the main features of the transformation of intimacy, according to Giddens.
3. Do information technologies threaten or enhance our family and intimate relationships?
4. Critically assess the usefulness of the concept of 'commodification' for understanding the contemporary changes in intimate life.
5. Explain how and why the sociology of families and intimacy has changed over the past 60 years.

14 Consuming culture

Drink a cup of tea or coffee and you instantly connect to the global marketplace. The list of world goods that arrives in this casual way is formidable and grows continuously. World goods are simultaneously produced in a multiplicity of locations, then purchased and experienced by people living in many different societies. As early as the 1990s, Firat (1995: 114) observed that what is really remarkable is not simply the sheer range of available global products but the fact that one can 'rent a Toyota, listen to Madonna and Sting tunes, enjoy a croissant for breakfast, and follow one's favourite soap opera on television' even in 'the remotest corners of the world'.

Our experience of living in the global marketplace is revealed particularly well in the case of food and beverages. Here are just a few examples:

- In 1993 in the British fast-food sector, fish and chip shops were outnumbered for the first time by Indian takeaways (James 1996: 81). Similarly, pizza and pasta became 'the most global of global foods', although both have only recently become recognized as national foods in Italy and many ingredients in Italian cuisine arrived initially from China (pasta) or the Americas (tomatoes and bell peppers) (James 1996: 76; Mariani 2011).
- Global cuisine could also be widely found in restaurants located in cities from New York to Manama, the capital of Bahrain, in the Persian Gulf. In the latter, according to Chase (1994: 84), one restaurant offered 'Arabic (Lebanese and Gulf items), Chinese, Indian, pizza and hamburger, and grills' all delivered by Filipina employees to the accompaniment of Greek music.
- The popularity of brand-named foods/beverages such as Pizza Hut, Kentucky Fried Chicken and the famous McDonald's burger had spread worldwide. For example, in 2010 Coca-Cola sold 1.6 billion of its various drinks each day in over 200 territories (www.thecoca-colacompany.com). Nearly half were drunk by consumers in Japan and the BRIC countries.

In this chapter we explore the globalization of consumption and consider its implications for how we now experience social and cultural life. Our central theme is the impact of what Sklair (2002: Ch. 7) calls 'the culture-ideology of consumerism' evidenced by many in the rich countries, but especially by those living in the developing countries. The adoption of this ideology has led some observers to fear that continued Western and more especially US domination of many industries, along with advertising and the mass media, is giving rise to a new kind of imperialism, one based not on political but on cultural control.

This process is said to be creating an increasingly homogeneous world in which Western lifestyles and brand goods are in danger of obliterating countless, unique local cultures. To examine this theory, we need first to explore the multidimensional character of consumerism as a universal activity along with its special features under global capitalism. Similarly, we need to consider the different perspectives – both pessimistic and optimistic – from which sociologists have viewed its contemporary implications.

CONSUMERISM AND EVERYDAY LIFE

As a central part of human experience, consumption has one foot squarely planted in the spheres of politics, economics and history and another rooted firmly in social life and culture. This has always been the case, but capitalist industrialization and globalization have deepened and accentuated these linkages in several ways:

1. Most people's contribution to economic life takes the form of self- or wage employment, helping to produce goods or services for sale. This is called 'commodity production'. Meanwhile, buyers satisfy their various needs by using their earnings to purchase things produced by vast numbers of people whom they do not know. This is quite different from the self- and family provisioning, supplemented by reciprocal sharing arrangements between kin and community members, characteristic of premodern societies.
2. The organization of production, transport and distribution through numerous companies and networks of exchange depends on certain national and worldwide institutional arrangements and laws. These facilitate financial investment and currency management, guarantee ownership rights and freedom of movement, and provide adequate systems of communication. Worldwide production and consumption also create a more interdependent global economy.
3. Social life shapes our consumption preferences and practices. We demonstrate our loyalties to others through such things as wearing special uniforms, public displays of hospitality, or generosity through giving gifts. Our consumer preferences and styles in everything from clothes and cars to household decorations say important things about who we are, or what claims to social status we would like to make.
4. Our possessions also carry various meanings. These are associated with the wider cultural beliefs, values and orientations we share with others. Drawing on this pool of common meanings enables us to communicate, make sense of the world around us, and express our shared identities and values.

Paralleling this bridging quality at the societal level is the dualistic nature of all goods (Douglas and Isherwood 1978), irrespective of whether we are talking about a premodern or capitalist society. Goods constitute the 'hardware' of social and cultural life. They possess an intrinsic materiality and utility, or what Marx called their 'use-value'; eating rice keeps you alive and clothes protect you from the weather. Yet, at the same time, even the most basic goods simultaneously act as the 'software' of everyday life. They express the meanings with which we have endowed them; they exercise a symbolic significance. Because these meanings are shared, others can read and decode our consumer practices. Archaeological evidence indicates that even the most basic utensils that prehistoric people used – such as clay water pots – were invariably embellished with decorations. These probably expressed family affiliations, social position or respect for religious deities. They also gave aesthetic pleasure.

In capitalist economies, this universal duality between function and form acquires a further characteristic because goods become commodities and assume an exchange value in the market. Moreover, as we shall see, the cultural meanings embedded in all goods become highly desirable forms of merchandise in their own right. Finally, because all goods contain symbolic as well as material qualities, it is virtually impossible, as some earlier writers suggested, to make a distinction between those that fulfil our 'real' survival *needs* and those that cater merely to our 'inessential' *wants*. No goods are inessential in cultural terms.

A PAUSE TO REFLECT

We have distinguished between the 'use-value' and the 'symbolic value' of consumer goods. Is this a similar distinction between 'a necessity' and 'a luxury'? Are luxuries culturally and historically determined? If so, can you think of different ways in which they vary across societies and across time?

THE MEANING OF CONSUMERISM

In contemporary successful economies, we enjoy a superfluity of goods and most are acquired through the market. Normally, private ownership defines our access to these goods. Also, in place of the rather durable non-commercialized meanings that formally adhered to products – derived from an accumulated cultural legacy – the meanings they hold today are often contrived, transitory and placed there for purposes of profit. To understand how and why this happens, we need to understand the semiotic or symbolic nature of goods. Contemporary sociological discussion of consumption often draws on the ideas of Ferdinand de Saussure (1857–1913) and Roland Barthes (1915–80). Saussure's book, *Course in General Linguistics* (1974), was put together by his colleagues from his lecture notes after his death. It became a classic text in semiotics. Saussure was mainly interested in language, the written words or spoken sounds that carry or signify meanings. We summarize some of his key ideas in Box 14.1.

SEMIOTICS

The study of signs and symbols in language and other means of communication.

BOX 14.1 Saussure's thinking about language and semiotics

In studying language, one of Saussure's key distinctions was between the signifier and the signified:

- The *signifier* is the vehicle or form by which meanings are conveyed. In language, signifiers are the actual words we either hear as sounds or read as particular letter combinations.

- The *signified* is the mental image or concept that is carried by the signifier.

- Together, the signifier and signified form the *sign*. We carry around learned knowledge of signs in our heads and this allows us to decode them.

- Thus, our ability to read signs enables us to engage in processes of *signification*, that is, to attribute meaning to signs.

In language, the relationship between actual words, or signifiers, and the meanings they convey, the signified, is arbitrary. The word for 'bird' could just as easily be 'splift' or 'mnenk'. The image conveyed of a feathery flying creature remains the same whatever 'sound image' (Strinati 1995: 91) we decide to use, providing we share it in common. Thus, the meanings of words do not derive from the actual objects to which they refer but from the overall structure of grammatical rules and elaborate systems of word differences that we call 'language'.

Contemporary sociologists and semiologists study all forms of representation to 'read' or decode their meanings. These exist, for example, in art, photographs, sounds, advertisements, logos, even the assortment of clothes that different subcultures, such as hippies, punks or goths, wear (Hall and Jefferson 1993; Hebdige 2003). In so doing, they adapt Saussure's basic scheme concerning the sign as made up by the combination of a signifier and signified.

Sources: Strinati (1995); Thwaites et al. (1994).

Barthes added to our understanding of signification (see Strinati 1995: Ch. 3; Thwaites et al. 1994: Chs 1, 2 and 3). Barthes argued that in other forms of cultural representation, such as advertisements and clothing, the link between the signifier and the signified is not arbitrary. This is because, unlike in language, signifiers are manifested through visible cultural items such as a national flag, a particular style of shoe, a photograph of a model X car, or a famous TV celebrity.

Because others exposed to the same culture have learned the same or similar codes, social conventions or ideologies, the messages carried and our ability to read them are not random happenings. Cultural meanings cluster together and tend to crystallize around certain dominant, clear messages that are embedded in particular shared histories and social conditions. In Britain, for example, a bouquet of white carnations usually means 'a wedding' and carries the message of fond congratulations. Other flowers and colours may suggest quite different things. For instance, red roses act as a signifier for an intimate declaration of romantic love. As Barthes pointed out, many signs are deliberately manufactured and spread by dominant interest groups and social classes – the Church, aristocratic elites or the rising capitalist bourgeoisie. Thus, signs are rarely innocent; rather, the messages they carry incorporate value preferences. We watch a TV news clip showing the coffin of a US marine draped in the Stars and Stripes being carried from a military plane amid a sombre scene. The president comforts bereaved relatives and uniformed dignitaries pay their respects against a backdrop of suitably doleful music. The decoded message is that the USA is proud to pay the price of exercising the global responsibility necessary to guarantee peace and civilized values in a troubled world.

However, such images and messages work to suppress alternative interpretations. These might lead us to ask why the USA engaged in military confrontations in Vietnam, Grenada, Somalia, Afghanistan and Iraq, and who benefited most from these activities. Thus, signs such as a military funeral prompt us to think that they depict unavoidable and 'natural' realities, but in fact they preclude other possible lines of enquiry and explanation. When this happens, the processes of signification assume the character of myth making. Myths acquire the status of timeless truths, but they also inhibit our ability to interpret cultural meanings.

Two important questions arise from this discussion:

1. How do we read the meanings advertisers attach to the commodities they want us to buy? On the one hand, we may be cultural dupes or dopes who passively decode these messages or signs exactly as the advertisers hope. On the other hand, we may be cultural heroes who are perfectly capable of disregarding such messages or imposing our own meanings irrespective of the advertisers' intentions (Slater 1997: 33–4).

2. What are the effects on our lives of the relentless volume of swirling messages, images and symbols to which we are subjected? These assail us every time we walk down the street, read a magazine, watch TV, visit the cinema, or attend a rock concert or football match where, inevitably, we are also exposed to advertising slogans and BRANDS.

> ### KEY CONCEPT
> A BRAND is much more powerful than an advertisement because it refers not to one product but to an entire range of goods sold by a company, and it promises consumers access to a whole way of life modelled on the vibrant grassroots cultures found in street life, among ethnic minorities, the urban poor, youth gangs and so on (see Klein 2001).

A CRITICAL PESSIMISTIC SCENARIO: CONSUMERS AS DOPES

To address some of the key arguments about consumption, we focus on two diametrically opposite viewpoints. First, we discuss the idea that consumers are innocents in the face of the onslaught of producers, advertisers and market managers. Then, we consider how consumers can strike back and, at least to some degree, assert their autonomy and capacity to innovate.

According to Marx, COMMODITY FETISHISM occurs when an inanimate object is treated as if it required a religious, or even sexual, devotion. In premodern societies, fetishes were handmade or rare natural objects thought to embody a spirit that protected the owner from misfortune or disease. Commodity fetishism arises under capitalism because the market system has become much more real and immediate to us than the underlying social relationships (based on inequality and exploitation) that made goods sold on the market possible in the first place.

COMMODITY FETISHISM

Employing one of his most powerful concepts – COMMODITY FETISHISM – Marx argued that commodity production creates a depersonalized economy. Clusters of unknown, hired workers and machines in different locations produce goods for unknown buyers. The capitalist system is so complex and impersonal that it is virtually impossible to understand or identify with it. Not only is there a 'distancing, both physical and imaginative, of production from consumption' (Brewer and Trentmann 2006: 3), but the surface world of commodity exchange often also conceals the hidden, real world of work. At the same time, the opportunity for self-realization through creative work and social cooperation is simultaneously denied and compensated for by the attractive possessions on sale in bazaars and shopping malls. We tend therefore to imbue our purchases with a meaning and significance they cannot possess. We fetishize them, that is, turn them into objects of devotion with magical features, when, in fact, a bottle of expensive perfume, for example, is only processed whale blubber with added drops of scent essence derived from skunks.

MASS CONSUMPTION

Many writers have been highly critical of the era of mass consumption associated with the rise of Fordist production, a theme we discussed in Chapter 4. Adorno and Horkheimer (1972), for example, argued that expanding Fordist production compelled businesses to feed our desire for more goods while persuading us to abandon still useful products in favour of newer ones. Here, the advertising industry played a major role by producing an endless stream of new meanings – images of exotica, nostalgia, desire, romance, beauty, or the good life. These meanings were then embedded in mundane products such as vacuum cleaners, soft drinks and soaps.

With these products quite incapable of fulfilling their promises, consumers tend to be seduced by false needs and impossible hopes. Brand 'Y' shampoos cannot actually improve your love life very much and refitting your living room with fashionable furniture is unlikely to fill a lonely, friendless life. Also, the meanings employed in mass consumer culture need to be simple and instantly accessible so that they speed up the turnover of huge volumes of goods. The harshest critics say this creates a homogenized world of standardized mass products and a bland, stupefying culture, lacking substance.

© MACDUFF EVERTON/CORBIS

FIGURE 14.1 Mexican girls with blocks of chewing gum

Blocks of *chicle* (chewing gum) are collected in remote parts of Latin America, including the forests of Yucatan in Mexico by Indian tappers (Redclift 2006). This helps to feed the endless appetites of Western consumers. The cost of cleaning chewing gum off London's streets was estimated at £10m in 2010.

SIGNIFYING CULTURE

In consumer culture, the subtle meanings that advertising and seductive packaging implant in goods – what Baudrillard (1988) called their 'sign-values' – become much more important to us than their material properties. Indeed, the intrinsic use value of goods may become detached from the advertisers' meanings altogether; the latter becoming free-floating. Either way, increasingly we live in a 'signifying culture', one that abounds with disconnected messages. It is these that we desire, not functional goods. In this scenario, what we buy bears less and less relation to our actual needs.

DEPTHLESSNESS

Another problem is the sheer quantity of signs circulating in our consumer culture. More-over, signs are inherently volatile. Their meanings often mutate or break free from the object or context they were originally intended to represent. They are also subject to media manip-ulation. Thus, despite the media and advertisers' emphasis on creating meanings in order to attract our attention, meaning actually eludes us. We are unable to find either self-realization or ourselves on the supermarket shelves. According to Jameson (1984), this gives life a shallow or 'depthless' quality: we lose our bearings and become disoriented.

KEY CONCEPT

SIMULACRA (singular simulacrum) are entities that have no original or no surviving original in the actual world, but are nonetheless thought to be 'real'. Cult followers, for example of Elvis Presley or characters in certain TV soaps, seek to emulate their simulacra perhaps by copying their appearance or supposed lifestyles, writing to them for personal advice, or even proposing marriage.

FANTASY BECOMES REALITY

The media-inspired fantasy world of TV soaps, films and adverts, where messages and symbols flourish, often seems more alive to us than the actual social world we inhabit. The latter shrinks in significance and, in a curious way, becomes far less real. Indeed, we may seek to imitate and build our lives around SIMULACRA. Baudrillard (1988) calls the condition in which fake or fantasy experiences become more real to us than our concrete everyday world 'hyperreality'.

Apart from the followings that grow up around certain films and TV programmes, another excellent example of hyperreality is the enor-mous popularity of Disney parks in the USA, Japan, Hong Kong and France. In 2009, these Disneyland theme parks attracted nearly 5 million visitors in Hong Kong, 25 million in Tokyo and almost 13 million in Paris (www.coastergrotto.com/theme-park-attendance.jsp). Disney parks offer spectacles based on a largely mythical or fairy-tale world of handsome princes and animals, such as Mickey Mouse, imbued with heroic or comical human characteristics. In Disney parks, visitors often mistake living birds and animals for plastic ones; the line between reality and fantasy has been lost. Bryman (1995: 172) speculated that: 'the fake worlds of the Disney parks, which represent a non-existent reality, become models for American society, so that a hyperreal America is being constructed which is based on a simulacrum'.

THE GLOBAL CONSUMPTION OF NOTHING

In Chapter 4 we discussed Ritzer's (2004a) work on the predictable, standardized character of the fast-food and other service industries and how this McDonaldization process has spread rapidly worldwide. More recently, Ritzer (2004b: 3–10) adapted this argument by suggesting that a vast number of products, from cars and watches to consumer services such as credit cards, entertainment and, of course, fast foods, are now relatively empty of the specific, detailed content and uniqueness that once came from their embeddedness in partic-ular local traditions and individualized production systems. Instead, they are bland, have little substantive content and lack distinction. Vast corporations, advertising agencies and banks control their production and merchandising centrally. People tend to consume these 'non-things' (Ritzer 2004b: 55) in 'non-places' (Augé 1995), such as shopping malls, airport lounges and supermarkets, which are anonymous, standardized locations to which it is impossible to feel any sense of personal attachment. Such 'nothing' consumer products and experiences lend themselves to being globalized – sold in vast quantities from huge emporia across many countries. This is in stark contrast to traditional individualized jewellery, or original, localized clothing produced by highly skilled artisans in tin shacks in Kenya, Senegal or Ghana, which are then transported in suitcases by air and bus through the informal 'African fashion network' (Augé 1995: 13) of individual marketers, designers and diasporic kin connections to locations such as the Los Angeles African market (Rabine 2002: Ch. 1).

AN OPTIMISTIC SCENARIO: CONSUMERS AS CREATIVE HEROES

The chief difficulty with the negative scenario is that it leaves little space for human agency. It also strongly implies that there is something inherently artificial and trivial about the meanings carried by goods under capitalism precisely because they are produced and sold for profit and obtained through market exchange. This renders them inferior as cultural forms and implicates them deeply in exploitation. There are several counterarguments to this view.

A PAUSE TO REFLECT

In this chapter we have distinguished between consumers as dopes or creative heroes. Perhaps this is a spectrum not a dichotomy. If you were to characterize your own consumer behaviour – buying clothes, choosing food, or listening to music – at which end of the spectrum do you find yourself?

PRODUCT DIFFERENTIATION

One of the most striking things about capitalist marketing techniques is the way companies attempt to promote their distinctive products. Consumers belong to quite different groups according to their class, education, religion, ethnicity, sexual orientation and type of family responsibilities. Each of these identities may generate marked variations in needs and taste. Then there is the question of what stage people have arrived at in their life course – whether they are adolescents, single people, couples with young children, middle-aged 'empty nesters', or the elderly. Thus, the preferences of different groups not only vary but each person's needs evolve and change over time. Further, people crave difference and distinction and expect the market to provide it. In other words, product differentiation and niche marketing are at the heart of contemporary capitalism.

ADVERTISING AND ITS LIMITATIONS

According to Sinclair (1987: 63), those employed in advertising are often highly sceptical about their influence on consumers and 'have learned to doubt the usefulness of advertising'. Certainly, as Warde (1992: 27) remarks: 'people (can only) play with the signs that they can afford'. Also, however appealing the images attached to goods, it seems absurd to suggest that we purchase them solely for their sign value. Tin openers, shoes and cars are useful objects and fulfil specific functions. In short, there is 'no necessary connection between the symbolic or ideological meaning of advertising and the behavioural responses which people make to it' (Sinclair 1987: 63). The messages transmitted are not necessarily the same as those the actual consumers receive.

THE SOCIAL SIEVE

In Global Thinkers 14 (see below), we say more about the key ideas of the leading late twentieth-century French sociologist Bourdieu, including his concept of 'habitus'. Here, however, it is important to mention his influential study of French lifestyles (Bourdieu 1984), where he argued that every aspect of consumer behaviour – from holidays and choice of wallpaper to food preferences and clothing styles – says important things about where we belong in society. 'Belonging' in this sense refers especially to our class, education, ethnicity, religion, generation and place of residence, namely city, suburb, region, small town or village. Shared tastes also provide access to membership of desired groups. Thus, each subgroup expresses its own special habitus, as in these examples:

- Urban factory workers may display art in their homes that sentimentalizes family life or romanticizes the rural past.
- Socially mobile business groups who enjoy first-generation wealth but little education may attend the opera and acquire antiques in an attempt to legitimize their economic gains and rub shoulders with more sophisticated people.
- Educated professionals are often relatively poor in terms of wealth, income and property but are able to compensate for this through their acquisition of cultural capital – an acquired body of discerning knowledge and taste, perhaps in jazz, nineteenth-century literature or cubist art.

Clearly, consumption patterns are deeply rooted in the soil of social life. The sign values attached to goods are not free to shape our needs without the mediation of strong countervailing forces.

CONSUMPTION AS LIFE ENHANCING

Many writers have pointed to the rise of a postmodern society in which consumers crave distinctiveness, personal service, originality and diversity. This is partly what has compelled businesses to move towards niche marketing and more flexible systems of manufacturing. The rise of postmodern sensibilities also means that consumption and leisure now play a more important role in the lives of contemporary citizens than they did during the era of early industrialization. Then, people were much poorer and work, class-consciousness, nationalism and deep loyalties to family and community loomed larger in their lives.

CONSUMER CREATIVITY

Far from being consumer dopes, some scholars (for example Featherstone 1987, 1990; Tomlinson 1991, 1999) argue that we have become skilled practitioners at decoding messages and altering their meanings by imposing our own interpretations on them. We also negotiate these meanings with others through the social webs in which we are entangled. Increasingly, we revel in plurality and difference. In these ways we weave meanings into changing patterns of personal identity. Consumerism has therefore become a vehicle through which to project individual and group affiliations into social space. Certainly, numerous subcultural youth groups appear to have done this ever since the 1950s by adopting a bricolage of clothing styles and a variety of fashions in a perpetually changing rock and pop scene. Thus, we are the masters not the servants of the consumer society. In addition, writers like Bennett (2004) and Foster (2008) suggest that consumerism also offers opportunities to display moral and ethical awareness, knowledge and power because informed spenders can engage in various degrees and kinds of boycotts and similar actions. Moreover, it can be argued that the shared lifestyles made possible by consumerism across

BRICOLAGE

An assembly of various apparently unconnected elements. The term was popularized by Claude Lévi-Strauss in *The Savage Mind* (1968).

the world may partly help to neutralize some of the cultural as well as economic divisions that currently undermine the formation of a stronger sense of global citizenship (Kenway et al. 2006; Urry 2000: 187).

Such postmodern arguments about the diverse opportunities shopping can provide reassure us that we are not consumer dopes. However, in displacing the earlier one-sided obsession with the compulsions of production and work as the primary source of meaning in people's lives, postmodernists seem to have substituted another equally skewed scenario in its place. Human creativity in the workplace is denied or devalued and reassigned almost entirely to the spheres of consumption and leisure. While shopping promises to turn our fantasies into realities, in fact, all too often expectations turn to disillusionment (Smart 2010: 147). Perhaps all this plays rather conveniently into the hands of capitalist interests and excludes those without the material means to enjoy consumer culture.

GLOBAL THINKERS 14 PIERRE BOURDIEU (1930–2002)

COURTESY OF CLAIRE GUTTINGER AT THE COLLEGE DE FRANCE

Agent–structure debates
Much of sociology has involved a debate between structuralists and constructivists. Bourdieu rejects both these approaches. Structuralism ignores how agents consciously interpret and sometimes resist the external structures they encounter while investing their lives with meaning, thereby often reinforcing those same structures, but not passively. In seeing society merely as an aggregate of millions of individual ways of thinking, constructivism neither explains the durability of social relations over time nor makes clear how agents obtained their thought categories in the first place (nor why some agents are more influential than others in determining these).

Bourdieu's key concepts
1. *Field:* Social life consists of many overlapping fields and subfields of social relations, such as religion, politics, art, production and education. Each field is rather like a game in which the players more or less know the rules and find it worthwhile to join with a view to pursuing their own interests.

2. *Different kinds of capital:* Fields of social activity are also regions of power where we use our different resources to improve or retain our position. These consist of different kinds of capital – economic, social, cultural or symbolic. We outlined these in Chapter 7.

3. *Habitus:* This comprises a set of cultural orientations or dispositions that result from each individual's specific life experiences and membership of a particular social subgroup. Through these we lean strongly towards displaying preferences for a cluster of distinctive tastes in consumption and lifestyles, although they are not completely fixed by social background. Thus, society forms us and we tend to act in ways that reproduce its structures of inequality. We do so as knowing agents simultaneously exercising some autonomy, and how we interpret and act out the meanings they carry partly governs our lives.

Relevance to global society and culture
Bourdieu's analysis was meant to apply to particular societies – in his case modern France. However, the concepts of field, different capitals and habitus could be usefully extended to global life (see main text). So too could the idea that the success of those who struggle to reduce the inequalities emerging in the global sphere might be improved if they could capture and redefine the dominant themes and assumptions (symbolic systems) concerning what is and might be the nature of modernity and/or the capitalism appropriate to a twenty-first-century integrated global life.

Sources: Bourdieu (1993); Bourdieu and Wacquant (1992); Schwartz (1997).

TOWARDS A HOMOGENEOUS, AMERICANIZED GLOBAL CULTURE?

The spectre of world cultural domination through the spread of Western consumerism and the rise of increasingly similar materialistic societies has concerned many observers. Consequently, several researchers (for example Canclini 1995; Howes 1996; Tomlinson 1991, 1999) have examined their worries in detail. The fear of Americanization, sometimes described as McDONALDIZATION, is often especially acute. McDonaldization specifically refers to the delivery of standardized products and their related systems of business control we discussed in Chapter 4 (Ritzer 1993, 2004a). Many businesses emulate the McDonald's franchising chain and its own worldwide appeal has certainly been enormous. During 1991 it opened 2.5 times more new restaurants abroad than in the USA. In 1992, China's first outlet opened in Beijing (Ritzer 2004a: 2–3) and by 2008 there were 960 McDonald's outlets across China employing 60,000 people (Smart 2010: 120). Worldwide, by 2009 McDonald's had over 33,000 outlets employing 1.5 million people in approximately 119 countries (www.mcdonalds.ca/ca/en/our_story/mcdonalds_worldwide.html).

Pointing to this fear of cultural domination, Hannerz (1992: 217) coined a similar term – the 'cocacolonization' of the world. Supposedly, what is at stake here is the destruction of once vibrant and unique religious, ethnic and national identities and not just local dietary customs and small industries. Interestingly, during the immediate postwar years, the fear of 'Yankee culture' was strong across Europe, especially in France. When Coca-Cola applied for a licence to begin local bottling in 1948, the French Communist Party won much public support when it implausibly argued that Coke's incursion should be resisted because the company doubled as a US spy network. Others maintained that it threatened French civilization and that advertising Coke exercised an 'intoxicating' effect on the masses (Pendergrast 1993: 241–3).

More recently, research has demonstrated that, by the late 1970s, US advertising agencies and media networks operating abroad earned half their incomes from these sources (Janus 1986: 127). Meanwhile, pushed by state initiatives, television ownership grew in many developing countries during the 1960s. The US radio and TV networks were then able to sell both US programmes and the technology required to establish communication facilities in developing countries (Sinclair 1987: 103).

Consequently, perhaps through direct TNC or advertising agency sponsorship of national radio and TV programmes and newspapers, there was a vast expansion in consumer demand for US products. This was especially evident in Latin America. For example, during the mid-1970s, TNCs bought between 20 and 50% of advertising space in Latin America's 22 largest newspapers. Thus, the media 'through commercial audience-maximizing systems built around advertising … encourage … high consumption patterns and the creation of expectations which can only be met by further incorporation into the world economy' (Cruise O'Brien 1979: 129).

In the former communist countries, the arrival of products like Big Mac burgers was eagerly welcomed in the 1990s. They were seen as powerful symbols that offered access to Western freedoms and consumer lifestyles as exemplified in the 'authentic taste of America' (James 1996: 83). Such instances appear to equate global culture explicitly with Americanization or Westernization. Are these merely extreme examples of a general stampede towards Western culture around the world, or are there reasons for thinking that the globalization of consumption will not necessarily lead to a homogeneous Americanized world?

KEY CONCEPT

The term McDONALDIZATION was first coined by Ritzer to refer to the irresistible dissemination of business systems associated with the US fast-food industry. These systems aimed to achieve intense control over workers and customers, and the supply of cheap, standardized, but quality products in pleasant surroundings. This drive for efficiency and predictability has now spread to many other economic activities and countries, so that the McDonald's burger franchise chain is merely the 'paradigm case' (Ritzer 1993: 1) of a much wider formula.

THE EXPERIENCED CONSUMER

People living in the advanced societies have been exposed for longer and more intensively than anywhere else to the attractions of a consumer society. As we have seen, there is a good case to make that the majority has not been turned into a gaggle of consumer dopes. With some possible exceptions, perhaps among children and adolescents, most of us impose our own interpretations on the goods we buy. Our membership of different groups also acts as a screening device through which to negotiate and alter meanings. This being so, it is hard to believe that people living in cultures vastly different from our own will not be equally or more capable of demonstrating creative responses. If anything, the potential for a mismatch between the advertisers' messages and the ways consumers read them is likely to be much greater. As Hannerz (1992: 243) argued, the meaning of any external cultural flow is 'in the eye of the beholder'.

DIVERSITY WITHIN THE HOMOGENIZING STATES

Apart from their native inhabitants, both Canada and the USA were formed out of cultural ingredients imported from many countries. Indeed, for much of the twentieth century, the USA has been described as the melting pot society par excellence. The dominant Protestant Anglo-Saxon groups made determined efforts since the 1900s to Americanize (or Anglicize) the masses arriving from Eastern Europe, Italy, Ireland, China, Japan, and, more recently, from other parts of Asia, the Middle East and Latin America – especially through the school system. Nevertheless, distinctive ethnic cores survive in many US cities. Most continue to celebrate their linguistic, religious and culinary legacies and retain connections through marriage and community with those descended from similar migrant backgrounds. In New York, for example, almost every conceivable cuisine, musical genre, ethnic art, style of dress, language, business form (complete with links into global networks), church and community can be experienced by those who have the desire to do so. With the growth of transnational identities (Chapter 12), homogenizing tendencies have become less effective in the USA and in European countries.

FIGURE 14.2 Mural in Cape Verde
This mural in Cape Verde celebrates the island heritage of Creole music. The *morna* is a distinctive product of Cape Verdean music and has been diffused by Cesária Évora, the best known of the islands' many musicians.

THE SURVIVAL OF LOCAL CULTURES

American consumer culture, from Hollywood to hamburgers, may be strongly present in every culture across the globe, but the reverse is equally true. Several generations of migrant cultural experience have survived prolonged exposure to intensive consumerist and media influences in wealthy and powerful countries. As de Mooij (2004: 9) suggests, homogeneous global markets 'exist only in the minds of international marketing managers and advertising people'. Consumer habits remain very different even within the advanced countries. In Japan, for example, the tradition of saving remained strong in the face of consumer culture until at least the 1970s and ambivalence towards rampant spending continues to this day (Garon 2006). This being so, it is not easy to understand why the availability of Kentucky Fried Chicken in Bombay or *Mad Men* in Egypt's villages is liable to destroy the entire cultural traditions of these or any other developing society. People in Lagos or Kuala Lumpur may drink Coke, wear Levi jeans and listen to North America pop artists, but this does not mean they are about to abandon their customs, family and religious obligations or national identities wholesale, even if they could afford to do so, which most cannot.

Even where certain types of clearly Western cultural commodities are imported more or less intact, local consumers invariably impose their own particular meanings, reinterpreting such products to reflect their special needs (de Mooij 2004). For example, Saldanha (2002) shows how teenage youths from wealthy elite families in Bangalore reject all the popular musical genres widely loved across India, including Bollywood film music (see below) and Indian pop, in favour of more or less undiluted imported Anglo-American rock/pop. However, in doing so, they are simultaneously rejecting all the signifiers of what they regard as the old Hindu, semi-colonized and still impoverished India – including the peasantry, caste, state bureaucracy, corruption and religious divisions. Their consumption of imported rock/pop, fast cars and other Western consumerist indulgences enables them to construct an Indian imaginary cleansed of all the traditions and constraints they believe have so far prevented India from fulfilling its potential to be a truly great power in the modern world while retaining its uniqueness.

REVERSE CULTURAL FLOWS

Significant reverse cultural flows to the West from Japan and developing countries located in all world regions are also increasingly evident. Many more are likely to occur in the future, especially when and if more non-Western countries achieve industrialization. We have already noted some examples such as world cuisine and the Japanese management ethos (Chapter 4). Another involves the spread to sizeable sections of the middle classes in Europe and North America of traditional Asian medicines, health and fitness practices and different approaches to mental health. Examples are yoga, tai chi, shiatsu, meditation, chromatherapy (derived from Ayurvedic medicine), acupuncture and some herbal remedies, as well as martial arts like karate, judo, capoeira, taekwando and kung fu. Jones and Leshkowich (2003) describe how traditional Asian garments have increasingly been making their mark on influential Western fashion houses. The economic prosperity of many East Asian countries helped the globalization of 'Asian chic', which increased rapidly in the 1990s through videos and films celebrating the music of Michael Jackson, Madonna and others, and through the interest that celebrity figures like the late Diana, Princess of Wales showed in wearing Asian dress items such as the salwar kameez – loose fitting trousers with a tunic (Craik 2009: 314–15). Consequently, indigenous dyed batik cloth from Sumatra in Indonesia, Indian saris, sarong skirts, kimono jackets, mandarin collars and much else besides became key elements in the global fashion industry as well as spreading between and cross-fertilizing the garment industries in these same Asian countries.

SHAPING GLOBAL CULTURE: THE ROLE OF THE LOCAL

Drawing on case studies by empirical sociologists, we now explore three types of response by local cultures to the supposedly homogenizing thrust of global consumerism – indigenization, reinvention and rediscovery, and creolization.

INDIGENIZATION

There have been several studies of how local groups capture global influences that they then incorporate into their indigenous traditions. Clammer (1992) argues that the Japanese in Japan are quintessentially postmodern in their concern to construct distinctive styles of dress and other forms of consumption and the need to express subjectivity through creating the right atmosphere at home. However, much of this is rooted in long-established Japanese traditions that have always delighted in selecting new avenues of cultural expression and prized aesthetic skills. The ancient Japanese tradition of giving and receiving gifts to a wide range of people still provides one of the 'essential ingredients of everyday culture' (Clammer 1992: 206), and the way in which the Japanese have incorporated Christmas into their cycle of gift giving and exchange, despite their adherence to quite different religions, is one such example of indigenization.

Since the mass media play such an important role in disseminating cultural values and consumerist expectations, it is worth noting that many developing countries have established their own TV and radio networks, film industries and much else besides. The Latin American TV networks' previous dependence on US programmes declined between 1972 and the early 1980s, and the development and rapid popularity of 'telenovelas' – locally made TV soaps that explore national problems and themes (Rogers and Antola 1985) and are also often sent to migrants and diasporic groups living overseas – partly facilitated this change.

The Indian film industry, or Bollywood, which is based in Mumbai, produced over 900 films a year in the mid-1990s (Kasbekar 1996), and is thought to exceed 1,000 per annum in 2011, double the output of Hollywood. It focuses on contemporary themes but also deals with traditional Hindu and other mythological matters such as dharma (duty) and kinship obligations, while drawing on ancient classical theatre and the love of epic dramas, dancing and spectacles. Nigeria's vibrant Lagos-based film industry, Nollywood, is less well known. Although often seen as another derivative of the US Hollywood model, in reality Nollywood films are 'distinctly different' from those made in the USA (Marston et al. 2007: 53). Nigeria produces around 1,000 films a year, mostly for the home video market rather than for cinemas, where they are watched on family TVs via video cassette recorders or compact disc players. Most are made in a house or compound – rather than in Western-type studios – on a shoestring budget by small, private companies and are often distributed through local networks and video clubs to a large African audience across the continent as well as to the Nigerian diaspora.

There are several favourite genres but central to them all is the desire for melodrama with a strong emphasis on emotionality, morality and many subplots that weave in and out of each film and may continue in sequels. Story lines demonstrate central concerns with good and evil, fate, family relationships and the tensions between tradition and modernity, while the emphasis is on long strings of dialogue rather than action. In this sense, these films follow 'African oral narrative patterns' and are readily 'accessible' and 'entirely familiar' to their African audiences (Marston et al. 2007: 57). Nigeria contains several hundred ethnic groups, and although the three main regional languages and English tend to predominate, Nollywood films are produced in many different languages. Marston et al. (2007) insist that given all these unique features and the fact that Nollywood is grounded in the technical, political and cultural conditions found only in Nigeria – although partly recognizable by and meaningful to people in other African nations – the only sense in which Nigeria's film industry is similar to Hollywood's is that both make films to sell.

REINVENTION AND REDISCOVERY

The supposedly homogenizing inrush of Western consumerism increases the possibility of rediscovering or reviving traditional or extinct cultures. This is especially likely in the case of cuisine. Visits to most bookshops to examine the cookery section will reveal just how massive and diverse the interest in global foods has become. Similarly, on most days one can watch a TV programme that explores global cuisine. However, the need to compete with the rising popularity of restaurants offering 'authentic' foreign dishes and imported fast foods does sometimes provoke a new interest in national and local culinary traditions.

Recently, 'resistance to heterogeneity' (James 1996: 89) has been particularly marked in the UK. Forgotten or neglected cheeses, sausages, preserves, beers, fruits or vegetables associated with particular localities have been rediscovered and reinstated in 'traditional' cookbooks. Meanwhile, items such as 'steamed puddings, pies and pastries, bread and butter pudding, tripe, authentic teacakes and muffins' have once again appeared 'on the menus of the more fashionable restaurants' (James 1996: 89). Chase (1994) offers another example from Istanbul, Turkey. The first hamburgers appeared in Turkish cities in the early 1960s and offered an 'all-enveloping American environment' (Chase 1994: 75). At the time she feared that it would destroy the vibrant local street trade in Middle Eastern dishes, but the variety, popularity and quality of local snacks and dishes from across Turkey has grown and burgeoned in bazaars, shops and cafés. Competition from Western foods has played a role in this revival, but so too has the growth in the city's busy working population in search of lunchtime sustenance at a time when rising inflation and worsening traffic congestion make it impossible to return home for the midday meal.

CREOLIZATION

KEY CONCEPT
CREOLIZATION describes how cross-fertilization takes place between different cultures when they interact. The locals select particular elements from incoming cultures, endow these with meanings different from those they possessed in the original culture, and then creatively merge these with indigenous traditions to create totally new forms. Although this definition serves most purposes, be warned that 'Creole' is used inconsistently in different settings.

Unlike indigenization, where the global is used to express essentially local cultural forms, the mixing of ingredients involved in CREOLIZATION generates altogether new, fused inventions. We can suppose that such creative blending has always occurred throughout human history. Creolization encompasses many cultural forms and not just consumerism. In southern Nigeria (and elsewhere in Africa), the absorption of Christianity has led to the fusion of African music and language with standard church liturgy and the incorporation of premodern concerns with health and the desire for magical protection against the ill wishes of others into ritual activity. Consequently, many Nigerian churches are very different from their European counterparts.

Turning to consumer culture, there are many example of creolization, both old and new, and here we explore three case studies.

Food

The Big Mac is eaten more or less everywhere. Yet, despite its immense commercial power through McDonald's franchise system and apparent iconic worldwide appeal as the quintessential signifier of everything 'American', in innumerable countries it has simultaneously been indigenized to meet local tastes and crossed with local food traditions so that it has, in effect, evolved into a new creolized entity. Thus:

- in India we find the Maharaja Mac (lamb mince served with cheese and lettuce in a sesame seed bun, with a vegetarian choice)
- Thailand offers a Samurai Pork Burger
- in New Zealand it may be served with a fried egg and sliced beetroot
- Japan offers a Teriyaki Mcburger served with green tea
- in Mexico there is the McBurrito a la Mexicana.

Capoeira

Capoeira is a form of martial arts that combines elements of dance and music, which Brazilian migrants and professionals introduced to the West where it attracts numerous local admirers and participants. Originating in the dances, musical forms and combat games of men from various parts of Africa, it was brought to Brazil through slavery and became especially important as a street game and contest in the Bahia region (Assunção 2010). The point to note about it is that, whether during the era of slavery, as part of the cycle of urban street life in twentieth-century Brazil, and right up to the present day, even in its role as a leisure export to the West, capoeira has always absorbed and merged with a diversity of cultural ingredients to form a ritualized but ever evolving 'intertextual bricolage' (Assunção 2010: 193). We see this in the widely diverse African origins of the musical instruments, rhythmic forms, songs and melodies that accompany its performance, in its ritualized body movements – kicks, blows, acrobatics, throws and so on – and in the merging of the contest with various religious practices, traditions and symbols imported through, among others, Catholic, Muslim and Jewish influences.

A PAUSE TO REFLECT

If capital generally flows from North to South, it seems that much popular culture flows the other way. Can you list all the types of music (for example samba, salsa and reggae), martial arts, food and dance that have now entered a global consumer market? How have they changed your life and the lives of the people around you?

Rock/pop music and rap

Perhaps more than any other aesthetic medium, music fosters creolization because so much of its repertoire flourishes without necessarily requiring text – or lyrics. Freed from the constraints of language and therefore particular cultural or historical referents, it flows unstoppably across borders. Classical composers borrowed national or regional peasant folk songs drawn from countries such as Russia, Scotland and Czechoslovakia for their symphonies and European folk music flowed to South America through migrants and became fused with the music of black slaves, helping to form genres such as the tango and samba. Similarly, not only did early twentieth-century African Americans living in the USA invent jazz in its various forms by drawing on African musical traditions, but the birth of rock/pop grew largely out of the marriage of jazz with country and western music. In turn, and since the 1950s, rock/pop's distinctive use of a strong beat coupled with electronic instruments, sound amplification techniques and vocal experimentation endowed it with a spontaneity and immediacy that has allowed it to spread across the world. Many other kinds of music have been compelled to accommodate it and incorporate some of its techniques and styles. There has been a 'pop-rockization of the world' (Regev 2002: 273). Yet, such altered indigenous musical forms have often flowed back from the South to Northern cities where rock/pop emerged, transported by diasporic musicians. They then utilized recording studios and sought minority audiences, thereby creating a rich melange of creolized styles, which add to the immense repertoire of 'world music' – neither completely Western nor indigenous/traditional (Figure 14.2).

Such creative combinations have continued until the present and have included further black cultural infusions including rap and hip hop from the USA. This appealed to youth who experienced it as a tool for reworking local identity (Mitchell 2001: 2; Peterson and Bennett 2004) in countries as diverse as Japan, Spain, Croatia, Australia, Senegal and Algeria. To take one instance, hip hop and rap became very popular among second-generation Turkish youth in Germany (Bennett 2000). Taken there originally by black soldiers serving with the US military forces stationed in the Frankfurt area, the young immigrants – and some native Germans – picked up the genre and the lyrics in nightclubs from listening to US forces radio programmes. Like black soldiers living in the USA, Turkish youths often felt like second-class citizens in white German society, even though they were born there. Their music reflected this sense of alienation and rejection. Interestingly, some Turkish rappers began to import traditional music from Turkey either through cassettes or via family or business trips. They then fused this imported music with African American rap while switching their song performances in German discos and clubs back into the Turkish language. This allowed them to rediscover their ethnic roots while remaining defiantly in a local German setting, but at the same time they created a hybrid musical form.

REVIEW

As a preliminary to examining global consumerism, we discussed two contrasting theoretical positions concerning the nature of contemporary consumer culture. We laid particular emphasis on the more positive scenario, arguing against the view that we are consumer dopes. Rather, we generally interpret and express the meanings implanted in goods by advertising in ways that reflect our personal lifestyle needs and participation in various social groups. Of course, there are other reasons for worrying about consumerism, especially its cumulative, environmental impact on the world's biosphere. We examine this issue in Chapter 19.

We also pointed out that although there is some evidence that Western or American consumer goods, and the values they carry, are spreading rapidly to the developing world, transnational cultural flows are neither one way nor do they totally swamp local cultural forms. Rather, the local normally find a way to capture, alter and mix external influences with indigenous ones or even to reinvent itself with the aid of new resources brought by the global.

Visit the companion website at www.palgrave.com/sociology/cohen3e for extra materials to check and expand your learning, including interactive self-test questions, mind maps making links between key themes, annotated web links to sociological research, data and key sociological thinkers, a searchable glossary and much more.

FURTHER READING

Mysteriously, writing on consumerism – something we all engage in every day – is not always easy to understand. However, D. Slater's *Consumer Culture and Modernity* (1997) is more accessible than most and provides a lively introduction to this subject. Try Chapters 1, 2 and 3.

Cross-cultural Consumption (1996), edited by D. Howes, includes some fascinating material. The introduction and Chapters 2, 4, 6 and 8 are especially useful.

J. Tomlinson's *Globalization and Culture* (1999) critically explores the Americanization thesis, while exploring other useful themes relevant to global culture.

Consumer Society: Critical Issues and Environmental Consequences (2010), by B. Smart, examines a range of contemporary issues relating to consumerism, including its effects on the environment and its spread to China, India and other countries.

QUESTIONS AND ASSIGNMENTS

1. Are we consumer dopes or consumer heroes?

2. Evaluate the main arguments for the proposition that the spread of consumerism leads to a homogeneous Americanized global culture.

3. In what ways does the local respond to the arrival of globalizing cultural forces?

4. To what extent have cultural and religious influences from outside Europe and North America affected Western social life since the 1970s?

15
Lifestyle and leisure

At its simplest, leisure consists of the pleasure and relaxation that comes both as an alternative to and a reward for work. Since the 1950s, for the great majority of ordinary citizens in the advanced economies and for many in the global South, expressing identity has become much more centred on the sphere of leisure (Crompton 2008: 20–1). The relatively greater significance many people attach to their leisure is linked to a swathe of socioeconomic and technological changes that we examine in other chapters. These include rising living standards after the Second World War, mass consumerism, a vibrant youth culture, the expansion of a diverse service industry, and the increased ease with which information, material objects and people move around the world (James 2005). Bauman (1993, 2000) draws attention to the process of individualization and the increasing social fluidity and class fragmentation it both engendered and followed. The shift towards postmodernism, with its hyperinflation of images and signifiers (Box 14.1), allowed many to see leisure, pleasure and play not merely as an alternative to and reward for work, but also as something that pervades all spheres of life.

The meaning and significance of leisure is inextricably linked to the question of lifestyle. It is difficult to disentangle one from the other. Whereas sociologists have always been interested in trying to define leisure and show how its meaning for social actors has changed (see Rojek 1995), the meaning of 'lifestyle' remains more slippery and attempts to pin it down are rarer. However, we can make two observations.

First, even more than leisure pastimes, lifestyle is closely tied – we might even say glued – to capitalism and commercialization. This is because the vast array of choices we need to make in order to construct our personal lifestyles can normally be satisfied only by the commodities we buy. Second, as we saw in Global Thinkers 5 and Chapter 2, **detraditionalization**, combined with the new uncertainties thrown up by globalization and a 'runaway world' (Giddens 2002), compels modern and postmodern social actors to construct their own life biographies. Central to any such life plan must be the forging of our individual lifestyles. This requires much more than a series of flippant and non-reflexive consumer purchases driven solely by fashion, advertising imagery or whim. Rather, we need to forge a set of integrated practices that enable us to achieve self-actualization, a coherent life narrative and a meaningful personal identity. Whatever else it involves, having and conducting a lifestyle is often a serious process and it intersects closely at many points with choosing and performing our leisure practices.

DETRADITIONALIZATION

This refers to the loosening of the ties of family, community, nation and class, a phenomenon noticed particularly in the twentieth century.

Many aspects of the leisure and lifestyle patterns that first developed in wealthy societies have become more widely disseminated, although reverse flows also occur from South to North, as we saw in Chapter 14. Thus, we now have global music, dance and film industries, fanzines and cults, as well as world celebrity figures across a spectrum of activities, international sport and entertainment. Powerful business and media corporations are eager to attract world audiences to visit their theme parks, watch their global TV networks, buy their sporting goods and other accessories, or indulge in one of their holiday packages.

GLOBAL THINKERS 15 JOHN URRY (1946–)

Urry's contribution to the sociology of tourism is discussed in this chapter. Here, we consider his work on the nature of capitalism under late or postmodern conditions, which he developed with Scott Lash. We also consider his more recent work on globalization.

From 'organized' to 'disorganized capitalism'

Urry, in conjunction with his colleague Scott Lash, discerned a major shift taking place from the 1960s away from nationally based economies where most wealth came from manufacturing carried out in vast integrated companies and urbanized regions. Businesses were supported by government protection, an expanding science and a middle-class technocracy. They existed alongside a huge manual labour force organized in trade unions and increasingly protected by state welfare. This increasingly gave way to a far less organized economy, an 'economy of signs and spaces', with several key characteristics. For example:

- Capital, whether as money and shares, investments, products or components, became increasingly free from national control.
- Economic life shifted towards relative dematerialization as the labour and physical content of many commodities shrank and the knowledge, design and sign content (Chapter 14) increased. A growing number of goods, like popular music, films and holidays, had an almost entirely aesthetic, expressive appeal.
- This led to the growing importance of lifestyle, leisure and consumption activities for most people in advanced societies and the rise of the new informational economy based on knowledge and the fusion of communications and computerization technologies.

The central components of globalization

Recently, Urry has expanded some of these ideas while incorporating many new and interesting arguments. Thus, at the core of global life, we find:

- Massive increases in the speed, intensity and quantity of *mobilities* of people (such as tourists, migrants and criminals), goods, images, money and signs. These are extremely diverse and they breach borders and spread in all directions.
- Accordingly, *networks* rather than territories and places provide a much more useful metaphor for exploring and explaining social life today.
- Mobilities are especially striking with respect to *cultural flows*. Fragments of cultures flow or are carried readily along the technological pathways provided by IT, travel and the media, but also through migration and investment flows.
- But flows also have a much wider reference. Urry adopts and applies the concept of *fluidity* to globalization. Thus, entities such as diseases, environmental waste, website messages, company brand images, icons and advertising images spread, seep and infiltrate everywhere like spilt liquids. Fluids are largely uncontainable and unpredictable.
- Social life is increasingly inconceivable without our dependence on technologies like the internet, mobile/smart phones, PCs, iPads, satellite TV, cars and aircraft.

Consequently, global life is hugely complex and could move, unpredictably, in many directions. Meanwhile the notion of 'society' is now highly dubious.

Sources: Lash and Urry (1987, 1994), Urry (2000, 2003).

From the many spheres of globalized leisure and lifestyle we might have chosen to explore, we have selected two – international tourism and sport. There are several reasons for our choice:

1. In common with virtually all forms of leisure and lifestyle construction, both depend crucially on huge financial investments and the creation of a worldwide market led by TNCs.
2. Both provide opportunities for those involved to attain a global consciousness. International tourists encounter members of the host society at first hand and, if they choose, they may learn something about their cultures and living conditions. Worldwide mass participation at global sporting events may also foster awareness of globality and the predicaments that citizens in other countries face.
3. They provide especially favourable opportunities for common social norms and patterns of behaviour. In the case of sport, professional associations have demanded a global consolidation of the codes and disciplines that every nation must adopt as a prerequisite for participation in world competitions. International tourism, by contrast, creates abundant opportunities, and provides considerable evidence, for the display and performance of very different kinds of tourist behaviours. Both sport and tourism have the potential to impact on host societies in starkly adverse or beneficial ways.

THE SCOPE OF INTERNATIONAL TOURISM

The World Tourism Organization (WTO), based in Madrid, collates statistics on the worldwide flows of people who holiday abroad. It defines 'international tourists' as those who remain in a country for at least 24 hours. The WTO includes people who visit in search of leisure and those engaged in business, because the two categories often coincide. It is intrinsic to the definition that both groups are financed from outside the host country. Workers commuting from nearby countries and visiting nationals who normally live abroad are not usually counted.

GROWTH AND REGIONAL DISTRIBUTION OF INTERNATIONAL TOURISM

The sheer numbers of overseas holidaymakers have increased at a breathtaking pace since the 1950s. Thus, international tourist arrivals grew by an astonishing 17 times between 1950 and 1990, although admittedly from a low base. Between 1990 and 2004, international tourism rose again by approximately two-thirds, but fell slightly in 2001/2, especially for the USA, following the events of 9/11. Remarkably, tourist arrivals continued to grow throughout the recession, reaching 980 million in 2011 (Figure 15.1). In 2010 tourism earned US$919bn, about 6% of world exports or nearly one-third of the total world earnings from the service industries (UNWTO 2012). Few other industries can match such sustained rates of growth.

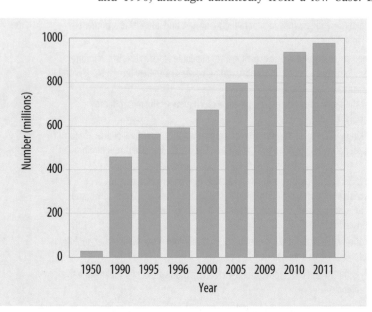

FIGURE 15.1 International tourist arrivals (selected years, in millions)
Sources: WTO (2005); UNWTO (2012).

There are several explanations for the rise in tourist numbers. With increasing affluence and paid leisure time, holidays and foreign travel have long ceased to be luxuries confined to the aristocratic and commercial elites, as they were until the late nineteenth century. Instead, the twentieth century witnessed the emergence of 'the holiday' as a social institution, along with the 'democratization of tourism' (Sharpley 1994: 83). The proliferation of cheaper cruise ships and especially long-haul jet air travel since the 1960s, the advent of the low-cost package holiday, and the attempt by ever more governments to promote their national tourist industries have further fostered internationalization.

A PAUSE TO REFLECT

Does one explanation for the growth of international tourism lie in the postmodern yearning to weave personal lifestyle identities around the signs and symbols associated with leisure and consumption? Is foreign travel seen as evidence of affluence, sophistication and an adventure-seeking spirit? Do foreign landscapes, climates, cuisine and customs offer new arenas and opportunities for people to 'score' sexually or socially? Does tourism provide an opportunity for fantasy and playing 'diverse social roles in exotic settings' (Turner 1994: 185)?

Since 1970 international tourism has itself become increasingly globalized. Until recently, a small number of rich Western countries dominated as the leading destinations, with the USA, Spain, France, Italy and the UK competing for rank order in the top five places. However, WTO statistics for 2010 show China in third place, having overtaken the UK, Italy and Spain (cited at Infoplease n.d.). These same statistics revealed that four countries from the global South were included in the top 10 destinations; in addition to China, these were Turkey, Malaysia and Mexico. (In 2003, Turkey was fifteenth and Malaysia seventeenth.) The combined share of world tourist arrivals for the rich Western countries has been slipping substantially. In the coming years, Africa and South Asia are also predicted to increase their share of a growing overall total (Table 15.1). Indeed, in 2010, one of the most notable features of the tourist statistics was that sub-Saharan Africa's tourist arrivals grew by 13% compared with 2009, far more than predicted by the WTO.

TABLE 15.1 Tourist destinations to selected regions, 1995 and 2020 (projected)

Region	Number of visitors, 1995 (millions)	Projected number of visitors, 2020 (millions)	Market share, 1995 (%)	Projected market share, 2020 (%)	Average annual growth rate (%)
The Americas	110	282	19.3	18.1	3.8
East Asia and Asia-Pacific	81	397	14.4	24.4	6.5
Europe	336	717	59.8	45.9	3.1
Middle East	14	69	2.2	4.4	6.7
South Asia	4	19	0.7	1.2	6.2
Africa	20	77	3.6	5.0	5.5

Source: Adapted from WTO (2005).

UNDERPINNING THE GLOBAL ECONOMY AND GLOBALITY

International tourism and globalization are inextricably connected in at least two overarching ways. One concerns the fact that tourism is 'big business' and plays a large role in the global economy. Especially in its international form, it depends on and fuels a vast and often corporatized set of commercial industries. Second, there are strong reasons for suggesting that international tourism also contributes to 'one worldism', or the growth of a global consciousness, although this effect may be particularly marked in visitors predisposed to cosmopolitan values. Tourism's contribution to the global economy can be noted in a number of ways:

1. Until recently, it was regarded as the third largest legitimate industry in the global economy after oil and vehicle production (Sinclair and Tsegaye 1990), but some observers believe that during the 1990s it became the world's largest, legal, money-spinner.

2. This huge growth in business potential has been accompanied by the increased involvement of TNCs competing as specialist tourist operators or as subsidiaries of larger corporations in the hotel business, resort development, transport provision or theme parks. By 2012, the hotel chain Accor, for example, had 4,591 hotels in over 90 countries with about 180,000 employees (http://www.accorhotels.com).

3. Like other forms of modernization, international tourism involves assigning a market price to a hitherto free good. 'Culture' is now wrapped and sold to tourists in the shape of ancient sites, ritual ceremonies and folk customs. Even the everyday life of ordinary people has been turned into a commodity to be sold to tourists.

4. In any single year, the sheer number of international travellers who holiday abroad has become vast and dwarfs all other comparable forms of transnational mobility, including long-term migrants, religious pilgrims, refugees from oppression, or seasonal workers.

5. International tourism clearly demonstrates what Sheller and Urry (2004: 6) call 'multiple networked mobilities'. Thus, for these vast numbers of tourists to be moved across borders and their numerous cultural, biological, physical, sensuous, emotional, sexual, communicative and other demands catered for, massive armies of people have be to deployed and mobilized, along with vehicles, signs, images, money and capital, information, foodstuffs, entertainments, sites of heritage and amusement, numerous artefacts such as surfboards and beachwear and much else besides.

6. International tourism has become a worldwide phenomenon, an inescapable 'international fact'. It encompasses virtually every country and penetrates most national regions and localities, however remote and inaccessible, while it 'makes itself felt at every level and in all sectors of collective life' (Lanfant et al. 1995: 25–6). In recent decades, even the declining, industrial rust-belt zones of North America and Europe have turned their rundown mills and furnaces, warehouses, canals and streets into industrial tourist sites.

7. Unlike the other fast-growing leisure industries (consumerism, the mass media, the arts and sports), international tourism necessarily involves the mass mobility of people who engage in direct social exchanges with hosts and who experience other societies at first hand. Also, international tourism is perhaps unique as a form of mass leisure in that, by definition, and unlike other forms, it requires that millions of people leave their homes and nations in order to enjoy their experience.

The combined impact of these features is that international tourism has

© LOUISE PSIHOYOS/CORBIS

FIGURE 15.2 Mickey Mouse
Walt Disney's success in marketing Mickey Mouse illustrates the capacity of corporations to turn images into commodities.

become what Lanfant (1995: 25) called a 'transmission belt' between different ways of life and a vehicle for increased global integration. It is possible to argue that tourism may also exercise a cumulative effect that is considerably greater than any other single agent of globalization. As Hannerz (1990: 239) argued, international tourism increasingly involves extensive interactions and social relationships unconfined by territorial boundaries. Wherever cultures are free to coexist and 'overlap and mingle' through transnational social networks, globalization is fostered. Many international tourists contribute to this growth of genuine multicultural understanding and the growing diversity of cultural choice.

CONTRASTING TOURIST STYLES

Various attempts have been made to distinguish between the varying types of tourist and we can treat these as an interesting device for exploring the different and changing forms of leisure and lifestyle preferences. A fundamental contrast is between 'mass charter' tourism and individual or small group holidays (Smith 1989: 12–13). Smith (1989: 13–14) describes mass tourism in this way:

> Charter tourists arrive *en masse* … and for every 747 planeload, there is a fleet of at least ten big buses waiting to transfer them from the airport to the designated hotel, in the lobby of which is a special Tour Desk to provide itineraries and other group services. … Charter tourists wear name tags, are assigned to numbered buses, counted aboard, and continually reminded: 'Be sure to get on the right bus.' … To avoid complaints tour operators and hotels have standardized the services to Western (or Japanese) tastes, and there are 'ice machines and soft drinks on every floor'. For Charter tourists, even the destination may be of little importance.

Like other commentators, Smith (1989: 11–12) contrasts these mass tourists with their rarer and presumably more discerning type. This species may comprise 'explorers' (in search of new experiences and unspoilt terrain) or 'off-beat' tourists (hoping to sample the exotic customs practised by remote societies): such groups either 'accept fully' or 'adapt well' to local customs, food and amenities (or lack of them). Indeed, endeavouring to 'fit in' may provide much of the attraction. We summarize this supposed contrast in Table 15.2. In doing so, we have utilized Sharpley's (1994: 84–5) rather tongue-in-cheek formulation of the 'good' and 'bad' tourist, with the implication that the latter is synonymous with mass tourism.

Increasingly, many writers question this distinction. This is because tourist markets are fragmenting, as promoters cater for a growing number of post-Fordist, flexible, specialist niche markets, such as the 'pink' or gay holiday (Binnie 2004), tours for the elderly or under thirties, and family holidays for people with young children. Linked to this is the reality that more and more people now live alone and travel singly. Also common is backpacking over a period of months or years by young adults, especially during their gap year between school and university. Australia alone received 580,000 backpackers in 2010/11, representing 11% of all its international visitors. More than a fifth of these came from the UK, but in addition to visitors from the USA and other European countries, especially Germany and France, 27,000 came from South Korea, with a further 26,000 from Japan (http://backpacker-tradenews.com.au). Hall and Weiler (1992: 4–6) show how 'special interest tourism' has also grown rapidly in recent years. This includes educational, adventure, health and sporting holidays, for example hang gliding, rock climbing or yachting, or vacations built around archaeological digs or attending fine arts festivals. A desire for self-development and knowledge and a conscious concern to enjoy holidays without inflicting permanent damage on the local culture, society or environment characterize these special interest holidays.

In this context, Feifer (1985) refers to the 'post-tourist' – someone who has acquired the reflexive capacity we described in Chapter 2. Feifer observes that other places and cultures metaphorically leap out of our TV sets virtually every day. Consequently, we are well informed

TABLE 15.2 Types of tourist and their likely impact on host societies

	The mass, traditional or 'bad' tourist	The alternative or 'good' tourist
Tourist flows and numbers involved	Large, steady or continuous flows (often seasonal) and may arrive en masse. High volume capacity	Small flows and numbers; usually travel individually or in family/friendship groups
Primary motivation for the 'sacred journey'	Recreation, recuperation, pleasure, fun. The 'four Ss' (sun, sand, sex and sea) plus tropical beaches, unclouded skies, cheap alcohol	Discovery of the self or values believed lost in home/industrial society. A search for authenticity, spiritual renewal and contact with nature
Specific goals and intentions	Seeks public places and crowds. Home plus the magical 'X' ingredient. Sports activities – swimming, surfing, water skiing. Sex tourism	Yearns to sample exotic cultures, peasant life and ancient sites; the 'culture', 'ethnic' or 'historical' tourist (Graburn 1989). Desires the curative properties of wilderness, remote regions; 'off-beat' (trekking, canoeing). 'Unusual' tourism, for example stays in Indian village (Smith 1989)
Tourist needs and expectations	Must have full quota of Western-type amenities as a 'right'. Desires the familiarities of home living as much as possible	Needs are relatively few; desires the unfamiliar and mostly tolerates rather poor local conditions and may prefer 'primitiveness' as part of the experience
Main orientation	Passive. Not very sensitive to host society. Social interaction with hosts is mostly confined to tipping the chambermaid or barman or bargaining with the souvenir traders. Relies heavily on the Westernized tour guide	Active, probing, well prepared. Highly reflexive, knowledgeable and perceptive of host problems. Participates in local culture and society where possible
Likely impact on host economy and society	Huge economic investment required for numbers and needs of visitors; hotel and beach complexes, airports. Disrupts local cultures because introduces new 'vices' (alcohol, drugs, beach nudity, gambling) and offers Western hedonistic role models likely to appeal especially to young people employed in tourist services. Large resorts engender adverse environmental effects	Tourist facilities needed are more evenly and thinly dispersed across host economy and more low key. Disposed to interact directly with locals and show interest in traditional culture. Fosters transnational exchange, cultural diversity and understanding. Generally supposed to create few undesirable environmental effects

about the many sites available to us and we realize that we can experience these without necessarily visiting them in person. Post-tourists have become much more self-aware. They often regard tourism as a game in which they are players who have the advantage of being able to read from a variety of ever changing scripts. All this involves 'playfulness', an ironic awareness of being participants in essentially a 'pseudo-event', for example at theme parks and museums (Sharpley 1994: 87).

SELLING NATIONAL ETHNIC CULTURES AND ITS POSSIBLE CONSEQUENCES

To attract visitors and compete in the growing global tourist market, central, regional or city governments and their agents need to give an account of what is special about their particular cultures and natural landscapes. Thus, 'there has been a frantic forging of signs of identity' everywhere (Lanfant 1995: 32) – an attempt to create and present appealing and easily recognizable images. Through skilful advertising, brochures and films, paradise regained appears on the beaches of Barbados, while a tropical, ancient, exotic wonderland emerges in Malaysia (King 1993: 108).

Urry's (1990a, 1990b, 1995) sociology of tourism is especially useful here. He suggested that central to holiday travel is the 'tourist gaze', where we seek and collect a series of new landscapes. Normally, these are 'captured through photographs, postcards, films, models and so on' (Urry 1990a: 3). However, to benefit from visitors' insatiable need to collect such signs – in addition to projecting their culture's uniqueness onto the global stage – national or regional tourist promoters, along with commercial tour operators and other professionals, construct a series of elaborate representations of different sites and tourist phenomena through glossy brochures, advertising and other media facilities. Accordingly, the tourist gaze is sign-posted by 'markers which identify the things and places worthy of our gaze' (Urry 1990a: 47). Meanwhile, the tourists themselves are trained to decipher these precise meanings.

Urry also makes a clear distinction between 'collective' and 'romantic' tourist gazers. The former generally seek holiday locations such as seaside resorts, theme parks or campsites where there are lots of people, even though this results in congestion and environmental stress, car parks, sewerage and piles of rubbish. Similarly, such sites attract a multiplicity of businesses from souvenir shops, restaurants and ice cream stalls to amusement arcades. Nevertheless, the collective gazer enjoys this mélange and only feels comfortable in a thoroughly commercialized milieu. The romantic gaze, in contrast, is sought by those more discerning travellers who go in search of supposedly untouched natural beauty off the beaten track, or 'traditional' village, farm, craft or religious life that is believed to survive unspoiled and unique, perhaps in faraway countries and regions. They try to escape from mass spectacles and commercialism and search for more idiosyncratic and personal experiences that offer better prospects of authenticity and emotional depth.

Nonetheless, this process of constructing representations of the local in order to attract visitors is likely to affect the society in question by challenging some of its traditions and undermining its authenticity. There are perhaps three main ways in which this may occur.

EXPOSURE TO OUTSIDE INFLUENCES

The arrival of tourists and their exercise of the tourist gaze, especially when they arrive en masse, exposes host societies to the outside world. In addition, as we have seen, the local tourist industry engages in promoting particular places as tourist sites through the representations they construct and the striking and repetitive visual signs they offer. They often create carefully staged events and fake authentic experiences in things such as theme parks, heritage sites and special musical, theatrical, dance or craft festivals. All this, however, may begin to alter the nature of host identities (Lanfant et al. 1995: 30–40). Partly, this is because the hosts attain greater self-awareness and reflexivity. This is hardly surprising, given that they are now in the business of recasting their identities.

THE NEED TO REINVENT TRADITIONS

A continuous process of interaction may take place between the locals involved in tourist promotion and various agents – not just visitors – from the outside world. Here, the former strive to retain their place in the global tourist market by adjusting to the inevitable changes in fashion and technology that constantly reshape tourist flows and to the concerns and perhaps demands of international organizations. One example from India is provided by Edensor (2004), who refers to 'reconstituting the Taj Mahal'. This has involved various interested local parties endlessly reinventing and rebranding a Muslim mausoleum built for the favourite wife of a Mogul emperor in the seventeenth century. The process involves the Agra city authorities and the Archaeological Survey of India, who are jointly responsible for the site, the government in Delhi, as well as pressure from a host of local interest groups whose livelihoods depend on the visitors – hotels, craft shops, markets and the operators of 'whistle stop tours' to adjacent areas of historical interest (Edensor 2004: 104).

THE LOSS OF AUTHENTICITY BOTH FOR LOCALS AND VISITORS

A further and perhaps even less beneficial consequence of all these interactions may be that both locals and visitors experience a substantial loss of authenticity with respect to the traditional culture they are performing or, in the case of visitors, trying to enjoy.

BOX 15.1   Sex tourism in Asia: can better branding help?

Tourism does not always bring advantages to local people, particularly in poor countries. Sex tourism is one such case. Since the 1980s, this has involved European paedophile rings organizing tour parties to the Philippines and Sri Lanka for gay men seeking sex with young boys. However, sex tourism is mainly associated with the exploitation of women and girls. This has been evident far longer and involves huge numbers of visitors.

In Thailand, tourism is the second highest foreign exchange earner and many visitors arrive specifically for the cheap and readily available sex. Phuket Island in southern Thailand was once a 'paradise beach', but the image soon turned sour when, in January 1984, a brothel was burned to the ground. The bodies of five young girls aged 9–14 were found in a locked basement. Subsequently, it was revealed that brothel keepers were in the habit of locking up or chaining young girls from the poor northern districts of the country for the delectation of Western, Japanese and Chinese tourists. The parents of two of the girls were eventually tracked down. The mother said in a low voice: 'We have ten children and we cannot feed them all. We had to send them to town; there was no other way' (Matsui 1989: 63).

The parents sell their children to 'flesh merchants', who drag them off to 'teahouses' in Chinatown or 'massage parlours' in Patpong Street (Bangkok) or Phuket. A virginal premenstrual girl brings a high price around Chinese New Year, when Chinese superstition holds that having sex with a child makes men younger. Thereafter, the young women are on a production line – force-fed birth control pills and typically serving about 1,000 customers a year. They are truly described as 'sex workers'.

Nuttavuthisit (2007) suggests that the negative image of Thailand as a honeypot for sex tourism should be changed by better branding. He draws attention to the ways in which particular places are positively marketed:

> For example, South Australia has the slogan 'Relax, Indulge, Discover, Enjoy' and the Maldives has the slogan 'The Sunny Side of Life'. The Thailand tourism campaign has been quite successful in terms of public awareness using the concept 'Amazing Thailand', particularly since many tourists enjoy the idea of experimenting with something new, exotic or different from their home environment or daily life.

Nuttavuthisit warns that the tourist authorities will need to choose their words carefully, as even the word 'exotic' needs to be avoided because it can convey a sexual attribute and trigger an impression of sex tourism. Instead, he counsels that words like 'warmth' and 'intimacy' would distinguish Thai sex workers from those in other countries, who are seen to be more driven by money. It is rather doubtful, however, that the harsh realities of Thai prostitution can be airbrushed by such naive appeals for better branding.

Sources: Matsui (1989); Nuttavuthisit (2007).

We can consider this loss of authenticity from both sides. From the host perspective, by the early 1970s, many observers (Greenwood 1972; Turner and Ash 1975) had become concerned that the business of promoting packaged, local cultures for economic gain, along with the influx of ever growing numbers of foreign tourists, threatened to degrade those very identities that attracted visitors in the first place. Mass tourism may be especially culpable. Thus, shared ancient meanings, religious beliefs and established social relations, which enable people to know who they are and to feel a pride in where they belong, were at risk of disintegrating and perhaps being replaced by a socially divisive, homogenizing, Western materialist ethos. This could be especially alarming in the case of already marginalized and sometimes repressed minorities who were being pushed by governments or driven by poverty to open their doors reluctantly to foreign guests. In fact, some recent studies have revealed a rather more positive picture, showing that, to a degree, some traditional cultures experience a partial revival precisely because of the impact and presence of international tourists. We summarize one such case for the Toraja people in Box 15.2.

We can also consider this question of a 'lost' authenticity from the tourists' perspective. Perkins and Thorns (2001) suggest that, in some situations, tourists may wish to become actively involved in the performance mounted on their behalf by the hosts. They give the example of New Zealand where large numbers of city dwellers organize their holidays around highly active outdoor pursuits such as mountaineering, horse riding, white-water canoeing or caving. However, many others – both international and domestic tourists – stay near Maori communities where, for a while, they become immersed in the latter's ancestral, cultural, spiritual and everyday life (Taylor 2001). While the rituals their Maori hosts perform for their benefit are obviously staged and therefore lack authenticity, both parties to the experience compensate for this by seeking interpersonal interaction behind the scenes where hosts and guests meet on equal terms and tourists are encouraged to 'reveal themselves' (Taylor 2001: 24).

BOX 15.2 The Toraja people of Bali, Indonesia

The Toraja people number around 300,000. Despite centuries of exposure to Hindu, Islamic and Christian influences (Volkman 1984: 153), they retained their ancient religious beliefs based on ancestor worship and the idea that the gods (their dead relatives), nature, living humans and the as yet unborn were linked together in one symbolic system. Everyday life was built around blood (kinship) and marriage ties, ancestral houses, and the enormous importance of elaborate funeral ceremonies, accompanied by singing, processions and dance, and the ritual slaughter of quantities of pigs and buffalo. Families invited to share the meat had to repay their 'debt' obligation in kind at some future time or risk a loss of social standing (Crystal 1989: 142–3). From 1906 onwards, a series of changes undermined Toraja traditional identity:

- the arrival of Dutch missionaries meant that their rituals and customs lost much of their earlier deep, religious content (Volkman 1984: 156–7) and were often reviled as 'primitive'
- Indonesia's attainment of independence from the Netherlands in 1949 led to the spread of schools and education and national policies to modernize and create national unity
- increased migration to Indonesia's growth centres for work brought new wealth from earnings and experiences of the wider world into Toraja society through returning, mostly young, migrants.

In 1975 roughly 2,500 tourists visited the Toraja region, but by 1985 this had risen to approximately 40,000. By 1986, the Toraja district was second only to Bali as Indonesia's most important tourist development region. It had a small airport, and bus services, hotels and restaurants had mushroomed across the island. Here, it is important to note that the tourists who visit remote societies and ancient cultures are sensitive to local needs and motivated primarily by the search for authentic traditions. They bring spending power and share a genuine fascination with exotic customs. How has international tourism further altered Toraja society?

1. The growing interest shown in its traditions by museums, archaeologists, antique dealers and TV companies around the world has placed Toraja society firmly on the international tourist and cultural map.

2. Tourist interest in gazing at exotic ceremonies and burial sites has promoted a 'pride in Toraja's unique and valuable heritage' and a self-conscious attempt to revive ancient religious identity 'as an image through which the outside world can perceive and come to know [the] Toraja' (Volkman 1984: 164).

3. Declining traditional crafts like basket weaving, wood carving and beadwork have been revived, bringing additional sources of wealth to local people along with the attempt to protect burial sites, rediscover funeral chants, and develop a historical and archaeological interest in Toraja culture.

4. Other groups in Indonesia once derided Toraja culture, but now they regard it as a vibrant component of national culture. Moreover, neighbouring peoples who once regarded the Toraja as 'savages' (Wood 1993: 62) now treat them with more respect.

5. Tourism has also brought less desirable consequences – family heirlooms are stolen, ancient burial sites are desecrated, and the less educated, poor residents and religious specialists who continue to participate in traditional life and culture may gain little from the new commercial advantages (Crystal 1989: 166–8).

Sources: Crystal (1989); Volkman (1984); Wood (1993).

Summarizing the discussion in this section, we arrive at three main conclusions:

1. *The reinvention of tradition:* Although tourism enables societies to retain something we might label as 'tradition' and even to regain a once threatened pride in their own identity,

the 'traditions' that survive are ones that have been reinvented. They are not the same as the original prototype.

2. *The inescapable tourist gaze:* Potentially everyone in the world has become a tourist product. There is no escape for any of us from the gaze of tourist visitors. Consequently, their search for leisure requires most of us to put on a performance at some time or other. But, by the same token, this means that everyone is now dependent, in part, on the tourist gaze to affirm and perpetuate their own identity.

3. *Retaining some kind of local identity despite embeddedness in global flows:* Not only does the tourist presence generate employment and valuable foreign exchange, but it also enables each country to 'guarantee … [its] paternity in the midst of an accelerating process of globalization … securing its present to its past' (Lanfant et al. 1995: 40). In short, in a curious kind of way, being exposed to the world and becoming thoroughly commercialized may be exactly what enables at least a version of the 'traditional' to survive.

SPORT IN A GLOBAL AGE

Sports activities demonstrate many interesting characteristics in respect to globalization. However, three closely linked features stand out as particularly relevant to this chapter on the sociology of leisure and lifestyle under globalizing conditions:

1. Sport has always formed and continues to form an intrinsic and often indispensable ingredient of leisure, especially for men. Alongside this it is closely bound up with our attitudes towards our bodies, especially male bodies, and how we wish to use, express and enjoy them.

2. As an activity, sport engenders competition, rivalry and strong team loyalties. When transposed onto a modern world stage, this competition is highly likely to develop into intense and sometimes overwhelming rivalries between nations – what Maguire (1999: 176) calls 'patriot games'.

3. Sport has always embodied features that render it eminently suited to becoming globalized, but even more so when the might of profit-seeking global entertainment, various corporations and the media intervene to exploit the possibilities it offers.

We now outline and briefly explore each of these overlapping themes before returning to expand on them in more detail later on.

SPORT AS A MAINSTREAM LEISURE ACTIVITY

Most contemporary sports originate in traditional folk games enjoyed, mainly by men, in preindustrial societies. These folk games often combined several social dimensions:

• They provided amusing pastimes and respite from work.
• They also brought people together in the celebration of community identity and sometimes health and fitness were part of the experience.
• Games often expressed the sensuous enjoyment of the body and were closely entwined with social rituals, particularly rites of passage from adolescence to adulthood.
• Alternatively, they tested the capabilities of the human body, as in wrestling, throwing or running contests.
• Moreover, folk games were usually characteristic of specific localities, ethnic groups or nations. A study by Renson et al. (1997) of folk games in Flanders, Belgium revealed more than 1,000 associations, each pursuing a type of traditional game. Most revolved around particular drinking haunts, localities or festivals. Similar games often flourished between villages or towns situated quite close together. For example, the study identified at least six different shooting games played with various kinds of bows.

All these characteristics are found in modern sports – social bonding often constructed around a notion of masculinity, maintaining collective identities, recreation, health, fitness, and friendly competition. Nevertheless, modern forms of sport have also taken on some additional characteristics that in some ways make them very different from 'traditional' folk games. One of these concerns the extent to which governments and political elites have intervened to reshape local community activities.

SPORT AND NATIONAL COMPETITION

People who are involved in sporting activities – whether as amateurs, professionals, individuals or teams – demonstrate certain universal characteristics. While sporting activities involve competition *between* players or teams, they normally arouse strong loyalties and emotions *within* the team and among its supporters. The latter, in turn, may help to support communal identities, whether these are to nations, regions, cities or districts. As Armstrong and Young (2000: 183) said in relation to football: 'it demands partisan involvement – it isn't an "egalitarian spectacle"'. Moreover, football as a kind of ritual warfare is the 'binary expression of a symbolic power which defines "us" – our lads, in our favour – against "the other" whose defeat is our priority' (Armstrong and Young 2000: 178).

However, precisely because sports are both intrinsically divisive and potentially unifying, governments and political elites often intervened during the era of modern nation building to foster certain nationally 'owned' or adopted sports. Consequently, these operated, like schooling and newspapers, as another source of the common intelligibility (Anderson 1983), binding citizens into an imagined national community while projecting national identity onto the world stage (see Bale and Sang 1996; Mangan 1996; Wagner 1990).

Britain was one of the first modernizing countries to engage in these politicizing and national activities with respect to sport. Indeed, Elias (1986) suggested that, in the mid-nineteenth century, Britain's aristocracy, the rising bourgeoisie and schoolmasters first formulated the ethos we now regard as fundamental to modern sport and then imposed it onto their own sons largely through the elite school system. The ethos was also taken up and eulogized by various poets and artists (Mangan 1981). Thus, fostering a team spirit and ideas of gentlemanly chivalry and moral responsibility to nation and empire were first worked through on Britain's school playing fields. Many of these young men then transferred these codes of sport practice to the top positions in the army, universities, professions and civil service. These same ideas also travelled to dominion countries like Australia and much of Asia and Africa, 'mainly on the back of British colonial expansion' (Stead and Maguire 1998: 54) through missionaries, military officers, colonial civil servants or teachers.

Some scholars (for example Dyreson 2003: 96; Mangan 1981) argue that British elites saw sport as a 'device' for maintaining 'British global power' and remaking 'the globe in their own image'. Indeed, their attempt to marry imperial and/or trading domination to the transmission of a unique sporting culture seems to have been extremely successful. The virtual worldwide take-up of football is the most outstanding example, although the adoption of rugby and cricket was more piecemeal. Nevertheless, cricket became widely adopted across Britain's dominions and in the South Asian and Caribbean colonies. Indeed, as early as the 1870s, the first Australian migrant cricket players came to play for English league teams, particularly in the northern county of Lancashire, while from the 1920s, black players like Learie Constantine from Trinidad arrived and soon became extremely popular (Hill 1994).

One of Britain's early colonies – the USA – became the 'biggest plunderer of the British tradition of imagining nationhood through sport' (Dyreson 2003: 96). Its political elites had always regarded national identity and patriotism as twin entities that could be fostered significantly through domestic sporting contests (Wilcox 1994). Nowhere is this more evident than in the Super Bowl football contests, which in recent decades have become the 'supreme performance' of a unique US identity and celebration of the 'aggressive masculinity' (Langman 2001: 202–3) considered necessary for a great world power. American elites have also used their own national sports, especially basketball, volleyball, baseball and football, as vehicles for trying to make the world 'more American' (Dyreson 2003: 97) and for constructing a 'second empire' (Miller et al. 2001: 15) more influential than Britain's. Thus, baseball won over football in Japan for many reasons, but especially because American cultural diplomacy strongly influenced Japan's elites in the early twentieth century (Horne 2000) and the top universities, whose graduates then shaped the country's wider economic and cultural life, favoured baseball.

CROSSING BORDERS: SPORT AS A POWERFUL GLOBALIZING ENTITY

Like music, dance and art, the enjoyment of sport does not depend on a shared language. Rather, sport comprises a kind of emotional language, the rules and procedures of which can usually be understood and appreciated by people from cultures outside the originating context. Thus, like music, dance and art, it readily crosses the borders between cultures and nations; sports are readily globalized. But there are at least three additional dimensions to the intrinsically globalizing nature of sport:

1. Many of the games originally embedded in particular localities – such as football, cricket, running or skiing – have not only become nationally popular but over the past 150 years have also undergone a process of SPORTIZATION (Elias 1986; Maguire 1999). Consequently, the celebratory, playful nature of movement cultures (Eichberg 1984) in preindustrial societies has been transformed into 'competitive, regularized, rationalized and gendered bodily exertions of achievement' (Maguire 2000: 364).

2. From the mid-twentieth century, we have also seen the 'corporatization' of achievement sport (Donnelly 1996: 246; McKay and Miller 1991) and a powerful process of 'turning sports into commodities' (Miller et al. 2001: 18). Thus, the American tendency to make sport dependent on business sponsorship and to turn it into an arena for multiple profit making has come to dominate world sport in general. Since the early 1990s, the continuing revolutions in the electronic mass media, especially digitalization and satellite TV, have further revolutionized sporting contests so that they have become 'global media spectacles' (Maguire 1999: 144) relayed and sold to billions of TV viewers worldwide. This process of the corporatization of global sport is discussed further below.

3. Given the existence of a global sports arena in which virtually all nations participate in various world sporting events, especially the Olympic Games and the World Cup, some observers have suggested that we can see the emergence of a sense of one worldness or a global consciousness – at least during those brief periods of play. Certainly, in terms of the participation in such key events through TV, the figures indicate a massive shared involvement by people across the world, although it is likely that much of this is driven equally, if not more so, by strongly patriotic sentiments. At the 2008 Beijing Olympics – appropriately signposted as 'One World, One Dream' – it is estimated that around 1 billion people, or 15% of the world's population, watched the opening ceremony (*Daily Telegraph*, 12 August 2008). The cumulative total for the entire games is said to have reached 4.7 billion, which is 20% higher than for the previous Olympic Games at Athens in 2004, although we need to remember that China's own huge population probably pushed these figures up. The World Cup is another example and here participation, measured in terms of TV viewing, is even more impressive. According to the International Federation of Association Football (cited at Goal.com n.d.), at the 2010 World Cup held in South Africa, more than 715 million people worldwide watched the final match (including later repeat views, mostly where the time frame was very different), while the cumulative total viewing figure for the tournament as a whole reached over 26 billion. The tournament was also broadcast in 214 countries.

KEY CONCEPT

SPORTIZATION is the term some scholars use to emphasize how once localized, community-based leisure practices involving some kind of sporting activity have become standardized and codified and then exported across the world – especially from Britain and America – culminating in the worldwide rise of competitive achievement sport and the disciplined, regulated sporting body.

In Box 15.3, we examine the idea that such events generate a sense of global togetherness and, with reference to the Olympic Games, a pride in belonging to a single humanity, although we also indicate some of the contradictions.

BOX 15.3 The Olympic Games: universal harmony?

Inspired by contests in ancient Greece, the first modern Olympic Games took place in Athens in 1896. The leading figure was a Frenchman, Pierre de Coubertin. He aspired to bring the youth of the world together every four years in a celebration of sporting endeavour. This would engender the goals of individual liberty and help replace warfare between nations with mutual understanding based on peaceful competition. From the outset, therefore, the organization of the Olympic Games was based on political as well as sporting principles (Guttman 1992). However, de Coubertin believed that nationality was also crucial to individual identity. Despite aspirations of fostering international peace, the Olympic Games were used as a platform for pursuing nationalist rivalries and they enabled politicians to manipulate patriotic sentiments. Instances of this are innumerable but here are just a few:

- As the president of the US Olympic Committee said in 1922, the primary goal in sending teams of US athletes to compete in international competitions was to 'sell the United States to the rest of the world' (cited in Dyreson 2003: 100). Other countries would perceive sporting success as an important indication of the superiority of American culture.

- On many occasions, governments – and cities – have plotted to win the bid to host a future Olympic Games competition. Common allegations have included offering bribes, sexual services, scholarships for children and much else besides to officials of the International Olympic Committee (Miller et al. 2001: 24).

- During the Cold War (1947–89), the Olympic Games and other world sporting events became arenas in which the USA and USSR strove to 'prove' the superiority of their way of life by the number of medals their champions could win. On occasions, they also scored political points by either boycotting or threatening to boycott the Olympic Games or other world sporting events. For example, the USA boycotted the Moscow Olympics in 1980 following the Soviet invasion of Afghanistan.

As with other international sports events such as the World Cup, Olympic ceremonies foster national feelings as much as they symbolize the ideal of a universal humanity. Miller et al. (2001: 61) demonstrate this clearly in the following description:

> For many spectators, the medal ceremony ... epitomizes national identification and affects. ... The athletes, their bodies draped in the colours and insignia of nation and corporation, are led to the ceremony by a functionary. ... They bend to receive their medals as in a military service, they turn their gaze to their national flags ... while the national anthem of the winning athlete/team reinforces visual supremacy with aural presence. ... At this point, athletes frequently cry ... moved perhaps by a sense of individual ... and national achievement and responsibility.

Andrews and Ritzer (2007: 35–6) also suggest that global events like the Olympic Games represent 'institutionalized and spectacularized paeans to sporting universalism'. Far from leading to a universal spirit, they lead to 'the particularization of universalsm'.

Sources: Andrews and Ritzer (2007); Dyreson (2003); Guttman (1992); Miller et al. (2001).

LEISURE, LIFESTYLE, THE BODY AND SPORT

Early sociologists rather neglected the importance of embodiment or corporeality – how human flesh impinges on social life and interaction. More recently, however, the discipline has taken a growing interest in the body as the focus of much human and social activity. Moreover, the technological advances associated with modernization, coupled with the post-modern and postindustrial character of social life today, make us increasingly aware of the role our bodies play in everyday social life. In particular, there is a powerful link between consumerism, commerce, leisure and self-realization and our ability to experience and enjoy our leisure lives and lifestyles, because these are often intricately bound up with issues closely relating to the human body. Indeed, the list of such topics keeps growing. It includes health and fitness, staying young and ageing, sexuality, the desire if not obsession to attain 'the body beautiful', disability, food and dieting as a self-discipline linked to knowledge and externally imposed 'standards' of an acceptable body shape (Evans and Lee 2002: 10). Added to these are modes of body enhancement such as piercing, tattoos, cosmetic surgery and dressing. The 'sporting body' is a particular variant of corporeality, one that is closely associated with commodification and feats of endurance.

A PAUSE TO REFLECT

A body is not only what we inherited from our parents; it is socially constructed. The leisure, entertainment, fashion and advertising industries construct a socially approved, desirable body (Evans and Lee 2002). Sportspersons are often seen to exemplify such bodies. Among your acquaintances, how many are preoccupied with their body appearance, size and shape? Which images of physical perfection portrayed in the media and by various elite celebrities are of interest to you? Can we distinguish between a 'fantasy body' and 'a real body', the real one being several sizes larger, considerably less shapely and less intricately adorned?

GLOBAL ACHIEVEMENT SPORT AND MODERN BODY CULTURE

Given that the human body is central to all sporting activities, the codification and globalization of sport rules have involved transforming the celebratory and playful nature typical of body cultures (Eichberg 1984) in preindustrial societies into a set of disciplined physical activities. This forms a central ingredient of the sportization process outlined earlier. Maguire (1993, 1999: 67–8) looks in detail at what was involved in the rise of the modern sporting body. One concern was the need to train the body through intensive, regulated exercise, often requiring the use of technologies combined with special diets. The bodies of leading sportspersons also express power and domination, certainly during competitive events, when mere spectators are awed by the strength, skill and endurance on display. The sporting body also provides a highly desirable model of perfectibility, health and, perhaps, beauty towards which we can aspire.

To illustrate the contrast between traditional and modern sporting activities and the rise and spread of achievement sport, we examine the fascinating example of athletics in connection with the rise of Kenya's runners to world renown as a case study. Bale and Sang (1996) observe that athletics is the most global of all sports because it attracts more national representatives than any other sport. In 2012, for example, 212 nations and territories were affiliated to the International Association of Athletics Federations. Bale and Sang (1996) describe how, since the 1960s, the stunning achievements of Kenyan athletes have attracted worldwide attention. Taking into account population size, it is possible to calculate each nation's per capita output of world-class athletes. In 1993, the Kenyan index was 9.87 compared with the male per capita index of 1.52 for Africa as a whole and 2.8 for the continent of America (Bale and Sang 1996: 26, 33). Unfortunately, this huge achievement has so far been so strongly gendered that the global index for Kenyan women was only 1.52 in 1993, although this was above the per capita average for African women as a whole of 0.84.

The first Kenyan men began to compete in world events in 1954 and by the mid-1960s were promising to become world beaters. However, Kenyan competition needed to make a gigantic leap before that became possible because the traditional sporting activities in precolonial Kenya were very different from those associated with modern world sport. Although this may reflect a bit of historical myth making, Bale and Sang (1996) argue that the games

younger men played before colonial times involved activities such as spear throwing or negotiating obstacles during running matches. These were often closely linked to hunting and
keeping wild animals at bay and tested military skills or were associated with initiation ceremonies into adult life or clan affiliation. Often these activities merged with dancing and other
sensuous cultural pursuits. Adventure, play and amusement were normally key elements,
while the competitive events were not recorded, standardized or regulated.

THE TRANSITION TO MODERN SPORTS CULTURE IN KENYA

All this changed dramatically when Britain colonized Kenya in the 1900s. Then, administrators, educators, missionaries, police and military personnel seized every opportunity to
encourage Kenyan school children, college students, police cadets, soldiers in training and
educated young employees to accept modernity, including learning the culture of modern
sport. They also instilled a very British version of modernity – team spirit, a respect for
friendly competitive rivalry, an understanding of the need for strict discipline, and the importance of setting high standards of sporting achievement. Gradually, therefore, between the
1920s and 1950s, a modern sport culture emerged from traditional practices, although for a
long time African and British sports coexisted uneasily.

How did traditional Kenyan body movement culture change between the 1920s and 1950s?

- Bodily movements associated with sports-like activities were transferred from the home-
stead, forest and village to the specially delineated sports field. Here, they were carefully
demarcated and separated in terms of time, space and kind of activity from the rest of
social life.
- The athletics running track and playing area constitute a 'territorialized space' that is
identical to all other such modern sport spaces across the world. Accordingly, a monolithic 'athletics space' replaced traditional African spatiality (Bale and Sang 1996: 98).
- This new space also required the imposition of 'starting and finishing lines' and 'geometrically arranged lane markings' (Bale and Sang 1996: 98–9). Thus, severe restriction and
the 'captured' body replaced the previous freedom of bodily movement.
- To this was added the new 'temporal tyranny of the stopwatch with races timed to a tenth
of a second' (Bale and Sang 1996: 99) and the need to fit in with a prearranged schedule
of different and specialized events.
- Careful records had to be kept so that individual and team events could be measured
against national or global indicators and new targets could be set. This contrasted markedly
with the oral traditions typical of premodern societies that were dependent on memory.
- Inculcating a modern sport ethos also required instilling the goal of 'maximum effort'
(Bale and Sang 1996: 90) and the desire to set high and continuously improving standards of individual achievement. This replaced the orientation towards pleasure, adventure and social solidarity.
- Thus, Kenyan athletes who aspired to attain world-class competence had to learn the
importance of obedience, drill and fitness, while imposing on themselves relentless and
punishing disciplines designed to raise their achievement to global levels. In effect, these
amount to a loss of individuality and a continuous submission of one's body to systems
of internal and external surveillance (from coaches, agents, rivals and media observers).

Bale and Sang (1996) argue that becoming socialized into the ideology of achievement
sport constructed around a particular body movement culture is inescapable because without
regulation and standardization, countries, teams or individuals cannot participate in global
sport. Also, this creates the possibility of shared experiences in world sporting events like the
World Cup for spectators and champions (Bale and Sang 1996: 107). Of course, the ability
to gain high financial rewards from the increasingly corporatized milieu of capitalist world
sporting events also presupposes acquiring this same culture.

KEY EFFECTS OF THE COMMERCIALIZED GLOBAL SPORTS INDUSTRY

Since at least the 1980s the process of 'turning sports into commodities' (Miller et al. 2001: 18) has been called 'corporatization'. Michael Jordan and David Beckham endorse a plethora of products, thereby projecting themselves as global sports icons. There is wide agreement that much of this corporatization and commercialization of global sport originated in, and spread from, the USA. This has given rise to the argument that the globalization of sport and the Americanization of the world economy as a whole – particularly in the past 30 years – are almost synonymous. As Donnelly (1996: 246) suggests, 'the American style of sport has become the international benchmark for corporate sport' and this has driven capitalism everywhere in the direction of corporatization.

First, sport has been turned into a highly individualized and competitive 'enterprise', with the key emphasis on the very few stars who win (see Figure 15.3). In most areas of sport, the amateur ethos based on respect for the game as an end in itself, once identified with the playing fields of Britain, has become less prevalent. Winning is now everything.

Second, every aspect of sport is systematically organized to maximize profit making. For Wilcox (1994: 74), sport is 'big business' and not just entertainment. For example, many sports organizations and teams have invested in their own business promotion activities, including arranging for the manufacture and marketing of team replica kits, flags, literature, videos and other local products, while some clubs have floated themselves as independent companies. Britain's Manchester United football club – which boasts thriving fanzines across many cities and nations – is but one example of a club taken over by a foreign entrepreneur (Porter 2008). In fact, nearly half of the English Premier League's 20 football clubs are under foreign ownership. Also, a vast international division of labour has been created to serve the sports goods industry organized through numerous global commodity chains (Chapter 4). These link homeworkers, small subcontractors and smaller enterprises across many countries to huge designing and marketing distributors based in the West such as Walmart. The sale of match broadcasting rights to public or private media companies has also become commonplace. Of course, these business sport activities now operate worldwide.

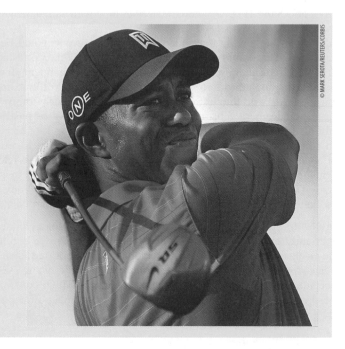

© MARK SEROTA/REUTERS/CORBIS

FIGURE 15.3 Tiger Woods at a tournament in Florida, USA
Woods refers to his ethnic make-up as 'Cablinasian' (a mixture of Caucasian, black, Indian and Asian). His ethnic ambiguity appears to have enhanced his international celebrity appeal. His self-confessed infidelity in 2009 led him to lose his winning streak, although he remains a formidable presence in golf, reputedly earning over US$90m in 2010.

Third, the commercial and competitive nature of sport means that most big events have become noisy spectacles (Maguire 1999: 149–50) or mega-events driven by the demands of glamorous 'show biz'-type commentators and audiences demanding 'record-setting superstar athletes' (Donnelly 1996: 246). It is therefore probable that sport is now more Americanized than other leisure activities, including films, television and music (Donnelly 1996: 246).

The corporatization of sport has also led to 'sports migration'. This now encompasses virtually every sport and nation from young African athletes recruited by American universities and South American footballers moving to Italian, French and British clubs. As an example, 433 leading Canadian ice hockey players migrated to Germany, Britain, Japan or elsewhere during the 1994/5 season alone (Maguire 1999: 107). Sports migration gives rise to stateless teams/clubs/players among the international superstars who have less need to demonstrate loyalty to their nations or cities of origin. This is gradually decoupling nationalism – for so long the beating heart of competition – from sporting achievement.

This loss of loyalty is also happening at a local level. For example, Harvey et al. (1996) describe the increasing dependence of Canadian ice hockey teams on corporate sponsorship, as public funding declines in the face of neoliberal economic policies along with increasing commercial pressures to achieve competitive success. In consequence, some teams have lost their former attachment to local communities. In Britain, too, Armstrong and Young (2000: 176, 202) describe how attempts to squeeze more profit out of football games led to selling key match coverage to media companies, pushing up ticket prices and 'extending' the football experience through such things as encouraging sales of club logos, replica clothing, videos and fanzine literature. Measures were also taken to 'curb' noisy match chanting and bodily swaying – long-established expressions of solidarity. These measures reduced the opportunities for young, working-class fans on low incomes to assert their traditional and local sense of togetherness.

REVIEW

Tourists are of global significance in terms of the steep rise in their numbers, their economic contribution and their cultural penetration of other societies. We have presented the 'good' and 'bad' leisure practices of international tourism and indicated some of their likely consequences. However, generalization is difficult now that so many people travel overseas, so we need to be wary of the distinction between the 'mass' and the 'alternative' tourist. Nevertheless, many travellers act like the battering rams of the rich, powerful states, while others seem more like pilgrims. Thus, they try to show their admiration for other cultures and thereby, perhaps, help to strengthen rather than weaken fragile traditions while enhancing multicultural understanding and awareness. As tourists and their hosts become aware of these capacities, they both become actors in the tourist transaction and perhaps recognize the ironies in their mutual situation. Yet others, like sex tourists, simply exploit weaker, poorer people.

Like tourism, today's globalized and corporatized sport practices have created both gains and losses. Among the former we might list the denationalization and delocalization of sports, leaving many supporters feeling they have lost their team and place identities. Again, we see the growing discrepancies between popular and less successful teams as the latter find their best players migrate, their ability to sell match tickets declines, and their activities are not attractive to the media. On the other side of the balance sheet, however, modern globalized sport helps create a more multicultural world in which the intermeshing of local and global sporting personalities, for example through sports migration, brings together different cultural experiences and, it is hoped, knits the nations of the world into greater interdependence. Commercial forces and competition also usually raise standards of performance and hopefully can provide more pleasure even if this also means the intensification of corporate interests. Last, the mass world audiences that participate in mega-sporting events like the Olympic Games may experience a kind of unity of feeling that contributes to our consciousness of the world as a single shared place.

Visit the companion website at www.palgrave.com/sociology/cohen3e for extra materials to check and expand your learning, including interactive self-test questions, mind maps making links between key themes, annotated web links to sociological research, data and key sociological thinkers, a searchable glossary and much more.

FURTHER READING

K. Meethan's *Tourism in Global Society* (2001) provides excellent coverage of the key debates on the sociology of international tourism. It is detailed, thoughtful, analytical and accessible to student readers.

Tourist Mobilities: Places to Play, Places in Play (2004), edited by M. Sheller and J. Urry, offers a generous compendium of lively research findings from many countries while exploring a range of tourist styles from ecotourism to websites and surfing.

J. Maguire's *Global Sport: Identities, Societies, Civilizations* (1999) provides an accessible and clear overview of the main themes relating to globalization and sport.

Football Culture: Local Contests, Global Visions (2000), edited by G. Finn and R. Giulianotti, contains some excellent chapters and spans a range of countries.

K. Woodward and D. Goldblatt edited an innovative special issue of the journal *Soccer & Society* (2011,12(1)) 'Football, Sounds and Things'.

Globalization and Sport (2007), edited by R. Giulianotti and R. Robertson, contains a number of important chapters on football and cricket and an intriguing one on why American baseball never went entirely global.

QUESTIONS AND ASSIGNMENTS

1. Evaluate the different ways in which tourism acts as a globalizing force.
2. 'We are all objects of a tourist gaze now.' What does this statement tell us about the relationship between the local and the global?
3. What are the main reasons why many sports have become globalized?
4. List the ways in which the sport body movement culture has changed with modernization. Then consider how and why this has also happened in other areas of social experience, such as public comportment in streets and neighbourhoods, at work and on holiday.

16 Media and the digital age

Marshall McLuhan (1962), the pioneer guru of contemporary media studies, had a disarmingly simple motto – 'the medium is the message'. How are we to understand this puzzling phrase? Systems of communication generally depend on:

- a speaker or author – 'a broadcaster'
- a listener, viewer or reader – 'an audience'
- a means of communication – the 'medium', 'media' in the plural, which links the broadcaster to the audience.

Traditionally, the people who disseminated the message saw themselves as all-important, with their capacities for inventive expression especially lionized and celebrated. Penetrating political speakers, evocative poets, amusing after-dinner speakers or astute writers are all still accorded high prestige. Nevertheless, however brilliant and original the message, it only becomes significant if critics, readers, viewers and listeners – the audience – recognize the broadcasters' claims and give them credibility or approval. In the past, the nature of the medium was generally disregarded as uninteresting or seen as inert.

McLuhan showed great insight in recognizing the power of the medium itself to change the message. Hitler and Goebbels had already demonstrated their ability to commandeer, monopolize and manipulate the radio as a propaganda device for state purposes. Since the discovery of printing, the typeface and phonetic alphabet have dominated most written communication. Yet, almost without us being conscious of its supersession, the TV screen took over from the book and newspaper as the most common medium of communication. This had profound consequences. Print favoured systematic exposition and sequential, deductive thinking, whereas TV is best suited, like many conversations, to impressionistic, contradictory or unstructured discourse (Castells 1996: 331–2). The central role of the medium can be seen in two simple examples:

1. Academics used to delivering scholarly papers to a respectful audience of colleagues or giving a lecture to an attentive class of students usually find themselves at sea in a TV studio, even though both are oral media and the intended message may be similar.
2. Listeners to a radio programme absorb highly selective messages. Sometimes they do this subconsciously; sometimes they choose what they want or need to hear in competition with other sounds, like a baby crying or the dog barking.

We can now begin to understand McLuhan's point. It matters a great deal through what means the message is conveyed, although his maxim that the 'medium *is* the message' needs to be seen as a device for making his meaning more powerful and intelligible. However, that the medium structures, constrains or amplifies the message and its reception is now well established in empirical studies.

The media foster globalization just as they are themselves changed by stepping up to a global scale. In this chapter we provide a definition and characterization of the media and also examine issues of ownership and content in relation to the growth of electronic media. We also discuss how the acceptance of the telephone as a mass consumer good and the arrival of linked computer networks has generated an 'informational' or (more simply) an information society. We also ask whether new possibilities for sharing information and interactive communication have promoted fresh democratic possibilities at local, national and global levels.

WHAT ARE 'THE MEDIA'?

The media are agencies and organizations that specialize in communicating ideas, information and images. They also project images about 'others' and their communities. Many journalists and media workers proclaim that all they are doing is collecting and disseminating these resources and are not responsible for the content of their reports or the consequences they might incur.

However, many commentators now regard such observations as naive (as do many in the audience) and believe, instead, that the media engage in other things besides reporting news neutrally, irrespective of whether or not the wider effects are intentional. The media certainly can be abused, for example by politicians who seek to monopolize them or influence their content, or by terrorists using threats against hostages to propagate their grisly messages. Owners of the media are often in a position to conceal or reveal subjects, depending on their preferences or interests. Often, too, below the surface message lies a hidden meaning, or an unintended consequence, in effecting communication. The media, in short, communicate values, emotions and opinions as well as ideas and information.

In the case of a newspaper, there is a nominal difference between the editorial columns (in the broadsheet newspapers they often appear in the centre of the newspaper) and the news pages. Tabloid newspapers, however, often run political or promotional campaigns on their front pages that elide the differences between advertising, editorial opinion and news. *The Sun*, a popular tabloid newspaper throughout the UK, is often accused of devising jingoistic and xenophobic headlines. When it briefly looked as if the Falklands/Malvinas War between Britain and Argentina might be averted in April 1982, the Argentine military government was urged to 'Stick It Up Your Junta'. When the British government urged NATO to bomb Serbia in March 1999, the tabloid's front page concurred, with the headline 'Clobba Slobba', a play on the name of Serbian leader Slobodan Milošević. In 2003, *The Sun* published a seemingly baseless story that asylum seekers in the UK were catching and eating swans in the parks. The headline was 'Swan Bake'.

The UK tabloids have also taken the opportunity to exploit marital discord in the British royal family and provide unsolicited advice on the future constitutional arrangements of the UK. Many newspapers paid vast sums of money to 'paparazzi' photographers for intimate pictures of Diana, Princess of Wales, caught in an unguarded moment. The mass waves of emotion (again communicated and amplified by the media) surrounding her untimely death in 1997 for a while shamed the most populist newspaper editors into reducing intrusive photography. Many seasoned observers correctly predicted that this uncharacteristic restraint would soon give way. So it proved. In May 2010 Sarah Ferguson, the estranged wife of Prince Andrew, was caught on camera in a sting operation taking money to introduce a fake businessman to Andrew. After accepting a substantial bribe from a *News of the World* reporter pretending to be an entrepreneur, she is recorded as saying: 'If you want to meet him in your business, look after me and he'll look after you … you'll get it back tenfold.'

This was a shocking moment for those who revered the royal family, but it also revealed the virtually unlimited level of moral laxity to which *News of the World* editors and reporters were prepared to sink. The lid was finally lifted off their practices in mid-2011 when a succession of stories revealed that celebrities, politicians and others (even a missing teenager who, it turned out, had been murdered) had their phones and emails hacked. Reporters at the same newspaper had paid police for stories and information. After 168 years of near continuous publication, the newspaper with the largest circulation in the English-speaking world closed on 10 July 2011. Rupert Murdoch, the owner, declared to a select committee of the British House of Commons that his appearance was 'the most humble day of his life'. This did not appear to dent his confidence at announcing a record profit for his worldwide media empire shortly thereafter. The combination of populist channels (like Fox News) and respectable newspapers like the *Wall Street Journal* and *The Times* have still left the disgraced media mogul in an enormously powerful position. He still has considerable holdings in his home base, Australia, owning some 150 publications (see Table 16.1 to see how the media moguls compare).

A PAUSE TO REFLECT

By the time of its demise, the *News of the World* still had 2.8 million readers each week, but this was a much smaller figure than at its height. Given the declining circulation of all newspapers, is it more important to understand media power as overwhelmingly an issue of digital control, rather than ownership of printed titles? Can McLuhan's aphorism that 'the medium is the message' be updated to a digital era?

BOX 16.1 Radios in Lebanon, blogs in Iran

Radios in Lebanon
While we might often denounce the sinister power of the media, they can also act as a force for democratization and 'progressive' social change. Lerner (cited in Kornblum 1988) examined a number of remote villages in Lebanon in the 1960s, when rural people had developed a passion for owning radios, which allowed them to access stories and information about the world outside. He demonstrated that when connectivity increased, the power of the village patriarchs declined; in other words, there was a major shift in power relations. With the arrival of television, women were able to see Western women in roles other than that of filial daughter, modest sister or devoted mother. The number wearing the veil dropped and there were other signs of women expressing more personal freedom in their lifestyles. The media also help to disseminate education more widely, offer some encouragement to literacy, and provide mass entertainment. Exposure to other people's cultures may nurture sentiments of common humanity, or at least get people to acknowledge the existence of cultural diversity.

Blogs in Iran
The development of blogs in Iran provides a more recent Middle Eastern example, with Hossein Derakhshan (editor myself) providing one of the most widely read blogs on Iranian politics and society. As Coleman (2005: 277–8) comments, blogs in Iran have fulfilled the following functions:

- they have provided first-hand reports of events like student protests
- young people have used them as a dating service (uncommon in Iran)
- parents have got to know their children's values
- they have informed Iranians abroad about events in their home country
- some bloggers have been hired by the newspapers
- politicians and policy-makers read and have responded to blogs

- they have greatly enhanced access to Persian-language sources and information
- they have enticed some web users away from chat rooms to a more serious engagement with politics
- e-zines (web magazines) have developed, some with many readers.

We can add that with the confrontation between the EU and the USA, on the one hand, and Iran, on the other, over the development of nuclear energy (which some think could be a prelude to nuclear weaponry), this blog provides a telling insight into attitudes in Iran.

Sources: Coleman (2005: 277–8); Lerner, cited in Kornblum (1988).

In short, the media jumbles information, news, emotions, values and opinions and these become confused in the minds of the audience. One possible consequence, which actors have reported, is that some fans fail to distinguish between a fictional TV soap character and the actor involved – a classic example of Baudrillard's simulacrum (Chapter 14). More seriously, in late January 2006, a Danish newspaper published a series of cartoons, one of which depicted Muhammad with a turban twisted into a bomb. The cartoons were not only hard-hitting, they also violated much Islamic teaching forbidding the creation of images of the prophet. The reproduction of these cartoons across Europe inflamed the Muslim world. Government policy towards Muslims, newspapers' right to free expression, and Western public opinion became hopelessly conflated in the minds of many Muslims, who were aghast at the insensitivity and ignorance of the newspapers and at what was seen as the West's attack on Islam. Riots and protests immediately followed in Indonesia, Gaza and elsewhere.

Broadly, the conventional media divide into the print media (books, magazines and newspapers) and the visual/aural media (films, radio and TV). As we shall see later, new and hybrid forms of media are emerging through digitalization. Hybridity also characterizes the conventional media. The media are mutually parasitical. Radio reports the headlines in the press or in 'What the papers say'. Newspapers list and review TV and radio programmes. Books are adapted into feature films. William Randolph Hearst (1853–1961), the reactionary and eccentric press mogul, provided the model for the classic film, *Citizen Kane*. The people in the media select each other as so-called 'celebrities'. 'Famous' journalists and broadcasters appear on quiz games and interview each other on chat shows. Many people who appear on TV today are, however, simply celebrities – famous for being famous – whereas, previously, talent and beauty shows in which hitherto 'unknown' people were discovered democratized celebrity culture.

CORPORATE OWNERSHIP OF THE MEDIA

The media's conflation of fact and fiction, or reason and emotion, is important not only in a trivial sense. Large media corporations may contrive to project images and ideas that serve their own interest rather than the national or international interest. This statement might be thought vastly exaggerated if not for the fact that some corporations have achieved an oligopolistic, complex and overlapping control of newspapers, film archives, TV networks, radio stations, cable companies, book publishers, music labels and satellite stations. We have already alluded to Rupert Murdoch's News Corporation, but this is true also of Walt Disney, Times Warner, Viacom and the Columbian Broadcasting Corporation (Table 16.1). The integration of programming, production, marketing and broadcasting in the hands of a small number of media corporations is increasingly evident. The combined ownership of different media gives such corporations enough global reach to enable media moguls to influence business, international agencies and national governments, which often attend to them as if they were suppliant courtiers presenting themselves for royal approval. We can allude to one example of media conglomerate power that caused considerable discussion in the USA. Early in 2004, the Walt Disney Company prevented its subsidiary, Miramax, from distributing Michael Moore's anti-war film, *Fahrenheit 9/11*. According to one report, the company was concerned that distributing the film 'would have endangered Disney's tax breaks for its theme parks in Florida, where the president's brother Jeb is governor' (Free Expression Policy Project 2012).

TABLE 16.1 Ownership of top five mass media conglomerates in 2009

Corporation and annual revenue (US$) in 2009	Sample of companies owned
Walt Disney (USA), $36bn	American Broadcasting Corporation (ABC) TV network, cable channels Disney and the History Channel, Miramax Films, 10 TV stations, many radio stations around the country, Disney theme parks
News Corporation (USA), $30.4bn	FOX Network, cable channels National Geographic, Fox News and Fox Movies, Sky satellite systems around the world, 20th Century Fox film studio, the *New York Post* and *Wall Street Journal*, HarperCollins book publishers, many TV stations in the USA
Time Warner (USA), $28.8bn	Warner Brothers films, Cable News Network (CNN), Turner Broadcasting System, Time-Life Books, *Fortune* and *Sports Illustrated*
Viacom (USA), $13.6bn	MTV Networks, Paramount Pictures, BET Network, various TV companies, including Comedy Central and Spike TV
Columbia Broadcasting Corporation (USA), $13bn	CW Television Network (with Times Warner), CBS Films, Simon & Schuster Publishing

Source: Free Expression Policy Project (2012).

The ownership and control of the infrastructure for communications – especially under-sea cables and satellites – is strategically and diplomatically vital, but it is also commercially and culturally important. Those who own the means of communications can link together vast audiences and potentially feed them with similar and selective messages. Billions saw the rites surrounding the death of the Princess of Wales and the marriage of Prince William and Kate Middleton. Individual sporting events also attract enormous global viewing figures. Figures from the International Federation of Association Football (cited at Goal.com n.d.) for the 2006 World Cup, for example, suggest that the cumulative viewing total over the entire tournament reached 26 billion – higher than the figures for the 2004 Olympics – with similar figures for the 2010 World Cup. To take one example, US viewing figures for the American football team were the highest they had ever been (over 24 million).

These major 'events' are atypical and illustrate only the latent dangers of the control of the airwaves. More gradual and perhaps more insidious are the ways in which internationally targeted TV soaps, like the pioneering 1980s' serial *Dallas*, were thought to convey a narrow, individualistic and materialist message. MTV's reality TV show *Cribs* has attracted similar criticisms – its emphasis on celebrity, consumerism and material possessions was thought by at least one youth worker in London to have prompted the widespread looting that took place in the capital in the summer of 2011 (Sydenham Town Forum 2010). As we see later, audience research on the 'consumption' of *Dallas* and similar soaps fails to support the presumption that there is a simple causal relationship between viewing and social behaviour.

TELECOMMUNICATIONS

The fear of control by governments and owners of large news corporations over the global media is partly offset where people can circumvent the media by direct lateral communication. This is particularly true of the telephone system and the internet. The global telephone network is now very dense and the cost of calls has declined rapidly. These are some of the key developments from 1965 to 2009:

1. In 1965, 85% of the world's telephone lines were in Europe and North America. There was just one transatlantic telephone cable that could handle 89 calls at a time. A three-minute call from the USA to Europe or Asia typically cost US$90.00 at 1995 prices.

2. By 1995, however, the global network comprised more than 600 million telephone lines and over 1.2 billion fixed-line telephones in 190 countries. The cable and satellite network across the Atlantic handled about 1 million simultaneous calls between the USA and Europe at a typical cost of US$3 for a three-minute call, one-thirtieth of the price 30 years earlier. Even that reduced price is massively marked up by the telephone companies whose costs per one-minute call across the Atlantic are a little over one US cent a minute.

3. By 2008 the number of fixed-line telephones had increased only slightly (to 1.27 billion) and in some countries the number was actually falling. This is largely explained by the phenomenal growth during the intervening years of mobile telephones (cell phones in the USA, Canada and other places) as an *alternative*. Whereas the cost of wiring dispersed rural areas for landline phones is often exorbitant, mobiles provide a cheaper, easier alternative. Moreover, indirect connections via low-cost local services, small businesses or NGOs will probably greatly enhance access to a mobile phone service, even for the very poor who cannot afford to own their own mobile. In many African countries, too, small kiosks selling phone cards and providing temporary access to a mobile connection have brought technology to many.

4. The explosive worldwide growth in the use of mobiles in the past 15 years has been so rapid that figures are often outdated by the time they are published. Bearing this in mind, here a few examples:

   - In 2005 the Telecom Regulatory Authority of India said that the country had 76 million mobile phone users. One researcher suggested that there were 526 million mobile users in 2011/12, a number projected to grow to 899 million to 2015/16, well over half the current Indian population (Indian Institute of Technology Kanpur n.d).
   - This story of hurtling growth is repeated in many countries, including China and South Africa.
   - China's Ministry of Industry and Information Technology (Marbridge Daily 2010) claims that China's mobile phone users reached 842 million in November 2010 (60% of the population) compared with only 10 million in 1997 (Branigan 2010), while fixed lines had risen to around 300 million.
   - As the most developed country in sub-Saharan Africa, South Africa's case is particularly interesting because it demonstrates the difficulties not only in collecting but also in interpreting statistics on the use of all kinds of communications technology. While the number of fixed-line telephones was only 5 million, by 2009 the ownership of mobile phones had reached around 70% of the population. But many more have access to mobile phones either through borrowing or the indirect techniques outlined in point 3 above. Thus, among high school students, even in poor localities, the number of users is probably nearer 98%, with over three-quarters owning a phone while the remainder use those of their fellow students. Because the costs involved in directly accessing the internet in most of Africa are around twenty times higher than those incurred by using a mobile, South African students use mobile phones as their primary access to the internet, and 68% do so every day (Czerniewicz 2010).

A PAUSE TO REFLECT

Given the costs, it seems likely that access to the internet for poor countries will be mainly through enhanced mobile phones rather than PCs attached to local area networks. What problems may this present in terms of the quality and variety of information available? Will this lead to a digital divide between those who have enriched, and those who have impoverished, content?

© CLIFF PARNELL

FIGURE 16.1 Homeless man with mobile phone

Fixed-line telephones are increasingly rare all over Africa, as the costs of installation and theft of copper telephone wire have escalated. By contrast, mobile networks have proliferated and even people of very modest means, including this homeless man, have managed to acquire mobile phones.

Outside South and North Africa, telephone connections were very sparse, perhaps about 4.6 million for the other 47 African countries in 2001. The cost of wiring up the continent and the theft of copper wire were major deterrents to extending landlines. Wireless phones have allowed Africa a benign 'later developer' effect. Many people of modest means can now access mobiles (see Figure 16.1). By late 2010, the number of mobile phones in Africa reached 500 million (Informa Telecoms & Media 2010).

THE COMPUTER AND THE INTERNET

By 1995, the internet covered no more than 2% of the world's population, but its exponential growth promised further rapid expansion and this has indeed occurred (see Table 16.2). Already, by 2004, the worldwide number of internet users had reached nearly 935 million, but by December 2011 this number had more than doubled to reach 2.26 billion (Internet World Stats 2012), or more than 28% of the world's population. Not surprisingly, the highest penetration rates for internet use are in North America, Europe and Japan, but the uptake since 2000 has been extremely rapid just about everywhere and has accelerated during the past five years. The internet links individual PCs through networks, broadband, wireless connections and modems. News groups and email lists can be set up out of the reach of the conventional media, while opinions, ideas and attitudes can be formulated in dialogue with other people linked to the internet, often on the other side of the globe. The media have attempted to get in on the act, with the production of digital versions of newspapers and digitally archived radio, but these have been notably unsuccessful in containing the explosion of information outside their control.

The recent growth of social networking, particularly Facebook and Twitter, has proved an especially vibrant development. Facebook has grown at an astonishing speed since its creator, Mark Zuckerberg, established it in 2004. By July 2010 there were over 500 million active users worldwide, more than two-thirds of whom were outside the USA. Further, the earnings for the site were expected to reach US$1bn in that year – up from US$550m in 2009. Evidence suggests that at least half of Facebook's users log on in any given day and the average number of friends contacted per user is around 130. Many of the national and regional markets for Facebook are growing annually at double-digit figures, and by 2011 the system had been translated into 100 languages (Inside Facebookgold 2010). In Table 16.2, we provide some basic data on the use and spread of the internet and Facebook for selected world regions and countries.

TABLE 16.2 Internet and Facebook users, 2000 and 2010: selected regions					
Region	Internet users, 2000 (millions)*	Internet users, June 2010 (millions)*	Internet users, 2010 (% population)	Facebook users, August 2010 (millions)*	Facebook users, 2010 (% population)
Africa	5	111	10.9	18	1.7
Asia	114	825	21.5	94	2.5
Europe	105	475	58.4	162	19.9
North America	108	266	77.4	149	43.4
World	**361**	**1967**	**28.7**	**518**	**7.6**

Note: *Numbers have been rounded up or down.
Source: Internet World Stats (2010).

The arrival and expansion of the internet in all its many forms and possibilities have drawn enormous interest from many observers, including academic researchers. From the outset, those involved in developing the technologies, systems and protocols that constitute the internet wished to create a structure of decentralized control built into the very system. From the perspective of the US Pentagon, which financed much of the early development, this was intended to prevent the possibilities of a Russian attack on the Pentagon permanently disabling all military communications. Computer to computer connections deliberately bypassed a central switching station, a model the universities and libraries of the world replicated, and rapidly connected to each other through unusual routes. However, many of the actual creators of the internet were idealists who were committed to this core principle of decentralization for other reasons. They wanted to reduce the constraints of physical distance and territory on human interaction, while enhancing democracy by enabling individuals to share information independently of governments, corporations and other powerful organizations. Some envisioned a future society of self-governing small communities linked in peaceful cooperation worldwide through cyberpower (Goldsmith and Wu 2006: Chs 2 and 3).

Such aspirations have continued to influence numerous experts, theorists, scholars, political activists and others. Gradually, though, anxieties were expressed about the internet's deployment and limitations, including the question of its democratizing possibilities. We now briefly list some of the main advantages of the internet but then consider some apparent limitations and even harmful effects.

THE INTERNET: A POSITIVE ASSESSMENT

At first, the absence of secure controls to prevent outsiders discovering credit card numbers, bank codes, personal identification numbers (PINs) and other sensitive information inhibited the internet's commercial use and this remains a serious problem. Nonetheless, the internet is used for billions of small sales and transactions. Ordering books, buying theatre tickets, selecting groceries for delivery, and interrogating bank accounts are now routine operations and this is clearly empowering for most people.

Despite the increased commercialization of the internet, there is little doubt that lateral links have proliferated faster than business interests predicted and that much of the internet will escape regulation and commercialization. The anarchist spirit underlying much communication on the internet has also been heartening to those who have felt oppressed by the global power of the large media corporations. Clearly, such links have provided a more democratic and less controlled form of communication between friends, families, businesses and professional associates across the world. The internet's partial capacity to thwart oppressive influences can also serve as a counter to government secrecy and/or abuses of power. The organization and intention behind WikiLeaks provides one obvious example of harnessing cyber and hacking skills to expose the secret actions, deals and mistakes of governments and their various bureaucracies. In Box 16.2, we explore some of the incidents surrounding the trajectory of this organization in more detail.

BOX 16.2 Cyberpolitics and WikiLeaks' defenders: a saga of twenty-first-century protest

On 27 January 2011, five young men aged 15–26 were arrested in a series of police raids across the UK and taken into custody. Were they urban terrorists, members of criminal gangs smuggling young women from Ukraine into prostitution against their will, or bankers who had fraudulently duped investors into buying toxic securities they knew would fail? No, their crimes were far more heinous. They were members of 'Anonymous', a group of online 'hacktivists' thought to number around 1,000 people. They claim to share the objective of protecting world citizens from government censorship irrespective of where it appears. The saga is complicated but the sequence of events went something like this:

1.   The group's members were prepared to break the law and risk arrest to defend WikiLeaks after politicians (especially in the US government), media people and others from across the world condemned it in November 2010 for releasing around 250,000 emails revealing previously hidden backstage diplomatic commentary that had passed between US officials and various embassies and other officials. Observers took very different views on the event, but Anonymous was convinced that WikiLeaks had been justified. What happened next?

2.   When the leaks were released, MasterCard, Visa and PayPal suspended their provision of financial services to their client, WikiLeaks, while Amazon and other companies withdrew their business support.

3.   Anonymous then moved to demonstrate its support for WikiLeaks by retaliating against these companies. It did so by overloading their websites with material and thus, for a short while, paralysing the internet operations of the companies concerned.

4.   Clearly, and irrespective of the motive for doing so, concerted attacks on websites with the deliberate intention of causing them to overload and collapse can be disruptive and obviously worries governments, businesses and other agencies. Indeed, such practices are illegal in the UK and subject to a hefty fine. This crime even has an official title: the 'distributed denial of services'. Not surprisingly, cooperation over law enforcement by agencies in the EU, the USA and the UK is being pursued in this and other cases.

5.   A few months after these events, in January 2011, Anonymous decided to lend its support to the surge of anti-government protest taking place on the streets of Tunisia and Egypt by paralysing government websites there, too, for a short while. It did so because the Tunisian and Egyptian governments were censoring information and blocking Facebook and Twitter in their countries – weapons deployed by protestors in their attempt to achieve political and regime change. *Plus ça change*?

Source: Adapted from Halliday (2011).

Facebook and Twitter have been widely credited with enhancing the effectiveness of political action taken against authoritarian governments. Such examples are Iran in 2009, Moldova in 2010, and Tunisia, Libya, Syria, Egypt and Yemen during the course of events in 2011 known as 'the Arab Spring'. These social networking tools enable political activists to rally friends quickly, to mobilize wider support, often from the diaspora abroad, to inform overseas and local journalists via photographic and other material, and to pass on immediate practical information concerning where, when and how to join movements in the streets. Moreover, participation in social networking may demonstrate or enhance a predisposition to empathize with and learn from others through shared experiences and thoughts, which may enhance globality as well as fire democratic aspirations. We should not, however, over-rate the potential of these cybertools.

The perceived advantages of the internet, as Webster (2008: 30) reminds us, may prompt the 'conceit' of 'presentism', which is to assume that today's transformations will fundamentally alter the human condition (for good, ill or both) to an extent that previous changes did not. Similarly, we should disregard a simplistic technological determinism that forgets that the current microelectronic revolution is grounded in capitalism's relentless, continuing drive for profit. Moreover, cybertools and social networking are neither the only nor always the most effective way of generating political momentum. Nevertheless, there is no doubt that they make an effective contribution to political action and in new ways (see Chapter 19 for a more detailed discussion and recent examples). In more democratic societies, too, politicians' lies and half-truths can be made to look hollow against the specialist knowledge and experiences of certain callers and bloggers. Values and social constructions of reality are also less amenable to manipulation by powerful interest groups.

SOME DISADVANTAGES OF THE INTERNET

Certain limitations of the internet for ordinary people have become apparent. For one thing, media moguls, software companies and businesses are now trying to control access to the internet by developing specialized software, search mechanisms ('browsers') and commercial gateways. They are also buying chunks of sensitive data and information and holding them in electronic stores that can only be accessed by codes, for which a consumer will have to pay. The success of the browser Google initially looked like a triumph for democratic control of the web.

A PAUSE TO REFLECT

Are the major search engines benign or neutral? Google's founders had promised famously 'to do no evil', yet in January 2006 they kowtowed to Chinese government censorship of their images and pages in exchange for access to the Chinese market and continued to do so for four years. Why did Google obey this demand? Are Google, Yahoo! and other search engines violating the rights of intellectual copyright holders (authors, artists and publishers) who depend on royalties to continue their creative work? Were the executives of Rupert Murdoch's News Corporation right in describing search engines as 'vampires', 'tapeworms' and 'content kleptomaniacs'?

However, authoritarian governments in Russia, China, Iran, Egypt and elsewhere have quickly learned how to block, manipulate and even turn the internet to their advantage in terms of gaining information about dissidents and suppressing political movements (Goldsmith and Wu 2006; Morozov 2011). The Chinese government has not been averse to abusing the internet in other ways too. Early in 2010, a number of Western companies operating in China were dismayed to discover that government-sponsored hackers had attempted to gain access to company computers to uncover details of the codes relating to their research, innovation and other key materials (Branigan and Arthur 2010).

Corporations, governments, transnational criminals, terrorists and sophisticated hackers with criminal intent are not the only abusers of the internet's potential. Increasingly, although ordinary people can, and do, use the internet in myriad ways as a way of improving the quality of their everyday lives, there is mounting evidence that many people employ its strengths in ways that harm themselves and/or others. We finish this section by briefly outlining a few instances of harm.

Internet addiction

More South Koreans are wired up to high-speed domestic internet connections than any other world citizens. Around 10% of these, mostly teenagers and young adults, are said to be web addicts who engage for long periods, if not continuously, in online role-playing games that plunge them into mythical and often violent worlds that many seem unable to leave. One psychologist fears that this addiction leaves many incapable of engaging in offline social relationships. One couple were jailed for starving their real baby through neglect while spending half their day game playing at a 24-hour internet café (McCurry 2010).

Grooming children for sexual abuse

It is common knowledge that national and sometimes international paedophile rings exploit the internet and Facebook as a device for gaining direct access to young children for purposes of sexual abuse or to distribute sexually explicit photographs of them. In 2003 the FBI closed a Texas-based website that had provided access to hundreds of child porn sites in Indonesia and Russia to a huge database of worldwide subscribers (Goldsmith and Wu 2006: 79–80). However, another alarming version of such practices recently came to light in the UK when police reports and court cases revealed that groups of young adult men had been using Facebook as a vehicle through which to groom vulnerable young teenage girls aged only 13–14 for an eventual meeting. Frequently, such practices lead to sexual exploitation, in which the men render the girls dependent through gifts, threaten to harm their families if they reveal what is happening, and even insist that they share their sexual favours with their co-conspirators.

Facebook narcissism

Some observers laud Facebook as a way of building online social communities. Others fear that it has more to do with 'self-promotion, narcissism and attention seeking' (Morozov 2011: 187) than with building enduring social relationships based on shared interests. What counts most for some users is being able to log more friends than other participants. Again, registering online political support for a cause is no substitute for genuine commitment – such as engaging in risky street demonstrations – and is often motivated by the desire to be seen supporting the group. Morozov refers to this sofa-based politics as 'slacktivism'. Equally, some researchers working on how people use Twitter, which is supposedly designed to permit small groups to broadcast short messages to specific individuals, have suggested that online debates sometimes degenerate into rival gangs insulting each other. Instead of discussion and learning through interaction, opinions are either merely reinforced around pre-existing positions or the majority follow opinion leaders (Harkin 2010). Clearly, we urgently need research that can clarify what is actually happening in these situations.

The social media and political extremism

Since there is nothing to enforce everyone's right to be treated with equal respect, anyone can legitimately utilize this resource for political purposes, including people holding extreme right-wing, nationalistic, even violent, racist or fascist opinions. The English Defence League (EDL), which was set up in 2009 to prevent, through violent means if necessary, what its members see as the Muslim takeover of Britain, is one such example. Its membership grew out of groups of rival football supporters, hooligan networks and extreme splinter Nazi groups, although others are also being recruited. During 2010, some of its members joined like-minded far right European groups for a rally in Germany and it seemed likely that an alliance would be forged with the US anti-Islam group. The EDL has also developed its own website, which passes information on to members from its various local and city divisions, plus video materials and adverts for similar events in other countries (Taylor 2010).

THE RISE OF THE INFORMATIONAL SOCIETY

Such is the level of internet activity and telecommunications traffic that the expression 'informational society' has been used to describe how important are the flows and links that crisscross the globe. Like some sociologists, **futurologists** and computer buffs are not known for their elegant use of language. Terms such as 'information superhighway', 'informatization', 'fourth generation language', 'ISDN' (integrated services digital network), 'hypertext', VoIP (Voice over Internet Protocol), 'Bluejacking' and so on are coined almost as fast as they are discarded for newer and often even more enigmatic vocabularies. Whatever the shifts in vocabulary, a persistent theme is that communication technologies and computer technologies are developing rapidly in their own right and converging into a set of shared information technologies.

FUTUROLOGISTS

They extrapolate from existing trends and make more or less sophisticated predictions about the future.

GLOBAL THINKERS 16   MANUEL CASTELLS (1942–)

© MAGGIE SMITH

Manuel Castells studied in Paris as a Spanish student. He was an assistant professor at the time of the 'events' of May 1968, when students and workers challenged the French state with creative expressions of revolutionary zeal. 'Be realistic: ask for the impossible', said one street poster, while another read: 'It is forbidden to forbid'. These 'events' failed to displace the government or produce lasting changes, but they informed Castells' view of how future challenges to the state were likely to emerge, focusing particularly on shifting communities of interest based on shared information.

Castells has published about 25 books, but undoubtedly his magnum opus is his trilogy *The Information Age: Economy, Society and Culture* (1996, 1997, 1998). Here, he recognized that information networks had created a new urban space, 'the informational city'. This had pushed cities onto a global scale as a distinctive and further stage in capitalism (Castells 1989), while creating 'a network society' and 'a space of flows'. In *The Rise of the Network Society* (1996: 412), Castells defines the latter as 'the material organization of time-sharing social practices that work through flows'. More concretely, three layers support the space of flows:

1. Microelectronics, computer processing, telecommunications and the like – the hardware.

2. The nodes and hubs where information is gathered, stored, exchanged and distributed – the network.

3. The spatial organization of the social actors who dominate the information flows and ensure that they are tilted asymmetrically in their favour – the organization of a new dominant class (Castells 1996: 412–18).

Castells conceded that this change was incomplete. Some, like Toyota's manufacturing plants, adapted to a network society and profited from earlier privileges and advantages (Castells 1996: 157–60). Others remained anchored in territorial-based identities and affiliations and reacted aggressively to the information society. As he explained (Castells 1996: 22):

New information technologies are integrating the world in global networks of instrumentality. Computer-mediated communication begets a vast array of virtual communities. Yet the distinctive social and political trend of the 1990s was the construction of social action and politics around primary identities, either ascribed, rooted in history and geography, or newly built in an anxious search for meaning and spirituality.

The result was to set up contradictions between cosmopolitans and locals, between virtual and place-based communities and, ultimately, between 'the net' and 'the self'.

Source: Castells (1983, 1989, 1996, 1997, 1998).

LUDDITES

English artisans who rioted rather than accept mechanical and technical changes. The term is used now to describe anyone who opposes technological change.

The convergence of communications and computer technologies can be seen in the often bewildering overlap of hitherto separated functions. One can send a fax from a PC via a modem or network. Some fax machines have sophisticated functions like copying, scanning, automatic switching between fax and voice calls, mechanisms for correcting telephone line noise, switching to alternative telephone networks and acting as a printer for a PC. Email messages sent over the internet can contain formatted files from PCs or networked file stores. Photographic images can be scanned, digitalized, altered, stored and transmitted. Voice, images and music are easily digitized, compressed, recorded and played back – a task familiar to the nearly 90 million users (as of January 2011) worldwide of the various iPhone and iPad models developed and marketed by Apple since 2007, as well as other similar devices.

Simply getting such technologies to work seamlessly and feeling comfortable with them is more than many of us can achieve. Some people have become technophobes or **Luddites** in order to maintain their sense of self-worth in the face of the incomprehensible. Castells (1996: 22–5) goes so far as to argue that even as 'information systems and networks augment human powers of organization and integration, they simultaneously subvert the traditional Western concept of a separate independent subject'. Communications and linked computer systems simulate in important respects a human brain. The 'artificial' in artificial intelligence is rapidly coming to resemble the real thing. It is perhaps not surprising that one patient in psychoanalysis saw in his dream an image of his head behind which was suspended a keyboard. He felt, he said, like a 'programmed head'. (We know the feeling.)

As the machine–human interface begins to naturalize through such emulative technologies as memory chips, virtual reality and artificial intelligence, humans will begin to lose the primacy of their own sensory perceptions. In the days of mass production, the notion of alienation was used to suggest that the social relations of production were artificial and that human nature was being altered to fit in with the rhythms of machines and assembly lines. Alienation in the informational society is even more profound. Whereas in the industrial age machines mimicked a person's physical characteristics (the clanking robot with arms and legs being emblematic), in the informational age the conscious mind itself is emulated and may eventually be relegated to a marginal status.

INFORMATIONAL SOCIETY: SOCIAL EFFECTS

Despite the positive possibilities and examples described earlier in Box 16.1, the negative (or presumed negative) effects of the mass media and mass communication worry many observers. Three of the principal effects often mentioned are:

- the effects of TV on patterns of violence, sexual mores and educational competence
- the growth of destructive consumerism
- the media's capacity to shape our identities.

NEGATIVE EFFECTS OF TV VIEWING

The first concern has some intuitive support in the upward trend in TV viewing hours. In US homes the TV is turned on for an average of seven hours a day. It is estimated that, by the age of 18, the average American child will have witnessed 18,000 simulated murders on TV (Watson 1998: 238). It is only reasonable that many parents, particularly those with young children, are disturbed at the thought of their children arbitrarily imitating images, ideas and behaviour patterns from the screen. However, the connection between lived violence and mediated violence is still uncertain. Some researchers point out that the most violent period in US history was between 1929 and 1933 when TV did not exist and that, in many poor countries, the level of violence experienced is high even where TV ownership is low (Watson 1998: 239). Clearly, violence is not *only* caused by TV. However, as Watson (1998: 238) avers, the argument cannot be dismissed lightly; 80 research studies affirm the connection between TV and actual violence. At the very least:

> the more we see of violence, the more we might become insensitive to it, and thus eventually immune to it. Either way it might confirm our view that out there is a dangerous and hostile world.

Beyond the issue of violence, long hours of watching TV might produce some kind of osmosis effect in which people, children in particular, are unable to distinguish fantasy from reality. Some postmodernists, of course, embrace this elision of a boundary between the imaginary and the real. Fortunately, there seems to be strong evidence that, despite the TV being on for so long each day, many people ignore routine programmes. The TV becomes like moving wallpaper – a mildly interesting and changing pattern, rather like the coloured wax blobs moving up and down in a lava lamp.

CONSUMERISM

We discussed the character of global consumerism in Chapter 14, but it is worth mentioning in this context how the global media effectively diffuse consumerism. The goods that are desirable, the music that is hip, the clothes that are fashionable, or the 'look' that is trendy are all rapidly absorbed through the power of the media. Perhaps surprisingly, this process of consumer imitation and emulation even had profound effects in fuelling the neoliberal opposition to state communism. The capacity of the media to suggest that there is a wonderful cornucopia of goods just waiting on the other side of the hill led many in the former communist countries to confuse the free market with political and social freedom. There is some evidence for this.

Drawing on research and informed observations, Morozov (2011: 61–72) argues that, in the 1980s, the communist government in the German Democratic Republic eventually relaxed its controls over access to satellite dishes because it came to the conclusion that exposure to the narcotizing effects of consumerism and popular culture from viewing Western TV programmes would very probably help to depoliticize its citizens. Indeed, young East Germans who lived in regions where Western TV was unavailable were more politicized and discontented with the regime than their more 'fortunate' young compatriots, and were thus more likely to apply for exit visas. It also became apparent that citizens were more interested in the escapism of American soap operas, and the fantasies a consumer culture conjured up, than in the world news or programmes on democratic politics. Moreover, not many people believed much of what they heard on the Western news channels. Morozov also claims that many authoritarian regimes, including Russia, China, Burma and others, have come to the same conclusion, whether with respect to the imported Western media or their own home-grown variety.

Turning to Western consumers, other countries and other cultures become mere objects for consumption. (Some more positive outcomes of mass consumption are also considered in Chapter 14.) The TV provides an endless stream of consumer and food programmes set in 'exotic' destinations. 'Holidays' are prizes given in fatuous competitions and dating programmes. The newspapers are full of travel writing and adverts for low-cost flights. Some companies, notably Disney, have brought together the consumption of goods, tourism and culture in a single setting (Disney World and Euro Disney). Children can graze on authentic American hamburgers, cokes, ice cream and popcorn while sitting on a mechanical boat going on a so-called 'Caribbean cruise'. Segments of historical reality are reordered for the purposes of this journey – pirates wave cutlasses, black actors sing 'Ol Man River', and young women perform belly dances in some sort of extraordinary pastiche of history, traditions and fake authenticity.

Thus, communications do not always lead to multicultural understanding and mutual respect for other peoples. Instead, the need to annex the media to consumerism leads to an appropriation of other cultures for profit. This double-edged feature of democratic openness yet commercial closure is also seen in the case of the humble phone. Although they can be used to foster lateral contacts outside the big media players and help to connect family members, they are also the stock in trade of transnational criminal gangs and terrorists (Chapter 11).

MEDIA DOMINATION AND IDENTITIES

Production, marketing and broadcasting may be integrated in the hands of a few media corporations but do we inevitably accept the messages they seek to disseminate? Morley and Robins (1995: 126–46) warn us against accepting what they call a 'hypodermic' model of media effects – the assumption that there are necessary cultural effects on all those who are 'injected'. The media are dominated by a few and this undoubtedly has far from negligible consequences. Yet, the results are also complex and more variable. Take the case of the TV soap *Dallas*, often cited as a classic example of Western media imperialism. Although this programme was broadcast from 1978 to 1991 (a new version is threatened in mid-2012), it has been intensely studied for its supposed model status. There were variable responses to the programme. Morley and Robins (1995: 120) cite an important study in the Netherlands, which found that Dutch women saw the programme 'through the grid of their own feminist agenda'. Far from seeing J. R. Ewing as successfully asserting his patriarchal power, respondents saw the women characters as making ironic jibes at the males' doomed bids for dominance. They did not see the males as offering credible macho characters; rather they were there, the Dutch women thought, to provoke a good laugh. Australian Aborigines, American, Russian, North African and Japanese audiences each saw the programme in a different way, through the differently tinted lenses of their own cultures, kinship patterns, social preferences, religions and norms.

'Complexity' is also at the heart of media consumption in a detailed ethnographic study of young Punjabi people living in Southall, London. Gillespie (1995) shows that the media had several distinctive effects on those she studied:

1. Parents often disapproved of their children watching Western soaps. Nevertheless, many did so, but programmes like *Neighbours* were 'embedded in family life', with aspirations for cultural change being negotiated within a context of shared family values.
2. Young people reacted to the TV news within a framework of being *both* British and Asian (Gillespie 1995: 128).
3. During the first Gulf War in 1991, the newspapers became triumphalist in tone, and Punjabis in general, but particularly Muslim ones, felt uncomfortably ambivalent. They saw through the obvious Western propaganda, yet had to thread their way uneasily through being pro-British (especially in the classroom) and not anti-Muslim (especially at home).

This rich study shows that the survival power of culture among many minority groups is high and the media can provide a means of asserting a minority identity. They also provide a means of affiliating to a cosmopolitan culture, and showing loyalty to the country of settlement, but without providing undue offence and provocation to the older generation's values and religious persuasions. The consumption of the media is, in short, a complex and ambiguous matter. We are neither the victims of an intrusive hypodermic needle nor 'semiotic guerrillas', accepting, discarding or refracting the message as we choose (Morley and Robins 1995: 127).

REVIEW

The media have assumed a relatively independent life because messages are significantly changed through the medium of communication. This gives special powers to technology and to those who own, work with or understand it. Although this is less evident in the print media, where there is more scope for the individual reader's judgement, the visual and aural media are more intrusive. In theory, looking away when passing an offensive advertising hoarding or switching off the TV set that others are also watching are perfectly possible, but in practice they demand continuous effort and attention, as well as a willingness to annoy others, qualities that most of us find difficult to muster continuously. It is hard to escape media influence, however reclusive or discriminating you are. This means that we need to understand media ownership patterns and appreciate what they are not, as well as what they are, telling us. Are they exercising an undue influence that distorts the democratic political order? Are they acting as missionaries for global capitalism, denigrating alternatives to the 'free market' for goods and ideas, as Herman and McChesney (1997) suggest? Do they misrepresent the lives and aspirations of women, ethnic minorities and other social groups?

On the revolution in communications and the growth of the information age, we have argued that the increased sophistication and use of the telephone and its adjunct technologies, as well as the internet and social media sites, have many democratic possibilities that are already being exploited. It is too early, however, to pass final judgement on their potential to bring benefits that outweigh their disadvantages. Nonetheless, these show that powerful corporate interests cannot monopolize everything. Detailed studies showing that we ignore much, challenge some and most commonly reconstitute the message of the broadcasters, according to our own shared values and cultures, offset our natural fear of media moguls and their pretensions. We have not *yet* been forced to bow down to the screen, the iPod and the incessant ring of mobile phones.

 Visit the companion website at www.palgrave.com/sociology/cohen3e for extra materials to check and expand your learning, including interactive self-test questions, mind maps making links between key themes, annotated web links to sociological research, data and key sociological thinkers, a searchable glossary and much more.

FURTHER READING

M. Castells' major work, *The Rise of the Network Society* (1996, rev. edn 2000), has a strong prologue and Chapters 1 and 2 are relevant to this chapter.

As media studies courses have proliferated, a number of student-friendly books and readers (reprints of already published articles) have battled for market share. Two established texts are G. Branston and R. Stafford's *The Media Student's Book* (2003) and A. Sreberny-Mohammadi et al. *Media in Global Context: A Reader* (1997).

E. Morozov's critique of the current celebration of social networking, *The Net Delusion: How Not to Liberate the World* (2011), may be pessimistic but he scrutinizes recent views, research projects and case studies in a highly accessible way.

QUESTIONS AND ASSIGNMENTS

1. What are the democratic possibilities of the advances in telecommunications?
2. Why is it important for us to know about the patterns of media ownership?
3. Is culture going to be 'dumbed down' to the lowest common denominator?
4. Can we argue that we live in an 'informational society'?
5. Compare and contrast the 'hypodermic needle' with the 'semiotic guerrilla' model.

17
Global religion

It is often difficult to separate strictly religious phenomena from other similar types of belief and behaviour. Rites, public ceremonials, superstitions, magic (and its subcategories of 'black magic' and sorcery) and myth are all closely associated with religion. For sociologists, the key issue is not whether religion is 'true' or 'false', but why it is manifested in all societies, what meanings are invested in it, and what social functions it provides. Other pertinent questions that a sociologist might ask include:

- Are particular religious convictions associated with special forms of conduct in the secular world? (A question that Weber, for example, posed was whether there was a link between Protestantism and capitalism.)
- Is there a long-term growth in secularization, or does the apparent revival of religiosity refute this thesis?
- Is Islam in general a threat to 'Western civilization'? And why have Islamic jihadists turned to terrorism to express their fervent beliefs?

In this chapter we examine all these themes but we also review what sociologists have contributed to the study of religion. Moreover, we continue the discussion of terrorism initiated in Chapter 11, this time concentrating on Islam.

EARLY SOCIOLOGISTS AND RELIGION: COMTE AND MARX

Historically, some sociologists were impatient with religious ideas and practices, seeing them as part of a pre-Enlightenment culture that would fade with the establishment of a secular rational culture. Auguste Comte (1883) reasoned that human thought passed through three historical stages. The first was a theological stage, seen in primitive and early society. The second was a metaphysical stage found in medieval society, while a third positive stage was seen in modern (for Comte this was the nineteenth-century) society. Animism gave way to monotheism, which, in turn, would give way to scientific, rational thinking based on logical presuppositions, experiment and evidence. In this way of thinking, religion could be seen as an irrational diversion or a residual survival of an outdated mode of seeing the world.

For Karl Marx, religion was similarly consigned to the category of 'false consciousness' and 'ideology'. He drew his major insight from the German materialist philosopher Ludwig Feuerbach (1957), who argued in *The Essence of Christianity* that God is the exterior projection of human beings' interior nature. God did not invent human beings, Feuerbach argued, rather, they invented God. It is always dangerous for a sociologist to overinterpret the force of personal circumstances in influencing a thinker's views. But it is interesting to note that while there were a number of rabbis among Marx's ancestors, Marx's father, a progressive-minded lawyer, changed his name from Hershel to Heinrich and converted to Lutherism. Subsequent to this embrace of Christianity, Heinrich's clients grew in number. But Karl Marx did not see his father's choice as opportunistic or hypocritical but simply as highly rational and Feuerbach's arguments as self-evident.

Compared with his writing on capitalism, Marx wrote very little on religion. However, he appreciated that poor, subordinated people turned to religion for solace. In 1844 he wrote:

> Religious distress is at the same time the expression of real distress and the protest against real distress. Religion is the sigh of the oppressed creature, the heart of a heartless world, just as it is the spirit of a spiritless situation. It is the opium of the people. (quoted in Bocock and Thompson 1985: 11)

In this quote Marx demonstrates more empathy with the need for religious expression than is usually ascribed to him. Moreover, when he observed that 'religion is the opium of the people', he did not mean that religion caused euphoria, but rather that it dulled the pain of existence (Aldridge 2000: 62).

A PAUSE TO REFLECT

What are the best ways to assess religiosity? Sociologists have sometimes used attendance at a place of worship as one measure, but does this adequately capture the intensity of belief or conviction? How can sociologists assess the functions of religion? Is it possible to have high levels of spirituality and moral cohesion without organized religion or even a belief in a divinity?

Comte also drew back from his secular conclusions in later work and sought to construct what we might nowadays see as a social movement in support of 'religious humanism', seeing the need to weld the 'warm' force of social cohesion that religion provided to his 'cold' quest for scientific understanding. Nonetheless, Comte's was the first voice in sociology that decisively opposed religion to science. This turned into a much wider debate after the publication in 1859 of Charles Darwin's book *On The Origin of Species*. Darwin's work challenged those who believed in the literal truth of the biblical account, in Genesis, of how humankind emerged. His account of natural selection was based on the variations in plant, animal, bird, insect and fish life, which he recorded through his international voyages and careful botanical studies. Darwin's prodigious powers of observation and analysis still fail to impress today's 'fundamentalists' and 'creationists' who continue to believe in the literal truth of the Bible. The angry debates that have accompanied this opposition between religion and science have not diminished in 150 years. As sociologists, we should recognize our limitations; we cannot provide major breakthroughs in the contestations between science and religion. Instead, we turn to more overtly sociological questions.

UNDERSTANDING RELIGIOUS EXPRESSION: RITUAL, TOTEM AND TABOO

Religion manifests itself in all societies. Usually, even determined efforts to suppress religion either fail or states are eventually compelled to accept compromises. For example, following the victory of the Communist Party of the Soviet Union in 1917, around 90% of the Russian Orthodox churches were closed or destroyed in the period to 1939 (Ramet 2005: ix). Moreover, bishops and priests were executed and religious instruction in schools was banned. Yet, even Stalin turned to the Orthodox Church in the Second World War in an attempt to arouse national patriotism against the Nazi invasion. When state communism ended (around 1989), the old Orthodox churches were openly reinstated in Russia and in the countries that emerged from the collapse of the Soviet Union. They quickly reverted to their former conservative, anti-liberal and anti-Western orientations, with each Orthodox Church identifying with its own nation-state as the Russian federation fractured into a number of independent states and ethno-national ideologies (Agadjanian and Roudometof 2005: 10–11).

To understand the pervasive quality of religion, we need to examine the phenomenon itself. We should not narrowly conflate 'religion' with a church, mosque, synagogue, temple or gurdwara. These are merely the places where religion is expressed, institutionalized or imbibed with doctrine. Increasing numbers of people are claiming to be religious or spiritual, but they do not necessarily attend places of worship or pay allegiance to particular faiths. Doctrine is the elaborated theology or system of ideas that scholars and religious thinkers have developed, often after centuries of discussions and arguments about sacred texts. For example, the Torah, the holy book of the Jewish religion, contains nearly 80,000 words, but the Babylonian Talmud – the extended commentary on the Torah – took 2,000 rabbis 1,200 years to complete and is more than 2.5 million words in length.

To appreciate some of the deeper structures of religion, which are features of all societies irrespective of the concrete forms or doctrines their religions manifest, it is helpful to examine their rituals, totems and taboos. Echoing Marx, this prompts many to explain religiosity through the argument that humans – with their doubts, insecurities and bewilderment at the inexplicable – need 'something' to give them comfort, calm their fears and address their anxieties.

RITUALS

Rituals occur in the moments when collective expressions of thanks, forgiveness, celebration or dedication are made. The naming of a newborn infant, the coming of age of a young man or woman, marriage, death, a funeral, military victory, the planting or harvesting of crops, the appearance or cessation of rain, lighting, earthquakes or volcanic activity – all these have been the objects of simple or elaborated rituals. Because these events are sometimes terrifying, or gratifying and often joyful, they are invested 'with the reverence and awe that characterize religious behaviour' (Chinoy 1967: 353). Of course, religions often appropriate rituals from elsewhere and absorb them into their doctrine and practice. The harvest festival, for example, which Christian churches all over Europe observe in September, is clearly a pre-Christian pagan ritual in celebration of the annual harvest. The 'corn dolly', in which the corn spirit was supposed to live or be reborn and which was kept until the following spring to ensure a good harvest, is another example of the appropriation of a non-Christian symbol into religious practice.

© ROBIN COHEN

FIGURE 17.1 A Candomblé religious statuette for sale in a Brazilian market
Candomblé is a syncretic religion combining Catholicism and West African religious traditions, white and black saints and gods being blended in a complex doctrine. There are about 2 million adherents, mainly based in Brazil, but also other South American countries.

TOTEM

> **TOTEM**
>
> An object, animal, fish or natural phenomenon endowed with supernatural qualities.

The idea of a **totem** is more contested. As with ritual, early ethnographers working among Melanesian and Polynesian islanders, Australian Aborigines and Native Americans noticed that these indigenous people often treated animals (sometimes domesticated, sometimes dangerous), plants, fish and even natural phenomena (rocky crags, ice, water) with a high degree of deference. They did not see them as divine; rather they saw the totems as both protecting the group and differentiating it from its enemies. For this reason, they either did not eat the flesh of totem animals or, if they did, only during elaborate ceremonies.

We should not, however, confuse this 'marker' or symbolic function of the totem with the deeper ties of sociality, habit, ritual and kinship that bind groups together. In fact, the French social anthropologist Lévi-Strauss (1963) questioned whether the role assigned to totemism was exaggerated, for it is easy to mistake symbol for substance. For example, few Americans actually believe that the names of fearsome animals they assign to more than one-third of their US sports teams really are grizzlies, hornets, tigers, bulls, panthers, bears, longhorns or coyotes, but nonetheless they serve as symbols of group identification and provide figurative threats to the opposing teams. Totemism thrives in contemporary society in the guise of amulets, charms and tokens. One good example, which arrived in the USA through African Americans, is the belief in the potency of rabbit feet. Ten million are sold each year in the USA where – as in other countries – they are associated with luck, quick-wittedness, the warding off of evil spirits, fertility and good fortune (Desai 2004). In short, we should understand totems from an interpretive perspective and not literally (see Chapter 1 on Weber's interpretative sociology).

TABOO

> **TABOO**
>
> A social practice that is forbidden, inaccessible or off limits.

Unlike a totem which refers to an object or animal, a **taboo** refers to a social practice that is socially prohibited. Key examples are the food prohibitions of many faiths. Pork and shellfish are outlawed by religious Jews; Muslims share the notion that pork is unclean and add a fierce condemnation of alcohol in nearly all its forms (but see below). Like the Jews, Mormons forbid shellfish; like the Muslims, they reject alcohol (to which they add other stimulants like tea and coffee). Catholics, by contrast, drink wine and ingest a wafer to symbolize the blood and flesh of Christ. Jews, Christians and Muslims all eat beef, which orthodox Hindus rebuff, treating the cow instead as sacred, a totem. That some taboos are shared while others differ markedly between faiths suggests that their significance for adherents lies in the meanings they ascribe to the act of rejection and even perhaps to the discipline required for self-abnegation. We should not, as Comte did, suppose that these prohibitions are a rational, instrumental response to premodern conditions where refrigeration was unavailable and rotting pork harboured dangerous diseases. Today, Jews and Muslims observe others eating breakfasts of bacon and eggs without harming anything but their cholesterol level. Yet, they often retain their taboo not for reasons of health but because it has acquired a spiritual and religious significance or acts as a marker of ethnic loyalty.

Despite the often contested interpretations of rituals, totems and taboo, they provide a way of understanding the underlying sentiments and therefore the building blocks of religious convictions. Freud deployed these notions to explain the roots of religious dissent in his book *Totem and Taboo* ([1913]1946). Here he argued that if people witnessing the violation of a taboo suppressed their resulting psychological anxieties and noticed that no retribution followed, they would venture more extensive violations of taboos until a secular outlook eventually emerged. We discuss more sociological explanations for secularization later.

Emile Durkheim is one of the founders of sociology. He held appointments at Bordeaux and the Sorbonne and established a formidable reputation on the basis of three books – *The Division of Labour in Society* (1933), *The Rules of Sociological Method* (1938) and his famous study on *Suicide* (1952). His early works set the ground rules by which most sociologists continue to operate. In distancing sociology from psychology, Durkheim (1938: 103) argued that:

Society is not a mere sum of individuals. Rather, the system formed by their association represents a specific reality that has its own characteristics. Of course, nothing collective can be produced if individual consciousnesses are not assumed, but this necessary condition is by itself insufficient. These consciousnesses must be combined in a certain way; social life results from this combination and is, consequently, explained by it.

This core idea led to three of his guiding concepts:

1. Societies evolved from a common set of ideas, norms and expectations that their members largely shared. This he called the *collective consciousness*.

2. In early prehistoric or agricultural forms of society, social cohesion was built on a common set of superstitions, social practices and rituals, often religious, resulting in what he deemed *mechanical solidarity* ('mechanical' is to be understood as 'accepted' or 'unquestioned').

3. *Organic solidarity*, which was based on a more complex division of labour between individuals, replaced mechanical solidarity in the more advanced, urban and industrial societies. Contract, impersonality and self-interest became more common, but Durkheim still strongly insisted that a powerful moral order underpinned modern societies.

Despite being an atheist, Durkheim was certain that religion played a vital function in social life. In *The Elementary Forms of Religious Life* ([1915]1976: 427), he concluded that: 'there can be no society which does not feel the need of upholding and reaffirming at regular intervals the collective sentiments and collective ideas which make its unity and its personality'. While meetings, reunions, assemblies and the like can be crucial, these tend to become routinized and part of everyday work, home and leisure life. Durkheim labelled such behaviour 'profane' and distinguished it from the 'sacred', where a sense of awe and reverence is induced and expressed. In this sense, the sacred was just as crucial for Australian Aborigines (one of his cases) as for contemporary Christians. Thus, all religions were systems of beliefs and practices, punctuated and cemented by rituals that drew believers into a moral community.

Source: Durkheim (1933, 1938, 1952, [1915]1976).

RELIGION AND CAPITALISM

Whereas Comte and Marx contrasted the practice of religion with secular, rational and scientific pursuits, Max Weber wondered whether there might be an important link between the world of mammon (the Christian representation of greed) and the world of God. In his incisive book, *The Protestant Ethic and the Spirit of Capitalism* ([1905]1977), Weber suggested that particular religious convictions could support the pursuit of material gain. Turning this around, he saw that Calvinist notions of predestination (in particular) could prompt hard work and generate patterns of accumulation consistent with successful entrepreneurship. Predestination suggested that God had already marked out the 'elect' for worldly success, but people who thought (or hoped) they were members of the elect could only demonstrate that they were to their family and peers if they acquired enough riches to do the good works to prove that they were indeed chosen by God. Rather than encouraging passivity, predestination (along with certain other Protestant assumptions) created a ceaseless quest for material achievement.

Weber suggested that Protestantism and capitalism have a particular affinity. How far, if at all, can we extend this argument? There were many important Muslim mathematicians and famous Chinese philosophers. Is it therefore possible to say that Islam has an affinity with mathematics or Confucianism with philosophy?

Weber did not say that Protestantism causes capitalism, or the other way around, but rather that there was 'an elective affinity' between them; they went hand in hand. He also focused on rational, calculative capitalism rather than on booty capitalism (characterized by plunder and despoliation) or what he called 'pariah capitalism' (such as moneylending). From his later studies of ancient Judaism, China and India, he deduced that it was not Protestantism per se that was important. Jainism and Zoroastrianism appealed to Indian traders and entrepreneurs, whereas orthodox Hinduism, with its stress on religious obedience and a passive acceptance of one's place in the caste hierarchy, constrained capitalism and permitted only slow intergenerational social mobility. Weber put forward equivalent arguments about Buddhism, Confucianism, Judaism and Islam. In each case, he was careful to allow deviant options and 'protestant-like' elements to emerge, which can accommodate an explanation of why, for example, India is currently such a resounding capitalist success. The role of the Tokugawa religion in providing the preconditions for Japanese industrialization is also consistent with a broad reading of the Weberian thesis (Bellah 1985).

The rise of evangelical Christianity in Central and Latin America, as well as in the many other parts of the world that have been experiencing economic growth since the 1970s, has lent additional weight to his thesis. In Brazil, for example, the Universal Church of the Kingdom of God, which was established in 1977, proved particularly attractive to destitute small farmers from the interior or the arid northeast who were driven by poverty to seek a livelihood in the shantytowns of São Paulo and other cities (Clarke 2006: 213–15). As a form of evangelical or Pentecostal Protestantism, this Church empowers its members to cope with the fragmentation of their former communities, while seeking a 'moral and ethical code for living in a more open-ended, less predictable world in which thrift and self-discipline are seen as the key to success' (Clarke 2006: 215). In a presentation commemorating the centenary of Weber's Protestant ethic thesis, Berger (2010: 5) strongly asserts its continuing relevance:

> One can observe a positive correlation with social mobility and with it a truly novel phenomenon in Latin America: a growing Protestant middle class, economically productive and increasingly assertive politically. Of course, Latin American Pentecostalism is not a monolithic phenomenon. There are strands which deviate from the Weberian concept (for example, groups that promote a so-called 'wealth gospel' wherein God provides benefits to people who have to make little effort beyond having faith). But the overall picture fits neatly with Weber's description of the Protestant ethic and its effects.

THE SECULARIZATION THESIS

Weber was also interested in the future of religion, which, he argued, would decline in influence as the 'legal-rational' claims of the bureaucracy of the modern state began to take over 'traditional' (by virtue of inherited office) and 'charismatic' (by virtue of personality) forms of authority. The 'iron cage' of bureaucracy was pitiless precisely because the modern state operated without passion or discrimination. Bryan Wilson (1966), who is the most widely cited proponent of the so-called 'secularization thesis' and draws heavily on Weber's work, believed that 'rationalization would sweep aside tradition and marginalize charisma' (quoted in Aldridge 2000: 73). Although Wilson made far wider claims for his arguments, he mainly based his observations on Anglicanism in England in the 1950s and 60s. Using various statistical indicators, he developed his thesis that Anglicanism was failing but set this within wider debates about the future of the Church.

Wilson believed that attempts to accommodate to secular society through such gestures as the ordination of women, a deference to laity, and ecumenical dialogues with other faiths were merely indicators of weakness and that such attempts to gain popularity would fail to stem declining church attendances. Meanwhile, clerical salaries were declining along with the prestige of parish priests and dwindling congregations were reluctant to pay for a professional service. Wilson (1966: 76) held that the high rates of church attendance in the USA did not compensate for the shallowness of religious conviction and the indirect forms of secularization that took place within formal religious adherence.

At a societal level, the connection between a faith and its following depended on personal contact between priest and parishioners in stable communities. But, the latter were disappearing with urbanization and the institutional differentiation between complementary but separate areas of social life. Indeed, the vast systems generated by state power, welfare provision, science and education, capitalism and money, among others, operated effectively irrespective of religion's influence while providing many of the needs that individuals once obtained from religious belief and membership (Beyer 2006: 86–8). Another consequence was that religion – at least in the advanced societies – was partly forced to retreat into the private sphere of individual thoughts and feelings. The global shares of adherents to a religion and those claiming no adherence are shown in Figure 17.2.

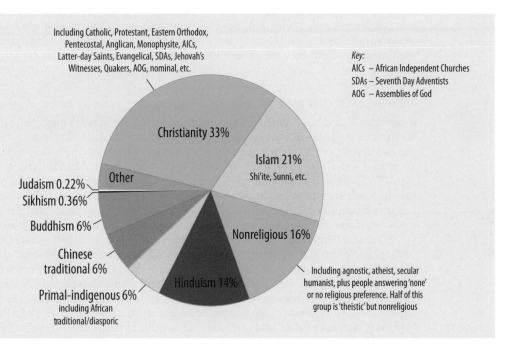

FIGURE 17.2 Global shares of religious adherents

Note: Totals add to more than 100% due to rounding.

Source: Adherents.com (2007).

In Figure 17.2, nonreligious people are estimated at 16% of the global population, but this is almost certainly a large underestimation. As Abrams et al. (2011: 1) note, people claiming no religious affiliation are, as a group, growing faster than any religious group. Moreover:

Americans without religious affiliation comprise the only … group growing in all 50 states; in 2008 those claiming no religion rose to 15 per cent nationwide, with a maximum in Vermont of 34 per cent. In the Netherlands, nearly half the population is religiously unaffiliated. (Abrams et al. 2011: 1)

Using dynamical systems and perturbation theory derived from engineering and mathematics, the model developed by Abrams et al., which has been applied to 85 countries, predicts the continuing growth of non-affiliation and even the eventual disappearance of formal religion.

CHALLENGES TO THE SECULARIZATION THESIS: RELIGIOSITY THRIVES

We must remember, however, that formal affiliation can be distinguished from religious sentiments and belief, and the latter still has considerable potency in shaping the lives of many people. Religions are also taking on new forms. The evidence indicates that:

- Christianity is surviving or only modestly declining in the advanced countries.
- Established religions and their churches may have declined in popularity, but there has been a surge of new religious movements (NRMs) across the world and these seem to be thriving.
- Virtually all religions – even those that resist modernization and Westernization – have become globalized and this points to some degree of resilience.

Some scholars, such as Agadjanian and Roudometof (2005: 4), even go so far as to suggest that religion not only remains 'mainstream', in that it provides valuable symbolic capital for humans, but that it has also been 'rediscovered as a constant and increasing agency'. Perhaps, they suggest, we can even talk of a world process of 'desecularization'.

RELIGIOUS SURVIVAL IN THE WEST

Through TV and radio channels and political organization, religious beliefs, practices and institutions are politically and publicly in the ascendant in the USA. Indeed, by the turn of the twenty-first century, the organized Christian right had become so important that many credited it with the election and re-election of George Bush Jr. Alternatively, it may be more plausible to argue that the Church is being mobilized for specific ideological purposes; for example, to back a political candidate who opposed abortion, wanted to be tough on terrorism or who supported 'family values'. The extent to which there has been a growth of religious sentiment and spirituality within the conventional churches is much less clear.

Stark and Bainbridge (1985) echoed Wilson's notion of a hidden secular consciousness underpinning the rise in church participation. Congregants are, in effect, using rational choice theory, which suggests that human beings seek to maximize their rewards and minimize their risks. Also compelling is the argument that the churches provide a series of concrete benefits for their congregants – superior educational opportunities, support in sickness, old age and misfortune (areas evacuated by the neoliberal state), and a network of fellow members 'who look after each other' and provide a warm circle of social acceptance. In Britain, where high-quality, state-supported schooling is at a premium, dual-supported Church schools (which are generally of better quality) have insisted that parents attend church if their children are to be considered for admission. Dutiful attendance at their local Anglican church by ambitious parents does not, however, prove that they have found the way of the Lord.

While instrumentality and rationality can partly explain the continued popularity of the established religions, the notable growth of fervent religious sentiment among the non-established churches is apparent. Take the Church of Jesus Christ of Latter-day Saints, or Mormons. Founded in the 1830s, the Mormons' scripture, *The Book of Mormon*, revealed to

Joseph Smith in Salt Lake City, had, by 1997, sold 78 million copies. With over 55,000 missionaries serving worldwide at any given time, the Church currently claims a growing membership of over 14.4 million. The Jehovah's Witnesses have about 7 million followers worldwide, many of whom read their publications, *Watchtower* and *Awake!* Their doctrine proclaims that Christ returned for his second coming in 1874 and was enthroned as king in 1878. All governments and churches were to be destroyed in 1914 and a worldwide paradise was to be ushered in. Despite this and other failed prophecies, the Jehovah's Witnesses continue to thrive; according to their own statistics, US membership, measured in terms of those attending Kingdom Hall churches to commemorate Christ's death at Easter, is 2.5 million (Jehovah's Witnesses 2011). Worldwide, the active membership seems to be growing at around 2.5% annually.

THE WORLDWIDE GROWTH OF NEW RELIGIOUS MOVEMENTS (NRMs)

Beyond established faiths and religious movements like the Mormons and Jehovah's Witnesses, there are many expressions of religion that fall into the categories of 'sects', 'cults', 'alternative religions' or 'new religious movements'. Beckford (1986: xv) sees the growth of such movements partly as critiques or renewals of older religions and partly as responses to the rapidity and ubiquity of social change, including globalization. He claims that they 'amount to social and cultural laboratories where experiments in ideas, feeling and social relations are carried out'. Clarke (2006) stresses the innovatory and experimental nature of NRMs, but sees these and other characteristics as applicable to a wide range of world religions, not just those linked to Christianity. He also insists that 'religious change is constituted differently in different religions and cultural settings' (Clarke 2006: xiv). Clarke (2006: 6–16) lists the following additional characteristics of NRMs:

- The core of NRMs involves the desire of individuals under modernizing and globalizing conditions to pursue a spirituality other than that based on external scriptural truth and doctrine or the divinely inspired word of God as mediated by a hierarchically organized church and priesthood (Clarke 2006: 8–10).
- Because this spirituality is crucially based on seeking direct, personal religious experience, it involves a quest for inner personal development and self-realization. This turning inwards to the self as the authority for belief constitutes, for Clarke, a religion for and of the 'True Self' (Clarke 2006: 8).
- For these reasons, NRMs are basically trying to combine the divine and the human in ways that are compelling and 'self-empowering' (Clarke 2006: 7). Equally, believers are trying to transform the world through developing their inner spirituality but without losing contact with the sacred, which they find in their own way.
- Typically, therefore, most NRMs contain a millenarian dimension. This is the belief that human life on earth can be transformed through spiritual means. Thus, instead of focusing entirely on securing salvation in the next world through engaging passively in appropriate religious rituals during life, they try to find truth and meaning in their present lives on earth. Interestingly, the earlier millenarian movements that sprang up in some countries during the colonial period were directed against alien rulers and sometimes led to acts of political insurrection.
- NRMs look upon evil more as ignorance than as domination by the devil or an indulgence in wilful egotistical personal behaviour. Consequently, there is a strong emphasis on acquiring the knowledge, skills and personal disciplines that enable adherents to escape from ignorance into a state of enlightenment.
- Not surprisingly, NRMs tend to reject priestly hierarchies, although many have gurus or masters who provide personal guidance. They are often tolerant of other religions and may allow members to follow other movements; their leaning towards experimentation tends to result in the adoption of aspects of belief and practice taken from other religions.

An astonishing number and range of NRMs have arisen worldwide in the past two centuries and many of these are very recent. The emphasis on developing a personal spirituality is usually more pronounced in the NRMs based in Western societies, whereas in the global South, where Buddhism and other religions predominate, the members of these movements tend to lean more towards 'communal, societal concerns' (Clarke 2006: xiv). Nevertheless, individual needs and orientations are also evident here, particularly in urban areas, and this trend is strengthening. In Box 17.1, we discuss two case studies that demonstrate this range and variation.

BOX 17.1 Case studies of NRMs, North and South

The People's Temple and the Jonestown mass suicide in Guyana

Jim Jones, the leader of the People's Temple, was born of humble origins in 1931. He showed an early interest in emotional religion (in this case Pentecostalism) and an ability to attract devotion and mistrust. In 1955 he established an NRM, which became known as the People's Temple Christian Church. It later moved to California. The movement drew together radical, often affluent, whites and marginal blacks to deliver social care to mentally disturbed and poor people.

After falling foul of the Californian tax authorities, the movement decamped to Guyana where it leased 4,000 acres in a remote area. Later, when Jones joined the settlement, it was renamed 'Jonestown'. Jones advocated a blend of faith healing, utopianism, Pentecostalism, communism and anti-racism, directed mainly at the USA. He demanded absolute obedience and claimed divine inspiration, haranguing the community on the public address system. Those who left were denounced as apostates and dismissed. Tim Stoen, a defector, returned to the USA and organized concerned relatives who accused Jones of brainwashing. They demanded a Congressional investigation.

When Congressman Leo Ryan eventually visited, the response was paranoiac and confused, and Ryan, three media people and a Temple member who wanted to leave were all killed at the airstrip at Port Kaituma. Others were wounded. When Jones realized that the US government would intervene, he shut the community down and proclaimed that their only option was 'revolutionary suicide'. This was eventually agreed. A cocktail of potassium cyanide and sedatives was prepared, which parents gave to their children before drinking it themselves (Hall 1987: 285). Jones, however, died of a gunshot wound – whether a result of murder or suicide was never determined. On 17 November 1978, the final death toll in Jonestown was 909, nearly a third of them children.

Postscript

Unsurprisingly, this horrific event and the rise of other exclusive, totalitarian movements prompted widespread concern. In the UK, Barker (1989) was commissioned to undertake a study of 500 NRMs to ascertain whether fears of 'brainwashing' and 'mind control' were justified. She concluded that the persuasion and socialization techniques they employed differed little from those used in families, schools, the armed forces and traditional religions (Barker 1989: 19).

An East Asian case: China's Falun Gong

Many NRMs have developed in East Asia. Some, like the Moonies in South Korea, have spread worldwide. Others are among the world's largest NRMs. Their dominant concerns can be political or religious, but nearly all are messianic or millenarian, in that they anticipate world transformation through engaging in some kind of self-realization strategy. Some have emerged out of the dominant religions of Confucianism, Daoism or Buddhism, while others have spread from abroad or were established by independent charismatic leaders. Sometimes elements from local folk religions or Christianity are also absorbed.

Li Hongzhi, a self-educated man from industrialized Manchuria, founded Falun Gong (also called Falun Dafa) in 1992. While influenced by the anti-Western ideas that the communist government upheld when he was young – he was born in 1951 – he also draws on conventional Buddhist and Daoist/Taoist teachings and qigong (chi gung). He believes that contemporary China demonstrates a moral decline similar to that of the West because of its rampant materialism and pro-scientific approach to modern life. Falun Gong predicts that degeneration will culminate soon in an apocalyptic catastrophe – as the present cycle of the universe reaches its close – followed by a new age of progress. This can only be avoided by conversion to the movement. This, in turn, requires participants to study and practise the texts Li Hongzhi wrote in 1992 (which have been widely translated), follow certain techniques to enhance health, personal calm and longevity (modern medicine is unhelpful), and live a morally upright life built around the principles of truthfulness, compassion and forbearance – even in the face of threats and persecution. These practices will allow individual members to develop a spirituality rendering them strong in mind and body while transforming the world.

In effect, the cult teaches that humans are capable of attaining a much higher state of existence than contemporary society permits. However, through correct spiritual practice, individuals can discover their original true selves before the world corrupted them and perhaps ultimately attain unity with Buddha. Falun Gong is popular in China (and elsewhere), suggesting the presence of widespread dissatisfaction among Chinese citizens. The rural migrants, who lost their jobs through economic restructuring in the early 1990s, are staunch supporters. Following a large demonstration in April 1999, the movement was banned as subversive and an agent of imperialism. Many members were imprisoned or – allegedly – placed in psychiatric institutions, while Li Hongzhi fled to the USA (Clarke 2006: 319–25).

Sources: Barker (1989); Chidester (2004); Clarke (2006); Hall (1987); Moore et al. (2004).

THE GLOBALIZATION OF RELIGION

In the global age, religions readily diffuse across every kind of border, flourish everywhere and often adopt elements from other religions. As Robertson (1992) rightly insisted, just like nations, states, economic systems, cultures, medical practices and other fields of human action, religions have become exposed to each other and cannot avoid interacting. Whether these relationships are hostile, sympathetic or a mixture of both, dialogue is unavoidable. Consequently, religions and their practitioners experience glocalization (see Chapter 2). In reacting to each other, they adapt, alter and mix fragments from other movements. This is as true of the older, traditional religions such as Christianity, Islam and Buddhism as it is of the movements that have emerged more recently. The case studies in Box 16.1 illustrate this well. Such mobility and diffusion, however, suggest that whatever changes may or may not be taking place in each church or movement as it adapts to modernity, science, capitalism and other aspects of its environment, and irrespective of the numbers of adherents it retains, some essential ingredients of what we can broadly define as 'religiosity' continue to appeal to many people across the world.

There is a further aspect to this. Partly because of the way globalization exposes us to everyone else's culture, it can also, as Robertson (1992) pointed out, propel us towards thinking not only about our shared humanity and questions of ethics but also about our own individual identity and purpose in a complex world – what it means to be human. All these are intrinsically religious concerns.

THE 'THREAT' FROM ISLAM

Embraced by just over one-fifth of humankind (see Figure 17.2), the expansion of Islam and the revival of militant versions of political Islam (we will call these 'jihadists') are viewed with considerable alarm, particularly in Western political circles. This notion of an Islamic threat to Western economic and political interests has gained particular credibility in the wake of the various terrorist attacks that have taken place in New York, Madrid and London since 11 September 2001.

In a climate marked by extreme ideological and military conflict, it is difficult to separate myth from reality (it has wisely been said that 'truth is the first casualty of war'), so we must be careful to assess the strength of the arguments and evidence claiming that Western and Islamic interests are heading for confrontation. The most prominent advocate of this position was Samuel Huntington, a conservative American writer, whose arguments in *The Clash of*

Civilizations (1998) have been echoed by presidents, politicians and journalists. Huntington forecast a future consisting of cultural conflict and bloody wars between rival 'civilizations'. His argument can be summarized as follows:

1. A 'civilization' consists of the broadest level of cultural identity shared by clusters of ethnic groups, nations or peoples based on common experiences, especially history, religion, language and customs. This yields perhaps seven or eight contemporary civilizations, although each contains important subdivisions.
2. In the post-Cold War era, while nation-states remain powerful actors, ideological conflicts, for example between communism and capitalism, and interstate conflicts are unlikely to shape global politics to the same extent as they did in the past. Rather, conflicts in future will increasingly develop along the 'fault lines' between civilizations, which political leaders and groups sometimes exploit in pursuing their own interests.
3. Such confrontations are most likely to take place between the West, now at the zenith of its global power, and a coalition of non-Western civilizations probably focused around an Islamic–Confucianist axis. The countries potentially drawn to this axis are rapidly increasing their military capability either through imports or the arms industries linked to their industrialization programmes.
4. Binding these and other non-Western civilizations together – although much also divides them – is a shared resentment about the West's past behaviour. They see the West as continuing to impose its version of modernity while using its control of international institutions such as the World Bank and the UN to further its interests. Western concern to prevent the further spread of military capability, especially nuclear weapons, can be readily understood against this background.

A PAUSE TO REFLECT

Huntington (1998) argues that there is an intensification of 'civilizational consciousness', generated by a reaction to globalization and modernization and a consequent yearning for lost identities. This latter is increasingly reflected, he suggests, in the revival of various forms of religious and cultural fundamentalism. Is this thesis sustainable or is it implausible to conceive a social unit as large as a 'civilization' attaining a collective consciousness?

In August 1998, President Clinton ordered a missile attack on alleged Islamic terrorist sites located in Sudan and Afghanistan. This followed the bombing by jihadist groups of US embassies in Kenya and Tanzania earlier that month. Were these events and the even more dramatic post-2000 bombings by jihadist terrorists in New York, Madrid and London manifestations of the civilizational wars that Huntington had predicted? Huntington publicly declared that they were and that his thesis had been proved. However, as we show below, not everyone agreed. The first three points are derived from Halliday's (1996) trenchant criticisms:

1. Like the idea of nationhood, the notion of 'civilization' assumes that it is possible to identify and represent a set of timeless traditions. However, traditions arise from conflicting interpretations of cultural creations concocted largely to suit the political interests of different elites. Thus, since it is impossible to demarcate such clearly distinctive entities as civilizations, the case for an actual or potential confrontation is largely a myth.
2. The idea of clearly differentiated civilizations is further undermined when we remember how cultures and peoples have always borrowed each other's technologies, art forms, religious symbolism and much else besides. Also, with globalization, these processes seem likely to intensify, not diminish.

3. The fragmentation and conflicts that have occurred within civilizations, such as inter-ethnic or state divisions, have been just as marked as those between them and often much more so. This has certainly been the case in Europe, which, despite sharing Christianity, was wracked for centuries by religious, civil and interstate wars. And these conflicts have not entirely abated – witness, for example, the Basque region of Spain, Northern Ireland and the former Yugoslavia in the early 1990s. The Islamic world is also deeply divided along national and sectarian lines, irrespective of some Westerners' attempts to project the image of a united Islam bent on destroying its ancient enemy (Hadar 1993).

4. The idea of an Islamic–Confucianist axis seems particularly unsustainable. Confucius defined five key relationships, all of which stressed duty and obligation. These were between ruler and ruled, husband and wife, parents and children, older and younger brothers, and among friends. Passivity, knowing one's place and obedience to one's parents lie at the heart of Confucian doctrine. It is difficult to square this with militant Islam or see the basis for some strategic alliance. It is likely that, seeing the economic rise of China and militant Islam as threats to US interests, Huntingdon yoked them together.

THE COMPLEXITY OF ISLAM

Western commentators often fail to distinguish between the many varieties of Islam. There is even some doubt among Islamic scholars whether Islam should be considered a religious faith, a political ideology, a personal conviction or a group identity (Ruthven 2000: 2). However, it is necessary to begin by clearly identifying the diversity that is Islam:

1. It is undeniable that there are a significant number of armed and trained jihadists who wish to defend and advance their faith by terrorist activities. Strictly, 'jihad' (meaning exertion or struggle) can be undertaken by the heart, tongue, hand or sword (Ruthven 2000: 116), so when Muslims protest that their religion is a peaceful one and sometimes that terrorist jihadists are not Muslims at all, it is quite legitimate to respond that a peaceful disposition may be true in their case and indeed in most cases, but classic Islamic doctrine *does* allow armed jihad against enemies that refuse to submit to persuasion.

2. Despite this explicit doctrinal support for violence, we must immediately recognize the quite contrary elements in Islamic historical practice. The Islamic record of government from the seventh to twentieth century showed considerable levels of tolerance. The 'people of the Book' (a term used to designate non-Muslim adherents to faiths that have a revealed scripture – Jews and Christians) were often left alone to practise their own faiths, while minorities in the Ottoman Empire and elsewhere were frequently given considerable autonomy (see Hourani 1991 for examples). What we see here, therefore, is that there are many strands in Islam, some pulling in difficult different directions.

3. *The Sunnis* comprise 85–90% of all Muslims. (After the Prophet's death in 632 CE, Islam split into the two main divisions of Sunni and Shi'a; and within the Sunnis there are many different sects.) Sunnis are akin to Protestants in that they rejected the attempts to fuse religious and political authority in the person of the caliph (just as Protestants rejected a similar synthesis by the Pope) and turned instead to the ulama (religious scholars). This turning to those who interpret the sacred texts, who are thereby removed from the realities of power and compromises needed to administer the caliphates, also led to religious conservatism. In fact, as Ruthven (2000: 59–60) suggests, but does not quite state, Sunni conservatism and Christian fundamentalism have a good deal in common.

4. *The Shi'a* (also known as Shi'ites) are followers of Ali, who was the Prophet Muhammad's cousin and son-in-law and one of his heirs apparent. (Muhammad did not clearly designate his successor.) Over the centuries, the Shi'a have followed both quietist and activist leaders. Shi'a Islam is the officially recognized religion in Iran, but it has a significant following in Iraq, Pakistan, Syria, Lebanon and the Gulf States as well.

5. *The Ismailis* form a significant minority within the Shi'a who both contest the line of succession between the different imams and have developed a distinctive doctrine involving 'hidden knowledge' that was passed from God to prophets and imams. Although at one point Ismailis were involved in assassinations of their enemies, their current imam (spiritual leader), who bears the Persian title of the Aga Khan, is a British citizen who was once married to a British model and then a German princess. He owns 600 racehorses, private jets and properties in five continents. His ownership of newspapers, an airline, hotels, factories and collections of jewellery and antiques would make him an unlikely ally of terrorist jihadists.

6. *The Sufis* are ascetic pietists who turned away from public pursuits to find inner conviction though an unusual combination of abstinence, purification, poverty and repentance, with quite wild ritual dancing, singing and music playing. The famous Whirling Dervishes (Figure 17.3) are Sufis.

© WARREN CLARKE/EPA/CORBIS

FIGURE 17.3 Whirling Dervishes
Known to all readers of the charming folk tales, *The Arabian Nights*, they tend to intervene on behalf of the underdog. They are also against jihad by the sword. During the Ottoman attack against the Habsburg Empire in 1690, they told Muslim troops to desert, because the Ottoman emperor and Frankish king were simply enjoying themselves at their troops' expense.

THE WEST'S INVASION OF 'MUSLIM LANDS'

For a religion that has expanded worldwide and has a strong deterritorialized notion of its religious community, the umma, it is perhaps remarkable that many Muslims are determined to expunge all non-Islamic elements from 'Muslim lands'. From the perspective of the contemporary Muslim world, particularly the Arab countries, the key threat was the foundation and recognition of the Israeli state. It has always been difficult to discern wider Arab opinions that may exist under the surface of the often powerful rhetoric that surrounds the continuing conflict in the Middle East. However, one pioneering survey covering the 'Arab elite' in nine Middle Eastern countries was published in a leading US journal. Suleiman (1973: 482–9) found that of the 363 respondents to his survey, 75% made a distinction between 'Jews' and 'Zionists', a strong indication that, at least among the elite (his sample was overwhelmingly middle and upper class in background), antagonism was not simply a matter of religion/ethnicity. This was reinforced by the crucial finding that over 91% of his Muslim sample (n = 254) (there were also some Christian respondents) saw Israel as harbouring ambitions to expand from the Nile to the Euphrates.

However, what complicated the Israeli–Palestinian conflict was that religious sensitivities became conflated with the political consolidation and later expansion of the Israeli state. This was apparent first in the declared status of Jerusalem, which Israeli leaders made clear was to be the permanent capital of the country, despite the fact that all three Abrahamic faiths had many holy sites in the city. Another key example is that many of the Israeli settlements in the West Bank from 1967 to the current day seem to be started and led by ultra-Orthodox Jews, while the Israeli state is doing very little to halt their expansion, despite the declarations of the UN that many of the settlements are illegal and the urgings of successive US administrations.

The perceived threat to Muslim lands has been reinforced by a number of military interventions by other powers. Under the aegis of a League of Nations mandate, France governed Lebanon from 1920 to 1946. In 1958, US marines were sent in briefly to Lebanon. The British and French occupied the Suez Canal in 1956 in a coordinated attack with Israel against Egypt. The list continues. The Soviets and then more recently the USA invaded Afghanistan. While few Muslims were enthusiastic about Iraq's occupation of Kuwait, the US-led counterstrike from its nearby bases in Saudi Arabia gave the 'infidel' an even stronger hold in the region. The 'US coalition of the willing' attacking, then occupying Iraq looked like the last straw. 'The West' (demonized as a single entity) was seen as mounting a sustained war against Islamic countries. Then, in the wake of the events of 11 September 2001, President Bush could hardly have said something more tactless when he warned that 'this **Crusade**, this war on terrorism, is going to take a while'. For many Muslims, this remark evoked their historical humiliation at the hands of Christian knights.

Militant Muslim anger against the West extends to those rulers in Arab and Muslim countries who are seen as conniving with Western interests. The Muslim Brotherhood in Egypt, Ennahda – the Islamic Renaissance Party in Tunisia, the Islamic Salvation Front in Algeria, Hizbollah in Lebanon, Hamas in the West Bank and Gaza, and the shadowy al-Qaeda networks that Osama bin Laden organized in Saudi Arabia and elsewhere are just some of the organizations that urge Arab rulers on to a more militant path. That such organizations are capable of achieving political power can be seen most notably in the Iranian revolution of 1979 when Ayatollah Khomeini, a Shi'a cleric, returned from his exile in Paris to install what looked superficially like a medieval Islamic theocracy. Yet, Iran's atavistic return to an old Islamic world was deceptive. Iran's ayatollahs revere the past, but to fight their cause they depend on advanced technology, ranging from TV, jet travel, selling their oil on the world market, to sophisticated armaments (Hadar 1993). Advancing their capacity to generate nuclear power (perhaps with a view to producing nuclear weapons) has become a major contention between Iran, the USA and Europe. A number of these developments will continue irrespective of the killing of Osama bin Laden in May 2011.

THE CRUSADES

They took place between the eleventh and thirteenth centuries and were a generally successful attempt to drive out Muslims from Christian holy places in the Holy Land. Many Christian feudal lords (knights), with their followers, responded to Pope Urban II's call to arms following his indignant outburst in 1095 that 'the Muslims have conquered Jerusalem'.

CAN THE WEST LIVE WITH ISLAM?

The question of whether the West can live with Islam cannot be answered definitively, yet there are pointers indicating a way forward. First, it is essential that Western political leaders distinguish in theory and in practice between the minority committed to violent jihad and the vast majority who see Islam as a peaceful religion able to coexist with other faiths and to accept a degree of internal pluralism. Esposito (1995: 250) puts this well:

> The focus on 'Islamic fundamentalism' as a global threat has reinforced a tendency to equate violence with Islam [and] fails to distinguish between illegitimate use of religion by individuals and the face and practice of the majority of the world's Muslims who, like believers in other religious traditions, wish to live in peace. To uncritically equate Islam and Islamic fundamentalism with extremism is to judge Islam only by those who wreak havoc, a standard not applied to Judaism or Christianity.

Second, Western political leaders need to avoid sending out mixed signals in contexts where peaceful electoral competition has resulted in victories for Islamic parties. The most notable example involved the Islamic Salvation Front in Algeria in 1991 when an Islamic party clearly won the election against the expectations of Algeria's secular leaders and their partners in France. Instead of accepting the outcome of the election, the Algerian army was encouraged to intervene and govern by military diktat. When democracy did not suit Western interests, it was simply abandoned.

Third, and more positively, NATO's attack on Serbia in defence of the Muslim Kosovars in March 1999 showed that Western leaders could take a principled stance on behalf of victimized Muslims. Indeed, in March 1999, this was noted in a number of editorials in the Pakistan newspaper *Dawn*, which called for the Muslim world to acknowledge that leading Western powers were defending Muslims against Christians. Other positive examples of Western humanitarian intervention include the Western powers' generous donations to the Muslim East Asian victims of the 2004 tsunami, the Muslim Kashmiris who suffered in the earthquakes of 2005, and the people of Pakistan affected by the floods of 2010.

Fourth, forms of modern 'civil Islam' allied closely to liberal democratic values are emerging in at least two strategically important countries. Hefner (2000) asks whether democracy and civil society can gain a foothold in Muslim societies. Can a public culture emerge that promotes tolerance, pluralism and public competition for office (Hefner 2000: 215)? He finds some ground for optimism in Indonesia (see also Mishra 2011), the country with the largest number of Muslims:

> In the independence era [Muslims] learned the language of democracy and constitutionality, and took enthusiastically to its forms. In matters of civic association, Muslims showed themselves second to no one. None of their rivals could match the breadth and vitality of their associations. Even under the New Order, Muslims were better able than others to resist state controls and nurture alternative ideas of the public good. (Hefner 2000: 217)

Muslim organizations played a central role in the overthrow of the Suharto regime, while the Islamic reform movement has repudiated an Islamic state and promoted women's rights. Turkey also gives grounds for cautious optimism, for it is where Atatürk vigorously promoted secularism as a way of modernizing the country. Turkey stands poised on the cusp between Europe and Asia, between a return to a dogmatic Islam or the evolution of a civil Islam. European politicians need to decide whether or not to admit Turkey to the EU. Their eventual choice could determine which way it turns.

Finally, the dissenting voices that demand the development of, or return to, an Islamic cosmopolitanism need outside support. There are many such voices, but one, Irshad Manji, has made a dramatic impact with her book, *The Trouble with Islam Today* (2004). She says her book is about 'why my faith community needs to come to terms with the diversity of ideas, beliefs and people in our universe, and why non-Muslims have a pivotal role in helping us get there' (https://www.irshadmanji.com/The-Trouble-with-Islam-Today). She wants to return to the pluralist traditions of eleventh-century Islam (when 135 varieties were on offer) and faces issues of Islamic anti-Semitism and women's rights in Muslim societies. Of course, there are many interfaith organizations and Muslim intellectuals, writers and artists who are making their own statements in a quiet way. The events surrounding the Arab Spring of 2011 suggest that the pluralist and secular voices will not have it all their own way. Indeed, the outcome of the elections in Egypt in late 2011 made the Muslim Brotherhood, which is strongly behind the Freedom and Justice Party, the biggest winner, with some 37% of the votes cast.

REVIEW

Religion is welded into the very fabric of human history and remains so in the current global age. But, by 'religion' we do not mean a particular faith, church or doctrine. Rather, we have explained how 'the building blocks' of religious sentiment and behaviour emerge from understanding rituals, totems and taboos.

Some sociologists were sceptical about the need for religion and thought it would decline as the rational, scientific Enlightenment took hold. Others, however, particularly Durkheim, soon realized that religion played a powerful and vital role as a form of social cement. Among contemporary sociologists, Turner (1991: 38–62) has emphasized the socially integrative role of religion. Christian churches in the USA, for example, have retreated from attacking the 'American way of life', choosing instead to celebrate the constitution, secular education, democracy, individualism and market capitalism.

Despite the capacity of organized religions to adapt to modernity and now globalization, there is a strong case for arguing that secularization is a growing reality, at least in the West. Yet, counterarguments also abound. For one thing, in the developing world, especially among the poor, traditional religions seem to retain much of their influence. Moreover, more unorthodox forms of religion along with innumerable new religious movements seem to be gaining adherents at the expense of the established faiths right across the world. We have tried to indicate why these movements attract so many followers even when governments repress them or they engage in unusual practices.

We have also explored the resurgence of militant forms of Islam, although fundamental sects have emerged in all the world's major religions. It seems that responding to the uncertainties of the global, postmodern world has often involved the reaffirmation of earlier traditions. Although armed jihadists have certainly created a frontal assault on liberal, pluralist, democratic values, we suggest that there are ways forward provided we appreciate the diversity within Islam and begin to cooperate with the many Muslims who are in favour of peaceful dialogue.

Visit the companion website at www.palgrave.com/sociology/cohen3e for extra materials to check and expand your learning, including interactive self-test questions, mind maps making links between key themes, annotated web links to sociological research, data and key sociological thinkers, a searchable glossary and much more.

FURTHER READING

B. Wilson's *Religion in Secular Society: A Sociological Comment* (1966) is the classic account of the secularization thesis.

One of many excellent reference books on religion is M. Fisher's *Living Religions* (1997), with substantive chapters on Hinduism, Jainism, Buddhism, Daoism and Confucianism, Shintoism, Zoroastrianism, Judaism, Christianity, Islam and Sikhism.

P. Clarke's *New Religions in Global Perspective* (2006) provides a clear analysis of new religious movements and discusses a large number of interesting case studies worldwide.

M. Ruthven's *Islam: A Very Short Introduction* (2000) packs an awful lot into a small number of words.

QUESTIONS AND ASSIGNMENTS

1. Has the secularization thesis been discredited or is secularization simply gaining ground more slowly than expected?

2. How do we learn to live with violent forms of Islam?

3. What are new religious movements and how and why are they different from traditional/ organized religions?

18
Urban life

For much of human history, life took place in the rural world. In the year 1800, 97% of the world's population lived in rural settlements of fewer than 5,000 people. In the year 2010, after a period of massive urbanization, 197 cities contained more than 2 million people; of these, 36 were in China, 21 in the USA and 15 in India. If we include smaller urban settlements, 395 cities housed more than 1 million people in 2010 and 782 housed more than 500,000 (Demographia 2011). These are very different in character, but many fall into these basic categories:

1. *Ancient cities* built on the ruins of settlements that once housed the great urban civilizations of the past. These include Baghdad, Cairo, Mexico City, Athens and Rome, where tourists try to capture some of the mysteries and glories of the past by picking over the remains of these great urban cultures.
2. *Colonial cities* that accompanied or followed colonial expansion. Their business districts and wealthy suburbs often resemble islands of privilege surrounded by seas of poverty. Examples are Caracas, Lagos, São Paulo and Bombay.
3. *Old established industrial cities* like Birmingham, Toronto, Frankfurt, Johannesburg, Chicago or Sydney. These became centres of industrial, commercial or financial activity during the period of modernity when the advanced economies were forming nation-states. They were also centres of major social change and immigration.
4. *New industrial and service cities* mushroomed in the developing world as these countries fast-tracked towards modernization. Some have sprung up out of long-established smaller towns offering religious, market or governmental services. Tianjin and Shenzhen in China, Yeosu and Gwangju in South Korea, and Bangalore in India are a few that fit this category.
5. *Global cities* that were equally important during the modern and/or colonial period but have now also assumed a particular social character and distinctive role in the processes of global change and integration. These include London, Paris, Tokyo, New York and Singapore (Figure 18.1).

Cities are, by definition, meeting places where new settlers arrive, new marketplaces spring up, new vocations are practised, and new sensibilities are formed. The culturally diverse cities in the ancient world like Athens gave us the word 'cosmopolis', while it was to Rome that all roads supposedly led. There were cities in the Chinese, Aztec, Ottoman and Holy Roman Empires. There were hundreds of cities before there were nation-states. Indeed, for many years, there were tensions between European cities and European states. Venice, Antwerp, Genoa and Amsterdam were often the economic and political rivals of kingdoms like Portugal, England and France. Eventually, some degree of 'mutuality' developed, which allowed big cities to play important administrative, military and economic roles in the evolution of the nation-state (Taylor 1995: 48–62). Their 'mutuality' was associated only with the period of modernity and essentially depended on the capacity of the state to act to secure its external boundaries, thereby protecting the functions of the major cities located within those boundaries.

Given their importance, urban forms of settlement became the terrains of study for some of the world's most eminent sociologists. Durkheim (1933), for example, described the rural–urban transition as the movement from 'mechanical' to 'organic' forms of solidarity (Chapter 17). The first was marked by customary, habitual modes of interaction, the second by social relations based on anonymity, impersonality and contract. Simmel (1950a) saw the city as a place where a distinctively modern culture emerged with new forms of 'mental life' and a complex web of group affiliations. High levels of individualism were not entirely counteracted by these social relations, so conflict and social pathologies were likely to erupt (see Global Thinker 18).

Urban sociology reached its heyday between the 1910s and 1930s when it was pivotal to the development of the discipline (Savage and Warde 1993: 7). The central role of urban sociology was reasserted in the 1970s with the recognition of the important global functions of certain cities. In this chapter we look first at colonial cities but bear in mind that today's developing cities in the global South frequently share characteristics with colonial cities. We then discuss the famous Chicago School of sociology, which developed a distinctive method of understanding the 'ecological patterning' and spatial distribution of urban groups in the older industrial cities of the North. However, we also need to consider the pattern of urban life today and predictions for likely future trends. What becomes apparent is that the world almost certainly faces a massive continuing trend towards rapid urbanization accompanied by urban sprawl and deepening inequality. Finally, and overlapping with this general scenario of current and future city life, we examine the specific evolution, characteristics and contradictions of global cities.

THE COLONIAL CITY

Perhaps the most obvious observation to make about colonial cities – and many of the fast emerging industrial/service cities in the developing world – is that they are characterized by extreme and often bizarre juxtapositions. As Roberts (1978: 5) puts it, 'modern skyscrapers, sumptuous shopping, office and banking facilities coexist with unpaved streets, squatter settlements and open sewage … the elegantly dressed are waylaid by beggars and street vendors; their shoes are shined and their cars are guarded by urchins from an inner-city slum', or, we could add, a squatter settlement.

© JAN HELTEN/ISTOCKPHOTO

FIGURE 18.1 Raffles Hotel, Singapore Tea is still served on the veranda of the Raffles Hotel, an important ritual surviving from colonial times. Raffles is now surrounded by the skyscrapers characteristic of Singapore's global city status.

In the colonial city there is no necessary association between urbanity and modernity. Unemployment is common, indeed normal, and self-employed forms of economic activity predominate. Although there is some full-time, blue-collar employment in factories and white-collar employment in government offices, banks and insurance companies, most people are located in what is known as the 'bazaar economy', or INFORMAL SECTOR. Self-employed craftsmen, carpenters, masons, tailors, taxi drivers, mechanics, 'market mammies' (women traders in cheap commodities) and even farmers raising small livestock are some typical occupations. When one of the authors lived in Nigeria, a self-proclaimed 'Doctor of Volkswagen' located at the side of the road serviced his car. Collecting the car was always time-consuming as the friendly mechanic extended his 'test drive' into a prolonged taxi service for the locals.

In short, people survive as best they can. While the rich enjoy lifestyles similar to the privileged groups in the advanced industrialized countries, the urban poor often face a combination of low incomes, minimal public services and poor housing. Many live in rundown public apartments, crowded tenements, and shantytowns made from cardboard, scrap wood, tin and thatch. Given the difficult life circumstances of the urban poor, sociologists have carefully investigated how far their social and political attitudes provide a threat to the established order. This has yielded rather different interpretations.

Research on Latin American cities has generated surprising evidence of a much more 'conservative' stance on the part of the urban poor than might perhaps be inferred from their deprivation. Those living in the shantytowns may either work in the formal sector or aspire to find a job there. Their shacks often are improved incrementally as bricks and corrugated iron roofs gradually replace the earlier rough materials. The urban poor also use the cultural and social resources at their disposal to improve their lives in creative ways (Roberts 1978: 141). Religious affiliations might provide emotional support; new ethnicities formed in the slums might be the basis for economic credit and political mobilization; while occasional forays by the conventional political parties in search of votes might provide a route into more conventional politics. Such is the weight of this push to the mainstream that Perlman (1976) has insisted that the 'marginality' of the urban poor is a myth. Moreover, despite their often precarious situation, women have often taken a lead in grassroots struggles to improve the lives of very poor people. We discussed one example of this in Chapter 8, namely the Self Employed Women's Association established in Bangladesh in 1972 (see also Sassen 2007: 118–22).

Recent observers, though, tend to offer a more sombre interpretation. Research conducted through the UN-HABITAT project (2003) suggests that around two-fifths of the economically active population in the South and their families depend on the informal economy for their livelihoods. Most live in cities. This kind of data, coupled with the widely held view that decades of neoliberal economic globalization have made most people's lives, especially those of the very poor, much less secure (see Chapter 4), has led some scholars to suggest that large numbers of the urban population are, in effect, 'cut off from the "mainstream" of economic life' (Standing 2009: 115). Drawing on the same UN data, Davis (2006: 174) argues that the cities these marginalized individuals inhabit operate partly as containers for the world's 'surplus humanity'. Moreover, instead of shantytown dwellers cooperating to improve their common situation – although doubtless this happens as well – he argues that chronic poverty and the intensely competitive struggle for a meagre livelihood undermines social solidarity and encourages the formation of rival gangs, often along racial, ethnic or religious lines, and open conflict (Davis 2006: 185). Beck (2000a) wonders whether the cities of the advanced economies are about to experience the emergence of informal economic sectors similar to those long evident in the global South. He refers to this as the 'Brazilianization' of the North.

A PAUSE TO REFLECT

Housing the poor coming to urban areas in the developing world presents a difficult challenge for urban authorities, as large-scale public housing is difficult to finance and often results in degraded housing a generation later. Should urban planners instead rely on self-improvement by shantytown dwellers? How can they facilitate the smooth political, economic and social incorporation of new migrants into already overcrowded cities?

THE INDUSTRIAL CITY AND THE CHICAGO SCHOOL

Robert Park, Ernest Burgess and their colleagues and successors at the University of Chicago, starting in the 1920s, undertook the most famous and far-reaching studies of industrial cities. Chicago provided the backdrop to their theories and field studies. For Park, writing in 1925 (cited in Kornblum 1988: 548–9):

> The city is more than a set of social conveniences – streets, buildings, electric lights, tramways, and telephones, etc., something more, also than a mere constellation of … courts, hospitals, schools, police, and civic functionaries of various sorts. The city is, rather, a state of mind, a body of customs and traditions … it is involved in the vital processes of the people who compose it; it is a product of nature and particularly of human nature.

As this quotation indicates, the Chicago School was vitally interested in the *meaning* of the city, or how an urban culture became constituted. Was the city the source of great evil or the fount of human civilization? What moral compromises would be necessary to live there and what conflicts arose between the longstanding residents and newcomers? How were the rival claims of individual achievement and community affiliation to be played out in the new setting? As Castells (1977: 77–8) recalls in a generous tribute to Louis Wirth, one of the key figures of the Chicago School, the main insights made were that the new forms of social life were structured around the axes of dimension, density and heterogeneity:

- *Dimension*: the bigger the city, the wider its spectrum of individual variation and social differentiation. This leads to the loosening of community ties, increased social competition, anonymity and a multiplication of interactions, often at low levels of intensity and trust. Direct participation and involvement in social affairs are no longer possible; instead, systems of representation have to evolve.
- *Density*: this reinforces differentiation because, paradoxically, the closer one is physically to one's fellow city dwellers, the more distant are one's social contacts. There is an increasing indifference to anything that does not fulfil individual objectives and this can lead to combative, aggressive attitudes.
- *Heterogeneity*: echoing Durkheim's observations, Wirth suggested that social heterogeneity, in ethnic and class terms, promotes rapid social mobility. Group membership is unstable because it is linked to the temporary interests of each individual. There is therefore a predominance of *association* (people linking up to further their rational goals) over *community* (a grouping based on descent, other affinities or long-held status).

In addition to its work on the character of urban culture, the Chicago School is also well known for its notion of HUMAN ECOLOGY, describing how humans related to the built environment.

> **KEY CONCEPT**
>
> Chicago sociologists normally used the expression 'ecology' without qualification, but because of its contemporary meaning – concern for the environment, especially nature – it is more explicit to allude to this key concept as HUMAN ECOLOGY, which refers to the initial idea that residents in a city cannot freely settle or manipulate spatial relationships. Their social actions and interactions are constrained by land values, planning restrictions, transport patterns, and features of the landscape. Human ecology thus alludes to the ways in which relationships and behaviour in cities are conditioned by the natural and built environment in which residents find themselves.

Essentially, Park, Burgess and their colleagues tried to show how physical space related to social space. They based their model on a set of concentric rings:

- In the centre, large stores, office blocks, theatres and hotels marked the central business district.
- The next ring was the 'zone of transition', with inner-city slums, small industry and areas of extreme urban decay (known in the USA as 'skid row').
- Moving out one ring and we have the zone of the respectable working class, with corner stores, modest but clean dwellings and schools.
- Better family residences and attractive, middle-priced apartment blocks marked the next ring.
- Finally, in a looser, surrounding zone, wealthier commuters lived in suburban settings with detached plots, often with big gardens.

We should not read the model developed by various members of the Chicago School too literally. Not every industrial city has exactly the same profile. For example, urban planners often augment other pressures to counteract inner-city decay by encouraging the building of high-income apartments in the central business district, a process known as GENTRIFICATION. Nonetheless, with some adaptation, the Chicago School's ecological zone model has continued to provide a useful sociological tool for understanding how big cities work and develop.

GLOBAL THINKERS 18   GEORG SIMMEL (1858–1918)

With Marx, Weber and Durkheim, Simmel is often declared to be one of the founders of sociology. Yet undoubtedly he is the least well known. He predicted this outcome, saying: 'I know I shall die without spiritual heirs' (quoted in Frisby 1978: 4). Among other factors, he suffered from late and partial translation of his work. He also wrote in an oddly disconnected way, drawing together grand generalizations, unusual examples and personal touches that suggested a pessimistic recognition of the ultimate futility of human striving.

It is this that seems to have touched a contemporary chord among some scholars and students. He connects personal intimacy and interpersonal relations. He is also a bridge between cultural and literary studies, psychology, philosophy and mainstream sociology. Since the full translation of his major work *The Philosophy of Money* (Simmel [1900]1978), his reputation has soared. There are large claims made for the complexity and depth of *The Philosophy of Money* and we cannot summarize it fully. Suffice to say that he saw that money could be understood in a far more profound way than simply as capital or as the means to exchange value. Money, he foresaw, leads to atomization and the fragmentation of experience as it leaches into social and cultural life. Money never rests; it speaks to 'the solitary ego', 'the deeply lonely soul' at the heart of industrial and metropolitan life (quoted in Frisby 1978: 29).

These views resonate closely with a twenty-first-century awareness that the commodification of everything reaches into the heart of our being and may destroy what we are. He explores this dynamic in a brilliant essay, 'The metropolis and mental life' (Simmel 1950b: 411–12), showing how producers supply goods sent to the metropolis for entirely unknown purchasers

> who never personally enter the producers' actual field of vision. Through this anonymity, the interest of each party acquires an unmerciful matter-of-factness; and the intellectually calculating economic egoism of both parties need not fear any deflection because of the imponderables of personal relationships.

Simmel shows here how strangeness and sociation, intimacy and anonymity, are held in a seemingly permanent and unbearable tension.

This abstract and impersonal quality of economic life, where actors from very different cultures interact over vast distances – partly through hugely complex formal and remote arrangements, partly through money and market competition, and partly via occasional co-present relations that neither require nor engender much mutual understanding – has probably become even more dominant with economic globalization.

Sources: Frisby (1978); Simmel (1950a, 1950b, [1900]1978).

BOX 18.1 African American migration to the north

Northern US cities gained importance at the turn of the twentieth century because of their industrial strengths. Chicago was the centre of the railways, the stockyards and meat-packing industries, while Detroit evolved into the main site of the motorcar and associated industries.

The social heterogeneity of such cities was based on immigration from many European countries and also from the US south. African Americans leaving the south is one of 'the largest and most rapid mass internal movements of people in history – perhaps the greatest not caused by the immediate threat of execution or starvation' (Lemann 1991: 6). This timeline outlines some of the reasons:

1865–1900   Jim Crow laws promoting segregation were passed after the civil war in the south. (Jim Crow was a derogatory name for a feeble-minded African American.) The basic mechanism for production (slavery) was destroyed, while embryonic cities in the south were devastated.

1900–30   This was the beginning of the boll weevil infestation, which affected cotton plants. The disease hit black farmers particularly hard as most were tenants and found it difficult to switch to alternative crops. Most African Americans were driven off their land – to the newly emerging cities of the south, to non-infested areas and finally to the north.

1920–30   Severe agricultural depression due to overproduction of cotton worldwide. Both blacks and whites were affected.

1930–50   Precipitous decline of agriculture. Bankruptcy for many farmers and even the big plantation owners. Tenants become part-time hands, or had to migrate north.

1950s–1970s   Displacement of agricultural workers through the spread of mechanical cotton picking.

Fortunately for the departing southern migrants, during the First World War there was a labour shortage in the industrial north – particularly in Chicago, in transport (where blacks were employed on the Pullman cars) and in the steelyards. African American songs of this period described the 'great black migration'. Here are verses from two:

> Some are coming on the passenger
> Some are coming on the freight
> Others will be found walking
> For none have time to wait.

> I'm tired of this Jim Crow; gonna leave this Jim Crow town
> Doggone my black soul, I'm sweet Chicago bound . . .

Of the 109,000 African Americans in Chicago in 1920, 90,000 were born in other states, most in the south.

Culturally, this migration led to the most important and influential musical expression since the development of European classical music. Think, for example, of jazz, bop, bebop, Motown (after the 'motor town' of Detroit) and urban blues – including the distinctive sounds of Chicago and Kansas City blues.

Sources: Fligstein (1981); Lemann (1991).

AN INCREASINGLY URBAN FUTURE

As we have seen, for at least 200 years, modernity and industrialization have been closely linked to growing urbanization. However, its pace worldwide seems to have accelerated since 1950 because many developing countries are following a trajectory that is similar to that formerly pursued by the advanced countries. In Chapter 6 we outlined research on urban poverty and slums that the UN commissioned in 2002/3 and that Davis (2006) discussed. Since then, an active world organization called the World Urban Forum (WUF) has emerged that brings together academics and policy-makers. In March 2010 it held its fifth annual conference at Rio de Janeiro in Brazil. The WUF is supported by UN-HABITAT – the UN's primary agency for research and policy relating to human settlements – and the UN's Department of Economic and Social Affairs (UNDESA). Significantly, the central theme discussed at WUF5 revolved around the implications of continuing worldwide urbanization. Based partly on the analysis provided by these two UN agencies, the following key themes were discussed at WUF5:

1. By 2009 the world became more urban than rural, with more than half the planet's inhabitants designated as living in urban locations (UN-HABITAT 2010).
2. Continuing urbanization was described as 'unstoppable'. Consequently, it is estimated that, by the middle of the twenty-first century, nearly 70% of the world's population will be urban dwellers. Drawing on data provided by the UN paper, *World Urbanization Prospects* (UNDESA 2010), Table 18.1 reveals this transformation over a 100-year period for selected regions of the global South and includes future projections. Table 18.1 demonstrates the varying degrees of urbanization across the global South over time. Yet, there is no mistaking the overall relentless pressure towards urbanization, or the tendency for the pace of urban growth to accelerate slightly for Asia and sub-Saharan Africa after 1990.

TABLE 18.1 Urbanization in selected world regions, 1950–2050 (%)				
	Latin America and the Caribbean	Asia	Sub-Saharan Africa	World
1950	41.4	16.3	11.0	28.8
1990	70.3	31.5	28.3	42.0
2010	79.6	42.2	37.2	50.5
2050	88.8	64.7	60.1	68.7

Source: UNDESA (2010).

3. The world's population growth – on the basis of current population growth rates of 1.8% annually – anticipated between now and 2050 will be an urban phenomenon. Along with continuing rural to urban migration, this means that the world's rural population will begin to decrease during the next decade or so. If this absolute (not relative) decline in the total rural world population occurs, it will be unprecedented, at least for the known period of human history.
4. Cities and urban regions (see below) have become the main sources of global wealth. For example, the UN cites one estimate suggesting that four-fifths of the world's GDP is generated by and within urban areas (UNDESA 2010: 14). Moreover, much of this flows back into rural areas especially through the remittances of international and local migrants to relatives or village agencies. Indeed, in many countries, most rural income now results from such remittances (reported by Vidal 2010b). No doubt, however, urban investment and spending – by governments, businesses or consumers – on rural products also contribute to the rural economy.
5. A fifth theme addressed at the WUF5 revolved around the emergence of an increasing number of 'megacities' or 'urban agglomerations'. Megacities are defined as those containing more than 10 million people. However, there is an increasing tendency to redesignate them as urban agglomerations because they contain huge populations living at very high densities but also their land areas and administrative jurisdictions tend to spill out into contiguous zones. Even more striking, some urban agglomerations tend to fuse with – or encompass – other nearby urban localities, forming corridors or vast urban sprawls. Tokyo is a prime example. It includes 87 surrounding towns and cities

(UNDESA 2010: 6). Eventually, these conurbations may form 'mega-urban regions' such as the one currently being created by merging Hong Kong, Shenzhen and Guangzhou in China. Several other mega-urban regions are emerging, especially in India, Brazil and West Africa (Vidal 2010b). In 2009 there were 21 such megacities or urban agglomerations, with several others just below the 10 million mark; 15 were situated in the global South, while Japan, Europe and the USA shared the remaining 6 – one being Los Angeles, whose particular history we outline later on. Taking the top 5 urban agglomerations in order of population size, we get the following list – Tokyo (nearly 37 million), Delhi (22.2 million), São Paulo (20.3 million), Mumbai (20 million), Mexico City (19.5 million) and New York/Newark (19.4 million). Although these 21 cities contain not quite 10% of the world's urban population, this proportion has increased rapidly and is predicted to continue rising (UNDESA 2010: 4). Although urbanization (irrespective of the size of the city) is of central concern to the UN and those participating in forums such as WUF5, megacities, urban agglomerations and mega-urban regions are a particular cause for worry. Not only do they contain reservoirs of deepening inequality and severe poverty – alongside growing wealth – but their transport needs worsen energy consumption, they accumulate vast amounts of waste, and their expansion eats up farm land (Vidal 2010b).

6. Finally, the WUF5 also emphasized the urgent need to prevent existing levels of urban inequality, poverty and squalor from getting any worse. In general, this requires much better urban planning and governance as well as policies tailored to empower disadvantaged groups, especially youth and women. Consequently, the WUF5 spoke of the 'right to the inclusive city'. Attention was paid to growing inequality within many cities and countries and the varying trends. For example, New York and Chicago are more unequal than Managua in Nicaragua or Brazzaville in Congo-Brazzaville (Vidal 2010b). There was also widespread acceptance that, left unchecked, rising urban inequality will result in deepening social tensions and political unrest. On the other hand, urban prosperity was often most apparent where steps were being taken to reduce inequality. Significantly, some of the Millennium Development Goals and targets set down in 2000 (see Chapter 6) were invoked at WUF5 as spurs to encourage participants to improve the lives of slum dwellers (UN-HABITAT 2010).

While there is no doubt about the centrality of cities to production and consumption, a UN-HABITAT (2010: 3) report noted that:

> they also create disease, pollution, crime, poverty and social unrest. In many cities, especially in developing countries, slum dwellers number more than 50 per cent of the population and have little or no access to shelter, water, sanitation, education or health services.

To state merely that the future for most of the world's inhabitants will be an urban one insufficiently addresses the issue of the kinds of conditions people in cities will be forced to live in. While it would be wonderful to associate the cities of the future with wealth and cosmopolitanism, the best we can realistically hope for is that they will be sustainable and tolerable for most of their inhabitants.

THE NOTION OF A GLOBAL CITY

The most important idea expressing the ways in which power has become spatially redistributed is the notion of a 'global city'. There is no significant distinction between the term 'world city', preferred by some authors, and 'global city', preferred by others, although the latter is now more common. John Friedman (1986) first helped to delineate the key characteristics of a world city. He argued that the spatial organization of the new international division of labour required a new way of understanding the role of certain cities. In particular, they embodied a key contradiction between the politics, which still operated on a territorial basis, and economics, which increasingly functioned at a global level. Social conflict arose within cities as a consequence of this tug of war. These initial ideas led Friedman to develop what he called a 'world city hypothesis', an intervention better described as a set of seven propositions:

1. It is not their absolute size in terms of population or land area that determines whether or not a given city can be defined as 'global', but rather the degree to which it is integrated into the wider world economy and is able to exercise influence over what happens beyond its borders. Friedman argued that this integration affects the physical form of the city and the nature of its labour and capital markets.
2. Global capital uses key cities throughout the world as 'basing points', with the cities arranged in a 'complex spatial hierarchy'.
3. World cities perform different 'control functions'.
4. World cities are sites for the concentration and accumulation of capital.
5. World cities are destination points for internal and international migrants.
6. Spatial and class polarization is likely in a world city.
7. The social costs generated in world cities exceed the fiscal (tax-raising) capacity of the domestic state.

Figure 18.2 shows the connections and tiered relationships between world cities as originally proposed by Friedman. Below we will see how his evaluation of where different cities belonged in this world hierarchy in the 1980s has changed in the past 25 years.

The world city hypothesis has generated considerable discussion in the literature, notably in Knox and Taylor (1995), Sassen (1991, 2000, 2002, 2007), and the contributors to Marcuse and van Kempen (2000). These authors have also considerably extended the notion of a global city in new directions. Their views can be summarized in the following propositions:

1. The corporate headquarters of the major TNCs are based in global cities. However, as we saw earlier in this book, TNCs are freeing themselves from their territorial origins, but there are nonetheless important advantages for a city that hosts the headquarters of a TNC. TNCs provide valuable employment, they attract important clients for conferences and business meetings, and there is a general political payoff in having a centre of power in a particular city.
2. In Friedman's original analysis, all the 'primary' cities were in rich industrial countries, with perhaps the most notable examples being New York, London, Paris and Tokyo, which formed a west–east axis of tremendous financial power through the strength of their markets. By 2010 the same four remained the most globalized cities in the world, but half of those listed in the top 10 were based in or near Asia – Hong Kong (5th), Singapore (8th), Sydney (9th), Seoul (10th) and, again, Tokyo (3rd) (*Foreign Policy* n.d.).
3. The location of the major banks, insurance houses and pension fund managers complements the presence of corporate headquarters and stock exchanges. A mutually reinforcing economic agglomeration develops in a global city.
4. Global cities are assigned a special place in the global international division of labour. This sometimes, but not necessarily, corresponds with their administrative centrality and current or former political power. For example, London, Paris, Tokyo, Seoul, Geneva, Stockholm, Copenhagen and Mexico City are both global and capital cities. However, the global city in Australia is Sydney, not Canberra. In South Africa it is Johannesburg, not Pretoria; in Canada, Toronto and Montreal are global cities, not Ottawa; in Italy, Milan qualifies but Rome does not. These disjunctures are important because they demonstrate the capacity of global capital to depart from the old political, religious and administrative logic that informed the choice of the capital city. Instead, global corporations and other global actors forge an intimate tie with the city with the most appropriate global features.
5. Some cities function primarily as corporate headquarters, some are financial centres, some are political capitals, and others are key national centres of economic activity. However, in the long run, global cities bring these functions together.

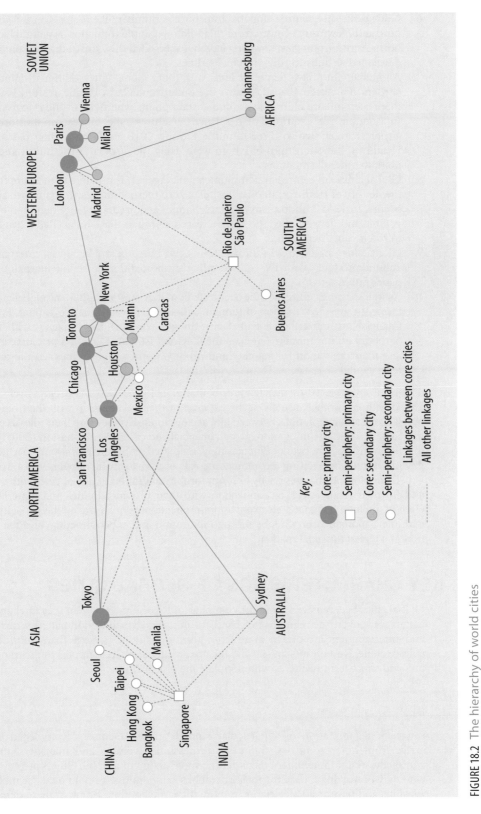

FIGURE 18.2 The hierarchy of world cities

Source: Friedman (1986). Copyright (1986) Wiley. Used with permission from J. Friedman, 'The world city hypothesis', *Development and Change*, John Wiley and Sons.

6. Global cities are centres of global transport. A number, like Hong Kong, Sydney, Singapore and New York, evolved from their old mercantile functions as natural harbours and ports. Air transport has, however, largely superseded this constraint and some cities have developed as hubs for the principal airlines.

7. All global cities have dense air links with other global cities. Although United Airlines clusters in Chicago, British Airways in London, and Cathy Pacific in Hong Kong, overall, there is an intense clumping around certain points where the traffic is extremely dense. In London, for example, planes leave Heathrow (the biggest of the three London airports) every two to three minutes. During 2010 some 66 million passengers used Heathrow – about a third of whom were using the airport as the transit and switching point to other destinations.

8. Global cities are centres of communications. Again it is possible to measure this through the density of traffic on phone, fax, telex and internet lines, and again the same pattern occurs. In 1985 London's six-digit telephones acquired a seventh digit, but by 1996 the volume and density of traffic had increased so much that one needed to push 11 digits to reach your friend's line.

9. Global cities are centres of information, news bureaux and agencies, entertainment and cultural products, with TV and recording studios, and major book, magazine and newspaper publishers.

10. As well as being centres for the accumulation of domestic capital, the global city becomes the centre for the attraction of foreign, although rarely speculative, capital. Typically, the financial institutions of a global city do not compete too brazenly with the known harbours of 'hot money' (such as the Cayman Islands, Bermuda or Curaçao) lest they lose their reputation for stability and probity. Rather, global cities tend to attract long-term capital investments from all over the world.

The result of these 10 further features is that global cities become progressively more integrated with each other, usually at the expense of their relationship with their hinterland. As transactions and interactions between global cities intensify, they lose their roles as administrative capitals while assuming more global, financial and cultural ones. Sassen (2007: 98) argues that this transurban network of increasingly integrated global cities amounts to a 'new geography of centrality' exercising a commanding role over virtually all dimensions of world life.

Technological changes partly account for the integration of global cities with one another and for their relative lack of connection with their provincial cities and hinterlands. Such changes include enhanced electronic communications, cheap travel, the capacity to deskill and internationalize certain jobs through relocation and subcontracting, and the consolidation of a global financial market.

SOME KEY CHARACTERISTICS OF GLOBAL CITIES

Global cities become even more international and cosmopolitan than they already were. The languages spoken, the religions practised, the outlooks, consumption patterns, forms of dress and entertainment are drawn more from a multiplicity of cultures than from the national culture alone. Restaurants, music and theatre are all designed to appeal to the transitory visitors and short-term residents who populate the global cities.

INWARD MIGRATION

International migration of a particular kind develops. 'Denizens' (privileged foreigners) arrive from other countries. Some are professional workers and managers, undertaking contract work for limited periods under the sponsorship of a TNC. Others are entrepreneurs who may be seeking a base for their operations but continue to hold dual (or multiple) citizenships and have residence rights in more than one country. Some of these denizen entrepreneurs have made spectacular inroads into the business elites of their countries of adoption. Egyptian-born Mohammed al-Fayed, whose son Dodi dated the late Princess Diana and was killed in a car accident with her, at one time owned Harrods, the famous store in London's Knightsbridge. Other notable denizens operating in London are Dickson Poon and David Tang (Box 18.2).

BOX 18.2 Wealthy Chinese and then Russian oligarchs take London by storm

The wealthy Chinese

Members of the new Chinese elite in London rather look down on the people of Chinatown as being of an unsophisticated earlier generation who sometimes cannot speak English. Their own English was learned in the posh schools of Hong Kong or the public (that is, private) schools of England.

Thomson (1997) reported that one of the leading Chinese cosmopolitans is Dickson Poon, the grandson of a rice farmer, the son of stockbrokers and a graduate of Uppingham public school, Rutland and the University of California. After borrowing half a million pounds from his father, he established the exclusive rights to import certain Western luxury goods to Hong Kong. Prior to Hong Kong's return to China from British colonial rule in 1997, its wealthy residents feared the austerity Beijing might impose. They spent money with wild abandon. By 1987 Poon, the owner of S. T. Dupont, the French manufacturer of gold pens and lighters, had profited mightily from this mood.

In 1991 he bought Harvey Nichols, the upper-class but loss-making British firm. With its distinctively restrained British style, the store has always been a Mecca for Hong Kongers of Poon's background. Turning this 'frayed-at-the-edges' store into 'Europe's most slickly packaged emporium in the middle of the recession is one of the great retail feats of the 1990s. It is also the work of a man who glides effortlessly between two worlds' (Thomson 1997). Poon has also started a chain of restaurants in London named after him. Conspicuously, he has avoided Chinatown, preferring instead to set out his wares in Covent Garden and near the City, where he can cater to high-spending 'City oafs'.

Someone with an even higher profile is David Tang, the grandson of one of Hong Kong's greatest magnates, S. K. Tang. While he was still a student in London in the 1970s, he lost his flat gambling in the Clermont Club, one of London's smart gambling clubs. By 1996 he had opened his own club in Beijing, which catered to the local yuppies. To launch the club in style he flew out 'the cream of London society'. He has more substantial talents too, having taught philosophy at Beijing University and given classical piano recitals for charity. Tang also managed to create a London fashion in colourful Mao Zedong jackets, made in velvet, which he sells in the Shanghai Tang shop in Hong Kong.

The Russian oligarchs

By the 1990s it was the turn of the Russian oligarchs. A number of them made their mark by buying into British popular culture. Roman Abramovich, for example, is the current owner of Chelsea Football Club and is the fifty-third richest person in the world, according to the 2011 Forbes rankings. As reported by Hollingsworth (2012), the managing director of Burgess Yachts says that the Russians have 'taken the yacht business by storm. From 10 to 20pc of our clients are Russians.' A yacht designer claimed that Russians are

> the biggest spenders. They want the very best design and materials. On the chartering market, they lease the very biggest and very best vessels for the longest periods of time. The Russians will charter a vessel that costs $100,000 a night, whereas the Americans will settle for a yacht that leases for $40,000 a night.

As Hollingsworth (2012) suggests:

> The advent of this gigantic geyser of foreign money has launched new industries and spawned huge profits while turning London into an immense club for those who can afford the membership fee. New jobs have appeared . . . chauffeurs, bodyguards, and gardeners are suddenly in great demand. London now boasts more butlers than it had in the time of Queen Victoria. Abramovich employed 28 servants at his Fyning Hill estate alone, while Oleg Deripaska's mansion on Belgrave Square was swarming with attendants all year round, though he rarely lived there himself.

Sources: Hollingsworth (2012); Thomson (1997).

By no means all immigrants from abroad are highly skilled or privileged. Entertainers, waiters and waitresses, prostitutes, maids, chauffeurs and nurses are also attracted to global cities. The indigenous labour force has deserted some of these occupations, but employers often prefer foreign workers because they can exploit them more. Cities like Miami, Sydney, New York, Los Angeles, Paris and London have more than a third of their populations born in foreign countries. Often these non-native born residents are from countries with no historical link to their destination. Most were doing jobs at the lowest range of the pay scale. For example, foreign born people carried out nearly half of all the cleaning work, refuse collection, labouring and domestic work in London (May et al. 2007). Students and visitors provide another segment. Many 'overstay' or ignore the entry conditions on their visas. Illegal entrants and asylum seekers may also be desperate to secure any kind of employment, however demeaning or badly paid. The fear that they may be reported to the immigration authorities gives the employers the whip hand in demanding compliance to their demands. Sometimes, the conditions in which illegal migrants work are little better than slavery.

CHANGES IN THE OCCUPATIONAL STRUCTURE

The new international division of labour generates important changes in the occupational structure in all regions, but many of these are more visible and more marked in global cities. In general, we see a strong shift from industrial to service and information-related employment.

Work is often informalized, subcontracted and increasingly carried out by migrants, women and underprivileged minorities (Sassen 2007: 117–18). Work in the unionized, high-wage sectors, by contrast, is gradually (or even dramatically) destroyed. Other changes are seen in the running down of nationalized or municipalized industries and public services in favour of consumer-led and insurance-supported services. These include private transport, healthcare, housing and education. Many schools have to secure business sponsorship to provide basic facilities like laboratories, while universities have to recruit fee-paying overseas students to maintain their libraries and pay their lecturers. Such is the extent of denationalization that, in several countries, prison and immigration services are subcontracted; for example, highly trained, state-certified air traffic controllers in the USA were fired to make way for cheaper, less qualified subcontractors.

The cumulative effects of these occupational changes became particularly visible in global cities from the 1970s onwards when substantial losses in manufacturing accompanied substantial gains in services (Table 18.2). Indeed, these transformations became even more pronounced in the decades that followed. For example, whereas in 1961 four times as many people were employed in London's manufacturing sector as in the city's business and professional sector, by 1999 the situation had been completely reversed and the latter's combined employment accounted for one-third of all jobs in the city (Hamnett 2003). A similar reversal took place during the same period in Helsinki and centred on the rise of Finland as a world class leader in IT businesses (Vaattovaara and Kortteinen 2003).

TABLE 18.2 Distribution of employment in New York, London and Tokyo, 1970s and 80s (% of total)

New York	1977	1981	1985
Manufacturing	21.9	18.7	15.4
Services	28.4	31.8	36.3
Wholesale/retail	19.4	20.2	20.2
London	1977	1981	1985
Manufacturing	22.0	19.2	16.0
Services	49.6	40.1	39.8
Wholesale/retail	13.5	19.2	20.5
Tokyo	1975	1980	1985
Manufacturing	25.1	23.5	22.0
Services	20.6	22.7	25.3
Wholesale/retail	27.5	28.5	28.4

Source: Sassen, Saskia: *The Global City* © 1991 Princeton University Press. Reprinted by permission of Princeton University Press.

THE FEMINIZATION OF EMPLOYMENT

The increased entry of women into the labour market is a feature of the global post-Fordist (Chapter 4) environment, but it is particularly notable in the global cities where the fashion, clerical and service occupations are concentrated. Even though they have gained a stronger foothold in employment, many women workers are paid less than their male equivalents and have highly insecure conditions of employment. One important example of the feminization of employment is in the garment and fashion industries, an activity that feeds off an international clientele. It is no coincidence that Hong Kong, Paris, London, New York and Milan are all global cities and the key global fashion centres with the most prestigious catwalks. The glamorous pictures of models reproduced in women's magazines have a seamy underside of sweatshops, low pay, exploitation (normally of women workers) and the hiring of illegal workers to reduce costs. Phizacklea (1992: 109) notes that homeworkers occupy the lowest rung in the clothing industry and

> serve a buffer function for contractors with an erratic flow of work. If there is a rush order or a full book they will receive work, if there is not, they receive nothing. Their rate of pay is exceedingly low. … The vast majority of homeworkers are women confined to the home because of domestic responsibilities, particularly the care of pre-school children. Most fail to recognize the hidden costs involved in homeworking, which include the purchase or hire of their own machine and running costs. Most homeworking is 'off the book' and a completely precarious occupation.

Homeworkers also address envelopes, perform routine clerical tasks via the internet, or act as remote outposts of 'call centres'. (Call centres are linked telephone networks providing directory enquiries and information on timetables, flight prices and products for sale.) Because the 'real' cost of telephone calls (as opposed to what the consumer pays) is now equalizing internationally, calls for big businesses are now often stacked globally, with homeworkers' numbers being activated in sequence wherever they happen to be. Bemused customers using their telephone in Milan and wanting to travel on British Airways from Bristol to Newcastle may find their bookings dealt with by a homeworker in New York or Mumbai.

A PAUSE TO REFLECT

As we have indicated, global cities have many functions and attributes that distinguish them from other cities. Have we overemphasized geographical, economic and sociological features compared with cultural issues? At the end of the day, is a global city simply 'buzzier', with more restaurants, art galleries, cinemas, theatres, outdoor concerts, lectures, bars and clubs? Is more choice the same thing as more cosmopolitan?

Some white-collar employment is also available to women as sales personnel in department stores and boutiques, office workers (particularly entering data) and in estate agencies, banks and advertising. Because women historically colonized office work (as typists, telephonists and clerks), with the switch to more information-related employment they are often at an advantage in the labour market. Although their pay and conditions do not often match those of male workers, in a number of global cities there are now more females than males in paid employment.

However, the main explosion of low-wage jobs in global cities occurs in the low-level service industries and these tend to be disproportionately done by women. This further pushes wages down (Sassen 2007: 118). Included in these low-paid occupations are domestic workers, cleaners, hotel and restaurant workers, or people at checkout counters. Yet, Sassen claims that women may gain several advantages from the informal and feminized character of much work in global cities, including homeworking. Thus, communities, neighbourhoods and households once more become 'important economic spaces' where local solidarities are possible and opportunities may emerge for low-grade female entrepreneurship, while women's paid work and a move into the public realm may enable them to challenge the male-dominated domestic culture (Sassen 2007: 119–21).

REGIONALIZATION AND THE GLOBAL CITY

Certain major cities tend to augment their *regional* role, which is something often overlooked in discussion of *global* cities. For many cities, at least in the medium term, geography is not yet history. Los Angeles remains the dominant entry point for trans-Pacific migrants, Mexicans and South Americans. New York receives many immigrants from the Caribbean archipelago. Berlin, particularly after the city's massive redevelopment, will form the hinge between Western and Eastern Europe, while 81% of Finnish emigrants head for Sweden, most of them for Stockholm. With the Channel Tunnel, London and Paris are conjoined in a single axial point in northern Europe, adding a new dimension to their roles as capital cities. Brussels links the Benelux countries. Miami has become the shopping capital and most desirable entry point for migrants from the Caribbean area, especially from the Spanish-speaking Caribbean – Latinos have more than doubled their share of the city's population in the last half-century and now form the majority. As Grosfoguel (1995: 164) ironically notes: 'today Miami is a bilingual city where you can find more stores with signs saying "We speak English" than those saying "*Se habla español*"'. In Miami's extensive neighbourhood of Little Havana – so named because of its reputation as the refuge for Cubans fleeing Castro's communist regime in the 1960s – 92% of residents identified themselves as of Hispanic or Latino origin in the 2000 census, including people from Central and South America, and not just Cuba (Price 2007: 97).

A PAUSE TO REFLECT

If some cities are providing global functions and others regional functions, what about the remainder? Will cities not linked to global or regional dynamics shrink into insignificance or find new roles? If continuous migration to cities fuels energy and innovativeness, can small cities offer incentives to migrants to relocate?

As some cities regionalize across frontiers, others, whether through accidental geographical proximity or by conscious design, blend their functions and dissolve their boundaries with other places. Randstad (the grouping of Amsterdam, Rotterdam, Utrecht and The Hague) is a good example of this development. The addition of Orange, San Bernardino, Riverside and Ventura counties to the core of Los Angeles, which now covers 53,136 square kilometres, is another (Waldinger and Bozorgmehr 1996: 5). The cities of Leeds, Bradford, Sheffield and Manchester in the north of England also form a continuous urban chain linked by motorways. We next consider the regional roles of Los Angeles as a case study in more detail.

LOS ANGELES: THE FRAGMENTED MEGA-URBAN REGION

Los Angeles (LA), 'the City of Angels', is almost twice as large as either New York, San Francisco, Chicago or Philadelphia and almost four times the size of Miami. Tourism, the Hollywood film industry, and thereafter a heavy manufacturing base – often depending on defence contracts – started the flow of immigrants to the city from other parts of the USA, from neighbouring Mexico and then from across the Pacific. In population terms, the result was spectacular. At the turn of the century, LA had 100,000 residents; by 1930 it had added another 2.2 million; 30 years on, in 1960, there were 6 million; and by 2010 there were nearly 13 million (UNDESA 2010: 6), not including the surrounding but linked districts.

LA partly evolved and was partly designed as a chain of low-density suburban settlements linking the valleys that mark the topography of the area. This form of urban settlement fascinated the prominent architects of the time who praised it for its human scale. However, the logic of a global city soon took over and a 'downtown' developed: insurance companies and banks moved in to create new skyscrapers. Much of this investment came from Japanese firms that were riding a massive boom in the 1980s. Indeed, there is no doubt that LA provides a key bridge from America across the Pacific to the global cities of Tokyo, Taipei, Hong Kong, Shanghai and Singapore, which the changing ethnic composition of the city reflects. For many years the city has been a magnet for migrants from Mexico, to which were added other Central Americans tempted by the lure of *el norte* (the North). From the 1980s, however, the city began to attract highly skilled, foreign-born arrivals ('denizens'), often from Asia. Waldinger and Bozorgmehr (1996: 16) describe the ethnic mix as follows:

> Starting from a relatively small base in 1970 the Asian population skyrocketed; as immigrants from China, the Philippines, Korea, Vietnam, and India (in that order) poured into the region. Asians emerged as LA's third largest group, outnumbering the previously established African American population. The newcomers transformed Los Angeles into the capital of contemporary Asian America, pushing it well beyond the other major Asian American centers of New York, San Francisco, Oakland and Honolulu. ... The new Asians became a source of extraordinary high-skilled labor, importing school levels that left natives far behind as well as other endowments like capital and entrepreneurial talents that gave them a competitive edge.

REVIEW

Many cities owe their significance to the rise of modernity in Europe while others were developed in the wake of colonial expansion. As people were pushed or walked off the land, the colonial cities swelled but often failed to provide the employment associated with mass industrialization: these 'cities of peasants' (Roberts 1978), as well as the successful industrial cites like Chicago, have provided the grist to many a sociologist's mill. It is likely that the economic, political and technological conditions characteristic of global cities will provide similarly important sites for sociological analysis. Nevertheless, the regional roles of global cities are also important, as we briefly demonstrated for Los Angeles, which has evolved to serve the Asia-Pacific region.

Global cities are not only important phenomena in their own right; they are where certain distinctive patterns of employment emerge – in particular the move from manufacturing to services. Employment often becomes 'feminized' as old male-dominated skills are discarded and new labour markets are formed. New kinds of people, from different ethnic backgrounds and with cosmopolitan outlooks and connections with several countries, enter the global city and often succeed in their quest for social mobility. By contrast, established racial or native minorities are often marginalized as in cities such as London or Detroit. The persistence of deprivation in the midst of successful immigrant entrepreneurship often fuels urban discontent expressed in the form of riots and demonstrations.

Visit the companion website at www.palgrave.com/sociology/cohen3e for extra materials to check and expand your learning, including interactive self-test questions, mind maps making links between key themes, annotated web links to sociological research, data and key sociological thinkers, a searchable glossary and much more.

FURTHER READING

J. Friedman's classic article, 'The world city hypothesis', in the journal *Development and Change* (1986, 17(2)), started the debate on global cities.

Globalizing Cities: A New Spatial Order? (2000), edited by P. Marcuse and R. van Kempen, contains a number of excellent chapters on different aspects of the debate on global cities.

The most accomplished and extensive work on the theme of global cities is S. Sassen's *The Global City: New York, London Tokyo* (1991).

More recently, S. Sassen's *A Sociology of Globalization* (2007) summarizes, condenses and updates much of her work on many key aspects of global cities over nearly 20 years.

QUESTIONS AND ASSIGNMENTS

1. What are the main differences between a colonial, industrial and global city, bearing in mind that individual cities might have 'migrated' across these categories?

2. Why were cities so important to pre-1945 sociologists?

3. To what extent and in what ways can global cities become detached from the national states in which they are found?

4. Why is employment becoming 'feminized' in some cities?

5. Why and in what ways is the future of human settlement likely to be increasingly an urban one?

PART 4
Dynamics and challenges

19

Global civil society and political activism

Much as transnational religious, ethnic, economic, artistic and other social relationships flourished across borders before the advent of the modern nation-state, so too have there been occasions when people from different countries have cooperated to resist a practice, advance a cause, or avert an event, as with the anti-slavery movement, feminism, and the First World War respectively. In this chapter we develop and contemporize the theme of transnational practices, but focus on those concerned in the broadest sense with pursuing 'emancipatory goals' (Kaldor 2008: 42) and strategies designed to 'make global processes visible and accountable to ordinary citizens who might otherwise be confined to national political arenas' (Batliwala and Brown 2006: xi). We therefore need to define and explain the links between three closely related phenomena while exploring, with the help of case studies, their recent contributions to shaping global social space. These are the rise of global civil society, the particularities of global social movements (GSMs), and the emergence of global public opinion.

First, we look at the characteristics of global civil society. We explore how and why it differs from national civil society, and we examine other major forms of transnational activity such as crime and business. We then identify the significant agents operating in global civil society and, in the process, pinpoint the special role and features of GSMs. We explore notable examples of recent global political activism choreographed by the Jubilee 2000 campaign and the Global Justice Movement. Finally, building on the discussion in Chapter 16, we consider what is involved in the emergence of global public opinion and assess the role the internet and social media plays in this process. The eruption of political insurgency across the Middle East and North Africa commencing in early 2011 provides a rich case study through which to explore and perhaps test debates on the changing nature of communication in shaping global public space.

© MARK MALLIAN/ZUMA PRESS/CORBIS

FIGURE 19.1 The *Fuerza Joven* ('Young Force') of Bolivia
Although an ambiguous category, the mobilization of 'youth' is a notable feature of civil society in Latin America, including Mexico and Venezuela. Here, the *Fuerza Joven* ('Young Force') of Bolivia are on the march in alliance with the indigenous people's movement. The election of Evo Morales, the son of a subsistence farmer, as president is a reflection of the recent radicalization of Bolivian society.

WHAT IS GLOBAL CIVIL SOCIETY?

The loose use of the expression 'civil society' can include numerous associations in myriad forms – in fact, everything from book clubs, choral societies and sports clubs to trade unions, professional associations and religious congregations. However, the 'civil society' appellation is used in a more specific sense to cover such associations only when they seek or engage in actions designed to affect some kind of political change and/or influence political forces. The same applies to civil society associations that have ceased to be entirely 'territorially bounded' (Kaldor 2008: 42). In this sense, all civil society actions involve actors pursuing various interests and concerns – as they see them – that engender bottom-up rather than top-down struggles (Kaldor 2008: 42). Moreover, these do not revolve around profit considerations and are basically nongovernmental in their organization: they are established by independent citizens who wish to retain this autonomy (Batliwala and Brown 2006: 2). Definitions by scholars working in the field differ slightly, but many draw on the classic work of Habermas (see Global Thinker 19).

Civil society activities of all sorts are lodged in the networks, affiliations and interactions that interlace family, community, state and market. However, as Keane (2003: 65) notes, global civil society includes the global economy and polity and global actors like TNCs. Because markets are always firmly entrenched in sociopolitical structures and relations, GLOBAL CIVIL SOCIETY could not exist without a money economy and the technological investments of large corporations in the communications and other resources that enable it to flourish.

Certainly, notable struggles in global civil society in recent years, like the Global Justice Movement and the Occupy Wall Street movement, focused on how to reform, abolish or humanize the way in which the global economy currently operates. The further discussions of global civil society used by Anheier and Themudo (2002), Batliwala and Brown (2006) and Kaldor (2008) contain considerable overlaps that we note below.

> **KEY CONCEPT**
>
> GLOBAL CIVIL SOCIETY includes all those social agents whose joint concerns and struggles stretch beyond the borders of their nation-states, as they try to shape the actions of a variety of powerful actors such as governments, IGOs and TNCs over issues and problems that cannot be tackled adequately, or at all, at any level other than the regional or global.

In all the above respects, global civil society associations are no different from those that operate within the confines of the nation-state. What makes them distinctive is that they engage in 'cross-border social activities' and operate 'outside the boundaries of governmental structures' (Keane 2003: 8, 9), irrespective of whether the interconnections they establish create 'thick' or 'thinly stretched networks, pyramids and hub-and-spoke clusters'. Although global civil society activities have many historical precedents, their 'sheer scale and scope' is new and the 'range and type of fields in which they operate has never been wider' (Anheier et al. 2005: 4).

Global civil society consists of a plurality of agents, which Batliwala and Brown (2006: 7) categorize under four headings. These are:

1. bureaucratic and hierarchical *organizations* such as Greenpeace or Amnesty International
2. loose *networks* of individuals and/or groups
3. *coalitions* or *campaigns*, such as the campaign against Nestlé's business practices in the developing world, the international campaign to ban landmines, the Jubilee 2000 anti-debt campaign and Via Campesina (see Chapter 21)
4. *social movements* engaged in 'sustained mobilization' for political ends.

Some, particularly networks, engage in temporary, short-lived or intermittent activities. A good example is the UK Tar Sands Network, which works with the Athabasca Chipewyan First Nation to prevent Shell Canada from extracting oil from Athabasca, a UNESCO heritage site. Others, which may be deemed 'true' INGOs, set up permanent organizations. These would include organizations like Oxfam or Save the Children. Then again, numerous global civil society actors do not quite fit these categories and fall somewhere in between. These comprise information networks, foundations, funds, 'grassroots organizations' such as diasporic groups, immigrant associations, 'internet-based organizations', and numerous informal hybrid associations (Anheier and Themudo 2002: 196).

The definition developed so far could include 'reactionary groups' with exclusive agendas (Kaldor 2008: 42) that oppose not only powerful groups, but also oppose people whose lifestyles and values differ from their own. An obvious example here would be certain kinds of Islamists, including terrorists, who, whatever other aims they possess, are resolutely opposed to aspects of modernity and are sometimes prepared to use violence to pursue their goals. Other examples are the neo-Nazi groups in the USA and EU (see Box 21.2), as well as the Christian right in the USA, which tries to disseminate its version of 'family values' worldwide (Khagram and Alvord 2006: 71) by opposing abortion, women's rights and homosexuality. The contributors to Batliwala and Brown's edited book deal with this problem by stating a preference to focus solely on 'progressive' civil society organizations, networks, campaigns and movements, groups whose members support the 'values and goals of tolerance, equity, nonviolence, and democratic participation' (Batliwala and Brown 2006: 5–6), and who do so in a spirit of social inclusion rather than exclusion. This definition would obviously encompass, among others, organizations working with women, workers, small farmers, peasants, indigenous peoples, marginalized ethnic or tribal minorities, the urban poor, and migrant groups facing discrimination. It would also include protecting the biosphere and cooperating with campaigns, movements and organizations, such as INGOs, that try to further the interests of these groups and pursue these goals. For the remainder of this chapter we follow this same preference.

A PAUSE TO REFLECT

There seems to be a considerable theoretical problem in arriving at a definition of 'civil society' that does not include right-wing or even violent groups. Is it legitimate to bypass this issue simply by declaring a preference for admitting only those associations with progressive and democratic aims into the civil society 'club'? Alternatively, does this core conceptual difficulty raise doubts about the value of the term 'civil society' and is there a better substitute term?

THE NEED FOR GLOBAL AND NOT JUST NATIONAL CIVIL SOCIETY

A cluster of key political issues that have increasingly come to the fore are also propelling the growing presence of global civil society actors. Mostly, they revolve around the absence, or inadequacies, of democratic practices within nations, but the spread of neoliberal economic globalization certainly aggravates them. There are perhaps four main ways in which this happening.

First, active participation in the conventional democratic political process – voting at elections or joining parties – has been declining in the advanced countries for some time. This is partly due to the 'democratic deficit', or, more precisely, voter disillusionment over the dwindling ability of elected governments, in the face of globalization and state support to the rich, to deliver full economic security and social protection to the wider community. Other factors are also doubtless at play here – squabbling party coalitions that fail to reach viable compromises, corruption and incompetent politicians, coupled with competition from the growing array of intellectually less demanding and far more glamorous distractions on offer from the mass media. Global civil society activism perhaps provides a way of not only calling governments to account but also of reviving some citizens' flagging interest in politics and 'revitalizing democracy' (Anheier et al. 2005: 15).

Second, despite the democratization of some African countries, the former Soviet Union and Latin America since the 1980s, much of it has yielded 'formal' rather than 'substantive' democratic government. Kaldor (2008: 35) defines formal democracy as one in which the institutions and procedures enable citizens to express their views and political party preferences freely. Such a society will also have an independent judiciary with a separation of government powers. While few would question the value of formal democracy, and everywhere those denied it desire its establishment, it lacks certain ingredients. Certainly, as we have just seen, formal democracy in the advanced countries seems to have lost its attraction for many citizens. A substantive democracy, however, would, in addition, 'maximise the opportunities for all individuals to shape their own lives and participate in and influence debates about public decisions that affect them' (Kaldor 2008: 35). Moreover, it also implies the determined pursuit of political processes and policies designed to reduce poverty and inequality. In short, existing democracies mostly fail to provide citizens with the economic security and fairness they crave.

National civil society groups – in both existing and newly established formal democracies – might enhance their chances of achieving such a transformation if they turned to the global sphere for assistance, and in this respect, the emergence of transnational advocacy networks augurs well. These are worldwide coalitions of informed public opinion and political pressure groups that exert pressure on oppressive governments from the outside (Keck and Sikkink 1998). For example, in the mid-1990s the Zapatistas rebelled against the Mexican government because they believed that its neoliberal economic policies were destroying their local economic and social life (Kiely 2005b: 205–6). The long road to freedom in South Africa (democratic elections were held there in 1994) was preceded by at least 40 years of struggle linking internal opposition forces to the African National Congress in exile and other anti-apartheid groups. A similarly long political struggle is unfolding in Burma (Myanmar), with Aung San Suu Kyi playing a similar role to Nelson Mandela. A final example is the linked international and national protests that occurred during the early months of 2011 when massive insurrection and protests erupted across the Middle East and North Africa. We return to this theme later.

Third, throughout this book we have alluded to problems that are partly or sometimes primarily global in nature and extent. These include climate change and worldwide pollution, the risk of pandemics, financial chaos, job insecurity and inequality in an ever more competitive global economy, the impact of transnational criminal gangs, and the increasing costs of water, food, energy and raw materials. It seems clear that such problems cannot be resolved by governments acting alone. Indeed, the existing layers of GLOBAL GOVERNANCE, drawing states into

> **KEY CONCEPT**
>
> GLOBAL GOVERNANCE is the fragile, inchoate and contested cluster of agreements, agendas, laws and institutional arrangements that have been put together by states, IGOs, INGOs, TNCs, GSMs, citizen networks, professional associations and others. It is the attempt to establish viable systems for managing world affairs, because no global sovereign government currently exists that is capable of attaining the same degree of order at the world level that individual states can guarantee within their own territories.

webs of legal, defence, diplomatic, trade and other policy collaboration, demonstrate how far this process of increased interdependence has already proceeded. However, this cooperation needs to proceed much further in terms of the range of spheres involved and the depth of collaboration required, and here national and global civil society activism can push governments much further in this direction.

Finally, the spread of neoliberal economic globalization since the early 1980s has driven numerous global civil society groups to retaliate and resist through a wide gamut of local, national, regional and global actions. We explore this in more detail in a later section in which we discuss the Global Justice Movement. Paradoxically, however, the increase in economic globalization has simultaneously strengthened the very resources that global civil society activists require – such as cheap mass transport and an improved ICT infrastructure – to confront the inequalities, insecurities and injustices that it caused or deepened in the first place (Anheier et al. 2005: 7).

FORGING GLOBAL CIVIL SOCIETY: INGOs AND PARALLEL SUMMITS

As we mentioned above, Batliwala and Brown (2006) suggest that we think of global civil society as consisting of four, albeit overlapping, types of actors – organizations, networks, campaigns and social movements. In Table 19.1 we provide a brief snapshot of the incidence, range and spread of global civil society activities that took place in just one month in April 2008. Since this was while the Olympic torch was being relayed across the world shortly before the Olympic Games were due to start in Beijing, all the events listed in the right-hand column in one way or another relate to the games. Despite this quirk, the chronology Timms (2009) put together for 2008 suggests that the activities taking place during this month were far from atypical.

Later, we look specifically at GSMs, but here we briefly provide some detail concerning the role of two key ways of contributing to global civil society, namely INGOs and parallel summits.

INTERNATIONAL NONGOVERNMENTAL ORGANIZATIONS (INGOs)

According to the Union of International Associations, which collects data on this topic, there were around 15,000 INGOs in the mid-1990s and by 2008/9 this number had risen to more than 21,000 (Katz 2009: 314–15). Estimates of the numbers, however, vary. The UNDP (2002) *Human Development Report* suggests that there were 37,000 INGOs by 2000, with huge growth since the mid-1990s. There are several important points to note about these organizations.

'True' INGOs like Oxfam or Amnesty International typically employ a core staff of permanent officials, have a large network of volunteer supporters, and operate worldwide through a federation of nationally based but globally cooperating offices and sister organizations that share global aims and concerns. Some of the larger ones cooperate with IGOs such as UN agencies or the World Bank, and some hold a consultancy status in these powerful organizations. Many INGOs participate in a number of global events and actions as advisers, participants or providers of local resources. For example, in addition to their regular work of providing famine relief, building up professional expertise and knowledge banks, or publicizing human rights abuses, they are often closely associated with and/or overlap other kinds of global social actors and activities. To cite one such instance, 155,000 delegates representing 6,872 organizations took part in the World Social Forum in 2005 (Fórum Social Mundial 2005) (see below). Also, they often run or participate in campaigns designed to shape government policies and public opinion and sometimes engage in overt protest (see Box 19.1).

TABLE 19.1 Global civil society events in April 2008

- Social forums and actions unconnected with the 2008 Olympic Games in China
- A mini-social forum in Melbourne on the theme of sustainable food, transport and urban policies
- On the International Day of Peasant Struggles (17 April) a series of events took place to show solidarity with farmers and social movements across the world. The demonstrations drew attention to how environmental damage – linked to the increased impact of corporate agribusinesses – is exacerbating the poverty, intimidation and violence to which farmers and peasants are increasingly subjected [Chapters 7 and 20]
- Activists blockaded Cargill (an agro-food company) in Ghent, Belgium to draw attention to rising food shortages worldwide. They accorded the shortages to the industrialization of farming (the use of pesticides, genetically modified food and monoculture) and the relentless removal of small farmers from the land
- A Brazilian youth social forum was held in the state of Florianopolis
- Campaigners for the rights of indigenous peoples in the Chittagong Hill Tracts areas of Bangladesh – local and international – demonstrated in support of the Jumma people, seven of whose villages had been burnt down by settlers from Bengal. These settlers were part of a government-backed programme of forcibly settling people in the region from outside the area but much of this had led to growing oppression of the local Jumma people

- Protests, rallies related to the movement of the Olympic torch across the world
- Uighur migrants in Kazakhstan (originally from Xinjiang, a huge autonomous region in northwest China) protested about the Chinese government's treatment of their people. Similar protests by Uighur migrants took place in Turkey
- Thousands of human rights activists and pro-Tibetan independence supporters demonstrated along the Olympic torch route in London. It later transpired that the security officials' heavy-handed reactions were carried out by members of the Chinese security service
- Banners appeared in key areas of Paris, including a Tibetan flag at the Hotel de Ville declaring: 'Paris defends Human Rights throughout the World'
- In San Francisco widespread demonstrations drew attention to China's human rights record in Tibet, Darfur in Sudan [Chapter 20] and towards the Falun Gong [Chapter 17]. 'Free Tibet' flags were displayed
- Similar protests occurred in Buenos Aires and Dar es Salaam (Tanzania), where Nobel peace laureate Wangari Maathai refused to participate in the Olympic procession because of human rights abuses in China
- In Islamabad, Pakistan, and New Dehli, pro-Tibet protestors (150,000 Tibetan exiles live in India) held mass demonstrations. Officials refused to ban the march despite China's request
- Pro-Tibetan and/or human rights protests followed the Olympic torch route through Bangkok, Kuala Lumpur, Jakarta in Indonesia (where the event was cancelled for security reasons), the Zenko-ji Buddhist temple in Japan, Seoul in South Korea, Pyongyang in North Korea and Ho Chi Minh City in Vietnam. In Kuala Lumpur and Seoul there were also pro-Chinese demonstrations
- Pro-Chinese protestors held a vigil (Manchester, UK) and demonstrated in Canberra, Australia for China's right to the take the Olympic torch worldwide

Source: Adapted from Timms (2009: 347–9).

Most INGOs (and of course NGOs) are geared towards ameliorating economic hardship and promoting human rights among women, the urban poor living in shantytowns, or tribal peoples whose livelihoods are being threatened by large development projects such as dams. They may be involved in disaster relief, providing short-term assistance in the event of floods, hurricanes or drought, and longer term programmes of development, such as providing new housing stock, road building, educational support, and the provision of water, sanitation and electricity. Often, INGOs seek substitutes for the top-down, commercially oriented structural adjustment programmes and development initiatives that Southern governments tend to promote, often with the backing of Western states, investors and IGOs like the World Bank.

Turning to NGOs, their numbers are much greater at local, grassroots and national levels. According to Fisher (1993: xi), by the early 1990s there were more than 100,000 such groups in the developing countries (the South), probably serving the needs of more than 100 million people. However, the numbers of locally operating NGOs has since leapt to much higher figures. There are now said to be more than 3 million in India – although most are probably very small and highly local in their reach – and more than 200,000 in Russia. Often, young professionals, either out of a sense of commitment to their fellow citizens or because they are unemployed so decide to work in a semi-voluntary capacity, staff both the grassroots and national NGOs operating in the South (Fisher 1993: viii). Many of these Southern NGOs enjoy links with INGOs that provide them with funds, technical expertise, international media coverage, and other kinds of external support.

PARALLEL SUMMITS

A notable example of a purposive and cooperative reaction to economic globalization is demonstrated by the rise of parallel summits. These occur when coalitions of groups organize mass participation at large public events in the expectation of gaining international media attention. The action is often timed to coincide with the official summit meetings of governments, IGOs or big businesses. These are not new but their incidence has drastically increased, especially since 1999. Also, the international mix of participants has tended to become more radical. Thus, in 2000 and 2001 alone, the incidence of parallel summits grew by nearly 40%. The social protest organized by global activists and timed to take place alongside the World Economic Forum of global business interests at Davos, Switzerland, in 2000, and the first alternative World Social Forum (WSF) held at Porto Alegre, Brazil, in 2001, are just two examples (Pianta 2001: 177). Since then and up until 2010, 10 WSFs have been held at different sites across the world. For example, the seventh took place in Nairobi, Kenya and explored the theme of 'people's struggles, people's alternatives'. More than 75,000 people attended from around 110 countries, while it is thought that probably 1,400 different organizations were represented (Timms 2008: 377). The ninth WSF, by contrast, held in 2009, took the form of a global day of action and mobilization at hundreds of local sites around the world (Vargas 2009). The central concern at all these WSFs has been the struggles of ordinary people to resist neoliberal capitalism (Chapters 4, 6 and 7).

GLOBAL SOCIAL MOVEMENTS

There are confusing similarities between discussions on civil society and discussions on social movements. Unfortunately, as you read more widely, you will find that many authors bury the one under the rubric of the other without much ado. The difference is this. Civil society alludes to the many voluntary bodies that underpin a healthy, functioning society. Everything from baby-sitting clubs, charities, book clubs, neighbourhood patrols and organized visits to the elderly are part of civil society. It gets more complicated when civil society organizations have political aims, for example the reform of the electoral system or abolishing the death penalty. Social movements are also 'political' in the general sense of that word, but seek to mobilize on a grand scale. They are, in other words, agencies of social transformation that galvanize their members to use various forms of active protest to challenge, reform, change or improve certain practices or institutions they believe harm social life. As such, they involve manifestations of popular sentiment and therefore overlap with numerous other kinds of social activities.

There are a plethora of definitions and descriptions. Wilson (1973: 8), for example, offers a rather prosaic one when he claims that 'a social movement is a conscious, collective, organized attempt to bring about or resist large-scale change in the social order by non-institutionalized means'. He adds that those who join social movements go 'beyond the customary resources of the social order to launch their own crusade against the evils of society; such actions may enable them to reach beyond themselves and become new men and women' (Wilson 1973: 5). A somewhat different definition is provided by Zirakzadeh (1997: 4–5), who suggests that a social movement:

- is a group of people who consciously attempt to build a radically new social order
- involves people of a broad range of social backgrounds
- deploys politically confrontational and socially disruptive tactics.

THE CHANGING NATURE OF SOCIAL MOVEMENTS SINCE THE 1960s

Many scholars argue that social movements changed markedly from the late 1960s onwards. This was probably linked to certain underlying changes that were then evident in the industrialized countries. Touraine (1981) tried to capture these changes with the term POSTINDUSTRIAL SOCIETY.

Touraine (1981) contrasted the 'old' labour and political movements with the 'new' social movements that represented the interests of those working in emerging occupations. The old labour movement was seen to be based on the dirty, dangerous jobs in mining, shipbuilding, stevedoring and construction. These occupations clearly demanded solidarity in the face of hazardous and exploitative environments. The question of whether there was a clear distinction between 'old' and 'new' movements was vigorously debated at the time, but we suggest that nearly all the changes were more of degree than of kind. Keeping this in mind, social movements are said to have changed in three main ways:

1. Early struggles were concerned with 'emancipatory politics' – gaining the freedoms of assembly, movement, opinion and equal political participation, and the right to form trade unions. Consequently, participants needed to gain some direct influence over the state (Giddens 1991: Ch. 7). To an extent, this remained a priority for civil rights activists in the USA and for women's, gay and disabled people's movements. However, in the 1980s the main focus shifted to causes relating to 'life politics' (Giddens 1991: 214–27). These are issues relating to self-realization, identity and what kinds of lifestyles and personal relationships we prefer.

2. Inglehart (1990) and others argued that growing affluence and material security, after the Second World War, plus welfare reforms brought a shift towards a concern with non-material values and the desire to prioritize personal fulfilment and identities, although recent economic changes have called this into question. Young people were often at the forefront of struggles like the anti-Vietnam War movement and much of this tended to overlap with hippie and drug cultures and the early green movement.

3. The spread of higher education and developments in communication technology, among other changes, have fuelled a demand for the democratization of decision-making and the right to be fully informed and consulted. We have also become more knowledgeable

FIGURE 19.2 An anti-war demo in London, 2011
The wars in Iraq and Afghanistan have galvanized the anti-war movement and generated significant protests. Here, demonstrators listen to a speech denouncing the continuing war in Afghanistan.

about science, technology and the management of economic life and their attendant risks (Beck 1992; Giddens 1991). Questioning authority has also characterized the internal running of most post-1960s social movements.

A PAUSE TO REFLECT

It now seems commonplace to assume that the international labour movement has dissipated in strength and been superseded by other global social movements – in particular the peace, human rights, women's and environmental movements. Have we been writing off the labour movement prematurely, particularly workers in the newer emerging economies, like China, Brazil, India and Nigeria? There also seems to be a more vigorous response by organized labour in the wealthy countries since 2007. What are the likely alliances between the labour movement and other social movements and what inhibits joint campaigning?

GLOBAL THINKERS 19 JÜRGEN HABERMAS (1929–)

COURTESY OF THE HOLBERG PRIZE, UNIVERSITY OF BERGEN/FLORIAN BREIEF

Jürgen Habermas is an eminent contemporary sociologist working in the tradition of the Frankfurt School of critical theory. The word 'critical' was essential to this group of scholars because it was a signal that, while they drew on core insights by Karl Marx, they also focused on the mass media, mass societies, mass cultures, and the psychological insights of Freud and others. The word also implied a preference for the interpretative understanding (*Verstehen*) of social affairs rather than a narrow belief in scientific and positivist methods – they saw rationality and irrationality as interlaced in human affairs. Habermas later became preoccupied with how to attain 'a rational society' and what rationality meant.

Unsurprisingly, members of the Frankfurt School (established in 1923) became concerned about irrationality when the Nazis seized power and many of them had to disperse. From 1931 to 1949 they were based largely in New York. After the Second World War, two scholars, Theodor Adorno and Max Horkheimer, re-established the school in Germany. In 1956, Habermas, then 27, became Adorno's assistant and so began a stream of powerful sociological works. Habermas produced about 15 major works, so we have to be selective in what follows. Here are just a few of his key ideas.

In *The Structural Transformation of the Public Sphere* (1989), he shows how an emerging European bourgeoisie began to take an interest in public affairs by starting up newspapers and constituting an informed reading public. However, in the twentieth century, the public sphere became fragmented and politicians were able to manipulate public opinion rather than be subject to its strictures (Outhwaite 1996: 7–8).

Despite a strong tendency towards public passivity, Habermas argues that there is a potential for rationality, in that human beings have an extended capacity for communicative competence. In *Towards a Rational Society* (1971) and *Communication and the Evolution of Society* (1979), he uses political theory, the study of language and linguistics, and notions of sociality and social action to show how people can oppose attempts to make them subject to the whims of elites. This more positive form of rationality may be deemed a 'humanizing rationality' – one that is different from the 'instrumental rationality' of states, the market, large organizations, corporations and the media.

Habermas thus wants to recover a role for the 'public sphere', 'civil society' and 'moral consciousness'. In this respect, he sees civil society as a complement rather than an alternative to formal politics. His work reveals a strong commitment to democracy and a fierce opposition to the tyranny of illegitimate state power. He took a hard-hitting stance against the 'war on terror' and the US invasion of Iraq.

Sources: Braaten (1991); Habermas (1971, 1979, 1989); McCarthy (1978); Outhwaite (1994, 1996).

WHY HAVE SOME SOCIAL MOVEMENTS BECOME GLOBALIZED?

Transnational collaboration was evident during the nineteenth century in movements opposing slavery and promoting peace, conservation, and the rights of women and workers. Similarly, the civil rights, anti-Vietnam War and student movements, as well as the Campaign for Nuclear Disarmament during the 1960s and the anti-cruise missile movement in the early 1980s, all spilled over national borders. Nevertheless, as we have seen, in the past 15 years there has been an upsurge in all kinds of global civil society activities, partly explained by the greater ease with which one can now organize global struggles than hitherto.

Certain mobilizing social movements, particularly those oriented towards labour, women, peace, the environment and human rights, are intrinsically global in their concerns and aims (Cohen and Rai 2000). Moreover, there are now good reasons to move towards global action. One factor, of course, is that increasing economic globalization is tying the fates of people together worldwide. In addition, as we mentioned in Chapters 4, 6 and 7, the impact of neoliberal economic policies in both North and South and the globalization of manufacturing have undermined nearly everyone's economic security. Thus, compared with previous upsurges of political action by excluded groups, the present one is 'truly transnational in its scale and scope [and] multidimensional in its thrust' (Oommen 1997: 51–2). There are other explanations for the upsurge in effective global action, but here we discuss changes in consciousness and changes in communications technology.

CHANGES IN CONSCIOUSNESS: TOWARDS GLOBAL THINKING

According to Hegedus (1989: 19), since the 1980s many individuals have undergone a 'planetization' of understanding. This is similar to Robertson's idea of an emerging global consciousness discussed in Chapter 2. Many realized that what threatens or concerns one person equally implicates everyone else; solutions are only meaningful if they involve joint struggles (Hegedus 1989: 33). The Live Aid rock song, 'We are the world', symbolized this sentiment and in the 1980s many rock groups became involved in raising funds for poverty and famine relief in Africa. This process was repeated with the Live 8 and Make Poverty History campaigns held simultaneously around the world during the summer of 2005. It is estimated that more than 1 million people attended the live music events held in eight countries in July 2005, while perhaps 2 billion watched them on TV.

Thus, empowering people in rich Western societies is only meaningful if poor people in the South are helped to assert their rights as well, an argument that is especially relevant to environmental problems. In fact, from the early 1980s, supporters of the peace movement in Europe and North America began to realize that simply putting pressure on one's own government to relinquish nuclear arms or curtail military expenditure was not enough. The range of actions had to be much wider, for example compelling arms-exporting countries to curtail their sales to repressive regimes and to divert arms industries into peaceful activities.

Many supporters of social movements also stopped focusing exclusively on self-realization and the reconstruction of cultural identities (Kennedy 2010: 234–6), and instead assumed a sense of 'personal responsibility for a collective future at a local, national and planetary level' (Hegedus 1989: 22). This links up with our earlier discussion of Giddens's notion of life politics, in which political matters invade the sphere of domestic/personal lives and relationships. But this can be a two-way process. When a myriad of tiny individual or household decisions are aggregated, they may lend their weight to the attainment of much broader, radical changes. The relative success of Jubilee 2000, outlined in Box 19.1, offers one example; the growth in ethical and green consumerism is another, as an increasing number of people are refusing to buy products from companies that engage in morally reprehensible activities.

BOX 19.1 The Jubilee 2000 campaign for debt relief for poor countries

The origins and development of the campaign

Jubilee 2000 began in 1996. It campaigned for debt relief on behalf of the 52 poorest countries – the so-called heavily indebted poor countries (HIPCs), whose debts were mostly to multilateral agencies like the IMF and the World Bank and the G7 governments. There were a number of reasons why these debts arose:

1. *Dollar surpluses:* during the 1970s a surfeit of dollars flowed into the recently deregulated international commercial banks. These came from, among other sources, US trade deficits and the surge in dollar earnings as a result of the huge oil price increases in 1974 and 1979.

2. *International support from 'responsible' agents:* with strong support from the G7 governments, the World Bank and the IMF, international banks were encouraged to lend this cash to indebted countries.

3. *Poor spending or corruption:* unfortunately, many governments spent these loans on unnecessary 'white elephant' development/status projects or military hardware. The returns from such projects were insufficient to repay the debt. Some funds also disappeared into the private Western bank accounts of corrupt politicians and officials.

The aim was to reduce these debts by the year 2000. In 1998 Jubilee 2000 brought together 50,000 people in Birmingham, UK to form a human chain around a G8 meeting, while a UK poll revealed that 69% supported debt cancellation. By 2000 there were groups in 68 countries – from Japan and the USA to Angola and Colombia. The use of the internet promoted global coordination. The intimate personal relations characteristic of local churches and their congregations provided a key vehicle for winning supporters.

Campaign organization and strategy

The organizers encouraged country groups to form autonomously and the added flexibility this provided enabled Jubilee 2000 to mobilize some 24 million people worldwide to sign a petition. The lack of centralization, however, made it difficult to reconcile the differences between more and less radical supporters. Also, a rift developed between Southern groups, which wanted a much broader agenda for world poverty, and supporters in the North.

The impact and successes of Jubilee 2000

The campaign succeeded in placing debt relief high on G7 governmental agendas and in educating the public. Yet, real debt reduction has proved difficult and has often been accompanied by conditions that make compliance difficult – such as further privatizations of public utilities and spending cuts. In 2005, the G8 nations agreed to cancel all IMF debt for 18 of the poorest HIPCs, while future cancellations will be partly offset against aid reduction. By 2011, a $55bn debt had been cancelled for 32 HIPCs and another 4 were in the final stages of the scheme. For those remaining, the process takes too long and the conditions remain onerous. The struggle continues.

Sources: Anheier and Themudo (2002); Kiely (2005b); Pettifor (2001); Reitan (2007).

CHANGES IN COMMUNICATIONS TECHNOLOGY

The contribution of communications technology to our emerging sense of a common global identity can be traced back to the late 1960s when important developments in satellite communications enabled vast numbers of people across the world to view images of planet earth for the first time on their home TVs. This coincided with various US voyages to the moon, which culminated in the first actual landing by humans in June 1969. These powerful images may have signalled a fundamental turning point in human experience. We became aware of the beauty of our planet and the need to preserve it at all costs as our only source of mutual sustenance in an otherwise bleak and infinitely vast universe. Similar emotions were activated in the early and mid-1980s when a series of computer-enhanced images taken from space gradually provided a body of clear and incontrovertible evidence of the extent to which the ozone layer (the band of gas encircling the planet 20–50 kilometres above the earth's surface) had become depleted, giving rise to the 'holes' that are especially noticeable over the polar regions in spring.

Of massive additional significance, however, is the development of electronic communications, particularly the internet, discussed in Chapter 16 and explored as a case study at the end of this chapter. These have provided new opportunities for achieving personal and small-group autonomy, circulating and sharing information, and challenging the claims and legitimacy of states and other powerful institutions. The internet also allows actors separated by vast distances to share their individual insights with ease and feed these into a kind of rapid cumulative learning experience. Other tactics may include galvanizing the support of consumers worldwide, capturing media attention, and lobbying sympathetic groups at the UN or other IGOs. The multiplicity of levels through which GSMs and INGOs now operate helps explain their much stronger presence in the world today. Assisted by the media and their close links to INGOs, GSMs can short-circuit the cumbersome processes that might otherwise be required if millions of people are to mount huge simultaneous protests across the word.

THE GLOBAL JUSTICE MOVEMENT: A CASE STUDY

Although global activists have come together to challenge official government and IGO agendas on several occasions – for example the street party protests against the G8 meeting in Cologne in June 1999 – the Global Justice Movement (also called the anti-globalization movement) first crystallized in the eyes of the world as a global force to be reckoned with in December 1999. Over a period of five days, 50,000 protestors from many countries succeeded in shutting down a major WTO conference in Seattle, USA. The protestors also received tacit support from some of the officials representing governments in Africa, Asia and Latin America who felt that the trade agreement being negotiated at the conference was unlikely to benefit poor countries and that the interests of wealthy G7 and OECD nations dominated the agenda. Between December 1999 and early 2002, there were 18 separate major mass protests against different IGO, EU or G8 meetings around the world involving demonstrations by various Global Justice Movement supporters; and this does not include events that had a more specific national focus. Two of the most momentous of these occurred during the IMF meeting in Prague in September 2000 and the G8 meeting in Genoa in July 2001, the latter attended by an estimated 300,000 protestors and accompanied by running street battles between some violent protestors and the Italian police.

The Global Justice Movement is a loose coalition of groups and networks that are willing to forge temporary alliances to oppose the 'global neoliberal project' (Kiely 2005b: 223), which the G7 governments, especially the USA, imposed on the world. Anheier et al. (2005: 7–10) list four possible responses to current forms of globalization – support them; reject them; advocate reform; or offer alternatives. Ignoring the first position, this classification now allows us to identify more clearly the different and sometimes divergent elements included in the Global Justice Movement and to make four observations:

1. All the many groups advocating the second, third and fourth responses have participated in the Global Justice Movement, apart from those with strong right-wing religious and nationalist leanings.
2. The majority of 'true' INGOs and many of the remaining actors in global civil society have campaigned as reformers; their intention is to transform global capitalism rather than abolish or escape from it.
3. We can see that strong strands of socialism, anarchism and environmentalism – each in turn breaking down into numerous subgroupings – have flourished within the Global Justice Movement alongside a wide spectrum of pro- and anti-globalization groups from both the North and South.
4. Both local and global inclinations are also found there, sometimes pulling together and at other times against each other.

The Global Justice Movement encountered various difficulties that limited its effectiveness. It has also been criticized on several counts. One criticism has been that its very diversity, flexibility, lack of hierarchy and openness – demonstrated by its reliance on networking, the accessible and interactive nature of its websites, and the ever changing constituent elements feeding into it – were a source of weakness as well as strength. Thus, its lack of coherence meant that it was less effective in fighting for global justice than it might otherwise have been (Kiely 2005b; Waterman and Timms 2004).

Second, the destruction of the twin towers in New York in September 2001, the spread of terrorism, and the Bush government's increasing assertion of unilateral military and political power in response posed a formidable challenge for the Global Justice Movement. Thus, to an extent, these events and the second Iraq War of 2003 distracted world opinion from the issues raised by the Global Justice Movement. They also highlighted the limits of GSMs in opposing determined and armed forces, state and non-state. Anderson and Rieff (2005: 35), for example, argue that 9/11 returned the issues of national security and sovereignty centre stage, while underlining the importance of the USA in shaping world responses. Certainly, 'the love affair between global civil society and international organizations' like the UN, which seemed to dominate much of international life during the 1990s and made global civil society seem more influential than perhaps it actually was, gave way to 'an international system under a specific challenge from the world's superpower' (Anderson and Rieff 2005: 36–7).

A PAUSE TO REFLECT

Movements based on networks and loose alliances have great advantages; they are flexible, democratic and responsive to new demands and issues. However, are the Global Justice Movement and the Occupy Wall Street movement simply convenient umbrellas rather than coherent social movements? Do some or all of the GSMs we have described require at least a modicum of permanent organization, leadership and an agreed set of goals?

Third, Kiely (2005b: 242) argues that not only have these events slightly sidelined issues of global economic justice in the past few years, but the Global Justice Movement and the anti-war movement have also often appeared confused about war, human rights and justice. Thus, being opposed to imperialist, self-seeking wars by an arrogant global superpower is one thing. However, simply refusing to counter any moves whatsoever against regimes that oppress their people in hideous ways if this happens to coincide with the views held by the USA undermines the 'principle of global solidarity' in the search for universal justice (Kiely 2005b: 248–9). This issue came to the fore again in early 2011 when civil unrest and insurgency spread across much of the Arab world and the question arose – especially over Libya – whether it was legitimate for the West to offer military and other assistance to the rebels.

Finally, a division emerged along North–South lines. At times, Southern activists accused Northern groups of adopting paternalistic attitudes in a 'one-way relationship' (Reitan 2007: 52–4). Sometimes, too, Southern NGOs and networks rejected Northern 'altruism' and preferred to organize protests with other Southern groups. Rifts of this kind also surfaced with Jubilee 2000, especially in 1999 when Southern groups rejected the promise of partial debt relief and reform wrung from G8 leaders because these gains fell 'far short' of what was necessary to improve the real lives of Southern people (Reitan 2007: 87). In fact, later in 1999, Jubilee 2000 split into a number of component groups including Jubilee South, representing campaigning groups in Africa, Asia and Latin America. Considered overall, Munck (2007: 55) also suggests that much of the discourse on global civil society demonstrates an 'irredeemably Eurocentric bias' that takes little account of the very different cultures and histories of non-European peoples.

GLOBAL COMMUNICATIONS AND THE SOCIAL MEDIA: THE ARAB SPRING

Communications and their capacity to stimulate debate and public opinion are an essential component of any effective, functioning, democratic civil society. While Habermas recognized the crucial role of an emerging public space in forging Europe's early moves towards representative government, communications make an equally important contribution towards the vibrancy of global civil society. Indeed, a key theme in the globalization literature, as we have seen (especially in Chapter 16 but also in Chapter 2), has been precisely the unprecedented extension and intensification of all forms of communication worldwide. These encompass newspapers, magazines, branded goods, advertising, television, radio, landlines and mobile phones, not to mention the exploding wealth of internet applications and links, including the social media. Yet, most observers believe that we should not allow its sheer magnitude and global character to lull us into assuming that, by itself, the unstoppable momentum of this worldwide communications revolution has unlimited potential to shape global public opinion and build a strong global civil society. We discussed some of the reasons for our scepticism in Chapters 10 and 16, but we list a few of the most crucial below:

1. The concentration of the global media in increasingly fewer hands narrows the range of opinions gaining expression (Deane 2008).
2. Widespread government censorship and moves to block information flows from Iran, Russia, China and the former Gaddafi regime in Libya (Goldsmith and Wu 2006; Morozov 2011) restrict the access of billons of people to global public opinion.
3. A number of people are disadvantaged by the tendency for English to dominate certain media, whereas the existence of a number of different languages fragments information flows in other respects (Albrow and Glasius 2008; Goldsmith and Wu 2006).
4. The multiplicity of voices and information flows needs to be accompanied by the equal possibility of being heard, which existing economic inequalities and political oppression obviously severely curtail (Albrow and Glasius 2008: 11).
5. In coping with the aftermath of the 9/11 bombings in New York, the US and other governments argued that the 'war on terror' necessitated some restrictions on freedom of expression (Albrow and Glasius 2008: 11).

Despite these limitations and restrictions, the global media, particularly the social media, have played a decisive role in the events in the Middle East and North Africa that have come to be known as 'the Arab Spring'. (By the way, the name derived from 'the Prague Spring', the period after 1968 when many in Czechoslovakia demanded democracy and wanted to escape from the dominance of the Soviet Union.) The Arab Spring began with massive street insurrections that rapidly spread across parts of the Arab world in the early months of 2011. They began in Tunisia, with Egypt, Bahrain, the Yemen and Libya following shortly thereafter. Commenting on the situation in Tunisia, Paul Rogers (2011), a professor of peace studies, presciently argued:

> The uprising has come from a complex mix of economic problems involving food-price rises and high unemployment together with a hatred of an autocratic and plutocratic regime that has exercised violent control of public order for decades. ...Tunisia may be significant because it is one of a cluster of countries that combine elitist regimes with rapid population growth and economic stagnation. This shared experience helps to explain the emergence of further unrest across the region.

By March, protests of varying degrees of intensity had spread to 16 other countries in the Middle East and North Africa, namely Algeria, Djibouti, Egypt, Iran, Iraq, Jordan, Kuwait, Mauritania, Morocco, Oman, the Palestinian territories (West Bank and Gaza), Saudi Arabia, Somalia, Sudan, Syria and Western Sahara. The demonstrations of street power were not always decisive, but they shook complacent, autocratic regimes to the core.

THE ROLE OF THE SOCIAL MEDIA

The strict controls that many governments in the region had exercised over political life, the mass media and the internet, reinforced by a vast security apparatus of terror and surveillance, meant that national civil society in the Arab world was very weak, although strikes by manual workers had not been uncommon, for example in Egypt. For similar reasons, linkages to global civil society were relatively limited until early 2011. In fact, the insurrections could be said to have filled the gap left by the relative absence of a civil society and to be a phenomenon that is likely to arise precisely because governments have persistently blocked its formation.

What role, then, did the internet, Twitter and Facebook play in these insurrections compared with other resources? There seems little doubt that the ability of protestors to use their mobile phones, notably using Twitter and Facebook, played a central role in these insurrections. Access to these resources facilitated organization – getting people onto the streets, coordinating their actions, and keeping them informed about the movements of security personnel. In fact, technology made it possible to mobilize thousands of protestors quickly and to get them to move to wherever the demonstrations would have the most impact at any one time. In addition, and perhaps prior to this, the same technology allowed protestors to stir others into joining the actions. The importance of visual material is obviously crucial here, too, since these often carry a meaning and impact that is far more immediate and powerful than words.

The social media performed additional and highly valuable functions that are perhaps less immediately obvious. Many of the protestors were young and relatively well educated. For these, and probably others, the internet, emails and the social media provided essential detailed information, not only on the unfolding events but also on the background to the uprisings. Their thirst for knowledge and information in countries where reliable, unbiased, nongovernmental ideas and news were scarce was considerable. Thus, the internet and social media were invaluable in supplementing the sources of information already available to them through interpersonal, co-present relations with 'harder', more up-to-date and independent sources. Given the weak civil society structure, it seems likely that the social media created a sense of participation and consolidated a sense of togetherness, a feeling that 'we are not alone'. This sense of strength in numbers constantly reinforced through Facebook and Twitter must, we suppose, have been essential to the protestors, given that they were risking their lives to challenge these highly oppressive regimes.

The vehicles and conduits through which social media operate to provide global connectivities clearly helped the protestors, for it quickly became evident that they were using their mobile phones along with Facebook, Twitter and no doubt other internet applications to relay videos, practical information, personal accounts and, probably, pleas for outside support to relatives and friends living in other Middle Eastern and North African countries and to members of the diasporic community working and studying in North America, Europe and elsewhere. These kinship and wider diasporic social networks helped to generate a contagion effect and deepened world interest in, and empathy for, the uprisings. This raised the level of wider international support and forced governments to react. By drawing on personal loyalties, international networks assisted not only in the simple dissemination of direct information to a much wider audience – including sympathetic student groups from other countries or the national media in the host society – but also in persuading others to provide moral if not political support to those organizing demonstrations outside embassies, at universities or outside government buildings in support of the protestors at home.

OTHER FORMS OF MOBILIZATION

We need to be cautious about giving too much credence to claims that what has been happening across the Arab world is tantamount to a 'twitter revolution', in which the sheer power of swarming internet messages has the potential to unravel oppressive hierarchies and structures. There are many reasons for circumspection and we end this chapter by outlining a few of the main ones.

As we have already seen, family, kin, friendship, neighbourhood and other intimate inter-personal affiliations, some of which operate across vast distances, can be activated and perhaps held together with the help of the internet's resources. Their power to command support and loyalty, however, exists and survives independently of the information technology. Moreover, at times, although not always, they can play a crucial role in emboldening and mobilizing members to engage in political actions. In Egypt, for example, during the mass protests of February 2011, it was evident that longstanding blood, marriage, religious, neighbourhood and friendship ties between factory workers and the people living in the urban city slums played an essential part in spreading the protests, for individuals called upon mutual loyalties and infused each other with the courage to join the insurrection. Similarly, there are strong indications that many of the young, educated protestors and their families were closely linked to people in other sectors of society.

Some determined governments, including China, have deployed Facebook and Twitter to identify protestors and their friends before spying on their activities or arresting them for subversion. One way of doing this is to encourage spoof 'friends' who are really government agents to join various Facebook networks (see Morozov 2011). Although they were rarely so sophisticated, the Egyptian and other Arab governments resorted to blocking mobile phone networks and the internet, thus rendering them nonoperational for a while. In response, the international protest site Avaaz mobilized its support to 'blackout-proof' protests – and claimed to have provided secure satellite modems and phones, tiny video cameras, portable radio transmitters, and support teams on the ground – to allow activists to broadcast live video feeds even during internet and phone blackouts.

Given these and other dangers, some will resort to more conventional media, of which radio and TV news channels are clearly options. Although these too may be subject to government censorship and bias, satellites may enable groups to access non-national sources. However, there are at least two other rather pedestrian but nevertheless effective resources that remain largely outside government control, which are capable of providing up-to-date information and empowering individuals. The old-fashioned leaflet, which anyone with access to a printer can produce cheaply, quickly and easily, is obviously one. Indeed, during the protests in Egypt and probably elsewhere, it seems that the mass circulation of simple leaflets proved highly effective in mobilizing the protests and in many ways were a near perfect substitute for the banned internet. Another important, albeit rather mundane and 'dated' technique to emerge across the Arab world involved people who had never before participated in any kind of political activity finding themselves gathering knowledge while acquiring skills, techniques, tactical knowledge and above all the ability to cooperate effectively with others. In effect, they were deepening their commitment just because they were caught up in the learning experience of praxis and actual events, actions and experiences on the streets. To illustrate these points, we end with two quotes taken from the real blogs of Egyptian protestors, published in *The Guardian* on 28 January 2011 under the heading 'The word on the street':

> The protests have drawn Egyptians from all walks of life, many of whom have never participated in demonstrations and feel they need to voice their opinion. Listening to the protestors, one gets the feeling that they have not been deterred by the severity of the beatings; rather, their resolve has been hardened. Before they head to another day of protest, they will have exchanged stories of heroism and courage, humanity and unity.

> Although I am not on the streets, the sentiments I am receiving in emails and messages from people on the ground are different from what I expected. They aren't talking about hope and what could be – instead, they are walking and marching for real change. And they are not withdrawing after government efforts to silence them through violence and even murder.

REVIEW

Over the past few decades we have seen the emergence of a tangible and proactive global civil society that is able to respond to, and is empowered by, a conjunction of wider currents of change. We have also, although less obviously, seen the early signs of a global public opinion emerging from the more widespread use of the various and often new lines of communication, each with its own advantages, limitations and risks. Campaigns and social movements, as well as the growing number of INGOs, which often serve as focal points around which other activities cohere, are key ingredients in the operation of global civil society. Although the political climate and availability of economic resources in the South place it in a less favourable position than the North, the various features of a global civil society have become very much more apparent there too. Thus, important cross-national, cross-issue and North–South linkages have been established, particularly over the wide-ranging impact that the imposition of neoliberal economic policies has had on the economies of the South. Crucial in this respect is the fact that there is now widespread recognition of the interconnected and universal nature of the problems we all confront, coupled with enhanced opportunities to engage in more effective strategies for global cooperation. Our understanding of the nature and activities of global civil society and movements has given sociologists the tools with which to examine how global society is emerging from below.

Visit the companion website at www.palgrave.com/sociology/cohen3e for extra materials to check and expand your learning, including interactive self-test questions, mind maps making links between key themes, annotated web links to sociological research, data and key sociological thinkers, a searchable glossary and much more.

FURTHER READING

Global Civil Society, the series of books edited by H. Anheier et al. and published every year from 2001 to 2009, provides a mine of detailed and interesting information, with up-to-date explanations for and debates on a host of themes and issues relating to global civil society.

R. Kiely's *The Clash of Globalizations: Neo-liberalism, the Third Way and Anti-globalization* (2005b) also offers a thoughtful and accessible exploration of the impact of neoliberalism on people worldwide and the struggles going on between the pro- and anti-globalizing forces in the world at present.

R. Munck's *Globalization and Contestation* (2007) is very readable and covers many recent debates on global social movements and related activities.

QUESTIONS AND ASSIGNMENTS

1. Define 'global civil society', and list and classify the main agencies involved in its generation. Using any case study, such as the UN, Médecins Sans Frontières, Jubilee 2000 or the Global Justice Movement, examine the roles this particular agent has played.

2. What factors explain the tendency over the past 15 or so years for social movements and NGOs to 'go global'? Assess their relative significance.

3. Why is it so important for people who want to elaborate a global sociology to study global social movements?

20
Towards a safe global environment

Until recently, the viability of nature, or the biosphere (Chapter 2), was not especially at risk from humans. However, the exploitation of the planet's resources in our relentless scramble for greater wealth is damaging the conditions that ultimately make material progress and, indeed, life itself possible. We start this chapter with a summary of the current scientific evidence suggesting that human action is harming the biosphere, particularly through global warming and the associated climate change to which it gives rise. We show how one needs to consider the risk of climate change alongside other impending dangers, especially energy insecurity, as the demand for fossil fuels increasingly exceeds the available supply of accessible stocks. We then briefly consider the controversies surrounding what kinds of technological and economic remedies might be available for limiting the destruction of the biosphere. This, in turn, leads us into an analysis of the changing nature of the green movement and the approaches, arguments and divisions it encompasses.

TRANSBOUNDARY ENVIRONMENTAL PROBLEMS

Some environmental crises are more or less confined to one location. A shocking instance of this was the release of methyl isocynate gas from a plant in Bhopal, India, in 1984. Others occur in one place but have a transnational impact, like the nuclear explosion at the Chernobyl plant in the Ukraine in 1986, which spread radioactive material over much of Europe. In contrast, many human actions impact on the planetary biosphere as a whole and not simply on the locality where they originate. The main examples of such environmental problems are global warming, ozone depletion, transboundary air pollution (especially acid rain), and the loss of biodiversity, namely the declining variety of species able to survive on our planet. Widespread deforestation and other kinds of commercial development are gradually eliminating the unique habitats in which insect, animal,

> ### ACID RAIN
> This is caused by the emission of toxic gases such as sulphur and nitrogen oxides, which are then carried by winds and rain.

bird and plant species have evolved. The relentless logging of tropical forests is especially worrying. They cover only 7% of the world's land but contain approximately half its species (Seager 1995: 16). As species diminish, so too does the storehouse of possible life forms we may need in future for medical or other purposes. At the same time, our aesthetic delight in the planet's infinite variety is despoiled.

There are several reasons why these phenomena are becoming increasingly global. First, the biosphere is intrinsically planetary and all-encompassing in its scope. Accordingly, winds and air flows, temperature changes, weather patterns, sea currents and tides all interact and traverse the globe from the poles to the tropics. Irrespective of where they actually occur, therefore, human activities feed into these gigantic systems and their impact is dispersed. Thus, the pollution-generating activities in which most people engage push wastes, gases, minute amounts of toxic poisons or radioactivity from nuclear power stations around the world into rivers, seas, landfill sites and the atmosphere. Moreover, as Beck (1992: 23, 38) observes, the perpetrators become the victims through what he calls the 'boomerang effect'. For example, chemical-intensive agriculture eventually leads to declining soil fertility and soil erosion and the disappearance of wild plants and animals. Meanwhile, the lead in our petrol, plus numerous other chemical traces, may turn up in breast milk consumed by babies in distant cities. Clearly, such actions affect the biosphere but do not respect national boundaries: they impact on everyone. Acting alone, states can no longer protect their citizens from environmental damage.

Second, growing international trade and global economic interdependence increase the volume of tankers and ships discharging oil and other substances into the oceans and fill the skies with air-polluting traffic. Some developing countries – for example in West Africa – have accepted hazardous wastes from rich countries. The most notorious case concerned an Amsterdam-based company, Trafigura, dumping considerable qualities of waste in Côte d'Ivoire, which newspapers and the BBC alleged had led to death and serious illnesses. The BBC's programme, *Newsnight*, was forced to withdraw some of its reports (19 December 2009) but insisted that the substance of its coverage was accurate. The need to generate foreign exchange for debt repayment has encouraged some developing countries to accelerate the rate at which their forests are being cut down. This, in turn, is reducing the planet's capacity to absorb carbon dioxide (CO_2).

A PAUSE TO REFLECT

With increased globalization, there appears to be a globalization of risk. Can enhanced cooperation between nation-states meet transboundary environmental issues, or do the scale of the problem and the sudden global effects of risk require a more permanent arm of global government concerned with managing global threats to the environment? If we think such a body is necessary, how can it be set up and how can democratic accountability be assured?

A third crucial factor is the globalization of industrial development. As more developing countries, especially the BRIC group, attain higher levels of economic growth, so world energy demand rises and the emissions of CO_2 and other greenhouse gases (see below) must also increase. By 2009, developing countries were already responsible for half of all global CO_2 emissions and unless serious attempts are made to counter this, the figure may reach 70% by 2030 (Giddens 2009: 201). China contributes the largest part. In fact, between 2007 and 2010, but probably in 2009 (Zhang 2008: 82), China pushed the USA into second place as the world's single largest CO_2 emitter. This is due not only to economic growth but also to China's considerable dependence on national coal deposits, although oil imports also doubled between 1999 and 2004 (Dennis and Urry 2009: 10). Unfortunately, coal emits higher amounts of CO_2 than the other two main sources of fossil fuel – oil and natural gas. Moreover, by 2010 China was building the equivalent of nearly two new coal-fired power stations every week (Giddens 2009: 185).China's population size is also crucial. Much the same is true of India, which, until recently, was only responsible for 3% of emissions. Again, however, rapid growth and a high dependence on coal, coupled with a vast population, are rapidly pushing up India's share of global emissions.

In the early 1990s, Durning (1992) defined the world's 'consuming class' – consisting at that time of the 1.1 billion people who were most responsible for energy consumption and pollution – in the following way. Its members eat meat and processed/packaged foods, depend on numerous energy-intensive gadgets, live in climate-controlled buildings supplied with abundant hot water, and travel in private cars and jet aeroplanes. They consume goods that are soon thrown away when fashions change. Most live in the advanced countries but the number also included about one-fifth of wealthy people living in the South. Building on Durning's work, Bentley (2003) estimated that, by 2003, the consuming class had grown to 1.7 billion members – around one-quarter of the world – but nearly half live in developing nations (48%). China and India alone provided over 20% of this group – 362 million individuals compared with 350 million in Western Europe.

BOX 20.1 Climate change: two African case studies

Climate change is already affecting many areas in Africa where droughts and floods have become more commonplace than previously.

Darfur

The annual rains in the semi-arid Sahel belt have become more irregular and are likely either to fail altogether in some years or to arrive in bursts that cause erosion, making farming difficult. The Darfur area of eastern Sudan has been particularly badly affected over the past 40 or so years and this has created difficulties and sometimes conflicts between traditional pastoral people seeking grass for their herds and settled farmers trying to preserve water. The long drought in this region has also caused neighbouring Lake Chad to dry up and the ensuing civil war led to armed migrants crossing the border into Darfur. The periodic droughts in the area have compounded land disputes between livestock herders and those who need even more water for sedentary agriculture. Added to this was the discovery of significant oil reserves in Darfur and its surrounding regions. According to the Sudanese authorities, new oil wells are due to come on stream in 2012 and the companies include China's biggest oil producer, China National Petroleum Company. According to the Sudanese government, the civil war, which commenced in 1991, resulted in the deaths of 19,500 civilians, while an NGO, the Coalition for International Justice, claimed in 2008 that the death toll had exceeded 400,000 people. As Neale (2008: 214) asserts: 'it was the intersection of the local war for grass and the global war for oil that created horror in Darfur'.

Uganda

Farmers in Uganda working their land on the banks of the Semliki River face a growing threat from the increased tendency of the river to swell with flood water and then overspill, thus indicating that its course is shifting. Sometimes, this alters the layout of farms so that land becomes stranded on the other side of the river in the neighbouring country, the Democratic Republic of the Congo (DRC), where the latter's government now exercises control over its use (Randerson 2010).

The impact of rising local temperatures

Increased flooding is directly linked to the impact of global warming on the Rwenzori mountains just north of the equator, which feed the waters of the Semliki River. Some of the mountains are over 5,000 metres high and are covered in snow for much of the year. Records from 1906 reveal that there were 43 glaciers flowing in six mountains. Now, only three mountains contain glaciers and those remaining have shrunk to less than one-quarter of their cover a century ago. Not only are melting snow and glaciers causing the Semliki River to flood but climate change has also increased the incidence of heavy rainfall, although the latter has also become more erratic.

Additional insecurities

1. With changes to seasons, farmers can no longer rely on a reasonably predictable climate. This makes it difficult for them to decide when to plant or harvest their crops.

2. Diseases such as malaria are spreading into areas where their impact was formerly limited or unknown.

3. The Semliki River marks the official border between Uganda and the DRC, so its movement creates uncertainty about both land ownership and political stability, especially since intense ethnic tensions characterize this border region.

4. In a country plagued by civil war, government and rebel forces had fought over the DRC territory only a few years earlier. The Ugandan farmers now fear that further political conflicts in the DRC, coupled with future border conflicts over land ownership and the river's moving banks may further threaten their struggles to grow food (Randerson 2010).

Sources: Neale (2008); Randerson (2010).

If we take cars as a significant indicator of this process, by 2005 China's burgeoning middle class was driving 21 million cars and China was already the world's second largest market for them (Dennis and Urry 2009: 24, 44). It is predicted that if per capita car ownership reaches US levels, there will eventually be around 970 million cars choking up China's roads (Dennis and Urry 2009: 24). Putting this another way, should every global inhabitant ultimately consume energy to the same degree as in North America today, world energy consumption will increase five times, as will greenhouse gases (Combarnous and Bonnet 2008: 16), and this takes no account of predicted world population growth.

THE EVIDENCE FOR GLOBAL WARMING AND CLIMATE CHANGE

Of all the threats to the biosphere, and therefore to human life, global warming is potentially the most damaging. Some of the gases making up the atmosphere encircling planet earth, particularly CO_2 and methane, but also water vapour, act as a shield to prevent much of the sun's energy from escaping although some is radiated back. These greenhouse gases keep the earth sufficiently warm to permit current life forms to flourish. However, with worldwide industrialization and the growing emissions of greenhouse gases, there is considerable scientific evidence to suggest that average global temperatures are rising. Moreover, the accumulation of greenhouse gases in the atmosphere as a result of behaviour that has already occurred means that temperatures will rise further even if we act to reduce emissions now. The real concern about global warming is that, as temperatures rise, world climatic patterns will become unpredictable, erratic and extreme. Climate change increases not only the risk of more frequent and intense storms and hurricanes, floods and droughts, but also the prospect of sea levels rising as a result of mountain glaciers, polar icecaps, previously frozen seas and the Siberian tundra gradually melting. This scenario, in turn, raises the spectre of food shortages and rising prices, increasingly uninhabitable coastal cities, chronic water shortages and spreading desert areas, failing states, and increased geopolitical conflicts over dwindling resources (see, for example, Dennis and Urry 2009: 138–41, 151–3).

GLOBAL WARMING

This is the process, which has been continuing since the Industrial Revolution, whereby increased emissions and accumulations of greenhouse gases in the atmosphere are trapping a greater proportion of the sun's heat than formerly, thereby leading to a rise in average planetary temperatures.

The prestigious scientists associated with the Intergovernmental Panel on Climate Change (IPCC) – formed in 1988 – originally came together to report the evidence of global warming to governments. By 1995 it included nearly 2,500 eminent scientists from about 40 countries. A minority of scientists – many funded by right-wing think tanks and/or heavy industries, including producers of fossil fuels (Rowell 1996) – continue to dispute the arguments put forward by the IPCC and environmental groups. However, most experts now consider the evidence of global warming irrefutable (Bunyard 2004) and 'unequivocal' (Amen et al. 2008: 50). Drawing partly on the findings discussed in the 2007 IPCC report, the evidence for global warming includes the following:

- The total amount of measurable CO_2 present in the earth's atmosphere is currently higher than at any time during the past 650,000 years.
- CO_2 emissions from human activity have risen by 80% since 1970 and are predicted to double within the next 20 years (Amen et al. 2008: 50).
- The world's average temperature has risen by 0.74^0C since around 1900. Given current trends, many governments and scientists now believe that, without drastic worldwide action to rein back CO_2 emissions, over the coming decades average global temperatures will almost certainly rise by at least 2^0C, possibly more. Of course, even this relatively small increase will endanger the lives of millions of people.
- Indeed, should this 2^0C target prove impossible, the temperature might increase by as much as 6^0C or more by 2100. This could trip yet further changes, such as releasing the vast methane gas deposits currently locked up in the frozen Siberian tundra, and push the earth's climate beyond any human capacity to take counteraction.
- Since the mid-1960s, space travel and communications technology have yielded ever more vivid images of earth. Satellites provide much more accurate evidence than ever before of the increasingly global extent of environmental destruction (Milton 1996: 177). For example, satellite data show that the Arctic sea ice is shrinking annually by almost 3% (Giddens 2009: 18–22).
- Indeed, data collected by the US National Snow and Ice Data Center on thinning Arctic ice shows that the summer ice cover is dwindling so rapidly that it may disappear in or before 2013 rather than around 2070 as was once thought (McKie 2008).
- Freak storms, hurricanes, unprecedented floods and other climatic events – including forest fires, droughts and heat waves – seem to have become everyday news items in recent years.

GLOBAL THINKERS 20   ULRICH BECK (1944–)

The risk society and different modernities
Beck's central interest has been the changing nature of social action and reflexivity as modernity unfolds against the background of increasing risks.

The era of the first or simple modernity
Capitalist industrialization involved detraditionalization – breaking with past institutions – but also the establishment of others such as the nuclear family, class solidarity, multigenerational working-class communities, nationhood and, eventually, social welfare. The prevailing logic involved overcoming scarcity through scientific rationality and capitalist efficiency and the struggle to achieve a more equitable redistribution of resources. Actors respected science while most risks generated by modernity were local and insurable through the calculation of probability.

The second/reflexive modernity and the world ecological risk society
It became increasingly obvious that the cumulative consequences of industrialization had spawned huge environmental 'side effects', such as nuclear contamination, chemical pollution, increasing greenhouse gas emissions and their link to global warming, the release of biogenetic organisms into farming, and a series of food scares such as 'mad cow disease'. None were predicted, their long-term impact is unknowable, they are often global in scope and they are uninsurable.

The wider scope of risk
Humanity faces additional risks and transformations:

- Social actors need to construct their own identities and life courses as the former safe structures of family, class and community weaken and the individual becomes the key social unit.

- Nowhere is this more evident than through the 'gender revolution' of the past 30 years. Now, most women expect to work and their ability to determine their identity and economic autonomy means they can demand much more equitable relationships.

- Continuing technological changes, economic globalization and the rise of post-Fordist flexible capitalism have combined to reduce job security and placed a downward pressure on wage levels and worker power.

Reflexive modernity and a new bottom-up politics

To cope with this world risk society, we need a new type of reflexivity based on 'self-confrontation'. This enables us to take personal responsibility for our private lives and the wider consequences of modernity. Globalization and individualization are like the two ends of a telescope; lone individuals across the world, and their actions, interpenetrate and shape each other's lives through interconnecting global forces. Dealing with all this requires the invention of a more radical, grassroots, transnational politics – confronting old institutions from both inside and outside.

Sources: Beck (1999a, 1999b, 2000a, 2000b); Beck and Beck-Gernsheim (2002).

GLOBAL WARMING AND ENERGY SECURITY

Climate change and its dangers are not the only global risks humans face. Many observers are claiming that energy security is equally crucial. In this section, we first examine the question of energy security and its implications, with particular reference to oil, before explaining how and why climate change and energy security are closely entwined issues that require joint responses.

OIL AND ENERGY SECURITY

Our main worry about energy security is that fossil fuels are either beginning to run out and/ or will become much more expensive. Three fossil fuels – oil, natural gas and coal – between them provide more that four-fifths of current world energy needs (Afgan 2008: 32); nuclear energy, hydroelectric power and renewables, such as wind, supply the remainder. There are several reasons why the issue of oil stocks is currently a major cause for concern.

OIL AND GLOBAL TRANSPORT

Oil underpins around 98% of all world transport, provides 20% of electricity consumption and the demand for it rises every year (Dennis and Urry 2009: 17). Modern armaments and warfare also depend on oil and it is crucial in agriculture (fertilizers and tractors) and for the manufacture of plastics, chemicals and many other materials. As Dennis and Urry (2009: 17–18) comment: 'the infrastructures of developed and developing countries are predicated on the plentiful supply of "cheap" oil to lubricate many areas of industrial, military and commercial life'.

WHEN WILL OIL PEAK?

Many commentators claim that oil production is about to peak or has already passed that point. The term 'peak oil' refers to a situation in which half of all possible oil reserves have already been extracted and future reserves become harder to find and much more expensive to obtain – such as the oil reserves located on deep ocean beds in the Gulf of Mexico, under the Atlantic icecap, or in the oil (tar) sands in Canada. This contrasts markedly with the vast, though diminishing, and relatively accessible oil reserves in Middle East countries such as Saudi Arabia, Iraq and Kuwait, which have so far provided the lion's share of world resources. Estimates differ but some experts fear that the oil peak occurred around five years ago (Dennis and Urry 2009: 14–15). Thus, the largest oilfields were discovered more than 40 years ago, while the quantities found recently tend to be smaller (Giddens 2009: 40–1). More than 60 oil-producing countries are known to have passed their peak production levels (Giddens 2009: 41). Nevertheless, the 'proven recoverable reserves of oil … including tar sand, are estimated to last approximately … 40 to 50 years' (Combarnous and Bonnet 2008: 5–6); similarly, the International Energy Authority claims that oil will not peak before 2030. However, the latter also observed that around $360bn per annum will need to be invested over the next 20 years to maintain current production levels and meet rising demand (Giddens 2009: 41).

FUTURE RISING OIL PRICES

Whoever proves correct on this issue, we can be certain that oil prices will rise, along with the global costs of food, heating, holidays, medical services and much else. Indeed, in 2008, prior to the world recession, oil prices rose to $147 a barrel compared with an average of $10 in the late 1990s. Prices retreated soon after as world output fell, but they were rising sharply again in late 2010, despite the tentative nature of the global economic recovery. In early 2012, the price of oil was around $100 per barrel.

THE SCRAMBLE FOR OIL AND GEOPOLITICAL TENSIONS

Intense competition between governments desperate to secure future access for their national economies is likely to generate geopolitical tensions and perhaps even the risk of open conflicts and wars. US involvement in Middle East politics (Chapter 5) is an obvious example of America's determination to gain access to future key world reserves, especially since its own fields began to decline in 1970. US support for oppressive governments, as in Saudi Arabia, and the war in Iraq are but two among many other consequences. The US intervention in the region, in turn, helped motivate extreme Islamic movements to set up worldwide terrorist networks. China has some of the worst polluted cites in the world (causing expensive health problems); acid rain blights one-third of its land; it faces an annual loss of between 3 and 8% of its GDP caused by environmental problems; and its land, water and air resources are all under pressure (Zhang 2008: 81–2). In effect, the Chinese government desperately needs to set in place a 'sustainable development framework' (Zhang 2008: 82). There is some evidence this is now happening, but China's need to scour the world for minerals and fuel, especially oil, is also strong. This has been particularly evident in Africa where China has poured in investment and supplied military equipment to several unpleasant regimes (Giddens 2009: 205–7). The genocidal war and mass murder that has blighted Darfur in Sudan is partly linked to climate change and prolonged drought, but the struggle to control the region's oil reserves also provided a central ingredient (see Box 20.1). For this reason, China formed an alliance with the Sudanese government, and provided finance, arms and military training (Neale 2008: 242–5). For a time, too, it refused to support the UN in condemning the Sudanese government's involvement in the Darfur war (Giddens 2009: 205).

TWIN RISKS: CLIMATE CHANGE AND ENERGY SECURITY

The risks associated with global warming and energy security are closely intertwined. After all, it is the growing consumption of oil, coal and natural gas that is causing global warming. The goal of energy security gives governments a strong additional incentive to reduce their dependence on fossil fuels, especially oil. In particular, it would help them avoid or reduce the 'threat of petro-political blackmail' (Dennis and Urry 2009: 17) from unpleasant oil (and natural gas) regimes, the possibility of interstate conflicts, or ever higher oil prices. Reducing their dependence on fossil fuels for energy would simultaneously limit greenhouse gas emissions. Dennis and Urry (2009: 13) explain how our lives depend on several vast interlocking systems all based on a carbon economy. This includes our obsession with owning private cars, the organization of fossil fuel production and distribution, with its links to transport, industry, agriculture and water supplies, and the threats to the biosphere from global warming. The way in which these systems interact suggests that a crisis in one is likely to trigger or worsen a failure or crisis in another. As Dennis and Urry (2009: 13) explain:

> various systems reverberate against each other. … It is the simultaneity of converging shifts that creates significant changes. Thus, resource depletion (peak oil) and climate change may come to overload a fragile global system, creating the possibility of catastrophic failure unless those carbon systems from the twentieth century have begun to be displaced.

FIGURE 20.1 Harbour Car Park, Sydney, Australia, showing our continuing love affair with the car
The numbers of motorists are set to rise massively in the BRIC countries. By 2005, Indian cars spewed out 219 million tonnes of carbon dioxide, an amount set to increase sevenfold by 2035 to 1470 million tonnes if the present car ownership trend in India continues (*The Guardian*, 11 June 2008).

TECHNOLOGY AND LIFESTYLE SOLUTIONS TO GLOBAL WARMING

Nobody denies that action to reduce global warming is urgently required. Just within the short period between 2007 and 2010, there were three major international conferences on the topic – in Bali, Copenhagen and Cancún, Mexico. These followed several earlier events on the same theme. The difficulty is to agree what changes in policy, national and international regulations, and the lifestyles of world citizens are most necessary to achieve this goal and – crucially – how the costs of ensuring environmental security are to be shared.

We now consider what technologies and lifestyle cultures are most appropriate for, and likely to procure, an environmentally safe future. There seem to be three possible strategies, each with its detractors and protagonists. These are:

1. Continue to depend on fossil fuels and other existing energy sources, such as nuclear power, but find ways to reduce their emissions and other dangers.

2. Rapidly replace fossil fuels with renewable energy sources that emit little or no green-house gases.

3. Move to a form of society that is less obsessed with the pursuit of economic growth and rising living standards, thereby reducing the dangers of a high carbon economy.

Obviously, these three strategies can be combined in various ways. This pertains especially to options 1 and 2 and most serious writing attempts to do just this. We now briefly highlight some of the current data and arguments relating to these three scenarios and their implications.

CLEAN UP CURRENT ENERGY SOURCES

Coal

Known oil and natural gas reserves are expected to last approximately 40–50 years, at current rates of consumption, although the cost of obtaining them will rise, probably hugely. Estimates of unexcavated coal reserves are much larger and might last several centuries at current consumption levels (Combarnous and Bonnet 2008: 5). Fossil fuels currently supply more than 80% of world energy needs; their consumption is rising fast and they are the main culprits in causing greenhouse gas emissions, with coal in the lead. Nuclear power, by contrast, emits no CO_2 or other gases and supplies of uranium are currently plentiful. As a possible substitute for fossil fuels, however, it incurs its own awesome risks. These include:

- the vast cost of building and eventually decommissioning nuclear power stations
- the long period before they produce electricity
- the possibility of terrorists or criminals gaining access to nuclear material
- the unimaginable destruction that would result from an accident
- the expense involved in disposing of nuclear waste, given that it constitutes a danger for many thousands of years.

For these reasons, there have been numerous campaigns committed to preventing further investment in this technology, and for this and other reasons the US and other governments – France being an exception – halted or slowed down their nuclear programmes from the 1970s. How, if at all, can these dilemmas be resolved?

Several technologies now exist that can separate and capture the carbon emitted when coal is burned, although it then has to be stored deep underground or in the seabed in deep parts of the ocean so that it cannot escape into the atmosphere. Given the world's huge coal reserves and their importance in generating electricity, improving carbon capture technologies and fostering their widespread use seems an obvious way forward. However, carbon capture technologies are very expensive and still experimental. Persuading the huge users of coal in the developing world, especially China and India, to adopt carbon capture on a large scale will not be easy, unless the advanced countries agree to subsidize the transfer of this – and other – carbon-reducing technologies. (In fact, just such an agreement appears to have been reached during the UN Climate Change Conference at Cancún in December 2010.) Experts suggest that the widespread adoption of carbon capture technologies could lead to a world emission reduction of between 70 and 85% (Kakaras et al. 2008: 246).

Nuclear power

Over the next two decades, it is anticipated that third and fourth generations of nuclear reactors will come on stream. There is confidence, too, that these will prove much safer than earlier models in terms of treating spent nuclear fuel, minimizing the generation of radioactive waste or its long-term disposal and storage (Cacuci 2008: 174–5). The continued public opposition to a revived nuclear power programme was given greater impetus by the disastrous events at the Fukushima Daiichi nuclear power plant in 2011. However, a significant body of scientists argue that only by investing in more advanced nuclear reactors can societies find an 'effective interim solution for stopping the ominous climate change before it is too late' (Hanjalić 2008: xx). Second, nuclear energy can serve as a stopgap measure helping to fill the energy gap until renewable energy sources come fully on stream. Giddens (2009: 132) shares this view, albeit with reservations. Writing about the UK, where the government is committed to an EU target involving reliance on renewable sources for 16% of its energy by 2020, he suggests that it is 'difficult' to see how this can be achieved if 'nuclear energy is allowed to lapse'. Most countries are in a similar position.

A PAUSE TO REFLECT

Many admired the bravery of the so-called 'Fukushima 50', the firefighters and workers who radiated themselves to protect the wider community in Japan and safeguard the environment after a tsunami destroyed the plant. Sociologists see such behaviour as an example of a 'gift relationship', whereby certain people at certain times give up their self-interest in favour of the greater good. Is the gift relationship more widespread than is sometimes thought? Is the health of the society indicated by acts of self-sacrifice?

REDUCE POWER/ENERGY NEEDS

Following the huge rises in oil prices during the 1970s, several countries, particularly Japan, started to invest in technologies that would reduce energy consumption. Over time, this has helped to slow carbon emissions. Consequently, in Japan – and elsewhere – the energy cost involved in producing steel has fallen by around 20% since the 1970s (Combarnous and Bonnet 2008: 15). Quite stringent gains have also been made in reducing the amount of energy needed both to manufacture and use vehicles. For example, in response largely to OPEC (Organization of the Petroleum Exporting Countries) oil price rises, in the 1970s the US federal government demanded that average car fuel consumption must be halved by 1984. Car manufacturers responded by doubling vehicle power output from the same input of fuel (Neale 2008: 142) and this has produced a fall of around one-quarter in fuel consumption. Other world car manufacturers, such as Toyota, took similar steps and many governments have responded with tiered car tax rates and other incentives encouraging owners to buy energy-efficient as well as less polluting cars (Combarnous and Bonnet 2008:15). Looking at the overall picture, the scope for further reducing energy consumption through cleaner technology over a vast span of goods and services – helped by digitization – offers one of the best strategies for reducing emissions.

© KOJI SASAHARA/AP/PRESS ASSOCIATION IMAGES

FIGURE 20.2 'No nukes' protest sign
A protester shows a 'No nukes' sign as they march during an anti-nuclear power demonstration in Tokyo, in the wake of the 2011 Fukushima disaster.

DEVELOP RENEWABLE ENERGY SOURCES

Because of the threats to energy security, even many of the sceptics about global warming recognize that developing renewable sources must become a long-term priority. However, such a programme is far from being unproblematic. In what follows, we cannot consider all possibilities. For example, the difficulties involved in harnessing energy from hydrogen are too complex to be discussed here (but see the discussion in van de Krol and Schoonman 2008). Nevertheless, we now examine some of the most promising renewable energies and their disadvantages.

Wind power

As a free energy source that emits no emissions – except when turbines are produced and installed – wind is an obvious candidate. Of course, in Europe and elsewhere, windmills were widely used for centuries to mill grain and pump water. Wind turbines currently constitute the fastest growing alternative energy source worldwide and have increased by around 30% a year since the 1970s. Nearly three-quarters of this occurred in Europe. It is estimated that wind power will provide around 12% of Europe's electricity by 2020. Mostly manufactured by a few TNCs, such as Siemens and General Electric, wind turbines have increased 10 times in size since 1990 and the largest sites will soon have an energy capacity similar to those of fossil fuel plants (van de Kuik et al. 2008). Among the drawbacks to wind power are the following:

*   Local communities unhappy about the blighting of countryside views and/or noisy turbines often oppose its use.
*   Because wind power is intrinsically intermittent, supplementary power sources are required to ensure continuity, although these could be renewables as well.
*   This also makes it difficult to link wind power into the electricity grid system, although this can be overcome.
*   Offshore wind power is much more cost-effective because generation is less often interrupted by falling winds, but it is also more expensive.
*   The current cost of wind power is considerably higher than that of fossil fuels, although this disadvantage diminishes with windy sites and very large turbines. This cost differential will reduce or disappear as the scale of operations rises.
*   Like other renewable energy sources, developing wind power has depended on government subsidies, guaranteed supply contracts and tax advantages. The 'carbon corporation' (Neale 2008: 138) lobby and/or free-market advocates can use these cost differences as an argument for inhibiting further wind power development (van de Kuik et al. 2008).

Geothermal energy

Geothermal energy involves harvesting the heat present in the rocks below the earth's surface; it is cheaper and easier to do where volcanic activity occurs near the surface, for example in Iceland. A technology is being developed that involves injecting water. This then heats up through contact with deep hot rocks before being brought back to the surface to drive electricity generation. Geothermal technology has potential but will require government support (Giddens 2009: 134).

Wave and tidal power

Wave and tidal power involve the installation of various gadgets at strategic locations to harness the flow of sea and river currents and tides that are then linked to electricity grid systems. Neither of these possibilities is cheap or easy and, like wind power, water flows fluctuate.

Solar energy

Solar energy may prove the most promising renewable energy source. It also forms the basis for fossil fuels, which originally depended for their creation on the sun's energy. So intense and universal are the solar rays hitting the earth that only 0.13% of the earth's surface could, in theory, supply the entire world's energy requirements, a calculation based on the use of solar panels of 10% efficiency for conversion into usable electric power (McEvoy and Grätzel 2008: 99–100). Indeed, there has been speculation that the installation of a vast network of the most advanced photovoltaic (PV) cells (which convert sunlight directly into electricity) across part of the Sahara could provide completely clean energy in volume and forever. However, this would require international corporate and government collaboration on a colossal scale. There are also other difficulties associated with solar power.

The sun's energy does not fall evenly or consistently on the planet. Even near the equator, cloud cover and humidity hinder absorption. There are also diurnal and seasonal fluctuations. Given its intermittent nature, there are questions concerning the need to store the energy gathered by PV cells so that its power is available all year round and on a large scale for industry and cities, although it is highly practical for small communities (Giddens 2009: 133–4). For this and other reasons, the current cost of generating electricity from solar energy is considerably higher than for fossil fuels. Europe has advanced furthest in harnessing solar power, particularly Germany, with 57% of the world's capacity – based partly on government assistance (McEvoy and Grätzel 2008: 117). Several conditions are necessary if solar power is to become more price competitive with fossil fuels:

- The price of the latter needs to continue rising, which seems highly likely.
- Government support for research and industry will remain essential, and this may be achieved more effectively where governments combine resources for long-term programmes, as in the EU.
- Further technological advance is needed so that the efficiency, reliability, lifetime duration of solar cells, problems of energy storage and links to grid systems are improved or resolved (McEvoy and Grätzel 2008: 99–101, 116–18).

Biofuels

There has been a massive expansion recently in investing in large-scale agricultural crops such as sugar cane, sunflowers, rape and oil palm for conversion to usable energy. Leading world exporters of crops for conversion to biofuels such as ethanol, which can be mixed with petrol or diesel, include the USA (corn), Brazil (sugar cane), Indonesia (palm oil) and China (oilseed). The rationale for expanding biofuel cultivation is that, like forests, growing crops absorb CO_2 and this cancels out the emissions produced when they are harvested, transported and converted into energy that can readily be utilized. In addition, unlike fossil fuels, biofuels are replaceable through continuous cultivation.

However, again, problems arise:

1. Transferring farm land to biofuels worldwide reduces the cultivation of staple food crops. Biofuel cultivation has been partly blamed for the rise in world food prices shortly before the 2008 recession. For example, 40% of the crop land currently used in the USA and Europe would be needed to satisfy 10% of vehicle fuel consumption in those two areas (Dennis and Urry 2009: 68–9). The risk of future food shortages is unlikely to disappear.
2. The vast agribusiness projects that increasingly manage biofuel farming, which governments often support, frequently end up displacing small farmers from their land. Recently, the UN claimed that perhaps up to 60 million indigenous people will become 'agro-fuel refugees' with expanding world acreage (cited in Dennis and Urry 2009: 68–9).
3. There are doubts about whether biofuels contribute much, if anything, to carbon emission reductions. For example, fossil fuels are needed to power tractors, provide fertiliz-

ers, as well as transport and later refine crops like sugar cane into ethanol. Similarly, where huge land areas are cleared for biofuel crops by cutting down savannah grasslands or engaging in massive deforestation, the fossil fuels needed to undertake such projects, coupled with the CO_2 released when vegetation is burned, generate more omissions than are saved by biocultivation (Neale 2008: 102–3).

In summary, long-term commitment and planning are required before renewables can seriously replace fossil fuels. This will be expensive, sometimes risky, have unforeseen consequences, and will certainly not happen on the scale required or with the urgency demanded unless considerable government support becomes available. Moreover, our dependence on fossil fuels – preferably with lower carbon-based technologies – and/or on nuclear energy may need to continue while we gradually develop renewable sources until they become the dominant form.

ADOPT A LOW CARBON ECONOMY AND A LESS MATERIALISTIC LIFESTYLE

Two very different approaches to adopting a low carbon economy and a less materialistic lifestyle can be identified, although there are overlaps. We might describe it as a 'soft' model of environmental responsibility, in which modernity remains fundamental to human life, or as a 'tough' and much more demanding approach in which nature's needs gain greater priority and societies are therefore required to undergo drastic change, probably involving some move away from modernity.

'Soft' environmental adaptation: modernity retained

With the 'soft' model of environmental responsibility, citizens' lifestyles will have to change in many respects, but will not require deep sacrifices and transformations. Giddens (2009: 65–7) suggests that the advanced economies will certainly have to recognize their 'overdevelopment' and slow down their pursuit of economic growth while concentrating more on improving the quality of life for citizens. This will give the poorer economies more chance to catch up, even though that will also involve further global warming. Nevertheless, societies will remain recognizably modern, more urban than rural, and dependent on science and technology, while utilizing a mix of state and market politics. Even this relatively modest degree of change, however, raises some difficult issues with respect to winning public support.

Take the case of killing whales, a practice that Japanese companies engage in ostensibly for scientific research, although campaigners insist that it is a cover for the commercial use of whale meat. The market for that meat is in any case diminishing in Japan, particularly among younger Japanese, so it would take little sacrifice to eliminate this food from the Japanese diet. Again, there are simple substitutes for chlorofluorocarbons, which pose a serious hazard to the ozone layer. Environmental campaigners or governments often find it difficult to 'package measures … in appealing and attractive terms where there are perceived threats to people's standards of living or freedom of choice' (Newell 2006: 90). The intergenerational implications of a situation in which the 'benefits of action will be felt in years to come but sacrifices have to be made now' (Newell 2006: 109) further complicate the problem.

Tough environmentalism: nature's needs gain greater prominence

At least since the 1970s, some radical 'deep green' groups within the environmental movement have demanded far more fundamental changes than voluntary changes in people's behaviour. The philosophical roots behind this kind of thinking lie partly in nineteenth-century European romanticism, where artists, poets and others led a reaction to the industrial and urban transformation then taking place. Thus, poets like William Wordsworth eulogized remote regions and rural life and depicted them as sources of spiritual regeneration. Indeed, the first environmental organizations set up in the mid-nineteenth century were committed to preserving areas of outstanding natural beauty and/or the protection of animals and birds. Campaigns were mounted to discourage people from buying fur coats and hats decorated with feathers. Interestingly, the first effective international conservationist NGO, the International Committee for Bird Protection, established in 1922, was concerned with European bird life (McCormick 1989: 23).

One variant of radical green thinking focuses on the pursuit of political or ethical agendas that extend well beyond concerns about global warming, for example the desire to construct a more equitable, democratic society built around localized production and small cooperative communities. Such views are often accompanied by an antipathy towards the state and large businesses, industrialism and powerful institutions. Other groups believe that nature possesses its own intrinsic value and rights and that its needs are of equal or even greater significance than those of humans. Not only should humans respect these as a precondition for resolving environmental risks but nature should also be accorded the central place in our lives because it is much vaster than human society and ultimately ensures our very existence. It also provides a standpoint from which to endow human affairs with meaning beyond our own ephemeral, selfish needs. In such circumstances, an almost 'mystical reverence' (Giddens 2009: 56) for the natural world takes over: we cross into a quasi-religious outlook in which our duty to preserve all living and inanimate things (including all plants, animals, rocks and the wilderness) takes precedence over human needs. Again, too, there is often a parallel distrust of modernity, science and technology, a strong preference for the instigation of low- or no-growth economic trajectories, and an insistence that continuous technological change is likely to incur risks to nature and human life. This being so, Giddens (2009: 53–4) suggests that we should refuse to harness new technologies unless they are proven beyond doubt not to impact adversely on nature.

BOX 20.2 Resisting genetically modified (GM) crops/foods: Europe and India

What are GM crops?

GM crops are those such as soya, maize and oilseed rape that have had their genetic structures modified by introducing specific genes (taken from unrelated life forms such as bacteria) into their genetic code. The two most common modifications involve implanting a gene that either gives crops resistance to certain insects without the use of chemical pesticides, or enables plants to remain healthy when exposed to herbicides so that only weeds are killed when these are applied.

Four TNCs – Syngenta, Bayer CropScience, Monsanto and Du Pont – dominate the agricultural biotech industry. Previous revolutions in agriculture, such as the postwar Green Revolution, harnessed science to farming by breeding higher yielding seeds and linking this to fertilizers and irrigation, but they did not use genetic modification.

The debate over GM crops

The biotech industry argues that GM seeds help farmers because they will need to spend less on pesticides and herbicides. It also claims that GM seeds can help overcome poverty because crops would be more abundant. These companies have cleverly linked their seeds – which can only be produced in laboratories, under licence, and so must be bought anew each year – to their production of herbicides and pesticides. If widely used, they would gain a monopolistic hold over the world's farmers and consumers.

Opponents in Europe

European opposition has focused mainly on three arguments:

1. There is a risk to health from consuming foods derived from GM crops. Consumers demand clearer labelling so they can identify such products.

2. GM cultivation creates huge risks, especially the possibility that cross-pollination by insects will spread the new genes and their properties uncontrollably into the wider environment. Rare butterflies and other insects might be especially liable to harm, thereby threatening biodiversity.

3. The biotech industry is unlikely to be interested in the crops grown by poor Southern farmers compared with the highly commercial crops like soya and maize grown for the meat industry, or for the processed foods consumed by the better off.

Resistance in India

In contrast to the mainly consumer and health-driven concerns of the urban-based anti-GM movement in Europe, the Indian protest focuses on different characteristics:

1. It grew out of much broader based and longstanding opposition to the Green Revolution but also to neoliberal globalization and the power of Western TNCs, particularly seed companies, to undermine farmers' autonomy.

2. Protest has demonstrated a strong rural dimension and small farmers have been at the forefront of campaigns alongside activists. Thus, farmers fear that if pests develop a resistance to the genetic component, they may need to buy more pesticides and so face rising costs and debts. Suicides among highly indebted cotton farmers have grown noticeably in recent years.

3. Like peasants and small farmers across the South, Indian farmers and activists are worried about food security both for their families and their nation but also about the threat of losing their land/livelihood and/or their independence in the face of relentless agricultural commercialization. This is being spearheaded by agribusinesses and governments anxious to accelerate economic growth and means that food crops such as beans, millets and legumes are replaced by commodities for export where large companies have a competitive advantage (Chapter 6).

Sources: Doyle and McEachern (2008: 104–5); Lynas (2004); Rowell (2003).

If these 'tough' environmentalist agendas were implemented, the socioeconomic conditions we have come to regard as 'normal' – and which many of the world's poor probably hope eventually to attain – would almost certainly require radical adjustment, including the acceptance of considerably lower living standards. Giddens's (2009: 49–57) thoughtful and balanced assessment of these issues is worth summarizing here. He suggests that some 'tough' agendas could and probably should be pursued. But this needs to be done in a moderate and careful way that prioritizes the primary goal of combating climate change. What, by contrast, is unhelpful is for deep green and/or radical groups to deploy these strategies as a way of achieving additional goals – such as placing the 'interests' of nature and wilderness areas above those of human beings, or using the environmental crisis as a pretext for seeking a return to a simpler, more decentralized, self-sufficient, equalitarian and democratic form of social life. These may be admirable and desirable goals in their own right and they might form the basis of future global public policies (Chapter 21). However, Giddens is concerned that they should not distract us from the immediate, practical and urgent task of reducing greenhouse gas emissions.

THE CHANGING ENVIRONMENTAL MOVEMENT

The environmental movement is a large and complex phenomenon, which we now briefly explore. We first outline some of the most salient themes in the literature on this important topic and then explore one of these in more detail.

With its evolving priorities, its ever changing character is a primary feature of the movement. For example, the nineteenth-century aesthetic and romantic preoccupation with preserving local wildernesses and rural life has partly given way to a contemporary focus on climate change as a manifestly global issue. The sheer fragmentation and complexity of the environmental movement, including the different priorities of the North and South, is another key theme. Thus, the movement draws on a shifting coalition of scientists, sympathetic government leaders and politicians, INGOs such as the United Nations Environment Programme, local and international NGOs, numerous fluctuating and overlapping local, national and global groups and networks, and clusters of individuals who sign petitions and take part in demonstrations, green consumer boycotts and much else (Doyle and McEachern 2008: 93–6). Not least of the dilemmas resulting from this complexity is the difficulty governments have in reconciling their national interests with the need to protect their citizens from environmental dangers that can only be tackled through intergovernmental cooperation. This problem has dogged repeated attempts by the UN to reach international agreements on capping greenhouse gas emissions at major conferences such as the Earth Summit in Rio in 1992, Kyoto in 1997 and Copenhagen in 2009.

A third theme centres on the movement's many internal divisions, whether over what issues deserve priority, who is mostly to blame for greenhouse gas emissions (and should shoulder most of the burden of resolving the problem), or what kinds of tactics will prove most efficacious. Focusing briefly on this question of tactics, we find that the range of possible actions is considerable and includes the following:

1. Engaging in mostly localized and sometimes illegal actions. One example would be the tree-spiking operations conducted by Earth First! against logging companies; others include a huge number of direct actions, such as blocking roads or invading land, by indigenous peoples, peasants and women in the South.
2. Mounting global spectacles designed to attract worldwide media attention and alter the policies of corporations and governments while inspiring public support. Examples would be Greenpeace's operations against French nuclear testing or whaling trawlers in the Pacific, or its capture of Shell's North Sea oil rig, Brent Spar, in 1995.
3. Building public support over long periods around specific concerns such as the preservation of endangered wildlife species through literature, leafleting, petitions and lobbying governments and businesses. The World Wildlife Fund is one obvious example, with its 5 million supporters active in more than 100 countries.
4. Establishing a long-term relationship with IGOs such as the World Bank or UN, and with governments or companies, which is what many NGOs in the North have done since the 1980s. This brings an NGO's expert knowledge directly to the attention of powerful bodies while attempting to effect policy change from the 'inside'. This approach might also attract funds for further campaigns and raise the group or organization's public profile. This, however, runs the risk of losing rather than gaining influence over powerful elites if the organization's actions are more widely perceived as helping to legitimize business interests and endorse rather than criticize government policy (Doyle and McEachern 2008: 128–30).

We now explore the significant theme of conflicts of interest and differences in perspective evident between the North and South and why these have arisen.

NORTH–SOUTH DIFFERENCES OVER TACKLING GREENHOUSE GAS EMISSIONS

Developing countries have argued, at least since the Earth Summit in Rio in 1992, that because the North is historically more culpable for the environmental problems than the South, it should shoulder most of the costs required to reduce the danger from greenhouse gas emissions. The North's high living standards are partly accredited to its exploitation of the South's raw materials and labour. Emissions in the South are often a direct consequence of the manufacture of goods destined for export to the North – in other words, a displacement of pollution.

Meanwhile, the South insists that its main priority must be to tackle poverty through economic development. Nonetheless, rapid industrialization in China and the other BRIC countries, with their huge populations and thirst for fossil fuels, means that their contribution to greenhouse gas emissions is fast becoming equivalent to, or greater than, those by the advanced countries. As we saw, China became the world's largest single polluter somewhere between 2007 and 2010. Thus, exempting the South from compulsory global targets for reducing emissions seems dangerously counterproductive and this has been a sticking point at climate change conferences. For example, in 2001 President Bush and the US Congress refused to ratify the targets agreed in the 1997 Kyoto Protocol on these grounds.

A PAUSE TO REFLECT

Poor countries do not want to meet emissions targets because their main focus is to propel more and more people out of poverty. Rich countries claim that the post-2007 recession means that they have to put their plans on hold. Can the environmental movement force a change in behaviour? Is the slow adoption of emission targets a reflection of the exaggerated doomsday predictions of certain scientists? Or have such scientists got it right, and we and our governments are just not listening?

One way out of this impasse would involve the North subsidizing the transfer of cleaner technologies to poorer countries so that they can industrialize without losing economic momentum or adding massively to global pollution. Similarly, governments in the South expect the North to create 'space' in the world economy for their economic development – what Giddens (2009: 64) refers to as a 'licence to pollute' – by slowing down or halting its rate of economic growth. They have also asked for financial compensation in return for agreeing to slow down the rate of deforestation or taking steps to preserve biodiversity. Following years of argument over several major conferences, it seems that progress on the issue of the subsidized transfer of clean technologies, and other topics, was achieved at the UN conference in Cancún in 2010 (Vidal and Goldenberg 2010).

Although they lobby governments and corporations and try to educate the public, environmental groups and NGOs operating in the South tend to direct their energy towards confronting local problems. According to Doyle and McEachern (2008: 144–6), they try to compensate poor communities in urban and rural areas for their governments' inadequate responses to neglected amenities and widespread poverty. In cities such as Mumbai, Bangkok and many others, some groups help shantytown dwellers build sewers or roads, clean up the locality, gain access to basic medical facilities, or improve housing. In addition to targeting local problems and communities and trying to fill the development 'void' (Doyle and McEachern 2008: 146) left by governments, NGOs in the South also 'build transnational networks with Northern and other Southern NGOs' (Doyle and McEachern 2008: 146) – partly to channel finance from the North into local projects while gaining international support. The motives for environmental protest and the kind of people who are most likely to become involved in direct actions also vary considerably between North and South, even with respect to the same issue. We explored the case of movements opposed to genetic engineering in Europe and India in Box 20.2.

Despite the 'immense gulf' (Doyle and McEachern 2008: 110) between environmental movements in the North and South over a range of issues and types of actors, there are indications that such differences can be overcome not only at governmental level – as with the agreement reached in 2010 at Cancún – but also with respect to the forms of and motives for political action. Thus, from the late 1990s, strong links were forged between the Global Justice Movement – a worldwide alliance of groups opposed to neoliberalism and unregulated capitalism (Chapter 19) – and many environmental groups in the South. This included the credo that millions of people in the South need both economic and 'climate' justice (Pettit 2004: 103), particularly given the evidence that climate change is already harming the poorest people in the world more than those who live in rich countries.

This unequal impact will accelerate if emission levels are not tackled much more stringently. Interestingly, around 80% of 'people of colour and indigenous peoples' (Newell 2006: 113) in the USA live in coastal regions. Indeed, this inequality was evident in 2005 when hurricane Katrina hit the area surrounding New Orleans and the people worst hit were those, mainly African Americans, who were too poor to escape because they did not own cars and/ or occupied houses in low-lying areas adjacent to the coastline. The Inuit people of Canada and Alaska and many Hispanics living in poor areas near coastlines face similar hazards. According to Newell (2006: 117), this link between a global politics of 'social justice ... and global injustice' will provide a way to 're-energise efforts' in the struggle to confront the enormous task of dealing with climate change. Doyle and McEachern (2008: 155) also see a growing coincidence of views over economic and environmental justice, and suggest that on this basis NGOs in the South may increasingly be 'driving the global green agenda'.

REVIEW

Environmental risks in the shape of climate change are becoming ever more evident. Increasingly, too, it is apparent that rapid economic growth in some developing countries, especially China and India, is accelerating the emission of greenhouse gases. Yet, the determination of these countries to prioritize the struggle against local poverty creates a worldwide dilemma in relation to climate change. If the advanced countries fail to assist developing economies in their drive to achieve faster but also more environmentally responsible development, then the former will also suffer certain consequences, not only through the impact of accelerated global warming but also the prospect of mass environmental migration and perhaps the spread of violence and crime far beyond national borders.

Another central issue relates to the debate on whether, when and how to phase out fossil fuels as the primary source of energy. While the benefits of this appear self-evident, in practice this is much harder than many advocates of a rapid switch to renewable energy sources imagine, although this does not mean that such a goal should not be attempted: quite the opposite. However, following this path will be extremely costly. It will also require a lot of government support, including tax concessions and guaranteed energy prices enabling renewable energy sources to compete with fossil fuels until their prices become competitive. At the international level, governments need to establish enforceable emission reduction targets in respect to each other and those agents whose actions fall within their sphere of national influence. So far this has proved difficult not least because of the diverging priorities of North and South.

Everyone bears some responsibility for green problems, albeit unequally, and most of us can help find solutions through accepting lifestyle changes. Persuading many ordinary citizens to accept such change, however, is fraught with difficulties at the present time. In the South people are locked into severe poverty while those in the North have grown accustomed to enjoying high-carbon economies. Nevertheless, presumably we all stand to gain from the preservation of a safe, vibrant natural world and a relatively stable climate. From this perspective, environmentalism may have a potentially universal appeal. In any case, as our shared biosphere shows ever greater symptoms of worldwide distress, so environmental movements have increasingly turned to transnational action. Nowhere is the mantra that global problems demand global solutions more appropriate than in the case of climate change.

Visit the companion website at www.palgrave.com/sociology/cohen3e for extra materials to check and expand your learning, including interactive self-test questions, mind maps making links between key themes, annotated web links to sociological research, data and key sociological thinkers, a searchable glossary and much more.

FURTHER READING

The Politics of Climate Change (2009), by A. Giddens, is a wide-ranging, thoughtful and accessible text. It also thoroughly dissects recent debates on every aspect of climate change.

T. Doyle and D. McEachern's *Environment and Politics* (3rd edn, 2008) offers an informative and clear account of the changing character of environmentalism and includes valuable material on the South.

After the Car (2009), by K. Dennis and J. Urry, is an interesting and provocative examination of climate change from the perspective of the car economy.

J. Neale's *Stop Global Warming: Change the World* (2008) provides a positive and passionate account of the benefits and opportunities available if we turn to renewable energy sources.

QUESTIONS AND ASSIGNMENTS

1. Examine the arguments for and against the continued but more responsible use of fossil fuels.

2. What are the drawbacks to prioritizing a switch to renewable energy sources? How far can these be overcome?

3. Using case studies, explain in what ways, how and why BRIC and other developing countries are increasingly contributing to global emissions. Briefly outline the wider implications of this.

4. Examine and explain the main ways in which the environmental movement has changed and evolved over the past 40 years.

21

Identities and belonging

We have seen how in different ways globalization can reshape people's life chances and existential and cultural experiences. Sometimes, the changes it brings deepen our economic and other insecurities, while at other times it offers opportunities to enrich our lives. It is important to remember that, despite being aware that global concerns and issues have penetrated our lives, we continue to remain partly or even predominantly bound into our local situation. Only a small minority of people in the world (about 3.3%) are first-generation migrants, in other words, living somewhere other than in their homeland, either temporarily or permanently. We might expect that this experience would incline them to become more open to new cultural influences but, as we argue below, even international migrants often seek some sense of ethnic particularity. As for the 96.7% who remain at home, their lives may be profoundly influenced by global flows of money, images, music and goods. They might participate in the global, for example by foreign travel, but this does not mean that their lives have been shaken to the roots.

We suggest that several overlapping entities form the continuing solidity of the local. These include the shared meanings derived from a sense of community, ethnic loyalty or national belonging. These generate the continuing pull of place, which remains important to most social actors, despite globalization. Accordingly, we explore two linked questions. First, how do social actors grapple with duality – the continuing need for and attachment to the local and their exposure to globalizing influences (see also Chapters 2, 4 and 6)? Second, what are the varying patterns of response through which actors resolve this dilemma?

We begin by pinpointing some of the factors that shape these different responses and then identify four possible outcomes. In each section we draw on case studies to look at these different patterns of response. This requires an examination of the main building blocks of social life – community, ethnicity, national identity and place – to show why and how they continue to exercise so much pulling power.

CONFRONTING THE LOCAL AND THE GLOBAL: KEY INFLUENCES

We suggest that several variables are likely to shape whether, to what extent and in what ways social actors cope with the competing demands of local belonging and global uncertainty. How these work out will influence, although not necessarily determine, their varying responses.

Sociologists and other academics are trained to acquire a critical insight, which gives them an outsider's view of human affairs and the wherewithal to construct rational knowledge and to do so with maximum objectivity, precisely because they view the world as external to their own lives. Although not necessarily having as much objectivity as trained social scientists, as we suggested in Chapter 2, some social actors have increasingly internalized the changes associated with globalization so that they are now incorporated into their ways of thinking, a process we called 'globality'. These shifts in consciousness include the growth of multicultural awareness, the empowerment of self-aware social actors, the broadening of identities, and a move towards greater cosmopolitanism.

However, it is unrealistic to imagine that globality is pervasive. Many social actors rely mostly on information that is taken for granted, so it is rarely examined or questioned. Poor or vulnerable people, in particular, may derive their consciousness from their immediate needs and from the familiar, commonsense, practical concerns they share with their neighbours. This might prompt us to conclude that few social actors probably have little detailed understanding of globalization, especially given that its operations are complex and its main determinants rather remote from their lives. A limited knowledge of the global situation is not, however, the only factor at work. Irrespective of their degree of understanding, we may also enquire whether most people care very much about global forces one way or another. Perhaps they are relatively indifferent to them. They may find their own local lives and affiliations not only easier to understand, but also more compelling, absorbing, familiar and emotionally rewarding. We argue that the inward pull of this influence affects virtually everyone to some extent, even those with strong cosmopolitan leanings.

In this chapter we consider the possibility that some individuals are better able than others to open their minds to influences, ideas and people from societies that are very different from their own, thereby perhaps beginning or accelerating a journey towards cosmopolitanism. Others, however, may perceive globalization as disturbing and likely to threaten their identity and sense of belonging. Consequently, they may entrench themselves more deeply in the local identities and affiliations with which they feel comfortable. There are, of course, numerous positions between these two extremes of cosmopolitan openness and fear of or hostility towards globalization.

In what forms of action might people engage who wish to resist aspects of globalization they find destructive? Again, a range of responses are possible. At one extreme, there are people who tend to project blame onto and, perhaps aggressively, close ranks against the relatively powerless minorities living within their social orbit. Yet others might seek national or transnational allies to help them resist the powerful agencies they perceive to be responsible for the destructive character of globalization. In doing so, they may be driven by an ethos that values social inclusiveness and the wish to benefit the majority. All in all, we can identify four modes, or patterns, of adaptation through which most of us juggle between the local and global, which we specify below:

1. *A relatively nonreflexive dependence on local belonging:* The vast majority of people in all societies, some by choice and others by necessity, are non-movers who feel little desire or need to explore alternative lifestyles. For them, identity and belonging are primarily local phenomena. Most probably have only a limited understanding of globalization, even though they cannot escape its impact on their lives. The latter include jobs being relocated overseas, rising food and fuel prices, the presence of migrants living next door, TV, internet and holiday glimpses of exotic music, fashion, customs and cuisines.

2. *An active, aggrieved search for relocalization:* Similar to the former in nearly all respects is a group that late modern globalization has affected, even harmed, but certainly marginalized. In industrialized economies these people are likely to be members of Standing's (2009) 'precariat', discussed in Chapter 7. Their experience may induce them either to resist globalization and/or to value and seek some kind of relocalization strategy, perhaps in ways that harm those whom they look upon as outsiders.

3. *Protecting localism through forging external alliances:* Another group of mostly poor social

actors are exposed to global forces that threaten to undercut their livelihoods, which reinforces their primary desire to protect their family, neighbourhood and village/regional culture. Yet, their response is mostly inclusive rather than exclusive, in that they turn outwards to enlist the support of potential allies.

4. *Constructing transnational/cosmopolitan, multi-level lives:* Although those who move overseas are likely to retain a sense of belonging and identity grounded in their native local society, they cannot entirely avoid exposure to cultures that differ from their own. Whether they are migrants, artists, professionals, retirees, students on exchange schemes or business entrepreneurs, they are likely to construct enduring transnational networks that straddle their home and host society. These experiences need not but often do propel them either towards developing cosmopolitan orientations of one kind or another and/or acquiring a multilayered social existence encompassing different identities.

We recognize that many people do not fit neatly into any of these analytical categories. Even where they appear closely to approximate a specific mode, few will do so completely. In any case, we stress that, however much we might try to remain encapsulated within our local identity and protect it from groups we presume are its enemies, it is difficult to escape entirely from the need to engage in a degree of reflexivity – or self-confrontation and learning (Beck 1994) – in a globalizing world where no society or individual can live in isolation but must take some account of the 'other'. This means that the scope for reinventing one's persona and habitus and for moving between these situations may be increasingly possible for many social actors.

THE RESILIENT LOCAL AS A CONTINUING SOURCE OF BELONGING

> ### KEY CONCEPT
>
> COMMUNITIES are units of belonging. They are marked by deep, familiar and cooperative ties between members supported by shared moral, aesthetic/expressive or cognitive meanings. In this sense, 'community' is close to Durkheim's idea of social solidarity, which emerges from a commitment to a shared set of values or 'the collective conscience'. A formal definition is given by Nisbet (1970: 47), who says that community 'encompasses all forms of relationship which are characterized by a high degree of personal intimacy, emotional depth, moral commitment, social cohesion and continuity in time'.

One sociologist (Scheff 1990: 4) has proposed that the maintenance of social bonds is 'our most crucial human motive'. These bonds take several forms, including kinship, but on a larger scale they are often formalized in associations such as COMMUNITIES.

Classical sociologists like Tönnies (Chapter 5) stressed that aspects of community would wither with modernization, although later writers such as Bendix (1967) suggested that communal relations remained significant in certain situations and life spheres. Nevertheless, compulsory and narrowly defined allegiances (Beck 2000a), based on descent (kinship), residence and/or locality, characterized most premodern and early modern communities. Their capacity to endure and exercise 'close surveillance' (Hannerz 2003: 26) over their members usually depended on their multi-purpose character and relied on face-to-face interactions. Most people faced restrictions on their movements, but the prospect of acquiring land, employment, mutual assistance, protection or charity from one's immediate kin offset whatever economic opportunities may have been available elsewhere.

A PAUSE TO REFLECT

Defining and understanding 'community' is at the heart of sociology. One simple way of understanding the evolution of community is that in the premodern period it was based on descent and kinship, in the modern period it was based on associations forged in a new place, while in the global era community is based on elective choice in a placeless world. Is this too schematic and, if so, why? Do earlier forms of community have a habit of resurrecting themselves?

Of course, modernity, postmodernity and globalization have reduced the need for communities to be based in particular locations and to engage in ongoing face-to-face relations with the same people. Also, many of the previous constraints on individual mobility have been removed. Nevertheless, although their character has changed, communities still meet the needs of their members and operate as units of belonging (Kennedy and Roudometof 2002). Thus, membership is often voluntarily chosen rather than ascribed by fixed criteria defined by birth or social position and is usually actively generated (Giddens 1994). Communities are also less all-embracing than hitherto and they usually depend more on symbolic, informational and cultural rather than material resources (Lash 1994: 161).

ETHNICITY

As we saw in Chapter 9, both race and ethnicity are socially constructed and their adherents sometimes assert their differences in ways that denigrate the 'other' or 'others' whom they define as outsiders. While race is built on presumed blood ties, biological descent and physical characteristics, especially skin colour and appearance, ethnic affiliation is usually based on social markers like culture, nationality, language or religion. Generally, this means that because ethnic differences rely on narratives, imagery and metaphors, the differences conjured up are more subtle and create scope for self-examination and flexibility. Nevertheless, for many people, ethnic ties are a matter of loyalty, pride, refuge, identity, acceptance and security and they engender strong feelings of belonging. They imply an unquestioned affinity and devotion purely on the basis of the intimacy of the tie (Allahar 1994). It is the closest form of association that a collectivity of humans can achieve. By embracing an ethnic identity, groups acknowledge that they are part of society and that their survival depends on forces bigger than the individual. The locality into which they were born is also likely to be an object of affection, a place shared with others of the same origin and likely fate.

Like feelings of national identity, ethnic ties have often proved to be much more resilient than many earlier observers predicted they would be. Their continuing strength testifies to the simultaneity of globalization and localization. This counteracts the common assumption of modernization theorists that with increasing secularization, urbanization, industrialization and rationalization, ethnicity and nationalism would recede in importance. It was surmised that as postcolonial developing nations moved towards modernity and liberal democracy, so the hold of ethnic or tribal affiliations over people's need to belong would diminish in significance. Marxist theorists were also largely dismissive of ethnic and national identities. They saw them as characteristics that capitalist and political elites cynically manipulated to exploit divisions in the working class and divert attention away from their capitalist oppression.

EPIPHENOMENON
Something that appears to be of great causal significance, but is really derived from some other primary basis. In overvaluing an epiphenomenon, observers mistake a symptom for a reason.

Ethnicity was merely an epiphenomenon, far less powerful as a form of association than class consciousness. However, class awareness is predominantly awareness of a common interest and, despite the mantras of Marxists and free marketeers, people live not only by interests alone but also by their emotions. They live by anger, grief, anxiety, jealousy, affection, fear and devotion – precisely those emotions that ethnic affiliations and local attachments harness.

BOX 21.1 Islamophobia and how to recognize it

Across Europe campaigns have been targeted against 'outsider' groups seen as threatening local identity, particularly people of Islamic origin. 'Islamophobia' is a newly coined world and means the dread and horror (from the Greek word 'phobia') of Muslim people.

The Runnymede Trust in the UK, set up to promote good race relations and the understanding of cultural diversity, established a special commission of academics, writers and religious figures to study the rise of Islamophobia (Stubbs 1997). They argued that unreasonable fear of Islam had seven telltale features:

- Muslim cultures are seen as monolithic and unchanging

- Muslim cultures are regarded as wholly different from other cultures

- Islam is seen as implacably threatening

- the Islamic faith is used, it is alleged, mainly for political or military advantage

- Muslim criticisms of Western cultures are rejected out of hand

- racist immigration restrictions are associated with Islam

- Islamophobia is assumed to be natural and unproblematic.

Each one of these supposed 'features' can be challenged by historical and comparative evidence. For example, as we explain in Chapter 17, Islam as practised in Iraq or Egypt is very different from the religion in Chechnya, Indonesia, Iran and Malaysia. There are also different interpretations of the Koran. As in the history of Christianity, different sects abounded. Moreover, Islamic civilization has closely interacted with Western civilization and made contributions in such diverse areas as architecture, philosophical thought, medicine and the numerals (1, 2, 3, 4) we all use in our daily life.

The debate about the place of Islam in Western societies is also being played out in the reactions to the proposal to build a mosque near Ground Zero in Manhattan, the site of the World Trade Center, which was so spectacularly bombed in the event known simply as 9/11. In fact, the proposed development, called 'Park51', is sited two blocks north of the World Trade Center and invisible from it. Park51 is to be a community centre that will include a mosque ('a prayer room'), but will also house a restaurant, a memorial to the victims of 9/11, classrooms and auditoria. While the city authorities, notably New York's Jewish mayor Bloomberg, have approved the project, arguing that the USA has had a long and notable tradition of religious liberty, Park51 has been strongly opposed by prominent Republicans (such as Newt Gingrich and Sarah Palin), influential Jewish lobby groups and many US citizens, who feel that building a mosque in that location is provocative.

Goodstein (2010) documents other protests against building mosques in a number of US cities. While initial protests often deployed neutral objections concerning parking, traffic and noise, now 'the gloves are off'. Protesters deploy explicit attacks on Islam, suggest that the birth rate for Muslims is unacceptably high, and argue that the political elements of the Islamic faith mean that Islam cannot evoke constitutional protection under the US Constitution.

Sources: Goodstein (2010); Stubbs (1997).

The survival of ethnic differences and loyalties are often explicable in terms of certain structural factors. Indeed, these may crystallize or intensify such affiliations. One involves the imposition or strengthening of certain legal and political restrictions that deny some groups access to particular rights, resources or occupations, so placing them in a subordinate position. One extreme example of this was the apartheid system that existed in South Africa until 1989. People designated as 'Bantu', 'white', 'coloured and 'Asian' were legally separated from one another, while the Bantu (black African) section of the population was subdivided into ethnicities like the Zulu, Tswana, Venda and Xhosa. These largely artificial ethnic distinctions were then legalized and given force in economic, educational, residential and occupational categories that set limits of opportunity to certain groups in terms of access to good housing, jobs or healthcare. Ethnic identities were, in short, not freely selected but imposed by law, regulation, police action and the threat of state violence.

At times, ethnic, racial and religious differences also come to the fore through coerced migration. During the eighteenth and nineteenth centuries, mercantile and colonial powers frequently imported different peoples to new settings in the Americas and elsewhere to work on their plantations or to further their commercial interests. For example, some 10 million African slaves were shipped across the Atlantic, while 1.4 million Indian indentured workers were sent to the sugar plantations. The governor of Dutch Indonesia even sent warships to capture mainland Chinese to help develop his colony. These involuntary migrations led to complex, often three-way interactions between indigenous, imported and colonial peoples. Over time, occupational categories became fused with ethnic identities, giving rise to 'ethno-

COOLIE/NAVVY

Originally an Urdu word for an unskilled day labourer, coolie was a description applied to the Indian indentured labourers and Chinese manual workers who were used in plantations and railway building in colonial territories and the USA. Navvy was short for a 'navigation engineer', generally referring to Irish men who dug the navigation canals in nineteenth-century Britain. Both expressions were used in a derogatory way.

occupations', such as 'Chinese traders', 'Indian coolies', 'Irish navvies', 'Lebanese middlemen' or 'Scottish engineers'.

NATIONAL IDENTITY

In Chapter 5, we saw that popular nationalism, as a force that engulfs most citizens and not just a few elites, is mostly built on an imagined national community, which its members experience as a sense of deep comradeship that overrides the many possible regional, religious, ethnic, generational, social class and other differences that might divide rather than unite them (Anderson 1983). Other entities, however, can and usually do buttress a sense of national belonging.

For example, the unity created around and by the nation-state is often crucial. This rests on the myth of a continuous legitimate authority of a single people, even though in reality most nation-states are diverse and plural. Modern states also insist on a shared language and construct a national educational system that socializes all children into believing in the myth of national unity, while inducting them into shared beliefs in a common history and destiny. Ceremonial rituals, along with flags, anthems, sporting teams, capital cities, grand buildings, icons and symbols all help to reinforce the nation builders' message. War, competitive trading relationships and imperialist rivalries might further consolidate the processes of national unification, while endowing symbols with substance.

For his part, Hannerz (2003: 69–70) argues that shared underlying cultural resources also sustain ethnic and national belonging but, to be effective, they do not always need to be grounded in myths about bloodlines, land rights or memories of the ancient defining battles to which Smith (1995) alludes. These cultural resources consist of all the ways of seeing, rules, tastes and preferences that constitute the cultural uniqueness of a given people. Hannerz calls them 'the forms of life' and they are present wherever people are brought into close proximity in 'households, work places [and] neighbourhoods' (Hannerz 2003: 69). They are continuously repeated and always 'massively present'. They provide the 'formative experiences' (Hannerz 2003: 69) of early life and so probably remain with people throughout their lives. These forms of life continue to shape the relatively exclusive sociocultural life of people in many countries. For example, 'for a great many people the idea of the nation ... still encompasses virtually all their social traffic' (Hannerz 2003: 90) even in the 'heartlands' of advanced Western nations where globalizing influences are most pronounced.

THE CONTINUING POWER OF PLACE

Most of us spend our lives in one locality at any one time. Each locality displays its own highly specific historical, architectural and cultural characteristics. It also possesses a particular microclimate plus a concatenation of flora and fauna coexisting with social life. All this survives even though incoming global forces are increasingly criss-crossing all localities. Indeed, each place remains unique just because it becomes the 'focus of a distinct *mixture* of wider and more local social relations' (Massey 1993: 68) that do not arise in exactly the same way anywhere else. For example, despite its partial McDonaldization, vast tourist flows, an invasion of TNCs, and its leading role as a global financial city, Paris continues to offer distinctive experiences that visitors cannot find in other global cities such as London or New York.

Because we have bodies with a range of physical, aesthetic and emotional needs, we have no option but to engage with place to live our embodied lives. Further, Bourdieu (2000: 135) reminds us that we need not just a 'physical space' but also a social space and therefore an arena within which our relationships can be played out. Without locality, we 'lack social existence' (Bourdieu 2000: 135). Our place of habitation is where we forge most of the exchanges that flow across the world and where we deal with incoming global influences. As Brenner

GLOBAL THINKERS 21 ZYGMUNT BAUMAN (1925–)

Zygmunt Bauman is emeritus professor of sociology at Leeds, having held chairs at Warsaw (he was born in Poland) and Tel Aviv. Bauman is a general social theorist of modernity and postmodernity. His writing moves seamlessly between Russian, Polish, French, German and English sources, and it seems that all Europe's predicaments – war, displacement, fragile boundaries, extermination, loss and resettlement – are saturated in his mind.

In his most controversial book, *Modernity and the Holocaust* (1991), he discounts as explanations for the Holocaust the peculiarities of German history and culture, the notion that Germans were authoritarian, or that the horrific events were an atavistic reversion to some barbarian and irrational past (Bauman 1991: 211–12). He holds that:

The Holocaust was as much a product, as it was a failure, of modern civilization. Like everything else done in the modern – rational, planned, scientifically informed, expert, efficiently managed, coordinated – way, the Holocaust left behind and put to shame all its alleged pre-modern equivalents, exposing them as primitive, wasteful and ineffective by comparison. (Bauman 1991: 89)

However, contrary to what many critics thought, Bauman was not trying to let the Germans 'off the hook' by displacing the 'blame' onto a system. He was clear that the ultra-modernist Nazis adopted a sinister intent to Gypsies and Jews because of their 'permanent and irremediable homelessness', which had formed such an integral part of Jewish identity 'from the beginning of their diasporic history' (Bauman 1991: 35).

The homeless nature of identity becomes a more general characteristic in the postmodern period. It becomes 'light' or 'liquid'. 'The search for identity', Bauman argues, 'is the ongoing struggle to arrest or slow down the flow, to solidify the fluid, to give form to the formless' (2000: 82–3). Elsewhere, he suggests that 'the problem of identity' is radically different under conditions of modernity and postmodernity. In the former, typified, say, by nation building, the problem is 'how to construct an identity and keep it solid and stable'. Under postmodernity, the problem is to 'avoid fixation and keep the options open' (Bauman 1995: 81).

Source: Bauman (1991, 1995, 2000).

(1999) contends, we need to reground the deterritorialized processes that link people across distance into other concrete places – housing estates, factories, airports and shopping centres – if much of what we understand by globalization is to make any sense.

All this gives localities a continuing 'stickiness', a distinctive logic that partly satisfies our need to belong. Paradoxically, this is revealed in the way we use IT, especially the internet. As we saw in Chapter 16, early innovators thought that IT would bring more open, accountable government, self-governing cybercommunities, and a massive reduction in the way geography and territorial borders had hitherto constrained human interaction. However, drawing on their research findings, Goldsmith and Wu (2006) argue that the internet's capacity to realize these aspirations has, so far, fallen short of earlier expectations and that the internet mostly caters to localized, bottom-up consumer demands and preferences and these normally operate within borders. Language is an obvious factor here, since the majority of internet customers wish to use their own language and few are proficient in any language other than their own (Goldsmith and Wu 2006: 50–1). In the late 1990s, English was the main internet language for 80% of users – who were mostly North Americans – but as markets have grown across Asia and elsewhere, consumers have turned to their own local languages: by 2005 only one-third of internet users were relying on English.

Nonetheless, language constitutes only one reason why most people's interests 'cluster by geography' (Goldsmith and Wu 2006: 52). Cultural tastes and needs reflect the enduring preferences concentrated in localities, regions, ethnic communities and countries. Commercial companies, like search engines, social networking sites and online marketplaces, respond by focusing their advertising in such a way as to maximize their appeal to different public tastes.

Whereas academics, intellectuals, students, artists, scientists and others with cosmopolitan leanings once monopolized the internet, it has since grown 'into an everyday tool for the masses'. Consequently, the 'average user' is unlikely to be someone who possesses 'overseas correspondents or interests in overseas or foreign-language content' (Goldsmith and Wu 2006: 57).

CASE STUDIES

Three UK sociologists interested in experiences of belonging and identity in a globalizing world (Savage et al. 2005) conducted research on individuals living in four different, but predominantly middle-class, districts around Manchester. We summarize some of their most salient findings and compare them with other European research:

1. Few respondents saw 'localness' as a condition that hinged on being born in a locality and remaining there for life. Instead, most regarded their attachment to the place in which they lived as something they had freely chosen while retaining connections to other localities. Yet, despite this 'elective belonging' (Savage et al. 2005: 53), they retained a strong sense of being at home and 'fixed places' played a central role in their lives.

2. Although most respondents had moved around, 80% of their mobility was confined to the Manchester area or neighbouring regions within 100 miles of the city. Moreover, well over half lived within fairly close regional reach of at least some of their immediate family. Only 12% had lived abroad, usually as a child or student and not for very long. This limited geographical mobility is widespread across Europe. Favell (2003) cites data suggesting that around 98% of Europeans remain in their country of origin and when they do venture overseas, they mostly remain encapsulated within expatriate social circles.

3. In all but one locality (undergoing gentrification and with a high proportion of graduates), most respondents expressed a strong 'local patriotism' for Manchester and disdain for London, which they regarded as crime-ridden, overcrowded and full of transients. Similarly, when asked about their preferred rural pastimes and landscapes, most strongly favoured the northern regions and few were interested in visiting, or had much knowledge of, rural parts of southern Britain (Savage et al. 2005: 94–104). As elsewhere in Europe, strong subregional loyalties accompanied by disinterest or even antagonism towards the capital city and other regions are clearly evident.

4. Only 4% of respondents demonstrated 'global reflexivity' (Savage et al. 2005: 191); they sometimes examined their experiences and expressed values from a comparative perspective that did not rely on 'English referents'. Interestingly, most of this tiny group were brought up abroad and moved to the UK later in life. Similarly, when the researchers compiled the respondents' cultural references – preferences in books, art, music, TV, internet sites and so on – they discovered that 70% depended on British sources while the remainder were mostly from the USA. Overall, less than 8% mentioned items involving products originating neither in Britain nor the USA and most of these were Australian or Canadian: only a few were European. Savage et al. (2005: 202) suggested that their sample mostly participated in a 'white English-speaking diaspora', with a strong cultural and linguistic basis in Anglo-Saxon influences rather than anything that could be justifiably labelled as 'cosmopolitan'.

A PAUSE TO REFLECT

The better educated, economically comfortable middle classes in the advanced countries are more likely than other social groups to possess an outward-looking, inclusive cosmopolitan orientation. Even then, the numbers with such preferences are small, as recent research in various European locations suggests that most people remain firmly ensconced in local, subregional, ethnic and/or national life worlds. How do we understand the continuing salience of a local sense of belonging?

Favell (2003) interviewed young EU migrants living in the three quintessentially European cities of Amsterdam, London and Brussels and found a similar scenario. Although non-nationals had penetrated national employment and housing markets and few had experienced discrimination with banking, legal, welfare and other bureaucratic systems, most found it difficult to gain entry to host society social networks. Consequently, their friends were mostly fellow nationals whom they had met overseas or other foreigners facing the same predicament. Likewise, Bozkurt (2006) studied young professionals in Helsinki and Stockholm who worked for TNCs in the mobile phone business and the respondents again revealed similar experiences of local middle-class culture. Indeed, they contrasted their own enjoyable experience of working in international teams of skilled professionals within these companies with being cut off from surrounding middle-class society (Bozkurt 2006), with its national 'homogeneity' and dominant parochial concerns.

In short, there are few indications here that most middle-class Europeans are particularly open to cultural difference or are willing to move far outside the comfort zone provided by local affiliations and identities.

AGGRESSIVE EXPRESSIONS OF RELOCALIZATION AND BELONGING

KEY CONCEPT

IDEOLOGY refers to a reasonably coherent set of assumptions and convictions shared by a particular social group. Pacifists and vegetarians share an ideology in this sense. For some social theorists, ideologies can be contrasted with reason or science, and are used deliberately by ruling groups to obscure real power relations in their own interest.

KEY CONCEPT

METANARRATIVES are 'grand' theories that offer an all-inclusive package of claims, which are designed to account for the truth of human experience. They often involve ideas concerning the inevitability of human progress. Examples are Marxism, communism, liberalism and nationalism.

We now take our argument a step further. Although most social actors appear to remain more or less bound within their local lives, neither resisting globalization nor showing much interest in it, others reassert their ethnic or national loyalties in ways that do, or might, endanger others. All too many examples of this have been evident since the bipolar IDEOLOGICAL struggle between 'capitalism' and 'communism'. Where ideological claims are all-encompassing, as in these cases, they are sometimes referred to as METANARRATIVES. Such struggles evaporated at the end of the Cold War and were partly replaced by the politics of identity and community. Unfortunately, these assertions have often led to fierce, large-scale struggles designed to divide once unified societies into separate ethnic entities or to exercise extreme forms of aggression to continue keeping people apart.

LARGE-SCALE ETHNO-CONFLICTS

Premdas (1996) estimated that there were 4,000 'ethnocultural' groups worldwide, uneasily enclosed (at that time) in 185 states and territories.

With migration, commerce and travel, nearly all states are now multi-ethnic to some degree: the few exceptions include Somalia, North and South Korea, Botswana and Swaziland. Some 40% of the world's states have more than five significant ethnic communities. In 1996, just seven years after the collapse of the Berlin Wall (the symbolic end of the Cold War), there were 100 ongoing subnational conflicts, with about 20 classified as 'high intensity'. To contain these conflicts, some of the peace dividend had to be spent on 70,000 UN peacekeepers, costing US$4bn each year to maintain.

Moreover, many observers have been alarmed at the increasingly militant demands for ethnic exclusivity, minority language education, religious separatism and exclusive territorial entities. The persistence or re-emergence of ethnic and religious differences are seen in the conflicts between Kosovars and Serbs in the Balkans, Hutus and Tutsis in Rwanda, Christians and Muslims in Lebanon and Pakistan, Jews and Arabs in the Middle East, Tamils and Sinhalese in Sri Lanka, Protestants and Catholics in Northern Ireland, rival clans in Somalia and many others.

FIGURE 21.1 Graffiti in Harlem
Artistically superior graffiti on a wall in Harlem, New York in 2010. The artist harks back to the 'Afro' haircuts of the 1960s and the 'black is beautiful' movement, when African Americans asserted a newfound sense of confidence in their appearance and identities.

Ethnicity is not, therefore, an irrelevant anachronism to the gathering pace of globalization but an observable reaction to it. The rapidity with which their known world dissolves encourages people to reach out for their 'groundings' in the habitual, namely in the communities where they find familiar faces, voices, sounds, smells, tastes and places. Much of this involves ethnicity. Confronted by the pace of globalization, they often need ethnicity more, not less. Confused by the effects of postmodernity and the relativism that globalization brings, they reaffirm and reify what they believe to be true (Hall 1991: 35–6).

Nationalism also seems to be on the increase while globalization runs apace. The number of UN-recognized nation-states has proliferated since the foundation of the UN in 1945 and now stands at 193. Despite this formal increase, a number of observers, as we have shown in Chapter 5, suggest that the autonomy of many nation-states has weakened. The nation-state may become the 'piggy in the middle', rushing from the global to the local level in an attempt to remain in the game. Others argue that the fears arising from global terrorism have forced us to recognize that we can only derive our security ultimately from strengthening the intelligence services, police and armed forces of existing nation-states, and giving greater weight to the need for nationwide social cohesion.

BLAMING OUTSIDERS FOR THREATS TO LOCAL BELONGING: MICRO-REACTIONS

Some expressions of ethnic and/or national belonging are linked to feelings of desperation and spill over into mass (as opposed to individual) acts of aggression and discrimination. They tend to stop short of escalating into large-scale conflict. One example is examined in Box 21.2.

As we saw in Chapters 6 and 7, members of the old industrial working class in advanced countries are among those whose livelihoods and feelings of local belonging are threatened by globalization and other changes. (Some lower middle-class people, especially in rural areas, have been similarly affected.) Although he is not referring only to this group, Bauman's (1998: 99) term 'enforced localization' captures their predicament. Once they engaged with their societies as workers and/or soldiers but now there is 'little need for mass industrial labour and conscript armies'. Instead, their primary function is to consume – if their credit limits allow that option. Change, including globalization, has exposed them to cumulative disadvantages, which leave them tied to their localities, where some family and community life may survive and where they remain eligible for dwindling social housing and welfare benefits. Meanwhile, migrants compete with them for insecure jobs, local housing and other resources, and the new, highly skilled middle classes have gentrified the surrounding urban locations, pushing up rents in the process.

One possible response to sociocultural fragmentation and economic decline has been to seek a 'return to roots' and to 'fixed identifications' that people suppose are immune from change (Friedman 1997: 77). This, in turn, may lead to the reassertion of an invented 'ethnic primordiality' (Friedman 1997: 71) and the revival of local, subnational or national affiliations. Indications of this have been apparent over the past three decades in many European countries and parts of the USA in the form of radical, populist, right-wing groups.

BOX 21.2   Reactions to enforced localization: nativism in the USA and the UK

US Patriot groups

In 2000, there were said to be 194 anti-government Patriot groups across the USA, although their membership level peaked in the mid-1990s (Southern Poverty Law Center 2001). Groups are usually armed and seek military training. Members are opposed to what they see as the augmentation of federal power and desire a return to more localism in government. They tend to cultivate conspiracy theories and resent the UN, which they regard as undermining US sovereignty. These anti-government sentiments were expressed in extreme form in 1996 when Timothy McVeigh, a Patriot, blew up the Oklahoma state building, killing 168 people and injuring more than 680.

Most supporters are youngish, white males living in small towns and rural areas. They tend to come from working-class or lower middle-class backgrounds or small farming communities. These are groups experiencing downward social mobility as their work opportunities become scarce and their limited qualifications bar them from entering more promising occupations. Most Patriot members have strong patriarchal family values and/or links to Christian fundamentalist sects. Racist attitudes and connections to neo-Nazi groups are also commonplace.

In the mid-term elections of November 2010, the Tea Party, a radical splinter group, which shares with the Patriots anti-immigration and anti-big government views, gained a number of seats in the Congress and Senate. They threatened to compel the Republican Partly to adopt a tough right-wing, nationalist line in future battles with President Obama and the Democrats.

The English Defence League (EDL)

The EDL emerged in 2009 and is committed to preventing what its members see as the Muslim takeover of Britain, sometimes through local violence. Membership sprang from rival football supporters, hooligan networks and extreme splinter Nazi groups. Most appear to come from the disaffected working class but a minority are being drawn from middle-class groups. By early 2011 the EDL had organized large demonstrations in several British cities. During 2010, some members joined similar far-right European groups for a rally in Germany and it seemed likely an alliance would be forged with the US anti-Islam group.

One danger with such populist right-wing groups is that blaming migrant communities for their situation, coupled with demands that the rights of the native population are given precedence, will spill over into violence and a situation in which there is little or no pretence at accepting everyone's right to be treated with equal respect. The EDL has also developed its own website, which passes on information to local and city divisions plus video materials and adverts for similar events in other countries (Taylor 2010). This is the downside of the internet and social networking (see Chapter 16), where those with undesirable agendas have equal access to the technology's advantages.

Sources: Castells (1997); Munck (2007); Southern Poverty Law Center (2001); Taylor (2010).

The core values that such groups demonstrate are a belief in nativism (the nation should be exclusively occupied by its original inhabitants), a desire to live in a highly ordered if not authoritarian society, and a marked preference for patriotic and commonsense knowledge rather than abstract intellectual thinking (Mudde 2007). Suspicion, if not hostility, is often shown towards minorities who are believed to threaten the nation from within, especially migrants who supposedly dilute native values, but also gays, feminists and established ethnic minorities. Many also fear that globalization is weakening the nation-state. Indeed, since the 1980s, globalization has contributed to growing electoral support across Europe for radical right populist parties, which, on average, gained 8% of votes during the 1990s (Liang 2007). These parties draw voting support from across the social spectrum, but working-class people may provide the main strength. For example, the Danish People's Party gained 12% of the votes in the national election of 2001 and 13.8% six years later (Andersen 2007: 103). In 2012, in the first round of voting in the French presidential election, Marine Le Pen took 19.9% of the vote – a stunning result for the far right. At times, radical populist right-wing groups move in potentially dangerous directions, as Box 21.2 suggests.

PROTECTING LOCALISM THROUGH FORGING EXTERNAL ALLIANCES

In Chapter 6 we considered the plight of social groups harmed by the realities of uneven world development. We now pick up this theme by looking in more detail at the situation that many people who are desperately poor and exposed to forces that destabilize their livelihoods face in the global South. We also explore their equal concern to retain their sociocultural identity and village/regional affiliations. But, instead of the aggressive demand for relocalization, leading to threats directed against vulnerable outsider groups, we find more inclusive forms of resistance. This involves attempts to enlist support from other local but very different groups facing similar dangers and/or from powerful transnational allies – an inclusive localism.

Several groups fit these criteria, including indigenous peoples, peasants and small farmers, and subordinate and oppressed women living in urban and rural areas. Despite their differences, they face common experiences in addition to their wish to retain their local belonging and unique cultural identity; for example:

• They are responding to forces adversely affecting their livelihoods, especially neoliberal economic globalization. For example, reduced state spending on health and education has damaged the livelihoods of many women in the global South.
• Although globalization has brought changes that threaten their situation, it has also brought resources they can harness in an attempt to resist the former.
• They face additional burdens, endemic to their local situation, which have a long history. For example, patriarchy and unequal gender relations inscribed in sociocultural life have long defined women as subordinate and undeserving of the same respect as men.

Peasants and small farmers in the South are exposed to a barrage of economic threats that have been undermining their independence and survival for decades (see Chapter 6), and many small farmers in advanced economies also struggle against the same forces. Moreover, like their counterparts in the South, the latter often fail to gain government assistance to alleviate their plight. Consequently, in 1993, despite their national, linguistic, North–South and other divides, peasant and farm leaders from 36 countries got together to set up an international peasant movement called Via Campesina (the Peasant Road), which pledged to represent the interests of rural women and indigenous people (Reitan 2007: 166–70). Since then, Via Campesina has played a key role at several important world events, including the WTO conference in Seattle in 1999, which presaged the formation of the Global Justice Movement. Years of transnational activism have failed to blunt the primary local attachments and concerns of peasants and small farmers worldwide, as the remarks of Nettie Wiebe, a former president of the National Farmers Union of Canada and later a Via Campesina activist, made abundantly clear during an interview in 2002:

If you actually ask what 'peasant' means, it means 'people of the land'. Are we Canadian farmers 'people of the land'? Well, yes, of course. …We too are peasants and it's the land and our relationship to the land and food production that distinguishes us. We're not part of the industrial machine. We're much more closely linked to places where we grow food and how we grow food, and what the weather is there. (cited in Edelman 2003: 187; see also www.viacampesina.org)

Drawing on recent research, we now look in more detail at indigenous peoples.

INDIGENOUS PEOPLES: CLASHING WITH MODERNIZATION

There are probably 5,000 separate **indigenous peoples** totalling around 350 million (Hall and Fenelon 2008: 6). They live in North and South America, Siberia, Africa, Australia, New Zealand and Asia. In India, they number around 84 million and belong to perhaps 600 distinctive communities. Most of them now farm marginal lands, although they were once forest people whom mining and logging had displaced. Indigenous cultures predate the establishment of modern nations when people from different nations occupied much of their ancestral lands and undermined their languages, religions and customs (Martin and Wilmer 2008). Against such threats, especially extensive settlement, agriculture and capitalist industrialization, indigenous peoples have struggled to preserve their unique cultures, ancestral lands and livelihoods for future generations.

Apart from their attempts to remain outside the modernization process, what is unique about these small-scale societies? First, their societies depend on 'intense local interactions' (Hall and Fenelon 2008: 2) based on kinship and small, largely self-sufficient communities. However, invasions of their lands and the imposition of modern national borders across their ancestral territories often split them between different nations. Consequently, members often cross illegally into foreign countries, bringing them into conflict with state authorities (Hall and Fenelon 2008; Schmidt 2007).

Second, they hold ontological beliefs (pertaining to the nature of being), values and priorities very different from those that emerged in the West and then spread to much of the world. Many indigenous peoples do not recognize private property and instead tend to work land on the principle of 'usufruct', which allows the working of land for useful purposes rather than for private ownership. It is relatively rare for land titles to exist; instead, land for cultivation or grazing is allocated by collective means or by a community leader. Although this generalization needs refinement, many indigenous peoples see the natural world of plants and animals as being as significant as humans, and their needs as equally deserving of consideration. Human rights are embodied in groups rather than individuals. They worship their ancestors, whom they believe should be buried in particular sacred places, which has brought them into conflict with governments and companies trying to extend farming or develop minerals.

And third, despite preserving their cultural identity, autonomy and ties to particular places, they have always responded to new opportunities and manoeuvred around the restrictions imposed on them by states and businesses (Schmidt 2007: 105). They have also adapted their livelihoods by acquiring the new skills brought by invaders such as the Spanish, including horse riding and sheep herding (Hall and Fenelon 2008: 3).

Indigenous peoples resisted attempts to undermine their local identity for centuries, but in the late nineteenth century, they started to seek alliances with national groups, especially workers and peasants. They also alerted national governments to their demands, although these were rarely successful, given their small numbers and the absence of democracy. The creation of the World Bank, the IMF and the UN after the Second World War, however, encouraged indigenous peoples to take advantage of the resulting world framework of institutions to appeal to a global public via the mass media and to win UN support for their agendas (Passy 1999: 149–50). UN conferences in 1977 and 1981 helped indigenous peoples to reach a consensus on their shared priorities. Later they established transnational networks (Passy 1999: 160–4).

INDIGENOUS PEOPLES

Because we all share a common ancestry in Africa, we are all ultimately migrants, so indigenous peoples are simply those whose descendants have lived in a particular area for a long time and who see themselves as firmly anchored there. Often, indigenous people have managed to remain relatively isolated (on islands or under forest cover).

Neoliberal policies such as opening forests to foreign companies or removing state protection from communal land further displaced indigenous peoples or undermined their autonomy. The Chiapas of southern Mexico fought back by forming the Zapatista National Liberation Army (EZLN) in 1994. After taking control of a radio station, several cities, a forest and an army barracks, they declared their region an autonomous zone. Their resistance is notable for many reasons, but perhaps the most significant is the extent to which the EZLN soon sought alliances with national and international organizations such as Amnesty International and Human Rights Watch. Then, helped by developments in IT, they forged additional links with universities, peace groups, anti-debt campaigns and other organizations across the world. The EZLN has attracted enormous worldwide scholarly interest (see Munck 2007; Solnit 2008; Stahler-Sholk 2007, among numerous others).

These events in Mexico were soon followed by the rise of the Global Justice Movement (Chapter 19) in the late 1990s against neoliberal globalization. Many indigenous peoples joined the Global Justice Movement's broad transnational coalition. Tellingly, though, their motives had little to do with reforming or replacing global capitalism with a socialist alternative. Rather, they wished to win international acceptance for retaining a 'political-cultural space to remain different' (Hall and Fenelon 2008: 2) while preserving their ancient cultures and livelihoods.

CONSTRUCTING BI-LOCAL OR MULTI-LOCAL TRANSNATIONAL LIVES

People who move overseas usually retain at least some of the sense of belonging and identity grounded in their native society, but cannot avoid becoming exposed to cultures that differ from their own. Whether they are migrants, professionals, students on exchange schemes, or business entrepreneurs, they are likely to construct enduring transnational networks that straddle home and host society (Chapter 12). These experiences need not but often do propel them towards developing cosmopolitan orientations and/or acquiring a multilayered social existence subject to different identities. In this section we examine two main innovative responses by such groups as they try to revive but also develop cosmopolitan and diasporic, multi-level identities. These expressions are explained further below.

DIASPORAS

While global cities contain important spatial vessels in which to accommodate plurality, the revival of a long-established social organization, a 'transnational diaspora', has come to symbolize how people subvert, transcend, or perhaps just parallel the nation-state. In Chapter 2 we defined a diaspora as the dispersion of peoples to a number of countries. People constitute a diaspora if they continue to evince a common concern for their 'homeland' (sometimes an imagined community) and come to share a sense of a common purpose with their own people, wherever they happen to be. The word 'diaspora' has particular associations with the Jewish (and later Armenian and African) peoples living out of their natal lands. These associations particularly evoke the idea of 'victims' – groups that were forcibly dispersed at one moment in history when a cataclysmic event happened. Nowadays, the concept is used more widely and imaginatively to include groups that are essentially voluntary migrants (Cohen 2008).

A diasporic consciousness is revived when a community still has links with its place of origin and does not feel the need for 'identificational assimilation' with the nation-state in which it currently resides. For many, reaffirming their diasporic connections is a positive choice, but sometimes the welcome accorded to them in a place of destination is so hostile or lukewarm that they feel impelled to reattach themselves to a transnational link. This is made easier by the ways in which 'home' and 'away' are connected by rapid transport, electronic communications and cultural sharing – part of the phenomena of globalization and transnationalism. It is now possible to have multiple localities and multiple identities.

A PAUSE TO REFLECT

Diasporas are rooted in a pre-national form of identification, yet they now seem to be ideally suited to bridging the national and the transnational. Can diasporic identities be helpful in creating paths for development in countries of origin or identification? Do diasporas have a more sinister side – allowing the growth of dissatisfied residents in host countries and the fomenting of civil conflict in home countries?

The revival of diaspora is also, however, based on a renewed search for 'roots', what Hall (1991) called a 'reach for groundings'. This need not imply a narrow localism, a retreat from global realities, or an inability to respond to the challenges of the ever widening marketplace and the new ethical and cultural demands stemming from globalization. Developing a meaningful identity and a flexible response to burgeoning opportunities requires a double-facing type of social organization and this is exactly what a diaspora can provide. However, diasporas have always been in a better position to act as a bridge between the particular and the universal, while equipping them to act as interlocutors in commerce, administration and other fields.

Many members of diasporic communities are bilingual or multilingual. They can spot 'what is missing' in the societies they visit or in which they settle. Often, they are better able to discern what their own group shares with other groups and when its cultural norms and social practices threaten majority groups. Being 'streetwise' may affect the very survival of the group itself. This need to be sensitive to prevalent currents means that, in addition to their achievements in trade and finance, diasporic groups are typically overrepresented in the arts, cinema, media and entertainment industries. Knowledge and awareness have enlarged to the point of cosmopolitanism or humanism. Yet, traditional cultural values, which sustain solidarity and have always supported the search for education and enlightenment, have not been threatened. Diasporas are able to interrogate the universal with the particular and can utilize transnational networks to press the limits of the local.

COSMOPOLITANISM AND THE CITY

As we saw in Chapter 18, cities predated the nation-state system and even during modernity continued as places where diversity rather than ethnic uniformity obtained. It may be that the city-state concept will be renewed in the global age (places like Singapore and Hong Kong play a comparable role with earlier city-states like Venice). But even if the city-state form does not take hold universally, 'the global city' within existing nation-states will increasingly contain the disparate elements moving from place to place, as travel, tourism, business links and the labour market become more organized on a global scale.

The social structure of global cities already operates to facilitate the international division of labour. For some living in these cities, identities are more fluid, situational, ambiguous and open. People may move through different zones or planes of belonging – perhaps combining residual attachments to a local community, a cross-ethnic partnership or marriage, and a transnational lifestyle in respect of leisure and cultural pursuits. Cosmopolitan practices and preferences are clearly a massive threat to those who claim that the only way to respond to globalization is to assert a determined loyalty to their ethnic group, nation or religion.

There are, however, critics of contemporary COSMOPOLITANISM. The liberal American historian Lasch (1995) suggested that cosmopolitans

KEY CONCEPT

The initial idea of COSMOPOLITANISM can be derived from its Greek roots. The important role of the city as a meeting place for people from across the world can be inferred from the words *kosmos* (world) and *polis* (city). As Vertovec and Cohen (2002: 1, 13) argue, cosmopolitanism now has four meanings: a vision of global democracy and world citizenship; the fostering of linkages between global social movements; a challenge to conventional notions of belonging, identity and citizenship; and a disposition to embrace diversity and to value behaviour and dispositions that support multiplicity, while respecting and enjoying cultural difference (for more on this, go to www.palgrave.com/sociology/cohen3e).

tend to be members of 'privileged classes' or 'elites' who no longer retain loyalty to the nation-state. Instead, they regard themselves as world citizens in a borderless world who have more in common with others of similar standing elsewhere than their own national populations. Accordingly, they do not need to accept, or they try to avoid, the normal obligations of national citizenship and, moreover, are sufficiently wealthy to opt out of public systems of education, health and welfare. Ironically, Lasch (1995: 47) argues, the 'cosmopolitanism of the favoured few … turns out to be a higher form of parochialism' or another kind of exclusiveness, separating people from others. In Chapter 7 we examined research findings on elites in global cities that reached similar conclusions (Butler 2003; Rofe 2003; Sassen 2007).

Others, by contrast, see the opportunities that cosmopolitanism might bring rather than its dangers (Beck 1998, 2006). Thus, cosmopolitan movements can transcend the appeal to national traditions and solidarities in favour of human values in every culture and religion. They may also address planetary concerns through new concepts, structures and organizations that can support the need to create transnationalism from below. For Beck, therefore, the notion of 'world citizenship' is to be embraced, not feared. Similarly, Hollinger (2002: 239) suggests that cosmopolitans help to sustain communities that engage with world problems affecting the entire human population and not just themselves.

In any case, the possibility of becoming a cosmopolitan or evolving further in the direction of greater openness to the cultural 'other(s)' and/or adopting some kind of moral responsibility for the world is available to many others besides privileged elites living in the flesh pots of global cities. Research has demonstrated that an increasing number of ordinary, educated, young middle-class individuals are also moving abroad for study or work. They provide a much more 'human face of global mobility' (Favell et al. 2006) and there is evidence that their experiences often propel them towards crossing cultural barriers and experimenting with multi-level identities (Kennedy 2007, 2010). We finish this discussion with a quote from one of the respondents interviewed in 2005 for Kennedy's (2007: 345) research on European migrants living in Manchester. Many of the other 60 respondents expressed similar views. Thomas was a language teacher in his early thirties from northern Spain. Asked whether living abroad had shaped his attitudes, he said:

> Well before, when I was living in Spain I didn't really have a big opinion about Europe. I think now I have a community of friends that are Europeans. And I see the links. … So now I'm against any kind of borders … at the end of the day we are all human, so we are supposed to share everything. So I never saw that when I was in Spain because I was never exposed to different cultures. Since I came to England I have also met so many South Americans and I can see the problems they have.

REVIEW

At the end of the Cold War, there were hopes of a 'new world order' and 'universal values' evolving from a single world culture based on mutual respect and understanding. Sadly, this has not happened. Despite exposure to numerous global influences, even educated people tend to remain tied to a sense of belonging to a place and to an ethnic or national attachment. This does not mean that they are oblivious to change; it merely means that coping with it has not, so far, rendered them more receptive to global understanding or involvement, although that may soon alter. Many political movements still try to resist multi-level transnational affiliations by creating new certainties and basing new states on a single ethno-nationality, as we saw with the disintegration of Yugoslavia. At worst, this can lead to 'ethnic cleansing' and even systematic attempts at genocide. Less overtly destructive, more sporadic and piecemeal are those situations in which groups damaged or even marginalized by globalization and other changes retreat behind local defences, resort to blaming vulnerable outsiders for their predicament, and reassert what they take to be their threatened native identity. By contrast, there are people in many parts of the global South who have responded to the assault that globalization has inflicted on their sense of local belonging not by closing ranks against outsiders but by joining forces with national and international agencies to resist those world forces that they believe endanger their local cultural integrity and economic survival.

At the same time, transnationalism and multi-level identities have begun to supersede national and/or ethnic identities in certain situations. Cities in general but global cities in particular provide a major stage for the increasing proliferation of subnational and transnational entities that cannot easily be contained in the nation-state system. The most important of these are diasporas and various kinds of cosmopolitan groups, although world religions could also be included here. Interestingly, they are all social formations that preceded the age of globalization by thousands of years. Transnationalism and cosmopolitanism are also evident in key shifts in attitude and behaviour; many people, not just those who can be called 'world citizens' or 'cosmopolites', are more willing to recognize and accept cultural and religious diversity. There is an increased knowledge and awareness of other cultures derived from the global media and travel. At times, knowledge and awareness lead to tolerance and respect for difference. We remind you of Perlmutter's (1991: 901) remark that now, for the first time in history: 'we have in our possession the technology to support the choice of sharing the governance of our planet rather than fighting with one another to see who will be in charge'. Our discussion provides both reasons to doubt and also to hope that more humans will take up this challenge.

Visit the companion website at www.palgrave.com/sociology/cohen3e for extra materials to check and expand your learning, including interactive self-test questions, mind maps making links between key themes, annotated web links to sociological research, data and key sociological thinkers, a searchable glossary and much more.

FURTHER READING

There are many readers and textbooks on ethnicity and nationalism. Among the most significant are A. D. Smith's *Ethnicity and Nationalism* (1992) and the same author's *Nations and Nationalism in a Global Era* (1995).

Two books on diasporas are R. Cohen's *Global Diasporas* (2008) and *Migration, Diasporas and Transnationalism* (1999), edited by S. Vertovec and R. Cohen, which contains 34 previously published articles.

R. Reitan's *Global Activism* (2007) includes useful material on the struggles of peasants, indigenous peoples and women in the face of global threats.

The readings in *Populist Radical Right Parties in Europe* (2007), edited by C. Mudde, provide a range of insights on attempts to reassert local affiliations across the EU.

QUESTIONS AND ASSIGNMENTS

1   How and why have communities changed with modernity and globalization?

2   Drawing on case study material, explain Bauman's concept of 'enforced localization', including how and why it is often applicable to workers in declining industrial regions.

3   To what extent have northern European countries failed in their quest to assimilate people of different cultures?

4   Do diasporas 'solve' the problem of bridging local sentiments and global imperatives?

22
Conclusion: global uncertainties and ways forward

In Chapter 2 we explored two concepts – 'globalization' (the objective worldwide processes of integration) and 'globality' (the subjective awareness of living in 'one world' with high levels of mutual interdependency). The extent to which these two processes have advanced remains contentious and besieged by uncertainties. Some anticipate that globalization and globality will be sufficiently vibrant phenomena to usher in a new global age and promote the construction of a generally benign global society. Others are gloomier. As we indicated in Chapter 21, attachment to local, ethnic and national sentiments remains strong and some scholars, who we might describe as 'globalization sceptics', strongly contest even the extent of globalization. The sceptical position needs enunciation, but provided we agree on what constitutes 'globalization', we can resolve the issue adequately by statistical means (see below). However, the pervasive global economic uncertainties that have followed the recession of 2007/8 have raised new doubts. The debate about the extent of globalization and whether it is slowing down, stabilizing or even reversing has been reignited. We should distinguish this issue from an essentially political or moral deliberation concerned with which people (or what organizations) promote, advocate, oppose, reject or wish to reform aspects of globalization and for what reasons. We also address these concerns.

In earlier chapters (especially Chapters 6 and 7), we probed the degree to which globalization was an uneven process, benefiting some, perhaps many, but also excluding and marginalizing others. We examine below whether the processes and dynamics of inclusion and exclusion have an underlying logic. We also need to address what can be done to reform some of the destructive aspects of market-led globalization, and whether some alternative ways of organizing our world can replace or repair some of the damage we see around us. After briefly defending the need to engage in some utopian thinking, we will focus on five possible trajectories that point to ways beyond our current crisis, namely: reviving mutuality; managing difference; creating greater equality; promoting a more pervasive democracy; and developing a sustainable environmental model. In our final remarks we reconsider the elements we have identified as constituting the building blocks of globality and the emergence of a global society. We argue that a more balanced relationship between societies, states and markets needs to evolve to stabilize the global order.

IS GLOBALIZATION NEW AND HOW EXTENSIVE IS IT?

One of the most persistent arguments developed by those with a sceptical turn of mind is that globalization is nothing new. Certainly, international trade is not new. As the leading economy for much of the nineteenth century, Britain's imports of raw materials rose by a factor of 20 between 1800 and 1875 (Dunning 1993: 110). The development of the commercial steamship, from approximately 1850, along with the telegraph, rapidly transformed trade opportunities in the last decades of the nineteenth century by reducing the previously prohibitive costs and risks involved in the movement of people and bulk goods. Moreover, since competition is intrinsic to capitalism, Britain and its emerging industrial rivals – the USA, Germany, France and eventually others – increasingly sought to export finished goods to each other's markets.

These countries also required reliable supplies of foodstuffs, raw materials and fuels for their expanding home markets and growing populations. This need for raw materials led to the scramble for captive colonies, imperial conquest, and the division of the world into rival spheres of trading interests, which each country then tried to monopolize. The net result of all this was that by 1914, on the eve of the First World War, a highly internationalized global economy had already emerged. Indeed, Hirst and Thompson's (1996: Ch. 2) boldest claim is that it was hardly less internationalized and open than the world economy in the early 1990s.

A similar case has been made for transnational flows of capital. Thus, foreign direct investment (FDI) by established home companies grew rapidly from about 1870. According to Dunning (1993: 116), by 1913 it had obtained an importance, proportionately, in the global economy that was not reached again until the mid-1950s. From about 1870, FDI also increasingly supplemented the investment role played by portfolio investment – where finance raised in a home country is used to acquire shareholding interests in a foreign government's or company's own projects rather than directly owned and managed businesses. Moreover, compared with the 1980s and 90s, when developing countries only received about 20% of FDI, before 1913 such flows were much more geographically dispersed – with two-thirds of the total directed to the colonies and dominions, especially Britain's overseas empire (Dunning 1993: 117–18).

So, the basic argument these sceptics make is that economic globalization is an old story and nothing special. However, there are several good reasons to doubt if the world economy was as open and integrated before the First World War as it is now. We will also present data showing the rapid acceleration in many indices of globalization since 1982. Considering only the economic dimension of globalization, we offer the following observations:

1. Far fewer countries were involved in international trade and FDI as major actors. For example, as Hirst and Thompson (1996: 22) concede, Britain and Germany between them supplied over half of the world's manufactured exports in 1913.
2. According to Dicken (1992: 27), whereas in the first quarter of this century only 8 countries supplied 95% of the world's manufacturing output, by 1986 the number producing this same share had risen to 25.
3. The lion's share of the capital outflows through FDI before 1914 was invested in such a way as to facilitate the export of raw materials, especially from the former colonies. Very little, only 15%, was directed towards manufacturing and most of this was located in Europe, America, Russia and Britain's dominions (Dunning 1993: Ch. 5).
4. Arguments that compare international trade in 1914 with the present period miss the crucial point that each country's trade (imports and exports) and the capital flows associated with the outward and inward FDI it experiences were, by the 1980s, fast becoming indistinguishable (Julius 1990). This is because their integrated global operations compel

TNCs to engage in intra-firm exchanges. A good part of a country's official declared imports and exports actually consists of the cross-border movement of components, semi-finished goods, production-related services and other 'products' between the various subsidiaries of foreign and locally based TNCs.

Although we readily accept that there were high levels of international trade in the period just before the First World War, we do not believe this significantly dents the argument that we are witnessing a new era of economic globalization. For one thing, prior to 1914 and for several decades after, overt and strongly nationalist pressures drove states towards protecting their home economies while seeking to dominate overseas spheres of imperialist influence. Also, in terms of scale, complexity, the number of actors involved (both state and non-state), and the integration of finance, manufacturing, services and investment, the economic globalization commencing in the late twentieth century has gone well beyond anything that existed in 1914.

RECENT MEASURES OF GLOBALIZATION IN GENERAL

Is it possible to measure the changes to and extent of globalization in a systematic way? This was the challenge taken up by two researchers at the University of Warwick. Lockwood and Redoano (2005) first divided the forms of globalization into three kinds – economic, social and political. Next, they sought to find reliable data sets that measured various variables within the three types of globalization. Thus:

1. *Economic globalization* was measured by these variables:
   - *trade* (exports plus imports of goods and services expressed as a proportion of GDP)
   - *FDI* (inflows plus outflows as a proportion of GDP)
   - *portfolio investment* (inflows and outflows as a proportion of GDP)
   - *income* (the amount crossing frontiers as a proportion of GDP).
2. *Social globalization* comprised two elements:
   - the 'people' variables were *stocks of foreigners* (as a proportion of a country's total population), *flows of foreigners* (again, as a proportion of total population), and *worker remittances* and *tourists* (arrivals)
   - the 'ideas' variables were *phone calls*, *internet users*, *films* (the number imported and exported), *books/newspapers* (value imported and exported) and *mail* (the number of international letters per capita).
3. *Political globalization* was measured by the following variables:
   - *embassies* (the number of foreign embassies in a country)
   - *UN missions* (the number of UN peacekeeping missions in which a country participates)
   - *organizations* (the number of memberships of international organizations).

The results of calculating and weighting all these variables are presented in many tables, but the crucial aggregated information is summarized in Table 22.1.

TABLE 22.1 Warwick world globalization index				
	1982	1992	2002	2004
Economic globalization	0.111	0.118	0.140	0.140
Social globalization	0.062	0.163	0.364	0.424
Political globalization	0.442	0.606	0.704	0.697
Overall globalization	**0.234**	**0.438**	**0.642**	**0.675**

Sources: Original article Lockwood and Redoano (2005); adapted from updated data at http://www2.warwick.ac.uk/fac/soc/csgr/index/.

Of course, statistical measures are not everything. There are certain activities that cannot be measured, or have only been measured in a sporadic fashion and are not therefore included. There may be disputes over the methodology, the selection of variables and the weighting between them. Perhaps more damagingly, because the researchers were forced to use country-based statistics (which is how they are collected), the data are stronger indications of the extent to which each country has become internationalized than the extent to which the world has become globalized. Nonetheless, by clustering the data both regionally and globally, we are able to gain the best measure yet of the extent to which globalization has indeed occurred, rather than has been said to have occurred by commentators and politicians. Within the stated parameters, the results are conclusive and even startling. While economic globalization and political globalization have proceeded apace, the growth of social globalization is staggering, and generally unrecognized. The headline news is that, by 2004, the world as a whole was nearly 2.9 times more globalized than it was 22 years earlier.

A PAUSE TO REFLECT

If globalization had an immanent purpose, a telos, then we could assume it will simply become stronger and stronger. However, we have argued in this book that globalization is made and furthered by the interests, energy, enthusiasm and organization of social actors – individuals, groups and corporations. Can globalization therefore be 'unmade', and are there intimations of a reverse movement of 'deglobalization'?

The data used in the indices of globalization are collected retrospectively, so it is difficult to measure the impact of the current global economic crisis. However, using 2008 data and measures comparable to the Warwick globalization index, the KOF Swiss Economic Institute (2011), a leading Swiss think tank, recorded a distinct slowdown in economic and social globalization in 2008 in its index of globalization. Only political globalization was on the rise, presumably as political institutions, agreements and connections proliferated in response to the economic slowdown. Despite this levelling off in economic and social measures of globalization, it is implausible to argue that globalization per se is unravelling. World trade continues to rise. The number of international tourists, students and migrants witnessed a brief slowing at the height of the recession, before the graph again continued upwards. There are denser than ever flows of internet and phone traffic, investments and remittances.

REACTING TO UNCERTAINTY

The continuing march of globalization should not conceal the fact that there have been enormous changes within the world system. After 2007/8, the idea that we can proceed on the basis of 'business as usual' has been seriously undermined. Business confidence in nearly all the established wealthy countries has been shaken to the roots. There are new democratic possibilities and epochal changes in the Middle East and North Africa. The power of the BRIC countries on the world stage is growing apace and has some unpredictable possibilities. Add to these the gyrations of the stock markets, the indebtedness of many countries, and the rapacious conduct of the banks and other financial institutions, all of which have driven massive stakes into the ideological heart of neoliberalism, the ideology that pumped the life-blood of economic globalization. Few observers now unreservedly accept the core neoliberal idea that a free market is both self-correcting and benign.

This ideological meltdown, together with continuing global changes and new global uncertainties, has produced differing reactions from people and organizations. These responses are contested and derive from differing political and ideological positions. Freely adapting the account of Anheier et al. (2001: 7–10) and relabelling their categories, these responses may be personified and classified into four clusters – supporters, detractors, reformers and outsiders.

SUPPORTERS

Supporters of current forms of globalization consist of TNCs and others who directly benefit from open economies. The 'others' may include highly skilled transnational migrants who are able to command high salaries and favourable work conditions by treating the world as a single labour market. The World Bank and the WTO are just two of the bodies promoting free trade and an open global capitalist economy. Banks and insurance and investment companies are also in favour of open borders because they profit by selling their services globally. At the social level, there is probably a consensus that student mobility, the global sharing of scientific data, and the transmission of films, DVDs, books and journals are 'a good thing'. A broadly positive view attaches to the internet and the opportunities for blogging, which have led to the democratization and internationalization of information and ideas, although we record some negative features of the internet in Chapter 16. Finally, at the political level, supporters of globalization may also be prepared to endorse interventions by strong states to enforce more benign regimes and protect human rights. Here the balance sheet is positive in some cases (Kosovo, Libya, Sierra Leone), negative in others (Somalia, Iraq), with some still undetermined outcomes, like Afghanistan.

DETRACTORS

Detractors seek to reverse globalization, preferring to return to a world in which nation-states exercise full sovereignty over the economic and political destinies of their own citizens. Such detractors include left-wing groups that are opposed to capitalism and wish to introduce some kind of socialist, collectivized economic life at the national level, largely decoupled from global financial flows. Also included in the detractor category are right-wing nationalist and religious interests that want to protect local markets, businesses and jobs from international competition and capital movements, or from 'foreign' faiths. Both left and right are suspicious of open borders, the growth of global governance, and giving increased power to the UN or its specialist agencies. Both also tend to romanticize or idealize the past. At the cultural and social level, enhanced intercourse with non-nationals is seen as threatening to national cultures and social cohesion, so detractors tend to be fiercely anti-immigration.

REFORMERS

Those we classify as 'reformers' see globalization as potentially beneficial because it can provide the technological means for fostering increased connectivity between different peoples and for bringing prosperity to more individuals, but they insist that these will remain only possibilities unless global capitalism is civilized or reformed. Thus, they demand fairer economic institutions and rules that are more clearly dedicated to spreading the benefits of economic development to the less advantaged. Politically, they demand much greater participation by ordinary people in setting global agendas at national and global levels, with respect to issues such as technological progress, debt relief, fair trade, controls on international business, and representation in international bodies. They are also likely to want stronger environmental protection, increased and more democratic global governance, and an international system for policing human rights. Unlike the 'supporters', the reformers would want the UN to be the sole body authorizing humanitarian interventions in support of human rights. It would probably be fair to argue that those who wish to reform globalization have failed so far to articulate a set of alternative principles that have commanded general acceptance. In a modest way, we make a number of suggestions to guide future global public policy later in this chapter.

OUTSIDERS

Finally, 'outsiders' see global changes as happening at one remove from them. They want to opt out and develop their own separate courses of action 'independently of government, international institutions and transnational corporations' (Anheier et al. 2001: 10). Such individuals or groups tend to operate very much at a local and grassroots level and are likely to prefer economic autarky and small-scale community organizations. Characteristically, outsiders will reject innovations like genetically modified foods or data collected on citizens, will be strongly committed to a simpler, less consumer-driven way of life, and are opposed to the powers wielded by TNCs and strong governments. When involved in protests and wider social movements, they tend to engage in striking and colourful activities with a strong central theme of reclaiming public spaces from all kinds of authority. Anarchists and those with strong green commitments are intertwined with global outsiders.

This fourfold division of reactions to globalization is imperfect, even crude. However, it serves to reinforce the point, already made in Chapter 2, that social actors are not simply helpless chaff, victims of an uncontrolled tornado of globalization that blows across the world. Individuals, groups, movements, institutions and governments can promote, defend and advance their own causes and preferences and so help to shape the nature and characteristics of globalization and globality. We will see below that human agency is also important in determining who is included and who is excluded from the current global order.

GLOBAL EXCLUSION AND INCLUSION

In Chapter 6 we showed that despite the claims by many writers (for example Wolf 2005) that 'globalization works', the contemporary world remains characterized by sharp inequalities, ubiquitous fears and uneven development. Particular countries, regions and selected groups – rural producers, refugees, famine victims, workers in deindustrializing areas, and the urban poor – were the focus of our attention. There are other groups – the disabled, those with major ailments like HIV/AIDS, and the elderly – that could also have been singled out for detailed discussion. Here, we ask the question whether there is some underlying logic or central insight that explains why social exclusion arises, why some are pushed to the edge of existence, and why others, at best, benefit only to a small degree from economic development.

Our hypothesis is that social exclusion is more likely to occur when the adoption of neoliberal economic practices is disengaged from public policy and legal-rational forms of political governance. Put more simply, a free market alone is neither an ethical good nor a practical solution to inequality or marginality if there is no simultaneous social reform or if dictatorial, inefficient or corrupt forms of politics are allowed to continue. This point can be illustrated at a country level, but more importantly it also forms the basis of a global discussion of social inclusion and exclusion – who wins and who loses. Let us take just one country as an example, namely the Russian Federation. There, the enthusiastic adoption of neoliberal economic blueprints after the end of communism triggered a near disintegration of society for about a decade and a half. Of course, some people benefited massively. Instead of lining up at the drab communist GUM (*Gosudarstvennyi Universalnyi Magazin*, state department store), the wealthy elite could now visit the Petrovsky Passage in Moscow (Figure 22.1). There they found boutiques selling labels like Moschino, Marina Rinaldi, Max Mara, La Perla, Nina Ricci, Mandarina Duck, Kenzo, Etro, Pomellato, Ermanno Scervino, Bosco Women and Bosco Men.

Other social and economic indicators of the new Russia are, however, less impressive. Without the protection of the old Soviet welfare state, the life expectancy of men fell to 58 years, while suicide rates climbed 60% in the 1989–99 period (Ciment 1999). An article in the authoritative UK medical journal, *The Lancet*, echoed these findings. Over the short period, 1989–2002, the mortality rates of men of working age (15–59) increased by a shocking 12.8% (Stuckler et al. 2009). The population rapidly declined, from 148 million in 1991 to a projected 130 million by 2030 (*The Economist*, 2005: 107). Corruption and crime were rife. When the recession hit, the Russian economy slumped, GDP shrinking 9.8% in the first quarter of 2009, while manufacturing fell by 23.5% in the same year, the largest contraction in 15 years (Le Blanc 2009). Again, in 2009, there was a 30% increase in recorded measures of poverty. It is true that the worst excesses of the decade after the end of communism are slowly ameliorating. By 2010, life expectancy rates for males rose to 63.04 and there is one important indication that expectations of the future are becoming more positive, namely the moderate increase in the birth rate. The suicide rate, however, remains double that of Western European societies. Despite reasonable expectations of an economic upturn (other countries need Russian oil and gas), the decade-long experience of Russia from 1989 is a grim warning of the socially corrosive possibilities of unregulated, free-market capitalism.

© PAVEL LOSEVSKY/FOTOLIA

FIGURE 22.1 Petrovsky Passage, Moscow
Petrovsky Passage is a refurbished architectural gem in Moscow, where luxury brands are concentrated. In 2008, with the onset of the recession, the 25 richest Russians lost $230bn between them. The number of Moscow's billionaires shrank from 74 to a mere 27. Russian imports of Bentley, Ferrari, Rolls-Royce and Lamborghini declined by 60% in 2009 (Le Blanc 2009).

THE 'GREAT TRANSFORMATION' AND SOCIAL EXCLUSION

In moving from the country level to a broadbrush global treatment of social exclusion, we can refer to Munck's (2005) stimulating discussion. Munck is not alone in spotting the renewed significance of Karl Polanyi's ([1957]2002) compelling work, *The Great Transformation*. The reissued version of Polanyi's work has a laudatory foreword by Joseph Stiglitz, Nobel laureate and former chief economist at the World Bank and now its principal gadfly. In brief, Polanyi's central insight was that there was no innate attribute explaining the rise of nineteenth-century economic liberalism. Contrary to claims of the free marketeers, the invisible hand of the market did not arise spontaneously or freely. As Polanyi (cited in Munck 2005: 146) wrote:

> There was nothing natural about *laissez faire*; free markets could never have come into being merely by allowing things to take their course … the road to the free market was

opened up and kept open by an enormous increase in continuous, centrally organized and controlled interventionism.

This apparently simple point carries enormous explanatory punch in our contemporary world. At a national level, it helps to explain farm subsidies to Midwest farmers and tax breaks to oil giants in the USA, illuminates the official banking/civil service/TNC alliance in Japan, and sheds light on 'Asian capitalism' in Singapore and Malaysia. It explains why state communism and capitalism are such compatible bedfellows in China. At a wider level, we can understand why banks in Europe and the USA were bailed out during 2008 and the salience of structural adjustment programmes, the WTO rules, and the TRIPS (Trade-Related Intellectual Property Rights) agreement. All these national and international measures were bribes or payoffs to particular interests, or measures agreed by governments under the influence of powerful companies and banks. As in the case of nineteenth-century liberalism, late twentieth-century neoliberalism, a virtual synonym for economic globalization, has come about not because of the mysterious workings of the free market, but because key social and political actors have determined that it should do so. And when things went wrong, increased taxes for the many were used to subsidize the tax benefits and bonuses for the rich. Even Warren Buffett (2011), one of the wealthiest people in the world, was constrained to complain (perhaps with his tongue in his cheek) to the *New York Times*:

> Our leaders have asked for 'shared sacrifice'. But when they did the asking, they spared me. I checked with my mega-rich friends to learn what pain they were expecting. They, too, were left untouched. While the poor and middle class fight for us in Afghanistan, and while most Americans struggle to make ends meet, we mega-rich continue to get our extraordinary tax breaks. Some of us are investment managers who earn billions from our daily labors but are allowed to classify our income as 'carried interest', thereby getting a bargain 15 percent tax rate. Others own stock index futures for 10 minutes and have 60 percent of their gain taxed at 15 percent, as if they'd been long-term investors. These and other blessings are showered upon us by legislators in Washington who feel compelled to protect us, much as if we were spotted owls or some other endangered species. It's nice to have friends in high places.

Buffett's intervention was seconded by 16 wealthy French citizens, including Liliane Bettencourt, the L'Oreal heiress (number 17 on the Forbes global billionaires list), who offered on the website of *Le Nouvel Observateur* to make a 'special contribution' to the French exchequer as an act of solidarity. Despite these unusual offers, the super-rich are generally content with the largess provided to them. Moreover, there has been a notable absence of a large-scale, coordinated opposition movement, equivalent to what Polanyi (2002) called a welfarist 'countermovement' in an earlier area. As Polanyi noted, nineteenth-century liberalism destroyed important socialities and cherished community values. Greed replaced need, individualism replaced social cohesion, neglect or indifference replaced caring, and contempt for the poor replaced charity. This is a characterization many would recognize as applying to our own situation. We can see numerous contemporary examples of states evacuating the social space needed to hold the fabric of society together. In some cases, this is a matter of choice or ideology. In others, where external forces determine spending patterns, national elites might reduce welfare spending with a good deal of reluctance, perhaps to help pay off massive deficits incurred in supporting the banks. Social exclusion is derivative of these large structural logics and forces. In developing his argument, Munck (2005: 25–6) argues that the notion of social exclusion can be used as a 'unifying perspective' linking varous forms of global deprivation, marginality and inequality for three reasons:

1. Globalization has brought all under the sway of capitalist market relations.
2. North and South are interpenetrated, with the people of the South (comprising poor immigrants and locals) found in urban slums in rich countries, and those of the North found in financial centres and gated communities in developing countries.

3. Neoliberalism has spread the ideology of the self-regulating market to all societies, even nominally communist ones like China.

We can add that, as the fiscal crisis beginning in 2007 ramifies, other aspects of global deprivation have become evident. Loans are denied to businesspeople, taxes and transport costs go up, unemployment rises, welfare payments go down, and the prices for the produce from developing countries fall. We are, in these respects, truly 'in it together'.

ELEMENTS OF A COUNTERMOVEMENT

Given the pervasive impact of neoliberalism on a global level, those arguing for social inclusion and seeking to advance a countermovement to the present social order are faced with the need to operate on a broad front. There is some ambiguity (given its structural starting point) about whether Polanyi's countermovement operates as an inevitable opposing force, rather along the lines of a Hegelian dialectic, or whether there needs to be organization to bring the countermovement into being and advance its course. We take the latter view, as it is consistent with Polanyi's prior argument that the free-market ideology was imposed and did not drop mysteriously from the skies. The countermovement (broadly described as the Global Justice Movement) remains highly fragmented, and principally comprises these active social agents:

1. progressive governments demanding reform of the international trading regime, for example pressing for 'fair trade, not free trade'
2. churches organizing programmes to protect the poor
3. global social movements, for example seeking to secure debt relief for poor countries or to restrict the environmentally destructive operations of some TNCs
4. consumer groups promoting the purchase of fair trade and ecologically friendly goods, as well as goods produced in factories where good labour conditions obtain
5. some governments and local authorities reinvigorating social welfare expenditure and policies
6. citizen groups demanding that deficit reduction programmes are funded by all, depending on income, and that tax evaders and avoiders be asked to pay their fair shares
7. corporations signing up to and actually delivering 'social responsibility' programmes, as opposed to simply massaging their public relations profile
8. labour/trade unions protecting their members from exploitation and helping to organize internationally
9. migrant organizations and those working on behalf of migrant organizations
10. intellectuals and journalists exposing the deficiencies of neoliberalism in theory and practice
11. protesters supporting movements like Occupy Wall Street, which from October 2011 was demanding that irresponsible financial institutions be brought to heel
12. members and supporters of radical social networking sites, like Avaaz, conducting an extensive range of campaigns (Avaaz had signed up some 10 million followers by the end of 2011).

We emphasize again that the countermovement to neoliberalism is still disjointed, weak and disorganized, although it has a plethora of enthusiasts and activists and operates on local, national and global scales. It is difficult to study such a global and dispersed countermovement, but we have shown throughout the book that global social movements like the civil rights, green and women's movements have episodically been successful in organizing the marginalized, dispossessed and excluded, drawing them into the mainstream through a process of confronting the established order and empowering the hitherto powerless (Chapters 19 and 20).

GLOBAL THINKERS 22 MARTIN ALBROW (1942–)

In *The Global Age* (1996), Albrow argues that, for 200 years, modernity and its assumptions – material progress steered by the nation-state and pursued through science and rational organization – have dominated our lives. However, we are now in a totally different situation. In particular, he highlights:

- the environmental limits to perpetual economic development
- the spread of weaponry that is too dangerous to use
- global systems of communication that overwhelm local cultures
- an integrated global economy
- increasingly reflexive individuals, critically aware of their own and others' actions.

The consequences of these five elements mean that:

- the nation-state no longer 'contains' all our aspirations or 'monopolizes' our attention
- for more and more people, the world is becoming the frame of reference, the object of concern and the reality that dominates our awareness (what we call 'globality')
- a world (although not yet a global) society is emerging, consisting of the totality of social relations that directly or indirectly involve actions having a global scope and intention
- we begin jointly to share values and take actions that are specifically designed to shape the global order.

Understanding everyday global life: sociospheres

Albrow also provides some useful concepts for making sense of global life. For example, we can conceptualize the totality of relations each person has under global conditions – spread over several locations and operated through virtual, imaginary and/or co-present relations – in terms of a 'sociosphere'. Each person's sociosphere is unique to them and many of those included in it may not know each other (your school and university friends are probably different from your work friends or your family). This concept is especially useful for analysing global life.

Socioscapes

He then adopts Appadurai's concept of 'scapes' (see Chapter 2). These are disjointed fragments of ethnic, media, technical, financial or ethical resources that flow around the world and out of which we build our own imagined lives. Albrow (1997) adds the idea of socioscapes to this repertoire. Wherever a cluster of individual's sociospheres come together in a particular location, we get a series of probably disconnected flows of social life forming something like a cavalcade (the people eating in the café when you are, those attending the same pop concert or strolling along a shopping mall). Like Appadurai's other scapes, technologies bring together a disjunctive set of social actors in a probably temporary but significant flow. Socioscapes do not constitute all our experience but with globalization they do become more prominent.

Source: Albrow (1987, 1996, 1997).

WAYS FORWARD FOR GLOBAL PUBLIC POLICY

While there has been some progress in the development and functioning of transnational initiatives to change the global order, there has been little headway made at the level of constructing an ideological alternative to neoliberalism. So far, reformers have failed to articulate a set of alternative principles that have commanded general acceptance. It would be arrogant for us to say we can provide the answers, but we will follow the latitude given to social scientists who are allowed, by convention, to venture further away from descriptive data to prescriptive comment in a final chapter. The famous raconteur Oscar Wilde (in Guy 2007: 247) once remarked that 'a map of the world that does not include Utopia is not worth even glancing at, for it leaves out the one country at which Humanity is always landing'. The collapse of cherished ideologies (like communism) and the near collapse of the certainties of neoliberalism have allowed some space for utopian thinking. As Tally (2011: 3) argues:

> As the spontaneous protests of Occupy Wall Street, the Arab Spring, and other restless movements agitating for change demonstrate, the utopian impulse remains powerfully vital today. Especially in its critical vocation, as it highlights the failings of the present system rather than sketching the concrete parameters of a future alternative, this utopian impulse is a forceful response to an intolerable status quo and to the anti-utopian strictures upon the imagination. That is, even within the apparently total system of globalization, other spaces are possible.

At the very least, policy inspired by some utopian impulse will give us some innovative outlooks and new modes of engagement. In particular, we argue that global public policy needs to develop in five areas:

- reviving mutuality
- managing difference
- creating greater equality
- promoting a more pervasive democracy
- developing a sustainable economic and environmental model.

REVIVING MUTUALITY

The extraordinary fact about the MUTUAL movement is that it is all around us, but has somehow remained rather invisible and escaped systematic sociological attention.

Mutuals include building societies, fishing cooperatives, housing associations, savings and loans clubs, cooperative banks, credit unions, friendly societies, healthcare providers, agricultural cooperatives, and insurance companies. Among other things, the cooperative movement in the UK, which has deep roots, can book your holiday, provide your groceries, bank your salary, advance you a loan, insure your house and car, and even bury you. The somewhat elusive quality of the mutual sector in the UK is illustrated by the fact that the movement's own publications variously estimated the size of the sector in 2010 as £33.2bn (http://www.uk.coop/economy/sectors) to over £100bn (Mutuo 2010: 4). If the latter is true (there are definitional issues as to what organizations are included), the mutual sector would feature in the top 30 in the FTSE list of leading companies, although, of course, it does not have a stock market listing. Beyond the UK, the International Co-operative Alliance claims that worldwide there are 800 million members and 100 million employees (employing 20% more people than all the TNCs combined). It is further claimed that the 300 largest mutuals are responsible for an aggregate turnover of US$1.1 trillion, which is equivalent to the size of the world's tenth economy – almost the size of the Spanish economy (Mutuo 2010: 5).

Even allowing for a little definitional stretch, the size of the mutual sector is impressively large and, moreover, it has proved much less vulnerable to the current fiscal crisis than quoted companies, which are plagued by shareholders demanding short-term profits, managers demanding large salaries and bonuses, and speculators who can buy or sell shares at a whim, following their own inclinations or the herd instinct. Mutuals generally invest in ethical products and companies, have a greater respect for the environment, and do not engage in the arms trade. They are regarded as good employers; indeed, employees often own shares in the organization. Given these virtues, it seems remarkable that potential consumers and members are still relatively unaware of where they can access cooperative goods or services. If millions or, better, hundreds of millions chose this option, the wild swings in the economy would be ameliorated and mutuals would contribute significantly to 'sustainable growth' (see below). Beyond consumer choice, if the mutuals are to

---

KEY CONCEPT

An easy way of defining the MUTUAL sector is that producers, consumers and partners have a strong stake in a collective organization, which is devoted to serving its members rather than producing profits for outsiders. There are no shareholders and the organization is not quoted on the equity market.

make a real impact, citizens would need to mobilize to ensure that demutualized building societies and savings clubs should be remutualized, that recently bailed-out banks should go the same way, and that legislatures enact regulations and tax breaks to encourage the mutual sector. Gradually, a larger and larger portion of the economy would be prised from the hands of those who triggered the biggest economic downturn since the 1930s and placed in the care of more responsible stewards of our wealth.

A PAUSE TO REFLECT

At first sight, reviving or promoting mutual or cooperatives seems to be a promising way of moderating the worst effects of a free market. But is the mutual movement merely a remnant of the past and the prospect of renewing it a burst of nostalgia? Cooperatives have to survive and operate in the wider capitalist market, so is it inevitable that they will themselves take on the coloration and practices of ordinary capitalist firms? Do you and your friends use cooperative services and can you see yourself joining or starting a mutual?

MANAGING DIFFERENCE

In Chapters 9, 12 and 17 we showed that enhanced connectivity and international migration serve to broaden and transnationalize identities, both of people who are moving and those with whom they come into contact. However, equally observable has been a simultaneous and reactive movement involving a return to old, familiar, comforting identities, be these of an ethnic, national or religious sort. At the extreme, the religious fundamentalist and the xenophobe are both symptoms of this tendency. In many places, but notably in the USA and Europe, the neoconservative and conservative right has seized the political moment afforded by the terrorist threat to question both the extent of migration and the degree of recognition afforded to migrants' home cultures, religions, languages and social practices. The attack on diversity and difference has been particularly fierce in the USA. Perhaps the most powerful academic voice on this question was that of Samuel P. Huntington (2004: 142–3), a professor of politics at Harvard and the director of security planning for the National Security Council in the Carter administration. In his *cri de cœur Who Are We? America's Great Debate*, he angrily denounced those in the USA who had discarded earlier notions that the USA was a 'melting pot'. He insisted on the primacy of the English-speaking, Protestant, eastern seaboard and deplored the 'deconstructionists' who sought to 'enhance the status and influence of subnational racial, ethnic and cultural groups', which, he (Huntington 2004: 142) claimed, has had deleterious effects on democratic values and liberties:

> They downgraded the centrality of English in American life and pushed bilingual education and linguistic diversity. They advocated legal recognition of group rights and racial preferences over the individual rights central to the American Creed. They justified their actions by theories of multiculturalism and the idea that diversity rather than unity or community should be America's overriding value. The combined effect of these efforts was to promote the deconstruction of the American identity that had been gradually created over three centuries.

The sneering use of 'they' – directed at a largely unidentified group of 'do-gooders' – leaps off the page. But does large-scale immigration really pose a threat to public order, economic prosperity, social wellbeing, or cultural cohesion? This is by no means an invariable outcome. However, in circumstances where the settled population is under threat or perceives a threat (of job loss, housing shortage or welfare rationing), the arrival of a large, culturally dissimilar group may well be resisted, even if the long-term effects may be benign (Goldin et al. 2011:

162–210). It is certainly more than possible that an ambitious or unscrupulous politician will fan the flames of xenophobia.

Public policy has yo-yoed in response to the growth of diversity or 'super-diversity'. In the global cities, enclave cultures have survived and even thrived under the banner of pluralism or multiculturalism. Again, some groups can seek to move between local, historical and transnational cultural affinities, a process we described in our discussion of diasporas and multi-level identities in Chapter 21. By contrast, the scope for tolerance of diversity has been significantly narrowed in many countries. In May 2008 thousands of foreigners fled from violence directed at them in South Africa by locals, only recently released from the bigotry of the apartheid regime. Routine racist attacks have become familiar in many European cities. Governments have been pressed into resurrecting quasi-assimilationist positions, demanding that migrants adopt local citizenships, speak the official language(s), and show courtesy and respect for the social practices and cultural norms expressed by the majority population.

To manage cultural difference, governments need to placate long-established communities, but not to such an extent that they fan the flames of extremism and racism. They need to recognize the legitimate claims of migrants to practise their religions or speak their languages, but again not to such a degree that a common understanding of citizenship and equality under the law becomes eroded. They need to convince all residents that the arrival of unfamiliar goods, ideas or artistic forms generally enriches rather than narrows the local repertoire of cultural resources by extending the opportunities to express indigenous traditions and lifestyles. In such situations, people can exercise selectivity and consciously mix the old with the new to create alternative (hybridized or creolized) forms of culture. This process of cultural borrowing and mixing is multidirectional and includes a variety of activities stretching from culinary, musical and artistic ones to practices and philosophies associated with health, sport and methods of business organization, to name but a few. By mixing and matching old with new, many people can create a novel home, a comforting locus, to express their uniqueness in the face of cultural fundamentalisms, imperialism or xenophobia. As those predicting the creolization of the world propose (see Glissant 1998; Hannerz 1987), the locals will select particular elements from incoming cultures, endow these with meanings different from those they possessed in the original culture and then creatively merge these with indigenous and other imported traditions to create totally new forms. In short, the flows and movements of ideas, images, capital and people will generate an original wave of syncretism, innovative cultures and different ways of being in the world.

CREATING GREATER EQUALITY

Arguing for greater equality has, historically, been a preoccupation of the left (in particular those advocating socialist or communist positions) or derives from a humanist or religious sense of what is 'fair' and 'just'. Remarkably, Wilkinson and Pickett (2010), two epidemiologists with social science backgrounds, have shown in their powerful book, *The Spirit Level: Why Equality is Better for Everyone*, that on purely utilitarian grounds, equality works not only for those who are disadvantaged, but for 'everyone'. 'Everyone' is perhaps something of an exaggeration, but in table after table covering, inter alia, mental health, drug use, life expectancy, crime, obesity, educational performance and incarceration, they are able to demonstrate that more equality produces better outcomes for most of the population. Their method is to deploy a simply presented statistical analysis. The x-axis is the index of inequality (measured by income) and the y-axis lists a particular health or social outcome. In Figure 22.2 their various measured outcomes are combined. The diagonal line is a regression line that shows the trend emerging between the data points. The data are startling – put bluntly, higher inequality leads to worse, often a lot worse, health and social problems. By way of illustration, in Figure 22.2, Portugal and the UK have much poorer outcomes than Japan or Sweden.

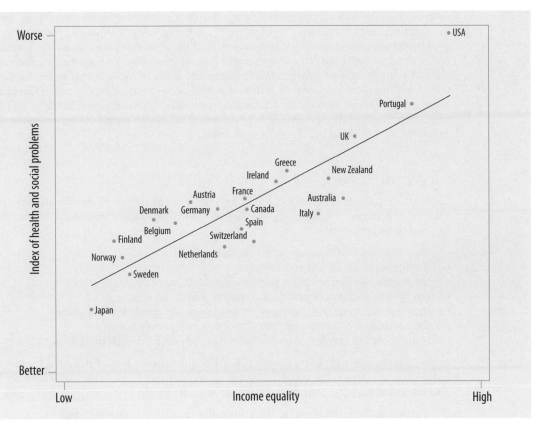

FIGURE 22.2 The relationship of health and social problems to income inequality

Source: Wilkinson and Pickett (2010: 20).

© Dr Kate Pickett and Professor Richard Wilkinson, 2009.

Wilkinson and Pickett's (2010) book has caused quite a sensation internationally, as well as a good deal of comment. Nonetheless, with some reservations, which the authors themselves often note, the analysis they provided looks remarkably secure. It covers 21 countries, all in the developed world. The data for the rest of the 172 countries in the UN are either not comparable or unavailable. It is doubtful that they would show such a consistent pattern. Wilkinson and Pickett have, however, armed themselves against the obvious refutation that statistics collected in different ways across countries and measures of health, poverty, educational performance and so on are likely to be culturally specific. They did this by including a complementary analysis of the 50 US states – where cultural specificity and statistical anomalies are minimized. A similar set of relationships was found, totally consistent with the international data.

What Wilkinson and Pickett have convincingly demonstrated is that at a certain level of wealth (not that reached by many developing countries), there are diminishing returns to welfare if growth is unaccompanied by measures to combat inequality. This affects the society at large, not merely the marginalized, excluded and poverty-stricken. To elaborate and give flesh to their argument, let us take crime as one example. More people are in prison in more unequal countries, a finding that is identical if considering more unequal states within the states of the USA (Wilkinson and Pickett 2010: 148–9). The growth in prison populations is often prompted by respectable citizens who demand longer and more custodial sentences for those who engage in property crimes or drug use. Taxes go up to pay for the prisons, while the number of repeat offenders rises as good rehabilitation schemes are difficult to fund from tax revenues. As recidivists reoffend, more police are needed, insurance premiums become more costly, and better locks, gates, fences, alarms and intruder lights need fitting. Some of the wealthier might move into expensive gated communities, with longer commuting times and distant schools. Moreover, it becomes more difficult to enjoy (or flaunt) one's wealth if a posh car might be 'keyed', or earrings might be snatched off one's ear lobes. We can now see the force of this type of analysis. More inequality leads to more crime, more taxes, and a fearful and insecure citizenry. In terms of public policy, even if policy-makers hold to the argument that social inequalities are 'natural' or helpful in encouraging initiative and enterprise, there is now sufficient evidence to suggest that happiness and the general good will be enhanced only by reducing income inequalities.

PROMOTING DEMOCRACY

Can mutuality, cultural enrichment or greater income equality be realized at an international level? This turns on the creation of an active, informed, engaged citizenry drawing on the following developments:

- the extension of democratic, civil and human rights
- the spread of education and literacy
- the provision of information and access to communications
- the growth of multicultural understanding and awareness
- the empowerment of women and other historically disadvantaged groups
- the promotion of environmentally friendly production systems
- the accomplishment of greater leisure, creativity and freedom from want.

At the heart of this wish list is the spread of Enlightenment ideas of freedom, human rights and democracy across the globe (Chapter 3). How is this to be achieved? There are those who insist that we must start with the nation-state. Bienefeld (1994: 122), for example, asks:

> Can we realistically hope, at the end of the twentieth century, to redefine and reconstruct political entities that would allow us to manage the increasingly destructive forces of global competition while providing individuals with the capacity to define themselves as social beings and while containing the risk of political conflict between such political entities?

A PAUSE TO REFLECT

How are ideas of freedom and democracy to be spread globally? Arguably, those who only wish to use a reformed nation-state do not adequately recognize how far disillusionment has already set in. In some 'hollowed out' or 'broken-backed' states, for example in Liberia, Sierra Leone, Myanmar or Somalia, the state imploded, leaving its former citizens at the mercy of gangs and warlords. But even in the industrialized states, has the belief in nationhood and formal democracy eroded? Do some democracies offer little more than a hollow administrative system for reaching decisions that do not begin to reach the needs or tap the energies of citizens living in our rapidly changing world?

We do not merely argue that there is still a need to develop more active national democracies with flourishing civil societies. In addition to and in some respects superseding the nation-state are transnational sites of political encounter and engagement. Let us just mention a few of these sites, which were discussed at greater length elsewhere in this book:

1. At the international level, courts have begun to make effective judgements that transcend domestic legislation, particularly those dealing with human rights and genocide. Dictators with blood on their hands have been held to account by the international community.

2. International governmental organizations, such as the UN and its agencies, have made some advances in acting on behalf of a global community, although the UN is still crucially dependent on the members of the Security Council and especially the USA.

3. A proliferation of regional bodies has developed, admittedly with a highly variable level of power and authority.

4   Transnational communities have developed through enhanced travel and communications. In particular, global diasporas and religions have resurfaced to bridge the gap between universalism and the need to link to one's past (Chapters 2, 17 and 21).

5. Global cities have evolved to service the needs of the world economy and its cosmopolitan citizens, a development discussed in Chapter 18.

6. Ideas of freedom and democracy have been spread across the airwaves through radio, TV and the internet (Chapter 16).

7. Global social movements have arisen to help build the global society of the future (Chapters 19 and 20).

The cumulative effect of these developments has been to energize the movement for democracy and freedom everywhere. During 2011 the action became concentrated on the Middle East and North Africa where ordinary citizens have joined marches and demonstrations, risked their lives for the ideals of the Enlightenment and, in some cases, taken up arms to overthrow autocratic and corrupt regimes. By late 2011, some 20 countries in the region had already been affected and there was little sign that the movement for democracy and freedom in the region had run out of steam. We should also not forget that there has been a significant democratic advance in Myanmar, so long a locus for authoritarianism, following the release in 2010 of Aung San Suu Kyi, the country's democratically elected leader who was placed under house arrest by the military junta. In April 2012 she won a seat in Myanmar's parliament and she plans to visit the UK and Norway in late 2012, the first time she will have left her country in 24 years.

DEVELOPING A SUSTAINABLE ENVIRONMENTAL MODEL

In Chapter 20 we distinguish between soft and tough environmentalism, the former involving a series of voluntary choices by an informed citizenry, the latter requiring intervention by the state and at the global level. To promote a greener world, consumers are being asked to make individual sacrifices, some small and some more challenging. These sacrifices range from taking shorter holiday journeys on fewer aeroplanes, eating less meat (because it requires such a large grain input in proportion to its calorific value) to insulating their houses more thoroughly. Our love affair with the private car is a key area in which most people are resistant to making radical lifestyle changes. Yet, 14% of worldwide emissions stem from vehicle transport and it has been estimated that 60% of all carbon emissions in the USA come from motor vehicles. This amounts to 45% of all world emissions coming from vehicles (Dennis and Urry 2009: 10).

It is difficult to imagine that a substantial move towards a relatively deindustrialized, low-energy economy will arise simply by voluntarily choice, although, of course, every little bit helps. How will the mass of world citizens, especially those who remain locked in extreme poverty, be persuaded of the need to accept such a scenario? We need to overcome the deep mistrust of science often articulated by green movements. This is because without recent advances in physics, chemistry and biology and their ever more sophisticated techniques, plus the development in satellite technology, we would possess little or no real understanding of the causes, character, or pace of environmental deterioration and would not be especially well equipped to combat it (Giddens 2009: 55). The development of alternative clean energy also relies strongly on scientific and technological experimentation, among other things.

Considered from a sociological perspective, nature and the biosphere are entities governed by their own objective, physical laws, which we can damage but not control. They are also subject to the social constructions imposed by human actions. Moreover, only humans have the capacity to create values concerned with our regard for nature. Even within the same society, people construct nature in very different ways. To take a simple example from research on a planning dispute over a new landfill site (MacNaghten 1993); while some groups pointed to the need to defend the location because of its untouched wilderness quality, others perceived the area as one that had long been farmed and altered through generations of human activity. It turned out that careful management of the new site would allow retention of the landscape quality.

The green movement needs both to harness the power of science and to move beyond a romantic defence of nature. Mouths need to be fed, houses built, food grown and jobs created. The role of state and local governments is essential in regulating the character and extent of economic growth and measuring and containing environmental damage. Beyond the nation-state, international cooperation is essential in controlling emissions, policing rogue companies, and cleaning up pollution. States need to cooperate in governing our future fragile planet.

REVIEW AND FINAL REMARKS

In concluding, we should note that not everything connected with the making of a global society brings advantages and gains to the human condition. A more integrated world is not necessarily a more harmonious or a more equal one. Rather, we face greater risks as well as opportunities. As we have seen throughout this book, some transnational activities are atavistic and potentially damaging to others – as in the case of neo-Nazi cells, crime gangs, terrorist networks, or drug syndicates that operate on an international basis. In poor countries, the shrinking of the sphere of society and the elevation of the market and the state have had profound effects. At first, structural adjustment programmes, enforced by the World Bank, stripped away subsidies to consumers and protection for farmers in poor countries. They too were required to kneel to the market. Then, the international agencies imposed doctrines of 'good governance' to strengthen fragile or reform corrupt states. The economic downturn since 2007 has left many governments vulnerable to violence and civil wars, especially where they manage resources like oil – Madagascar, the eastern Congo and Guinea Bissau provide examples. Globalization has not substantially diminished the blight of poverty and wretchedness in which about 1 billion of the world's inhabitants are forced to live (Collier 2007). And social movements have yet to prove effective in mobilizing efforts to reduce global inequalities. Thus, we are not dealing with a teleological, unilinear process that will inevitably take us to a better world.

Despite this recognition of the validity of the many critiques of globalization, we nonetheless argue that globalization has become irreversible and is taking on new forms not previously encountered. Moreover, although the direction in which it may evolve is unclear and certainly not fixed, some global changes are very positive. They provide a greater potential than ever before for the world's inhabitants to forge new understandings, alliances and structures – both from below and in alliance with elite institutions – in the pursuit of more harmonious, environmentally sustainable and humanitarian solutions to local and global problems. The world of work has been transformed and for many lucky citizens the possibilities for a creative engagement with global changes are much enhanced. In itself, globalization will lead neither to a dystopia nor a utopia. The future directions of global society depend on us as ordinary world citizens, on what moral positions we choose and what battles we are prepared to fight.

As democracy spreads, we expect to see the restarting or strengthening of institutions of mutuality – such as savings clubs, burial societies, health benefit unions, credit unions, building societies or cooperatives. We anticipate the development of common programmes by key social movements – labour, women's, environmental, human rights. We expect a renewal in a sense of place and locality as neighbours cooperate in growing their own food, extending allotments and swapping non-monetized skills and services. Through new and more powerful means of communication, principally the internet and social media, virtual and networked communities can be formed and exert their power through consumer choice, disengagement from the more odious players in the market, or political action. Low growth or sustainable development models may be forced upon many countries by the recession, but they can also be deployed for good environmental ends. We anticipate a massive programme of renewable energy, clean transport and recycling initiatives, much of this already prefigured in the speeches of the US administration and other leaders. This will have profound effects on the organization of society. For those countries that are experiencing strong growth, there remain important problems of housing, feeding and educating their populaces and providing them with a degree of social protection. The BRIC countries, Australia and other countries that have weathered the economic storm well will also inherit profound responsibilities on a global scale as their influence grows and a plural world emerges.

A 'global ecumene', 'a universal humanism', a 'shared planet', a 'cosmopolitan democracy', 'an erosion of cultural difference' – these notions are not fully developed realities, but possibilities and aspirations. The world remains lopsided. Many powerful and wealthy actors profit disproportionately from global changes. Throughout this book we have shown how 'global winners' use their privileged access to power, wealth and opportunity to feather their own nests. The TNCs, crime syndicates, rich tourists, skilled migrants and others are all major beneficiaries of the opportunities for transnational activity. We remind you also of the many 'global losers' – the refugees, poor peasants, famine and AIDS victims, and the underclasses of the collapsing cities – who still peer through the bars at the gilded cages of the rich and powerful. The key social challenge of the twenty-first century is to prise open the bars for these disadvantaged people so that they can discover the transformatory possibilities that globalization has generated. A vibrant civil society, creative cultural achievements and active global social movements provide far-off glimpses of that benign future. However distant, we hope we have encouraged you to envisage some of the many possibilities for social engagement, cooperation and positive change.

 Visit the companion website at www.palgrave.com/sociology/cohen3e for extra materials to check and expand your learning, including interactive self-test questions, mind maps making links between key themes, annotated web links to sociological research, data and key sociological thinkers, a searchable glossary and much more.

FURTHER READING

An articulate and coherent critique of globalization from a Marxist point of view is provided by R. Burbach et al. in *Globalization and its Discontents: The Rise of Postmodern Socialisms* (1997).

Although written by an anthropologist rather than a sociologist, U. Hannerz's *Cultural Complexity* (1992) provides an insightful account of cultural and social change in many settings.

R. Wilkinson and K. Pickett's *The Spirit Level: Why Equality is Better for Everyone* (2010) provides a masterclass in how international and governmental statistics can be used to construct a compelling social scientific argument.

M. Albrow's *The Global Age* (1996) remains an incisive introduction to global thinking.

QUESTIONS AND ASSIGNMENTS

1. 'The degree to which the world economy has become integrated is no greater than it was before the First World War.' Discuss.

2. How can socially marginalized and excluded people improve their situation?

3. Is the world likely to become more culturally creolized or will cultural differences continue to blight social relations?

4. Using the material in this chapter and any other sources you like, construct an optimistic scenario for an emergent global society, followed by a critique that traces the possible parallel dangers and difficulties.

References

Abrams, D. M., Yaple, H. A. and Wiener, R. J. (2011) 'A mathematical model of social group competition with application to the growth of religious non-affiliation', *Physics and Society*, http://arxiv.org/pdf/1012.1375.pdf.

Abu-Lughod, J. (1989) *Before European Hegemony: The World System, AD 1250–1350*, New York: Oxford University Press.

Adam, B. and Frost, J. (eds) (2005) *The Handbook of World Families*, London: Sage.

Adherents.com (2007) 'Major religions of the world ranked by number of adherents', http://www.adherents.com/Religions_By_Adherents.html (accessed June 2011).

Adorno, T. and Horkheimer, M. (1972) *Dialectic of Enlightenment*, New York: Herder.

Afgan, N. H. (2008) 'Sustainability concept for energy use, water and environmental systems', in Hanjalić, K., van de Krol, R. and Lekić, A. (eds) *Sustainable Energy Technologies: Options and Prospects*, Dordrecht: Springer, 25–50.

Agadjanian, A. and Roudometof, V. (2005) 'Introduction: Eastern Orthodoxy in a global age – preliminary considerations', in Roudometof, V., Agadjanian, A. and Pankhurst, J. (eds) *Eastern Orthodoxy in a Global Age: Tradition Faces the Twenty-first Century*, Walnut Creek, CA: Rowman & Littlefield, 1–26.

Aglietta, M. (1979) *A Theory of Capitalist Regulation*, London: New Left Books.

Alavi, H. (1972) 'The state in post-colonial societies: Pakistan and Bangladesh', *New Left Review*, 74, 59–81.

Albrow, M. (1987) 'Sociology for one world', *International Sociology*, 2, 1–12.

Albrow, M. (1990) 'Globalization, knowledge and society: an introduction', in Albrow, M. and King, E. (eds) *Globalization, Knowledge and Society*, London: Sage, 3–13.

Albrow, M. (1996) *The Global Age*, Cambridge: Polity.

Albrow, M. (1997) 'Travelling beyond local cultures: socioscapes in a global city', in Eade, J. (ed.) *Living the Global City: Globalization as a Local Process*, London: Routledge, 37–55.

Albrow, M. and Glasius, M. (2008) 'Introduction: democracy and the possibility of a global public sphere', in Albrow, M., Anheier, H., Glasius, M. et al. (eds) *Global Civil Society 2007/8*, London: Sage, 1–19.

Alcock, P. (1997) *Understanding Poverty* (2nd edn), Basingstoke: Macmillan – now Palgrave Macmillan.

Aldridge, A. (2000) *Religion in the Contemporary World: A Sociological Introduction*, Cambridge: Polity.

Alexander, D. (2002) 'Nature's impartiality, man's inhumanity: reflections on terrorism and world crisis in a context of historical disaster', *Disasters*, 26(1), 1–9.

Ali, T. (2010) *The Obama Syndrome: Defender at Home, War Abroad*, London: Verso.

Alkire, S. and Santos, M. E. (2010) 'Acute multidimensional poverty: a new index for developing countries', *OPHI Working Paper No. 38*, 1–131.

Allahar, A. (1994) 'More than an oxymoron: ethnicity and the social construction of primordial attachment', unpublished paper, Department of Sociology, University of Western Ontario, Canada.

Allen, J., Braham, P. and Lewis, P. (eds) (1992) *Political and Economic Forms of Modernity*, Cambridge: Polity.

Altman, D. (1996) 'On global queering', *Australian Humanities Review*, 2, http://www.australian humanitiesreview.org/archive/Issue-July-1996/altman.html.

Altman, D. (2001) *Global Sex*, Chicago, IL: Chicago University Press.

Amen, M., Bosman, M. M. and Gills, B. K. (2008) 'Editorial: the urgent need for global action to combat climate change', *Globalizations*, 5(1), 49–52.

Amin, A. (ed.) (1994) *Post-Fordism: A Reader*, Oxford: Blackwell.

Amin, A. (2002) *Ethnicity and the Multicultural City: Living with Diversity*, Report for the DTLR/ESRC Cities Initiative, Swindon: ESRC.

Amin, S. (1974) *Accumulation on a World Scale* (2 vols), New York: Monthly Review Press.

Andersen, J. G. (2007) 'Nationalism, new right and new cleavages in Danish politics: foreign and security policy of the Danish People's Party', in Liang, C. S. (ed.) *Europe for the Europeans: The Foreign and Security Policy of the Populist Radical Right*, Aldershot: Ashgate, 103–24.

Anderson, B. (1983) *Imagined Communities: Reflections on the Origins and Spread of Nationalism*, London: Verso.

Anderson, K. and Rieff, D. (2005) '"Global civil society": a sceptical view', in Anheier, H., Glasius, M. and Kaldor, M. (eds) *Global Civil Society 2004/05*, London: Sage, 26–39.

Andersson, M. (2005) 'Individualized and collectivized bases for migrant youth identity work', in Andersson, M., Lithman, Y. G. and Sernhede, O. (eds) *Youth, Otherness and the Plural City: Modes of Belonging and Social Life*, Göteborg: Bokförlaget Daidalas, 27–51.

Andrae, G. and Beckman, B. (1985) *The Wheat Trap: Bread and Underdevelopment in Nigeria*, London: Zed Books/Scandinavian Institute of African Studies.

Andreas, P. (2000) *Border Games: Policing the US–Mexico Divide*, Ithaca, NY: Cornell University Press.

Andreas, P. (2002) 'Transnational organized crime and economic globalization', in Berdal, M. and Serrano, M. (eds) *Transnational Organized Crime and International Security*, Boulder, CO: Lynne Rienner, 37–52.

Andreas, P. and Nadelmann, E. (2009) 'The internationalization of crime control', in Friman, H. R. (ed.) *Crime and the Global Political Economy*, Boulder, CO: Lynne Rienner, 21–34.

Andrews, D. L. and Ritzer, G. (2007) 'The grobal in the sporting glocal', in Giulianotti, R. and Robertson, R. (eds) *Globalization and Sport*, Oxford: Blackwell, 28–45.

Anheier, H. and Themudo, N. (2002) 'Organisational forms of global civil society: implications of going global', in Glasius, M., Kaldor, M. and Anheier, H. (eds) *Global Civil Society 2002*, Oxford: Oxford University Press, 191–216.

Anheier, H., Glasius, M. and Kaldor, M. (eds) (2001) *Global Civil Society 2001*, Oxford: Oxford University Press.

Anheier, H., Glasius, M. and Kaldor, M. (eds) (2002) *Global Civil Society 2002*, Oxford: Oxford University Press.

Anheier, H., Glasius M. and Kaldor, M. (2005) 'Introducing global civil society', in Anheier, H., Glasius, M. and Kaldor, M. (eds) *Global Civil Society 2004/05*, London: Sage, 3–22.

Anthias, F. (2005) 'Social stratification and social inequality: models of intersectionality and identity', in Devine, F., Savage, M., Scott, J. and Crompton, R. (eds) *Rethinking Class: Culture, Identities and Lifestyle*, Basingstoke: Palgrave Macmillan, 24–44.

Appadurai, A. (1990) 'Disjuncture and difference in the global cultural economy', in Featherstone, M. (ed.) *Global Culture: Nationalism, Globalization and Modernity*, London: Sage, 295–310.

Appadurai, A. (1991) 'Global ethnoscapes: notes and queries for a transnational anthropology', in Fox, R. G. (ed.) *Recapturing Anthropology: Working in the Present*, Sante Fe, NM: School of American Research Press, 191–200.

Armstrong, G. and Young, M. (2000) 'Fanatical football chants: creating and controlling carnival', in Finn, G. P. and Giulianotti, R. (eds) *Football Culture: Local Contests, Global Visions*, London: Frank Cass, 173–211.

Arrighi, G. (1994) *The Long Twentieth Century*, New York: Verso.

Asad, T. (ed.) (1974) *Anthropology and the Colonial Encounter*, London: Ithaca Press.

Asfah, H. (ed.) (1996) *Women and Politics in the Third World*, London: Routledge.

Assunção, M. R. (2010) 'Capoeira: the Brazilian marshal art', in Cohen, R. and Toninato, P. (eds) *The Creolization Reader: Studies in Mixed Identities and Cultures*, London: Routledge, 185–200.

Atkinson, R. D. (2005) 'Inequality in the new knowledge economy', in Giddens, A. and Diamond, P. (eds) *The New Egalitarianism*, Cambridge: Polity, 52–68.

Augé, M. (1995) *Non-places: Introduction to an Anthropology of Supermodernity*, London: Verso.

Auger, P., Devinney, T. M. and Louviere J. J. (2010) 'Global segments of socially conscious consumers: do they exist?', in Craig Smith, N., Bhattacharya, C. B., Vogel, D. and Levine, D. I. (eds) *Global Challenges in Responsible Business*, Cambridge: Cambridge University Press, 135–60.

Avineri, S. (1968) *The Social and Political Thought of Karl Marx*, Cambridge: Cambridge University Press.

Badham, R. (1986) *Theories of Industrial Society*, London: Croom Helm.

Bagchi, A. K. (1982) *The Political Economy of Underdevelopment*, Cambridge: Cambridge University Press.

Bale, J. and Sang, J. (1996) *Kenyan Running: Movement Culture, Geography and Global Change*, London: Frank Cass.

Bales, K. (1999) *Disposable People: New Slavery in the Global Economy*, Berkeley, CA: University of California Press.

Bales, K., Trodd, Z. and Kent Williamson, A. (2009) *Modern Slavery: The Secret World of 27 Million People*, Oxford: Oneworld.

Banton, M. (1994) 'UNESCO', in Ellis Cashmore, E. (ed.) *Dictionary of Race and Ethnic Relations* (3rd edn), London: Routledge, 336–7.

Barker, E. (1989) *New Religious Movements: A Practical Introduction*, London: HMSO.

Basch, L., Glick Schiller, N. and Blanc, C. S. (1994) *Nations Unbound: Transnational Projects, Postcolonial Predicaments and Deterritorialized Nation States*, New York: Gordon & Breach.

Basu, A. (ed.) (1995) *The Challenge of Local Feminisms*, Boulder, CO: Westview Press.

Batliwala, S. and Brown, D. L. (2006) 'Introduction: why transnational civil society matters', in Batliwala, S. and Brown, D. L (eds) *Transnational Civil Society: An Introduction*, Bloomfield, CT: Kumarian Press, 1–15.

Baudrillard, J. (1988) *Selected Writings* (ed. Poster, M.) Cambridge: Polity.

Bauman, Z. (1991) *Modernity and the Holocaust*, Cambridge: Polity.

Bauman, Z. (1993) *Postmodern Ethics*, Oxford: Blackwell.

Bauman, Z. (1995) *Life in Fragments: Essays in Postmodern Morality*, Oxford: Blackwell.

Bauman, Z. (1998) *Globalization: The Human Consequences*, Cambridge: Polity.

Bauman, Z. (2000) *Liquid Modernity*, Cambridge: Polity.

Baxi, P., Rai, S. M. and Ali, S. S. (2006) 'Legacies of common law: "crimes of honour" in India and Pakistan', *Third World Quarterly*, 27(7), 1239–53.

Beck, U. (1992) *The Risk Society: Towards a New Modernity*, London: Sage.

Beck, U. (1994) 'The reinvention of politics: towards a theory of reflexive modernization', in Beck, U., Giddens, A. and Lash, S. (eds) *Reflexive Modernization: Politics, Tradition and Aesthetics in the Modern Social Order*, Cambridge: Polity, 1–55.

Beck, U. (1998) 'The cosmopolitan manifesto', *New Statesman*, 20 March, 28–30.

Beck, U. (1999a) *World Risk Society*, Cambridge: Polity.

Beck, U. (1999b) *The Reinvention of Politics: Rethinking Modernity in the Global Social Order*, Cambridge: Polity.

Beck, U. (2000a) *What is Globalization?* Cambridge: Polity.

Beck, U. (2000b) *Brave New World of Work*, Cambridge: Polity.

Beck, U. (2006) *The Cosmopolitan Vision*, Cambridge: Polity.

Beck, U. and Beck-Gernsheim, E. (2002) *Individualization: Institutionalized Individualism and its Social and Political Consequences*, London: Sage.

Beck, U., Giddens, A. and Lash, S. (eds) (1994) *Reflexive Modernization: Politics, Tradition and Aesthetics in the Modern Social Order*, Cambridge: Polity.

Beckford, J. A. (1986) *New Religious Movements and Rapid Social Change*, London: Sage for UNESCO.

Bell, D. (1960) *The End of Ideology*, Glencoe, IL: Free Press.

Bell, D. (1973) *The Coming of Post-industrial Society: A Venture in Social Forecasting*, Harmondsworth: Penguin.

Bellah, R. N. (1985) *Tokugawa Religion: The Cultural Roots of Modern Japan*, New York: Free Press.

Bello, W. (1994) *Dark Victory: The United States, Structural Adjustment and Global Poverty*, London: Pluto Press.

Bello, W. (2001) *The Future in the Balance: Essays on Globalization and Resistance*, Oakland, CA: Food First Books.

Bello, W. (2002) *Deglobalization: Ideas for a New World Economy*, London: Zed Books.

Benantar, A. (2011) 'Arab democratic uprisings: domestic, regional and global implications', *New Global Studies*, 5(1), 1–7.

Bendix, R. (1967) 'Tradition and modernity reconsidered', *Comparative Studies in Society and History*, 9(2), 292–346.

Bennett, A. S. (2000) *Popular Music and Youth Culture: Music, Identity and Place*, Basingstoke: Macmillan – now Palgrave Macmillan.

Bennett, W. L. (2004) 'Branded political communication: lifestyle politics, logo campaigns, and the rise of global citizenship', in Føllesdal, A., Micheletti, M. and Stolle, D. (eds) *Politics, Products and Markets: Exploring Political Consumerism Past and Present*, New Brunswick, NJ: Transaction Books, 101–25.

Bentley, M. (2003) 'Sustainable consumption: ethics, national indices and international relations', unpublished PhD, American Graduate School of International Relations and Diplomacy, Paris.

Berger, P. L. (2010) 'Max Weber is alive and well, and living in Guatemala: the Protestant ethic today', *The Review of Faith & International Affairs*, 8(4), 3–9.

Bergesen, A. (1990) 'Turning world-system theory on its head', in Featherstone, M. (ed.) *Global Culture: Nationalism, Globalization and Modernity*, London: Sage, 67–82.

Bergesen, A. J. and Lizardo, O. (2004) 'International terrorism and the world-system', *Sociological Theory*, 22(1), 38–52.

Beyer, P. (2006) *Religions in Global Society*, London: Routledge.

Beynon, H. (1973) *Working for Ford*, Harmondsworth: Allen Lane.

Bienefeld, M. (1994) 'Capitalism and the nation state in the dog days of the twentieth century', in Miliband, R. and Panitch, L. (eds) *Socialist Register: Between Globalism and Nationalism*, London: Merlin Press, 94–129.

Bienefeld, M. (2007) 'Suppressing the double movement to secure the dictatorship of finance', in Buğra, A. and Ağartan, K. (eds) *Reading Karl Polanyi for the Twenty-first Century: Market Economy as a Political Project*, Basingstoke: Palgrave Macmillan, 13–32.

Binnie, J. (2004) *The Globalization of Sexuality*, London: Sage.

Black, D. (2004) 'The geometry of terrorism', *Sociological Theory*, 22(1), 14–25.

Bloch, A. (2010) 'Intimate circuits: modernity, migration and marriage among post-Soviet women in Turkey', *Global Networks*, 11(4), 502–21.

Blythman, J. (2007) *Shopped: The Shocking Power of Britain's Supermarkets*, London: Harper Perennial.

Bocock, R. and Thompson, K. (1985) *Religion and Ideology: A Reader*, Manchester: Open University Press.

Booth, C. (1889–91) *Labour and Life of the People*, 2 vols, London: Williams and Norgate.

Boris, E. and Prugl, E. (eds) (1996) *Homeworkers in Global Perspective: Invisible No More*, New York: Routledge.

Boserup, E. (1970) *Women's Role in Economic Development*, London: Allen & Unwin.

Bourdieu, P. (1984) *Distinction: A Social Critique of the Judgement of Taste*, Cambridge, MA: Harvard University Press.

Bourdieu, P. (1993) *Sociology in Question*, London: Sage.

Bourdieu, P. (2000) *Pascalian Meditations*, Cambridge: Polity.

Bourdieu, P. and Wacquant, L. J. (1992) *An Invitation to Reflexive Sociology*, Cambridge: Polity.

Bozkurt, Ö. (2006) 'Highly skilled employment and global mobility in mobile telecommunications multinationals', in Smith, M. P. and Favell, A. (eds) *The Human Face of Global Mobility*, New Brunswick, NJ: Transaction, 247–74.

Braaten, J. (1991) *Habermas's Critical Theory of Society*, Albany, NY: State University of New York Press.

Bradsher, K. and Dempsey, J. (2010) 'China passes Germany as world's top exporter', *New York Times*, www.nytimes.com/2010/02/10/business/global/10export.html (accessed October 2010).

Branigan, T. (2010) 'China's mobile superpower poised to make international connections', *The Guardian*, 12 January, 26–7.

Branigan, T. and Arthur, C. (2010) 'Playing the wall game', *Media Guardian*, 18 January, 1.

Branston, G. and Stafford, R. (2003) *The Media Student's Book*, London: Routledge.

Brautigam, D. (2010) *The Dragon's Gift: The Real Story of China in Africa*, New York: Oxford University Press.

Braverman, H. (1974) *Labour and Monopoly Capital*, New York: Monthly Review Press.

Brennan, D. (2004) *What's Love Got to Do with It? Transnational Desires and Sex Tourism in the Dominican Republic*, Durham, NC: Duke University Press.

Brenner, N. (1999) 'Beyond state-centrism: space, territoriality, and geographical scale in globalization studies', *Theory and Society*, 28(1), 39–78.

Brenner, R. (2002) *The Boom and the Bubble: The US in the World Economy*, London: Verso.

Brett, E. A. (1985) *The World Economy Since the War: The Politics of Uneven Development*, Basingstoke: Macmillan.

Brewer, J. and Trentmann, F. (2006) 'Introduction: space, time and value in consuming cultures', in Brewer, J and Trentmann, F. (eds) *Consuming Cultures. Global Perspectives: Historical Trajectories, Transnational Exchanges*, Oxford: Berg, 1–18.

Brickell, K. and Chant, S. (2010) '"The unbearable heaviness of being": expressions of female altruism in Cambodia, Philippines, the Gambia and Costa Rica', *Progress in Development Studies*, 10(2), 145–59.

Brubaker, R. (1991) *The Limits of Rationality: An Essay on the Social and Moral Thought of Max Weber*, London: Routledge.

Bruegel, I. (1988) 'Sex and race in the labour market', paper given at the Socialist Feminist Forum, London.

Bryman, A. (1995) *Disney and his World*, London: Routledge.

Buffett, W. E. (2011) 'Warren Buffett says the super-rich pay lower tax rates than others', *New York Times*, 14 August.

Bunch, C., Antrobus, P., Frost, S. and Reilly, N. (2001) 'International networking for women's human rights', in Edwards, M. and Gaventa, J. (eds) *Global Citizen Action*, London: Earthscan, 217–30.

Bunyard, P. (2004) 'Crossing the threshold', *The Ecologist*, 34(1), 55–9.

Burbach, R., Núñez, O. and Kagarlitsky, B. (1997) *Globalization and its Discontents: The Rise of Postmodern Socialisms*, London: Pluto Press.

Burawoy, M. (2005) '2004 American Sociological Association presidential address: for public sociology', *British Journal of Sociology*, 56(2), 259–94.

Bush, R. (1996) 'The politics of food and starvation', *Review of African Political Economy*, 23(68), 169–95.

Butler, T. (2003) 'Living in the bubble: gentrification and its "others" in North London', *Urban Studies*, 41(1), 2469–86.

Cabezas, A. (2004) 'Between love and money: sex, tourism, and citizenship in Cuba and the Dominican Republic', *SIGNS*, 29(4), 987–1015.

Cacuci, D. G. (2008) 'Current international initiatives for sustainable nuclear energy', in Hanjalić, K., van de Krol, R. and Lekić, A. (eds) *Sustainable Energy Technologies: Options and Prospects*, Dordrecht: Springer, 159–76.

Calhoun, C. (2002) 'The class consciousness of frequent travellers: towards a critique of actually existing cosmopolitanism', in Vertovec, S. and Cohen, R. (eds) *Conceiving Cosmopolitanism: Theory, Context and Practice*, Oxford: Oxford University Press, 86–119.

Campbell, D. and Bowcott, O. (2008) 'Drug cartels running rampant, says UN', *The Guardian*, 5 March, 19.

Canclini, N. G. (1995) *Hybrid Cultures: Strategies for Entering and Leaving Modernity*, Minneapolis, MN: University of Minneapolis Press.

Captain, S. (2011) 'The demographics of Occupy Wall Street', www.fastcompany.com/1789018/occupy-wall-street-demographics-statistics (accessed October 2010).

Cardoso, F. H. and Faletto, E. (1969) *Dependency and Development in Latin America*, Berkeley, CA: University of California Press.

Carr, M. (2004) 'Lessons learned', in Carr, M. (ed.) *Linking Women Producers and Workers with Global Markets*, London: Commonwealth Secretariat, 197–214.

Carroll, B. A. (1989) '"Women take action!" Women's direct action and social change', *Women's Studies International Forum*, 12(1), 3–24.

Carroll, W. K. and Carson, C. (2003) 'The network of global corporations and elite policy groups: a structure for transnational capitalist formation?', *Global Networks: A Journal of Transnational Affairs*, 3(1), 29–58.

Cashmore, E. (2004) *Encyclopedia of Race and Ethnic Studies*, London: Routledge.

Cass, N., Shrove, E. and Urry, J. (2005) 'Social exclusion, mobility and class', *The Sociological Review*, 53(3), 539–55.

Cassidy, J. (2009) 'The bosses who break their banks', *The Guardian*, 25 November, 6.

Castells, M. (1977) *The Urban Question: A Marxist Approach*, London: Edward Arnold.

Castells, M. (1983) *The City and the Grassroots: A Cross-cultural Theory of Urban Social Movements*, London: Edward Arnold.

Castells, M. (1989) *The Informational City: Information Technology, Economic Restructuring and the Urban-Regional Process*, Oxford: Blackwell.

Castells, M. (1996) *The Rise of the Network Society*, vol. 1, Castells, M., *The Information Age: Economy, Society and Culture*, Oxford: Blackwell (rev. edn 2000).

Castells, M. (1997) *The Power of Identity*, vol. 2, *The Information Age: Economy, Society and Culture*, Oxford: Blackwell (rev. edn 2000).

Castells, M. (1998) *End of Millennium*, vol. 3, *The Information Age: Economy, Society and Culture*, Oxford: Blackwell (rev. edn 2000).

Castles, S. and Miller, M. (2009) *The Age of Migration: International Population Movements in the Modern World* (4th edn), Basingstoke: Palgrave Macmillan.

Castree, N., Coe, M., Ward, K. and Samers, M. (2004) *Spaces of Work: Global Capitalism and Geographies of Labour*, London: Sage.

Chamberlain, G. (2010) 'How the love commandos rescue India's young lovers', *The Observer*, 10 October, 36–7.

Chang, G. (2000) *Disposable Domestics: Immigrant Women Workers in the Global Economy*, Cambridge, MA: South End Press.

Chang, H.-J. (2008) *Bad Samaritans: The Guilty Secrets of Rich Nations and the Threat to Global Prosperity*, Croydon: Random Books.

Chant, S. (2008) 'Beyond incomes: a new take on the "feminisation of poverty"', *Poverty in Focus*, 13, 26–7.

Chant, S. (2009) 'The "feminisation of poverty" in Costa Rica: to what extent a conundrum?', *Bulletin of Latin American Research*, 28(1), 19–43.

Chapman, D. (2005) 'Derivatives disaster, hedge fund monster?', www.safehaven.com/article/4099 (accessed June 2010).

Chase, H. (1994) 'The *Meyhane* or the McDonald's? Changes in eating habits and the evolution of fast food in Istanbul', in Zubaida, S. and Tapper, R. (eds) *Culinary Cultures of the Middle East*, London: I.B. Tauris, 73–86.

Cheah, P. and Robbins, B. (eds) (1998) *Cosmopolitics: Thinking and Feeling Beyond the Nation*, Minneapolis, MN: University of Minnesota Press.

Chen, S. and Ravallion, M. (2008) *The Developing World is Poorer Than We Thought, But no Less Successful in the Fight Against Poverty*, Washington, DC: World Bank Development Research Group.

Chen, S. and Ravallion, M. (2009) 'The impact of the global financial crisis on the world's poorest', http://www.voxeu.org/index.php?q=node/3520 (accessed August 2010).

Cherlin, A. (2004) 'The de-institutionalization of American marriage', *Journal of Marriage and the Family*, 66(4), 848–61.

Chidester, D. (2004) *Salvation and Suicide: An Interpretation of Jim Jones, the People's Temple, and Jonestown*, Bloomington, IN: Indiana University Press.

Chinoy, E. (1967) *Society: An Introduction to Sociology*, New York: Random House.

Chomsky, N. (2003) *Hegemony or Survival: America's Quest for Global Dominance*, London: Penguin.

Chu, Y. K. (2002) 'Global triads: myth or reality?', in Berdal, M. and Serrano, M. (eds) *Transnational Organized Crime and International Security*, Boulder, CO: Lynne Rienner, 183–93.

CIA (Criminal Investigation Agency) (2010) *CIA World Factbook*, Washington, DC: CIA.

CIA (2011) *CIA World Factbook*, Washington, DC: CIA.

Ciment, J. (1999) 'Life expectancy of Russian males falls to 58', *British Medical Journal*, 319, 468.

Clammer, J. (1992) 'Shopping in Japan', in Shields, R. (ed.) *Lifestyle Shopping*, London: Routledge, 195–213.

Clark, A. (2009) 'Goldman Sachs breaks record with $16.7bn bonus pot', *The Guardian*, 16 October, 30.

Clark, A. (2010) 'Goldman Sachs charged with $1bn fraud over toxic sub-prime securities', *The Guardian*, 16 April.

Clarke, P. (2006) *New Religions in Global Perspective*, London: Routledge.

CNNMoney (n.d.) 'Global 500: our annual ranking of the world's largest corporations', money.cnn.com/magazines/fortune/global500/2010/full_list (accessed October 2010).

Cohen, G. A. (1978) *Karl Marx's Theory of History: A Defence*, Oxford: Oxford University Press.

Cohen, R. (1987) *The New Helots: Migrants in the International Division of Labour*, Aldershot: Gower.

Cohen, R. (2006) *Migration and its Enemies: Global Capital, Migrant Labour and the Nation-state*, Aldershot: Ashgate.

Cohen, R. (2008) *Global Diasporas: An Introduction* (2nd edn), London: Routledge.

Cohen, R. (2011) 'On the move: the migration imperative', http://www.imi.ox.ac.uk/pdfs/on-the-move-the-migration-imperative-1 (accessed April 2012).

Cohen, R. and Rai, S. (eds) (2000) *Global Social Movements*, London: Athlone.

Cohen, S. (1972) *Folk Devils and Moral Panics*, London: MacGibben & Kee.

Cohen, S. (1985) *Visions of Social Control: Crime, Punishment and Classification*, Cambridge: Polity.

Coleman, S. (2005) 'Blogs and the new politics of listening', *Political Quarterly*, 76(2), 273–80.

Collier, P. (2007) *The Bottom Billion: Why the Poorest Countries are Failing and What Can Be Done About It*, Oxford: Oxford University Press.

Combarnous, M. and Bonnet, J.-F. (2008) 'World thirst for energy: how to face the challenge', in Hanjalić, K., van de Krol, R. and Lekić, A. (eds) *Sustainable Energy Technologies: Options and Prospects*, Dordrecht: Springer, 3–24.

Comte, A. (1853) *The Positive Philosophy of Auguste Comte, Freely Translated and Condensed by Harriet Martineau*, London: John Chapman.

Constable, N. (2009) 'The commodification of intimacy: marriage, sex, and reproductive labor', *Annual Review of Anthropology*, 38, 49–64.

Cooper, R. (1985) *The Baha'is of Iran*, London: Minority Rights Group.

Coser, L. A. and Rosenberg, B. (eds) (1976) *Sociological Theory: A Book of Readings* (2nd edn), New York: Macmillan.

Coward, R. (1978) 'Sexual liberation and the family', *m/f*, 1, 7–24.

Cragg, W. (2005) 'Ethics, globalization and the phenomenon of self-regulation: an introduction', in Cragg, W. (ed.) *Ethics, Codes, Corporations and the Challenge of Globalization*, Cheltenham: Edward Elgar, 1–19.

Craig Smith, N., Bhattacharya, C. B., Vogel, D. and Levine, D. I. (2010a) 'Introduction: corporate responsibility and global business', in Craig Smith, N., Bhattacharya, C. B., Vogel, D. and Levine, D. I. (eds) *Global Challenges in Responsible Business*, Cambridge: Cambridge University Press, 1–9.

Craig Smith, N., Bhattacharya, C. B., Vogel, D. and Levine, D. I. (eds) (2010b) *Global Challenges in Responsible Business*, Cambridge: Cambridge University Press.

Craik, J. (2009) *Fashion: Key Concepts*, Oxford: Berg.

Crompton, R. (2008) *Class and Stratification* (3rd edn), Cambridge: Polity.

Crow, G. (1997) *Comparative Sociology and Social Theory*, Basingstoke: Macmillan – now Palgrave Macmillan.

Cruise O'Brien, R. (1979) 'Mass communications: social mechanisms of incorporation and dependence', in Villamil, J. (ed.) *Transnational Capitalism and National Development*, Atlantic Highlands, NJ: Humanities Press, 129–43.

Crystal, E. (1989) 'Tourism in Toraja (Sulawesi, Indonesia)', in Smith, V. L. (ed.) *Hosts and Guests: The Anthropology of Tourism* (2nd edn), Philadelphia, PA: University of Pennsylvania Press, 139–68.

Curtin, P. (1969) *The Atlantic Slave Trade: A Census*, Madison, WI: University of Wisconsin Press.

Czerniewicz, L. (2010) 'Mobile is my soul: more about cell phones in the south of Africa', http://mfeldsten.com/mobile-is-my-soul-cell-phones-in-south-africa/ (accessed January 2010).

Darwin, C. (1859) *On The Origin of Species*, London: John Murray.

Davis, M. (2006) *Planet of Slums*, London: Verso.

Deane, J. (2008) 'Democratic advance or retreat? Communicative power and current media developments', in Albrow, M., Anheier, H., Glasius, M. et al. (eds) *Global Civil Society 2007/8*, London: Sage, 144–65.

De Bree, J., Davids, T. and de Haas, H. (2010) 'Post-return experiences and transnational belonging of return migrants: a Dutch-Moroccan case study', *Global Networks: A Journal of Transnational Affairs*, 10(4), 489–509.

Delanty, G. (2000) *Citizenship in a Global Age: Society, Culture, Politics*, Buckingham: Open University Press.

Demographia (2011) '*Demographia World Urban Areas*', www.demographia.com/db-worldua. pdf (accessed December 2010).

De Mooij, M. (2004) *Consumer Behavior and Culture: Consequences for Global Marketing and Advertising*, London: Sage.

Dennis, K. and Urry, J. (2009) *After the Car*, Cambridge: Polity.

De Rivero, O. (2001) *The Myth of Development*, London: Zed Books.

Dermott, E. (2003) 'The "intimate father": defining paternal involvement', *Sociological Research Online*, 8(4), http://www.socresonline.org.uk/8/4/dermott.html (accessed December 2010).

Dermott, E. (2008) *Intimate Fatherhood*, London: Routledge.

Desai, S. (2004) 'Lucky foot? Unlucky rabbit', http://www.buzzle.com/editorials/5-16-2004-54202 (accessed December 2010).

Deslatte, M. (2010) 'Oil spill has Gulf candidates walking tightrope', Associated Press, 29 October.

Desroches, F. J. (2003) 'Drug trafficking and organized crime in Canada: a study of high-level drug networks', in Beare, M. E. (ed.) *Critical Reflections on Transnational Organized Crime, Money Laundering, and Corruption*, Toronto: University of Toronto Press, 237–55.

Devine, F. and Savage, M. (2005) 'The cultural turn, sociology and class analysis', in Devine, F., Savage, M., Scott, J. and Crompton, R. (eds) *Rethinking Class: Culture, Identities and Lifestyle*, Basingstoke: Palgrave Macmillan, 1–22.

Dicken, P. (1992) *Global Shift: The Internationalization of Economic Activity*, London: Paul Chapman.

Dicken, P. (2003) *Global Shift: Reshaping the Global Economic Map in the 21st Century*, London: Sage.

Dicken, P. (2007) *Global Shift: Mapping the Changing Contours of the World Economy* (5th edn), London: Sage.

Dohse, K., Jürgens, U. and Malsch, T. (1985) 'From Fordism to Toyotism', *Politics and Society*, 14(2), 115–46.

Donnelly, P. (1996) 'The local and the global: globalization in the sociology of sport', *Journal of Sport and Social Issues*, 20(3), 239–57.

Dore, R. (1958) *City Life in Japan: A Study of a Tokyo Ward*, London: Routledge & Kegan Paul.

Dore, R. (1959) *Land Reform in Japan*, London: Oxford University Press.

Dore, R. (1965) *Education in Tokugawa Japan*, London: Routledge & Kegan Paul.

Douglas, M. and Isherwood, B. (1978) *The World of Goods: Towards an Anthropology of Consumption*, New York: W. W. Norton.

Doward, J. (2003) 'Rappers put the bling into business', *The Observer*, 11 November, 8.

Doyle, T. and McEachern, D. (2008) *Environment and Politics* (3rd edn), London: Routledge.

Dreze, J. and Sen, A. (1989) *Hunger and Public Action*, Oxford: Clarendon Press.

Duncombe, J. and Marsden, D. (1993) 'Love and intimacy: the gender division of emotion and emotion work', *Sociology*, 27(2), 221–41.

Dunning, J. H. (1993) *The Globalization of Business*, London: Routledge.

Durkheim, E. (1933) *The Division of Labor in Society* (2nd edn), New York: Macmillan.

Durkheim, E. (1938) *The Rules of Sociological Method*, Chicago, IL: Chicago University Press.

Durkheim, E. (1952) *Suicide: A Study in Sociology*, London: Routledge.

Durkheim, E. ([1915]1976) *The Elementary Forms of Religious Life*, London: George Allen & Unwin.

Durning, A. T. (1992) *How Much is Enough? The Consumer Society and the Future of the Earth*, London: Earthscan.

Dyreson, M. (2003) 'Globalizing the nation-making process: modern sport in world history', *International Journal of the History of Sport*, 20(1), 91–106.

Eade, J. and Garbin, D. (2006) 'Competing visions of identity and space: Bangladeshi Muslims in Britain', *Contemporary South Asia*, 15(2), 181–93.

Ebbe, O. N. (2008) 'The nature and scope of trafficking in women and children', in Ebbe, O. N. and Das, D. K. (eds) *Global Trafficking in Women and Children*, Boca Raton, FL: Taylor & Francis, 17–32.

Edelman, M. (2003) 'Transnational peasant and farm movements and networks', in Anheier,

H., Glasius, M. and Kaldor, M. (eds) *Global Civil Society 2003*, Oxford: Oxford University Press, 185–218.

Edensor, T. (2004) 'Reconstituting the Taj Mahal: tourist flows and glocalization', in Sheller, M. and Urry, J. (eds) *Tourism Mobilities: Places to Play, Places in Play*, London: Routledge, 103–15.

Edgell, S. (2005) *Sociological Analysis of Work: Change and Continuity in Paid and Unpaid Work*, London: Sage.

Edgell, S. (2012) *The Sociology of Work: Continuity and Change in Paid and Unpaid Work* (2nd edn), London: Sage.

Ehrenreich, B. and Hochschild, A. (eds) (2003) *Global Woman: Nannies, Maids and Sex Workers in the New Economy*, New York: Holt/Metropolitan Books

Eichberg, H. (1984) 'Olympic sport: neocolonialism and alternatives', *International Review for the Sociology of Sport*, 19, 97–105.

Elger, T. and Smith, C. (eds) (1994) *Global Japanization? The Transnational Transformation of the Labour Process*, London: Routledge.

Elias, J. (2004) *Fashioning Inequality: The Multinational Company and Gendered Employment in a Globalizing World*, Aldershot: Ashgate.

Elias, N. (1978) *What is Sociology?* London: Hutchinson.

Elias, N. (1986) 'Introduction', in Elias, N. and Dunning, E. (eds) *Quest for Excitement: Sport and the Civilizing Process*, Oxford: Basil Blackwell, 19–62.

Elias, N. (1994) *The Civilizing Process*, Oxford: Blackwell.

Elliot, L. (2010) 'FactFile UK, Economy', *The Observer*, 25 April, 12.

Elliot, L. and Atkinson, D. (2008) *The Gods that Failed: How Blind Faith in Markets Has Cost Us Our Futures*, London: Bodley Head.

Enloe, C. (1989) *Bananas, Beaches and Bases: Making Feminist Sense of International Politics*, Berkeley, CA: University of California Press.

Enloe, C. (2000) *Maneuvers: The International Politics of Militarizing Women's Lives*, Berkeley, CA: University of California Press.

Esposito, J. L. (1995) *The Islamic Threat: Myth or Reality?* Oxford: Oxford University Press.

Ethical Consumer Research Association (2007) *The Ethical Consumer Report for the Co-operative Bank*, Manchester: The Co-operative Bank.

Ethical Investment Research Service (2009) *Key Ethical/Socially Responsible Investments (SRI) Statistics*, www.eiris.org.

Evans, M. and Lee, E. (eds) (2002) *Real Bodies: A Sociological Introduction*, Basingstoke: Palgrave – now Palgrave Macmillan.

Facebook (n.d.) 'Newsroom: fact sheet', http://newsroom.fb.com/content/default.aspx?NewsAreaId=22 (accessed April 2012).

Faist, T. (2000) *The Volume and Dynamics of International Migration and Transnational Society*, Oxford: Clarendon Press.

Fanon, F. (1967) *The Wretched of the Earth*, Harmondsworth: Penguin.

Favell, A. (2003) 'Games without frontiers? Questioning the transnational social power of migrants in Europe', *European Journal of Sociology*, 44(3), 397–427.

Favell, A., Feldblum, M. and Smith, M. P. (2006) 'The human face of global mobility: a research agenda', in Smith, M. P. and Favell, A. (eds) *The Human Face of Global Mobility*, New Brunswick, NJ: Transaction, 1–25.

Fawcett Society/UNISON (2007) '£4000 cheaper: a Fawcett Society/Unison briefing on equal pay', Fawcett Society.

Featherstone, M. (1987) 'Lifestyle and consumer culture', *Theory, Culture and Society*, 4, 55–70.

Featherstone, M. (1990) 'Global culture: an introduction', in Featherstone, M. (ed.) *Global Culture: Nationalism, Globalization and Modernity*, London: Sage, 1–14.

Featherstone, M. (1992) *Consumer Culture and Postmodernism*, London: Sage.

Feifer, M. (1985) *Going Places: The Ways of the Tourist from Imperial Rome to the Present*, Basingstoke: Macmillan.

Feuerbach, L. (1957) *The Essence of Christianity*, New York: Harper & Row.

Finch, L. and Bowers, S. (2009) 'Executive pay keeps rising', *The Guardian*, 14 September.

Finn, G. P. and Giulianotti, R. (eds) (2000) *Football Culture: Local Contests, Global Visions*, London: Frank Cass.

Firat, A. F. (1995) 'Consumer culture or culture consumed?', in Costa, J. A. and Bamossy, G. J. (eds) *Marketing in a Multicultural World*, London: Sage, 105–25.

Fisher, J. (1993) *The Road from Rio: Sustainable Development and the Non-governmental Movement in the Third World*, Westport, CN: Praeger.

Fisher, M. P. (1997) *Living Religions*, London: Prentice Hall.

Fligstein, N. (1981) *Going North: Migration of Blacks and Whites from the South, 1900–1950*, New York: Academic Press.

Flusty, S. (2004) *De-Coca-Colonization: Making the Globe from the Inside Out*, London: Routledge.

Ford, J. (2008) 'A greedy giant out of control', *Prospect*, 152, 22–9.

Ford, J. and Larsen, P. T. (2009) 'How to shrink the banks', *Prospect*, 165, 50–3.

Foreign Policy (n.d.) 'The Global Cities Index 2010', http://www.foreignpolicy.com/node/373401 (accessed December 2010).

Fortune 500 (2010) 'Our annual ranking of America's largest corporations', http://money.cnn.com/magazines/fortune/fortune500/2010/ (accessed December 2011).

Fórum Social Mundial (2005) 'World Social Forum 2005 Memorial', http://www.forumsocialmundial.org.br/main.php?id_menu=14_5&cd_language=2 (accessed December 2010).

Foster, R. J. (2008) *Coca-Globalizaton: Following Soft Drinks from New York to New Guinea*, Basingstoke: Palgrave Macmillan.

Foucault, M. (1973) *Birth of the Clinic*, London: Routledge.

Foucault, M. (1977) *Discipline and Punish: The Birth of the Prison*, London: Allen Lane.

Foucault, M. (2008) *The Birth of Biopolitics: Lectures at the Collège de France, 1978–1979* (ed. M. Senellart, trans. G. Burchell), Basingstoke: Palgrave Macmillan.

Foucault, M. (2009) *Security, Territory, Population: Lectures at the Collège de France 1977–1978*, New York: Picador.

France, P. (1996) *Hermits: The Insights of Solitude*, London: Chatto & Windus.

Frank, A. G. (1967) *Capitalism and Underdevelopment in Latin America*, New York: Monthly Review Press.

Frank, A. G. (1969) *Latin America: Underdevelopment or Revolution*, New York: Monthly Review Press.

Freedland, J. (1999) 'Shangri-la: it's quite a European place-name, the way it splits in two', *The Guardian*, 24 March.

Freedland, J. (2009) 'Obama is not the saviour of the world: he's still an American president', *The Guardian*, 16 December, 29.

Free Expression Policy Project, The (2012) 'Fact sheets on media democracy', http://www.fepproject.org/factsheets/mediademocracy.html (accessed April 2012).

Freeman, R. B. (2007) 'The challenge of the growing globalization of labor markets to economic and social policy', in Paus, E. (ed.) *Global Capitalism Unbound: Winners and Losers in Offshore Outsourcing*, Basingstoke: Palgrave Macmillan, 23–40.

Freidberg, S. (2001) 'On the trail of the global green bean: methodological considerations in multi-site ethnography', *Global Networks*, 1(4), 353–68.

Freire-Medeiros, B. (2009) 'The favela and its touristic transits', *Geoforum*, 40(4), 580–8.

Freud, S. ([1913]1946) *Totem and Taboo: Resemblances between the Psychic Lives of Savages and Neurotics*, New York: Vintage.

Friberg, M. and Hettne, B. (1988) 'Local mobilization and world system politics', *International Journal of Social Science*, 40(117), 341–60.

Friedman, E. (1995) 'Women's human rights: the emergence of a movement', in Peters, J. and Wolper, A. (eds) *Women's Rights, Human Rights: International Feminist Perspectives*, New York: Routledge, 18–35.

Friedman, J. (1986) 'The world city hypothesis', *Development and Change*, 17(2), 69–83.

Friedman, J. (1997) 'Global crises, the struggle for cultural identity and intellectual porkbarrelling: cosmopolitans versus locals, ethnics and nationals in an era of de-hegemonisation', in Werbner, P., and Modood, T. (eds) *Debating Cultural Hybridity: Multi-cultural Identities and the Politics of Anti-racism*, London: Zed Books, 70–89.

Frisby, D. (1978) 'Translator's introduction', in Simmel, G., *The Philosophy of Money* (trans. T. Bottomore and D. Frisby), London: Routledge & Kegan Paul.

Fröbel, F., Heinrich, J. and Kreye, O. (1980) *The New International Division of Labour*, Cambridge: Cambridge University Press.

Garon, S. (2006) 'Japan's post-war "consumer revolution", or striking a "balance" between consumption and saving', in Brewer, J. and Trentmann, F. (eds) *Consuming Cultures. Global Perspectives: Historical Trajectories, Transnational Exchanges*, Oxford: Berg, 189–218.

Gentleman, A. (2010) 'Unequal Britain: richest 10% are now 100 times better off than the poorest', *The Guardian*, 27 January, 4.

Gerschenkron, A. (1966) *Economic Backwardness in Historical Perspective*, Cambridge, MA: Harvard University Press.

Gerth, H. H. and Mills, C. W. (1946) *From Max Weber: Essays in Sociology*, New York: Oxford University Press.

Giddens, A. (1985) *The Nation-state and Violence*, Cambridge: Polity.

Giddens, A. (1990) *The Consequences of Modernity*, Cambridge: Polity.

Giddens, A. (1991) *Modernity and Self-identity: Self and Society in the Late Modern Age*, Stanford, CA: Stanford University Press.

Giddens, A. (1992) *The Transformation of Intimacy*, Cambridge: Polity.

Giddens, A. (1994) 'Living in a post-traditional society', in Beck, U., Giddens, A. and Lash, S. (eds) *Reflexive Modernization: Politics, Tradition and Aesthetics in the Modern Social Order*, Cambridge: Polity, 56–108.

Giddens, A. (2002) *Runaway World: How Globalisation is Reshaping our Lives* (2nd edn), London: Profile Books.

Giddens, A. (2009) *The Politics of Climate Change*, Cambridge: Polity.

Gillespie, M. (1995) *Television, Ethnicity and Cultural Change*, London: Routledge.

Giulianotti, R. and Robertson, R. (eds) (2007) *Globalization and Sport*, Oxford: Blackwell.

Glick Schiller, N. (2007) 'Beyond the nation state and its unitary analysis: towards a new research agenda for migration studies', paper presented at the conference 'Transnationalisation and Development(s): Towards a North-South Perspective', Centre for Interdisciplinary Research, Bielefeld, Germany, 31 May–1 June.

Glissant, E. (1998) 'Creolization du monde', in Ruano-Borbalan, J. C. (ed.) *L'Identité: L'Individu, le Groupe, la Société*, Auxerre: Sciences Humaines Editions.

Goal.com (n.d.) 'World cup viewing figures prove that this really is the world's game', http://www.goal.com/en/news/1863/world-cup-2010/2010/05/29/1947801/world-cup-viewing-figures-prove-that-this-really-is-the-world's-game (accessed April 2012).

Godrej, D. (2004) 'Smoke gets in your eyes', *New Internationalist*, 369, 9.

Goldin, I., Cameron, G. and Balarajan, M. (2011) *Exceptional People: How Migration Shaped our World and Will Define our Future*, Princeton: Princeton University Press.

Goldsmith, J. and Wu, T. (2006) *Who Controls the Internet? Illusions of a Borderless World*, Oxford: Oxford University Press.

Goldthorpe, J. H. with Llewellyn, C. and Payne, C. (1980) *Social Mobility and Class Structure in Modern Britain*, Oxford: Clarendon.

Goodstein, L. (2010) 'Across nation, mosque projects meet opposition', *New York Times*, 7 August.

Gould, W. T. (2008) *Population and Development*, New York: Routledge.

Gowan, P. (1999) *The Global Gamble: Washington's Faustian Bid for World Dominance*, London: Verso.

Gowan, P. (2009) 'Crisis in the heartlands: consequences of the new Wall Street system', *New Left Review*, 55, 5–28.

Graburn, N. H. (1989) 'The sacred journey', in Smith, V. L. (ed.) *Hosts and Guests: The Anthropology of Tourism*, Philadelphia, PA: University of Pennsylvania Press, 21–36.

Granovetter, M. (1983) 'The strength of weak ties: a network theory revisited', *Sociological Theory*, 1, 201–33.

Greenwood, D. J. (1972) 'Tourism as an agent of change: a Spanish Basque case', *Ethnology*, 11, 80–91.

Grosfoguel, R. (1995) 'Global logics in the Caribbean city system: the case of Miami', in Knox, P. L. and Taylor, P. J. (eds) *World Cities in a World System*, Cambridge: Cambridge University Press, 156–70.

Guardian, The (2011) 'The word on the street', 28 January, G2, 6–9.

Gugler, J. (1995) 'The urbanization of the globe', in Cohen, R. (ed.) *The Cambridge Survey of World Migration*, Cambridge: Cambridge University Press, 541–5.

Gunson, P. (1996) 'Indians run for their lives', *The Observer*, 29 September.

Guttman, A. (1992) *The Olympics: A History of the Modern Games*, Urban, IL: University of Illinois Press.

Guy, J. (ed.) (2007) *The Complete Works of Oscar Wilde*, vol. 4, Oxford: Oxford University Press (includes Wilde's *The Soul of Man under Socialism*) (first published in 1895).

Habermas, J. (1971) *Towards a Rational Society*, London: Heinemann.

Habermas, J. (1979) *Communication and the Evolution of Society*, London: Heinemann.

Habermas, J. (1989) *The Structural Transformation of the Public Sphere*, Cambridge: Polity.

Hadar, L. T. (1993) 'What green peril?' *Foreign Affairs*, 72(2), 27–42.

Hale, A. (2004) 'Globalised production and networks of resistance: Women Working Worldwide and new alliances for the dignity of labour', *Journal of Interdisciplinary Gender Studies*, 8(1/2), 153–170.

Hall, C. M. and Weiler, B. (1992) *Special Interest Tourism*, London: Belhaven Press.

Hall, J. R. (1987) *Gone from the Promised Land: Jonestown in American Cultural History*, New Brunswick: Transaction Books.

Hall, S. (1991) 'The local and the global: globalization and ethnicity', in King, A. D. (ed.) *Culture, Globalization and the World System: Contemporary Conditions for the Representations of Identity*, Basingstoke: Macmillan – now Palgrave Macmillan, 19–40.

Hall, S. (1992) 'New ethnicities', in Donals, J. and Rattansi, A. (eds) *Race, Culture and Difference*, London: Sage/Open University Press, 252–9.

Hall, S. and Gieben, B. (eds) (1992) *Formations of Modernity*, Cambridge: Polity/Open University Press.

Hall, S. and Jefferson, T. (1993) *Resistance through Rituals: Youth Subcultures in Post-war Britain*, London: Routledge.

Hall, T. D. (1996) 'World-system theory', in Kuper, A. and Kuper, J. (eds) *The Social Science Encyclopaedia* (2nd edn), London: Routledge, 922–3.

Hall, T. H. and Fenelon, J. V. (2008) 'Indigenous movements and globalization: What is different? What is the same?', *Globalizations*, 5(1), 1–12.

Halliday, F. (1994) *Rethinking International Relations*, Basingstoke: Macmillan – now Palgrave Macmillan.

Halliday, F. (1996) *Islam and the Myth of Confrontation*, London: I.B. Tauris.

Halliday, J. (2011) 'Police arrest five over anonymous WikiLeaks attacks', *The Guardian*, 28 January, 15.

Hamnett, C. (2003) 'Gentrification and the middle-class remaking of inner London 1961–2001', *Urban Studies*, 40(12), 2401–26.

Handzic, K. (2010) 'Is legalized land tenure necessary in slum upgrading? Learning from Rio's land tenure policies in the Favela Bairro Program', *Habitat International*, 34(1), 11–17.

Hanjalić, K. (2008) 'Introduction', in Hanjalić, K., van de Krol, R. and Lekić, A. (eds) *Sustainable Energy Technologies: Options and Prospects*, Dordrecht: Springer, xvii–xxiii.

Hannerz, U. (1987) 'The world in creolization' *Africa*, 57, 546–59.

Hannerz, U. (1990) 'Cosmopolitans and locals in world culture', in Featherstone, M. (ed.) *Global Culture: Nationalism, Globalization and Modernity*, London: Sage, 237–53.

Hannerz, U. (1992) *Cultural Complexity: Studies in the Social Organization of Meaning*, New York: Columbia University Press.

Hannerz, U. (2003) *Transnational Connections: Culture, People, Places*, London: Routledge.

Harcourt, W. (2005) 'The body politic in global development discourse: a woman and the politics of place perspective', in Harcourt, W. and Escobar, A. (eds) *Women and the Politics of Place*, Bloomfield, CT: Kumarian Press, 32–47.

Harcourt, W. and Escobar, A. (2005) *Women and the Politics of Place*, Bloomfield, CT: Kumarian Press, 1–17.

Hardt, M. and Negri, A. (2000) *Empire*, Cambridge, MA: Harvard University Press.

Hargreaves, C. (1992) *Snowfields: The War on Cocaine in the Andes*, London: Zed Books.

Harkin, J. (2010) 'When the net's wisdom of crowds turns into an online lynch mob', *The Observer*, 29 February, 31.

Harris, N. (1983) *Of Bread and Guns: The World Economy in Crisis*, Harmondsworth: Penguin Books.

Harrison, P. (1981) *Inside the Third World*, Harmondsworth: Penguin Books.

Hart, R. P. and Childers, J. P. (2005) 'The evolution of candidate Bush: a rhetorical analysis', *American Behavorial Scientist*, 49(2), 180–97.

Harvey, D. (1982) *The Limits to Capital*, Oxford: Blackwell.

Harvey, D. (1985) *Consciousness and the Urban Experience*, Oxford: Blackwell.

Harvey, D. (1989) *The Condition of Postmodernity: An Enquiry into the Origins of Cultural Change*, Oxford: Blackwell.

Harvey, D. (2003) *The New Imperialism*, Oxford: Oxford University Press.

Harvey, J., Rail, G. and Thibault, L. (1996) 'Globalization and sport: sketching theoretical models for empirical analyses', *Journal of Sport and Social Issues*, 23, 358–77.

Hayashi, Y. (2008) 'In Japan, temporary workers leave a lasting mark on economy', *Wall Street Journal*, 406, 14–15.

Hebdige, R. (2003) *Subculture: The Meaning of Style*, London: Routledge.

Hefner, R. W. (2000) *Civil Islam: Muslims and Democratization in Indonesia*, Princeton: Princeton University Press.

Hegedus, Z. (1989) 'Social movements and social change in self-creative society: new civil initiatives in the international arena', *International Sociology*, 4(1), 19–36.

Held, D. (1989) 'The decline of the nation state', in Hall, S. and Jacques, M. (eds) *New Times*, London: Lawrence & Wishart, 191–204.

Held, D. and McGrew, A. (2002) *Globalization/Anti-globalization*, Cambridge: Polity.

Hendrickson, M. K. and Heffernan, W. D. (2002) 'Opening spaces through relocalization: locating potential resistance in the weaknesses of the global food system', *Sociologia Ruralis*, 42(4), 347–69.

Herman, E. S. and McChesney, R. W. (1997) *The Global Media: The New Missionaries of Global Capitalism*, London: Cassell.

Herrnstein, R. J and Murray, C. (1994) *The Bell Curve: Intelligence and Class Structure in American Life*, New York: Free Press.

Hill, J. (1994) 'Cricket and the imperial connection: overseas players in Lancashire in the inter-war years', in Bale, J. and Maguire, J. (eds) *The Global Sports Arena: Athletic Talent Migration in an Interdependent World*, London: Frank Cass, 49–62.

Hill Collins, P. (2000) *Black Feminist Thought: Knowledge, Consciousness and the Politics of Empowerment* (2nd edn), New York: Routledge.

Hill Collins, P. (2005) *Black Sexual Politics: African Americans, Gender and the New Racism*, New York: Routledge.

Hill Collins, P. and Solomos, J. (eds) (2010) *The Handbook of Race and Ethnic Studies*, London: Sage.

Hirschland, M. J. (2006) *Corporate Social Responsibility and the Shaping of Global Public Policy*, Basingstoke: Palgrave Macmillan.

Hirst, P. and Thompson, G. (1996) *Globalization in Question: The International Economy and the Possibilities of Governance*, Cambridge: Polity.

Hobsbawm, E. J. (1994) *Age of Extremes: The Short Twentieth Century, 1914–1991*, London: Michael Joseph.

Hochschild, A. R. (1983) *The Managed Heart: The Commercialization of Human Feeling*, Berkeley, CA: University of California Press.

Hochschild, A. R. (2000) 'Global care chains and emotional surplus value', in Hutton, W. and Giddens, A. (eds) *On the Edge: Living with Global Capitalism*, London: Jonathan Cape, 130–46.

Hochschild, A. R. (2003) 'Love and gold', in Hochschild, A. R., *The Commercialization of Intimate Life: Notes from Home and Work*, Berkeley, CA: University of California Press, 195–97.

Hochschild, A. R. and Machung, A. (1989) *The Second Shift: Working Parents and the Revolution at Home*, New York: Viking Penguin.

Hoenig, J. (2010) 'Sogo Shosha – great promise, zero buzz', www.smartmoney.com/invest/stocks/sogo-shosha-great-promise-zero-buzz (accessed March 2012).

Hoggart, S. (1996) 'The hollow state', *The Guardian*, 26 October.

Hollinger, D. A. (2002) 'Not universalists, not pluralists: the new cosmopolitans find their way', in Vertovec, S. and Cohen, R. (eds) *Conceiving Cosmopolitanism: Theory, Context, and Practice*, Oxford: Oxford University Press, 227–39.

Hollingsworth, M. (2012) 'Londongrad: from Russia with cash', http://www.telegraph.co.uk/sponsored/russianow/society/8476412/Why-are-Russians-moving-to-Britain.html (accessed April 2012).

Holmes, M. (2006) 'Love lives at a distance: distance relationships over the lifecourse', *Sociological Research Online*, 11(3), http://www.socresonline.org.uk/11/3/holmes.html (accessed April 2012).

Holton, R. J. (2009) *Cosmopolitanism: New Thinking and New Directions*, Basingstoke: Palgrave Macmillan.

Holton, R. J. (2011) *Globalization and the Nation-state* (2nd edn), Basingstoke: Palgrave Macmillan.

Hoogvelt, A. M. (1997) *Globalization and the Post-colonial World: The New Political Economy of Development*, Basingstoke: Macmillan – now Palgrave Macmillan.

Hopkins, A. G. (1973) *An Economic History of West Africa*, London: Longman.

Horne, J. (2000) 'Soccer in Japan: is *Wa* all you need?' in Finn, G. P. and Giulianotti, R. (eds) *Football Culture: Local Contests, Global Visions*, London: Frank Cass, 212–29.

Horst, H. (2006) 'The blessings and burdens of communication: cell phones in Jamaican transnational social fields', *Global Networks*, 6(2), 143–59.

Hourani, A. H. (1991) *A History of the Arab Peoples*, London: Faber and Faber.

Howes, D. (ed.) (1996) *Cross-cultural Consumption: Global Market, Local Realities*, London: Routledge.

Hu T., Mao, Z., Shi, J. and Chen, W. (2008) *Tobacco Taxation and its Potential Impact in China*, Paris: International Union Against Tuberculosis and Lung Disease.

Huang, Y. (2008) *Capitalism with Chinese Characteristics: Entrepreneurship and the State*, Cambridge: Cambridge University Press.

Huntington, S. P. (1998) *The Clash of Civilizations and the Remaking of World Order*, London: Touchstone.

Huntington, S. P. (2004) *Who Are We? America's Great Debate*, London: Simon & Schuster.

Hutton, W. (1998) 'World must wake up to this disaster', *The Observer*, 30 August.

Hutton, W. (2007) *The Writing on the Wall: China and the West in the 21st Century*, London: Abacus.

Hutton, W. (2010) 'Now we know the truth: the financial meltdown wasn't a mistake – it was a con', *The Observer*, 18 April, 28.

Illouz, E. (2007) *Cold Intimacies: The Making of Emotional Capitalism*, Cambridge: Polity.

ILO (International Labour Office) (2008) 'Income inequalities in the age of financial globalization', *World of Work Report 2008*, Geneva: ILO.

Indian Institute of Technology Kanpur (n.d.) 'The diffusion of mobile phones in India', http://home.iitk.ac.in/~sanjay/skspresentation.ppt, slide 16 (accessed April 2012).

INET (Institute for New Economic Thinking) (2010) 'Economics in crisis and the crisis in economics', Conference summary, http://ineteconomics.org/blog/institute-new-economic-thinking-conference-summary%E2%80%9D-%E2%80%9Ceconomics-crisis-and-crisis-economics%E2%80%9D (accessed April 2012).

Infoplease (n.d.) 'The world's top tourism destinations', www.infoplease.com/ipa/A0198352.htm (accessed April 2012).

Informa Telecoms & Media (2010) 'Press release: Africa crosses 500 million mobile subscriptions', T. Mbongue, 10 November, http://blogs.informatandm.com/1388/press-release-africa-crosses-500-million-mobile-subscriptions-mark/ (accessed April 2012).

Inglehart, R. (1990) *Culture Shift in Advanced Industrial Society*, Princeton, NJ: Princeton University Press.

Inside Facebookgold (2010) 'Learn more', http://gold.insidenetwork.com/facebook/learn-more (accessed January 2011).

Internet World Stats (2010) 'New Facebook statistics', http://www.internetworldstats.com/pr/edi058.htm, 'Internet users in the world', httm://www.internetworldstats.com/stats.htm (accessed January 2011).

IPCC (Intergovernmental Panel on Climate Change) (2007) *Climate Change 2007*, the Fourth Assessment Report (AR4) of the United Nations, Cambridge: Cambridge University Press.

Ishii-Kuntz, M., Makino, K., Kuniko, K. and Tsuchiya, M. (2004) 'Japanese fathers of preschoolers and their involvement in child care', *Journal of Marriage and the Family*, 66(3), 779–91.

Jacobs, S. (2004) 'New forms, longstanding issues, and some successes: feminist networks and organizing in a globalising era', *Journal of Interdisciplinary Gender Studies*, 8(1/2), 171–93.

Jacobs, S., Jacobson, R. and Marchbank, J. (eds) (2000) *States of Conflict: Gender, Violence and Resistance*, London: Zed Books.

Jacobson, R., Jacobs, S. and Marchbank, J. (2000) 'Introduction: states of conflict', in Jacobs, S., Jacobson, R. and Marchbank, J. (eds) *States of Conflict: Gender, Violence and Resistance*, London: Zed Books.

Jaising, I. (1995) 'Violence against women: the Indian perspective', in Peters, J. and Wolper, A. (eds) *Women's Rights, Human Rights: International Perspectives*, New York: Routledge, 51–6.

James, A. (1996) 'Cooking the books: global or local identities in contemporary food cultures', in Howes, D. (ed.) *Cross-cultural Consumption: Global Markets, Local Realities*, London: Routledge, 77–92.

James, P. (2005) 'Arguing globalizations: propositions towards an investigation of global formation', *Globalizations*, 2(2), 193–209.

Jameson, F. (1984) 'Postmodernism or the cultural logic of late capitalism', *New Left Review*, 146, 53–92.

Jamieson, L. (1998) *Intimacy: Personal Relationships in Modern Societies*, Cambridge: Polity.

Jamieson, L., Anderson, M., McCrone, D. et al. (2002) 'Cohabitation and commitment: partnership plans of young men and women', *Sociological Review*, 50(3), 354–75.

Janus, N. (1986) 'Transnational advertising: some considerations on the impact of peripheral societies', in Atwood, R. and McAnany, E. G. (eds) *Communications and Latin American*

Society: Trends in Critical Research 1960–85, Madison, WI: University of Wisconsin Press, 127–42.

Jehovah's Witnesses (2011) 'Statistics: 2011 Report of Jehovah's Witnesses Worldwide', http://www.watchtower.org/e/statistics/worldwide_report.htm (accessed April 2012).

Jenson, A. (1969) 'How much can we boost IQ and scholastic achievement', *Harvard Educational Review*, 39, 1–123.

Jones, C. and Leshkowich, A. M. (2003) 'Introduction: the globalization of Asian dress: re-orienting fashion or re-orientalizing Asia?', in Niessen, S., Leshkowich, A. M. and Jones, C. (eds) *The Globalization of Asian Dress: Re-orienting Fashion*, Oxford: Berg, 1–48.

Jones, E. L. (1988) *Growth Recurring: Economic Change in World History*, Oxford: Clarendon Press.

Jones, S. (1993) *The Language of the Genes: Biology, History and the Evolutionary Future*, London: HarperCollins.

Jordan, B. and Düvell, F. (2003) *Migration: Boundaries of Equality and Justice*, Cambridge: Polity.

Juergensmeyer, M. (2003) *Terror in the Mind of God: The Global Rise of Religious Violence*, Berkeley, CA: University of California Press.

Julius, D. (1990) *Global Companies and Public Policy*, London: Pinter.

Kakaras, E., Doukelis, A., Giannakopoulos, D. and Koumanakos, A. (2008) 'CO_2 mitigation options for retrofitting Greek low-quality coal-fired power plants', in Hanjalić, K., van de Krol, R. and Lekić, A. (eds) *Sustainable Energy Technologies: Options and Prospects*, Dordrecht: Springer, 239–50.

Kaldor, M. (2008) 'Democracy and globalisation', in Albrow, M., Anheier, H., Glasius, M. et al. (eds) *Global Civil Society 2007/8*, London: Sage, 34–45.

Kamano, S. and Khor, D. (2008) 'How did you two meet? Lesbian partnerships in present day Japan', in Jackson, S., Jieyu, L. and Juhyun, W. (eds) *East Asian Sexualities: Modernity, Gender and New Sexual Cultures*, London: Zed Books, 161–77.

Kandiyoti, D. (1997) 'Bargaining with patriarchy', in Visvanathan, N., Duggan, L., Nissonoff, L. and Wiegersmal, N. (eds) *The Women, Gender and Development Reader*, London: Zed Books, 86–99.

Kasbekar, A. (1996) 'An introduction to Indian cinema', in Nelmes, J. (ed.) *An Introduction to Film Studies*, London: Routledge, 365–92.

Katz, H. (2009) 'Data programme', in Kumar, A., Scholte, J. A., Kaldor, M. et al. (eds) *Global Civil Society 2009*, London: Sage, 252–337.

Keane, J. (2003) *Global Civil Society?* Cambridge: Cambridge University Press.

Keck, M. E. and Sikkink, K. (1998) *Activists Beyond Borders: Advocacy Networks in International Politics*, Ithaca, NY: Cornell University Press.

Keen, D. (1994) *The Benefits of Famine: A Political Economy of Famine and Relief in Southwestern Sudan, 1983–89*, Princeton, NJ: Princeton University Press.

Keen, S. (2001) *Debunking Economics: The Naked Emperor of the Social Sciences*, Sydney: Pluto.

Kegley, C. W. and Wittkopf, E. R. (2004) *World Politics: Trend and Transformation* (9th edn), Belmont, CA: Thomson & Wadsworth.

Kelly, L. (2000) 'Wars against women: sexual violence, sexual politics and the militarized state', in Jacobs, S., Jacobson, R. and Marchbank, J. (eds) *States of Conflict: Gender, Violence and Resistance*, London: Zed Books, 45–65.

Kennedy, P. (2004) 'Making global society: friendship networks among transnational professionals in the building design industry', *Global Networks: A Journal of Transnational Affairs*, 4(2), 157–79.

Kennedy, P. (2007) 'The subversive element in interpersonal relations – cultural border crossings and third spaces: skilled migrants at work and play in the global system, *Globalizations*, 4(3), 341–54.

Kennedy, P. (2010) *Local Lives and Global Transformations: Towards World Society*, Basing-stoke: Palgrave Macmillan.

Kennedy, P. and Roudometof, V. (2002) 'Transnationalism in a global age', in Kennedy, P. and Roudometof, V. (eds) *Communities Across Borders: New Immigrants and Transnational Cultures*, London: Routledge, 1–26.

Kenway, J., Kraack, A. and Hickey-Moody, A. (2006) *Masculinity Beyond the Metropolis*, Basingstoke: Palgrave Macmillan.

Khagram, S. and Alvord, S. (2006) 'The rise of civic transnationalism', in Batliwala, S. and Brown, D. L. (eds) *Transnational Civil Society: An Introduction*, Bloomfield, CT: Kumarian Press, 65–81.

Kidron, M. and Segal, R. (1995) *The State of the World Atlas*, London: Penguin.

Kiely, R. (2005a) *Empire in the Age of Globalisation: US Hegemony and the Neoliberal Disorder*, London: Pluto Press.

Kiely, R. (2005b) *The Clash of Globalizations: Neo-liberalism, the Third Way and Anti-globalization*, Leiden: Brill.

Kiernan, V. (1995) *The Lords of Human Kind: European Attitudes to Other Cultures in the Imperial Age*, London: Serif.

King, V. T. (1993) 'Tourism and culture in Malaysia', in Hitchcock, M., King, V. T. and Parnwell, J. G. (eds) *Tourism in South-East Asia*, London: Routledge, 99–116.

Klein, N. (2001) *No Logo: No Space, No Choice, No Jobs*, London: Flamingo.

Klesse, C. (2007) *The Spectre of Promiscuity*, Aldershot: Ashgate.

Knox, P. L. and Taylor, P. J. (eds) (1995) *World Cities in a World-system*, Cambridge: Cambridge University Press.

KOF Swiss Economic Institute (2011) 'Press release', 18 March, http://globalization.kof.ethz.ch/static/pdf/press_release_2011_en.pdf (accessed April 2012).

Kornblum, W. (1988) *Sociology in a Changing World*, New York: Holt, Rinehart & Winston.

Kothari, S. and Harcourt, W. (2005) 'Women displaced: democracy, identity and development in India', in Harcourt, W. and Escobar, A. (eds) *Women and the Politics of Place*, Bloomfield, CT: Kumarian Press, 115–28.

Kreis, S. (2000) 'The age of ideologies: the world of Auguste Comte', http://www.historyguide.org/intellect/lecture25a.html (accessed April 2012).

Kumar, R. (1995) 'From Chipko to Sati: the contemporary Indian women's movement', in Basu, A. (ed.) *The Challenge of Local Feminisms*, Boulder, CO: Westview Press, 58–86.

Kumaranayake, L. and Lake, S. (2002) 'Global approaches to private sector provision: where is the evidence?' in Lee, K., Buse, K. and Fustukian, S. (eds) *Health Policy in a Globalising World*, Cambridge: Cambridge University Press, 78–96.

Kwan Lee, C. (2007) *Against the Law: Labour Protests in China's Rustbelt and Sunbelt*, Berkeley, CA: University of California Press.

Lanfant, M. F. (1995) 'International tourism, internationalisation and the challenge to identity', in Lanfant, M. F., Allcock, J. B. and Bruner, E. M. (eds) *International Tourism: Identity and Change*. London: Sage, 24–43.

Lanfant, M. F., Allcock, J. B. and Bruner, E. M. (eds) (1995) *International Tourism: Identity and Change*, London: Sage.

Langman, L. (2001) 'Globalization and national identity rituals in Brazil and the USA: the politics of pleasure versus the politics of protest', in Kennedy, P. and Danks, C. J. (eds) *Globalization and National Identities: Crisis or Opportunity?* Basingstoke: Palgrave – now Palgrave Macmillan, 190–209.

Lasch, C. (1995) *The Revolt of the Elites and the Betrayal of Democracy*, New York: W. W. Norton.

Lash, S. (1994) 'Reflexivity and its doubles: structure, aesthetics, community', in Beck, U., Giddens, A. and Lash, S. (eds) *Reflexive Modernization: Politics, Tradition and Aesthetics in the Modern Social Order*, Cambridge: Polity, 110–75.

Lash, S. and Urry, J. (1987) *The End of Organised Capitalism*, Cambridge: Polity.

Lash, S. and Urry, J. (1994) *Economies of Signs and Space*, London: Sage.

Lauricella, T. and Kansas, D. (2010) 'Currency trading soars', 31 August, http://online.wsj.com/article/SB10001424052748704421104575463901973510496.html.

Le Blanc, H. (2009) 'Russia: going from sprint to marathon', http://luxurysociety.com/articles/2009/10/russia-going-from-sprint-to-marathon (accessed April 2012).

Lee, E. and Jackson, E. (2002) 'The pregnant body', in Evans, M. and Lee, E. (eds) *Real Bodies: A Sociological Introduction*, Basingstoke: Palgrave – now Palgrave Macmillan, 115–32.

Lemann, N. (1991) *The Promised Land: The Great Black Migration and How it Changed America*, New York: Alfred S. Knopf.

Lenin, V. I. (1988) *Imperialism, the Highest Stage of Capitalism: A Popular Outline*, New York: International Publishers.

Lett, D., Hier, S. and Walby, K. (2010) 'CCTV surveillance and the civic conversation: a study in public sociology', *Canadian Journal of Sociology*, 35(3), 437–62.

Lévi-Strauss, C. (1963) *Totemism* (trans. R. Needham), Boston, MA: Beacon Press.

Lévi-Strauss, C. (1968) *The Savage Mind*, Chicago, IL: Chicago University Press.

Lewis, D. (1973) 'Anthropology and colonialism', *Current Anthropology*, 14(5), 581–602.

Liang, C. S. (2007) 'Europe for the "Europeans": the foreign and security policy of the populist radical right', in Liang, C. S. (ed.) *Europe for the Europeans: The Foreign and Security Policy of the Populist Radical Right*, Aldershot: Ashgate, 1–32.

Lilley, P. (2006) *Dirty Dealing*, London: Kogan Page.

Lipietz, A. (1987) *Mirages and Miracles: The Crisis of Global Fordism* (trans. D. Macey), London: Verso.

Lipsitz, G. (1997) *Dangerous Crossroads: Popular Music, Postmodernism, and the Poetics of Place*, London: Verso.

Lister, R. (1997) *Citizenship: Feminist Perspectives*, Basingstoke: Macmillan – now Palgrave Macmillan.

Lithman, Y. G. and Andersson, M. (2005) 'Introduction', in Andersson, M., Lithman, Y. G. and Sernhede, O. (eds) *Youth, Otherness and the Plural City: Modes of Belonging and Social Life*, Göteborg: Bokförlaget Daidalas, 1–24.

Livi-Bacci, M. (2006) *A Concise History of World Population* (4th edn), Oxford: Blackwell.

Lockwood, B. and Redoano, M. (2005) 'The CSGR globalisation index: an introductory guide', Centre for the Study of Globalisation and Regionalisation, University of Warwick, Working Paper 155/04.

Loomis, C. J. (2010) 'The $600 billion challenge', *Fortune Magazine*, 16 June.

Luxemburg, R. (1972) *Imperialism and the Accumulation of Capital*, London: Allen Lane.

Lynas, M. (2004) 'If they plant them, we'll pull them up', *The Ecologist*, 34(3), 26–30.

McCarthy, T. (1978) *The Critical Theory of Jürgen Habermas*, Cambridge: Polity.

Macionis, J. J. and Plummer, K. (2008) *Sociology: A Global Introduction* (4th edn), Harlow: Pearson.

McCormick, J. (1989) *The Global Environmental Movement*, London: Bellhaven.

McCurry, J. (2010) 'Addicted to the internet: how virtual worlds have trapped 2 million in their web', *The Guardian*, 14 July, 21.

McDougall, C. (2009) 'The painful truth about trainers: Are running shoes a waste of money?', *Mail Online*, 15 April.

McEvoy, A. J. and Grätzel, M. (2008) 'Photovoltaic cells for sustainable energy', in Hanjalić, K., van de Krol, R. and Lekić, A. (eds) *Sustainable Energy Technologies: Options and Prospects*, Dordrecht: Springer, 99–120.

McKay, J. and Miller, T. (1991) 'From old boys to men and women of the corporation: the Americanization and commodification of Australian sport', *Sociology of Sport Journal*, 8(1), 86–94.

McKie, R. (2008) 'Arctic "could be free of ice in five years"', *The Observer*, 10 October, 17.

McLuhan, M. (1962) *The Gutenberg Galaxy: The Making of Typographical Man*, Toronto: University of Toronto Press.

McMichael, P. (2000) *Development and Social Change: A Global Perspective* (2nd edn), Thousand Oaks, CA: Pine Forge.

McMurray, C. and Smith, R. (2001) *Diseases of Globalization: Socioeconomic Transitions and Health*, London: Earthscan.

MacNaghten, P. (1993) 'Discourses of nature: argumentation and power', in Burman, E. and Parks, I. (eds) *Discourse Analytical Research*, London: Routledge, 52–71.

McNeill, W. H. (1971) *A World History*, Oxford: Oxford University Press.

Maguire, J. (1993) 'Bodies, sports cultures and societies: a critical review of some theories in the sociology of the body', *International Review for the Sociology of Sport*, 28(1), 33–52.

Maguire, J. (1999) *Global Sport: Identities, Societies, Civilizations*, Cambridge: Polity.

Maguire, J. (2000) 'Sport and globalization', in Oakley, J. and Dunning, E. (eds) *Handbook of Sport Studies*, London: Sage, 356–69.

Malik, K. (1996) *The Meaning of Race: Race History and Culture in Western Society*, Basingstoke: Macmillan – now Palgrave Macmillan.

Malthus, T. (1798) *Essay on the Principle of Population*, London: J. Johnson.

Mangan, J. A. (1981) *Athleticism in the Victorian and Edwardian Public Schools*, Cambridge: Cambridge University Press.

Mangan, J. A. (1996) 'Duty unto death: English masculinity and militarism in the age of the new imperialism, in Mangan, J. A. (ed.) *Tribal Identities: Nationalism, Sport and Europe*, London: Frank Cass, 10–38.

Manji, I. (2004) *The Trouble with Islam Today: A Muslim's Call for Reform in her Faith*, New York: St Martin's Press.

Mansoor, A. and Quillan, B. (2006) *Migration and Remittances: Eastern Europe and the Former Soviet Union*, Washington, DC: World Bank.

Marbridge Daily (2010) 'MIIT announces October 2010 telecom statistics', http://www.marbridgeconsulting.com/marbridgedaily/2010-11-24/article/41168/miit_announces_october_2010_telecom_statistics (accessed 9 April 2012).

Marcuse, P. and van Kempen, R. (2000) *Globalizing Cities: A New Spatial Order?* Oxford: Blackwell.

Mariani, J. F. (2011) *How Italian Food Conquered the World*, Basingstoke: Palgrave Macmillan.

Marsh, I., Keating, M., Eyre, A. et al. (eds) (1996) *Making Sense of Society: An Introduction to Sociology*, Harlow: Addison Wesley Longman.

Marshall, T. H. (1950) *Citizenship and Social Class*, Cambridge: Cambridge University Press.

Marston, S. A., Woodward, K. and Jones, J. P. III (2007) 'Flattening ontologies of globalization: the Nollywood case', *Globalizations*, 4(1), 45–64.

Martin, H. P. and Schuman, H. (1997) *The Global Trap: Globalization and the Assault on Democracy and Prosperity*, London: Zed Books.

Martin, P. and Wilmer, F. (2008) 'Transnational normative struggles and globalization: the case of indigenous peoples in Bolivia and Ecuador', *Globalizations*, 5(4), 583–98.

Marx, K. (1976) *Capital: A Critique of Political Economy*, vol. 1, Harmondsworth: Penguin Books.

Marx, K. and Engels, F. ([1848]1967) *The Communist Manifesto*, Harmondsworth: Penguin.

Massey, D. B. (1993) 'Power-geometry and a progressive sense of place', in Bird, J., Curtis, B., Putnam, T. et al. (eds) *Mapping the Futures: Local Cultures, Global Change*, London: Routledge, 59–70.

Massey, D. B. (2005) *For Space*, London: Sage.

Massey, D. S. and Denton, N. A. (1993) *American Apartheid: Segregation and the Making of the Underclass*, Cambridge, MA: Harvard University Press.

Matsui, Y. (1989) *Women's Asia*, London: Zed Books.

May, J., Wills, J., Datta, K. et al. (2007) 'Keeping London working: global cities, the British state and London's new migrant division of labour', *Urban Studies*, 32, 151–67.

Mayer, J. A. (1983) 'Notes towards a working definition of social control in historical analysis', in Cohen, S. and Scull, A. (eds) *Social Control and the State*, Oxford: Martin Robertson, 17–38.

Mayhew, H. (1864) *London Labour and the London Poor: The Condition and Earnings of Those that Will Work, Cannot Work, and Will Not Work*, London: C. Griffin.

Medilinks (2001) 'Africa: five million grandparents looking after orphans', *Health News*, http://medilinkz.org/old/news/news2.asp?page=648&NewsID=330 (accessed April 2012).

Meernik, J. (1996) 'United States military intervention and the promotion of democracy', *Journal of Peace Research*, 33(4), 391–402.

Meethan, K. (2001) *Tourism in Global Society: Place, Culture, Consumption*, Basingstoke: Palgrave – now Palgrave Macmillan.

Mercer, C., Page, B. and Evans, M. (2009) 'Unsettling connections: transnational networks, development and African home associations', *Global Networks: A Journal of Transnational Affairs*, 9(2), 141–61.

Miko, F. T. (2007) 'International human trafficking', in Thachuk. K. L. (ed.) *Transnational Threats: Smuggling and Trafficking in Arms, Drugs and Human Life*, Westport, CT: Praeger Security International, 36–52.

Milanovic, B. (2007) 'Globalization and inequality', in Held, D. and Kaya, A. (eds) *Global Inequality: Patterns and Explanations*, Cambridge: Polity, 26–49.

Miles, A. (1996) *Integrative Feminisms: Building Global Visions, 1960s–1990s*, New York: Routledge.

Miles, R. (1989) *Racism*, London: Routledge.

Millar, J. and Salt, J. (2008) 'Portfolios of mobility: the movement of expertise in transnational corporations in two sectors – aerospace and extractive industries', *Global Networks*, 8(1), 25–50.

Miller, T., Lawrence, G., McKay, J. and Rowe, D. (2001) *Globalization and Sport: Playing the World*, London: Sage.

Millet, K. (1977) *Sexual Politics*, London: Virago.

Milton, K. (1996) *Environmentalism and Cultural Theory*, London: Routledge.

Mishra, P. (2011) 'To see Muslim discourse in politics as a vicious anachronism is to see very little', *The Guardian*, 6 January, 31.

Mitchell, K. (1995) 'Flexible circulation in the Pacific Rim: capitalism in cultural context, *Economic Geography*, 71(4), 364–82.

Mitchell, T. (2001) 'Another root: hip-hop outside the USA', in T. Mitchell (ed.) *Global Noise: Rap and Hip-Hop Outside the USA*, Middletown, CT: Wesleyan University Press, 1–38.

Mittelman, J. H. (2009) 'Social research, knowledge and criminal power', in Friman, H. R. (ed.) *Crime and the Global Political Economy*, Boulder, CO: Lynne Rienner, 159–76.

MoD (Ministry of Defence) Joint Doctrine and Concept Centre (2005) *Strategic Trends*, www.jdcc-strategictrends.org.

Moghadam V. M. (2007) *From Patriarchy to Empowerment*, Syracuse, NY: Syracuse University Press.

Molyneux, M. (2001) *Women's Movements in International Perspective: Latin America and Beyond*, Basingstoke: Palgrave – now Palgrave Macmillan.

Monnier, C. (2010) 'Family concepts & structures', https://globalsociology.pbworks.com/w/page/14711176/Family (accessed April 2012).

Moore, B. (1967) *Social Origins of Dictatorship and Democracy: Lord and Peasant in the Making of the Modern World*, Harmondsworth: Penguin.

Moore, B. (1972) *Reflections on the Causes of Human Misery and upon Certain Proposals to Eliminate Them*, London: Allen Lane.

Moore, R., Pinn, A. B. and Sawyer, M. R. (eds) (2004) *People's Temple and Black Religion in America*, Bloomington, IN: University of Indiana Press.

Moore, W. E. (1966) 'Global sociology: the world as a singular system', *American Journal of Sociology*, 71(5) 475–82.

Morgan, D. H. (1996) *Family Connections*, Cambridge: Polity.

Morley, D. and Robins, K. (1995) *Spaces of Identity: Global Media, Electronic Landscapes and Cultural Boundaries*, London: Routledge.

Morozov, E. (2011) *The Net Delusion: How Not to Liberate the World*, London: Allen Lane.

Mudde, C. (2007) *Populist Radical Right Parties in Europe*, Cambridge: Cambridge University Press.

Munck, R. (2005) *Globalization and Social Exclusion: A Transformationalist Perspective*, Bloomfield, CT: Kumerian Press.

Munck, R. (2007) *Globalization and Contestation*, London: Routledge.

Murie, A. and Musterd, S. (2004) 'Social exclusion and opportunity structures in European cities and neighbourhoods', *Urban Studies*, 41(8), 1441–59.

Mutuo (2010) *Britain Made Mutual: Mutuals Yearbook*, Borehamwood: Mutuo.

Naito, T. and Gielen, U. P. (2005) 'The changing Japanese family: a psychological portrait', in Roopnarine, J. and Gielen, U. P. (eds) *Families in Global Perspective*, Boston, MA: Pearson.

Nakatani, A. (2006) 'The emergence of nurturing fathers: discourses and practices of fatherhood in contemporary Japan', in Rebick, M. and Takanake, A. (eds) *The Changing Japanese Family*, New York: Routledge, 94–109.

Napoleoni, L. (2004) *Terror Inc: Tracing the Money behind Global Terrorism*, London: Penguin Books.

Nardi, P. M. (1998) 'The globalization of the gay and lesbian socio-political movement', *Sociological Perspectives*, 41(3), 569–85.

National Counterterrorism Center (2010) 'Worldwide Incidents Tracking System, 2010', https://wits.nctc.gov/FederalDiscoverWITS/index.do?N=0 (accessed August 2011).

Neale, J. (2008) *Stop Global Warming: Change the World*, Cambridge: Bookmarks.

Needham, J. (1969) *The Grand Titration: Science and Society in East and West*, Toronto: University of Toronto Press.

Nemoto, K. (2008) 'Postponed marriage: exploring women's views of matrimony and work in Japan', *Gender and Society*, 22(2), 219–37.

Newell, P. (2006) 'Climate for change? Civil society and the politics of global warming', in Glasius, M., Kaldor, M. and Anheier, H. (eds) *Global Civil Society 2005/06*, London: Sage, 90–120.

Nicholls, D. (1995) 'Population and process: Parson Malthus', *Anglican Theological Review*, 77(3), 321–34.

Nisbet, R. A. (1970) *The Sociological Tradition*, London: Heinemann Educational Books.

Novicka, M. and Rovisco, M. (eds) (2009) *Cosmopolitanism in Practice*, Aldershot: Ashgate.

Nuttavuthisit, K. (2007) 'Branding Thailand: correcting the negative image of sex tourism', *Place Branding and Public Diplomacy*, 3(1), 21–30.

Nye, J. S. (2002) *The Paradox of American Power: Why the World's Superpower Can't Go It Alone*, New York: Oxford University Press.

Nye, J. S. (2004) *Soft Power: The Means to Success in World Politics*, New York: Public Affairs.

Obama, B. (2004) Video of speech to the Democratic National Convention, http://www.youtube.com/watch?v=eWynt87PaJ0&feature=related 2004 (accessed April 2012).

O'Brien, M., Penna, S. and Hay, C. (eds) (1999) *Theorising Modernity: Reflexivity, Environment and Identity in Giddens' Social Theory*, New York: Longman.

O'Byrne, D. (2003) *Human Rights: An Introduction*, Harlow: Pearson Education.

O'Connell Davidson, J. N. and Sanchez Taylor, J. (1999) 'Fantasy islands: exploring the demand for sex tourism', in Kempadoo, K. (ed.) *Sun, Sex and Gold: Tourism and Sex Work in the Caribbean*, Boulder, CO: Rowman & Littlefield.

O'Connor, A. (2002) 'Punk and globalization: Mexico City and Toronto', in Kennedy, P. and Roudometof, V. (eds) *Communities Across Borders: New Immigrants and Transnational Cultures*, London: Routledge, 143–55.

Ohmae, K. (1994) *The Borderless World: Power and Strategy in the International Economy*, London: Collins.

ONS (Office for National Statistics) (2011) *Divorces in England and Wales, 2009*, Statistical Bulletin, Newport: ONS.

Oommen, T. K. (1997) 'Social movements in the Third World', in Lindberg, S. and Sverrisson, A. (eds) *Social Movements in Development: The Challenges to Globalization and Democratization*, Basingstoke: Macmillan – now Palgrave Macmillan, 46–66.

Outhwaite, W. (1994) *Habermas: A Critical Introduction*, Cambridge: Polity.

Outhwaite, W. (ed.) (1996) *The Habermas Reader*, Cambridge: Polity.

Padilla, M., Hirsh, J. S., Munoz-Laboy, M. et al. (eds) (2007) *Love and Globalization: Transformations of Intimacy in the Contemporary World*, Nashville, TN: Vanderbilt University Press.

Pahl, J. (1989) *Money and Marriage*, Basingstoke: Macmillan.

Palan, R. (2009) 'Crime, sovereignty and the offshore world', in Friman, H. R. (ed.) *Crime and the Global Political Economy*, Boulder, CO: Lynne Rienner, 35–48.

Parsons, T. (1971) *Societies: Evolutionary and Comparative Perspectives*, Englewood Cliffs, NJ: Prentice Hall.

Parsons, T. and Bales, R. F. (eds) (2003) *Family Socialization and Interaction Process*, London: Routledge.

Passel, J. (2005) 'Unauthorised, immigration agencies', *Migration News*, http://migration.ucdavis.edu/mn/more.php?id=3087_0_2_0 (accessed April 2012).

Passy, F. (1999) 'Supranational political opportunities as a channel of globalization of political conflicts: the case of the rights of indigenous peoples', in della Porta, D., Hanspeter, K. and Rucht, D. (eds) *Social Movements in a Globalizing World*, Basingstoke: Macmillan – now Palgrave Macmillan, 148–69.

Patterson, O. (1982) *Slavery and Social Death: A Comparative Study*, Cambridge, MA: Harvard University Press.

Paus, E. (ed.) (2007) *Global Capitalism Unbound: Winners and Losers from Offshore Outsourcing*, Basingstoke: Palgrave Macmillan.

Pearce, F. and Tombs, S. (1993) 'US capital vs. the third world: Union Carbide and Bhopal', in Pearce, F. and Woodiwiss, M. (eds) *Global Crime Connections: Dynamics and Control*, Toronto: University of Toronto Press, 187–211.

Pearse, A. (1980) *Seeds of Plenty, Seeds of Want: Social and Economic Implications of the Green Revolution*, Oxford: Clarendon Press.

Pendergrast, M. (1993) *For God, Country and Coca-Cola*, New York: Charles Scribner & Sons.

Perkins, H. C. and Thorns, D. C. (2001) 'Gazing or performing? Reflections on Urry's tourist gaze in the context of contemporary experience in the Antipodes', *International Sociology*, 16(2), 185–204.

Perlman, J. E. (1976) *The Myth of Marginality: Urban Poverty and Politics in Rio de Janeiro*, Berkeley, CA: University of California Press.

Perlman, J. E. (2010) *Favela: Four Decades of Living on the Edge of Rio de Janeiro*, Oxford: Oxford University Press.

Perlmutter, H. (1991) 'On the rocky road to the first global civilization', *Human Relations*, 44(9), 897–1010.

Peters, J. and Wolper, A. (eds) (1995) *Women's Rights, Human Rights: International Feminist Perspectives*, New York: Routledge.

Peterson, R. A. and Bennett, A. (2004) 'Introducing music scenes', in Bennett, A. and Peterson, R. A. (eds) *Music Scenes: Local, Translocal, and Virtual*, Nashville, TN: Vanderbilt University Press, 1–30.

Peterson, V. S. and Runyan, A. S. (1993) *Global Gender Issues*, Boulder, CO: Westview Press.

Pettifor, A. (2001) 'Why Jubilee 2000 made an impact', in Anheier, H., Glasius, M. and Kaldor, M. (eds) *Global Civil Society 2004/05*, London: Sage, 62–3.

Pettit, J. (2004) 'Climate justice: a new social movement for atmospheric rights', *IDS Bulletin*, 35(3), 102–6.

Phizacklea, A. (1992) 'Jobs for the girls: the production of women's outerwear in the UK', in Cross, M. (ed.) *Ethnic Minorities and Industrial Change in Europe and North America*, Cambridge: Cambridge University Press, 94–110.

Pianta, M. (2001) 'Parallel summits of global civil society', in Anheier, H., Glasius M. and Kaldor, M. (eds) *Global Civil Society 2001*, Oxford: Oxford University Press, 169–94.

Pogge, T. W. (2007) 'Why inequality matters', in Held, D. and Kaya, A. (eds) *Global Inequality: Patterns and Explanations*, Cambridge: Polity, 132–47.

Polanyi, K. ([1957]2002) *The Great Transformation: The Political and Economic Origins of Our Time*, Foreword by J. E. Stiglitz, New York: Beacon Books.

Porter, C. (2008) 'Manchester United, global capitalism and local resistance', *Belgeo*, 2, 181–91.

Portes, A. (1997) 'Globalization from below: the rise of transnational communities', Working Paper Series No. 1 of the Transnational Communities Project at the Faculty of Anthropology and Geography, Oxford University.

Premdas, R. (1996) 'Ethnicity and elections in the Caribbean', Working Paper No. 224, Kellogg Institute, University of Notre Dame.

Price, P. L. (2007) 'Cohering culture on *Calle Ocho*: the pause and the flow of *Latinidad*', *Globalizations*, 4(1), 81–99.

PricewaterhouseCoopers (2008) 'Vietnam may be fastest growing emerging economy', http://www.pwc.com/vn/en/releases2008/vietnam-may-be-fastest-growing-emerging-economy.jhtml (accessed April 2012).

Pries, L. (ed.) (2001) *New Transnational Social Spaces: International Migrations and Transnational Companies in the Early 21st Century*, London: Routledge.

Probyn, E. (1995) 'Lesbians in space: gender, sex and the structure of missing', *Gender, Place and Culture*, 2(1), 77–84.

Pugh, M. (2002) 'Maintaining peace and security', in Held, D. and McGrew, A. (eds) *Governing Globalization: Power, Authority and Global Governance*, Cambridge: Polity Press, 209–33.

Putnam, R. D. (1995) 'Bowling alone: America's declining social capital', *Journal of Democracy*, 6(1), 65–78.

Putnam, R. D. (2007) 'E pluribus unum: diversity and community in the twenty-first century', *Scandinavian Political Studies*, 30(2), 137–74.

Rabine, L. W. (2002) *The Global Circulation of African Fashion*, Oxford: Berg.

Radford, J. (2000) 'Theorizing commonalities and differences: sexual violence, law and feminist activism in India and the UK', in Radford, J., Friedberg, M. and Harne, L. (eds) *Women, Violence and Strategies for Action: Feminist Research, Policy and Practice*, Buckingham: Open University Press, 167–84.

Rajeev, D. (2005) 'India: everything gets worse with Coca-Cola', *Inter Press Service*, India, 22 August.

Ramet, S. P. (2005) 'Foreword', in Roudometof, V., Agadjanian, A. and Pankhurst, J. (eds) *Eastern Orthodoxy in a Global Age: Tradition Faces the Twenty-first Century*, Walnut Creek, CA: Rowman & Littlefield, vii–xii.

Randerson, J. (2010) 'Losing my land is breaking my heart', *The Guardian*, G2, 8 December, 10–11.

Ratha, D. (2009) 'Remittance flows to developing countries are estimated to exceed $300 billion in 2008', http://peoplemove.world bank.org/en/comment/reply130 (accessed April 2009).

Raworth, K. (2005) *Trading Away our Rights: Women Working in Global Supply Chains*, Oxford: Oxfam International.

Rebick, M. and Takenaka, A. (eds) (2006) *The Changing Japanese Family*, New York: Routledge.

Redclift, M. R. (2006) 'Chewing gum: mass consumption and the 'shadow-lands of the

Yucatan', in Brewer, J. and Trentmann, F. (eds) *Consuming Cultures. Global Perspectives: Historical Trajectories, Transnational Exchanges*, Oxford: Berg, 167–88.

Regev, M. (2002) 'The "pop-rockization" of popular music', in Hesmondalgh, D. and Negus, K. (eds) *Popular Music Studies*, London: Arnold, 251–74.

Reitan, R. (2007) *Global Activism*, London: Routledge.

Renson, R., de Cramer, E. and de Vroede, E. (1997) 'Local heroes: beyond the stereotype of the participants in traditional games', *International Review for the Sociology of Sport*, 32(1), 59–68.

Rex, J. (1986) *Race and Ethnicity*, Milton Keynes: Open University Press.

Rice, X. (2008) 'They risk everything to escape', *The Guardian, G2*, 21 April, 2.

Ritzer, G. (1993) *The McDonaldization of Society: An Investigation into the Changing Character of Social Life*, Thousand Oaks, CA: Pine Forge Press.

Ritzer, G. (1998) *The McDonaldization Thesis: Explorations and Extensions*, London: Sage.

Ritzer, G. (2004a) *The McDonaldization of Society*, Thousand Oaks, CA: Pine Forge Press (revised New Century edn).

Ritzer, G. (2004b) *The Globalization of Nothing*, Thousand Oaks, CA: Pine Forge Press.

Roberts, B. (1978) *Cities of Peasants: The Political Economy of Urbanization in the Third World*, London: Edward Arnold.

Roberts, J. M. (1992) *History of the World*, Oxford: Helicon.

Robertson, R. (1992) *Globalization: Social Theory and Global Culture*, London: Sage.

Robertson, R. (1995) 'Glocalization: time–space and homogeneity–heterogeneity', in Featherstone, M., Lash, S. and Robertson, R. (eds) *Global Modernities*, London: Sage, 25–44.

Robertson, R. (2001) 'Globalization theory 2000+: major problematics', in Ritzer, G. and Smart, B. (eds) *Handbook of Social Theory*, London: Sage, 458–71.

Robinson, W. I. (2002) 'Capitalist globalization and the transnationalization of the state', in Rupert, M. and Smith, H. (eds) *Historical Materialism and Globalization*, London: Routledge, 210–29.

Robinson, W. I. and Harris, J. (2000) 'Towards a global ruling class? Globalization and the transnational capitalist class', *Science and Society*, 64(1), 11–54.

Roche, M. (1992) *Rethinking Citizenship: Welfare, Ideology and Change in Modern Society*, Cambridge: Polity.

Rock, P. (1996a) 'Deviance', in Kuper, A. and Kuper, J. (eds) *The Social Science Encyclopaedia*, London: Routledge, 182–5.

Rock, P. (1996b) 'Symbolic interactionism', in Kuper, A. and Kuper, J. (eds) *The Social Science Encylopedia*, London: Routledge, 859–60.

Rofe, M. W. (2003) '"I just want to be global": theorising the gentrifying class as an emergent elite global community', *Urban Studies*, 40(12), 2511–26.

Rogers, E. M. and Antola, L. (1985) 'Telenovelas in Latin America', *Journal of Communications*, 35, 24–35.

Rogers, P. (2011) 'Tunisia and the world: roots of turmoil', 24 January, http://www.open democracy.net/paul-rogers/tunisia-and-world-roots-of-turmoil (accessed February 2011).

Rohatyn, F. (2002) 'The betrayal of capitalism', *New York Review of Books*, 49(3), 6–8.

Rojek, C. (1995) *Decentring Leisure: Rethinking Leisure Theory*, London: Sage.

Roopnarine, J. and Gielen, U. P. (eds) (2005) *Families in Global Perspective*, Boston, MA: Pearson.

Rosenau, J. N. (1990) *Turbulence in World Politics: A Theory of Change and Continuity*, Princeton, NJ: Princeton University Press.

Ross, A. (ed.) (1997) *No Sweat*, London: Verso.

Rothkopf, D. (2008) 'Tax cuts and world trade widens US gap between rich and poor', *Financial Times*, 9 April, 9.

Rowbotham, S. (1993) *Homeworkers Worldwide*, London: Merlin Press.

Rowbotham, S. and Linkogle, S. (2001) 'Introduction', in Rowbotham, S. and Linkogle, S.

(eds) *Women Resist Globalization: Mobilizing for Livelihood and Rights*, London: Zed Books, 1–12.

Rowell, A. (1996) *Green Backlash: Global Subversion of the Environmental Movement*, London: Routledge.

Rowell, A. (2003) 'Debate, what debate?' *The Ecologist*, 33(6), 26–36.

Royal Commission on Environmental Pollution (2011) *Demographic Change and the Environment*, London: TSO.

Runciman, W. G. (1990) 'How many classes are there in contemporary society?' *Sociology*, 24, 377–96.

Ruthven, M. (2000) *Islam: A Very Short Introduction*, Oxford: Oxford University Press.

Saldanha, A. (2002) 'Music, space, identity: geographies of youth culture in Bangalore', *Cultural Studies*, 16(3), 337–50.

Sampson, E. E. (1993) *Celebrating the Other: A Dialogic Account of Human Nature*, Hemel Hempstead: Harvester Wheatsheaf.

Sassen, S. (1991) *The Global City: New York, London, Tokyo*, Princeton, NJ: Princeton University Press.

Sassen, S. (2000) *Cities in a World Economy*, Thousand Oaks, CA: Pine Forge Press.

Sassen, S. (2002) 'Introduction: locating cities on global circuits', in Sassen, S. (ed.) *Global Networks: Linked Cities*, New York: Routledge, 1–37.

Sassen, S. (2007) *A Sociology of Globalization*, New York: W.W. Norton.

Saunders, D. (2011) *Arrival City: How the Largest Migration in History is Reshaping the World*, New York: Pantheon.

Saussure, F. de (1974) *Course in General Linguistics*, London: Fontana/Collins.

Savage, M. and Warde, A. (1993) *Urban Sociology, Capitalism and Modernity*, Basingstoke: Macmillan – now Palgrave Macmillan.

Savage, M., Bagnall, G. and Longhurst, B. (2005) *Globalization and Belonging*, London: Sage.

Schechter, D. (2000) *Falun Gong's Challenge to China: Spiritual Practice or 'Evil Cult'*, New York: Akashic Books.

Scheff, T. J. (1990) *Microsociology: Discourse, Emotion and Social Structure*, Chicago, IL: University of Chicago Press.

Schmalzbauer, L. (2008) 'Family divided: the class formation of Honduran transnational families', *Global Networks: A Journal of Transnational Affairs*, 8(3), 329–46.

Schmidt, E. (2007) 'Whose "culture": globalism, localism and the expansion of tradition: the case of the Hñähñu of Hidalgo, Mexico and Clearwater, Florida', *Globalizations*, 4(1), 101–14.

Scholte, J. A. (2005) *Globalization: A Critical Introduction*, Basingstoke: Palgrave Macmillan.

Schwartz, D. (1997) *Culture and Power: The Sociology of Pierre Bourdieu*, Chicago, IL: University of Chicago Press.

Scott, J. (2004) *Social Theory: Central Issues in Sociology*, London: Sage.

Seager, J. (1995) *The New State of the Earth Atlas*, New York: Simon & Schuster.

Seagrave, S. (1995) *Lords of the Rim: The Invisible Empire of the Overseas Chinese*, New York: G. P. Putnam's Sons.

Seckinelgin, H. (2002) 'Time to stop and think: HIV/AIDS, global civil society and people's politics', in Glasius, M., Kaldor, M and Anheier, H. (eds) *Global Civil Society 2002*, Oxford: Oxford University Press.

Seidman, S. (1983) *Liberalism and the Origins of European Social Theory*, Oxford: Blackwell.

Sen, A. (1981) *Poverty and Famine: An Essay on Entitlement and Deprivation*, Oxford: Clarendon Press.

Sernhede, O. (2005) '"Reality is my nationality": the global tribe of hip hop and immigrant youth in "The New Sweden"', in Andersson, M., Lithman, Y. G. and Sernhede, O. (eds) *Youth, Otherness and the Plural City: Modes of Belonging and Social Life*, Göteborg: Bokförlaget Daidalas, 271–89.

Serrano, M. (2002) 'Transnational organized crime and international security: business as usual?', in Berdal, M. and Serrano, M. (eds) *Transnational Organized Crime and International Security*, Boulder, CO: Lynne Rienner, 13–36.

Serrano, M. and Toro, M. C. (2002) 'From drug trafficking to transnational organized crime in Latin America', in Berdal, M. and Serrano, M. (eds) *Transnational Organized Crime and International Security*, Boulder, CO: Lynne Rienner, 155–182.

Sharpley, R. (1994) *Tourism, Tourists and Society*, Huntingdon: Elm.

Shaw, M. (1994) *Global Society and International Relations: Sociological Concepts and Political Perspective*, Cambridge: Polity.

Shaw, M. (1997) 'The state of globalization: towards a theory of state transformation', *Review of International Political Economy*, 4(3), 497–513.

Sheller, M. and Urry, J. (eds) (2004) *Tourism Mobilities: Places to Play, Places in Play*, London: Routledge.

Shelley, L. I. (2007) 'The rise and diversification of human smuggling and trafficking into the United States', in Thachuk, K. L. (ed.) *Transnational Threats: Smuggling and Trafficking in Arms, Drugs and Human Life*, Westport, CT: Praeger Security International, 194–210.

Sheridan, A. (1980) *Michel Foucault: The Will to Truth*, London: Tavistock.

Simmel, G. (1950a) *The Sociology of Georg Simmel* (trans. and ed. K. H. Wolff), New York: Free Press.

Simmel, G. (1950b) 'The metropolis and mental life', in Wolff, K. H. (ed. and trans.), *The Sociology of Georg Simmel*, New York: Free Press, 409–24.

Simmel, G. ([1900]1978) *The Philosophy of Money* (trans. T. Bottomore and D. Frisby), London: Routledge & Kegan Paul.

Sinclair, J. (1987) *Images Incorporated: Advertising as Industry and Ideology*, London: Croom Helm.

Sinclair, M. T. and Tsegaye, A. (1990) 'International tourism and export instability', *Journal of Development Studies*, 26(3), 487–504.

Skeggs, B. (2005) 'The re-branding of class: propertising culture', in Devine, F., Savage, M., Scott, J. and Crompton, R. (eds) *Rethinking Class: Culture, Identities and Lifestyle*, Basingstoke: Palgrave Macmillan, 46–67.

Sklair, L. (1970) *The Sociology of Progress*, London: Routledge & Kegan Paul.

Sklair, L. (1991) *Sociology of the Global System*, Hemel Hempstead: Harvester Wheatsheaf.

Sklair, L. (1995) *Sociology of the Global System*, London: Prentice Hall (rev. and expanded edn).

Sklair, L. (1997) 'Social movements for global capitalism: the transnational capitalist class in action', *Review of International Political Economy*, 4(3), 514–38.

Sklair, L. (2001) *The Transnational Capitalist Class*, Oxford: Blackwell.

Sklair, L. (2002) *Globalization, Capitalism and its Alternatives*, Oxford: Oxford University Press.

Sklair, L. (2005) 'The transnational capitalist class and contemporary architecture in globalizing cities', *International Journal of Urban and Regional Research*, 29(3), 485–500.

Skocpol, T. (1979) *States and Social Revolutions: A Comparative Analysis of France, Russia and China*, Cambridge: Cambridge University Press.

Slater, D. (1997) *Consumer Culture and Modernity*, Cambridge: Polity.

Smart, B. (2010) *Consumer Society: Critical Issues and Environmental Consequences*, London: Sage.

Smith, A. D. (1991) *National Identity*, London: Penguin.

Smith, A. D. (1992) *Ethnicity and Nationalism*, Leiden: Brill.

Smith, A. D. (1995) *Nations and Nationalism in a Global Era*, Cambridge: Polity.

Smith, D. and Bræin, A. (2003) *The State of the World Atlas*, London: Earthscan.

Smith, J. L., Adhikari, A., Tondkar, R. H. and Andrews, R. L. (2010) 'The impact of corporate social disclosure on investment behavior: a cross-national study', *Journal of Accounting and Public Policy*, 29, 177–92.

Smith, R. C. (1998) 'Transnational localities: community, technology and the politics of membership within the context of Mexico and US migration', in Smith, M. P. and Guarnizo, L. E. (eds) *Transnationalism from Below*, New Brunswick, NJ: Transaction, 196–238.

Smith, V. L. (ed.) (1989) *Host and Guests: The Anthropology of Tourism* (2nd edn), Philadelphia, PA: University of Pennsylvania Press.

Solnit, R. (2008) 'Revolution of the snails: encounters with the Zapatistas', http://www.tomdispatch.com/post/174881 (accessed April 2012).

Solzhenitsyn, A. (1998) *Russia in the Abyss*, not yet published in English.

Sontag, D. (1993) 'Increasingly, two-career family means illegal immigrant help', *New York Times*, 24 January, A6.

Southern Poverty Law Center (2001) Intelligence Report: 'the rise and decline of the "patriots"', http://www.splcenter.org/intel/intelreport/article.jsp?aud=195 (accessed February 2009).

Spencer, H. (1902) *The Principles of Sociology*, London: Williams & Norgate.

Spicker, P. (2005) *An Introduction to Social Policy*, Aberdeen: The Robert Gordon University.

Sreberny-Mohammadi, A., Winseck, D., McKenna, J. and Boyd-Barrett, O. (eds) (1997) *Media in Global Context: A Reader*, London: Edward Arnold.

Srinivas, M. N. (1952) *Religion and Society among the Coorgs of South India*, Oxford: Oxford University Press.

Stahler-Sholk, R. (2007) 'Resisting neoliberal hegemonization: the Zapatista Autonomy Movement', *Latin American Perspectives*, 34, 48–63.

Standing, G. (2007) 'Labour recommodification in the global transformation', in Buğra, A. and Ağartan, K. (eds) *Reading Karl Polanyi for the Twenty-first Century: Market Economy as a Political Project*, Basingstoke: Palgrave Macmillan, 67–94.

Standing, G. (2009) *Work after Globalization: Building Occupational Citizenship*, Cheltenham: Edward Elgar.

Stark, R. and Bainbridge, W. S. (1985) *The Future of Religion: Secularization, Revival and Cult Formation*, Berkeley, CA: University of California Press.

Stead, D. and Maguire, J. (1998) 'Cricket's global "finishing school": the migration of overseas cricketers into English county cricket', *European Physical Education Review*, 4(1), 54–69.

Stephan, N. (1982) *The Idea of Race in Science: Great Britain, 1800–1960*, Basingstoke: Macmillan.

Stienstra, D. (1994) *Women's Movements and International Organizations*, New York: St Martin's Press.

Stiglitz, J. E. (2002) *Globalization and its Discontents*, London: Allen Lane.

Strange, S. (1986) *Casino Capitalism*, Oxford: Basil Blackwell.

Strange, S. (1996) *The Retreat of the State: The Diffusion of Power in the World Economy*, Cambridge: Cambridge University Press.

Strinati, D. (1995) *An Introduction to Theories of Popular Culture*, London: Routledge.

Stubbs, S. (1997) 'The hooded hordes of prejudice', *New Statesman*, 28 February, 10.

Stuckler, D., King, L. and McKee, M. (2009) 'Mass privatization and the post-communist mortality crisis: a cross-national analysis', *Lancet*, 373(9661), 399–407.

Suleiman, M. W. (1973) 'Attitudes of the Arab elite to Palestine and Israel', *American Political Science Review*, 67(2), 482–9.

Sutcliffe, B. (2007) 'The unequalled and unequal twentieth century', in Held, D. and Kaya, A. (eds) *Global Inequality: Patterns and Explanations*, Cambridge: Polity, 50–72.

Sydenham Town Forum (2010) 'My take on London's riots', http://sydenham.org.uk/forum/viewtopic.php?f=1&t=6558 (accessed April 2012).

Szerszynski, B. and Urry, J. (2006) 'Visuality, mobility and cosmopolitanism: inhabiting the world from afar', *British Journal of Sociology*, 57(1), 113–32.

Tally, R. T. (2011) 'Other spaces are still possible: Marcuse, theory and "the end of utopia" today', paper to the Critical Refusals Conference, Philadelphia, 29 October.

Taylor, J. P. (2001) 'Authenticity and sincerity in tourism', *Annals of Tourism Research*, 28(1), 7–26.

Taylor, M. (2010) 'The new wave of extremists plotting summer of unrest', *The Guardian*, 29 May, 20–1.

Taylor, P. J. (1995) 'World cities and territorial states: the rise and fall of their mutuality', in Knox, P. L. and Taylor, P. J. (eds) *World Cities in a World System*, Cambridge: Cambridge University Press, 48–62.

Teschke, B. and Heine, C. (2002) 'The dialectics of globalization: a critique of social constructivism', in Rupert, M. and Smith, H. (eds) *Historical Materialism and Globalization*, London: Routledge, 165–88.

Tett, G. (2009) *Fool's Gold: How Unrestrained Greed Corrupted a Dream, Shattered Global Markets and Unleashed a Catastrophe*, London: Little, Brown.

Thachuk, K. L. (ed.) (2007) *Transnational Threats: Smuggling and Trafficking in Arms, Drugs and Human Life*, Westport, CT: Praeger Security International.

The Allegiant.org (2011) 'Top 10 most profitable crimes in the world', http://www.theallegiant.org/top-5-most-profitable-crimes-in-the-world (accessed April 2012).

Therborn, G. (2004) *Between Sex and Power: Family in the World 1900–2000*, London: Routledge.

Thomson, D. (1997) 'Hong Kong on the Thames', *Telegraph Magazine*, 12 April, 38–42.

Thrift, N. (2004) 'Movement–space: the changing domains of thinking resulting from the development of new kinds of spatial awareness', *Economy and Society*, 34(4), 482–604.

Thwaites, T., Davis, L. and Mules, W. (1994) *Tools for Cultural Studies: An Introduction*, South Melbourne: Macmillan Education.

Tilly, C. (ed.) (1975) *The Formation of Nation States in Western Europe*, Princeton, NJ: Princeton University Press.

Tilly, C. (2004) 'Terror, terrorism, terrorists', *Sociological Theory*, 22(1), 5–13.

Timms, J. (2008) 'Chronology of global civil society events', in Albrow, M., Anheier, H., Glasius, M. et al. (eds) *Global Civil Society 2007/8*, London: Sage, 368–80.

Timms, J. (2009) 'Chronology of global civil society events', in Kumar, A., Scholte, J. A., Kaldor, M. et al. (eds) *Global Civil Society 2009*, London: Sage, 338–49.

Tomlinson, J. (1991) *Cultural Imperialism: A Critical Introduction*, London: Pinter.

Tomlinson, J. (1999) *Globalization and Culture*, Cambridge: Polity.

Tönnies, F. ([1887[1971) *Ferdinand Tönnies on Sociology: Pure, Applied and Empirical: Selected Writings*, Chicago, IL: University of Chicago Press.

Touraine, A. (1981) *The Voice and the Eye: An Analysis of Social Movements*, Cambridge: Cambridge University Press.

Travis, A. (2007) 'Migrants – the verdict: hardworking and skilled but with social problems in tow', *The Guardian*, 17 October.

Trifiletti, R. (2006) 'Different paths to welfare: family transformations, the production of welfare, and future prospects for social care in Italy and Japan', in Rebick, M. and Takanake, A. (eds) *The Changing Japanese Family*, New York: Routledge, 177–205.

Turner, B. (1991) *Religion and Social Theory*, London: Sage.

Turner, B. (1994) *Orientalism, Postmodernism and Globalism*, London: Routledge.

Turner, L. and Ash, J. (1975) *The Golden Hordes: International Tourism and the Pleasure Periphery*, London: Constable.

UN (United Nations) (1995) *The Copenhagen Declaration and Programme of Action: World Summit for Social Development (6–12 March 1995)*, New York: UN Department of Publications.

UN (2004) *World Population Prospects: The 2002 Revision*, New York: UNDESA.

UN (2009) *The Millennium Development Goals Report 2009*, New York: UNDESA.

UNCTAD (UN Conference on Trade and Development) (2009) *World Investment Report 2009: Transnational Corporations, Agricultural Production and Development*, http://archive.unctad.org/en/docs/wir2009_en.pdf (accessed March 2012).

UNCTAD (2010) *World Investment Report 2010: Investing in a Low-carbon Economy*, http://archive.unctad.org/en/docs/wir2010_en.pdf (accessed March 2012).

UNDESA (UN Department of Economic and Social Affairs) (2010) *World Urbanization Prospects: The 2009 Revision*, New York: UNDESA.

UNDESA (2011) *World Population Prospects: The 2010 Revision*, http://esa.un.org/unpd/wpp/index.htm (accessed 5 August 2011).

UNDP (United Nations Development Programme) (2002) *Human Development Report 2002: Deepening Democracy in a Fragmented World*, UNDP, New York: Oxford University Press.

UN-HABITAT (UN Human Settlements Programme) (2003) *Global Report on Human Settlements 2003: The Challenge of Slums*, London: Earthscan.

UN-HABITAT (2010) *State of the World's Cities 2010/11 – Cities for All: Bridging the Urban Divide*, http://www.unhabitat.org/pmss/listItemDetails.aspx?publicationID=2917 (accessed April 2012).

UNHCR (UN High Commission for Refugees) (2005) *Global Refugee Trends*, Geneva: UNHCR.

UNHCR (2011) *Global Appeal 2011 (Update): Populations of Concern to UNHCR*, http://www.unhcr.org/4cd91dc29.html (accessed August 2011).

UNODC (UN Office on Drugs and Crime) (2005) *World Drug Report 2005*, New York: UNODC.

UNODC (2011) *World Drug Report 2011*, New York: UNODC.

UNRISD (UN Research Institute for Social Development) (1995) *States of Disarray: The Social Effects of Globalization*, Geneva: UNRISD.

UNWTO (UN World Tourism Organization) (2012) *UN World Tourism Barometer*, http://dtxtq4w60xqpw.cloudfront.net/sites/all/files/pdf/unwto_barom12_02_march_excerpt.pdf (accessed December 2011).

Urry, J. (1990a) *The Tourist Gaze*, London: Sage.

Urry, J. (1990b) 'The "consumption" of tourism', *Sociology*, 24(1), 23–34.

Urry, J. (1995) *Consuming Places*, London: Routledge.

Urry, J. (2000) *Sociology Beyond Societies: Mobilities for the Twenty-first Century*, London: Routledge.

Urry, J. (2003) *Global Complexity*, Cambridge: Polity.

Uy-Tioco, C. (2007) 'Overseas Filipino workers and text messaging: reinventing transnational mothering', *Continuum: Journal of Media & Cultural Studies*, 21(2), 253–65.

Vaattovaara, M. and Kortteinen, N. (2003) 'Beyond polarisation versus professionalism? A case study of the development of the Helsinki region, Finland', *Urban Studies*, 40(11), 2127–45.

Valentine, G. (2006) 'Globalizing intimacy: the role of information and communication technologies in maintaining and creating relationships', *Women's Studies Quarterly*, 34(1/2), 365–93.

Van de Krol, R. and Schoonman, J. (2008) 'Photo-electrochemical production of hydrogen', in Hanjalić, K., van de Krol, R. and Lekić, A. (eds) *Sustainable Energy Technologies: Options and Prospects*, Dordrecht: Springer, 121– 42.

Van de Kuik, G., Ummels, B. and Hendricks, R. (2008) 'Perspectives on wind energy', in Hanjalić, K., van de Krol, R. and Lekić, A. (eds) *Sustainable Energy Technologies: Options and Prospects*, Dordrecht: Springer, 75–98.

Van den Berghe, P. (1994) 'Intelligence and race', in Cashmore, E. (ed.) *Dictionary of Race and Ethnic Relations* (3rd edn), London: Routledge, 150–2.

Van Doorn-Harder, P. (2006) *Women Shaping Islam: Reading the Qur'an in Indonesia*, Chicago, IL: University of Illinois.

Vargas, V. (2009) 'The World Social Forum', in Kumar, A., Scholte, J. A., Kaldor, M. et al. (eds) *Global Civil Society 2009*, London: Sage, 222–5.

Vertovec, S. (2004) 'Cheap calls: the social glue of migrant transnationalism', *Global Networks*, 4(2), 219–24.

Vertovec, S. (2007) 'Super-diversity and its implications', *Ethnic and Racial Studies*, 30(6), 1024–56.

Vertovec, S. (2009) *Transnationalism*, London: Routledge.

Vertovec, S. and Cohen, R. (eds) (1999) *Migration, Diasporas and Transnationalism*, Cheltenham: Edward Elgar.

Vertovec, S. and Cohen, R. (eds) (2002) *Conceiving Cosmopolitanism: Theory, Context and Practice*, Oxford: Oxford University Press.

Vidal, J. (2010a) 'How food and water drive a new foreign land grab in Africa', *The Observer*, 7 March, 28–9.

Vidal, J. (2010b) 'Urbanisation is unstoppable, says UN', *The Guardian*, 23 March, 22.

Vidal, J. and Goldenberg, S. (2010) 'UN deal binds all nations to cut emissions', *The Observer*, 12 December, 5.

Villabos, J. R., Smith, B., Lazzarotto, A, and Restori, M. (2004) 'Inbound for Mexico', *Industrial Engineer*, 36(4), 48–51.

Vogler, C. (2005) 'Cohabiting couples: rethinking money in the household at the beginning of the twenty-first century', *The Sociological Review*, 53(1), 1–29.

Volkman, T. A. (1984) 'Great performances: Toraja cultural identity in the 1970s', *American Ethnologist*, 11(1), 152–68.

Wade, R. (2004) 'Is globalization reducing poverty and inequality?', *World Development*, 32(4), 567–89.

Wade, R. (2007) 'Should we worry about income inequality?', in Held, D. and Kaya, A. (eds) *Global Inequality: Patterns and Explanations*, Cambridge: Polity, 104–131.

Wagner, E. A. (1990) 'Sport in Asia and Africa: Americanization or mundialization?', *Sociology of Sport Journal*, 7(4), 399–402.

Walby, S. (1990) *Theorizing Patriarchy*, Oxford: Blackwell.

Waldinger, R. and Bozorgmehr, M. (eds) (1996) *Ethnic Los Angeles*, New York: Russell Sage Foundation.

Waldinger, R. and Fitzgerald, D. (2004) 'Transnationalism in question', *American Journal of Sociology*, 109(5), 1177–95.

Walker, J. (1999) 'Measuring the extent of international crime and money laundering', paper given at the Budapest conference, 'KriminálExpo', June.

Wallerstein, I. (1974) *The Modern World-system I: Capitalist Agriculture and the Origins of the European World-economy in the Sixteenth Century*, New York: Academic Press.

Wallerstein, I. (1979) 'The rise and future demise of the world capitalist system: concepts for comparative analysis', in Wallerstein, I. (ed.) *The Capitalist World-economy*, Cambridge: Cambridge University Press, 3–36.

Wallerstein, I. (1989) 'Culture as the ideological battleground of the modern world-system', *Hitotsubashi Journal of Social Studies*, 21(1), 5–22.

Wallerstein, I. (1991) *Geopolitics and Geoculture*, Cambridge: Cambridge University Press.

Wallerstein, I. (1996) *Open the Social Sciences: Report of the Gulbenkian Commission on the Restructuring of the Social Sciences* (ed. V.Y. Mudimbe), Stanford: Stanford University Press.

Warde, A. (1992) 'Notes on the relationship between production and consumption', in Burrows, R. and Marsh, C. (eds) *Consumption and Class: Divisions and Change*, Basingstoke: Macmillan – now Palgrave Macmillan, 15–31.

Waterman, P. and Timms, J. (2004) 'Trade union internationalism and a global civil society in the making', in Anheier, H., Glasius, M. and Kaldor, M. (eds) *Global Civil Society 2004/05*, London: Sage, 178–202.

Waters, M. (1995) *Globalization*, London: Routledge.

Watson, J. (1998) *Media Communication: An Introduction to Theory and Practice*, Basingstoke: Macmillan – now Palgrave Macmillan.

Watt, P. (2006) 'Respectability, roughness and 'race': neighbourhood place images and the making of working-class social distinctions in London', *International Journal of Urban and Regional Research*, 30(4), 776–97.

Wearden, G. and Stanway, D. (2008) 'China slowdown: after years of boom', *The Guardian*, 21 October, 8.

Weber, M. (1976) 'Subjective meaning in the social situation', in Coser, L. A. and Rosenberg, B. (eds) *Sociological Theory: A Book of Readings*, Basingstoke: Macmillan, 209–20.

Weber, M. ([1905]1977) *The Protestant Ethic and the Spirit of Capitalism*, London: Allen & Unwin.

Weber, M. (1978) *Economy and Society*, Berkeley, CA: University of California Press.

Webster, F. (2002) *Theories of the Information Society*, London: Routledge.

Webster, F. (2008) 'Understanding the information domain: the uneasy relations between sociology and cultural studies and the peculiar absence of history', in Boyd Rayward, W. (ed.) *European Modernism and the Information Society*, Aldershot: Ashgate, 27–45.

WHO (World Health Organization) (2005) *WHO Multi-country Study on Women's Health and Domestic Violence Against Women*, Geneva: WHO.

Wight, M. (1977) *Systems of States*, Leicester: Leicester University Press.

Wilcox, R. C. (1994) 'Of fungos and fumbles: explaining the cultural uniqueness of American sport, or a paradoxical peek at sport American style', in Wilcox, R. C. (ed.) *Sport in the Global Village*, Morgantown, WV: Fitness Information Technology, 73–102.

Wilding, R. (2006) '"Virtual" intimacies: families communicating across transnational contexts', *Global Networks*, 6(2), 125–42.

Wilkinson, R. and Pickett, K. (2010) *The Spirit Level: Why Equality is Better for Everyone*, London: Penguin.

Williams, E. E. (1972) *Capitalism and Slavery*, London: André Deutsch.

Williams, P. and Baudin-O'Hayon, G. (2002) 'Global governance, transnational organized crime and money laundering', in Held, D. and McGrew, A. (eds) *Governing Globalization: Power, Authority and Global Governance*, Cambridge: Polity: 127–44.

Wills, J. and Hale, A. (2005) 'Threads of labour in the global garment industry, in Hale, A. and Wills, J. (eds) *Threads of Labour*, Oxford: Blackwell, 1–15.

Wilson, B. (1966) *Religion in Secular Society: A Sociological Comment*, London: Watts.

Wilson, J. (1973) *Introduction to Social Movements*, New York: Basic Books.

Wimberley, E. T. (2009) *Nested Ecology: The Place of Humans in the Ecological Hierarchy*, Baltimore: Johns Hopkins University Press.

Wimmer, A. and Glick Schiller, N. (2002) 'Methodological nationalism and beyond: nation-state building, migration and the social sciences', *Global Networks: A Journal of Transnational Affairs*, 2(4), 301–34.

Wolf, M. (2005) *Why Globalization Works: The Case for the Global Market Economy* (2nd edn), New Haven, CT: Yale University Press.

Wood, R. E. (1993) 'Tourism, culture and the sociology of development', in Hitchcock, M., King, V. T. and Parnwell, M. J. (eds) *Tourism in South-East Asia*, London: Routledge, 48–70.

Woodward, K. and Goldblatt, D. (2011) 'Introduction to special issue: football, sounds and things, *Soccer & Society*, 12(1), 1–8.

World Bank (2004a) *World Development Indicators*, Washington, DC: World Bank.

World Bank (2004b) 'Global poverty down by half since 1981 but progress uneven as economic growth eludes many countries', press release, Washington, DC: World Bank, 23 April.

World Bank (2009) *World Development Indicators*, Washington, DC: World Bank.

World Bank (2010) *World Development Indicators*, Washington, DC: World Bank.

Worsley, P. (1967) *The Third World*, London: Weidenfeld & Nicolson.

Wright, E. O. (1985) *Classes*, London: Verso.

WTO (World Tourism Organization) (2005) *Yearbook of Tourism Statistics*, Madrid: WTO.

Yamada, M. (1999) *The Age of Parasite Singles*, Tokyo: Chikuma Shobo.

Yearley, S. (1996) *Sociology, Environmentalism, Globalization: Reinventing the Globe*, London: Sage.

Yeates, N. (2004) 'Global care chains: critical reflections and lines of enquiry', *International Feminist Journal of Politics*, 6(3), 369–91.

Yeon Choo, H. and Marx Ferree, M. (2010) 'Practising intersectionality in social research: a critical analysis of inclusions, interactions, and institutions in the study of inequalities', *Sociological Theory*, 28(4), 129–49.

Yuval-Davis, N. (2009) 'Intersectionality and stratification', paper presented at the conference 'Celebrating Intersectionality: Debates on a Multi-faceted Concept in Gender Studies', Goethe University, Frankfurt.

Yuval-Davis, N. and Anthias, F. (eds) (1989) *Woman–Nation–State*, Basingstoke: Macmillan.

Zalewski, M. (1993) 'Feminist theory and international relations', in Bowker, M. and Brown, R. (eds) *From Cold War to Collapse: Theory and World Politics in the 1980s*, Cambridge: Cambridge University Press, 115–44.

Zelizer, V. (2005) *The Purchase of Intimacy*, Princeton: Princeton University Press.

Zhang, S. (2008) 'China: facing the challenges to link climate change responses with sustainable development and local environmental protections', *Globalizations*, 5(1), 81–8.

Zhou, Y. and Tseng, Y. F. (2001) 'Regrounding the "ungrounded empires": localization as the geographical catalyst for transnationalism', *Global Networks: A Journal of Transnational Affairs*, 1(2), 131–54.

Zirakzadeh, C. E. (1997) *Social Movements in Politics: A Comparative Study*, London: Longman.

Zolberg, A. R., Suhrke, A. and Aguayo, S. (1989) *Escape from Violence: Conflict and the Refugee Crisis in the Developing World*, New York: Oxford University Press.

Zukin, S. (1981) *Loft Living*, London: Hutchinson/Radius.

Name index

Subject index

THE HENLEY COLLEGE LIBRARY